FIFTH EDITION
social
PROBLEMS

For B. D. S. and B. W. S.

SAGE was founded in 1965 by Sara Miller McCune to support the dissemination of usable knowledge by publishing innovative and high-quality research and teaching content. Today, we publish more than 850 journals, including those of more than 300 learned societies, more than 800 new books per year, and a growing range of library products including archives, data, case studies, reports, conference highlights, and video. SAGE remains majority-owned by our founder, and after Sara's lifetime will become owned by a charitable trust that secures our continued independence.

Los Angeles | London | New Delhi | Singapore | Washington DC

FIFTH EDITION

social
PROBLEMS

Community, Policy, and Social Action

ANNA LEON-GUERRERO

Pacific Lutheran University

Los Angeles | London | New Delhi
Singapore | Washington DC

Los Angeles | London | New Delhi
Singapore | Washington DC

FOR INFORMATION:

SAGE Publications, Inc.
2455 Teller Road
Thousand Oaks, California 91320
E-mail: order@sagepub.com

SAGE Publications Ltd.
1 Oliver's Yard
55 City Road
London EC1Y 1SP
United Kingdom

SAGE Publications India Pvt. Ltd.
B 1/I 1 Mohan Cooperative Industrial Area
Mathura Road, New Delhi 110 044
India

SAGE Publications Asia-Pacific Pte. Ltd.
3 Church Street
#10-04 Samsung Hub
Singapore 049483

Acquisitions Editor: Jeff Lasser
Senior Development Editor: Nathan Davidson
eLearning Editor: Gabrielle Piccininni
Editorial Assistant: Alexandra Croell
Production Editor: Laura Barrett
Copy Editor: Rachel Keith
Typesetter: C&M Digitals (P) Ltd.
Proofreader: Theresa Kay
Indexer: Teddy Diggs
Cover/Interior Designer: Scott Van Atta
Marketing Manager: Erica DeLuca

Printed in Canada

ISBN 978-1-4833-6937-2

This book is printed on acid-free paper.

15 16 17 18 19 10 9 8 7 6 5 4 3 2 1

BRIEF CONTENTS

DETAILED CONTENTS

Chapter 4. Gender   98

Chapter 5. Sexual Orientation   122

Chapter 6. Age and Aging   146

PREFACE

I wrote this text with two goals in mind: to offer a better understanding of the social problems we experience in our world and to begin working toward real solutions. In the pages that follow, I present three connections to achieve these goals. The first connection is between sociology and the study of social problems. Using your sociological imagination (which you'll learn more about in Chapter 1), you will be able to identify the social and structural forces that determine our social problems. I think you'll discover that this course is interesting, challenging, and sometimes frustrating (sort of like real-life discussions about social problems). After you review these different social problems, you may ask, "What can be done about all this?" The second connection is between social problems and their solutions. In each chapter, we review selected social policies along with innovative programs that attempt to address or correct these problems. The final connection is one that I ask you to make yourself: recognizing the social problems in your community and identifying how you can be part of the solution.

LEARNING FEATURES OF THIS TEXT

The three connections are made evident in each chapter and throughout the text through a variety of specific learning features:

- **A focus on the basis of social inequalities.** Using a sociological perspective, we examine how race and ethnicity, gender, social class, sexual orientation, and age determine our life chances. Chapters 2 through 6 focus specifically on these bases of social inequality and how each contributes to our experience of social problems.
- **A focus on the global experience of social problems.** Throughout the text, the consequences of social problems throughout the world are highlighted, drawing upon data and research from international scholars and sociologists. In a boxed chapter feature, Taking a World View, specific social problems or responses are examined from a global perspective. We look at China's aging population (Chapter 6), Japan's educational tracking system (Chapter 8), Mexico's maquiladoras (Chapter 9), India's all-female international news organization (Chapter 11), and marijuana legalization in other countries (Chapter 12).
- **A focus on social policy and social action.** Each chapter includes a discussion on relevant social policies or programs. In addition, each chapter highlights how individuals or groups have made a difference in their community. The chapters include personal stories, some from professionals in their field, others from ordinary individuals who accomplish extraordinary things. Several feature those who began their activism as young adults or college students. For

example, in Chapter 8, you'll meet Wendy Kopp, the woman behind the Teach for America program; in Chapter 13, you'll meet Max Kenner, founder of the Bard Prison Initiative, an educational program for prisoners; and in Chapter 17, you'll read the story of Camila Vallejo, who began her activism while she was a student at the University of Chile. The text concludes with a chapter titled "Social Problems and Social Action" that identifies ways you can become more involved.

- **"What Does It Mean to Me?" exercises.** Each chapter includes questions or activities that can be completed by small student groups or on your own. Though some questions require you to collect data and information on what is going on in your own state, city, or campus, most of the exercises ask you to reflect on the material and consider how the social problem affects you. These exercises take you out of the classroom, away from the textbook, and into your community!

HIGHLIGHTS OF THE FIFTH EDITION

I have made a number of revisions in response to comments and feedback from the many instructors who adopted the earlier editions and from other interested instructors and their students.

- **Expanding the sociological perspectives.** Four theoretical perspectives (functionalist, conflict, feminist, and interactionist) are presented in each chapter, identifying how each perspective defines the causes and consequences of specific problems. Additional material has been incorporated in Chapter 3 (the 1.5 generation), Chapter 7 (cultural norms and sex education), Chapter 9 (the living wage movement), Chapter 11 (the boundary-less workplace), Chapter 13 (racial profiling), and Chapter 15 (climate change). In Chapter 1, I've included a general overview of basic sociological terms and concepts.
- **Keeping it current.** The focus of this text is unlike most other social problems texts, featuring a strong emphasis on social policy and action. It is necessary with each edition to provide an update on significant social policy decisions and debates. In this edition, the following social policy discussions have been updated: immigration (Chapter 3); same-sex marriage rights, including the U.S. Supreme Court's 2013 ruling (Chapter 5); and an expanded discussion on the Affordable Care Act (Chapter 10).
- **Data matters.** Data are important for understanding the extent of our social problems and recognizing populations vulnerable to them. In each revision I update data sources and incorporate new research findings. In this edition, each chapter includes a new feature, Exploring Social Problems, offering a closer empirical examination of social problems like HIV/AIDS, teen pregnancy, minimum-wage employment, and health care access.

- **Life after college.** What can you do with a sociology undergraduate degree? Almost anything. And to prove it to you, each chapter includes a new Sociology at Work feature, reviewing the invaluable workplace skills that you'll develop as a sociology major and presenting stories of sociology graduates who continue to rely on their sociological imaginations in their field of work.

I wanted to write a book that captured the experiences that I've shared with students in my own social problems course. I sensed the frustration and futility that many felt by the end of the semester—imagine all those weeks of discussing nothing else but "problems"! I decided that my message about the importance of *understanding social problems* should be complemented with a message on the importance of *taking social action.*

Social action doesn't happen just in Washington, DC, or in your state's capital, and political leaders aren't the only ones engaged in such efforts. Social action takes place on your campus, in your neighborhood, in your town, in whatever you define as your "community."

There were stories to be told by ordinary people—community, church, business, or student leaders—who recognized that they had the power to make a difference in the community. No act is too small to make a difference. Despite the persistence and severity of many social problems, members of our community have not given up.

I hope that by the time you reach the end of this text, with your newfound sociological imagination, you will find your own path to social action. Wherever it leads you, I wish you all the best.

ANCILLARIES

$SAGE edge™

edge.sagepub.com/leonguerrero5e

SAGE edge for Instructors supports your teaching by making it easy to integrate quality content and create a rich learning environment for students.

- **Test banks** provide a diverse range of pre-written options as well as the opportunity to edit any question and/or insert your own personalized questions to effectively assess students' progress and understanding
- **Learning objectives** reinforce the most important material
- **Sample course syllabi** provide suggested models for structuring your courses
- Editable, chapter-specific **PowerPoint®** slides offer complete flexibility for creating a multimedia presentation for your course

- **Lecture notes** summarize key concepts by chapter to help you prepare for lectures and class discussions
- **Course cartridges** for easy LMS integration
- **Chapter activities** are specially designed to accompany each chapter for professors to use in and out of the classroom
- **Web Exercises,** comprised of web resources and critical thinking questions to apply your knowledge of the chapter perspectives.
- Chapter-specific **discussion questions** prompt students to engage with the material and by reinforcing important content
- Carefully selected chapter-by-chapter **Video and Multimedia** content which enhance classroom-based explorations of key topics
- EXCLUSIVE! Access to full-text **SAGE journal articles and readings** that have been carefully selected to support and expand on the concepts presented in each chapter

SAGE edge for Students provides a personalized approach to help students accomplish their coursework goals in an easy-to-use learning environment.

- Mobile-friendly **eFlashcards** strengthen understanding of key terms and concepts
- Mobile-friendly practice **quizzes** allow for independent assessment by students of their mastery of course material
- **Web exercises** and meaningful web links facilitate student use of Internet resources, further exploration of topics, and responses to critical thinking questions
- Chapter-specific **discussion questions** help launch classroom interaction by prompting students to engage with the material and by reinforcing important content
- Carefully selected chapter-by-chapter **Video and Multimedia** content which enhance classroom-based explorations of key topics.
- EXCLUSIVE! Access to full-text **SAGE journal articles and readings** that have been carefully selected to support and expand on the concepts presented in each chapter
- Chapter-by-chapter **study questions** to help you prepare for quizzes and tests

ACKNOWLEDGMENTS

Social Problems: Community, Policy, and Social Action represents a deeply personal and professional journey. My heartfelt thanks to Jerry Westby for being the first to recognize and support my vision. Along with Denise Simon, Jerry guided me through the first three editions of this text, sharing my commitment to my message of social action. For this edition, I was fortunate to work with Jeff Lasser and Nathan Davidson. They challenged and encouraged me to reimagine the content and instructional features of this text. My thanks to both of them for their unwavering support.

I am indebted to Laura Barrett for her fine production support, to Rachel Keith for her thorough and thoughtful copyediting, and to Gabrielle Piccininni for her work on the ancillary materials and features.

The following sociologists served as the first audience and reviewers for this text. Thank you all for your encouragement and for your insightful comments and suggestions, many of which have been incorporated in this fifth edition.

For the fifth edition:

Karen Allen, *Arkansas State University*

Todd Michael Callais, *University of Cincinnati–Blue Ash*

Robert M. Clark, *Pennsylvania Highlands Community College*

Kate D'Arcy, *University of Bedfordshire, Applied Social Studies*

Sue Dowden, *El Camino College*

John J. Errigo, III, *Chestnut Hill College*

Aimee E. Huard, *Nashua Community College*

Linda L. Jasper, *Indiana University Southeast*

Rosalind Kopfstein, *Western Connecticut State University*

For the fourth edition:

Kathleen Baldwin, *Olympic College*

Angela Jones, *Elon University*

Thomas R. Lake, *SUNY Dutchess Community College*

Minu Mathur, *College of San Mateo*

Johnny Underwood, *Carteret Community College*

For the third edition:

Doug Degher, *Northern Arizona University*

Mark J. Guillette, *Valencia Community College–Osceola Campus*

Eric Jorrey, *Bowling Green State University*

Amanda Jungels, *Georgia State University*

Mary Kniskern, *University of Maryland, Virginia–Maryland Regional College of Veterinary Medicine*

Sandy Martinez, *Central Washington University*

Sophie Nathenson, *The University of Utah*

Bob Parker, *University of Nevada School of Medicine*

Matthew Sargent, *Madison Area Technical College–Downtown*

Athena Smith, *Hillsborough Community College–Dale Mabry Campus*

Annie Tuttle, *The Florida State University College of Law*

Mike Victor, *The University of Texas Science Health Center at Tyler*

For the second edition:

Donna Abrams, *Georgia Highlands College*
Brian C. Aldrich, *Winona State University*
Carl Backman, *Auburn University*
Janet Cosbey, *Eastern Illinois University*
Janine Dewitt-Heffner, *Marymount University*
Ronald Ferguson, *Ridgewater College*
Mark J. Guillette, *Valencia Community College*
Gaetano Guzzo, *Wright State University*
Jason Hendrickson, *State University of New York at Albany*
Judith Hennessy, *Central Washington University*
Ronald Huskin, *Del Mar College*
Richard Jenks, *Indiana University Southeast*
Rohald Meneses, *University of Florida*
Paul Mills, *University of Alabama*
Adam Moskowitz, *Columbus State Community College*
Wendy Ng, *San Jose State University*
Robert Parker, *University of Nevada Las Vegas*
James Roberts, *University of Scranton*
Katherine R. Rowell, *Sinclair Community College*
Rita Sakitt, *Suffolk County Community College*
Frank Salamone, *Iona College*
Jim Sikora, *Illinois Wesleyan College*

For the first edition:

Arfa Aflatooni, *Linn-Benton Community College*
Joanne Ardovini, *Sam Houston State University*
Bernadette Barton, *Morehead State University*
Allison Camelot, *California State University, Fullerton*
Janine Dewitt-Heffner, *Marymount University*
Dan Dexheimer, *University of Florida*
Woody Doane, *University of Hartford*
Joe Dupris, *California State University, Humboldt*
Rachel Einwohner, *Purdue University*
Heather Smith Feldhaus, *Bloomsburg University*
Jim Fenelon, *California State University, San Bernardino*
Bobbie Fields, *Central Piedmont Community College*
Debbie Franzman, *Allan Hancock College*
Marcie Goodman, *University of Utah*
George Gross, *Northern Michigan University*
Mark J. Guillette, *Valencia Community College*

Julia Hall, *Drexel University*

Dan W. Hayden, *University of Southern Indiana*

Chuck Hohm, *San Diego State University*

Leslie Houts, *University of Florida*

James R. Hunter, *Indiana University–Purdue University at Indianapolis*

K. Land, *Duke University*

Nick Larsen, *Chapman University*

Kari Lerum, *Seattle University*

Stephen Light, *SUNY Plattsburgh*

Dennis Loo, *Cal Poly Pomona*

Scott Lukas, *Lake Tahoe Community College*

Christina Myers, *Oklahoma State University*

Paul Roof, *San Juan College*

Kim Saliba, *Portland Community College*

Norma K. Simmons, *Washington State University*

Deborah Sullivan, *Arizona State University*

Mary Texeira, *California State University, San Bernardino*

Linda A. Treiber, *North Carolina State University*

Gailynn White, *Citrus College*

Anthony W. Zumpetta, *West Chester University*

My thanks to my AKD colleagues Michele Kozimor-King, Erik Larsen, and Amy Orr for connecting me with their star alums. And to each sociology alum, thank you for sharing your amazing stories of success, vocation, and sociology with me and my readers.

I dedicate this book to the two people who have been with me from the beginning of this journey: to my mentor, Byron D. Steiger, and to my husband, Brian W. Sullivan. From Byron, I learned the importance of loving one's work. Thank you for showing me what an excellent teacher can and should be. From Brian, I learned the value of caring for one's community and the environment. Thank you for all that you do—this book would not have been possible without you.

Michael Clark

Anna Leon-Guerrero is a professor of sociology at Pacific Lutheran University in Tacoma, Washington. A recipient of the university's Faculty Excellence Award and the K. T. Tang Award for Excellence in Research, she teaches courses on statistics, sociological theory, and social problems. As a social service program evaluator and consultant, she has focused her research on welfare reform, employment strategies for the working poor, and program assessment. She is the coauthor of *Social Statistics for a Diverse Society* and *Essentials of Social Statistics for a Diverse Society* (with Chava Frankfort-Nachmias).

Sociology and the Study of Social Problems

If I asked everyone in your class what they believe is the most important social problem facing the United States, there would be many different answers: the economy, immigration, health care, unemployment. Most would agree that some or all of these are social problems. But which is the most important, and how would we solve it?

Suppose I asked the same question in a South African college classroom. AIDS is likely to be one of the responses from South African college students. According to UNAIDS (2014), 35 million adults and children worldwide were living with HIV in 2013. Africa remains the epicenter of the pandemic, with more than 25 million HIV-infected adults and children (refer to Figure 1.1). The prevalence of HIV is predicted to triple during the next decade, especially in Africa, but also in the former USSR, China, and India. The AIDS pandemic has been described as a threat to global stability (Lichtenstein 2004). However, effective risk-reduction strategies, along with new treatments for HIV/AIDS, have saved countless lives in the United States. During the early 1980s, nearly 150,000 Americans were infected with the disease each year, but by the early 1990s, the number of new infected cases had dropped to 50,000 per year, where it remains today (Centers for Disease Control and Prevention 2007, 2013).

Figure 1.1   Number of individuals living with HIV, regional data for 2013

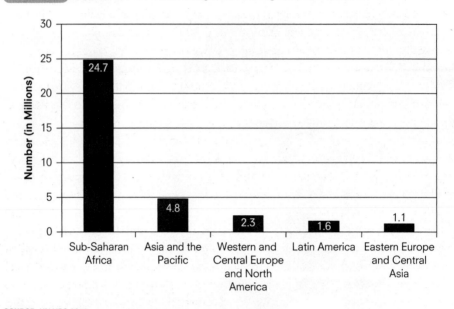

SOURCE: UNAIDS 2014.

NOTE: The total number of HIV infections is 35 million. HIV infection data for the Caribbean (250,000) and Middle East and North Africa (230,000) are not reported in the figure.

Globalization, defined as the process of increasing transborder connectedness (Hytrek and Zentgraf 2007)—whether economically, politically, environmentally, or socially—poses new challenges and opportunities for understanding and solving social problems. We cannot understand the nature of social problems by simply taking a national or local perspective. Taking a global perspective allows us to look at the interrelations between countries and their social problems (Heiner 2002). We are not the only country to experience social problems. Knowledge based on research to understand and policies to address social problems here could be applied in other countries, and what other countries have learned based on their social problems could be applied in the United States. Finally, we all need a little help from our neighbors—we can increase our connectedness and goodwill with other countries through implementing solutions collaboratively rather than alone. So what do you think? Is HIV/AIDS in South Africa a problem only for South Africans, or is it also a problem for those living in the United States?

Globalization:
A process of increasing transborder connectedness; the basis may be economic, political, environmental, or social

· ·

What Does It Mean to Me?

What would be at the top of your social problems list? Would your list include AIDS? Why or why not?

· ·

The Origin of AIDS

This is how we spend much of our public conversation—on the Senate floor, on afternoon talk shows, at work, or in the classroom—arguing, analyzing, and just trying to figure out which problem is most serious and what needs to be done about it. In casual or sometimes heated conversations, we offer opinions about the economy, the wars in the Middle East, the Affordable Care Act, or appropriate policies for the African AIDS pandemic. Often, these explanations are not based on firsthand data collection or on an exhaustive review of the literature. For the most part, they are based on our opinions and life experiences, or they are just good guesses.

What this text and your course offer is a sociological perspective on social problems. Unlike any other discipline, sociology provides us with a form of self-consciousness, an awareness that our personal experiences are often caused by structural or social forces. **Sociology** is the systematic study of individuals, groups, and social structures. A sociologist examines the relationship between individuals and society, which includes such social institutions as the family, the military, the economy, and education. As a social science, sociology offers an objective and systematic approach to understanding the causes of social problems. From a sociological perspective, problems and their solutions don't just involve individuals; they also have a great deal to do with the social structures in our society. C. Wright Mills ([1959] 2000) first promoted this perspective in his 1959 essay, "The Promise."

USING OUR SOCIOLOGICAL IMAGINATION

According to Mills, the sociological imagination can help us distinguish between personal troubles and public issues. The **sociological imagination** is the ability to link our personal lives and experiences with our social world. Mills ([1959] 2000) describes how personal troubles occur within the "character of the individual and within the range of his immediate relationships with others" (p. 8), whereas public issues are a "public matter: some value cherished by publics is felt to be threatened" (p. 8). As a result, the individual, or those in contact with that individual, can resolve a trouble, but the resolution of an issue requires public debate about what values are being threatened and the source of such a threat.

Let's consider unemployment. One man unemployed is his own personal trouble. Resolving his unemployment involves reviewing his current situation, reassessing his skills, considering his job opportunities, and submitting his résumés or job applications to employers. Once he has a new job, his personal trouble is over. However, what happens when your city or state experiences high levels of unemployment? What happens when there is a nationwide problem of unemployment? This affects not just one person but, rather, thousands or millions. A personal trouble has been transformed into a public issue. This is the case not just because of how many people it affects; something becomes an issue because of the public values it threatens. Unemployment threatens our sense of economic security. It challenges our belief that everyone can work hard to succeed. Unemployment raises questions about society's obligations to help those without a job.

Sociology: The systematic study of individuals and social structures

Sociological imagination: The ability to link our personal lives and experiences with our social world

 College Costs and Alternatives

A key distinction between a personal trouble and a public issue is how each one can be remedied. According to C. Wright Mills, an individual may be able to solve a trouble, but a public issue can only be resolved by society and its social structures.

We can make the personal trouble–public issue connection with regard to another issue, one that you might already be aware of—the cost of higher education. In 2014, during a rally in Florida's Coral Reef High School, President Barack Obama announced an initiative to help students complete the federal student aid application form, part of an effort to broaden access to higher education. Coral Reef senior David Scherker, an aspiring filmmaker, was in the audience. At the time, David was waiting to hear about the status of his admission to several colleges and universities, including Florida State University and USC. He worried about his financial aid offers and whether he would be able to attend the school of his choice (NPR 2014). Is this a personal trouble facing only David? Or is this a public issue?

College cost has become a serious social problem because the "barriers that make higher education unaffordable serve to erode our economic well being, our civic values, and our democratic ideals" (Callan and Finney 2002:10). Although most Americans still believe that a college education is essential for one's success, increasingly they also believe that qualified and motivated students do not have the opportunity to attend college (National Center for Public Policy and Higher Education and Public Agenda 2010). The data support this. Nearly one half of all college-qualified, low- and moderate-income high school graduates are unable to afford college and have lower rates of bachelor's degree attainment than their middle- and high-income peers (Advisory Committee on Student Financial Assistance 2006). Though only about a third of students pay the published tuition or sticker price, the cost of tuition has risen at a faster rate than family income or student financial aid. At a four-year public institution, for academic year 2013–2014, in-state total fees (tuition, room, and board) were $18,391 (a 3.2% increase from 2012–2013); at four-year private institutions, the average cost was $40,917 (a 3.7% increase from 2013–2014) (College Board 2014).

The majority of students receive some form of assistance through scholarships, federal grants, or state aid. The financial burden of a college education is unevenly distributed, with low- and moderate-income students and families experiencing the burden most. In 2007, even after grant aid, low-income families paid or borrowed an amount equivalent to 72% of their family income to cover one year of tuition. In contrast, families with incomes between $54,001 and $80,400 had to finance the equivalent of 27% of their family income for tuition. The percentage was lowest for families with incomes over $115,400 at 14% (Education Trust 2009). The average indebtedness for a graduating college senior was $28,400 for 2013 (Institute for College Access & Success 2014).

 Rising College Costs

As Mills explains, "to be aware of the ideal of social structure and to use it with sensibility is to be capable of tracing such linkages among a great variety of milieus. To be able to do that is to possess the sociological imagination" (Mills [1959] 2000:10–11). The sociological imagination challenges the claim that the problem is "natural" or based on individual failures, instead reminding us how the problem is rooted in society, in our social structures themselves (Irwin 2001). For example, can we solve unemployment by telling every unemployed person to work harder? Can David solve his tuition problem by taking out student loans? Or will this create additional problems? The sociological imagination emphasizes the structural bases of social problems, making us aware of the economic, political, and social structures that govern employment and unemployment trends and the cost of higher education. Individuals have may agency, the ability to make their own choices, but their actions and even their choices may be constrained by the realities of the social structure. Throughout this text, we apply our sociological imagination to the study of social problems. Before we proceed, we need to understand what a social problem is.

....

What Does It Mean to Me?

What is the annual cost of attending your college or university? What did you and/or your family consider before making your final school decision? How much were finances included in your considerations?

....

WHAT IS A SOCIAL PROBLEM?

The Negative Consequences of Social Problems

A **social problem** is a social condition or pattern of behavior that has negative consequences for individuals, our social world, or our physical world. A social problem such as unemployment, alcoholism, drug abuse, or HIV/AIDS may negatively affect a person's life and health, along with the well-being of that person's family and friends. Problems can threaten our social institutions, for example, the family (spousal abuse), education (the rising cost of college tuition), or the economy (unemployment). Our physical and social worlds can be threatened by problems related to urbanization (lack of affordable housing) and the environment (climate change). You will note from the examples in this paragraph that social problems are inherently social in their causes, consequences, and solutions.

Objective and Subjective Realities of Social Problems

A social problem has objective and subjective realities. A social condition does not have to be personally experienced by every individual to be considered a social problem. The **objective reality** of a social problem comes from acknowledging that a particular social condition does exist. Objective realities of a social problem can be confirmed by

Social problem: A social condition that has negative consequences for individuals, our social world, or our physical world

Objective reality: Actual existence of a particular condition

Unemployment and the Great Recession

collection of data. For example, we know from the Centers for Disease Control and Prevention (CDC) (2013) that more than 1.1 million Americans are living with HIV/AIDS. Refer to this chapter's Exploring Social Problems feature for more information about HIV infections in the United States. You or I do not have to have been infected with HIV to know that the disease is real, with real human and social consequences. We can confirm the realities of HIV/AIDS by observing infected individuals and their families in our own community, at AIDS programs, shelters, or hospitals.

The **subjective reality** of a social problem addresses how a problem becomes defined as a problem. This idea is based on the concept of the **social construction of reality**. Coined by Peter Berger and Thomas Luckmann (1966), the term refers to how our world is a social creation, originating and evolving through our everyday thoughts and actions. Most of the time, we assume and act as though the world is a given, objectively predetermined outside our existence. However, according to Berger and Luckmann, we also apply subjective meanings to our existence and experience. In other words, our experiences don't just happen to us. Good, bad, positive, or negative—we attach meanings to our reality.

From this perspective, social problems are not objectively predetermined. They become real only when they are subjectively defined or perceived as problematic. This perspective is known as **social constructionism**. Recognizing the subjective aspects of social problems allows us to understand how a social condition may be defined as a problem by one segment of society but be completely ignored by another. For example, do you believe AIDS is a social problem? Some may argue that it is a problem only if you are the one infected with the disease or if you are morally corrupt or sexually promiscuous. Actually, some would not consider AIDS a problem at all, considering the medical and public health advances that have successfully reduced the spread of the disease in the United States. Yet others would argue that AIDS still qualifies as a social problem.

Sociologist Denise Loseke (2003) explains, "Conditions might exist, people might be hurt by them, but conditions are not social problems until humans categorize them as troublesome and in need of repair" (p. 14). To frame their work, social constructionists ask the following set of questions:

> What do people say or do to convince others that a troublesome condition exists that must be changed? What are the consequences of the typical ways that social problems attract concern? How do our subjective understandings of social problems change the objective characteristics of our world? How do these understandings change how we think about our own lives and the lives of those around us? (Loseke and Best 2003:3–4)

The social constructionist perspective focuses on how a problem is socially defined, in a dialectic process between individuals interacting with each other and with their social world. In the next section, we'll learn how the problem of HIV/AIDS was socially constructed.

Subjective reality: Attachment of meanings to our reality

Social construction of reality: The world regarded as a social creation

Social constructionism: Subjective definition or perception of conditions

HIV and AIDS

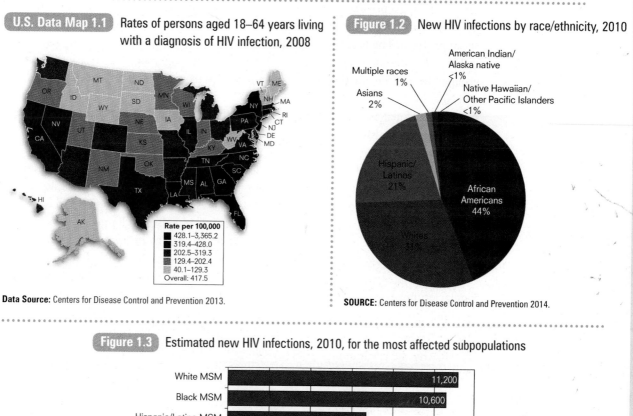

U.S. Data Map 1.1 Rates of persons aged 18–64 years living with a diagnosis of HIV infection, 2008

Rate per 100,000
- 428.1–3,365.2
- 319.4–428.0
- 202.5–319.3
- 129.4–202.4
- 40.1–129.3
Overall: 417.5

Data Source: Centers for Disease Control and Prevention 2013.

Figure 1.2 New HIV infections by race/ethnicity, 2010

Multiple races 1%
Asians 2%
American Indian/ Alaska native <1%
Native Hawaiian/ Other Pacific Islanders <1%
Hispanic/ Latinos 21%
African Americans 44%
Whites 31%

SOURCE: Centers for Disease Control and Prevention 2014.

Figure 1.3 Estimated new HIV infections, 2010, for the most affected subpopulations

Subpopulation	Number of New HIV Infections
White MSM	11,200
Black MSM	10,600
Hispanic/Latino MSM	6,700
Black Heterosexual Women	5,300
Black Heterosexual Men	2,700
White Heterosexual Women	1,300
Hispanic/Latino Heterosexual Women	1,200
Black Male IDUs	1,100

Legend: ■ Men ■ Women

Number of New HIV Infections

SOURCE: Centers for Disease Control and Prevention 2014.

NOTE: MSM stands for "men who have sex with men." IDU stands for "injecting drug user."

WHAT DO YOU THINK?

More than 1.1 million Americans are living with HIV/AIDS (Centers for Disease Control and Prevention 2013).

Despite representing 12% of the U.S. population, African Americans accounted for 44% of all new HIV infections among adults and adolescents (13 years or older) in 2010 (refer to Figure 1.2). Gay and bisexual men account for most of the new infections among whites and African Americans. Men who have sex with men (MSM) are most at risk for HIV infections (refer to Figure 1.3).

How should health programs or policies address the risk factors for these populations? What structural barriers might make these populations difficult to reach?

Which groups have the lowest number of new HIV infections?

The History of Social Problems

Problems don't appear overnight; rather, as Malcolm Spector and John Kituse (1987) argue, the identification of a social problem is part of a subjective process. Spector and Kituse identify four stages to the process. Stage 1 is defined as a transformation process: taking a private trouble and transforming it into a public issue. In this stage, an influential group, activists, or advocates call attention to and define an issue as a social problem. The first HIV infection cases were documented in the United States in 1979. The disease was originally referred to as the "gay plague" because the first group to be identified with the disease was gay men from San Francisco, Los Angeles, and New York. The association of HIV/AIDS with this specific population led to its first being defined as a sexual epidemic rather than a public health threat. Gay activists and public health officials mobilized to increase awareness and began to change the public's perception of the disease in the early 1980s.

Stage 2 is the legitimization process: formalizing the manner in which the social problems or complaints generated by the problem are handled. For example, an organization or public policy could be created to respond to the condition. An existing organization, such as a federal or state agency, could also be charged with taking care of the situation. In either instance, these organizations begin to legitimize the problem by creating and implementing a formal response. In the early 1980s, HIV/AIDS task forces were created in the CDC and the World Health Organization. Similar groups were convened in the United Kingdom, France, and other countries. Although no single organization or country was in charge, all were intent on identifying the disease and finding a cure. Activists looked for public legitimization of the disease from then President Ronald Reagan. But Reagan did not acknowledge AIDS until 1985, when he was asked directly about the disease during a press conference. His first public statement about the disease came in 1987 at the Third International Conference on AIDS. By then, nearly 36,000 Americans had been diagnosed with AIDS and more than 20,000 had died. AIDS advocates blamed Reagan's slow and ineffective response for these deaths and the increasing spread of the disease.

Stage 3 is a conflict stage, when Stage 2 routines are unable to address the problem. During Stage 3, activists, advocates, and victims of the problem experience feelings of distrust and cynicism toward the formal response organizations. Stage 3 activities include readjusting the formal response system: renegotiating procedures, reforming practices, and engaging in administrative or organizational restructuring. Many early public health protocols were revised in response to increased understanding about how HIV/AIDS is spread and treated. For example, patient isolation was common during the first stages of the disease. Teenager Ryan White had to petition for the right to attend public school with his classmates. Ryan and his mother's experiences also shed light on the difficulties faced by low-income, uninsured, or underinsured individuals and families living with HIV/AIDS. After his death in 1990, the U.S. Congress passed the Ryan White CARE Act to provide for the unmet health needs of individuals with HIV/AIDS. The act continues to provide support for nearly

TAKING A WORLD VIEW

IDENTIFYING THE GREATEST THREAT TO THE WORLD

In 2014, the Pew Research Center asked residents in 44 countries what they perceived as the greatest threat to the world. According to the Center, "across the nations surveyed, opinions on which of the five dangers is the top threat to the world vary greatly by region and country, and in many places there is no clear consensus." Results are grouped in six regions presented in Table 1.1.

Inequality was more likely to be identified by citizens of advanced economies. More than a quarter of surveyed Americans and a third of surveyed Europeans selected inequality as the greatest threat. The EU country with the highest level of concern was Spain (54%). Inequality was of less concern in the other reported world regions—the Middle East, Asia, Latin America, and Africa.

Note how AIDS and other diseases are of great concern to African residents (29%), but of lowest concern in the United States (7%) and Europe (5%). Religious and ethnic hatred was identified as the top threat to the world by citizens in Middle Eastern countries (34%). Nuclear weapons (26%) and pollution (25%) were the greatest threats for Latin American respondents.

Which of these do you think is the greatest threat to the world?

Table 1.1 2014 global threats by world region (median percentage saying each is a major threat to the world)

Item	Middle East	Europe	Asia	Latin America	Africa	U.S.
Religious and ethnic hatred	34	15	13	9	24	24
Inequality	18	32	18	18	18	27
Pollution and environment	9	14	22	25	7	15
Nuclear weapons	20	19	21	26	22	23
AIDS and other diseases	10	5	12	19	29	7

SOURCE: Pew Research Center 2014.

500,000 individuals annually, making it the largest federal government program for those living with the disease.

Finally, Stage 4 begins when groups believe that they can no longer work within the established system. Advocates or activists are faced with two options: to radically change the existing system or to work outside the system. As an alternative to the

IN FOCUS

A REVIEW OF SOCIOLOGY

According to Jeanne Ballantine and Keith Roberts (2012), sociologists examine the software and hardware of society. A *society* consists of individuals who live together in a specific geographic area, who interact with each other, and who cooperate for the attainment of common goals.

The software is our *culture*. Each society has a culture that serves as a system of guidelines for living. A culture includes *norms* (rules of behavior shared by members of society and rooted in a value system), *values* (shared judgments about what is desirable or undesirable, right or wrong, good or bad), and *beliefs* (ideas about life, the way society works, and where one fits in).

The hardware comprises the enduring social structures that bring order to our lives. This includes the positions or *statuses* that we occupy in society (student, athlete, employee, roommate) and the social *groups* to which we belong and identify with (our family, our local place of worship, our workplace). *Social institutions* are the most complex hardware. Social institutions, such as the family, religion, or education, are relatively permanent social units of roles, rules, relationships, and organized activities devoted to meeting human needs and to directing and controlling human behavior (Ballantine and Roberts 2012).

government and public health agencies' response to HIV/AIDS, numerous independent advocacy and research groups were formed. One such group is AIDS United (first called AIDS Action), formed in 1984 by a coalition of AIDS service organizations. In an effort to end AIDS in our country, AIDS United embraced a multi-strategy of research, granting funding, policy making, and advocacy. Through its Access to Care program, AIDS United supports innovative, evidence-based, collaborative programs serving low-income and marginalized individuals living with HIV. Access to Care not only supports the health and care of HIV patients, but also provides job training, housing stabilization, and peer support (AIDS United 2014).

Theory: A set of assumptions and propositions used for explanation, prediction, and understanding

Macro level of analysis: Societal level of analysis

Micro level of analysis: Individual level of analysis

UNDERSTANDING THE SOCIOLOGICAL PERSPECTIVE

The way sociologists conduct sociology and study social problems begins first with their view on how the world works. Based on a **theory**—a set of assumptions and propositions used for explanation, prediction, and understanding—sociologists begin to define the relationship between society and individuals and to describe the causes and consequences of social problems.

Theories vary in their level of analysis, focusing on a **macro** (societal) or a **micro** (individual) **level of analysis**. Theories help inform the direction of sociological research and data analysis. In the following section, we review four theoretical perspectives—functionalist, conflict, feminist, and interactionist—and how each perspective explains and examines social problems. Research methods used by sociologists are summarized in the next section.

Functionalist Perspective

Among the theorists most associated with the functionalist perspective is French sociologist Émile Durkheim. Borrowing from biology, Durkheim likened society to a human body. As the body has essential organs, each with a specific function, he theorized that society has its own organs: institutions such as the family, religion, education, economics, and politics. These organs or social structures have essential and specialized functions. For example, the institution of the family maintains the health and socialization of our young and creates a basic economic unit. The institution of education provides knowledge and skills for women and men to work and live in society. No other institution can do what the family or education does.

Durkheim proposed that the function of society is to civilize or control individual actions. He wrote, "It is civilization that has made man what he is; it is what distinguishes him from the animal: man is man only because he is civilized" (Durkheim [1914] 1973:149). The social order can be threatened during periods of rapid social change, such as industrialization or political upheaval, when social norms

Jane Addams' (center) sociological perspective informed her connection to her Chicago community and led her to a life of social action. She developed programs to assist the poor and advocated for legislative and political reforms.

and values are likely to be in transition. During this state of normlessness or **anomie**, Durkheim believed, society is particularly prone to social problems. As a result, social problems cannot be solved by changing the individual; rather, the problem has to be solved at the societal level. The entire social structure or the affected part of the social structure needs to be repaired.

The **functionalist perspective**, as its name suggests, examines the functions or consequences of the structure of society. Functionalists use a macro perspective, focusing on how society creates and maintains social order. Social problems are not analyzed in terms of how "bad" they are for society. Rather, a functionalist asks, how does the social problem emerge from society? Does the social problem serve a function?

The systematic study of social problems began with the sociologists at the University of Chicago. Part of what has been called the Chicago School of Sociology,

Anomie: State of normlessness

Functionalist perspective: A theoretical perspective that examines the functions or consequences of the structure of society; functionalists use a macro perspective, focusing on how society creates and maintains social order

 Diversity as Dysfunction

scholars such as Ernest W. Burgess, Homer Hoyt, Robert E. Park, Edward Ullman, and Louis Wirth used their city as an urban laboratory, pursuing field studies of poverty, crime, and drug abuse during the 1920s and 1930s. Through their research, they captured the real experiences of individuals experiencing social problems, noting the positive and negative consequences of urbanization and industrialization (Ritzer 2000). Taking it one step further, sociologists Jane Addams and Charlotte Gilman studied urban life in Chicago and developed programs to assist the poor and lobbied for legislative and political reform (Adams and Sydie 2001).

According to Robert Merton (1957), social structures can have positive benefits as well as negative consequences, which he called **dysfunctions**. A social problem such as homelessness has a clear set of dysfunctions but can also have positive consequences or functions. One could argue that homelessness is clearly dysfunctional and unpleasant for the women, men, and children who experience it, and for a city or community, homelessness can serve as a public embarrassment. Yet, a functionalist would say that homelessness is beneficial for at least one part of society, or else it would cease to exist. The population of the homeless supports an industry of social service agencies, religious organizations, and community groups and service workers. In addition, the homeless also highlight problems in other parts of our social structure, namely, the problems of the lack of a livable wage or affordable housing.

Conflict Perspective

Like functionalism, conflict theories examine the macro level of our society, its structures and institutions. Whereas functionalists argue that society is held together by norms, values, and a common morality, those holding a **conflict perspective** consider how society is held together by power and coercion (Ritzer 2000) for the benefit of those in power. In this view, social problems emerge from the continuing conflict between groups in our society—based on social class, gender, race, or ethnicity—and in the conflict, the dominant groups usually win. There are multiple levels of domination; as Patricia Hill Collins (1990) describes, domination "operates not only by structuring power from the top down but by simultaneously annexing the power as energy of those on the bottom for its own ends" (pp. 227–28).

As a result, this perspective offers no easy solutions to social problems. The system could be completely overhauled, but that is unlikely to happen. We could reform parts of the structure, but those in power would retain their control. The biggest social problem from this perspective is the system itself and the inequality it perpetuates.

The first to make this argument was German philosopher and activist Karl Marx. Conflict, according to Marx, emerged from the economic substructure of capitalism, which defined all other social structures and social relations. He focused on the conflict based on social class, created by the tension between the **proletariat** (workers) and the **bourgeoisie** (owners). Capitalism did more than separate the haves and the have-nots. Unlike Durkheim, who believed that society created a civilized man, Marx argued that a capitalist society created a man alienated from his **species being**,

Dysfunctions: Negative consequences of social structures

Conflict perspective: A theoretical perspective that considers how society is held together by power and coercion for the benefit of those in power (based on social class, gender, race, or ethnicity)

Proletariat: The working class in a capitalist economy

Bourgeoisie: Capitalist ruling class; owners of businesses

Species being: A human being's true self

Alienation: Separation from one's true self; alienation occurs on multiple levels—from one's work, the product of one's work, other workers, and one's human potential from his true self. **Alienation** occurred on multiple levels: man would become increasingly alienated from his work, the product of his work, other workers, and, finally, his own human potential. For example, a salesperson might be so involved in the process of her work that she doesn't spend quality time with her coworkers, talk with her customers, or stop and appreciate the merchandise. Each sale transaction is the same; all customers and workers are treated alike. The salesperson cannot achieve her human potential through this type of mindless unfulfilling labor. According to Marx, workers needed to achieve a **class consciousness**, an awareness of their social position and oppression, so they could unite and overthrow capitalism, replacing it with a more egalitarian socialist and eventually communist structure.

Widening Marx's emphasis on the capitalist class structure, contemporary conflict theorists have argued that conflict emerges from other social bases, such as values, resources, and interests. Mills ([1959] 2000) argued the existence of a "power elite," a small group of political, business, and military leaders who control our society. Ralf Dahrendorf (1959) explained that conflict of interest is inherent in any relationship because those in powerful positions will always seek to maintain their dominance. Lewis Coser (1956) focused on the functional aspects of conflict, arguing that conflict creates and maintains group solidarity by clarifying the positions and boundaries between groups. Conflict theorists may also take a social constructionist approach, examining how powerful political, economic, and social interest groups subjectively define social problems.

http://upload.wikimedia.org/wikipedia/commons/0/0a/Marx7.jpg

From a conflict perspective, all social problems could be traced back to the economic substructure of capitalism. According to Karl Marx, the organization of capitalist labor eroded one's human potential or what he refered to as species being.

Feminist Perspective

Rosemarie Tong (1989) explains that "feminist theory is not one, but many, theories or perspectives and that each feminist theory or perspective attempts to describe women's oppression, to explain its causes and consequences, and to prescribe strategies for women's liberation" (p. 1). By analyzing the situations and lives of women in society, the **feminist perspective** defines gender (and sometimes race or social class) as a source of social inequality, group conflict, and social problems. For feminists, the patriarchal society is the basis of social problems. **Patriarchy** refers to a society in which men dominate women and justify their domination through devaluation; however, the definition of patriarchy has been broadened to include societies in which powerful groups dominate and devalue the powerless (Kaplan 1994).

Patricia Madoo Lengermann and Jill Niebrugge-Brantley (2004) explain that feminist theory was established as a new sociological perspective in the 1970s, largely because

Class consciousness: Awareness of one's social position

Feminist perspective: A theoretical perspective that defines gender (and sometimes race or social class) as a source of social inequality, group conflict, and social problems

Patriarchy: Society in which the powerful (often men) dominate the powerless (often women)

Misogyny in the Music Industry

Individuals come together in public rallies to voice their concerns about HIV/AIDS policies and funding. These demonstrations galvanize the efforts of advocacy and activist groups, as well as educate the public about HIV/AIDS.

of the growing presence of women in the discipline and the strength of the women's movement. Feminist theory treats the experiences of women as the starting point in all sociological investigations, seeing the world from the vantage point of women in the social world and seeking to promote a better world for women and for humankind.

Although the study of social problems is not the center of feminist theory, throughout its history, feminist theory has been critical of existing social arrangements and has focused on such concepts as social change, power, and social inequality (Madoo Lengermann and Niebrugge-Brantley 2004). Major research in the field has included Jessie Bernard's ([1972] 1982) study of gender inequality in marriage, Collins's (1990) development of Black feminist thought, Dorothy Smith's (1987) sociology from the standpoint of women, and Nancy Chodorow's (1978) psychoanalytic feminism and reproduction of mothering. Although sociologists in this perspective may adopt a conflict, functionalist, or interactionist perspective, their focus remains on how men and women are situated in society, not just differently but also unequally (Madoo Lengermann and Niebrugge-Brantley 2004).

Interactionist Perspective

Interactionist perspective: A micro-level perspective that highlights what we take for granted: the expectations, rules, and norms that we learn and practice without even noticing; interactionists maintain that through our interaction, social problems are created and defined

An **interactionist perspective** focuses on how we use language, words, and symbols to create and maintain our social reality. This micro-level perspective highlights what we take for granted: the expectations, rules, and norms that we learn and practice without even noticing. In our interaction with others, we become the products and creators of our social reality. Through our interaction, social problems are created and defined.

More than any other perspective, interactionists stress **human agency**—the active role of individuals in creating their social environment (Ballantine and Roberts 2012).

George Herbert Mead provided the foundation of this perspective. Also a member of the Chicago School of Sociology, Mead ([1934] 1962) argued that society consists of the organized and patterned interactions among individuals. As Mead defined it, the self is a mental and social process, the reflective ability to see others in relation to ourselves and to see ourselves in relation to others. Our interactions are based on language, based on words. The words we use to communicate with are symbols, representations of something else. The symbols have no inherent meaning and require human interpretation. The term **symbolic interactionism** was coined by Herbert Blumer in 1937. Building on Mead's work, Blumer emphasized how the existence of mind, self, and society emerge from interaction and the use and understanding of symbols (Turner 1998).

How does the self emerge from interaction? Consider the roles that you and I play. As a university professor, I am aware of what is expected of me; as university students, you are aware of what it means to be a student. There are no posted guides in the classroom that instruct us where to stand, how to dress, or what to bring to class. Even before we enter the classroom, we know how we are supposed to behave and even our places in the classroom. We act based on our past experiences and based on what we have come to accept as definitions of each role. But we need each other to create this reality; our interaction in the classroom reaffirms each of our roles and the larger educational institution. Imagine what it takes to maintain this reality: consensus not just between a single professor and his or her students but between every professor and every student on campus, on every university campus, ultimately reaffirming the structure of a university classroom and higher education.

So, how do social problems emerge from interaction? First, for social problems such as juvenile delinquency, an interactionist would argue that the problem behavior is learned from others. According to this perspective, no one is born a juvenile delinquent. Like any other role we play, people learn how to become juvenile delinquents. Although the perspective does not answer the question of where or from whom the first delinquent child learned this behavior, it attempts to explain how deviant behavior is learned through interaction with others.

Second, social problems emerge from the definitions themselves. Objective social problems do not exist; they become real only in how they are defined or labeled. A sociologist using this perspective would examine who or what group is defining the problem and who or what is being defined as deviant or a social problem. As we have already seen with the HIV/AIDS epidemic in the United States, the problem became real only when activists and public health workers called attention to the disease.

Third, the solutions to social problems also emerge from our definitions. Helen Schneider and Anne Ingram (1993) argued that the social construction of target populations influences the distribution of policy benefits or policy burdens. Target populations are groups of individuals experiencing a specific social problem; these groups gain policy attention through their socially constructed identity and political power. The authors identified four categories: advantaged target populations are

Human agency: The active role of individuals in creating their social environment

Symbolic interactionism: Theoretical perspective that examines how we use language, words, and symbols to create and maintain our social reality

Table 1.2 Summary of sociological perspectives: A general approach to examining social problems

	Functionalist	Conflict/Feminist	Interactionist
Level of analysis	**Macro**	**Macro**	**Micro**
Assumptions about society	Order. Society is held together by a set of social institutions, each of which has a specific function in society.	Conflict. Society is held together by power and coercion. Conflict and inequality are inherent in the social structure.	Interaction. Society is created through social interaction.
Questions asked about social problems	How does the problem originate from the social structure? How does the problem reflect changes among social institutions and structures? What are the functions and dysfunctions of the problem?	How does the problem originate from the competition between groups and from the social structure itself? What groups are in competition and why?	How is the problem socially constructed and defined? How is problem behavior learned through interaction? How is the problem labeled by those concerned about it?

positively constructed and politically powerful (likely to receive policy benefits), contenders are politically powerful yet negatively constructed (likely to receive policy benefits when public interest is high), dependent target populations have positive social construction but low political power (few policy resources would be allocated to this group), and deviant target populations are both politically weak and negatively constructed (least likely to receive any benefits).

Jean Schroedel and Daniel Jordan (1998) applied the target population model to U.S. Senate voting patterns between 1982 and 1992, examining the allocation of federal funds to four distinct HIV/AIDS groups. As Schneider and Ingram's (1993) theory would predict, the groups receiving the most funding were those in the advantaged category (war veterans and health care workers), followed by contenders (gay and bisexual men and the general population with AIDS), dependents (spouses and the public), and, finally, deviants (IV drug users, criminals, and prisoners).

- -

What Does It Mean to Me?

A summary of these sociological perspectives is presented in Table 1.2. These sociological perspectives are reintroduced in each chapter as we examine a new social problem or set of problems. As you review each perspective, do not attempt to classify one as the definitive explanation. Consider how each perspective focuses on different aspects of society and its social problems. Which perspective(s) best fits with your understanding of society or your understanding of social problems?

- -

THE SCIENCE OF SOCIOLOGY

Sociology is not commonsense guessing about how the world works. The social sciences rely on "scientific methods to investigate individuals, societies, and social process" and encompass "the knowledge produced by these investigations" (Schutt 2012:9).

Sociological research is divided into two areas: basic and applied. The knowledge we gain through **basic research** expands our understanding of the causes and consequences of a social problem, for example, identifying the predictors of HIV/AIDS or examining the rate of homelessness among AIDS patients. Conversely, **applied research** involves the pursuit of knowledge for program application or policy evaluation (Katzer, Cook, and Crouch 1998); effective program practices documented through applied research can be incorporated into social and medical programs serving HIV/AIDS patients.

Some social scientists disagree about the applied use of data, arguing that the role of science is to describe the world as it is. Others (like me) acknowledge how research and data can inform our understanding of a social problem and consequently identify a solution or a path to some desired change. While the goal of research is to achieve an empirical understanding of our social world, it is not to say that values do not influence the research process. Max Weber, one of the discipline's founders, described how research should have value-relevance. Though he believed that data collection and data analysis should be objectively conducted, Weber noted how "the choice of objects to study would be made on the basis of what is considered important in the particular society in which the researchers live" (Ritzer 2008: 123). Social problems research is important, not only for expanding what we know about the causes and consequences of problems, but also for identifying what can be done to address them.

All research begins with a theory to help identify the phenomenon we're trying to explain and provide explanations for the social patterns or causal relationships between variables (Frankfort-Nachmias and Leon-Guerrero 2013). **Variables** are a property of people or objects that can take on two or more values. For example, as we try to explain HIV/AIDS, we may have a specific explanation about the relationship between two variables—social class and HIV infection. Social class could be measured according to household or individual income, whereas HIV infection could be measured as a positive test for the HIV antibodies. The relationship between these variables can be stated in a **hypothesis**, a tentative statement about how the variables are related to each other. We could predict that HIV infection would be higher among lower-income men and women. In this hypothesis statement, we've identified a **dependent variable** (the variable to be explained, HIV infection) along with an **independent variable** (the variable expected to account for the cause of the dependent variable, social class). Data, the information we collect, may confirm or refute this hypothesis.

Basic research: Exploration of the causes and consequences of a social problem

Applied research: Pursuit of knowledge for program application or policy evaluation

Variables: A property of people or objects that can take on two or more values

Hypothesis: Statement of a relationship between variables

Dependent variable: The variable to be explained

Independent variable: The variable expected to account for the cause of the dependent variable

VOICES IN THE COMMUNITY

JUDITH AUERBACH

Since earning her PhD in Sociology from the University of California, Berkeley, Judith Auerbach has been working outside academia on HIV/AIDS medical research and health policy issues related to women. Throughout her career, Auerbach has had many distinguished appointments—assistant director for social and behavioral sciences in the White House Office of Science and Technology Policy, senior program officer at the Institute of Medicine of the National Academy of Sciences, director of the Behavioral and Social Science Program and HIV prevention science coordinator in the Office of AIDS Research at the National Institutes of Health, and vice president for public policy and program development at amfAR. Currently Auerbach is an adjunct professor in the School of Medicine at the University of California, San Francisco.

In 2011, Auerbach described her role as a public sociologist:

I have a PhD in sociology, but I have chosen to work outside of academia almost all of my career—in government, research, policy, advocacy and community-based organizations. In all these domains, I have attempted to bring the insights of sociology to bear on medical research and health policy deliberations focused on HIV/AIDS, women's health

and gender equity. (quoted in International AIDS Society 2011)

This has sometimes been a challenging role, as I am usually the lone social scientist in the biomedical conversation, particularly around so-called "biomedical technologies" for HIV prevention. Having to constantly educate and convince others about the existence and contributions of social science is exhausting and frustrating. It boggles me that I still have to make the case for understanding the relational and contextual nature of HIV transmission and the need to recognize that people and technologies are interactive and interdependent. But, I have seen progress in recent years, so I'm happy to keep playing the social science missionary through my publications, presentations, and inputs at meetings and conferences. (quoted in Mapping Pathways 2011)

Auerbach and her research colleagues are collecting qualitative data on women's attitudes and knowledge about taking a daily oral pill as part of an HIV prevention protocol. They advocate shifting the HIV/AIDS public health response "from an 'emergency' approach to a longer-term response" (quoted in Mapping Pathways 2011) addressing the maintenance of the disease and its transmission.

What other social problems could a public sociologist study?

Quantitative methods: Research methods that rely on the collection of statistical data and require the specification of variables and scales collected through surveys, interviews, or questionnaires

Research methods can include quantitative or qualitative approaches or a combination. **Quantitative methods** rely on the collection of statistical data. They require the specification of variables and scales collected through surveys, interviews, or questionnaires. **Qualitative methods** are designed to capture social life as participants experience it. These methods involve field observation, depth interviews, or focus groups. Following are definitions of each specific method.

Survey research: This is data collection based on responses to a series of questions. Surveys can be offered in several formats: a self-administered mailed survey, group surveys, in-person interviews, or telephone surveys. For example, information from HIV/AIDS patients may be collected by a survey sent directly in the mail or by a telephone or in-person interview (e.g., Simoni et al. 2006; Sambisa, Curtis, and Mishra 2010).

Qualitative methods: This category includes data collection conducted in the field, emphasizing the observations about natural behavior as experienced or witnessed by the researcher. Methods include participant observation (a method for gathering data that involves developing a sustained relationship with people while they go about their normal activities), focus groups (unstructured group interviews in which a focus group leader actively encourages discussion among participants on the topics of interest), or intensive (depth) interviewing (open-ended, relatively unstructured questioning in which the interviewer seeks in-depth information on the interviewee's feelings, experiences, and perceptions). Sociologists have used various qualitative methods in HIV/AIDS research—collecting data through participant observation at clinics or support groups and focus groups or depth interviews with patients, health care providers, or key informants (e.g., Chakrapani et al. 2007; Akintola 2010).

Historical and comparative methods: This is research that focuses on one historical period (historical events research) or traces a sequence of events over time (historical process research). Comparative research involves multiple cases or data from more than one time period. For example, researchers have examined the effectiveness of HIV/AIDS treatments over time (e.g., Fumaz et al. 2007) and compared infection rates between men and women (e.g., Ballesteros et al. 2006).

Secondary data analysis: Secondary data analysis usually involves the analysis of previously collected data that are used in a new analysis. Large public survey data sets, such as the U.S. Census, the General Social Survey, the National Election Survey, or the International Social Survey Programme, can be used, as can data collected in experimental studies or with qualitative data sets. For HIV/AIDS research, a secondary data analysis could be based on existing medical records (e.g., Tabi and Vogel 2006) or a routine health survey (e.g., Sambisa et al. 2010). The key to secondary data analysis is that the data were not originally collected by the researcher but were collected by another researcher and for a different purpose.

THE TRANSFORMATION FROM PROBLEM TO SOLUTION

Although Mills identified the relationship between a personal trouble and a public issue, less has been said about the transformation of issue to solution. Mills leads us in the right direction by identifying the relationship between public issues and social institutions. By continuing to use our sociological imagination and recognizing the role of larger social, cultural, and structural forces, we can identify appropriate measures to address these social problems. Mills ([1959] 2000) suggests that "the

Qualitative methods: Research methods designed to capture social life as participants experience it

AP Photo/Wichita Falls Times Record News, Torin Halsey

With more than 70 national organizations around the world, Habitat for Humanity is supported primarily by local volunteers. In this photo, volunteers from the Rochester Institute of Technology are building a home during their spring break in Wichita Falls, Texas.

educational and political role of social science in a democracy is to help cultivate and sustain publics and individuals that are able to develop, to live with, and to act upon adequate definitions of personal and social realities" (p. 192).

Modern history reveals that Americans do not like to stand by and do nothing about social problems. Actually, most Americans support efforts to reduce homelessness, improve the quality of education, or find a cure for HIV/AIDS. In some cases, there are no limits to our efforts. Helping our nation's poor has been an administrative priority of many U.S. presidents. President Franklin Roosevelt proposed sweeping social reforms during his New Deal in 1935, and President Lyndon Johnson declared the War on Poverty in 1964. President Bill Clinton offered to "change welfare as we know it" with broad reforms outlined in the Personal Responsibility and Work Opportunity Reconciliation Act of 1996. In 2003, President George W. Bush supported the reauthorization of the 1996 welfare reform bill. During his term in office, President Obama addressed poverty through community development programs like the Promise Zones Initiative. No president or Congress has ever promised to eliminate poverty; instead, each promised only to improve the system serving the poor or to reduce the number of poor in our society.

Solutions require social action—in the form of social policy, advocacy, and innovation—to address problems at their structural or individual levels. **Social policy** is the enactment of a course of action through a formal law or program. Policy making usually begins with identification of a problem that should be addressed; then, specific guidelines are developed regarding what should be done to address the problem. Policy directly changes the social structure, particularly how our government,

Social policy:
Enactment of a course of action through a formal law or program

an organization, or our community responds to a social problem. In addition, policy governs the behavior and interaction of individuals, controlling who has access to benefits and aid (Ellis 2003). Social policies are always being enacted. According to Jacob Lew, President Barack Obama's budget director, "the [federal] budget is not just a collection of numbers, but an expression of our values and aspirations" (as quoted in Herbert 2011:11).

Social advocates use their resources to support, educate, and empower individuals and their communities. Advocates work to improve social services, change social policies, and mobilize individuals. During his first presidential campaign, Barack Obama recalled his work as a community organizer for the Developing Communities Project in Chicago's far South Side. The church-based organization served White, Black, and Latino blue-collar neighborhoods addressing education, public safety, and housing issues.

Service and volunteer opportunities are available to college and university students in the United States and abroad. This student is doing her service work in Kingston, Jamaica, through Emory University's nursing program.

Social innovation may take the form of a policy, a program, or advocacy that features an untested or unique approach. Innovation usually starts at the community level, but it can grow into national and international programming. Millard and Linda Fuller developed the concept of "partnership housing" in 1965, partnering those in need of adequate shelter with community volunteers to build simple interest-free houses. In 1976, the Fullers' concept became Habitat for Humanity International, a nonprofit, ecumenical Christian housing program responsible for building more than 1 million houses worldwide. When Millard Fuller was awarded the Presidential Medal of Freedom, the nation's highest civilian honor, President Clinton described Habitat for Humanity as "the most successful continuous community service project in the history of the United States" (Habitat for Humanity 2004).

MAKING SOCIOLOGICAL CONNECTIONS

In his book *Social Things: An Introduction to the Sociological Life*, Charles Lemert (1997) tells us that sociology is often presented as a thing to be studied. Instead, he argues that sociology is something to be "lived," becoming a way of life. Lemert (1997) writes,

> To use one's sociological imagination, whether to practical or professional end, is to look at the events in one's life, to see them for what they truly are, then to figure out how the structures of the wider world make social things the way they are. No one is a sociologist until she does this the best she can. (p. 105)

Social innovation: Policy, program, or advocacy that features an untested or a unique approach

 Young and Homeless

We can use our sociological imagination, as Lemert (1997) recommends, but we can also take it a step further. As Marx (1972) maintained, "the philosophers have only interpreted the world, in various ways; the point, however is to change it" (p. 107).

Throughout this text, we explore three connections. The first connection is the one between personal troubles and public issues. Each sociological perspective—functionalist, conflict, feminist, and interactionist—highlights how social problems emerge from our social structure or social interaction. While maintaining its primary focus on problems within the United States, this text also addresses the experience of social problems in other countries and nations. The comparative perspective will enhance your understanding of the social problems we experience here.

The sociological imagination will also help us make a second connection: the one between social problems and social solutions. Mills believed that the most important value of sociology was in its potential to enrich and encourage the lives of all individuals (Lemert 1997). In each chapter, we review selected social policies, advocacy programs, and innovative approaches that attempt to address or solve these problems.

Textbooks on this subject present neat individual chapters on a social problem, reviewing the sociological issues and sometimes providing some suggestions about how it can and should be addressed. This book follows the same outline but takes a closer look at community-based approaches, ultimately identifying how *you* can be part of the solution in your community.

I should warn you that this text will not identify a perfect set of solutions to our social problems. Individual action may be powerless against the social structure. Some individuals or groups will have more power or advantage over others. Solutions, like the problems they address, are embedded within complex interconnected social systems (Fine 2006). Sometimes solutions create other problems. For example, United Nations Children's Fund (UNICEF) Chief of Health Mickey Chopra reports that as countries, such as the United States, have focused their attention and funding on the AIDS epidemic worldwide, deaths due to preventable or treatable diseases (e.g., diarrhea and pneumonia) have increased. Diarrhea kills 1.5 million children a year in developing countries, more than AIDS, malaria, and measles combined (Dugger 2009). A program may have worked, but it might no longer exist because of lack of funding or political and public support. Programs and policies are never permanent; they can be modified. Consistent with standards established in many European countries, in 2014 the U.S. Food and Drug Administration lifted the prohibition on blood donation from gay and bisexual men, but kept the prohibition in place for men who have had sex with a man in the last year.

In communities such as yours and mine, individuals and community groups are taking action against social problems. They are women, men, and children, common citizens and professionals, from different backgrounds and experiences. Whether they are working within the system or working to change the system, these individuals are part of their community's solution to a problem. The goal might be to solve one social problem or several or to create what Joel Feagin (2002) describes as a "new global system that reduces injustice, is democratically accountable to

 Solving Problems

SOCIOLOGY AT WORK

DOING SOCIOLOGY

At the end of each chapter, the Sociology at Work feature will examine how your sociological imagination and skills can be used in the workplace.

You may be most familiar with how your sociology professors use their sociological imagination as teachers and researchers. Yet sociology is practiced in a variety of ways and settings beyond academia. Hans Zetterberg, in his 1964 article "The Practical Use of Sociological Knowledge," identified five roles for sociologists: decision maker, educator, commentator/critic, researcher, and consultant. Notice that none of these roles includes *sociologist* in the title. Yet people are doing sociology, using sociological methods and skills or applying their sociological imagination in their work, even though sociology or sociologist is not part of their job description.

According to the U.S. Bureau of Labor Statistics (2014), many Sociology bachelor's degree holders find positions in related fields, such as social services, education, or public policy. Based on their survey of recent bachelor's degree graduates, the American Sociological Association (Spalter-Roth and Van Vooren 2008) reported that about one quarter of full-time working graduates were employed in social service and counseling occupations. Almost 70% of graduates who reported that their jobs were closely related to their Sociology major were very satisfied with their jobs.

In Chapters 2 through 5, we will review how your sociology learning experiences and skill development will be important for your post-college work life. Specific occupations will be examined in Chapters 6 through 15, including social work, criminal justice, public health, education, and medicine. Told through stories of Sociology alumni, these features highlight how sociology can be used in the workplace. In Chapter 16, we'll discuss opportunities in the global job market, and we'll conclude with a discussion on postgraduate study in Chapter 17.

all people, offers a decent standard of living for all, and operates in a sustainable relation to earth's other living systems" (p. 17). As Gary Fine (2006) observes, "those who care about social problems are obligated to use their best knowledge to increase the store of freedom, justice and equality" (p. 14). In the end, I hope you agree that it is important that we continue to do something about the social problems we experience.

In addition, I ask you to make the final connection to social problems and solutions in your community. For this quarter or semester, instead of focusing only on problems reported in your local newspaper or the morning news program, start paying attention to the solutions offered by professionals, leaders, and advocates. Through the Internet or through local programs and agencies, take this opportunity to investigate what social action is taking place in your community. Regardless of whether you define your "community" as your campus, your residential neighborhood, or the city where your college is located, consider what avenues of change can be taken and whether you can be part of that effort.

What Does It Mean to Me?

What Feagin (2002) describes has also been referred to as social justice. Though the term is widely used, there is no single definition. Social justice has different meanings and will vary depending on one's ideology, discipline, and experience. One way to think of social justice is to consider what constitutes a "perfect" society and what it takes to make that happen. How would you define social justice? What is your "perfect" society?

I often tell my students that the problem with being a sociologist is that my sociological imagination has no "off" switch. In almost everything I read, see, or do, there is some sociological application, a link between my personal experiences and the broader social experience that I share with everyone else, including you. As you progress through this text and your course, I hope that you will begin to use your own sociological imagination and see connections between problems and their solutions that you never saw before.

CHAPTER REVIEW

1.1 Define the sociological imagination

The sociological imagination is the ability to recognize the links between our personal lives and experiences and our social world.

1.2 Identify the characteristics of a social problem

A social problem is a social condition that has negative consequences for individuals, our social world, or the physical world. A social problem has objective and subjective realities. The identification of a social problem is a process that happens over time.

1.3 Compare the four sociological perspectives

A functionalist considers how the social problem emerges from society itself. From a conflict perspective, social problems arise from conflict based upon social class or competing interest groups. By analyzing the situations and lives of women in society, feminist theory defines gender (and sometimes race or social class) as a source of social inequality, group conflict, and social problems. An interactionist focuses on how we use language, words, and symbols to construct and define social problems.

1.4 Explain how sociology is a science

Sociologists rely on scientific methods of qualitative and quantitative data collection and analyses to investigate individuals, social processes, and structures.

1.5 Explain the roles of social policy, advocacy, and innovation in addressing social problems

Solutions require social action—in the form of social policy, advocacy, and innovation—to address problems at their structural or individual levels. Social policy is the enactment of a course of action through a formal law or program. Social advocates use their resources to support, educate, and empower individuals and their communities. Social innovation may take the form of a policy, a program, or advocacy that features an untested or unique approach. Innovation usually starts at the community level, but can be applied to national and international programming.

KEY TERMS

alienation, 14

anomie, 13

applied research, 19

basic research, 19

bourgeoisie, 14

class consciousness, 15

conflict perspective, 14

dependent variable, 19

dysfunctions, 14

feminist perspective, 15

functionalist perspective, 13

globalization, 4

human agency, 17

hypothesis, 19

independent variable, 19

interactionist perspective, 16

macro level of analysis, 12

micro level of analysis, 12

objective reality, 7

patriarchy, 15

proletariat, 14

qualitative methods, 21

quantitative methods, 20

social construction of reality, 8

social constructionism, 8

social innovation, 23

social policy, 22

social problem, 7

sociological imagination, 5

sociology, 5

species being, 14

subjective reality, 8

symbolic interactionism, 17

theory, 12

variables, 19

STUDY QUESTIONS

1. How does the sociological imagination help us understand social problems?

2. Select two of the sociological perspectives introduced in this chapter. Compare and contrast how each defines a social problem. What solutions does each perspective offer?

3. Identify the objective and subjective realities of the increasing cost of college.

4. Apply your sociological imagination to the problem of the increasing cost of college. Is this a personal problem only for students who can't afford tuition? Or is the increasing cost of tuition a public issue?

5. Using the social constructionist perspective, analyze how the primary messages in the

2012 presidential campaign (and leading up to the 2016 campaign) were defined by the candidates, political leaders, the media, and public interest groups. In your opinion, what was defined as a social problem?

6. Explain how science and the scientific method help us understand social problems. How is this different from a commonsense understanding of social problems?

7. Select two research methods and explain how each could be used to examine the impact of the rising cost of college on students, their families, and the institution of higher education.

8. What is the relationship among social advocacy, innovation, and policy?

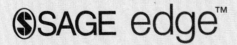

Sharpen your skills with SAGE edge at **edge.sagepub.com/leonguerrero5e**

SAGE edge provides a personalized approach to help you accomplish your coursework goals in an easy-to-use learning environment.

PART I | The Bases of Inequality

Sociologists use the term *social stratification* to refer to the ranking of individuals into social strata or groups. We are divided into groups such as women versus men or African Americans versus Asian Americans. Our lives are also transformed because of our group membership. In U.S. society, being different has come to mean that we are unequal.

The differences between social strata become more apparent when we recognize how some individuals are more likely to experience social problems than others are. Attached to each social position are *life chances*, a term Max Weber used to describe the consequences of social stratification, how each social position provides particular access to goods and services such as wealth, food, clothing, shelter, education, and health care. Sociologists refer to the unequal distribution of resources, services, and positions as social inequality.

In the next five chapters, we will explore two basic sociological questions: Why does social inequality exist, and how are we different from one another? We will review sociological theories that attempt to explain and examine the consequences of social inequality. Although the five bases of inequality are discussed in separate chapters, real life happens at the intersection of our social class, racial and ethnic identity, gender, sexual orientation, and age. These bases of inequality simultaneously define and affect us. We need to recognize how each social characteristic (class, race, ethnicity, gender, sexual orientation, or age) shapes the history, experiences, and opportunities of men, women, and children in the United States (Shapiro 2004) and throughout the world. Your life experience may have less to do with your ability or your hard work and more to do with how (well) you are positioned in society. Ultimately, this includes your experience of social problems.

If this is your first sociology course, these chapters will provide you with an overview of several core sociological concepts. If you have already had a sociology course, welcome back; these chapters should provide a good review.

Social Class

The United States is perceived as one of the world's richest countries. Nonetheless, economic inequality is one of the most important and visible of America's social problems (McCall 2002). President Barack Obama identified "the combined trends of increased inequality and decreasing mobility" as "the defining challenge of our time" (White House 2013). Sociologists Steve McNamee and Robert Miller (2014) observe:

Opinion polls consistently show that Americans continue to embrace the American Dream. But as they strive to achieve it, they have found that it has become more difficult simply to keep up and make ends meet. Instead of "getting ahead", Americans often find themselves working harder just to stay in place, and despite their best efforts, many find themselves "falling behind"—worse off than they were earlier in their lives or compared to their parents at similar points in their lives. (p. 217)

Many Americans believe that their economic status is declining or not improving at all and that there is increasing tension between the rich and the poor (Pew Research Center 2008; Drake 2013). Almost 80% of those surveyed by the Pew Research Center (2008) said that it had been more difficult over the past five years for middle-class people to maintain their standard of living. About two thirds of the 2012 Pew Research Center sample agree that the rich are getting richer and the poor are getting poorer, and more than half believe it is a bad thing for our society (Drake 2013).

In this chapter, we will examine how the overall distribution of wages and earnings has become more unequal and how the distance between the wealthy and the poor has widened considerably in recent decades and worsened during the Great Recession of 2007–2009. The Occupy Wall Street movement highlighted wealth and income inequality through its central protest question: Are you a member of the wealthy 1% or part of the remaining 99%? Martin Marger (2002) writes, "Measured in various ways, the gap between rich and poor in the United States is wider than [in] any other society with comparable economic institutions and standards of living" (p. 48).

According to the U.S. Census, for 2013 the median income was $51,939 (DeNavas-Walt and Proctor 2014). The U.S. Census examines income distribution by dividing the U.S. household population into fifths or quintiles. If all U.S. income were equally divided, each quintile would receive one fifth of the total income. However, based on U.S. Census data for 2013, 51% of the total U.S. income was earned by households in the highest quintile or among households making an average of $185,206. The lowest 20% of households (earning an average of $11,651 per year) had 3.2% of the total income (DeNavas-Walt and Proctor 2014). Inequality first grew between 1973 and 1999, when the top fifth of the distribution began to increase its share of aggregate income, while the bottom four fifths began to lose their share (Jones and Weinberg 2000). A report by the U.S. Congressional Budget Office (2011) revealed that the income for the top 1% increased by 275% from 1979 to 2007. (Refer to Table 2.1.)

Wealth, rather than income, may be more important in determining one's economic inequality. Wealth is usually defined as the value of assets (checking and savings accounts, property, vehicles, and stocks) owned by a household (Keister and Moller 2000) at a point in time. Wealth is measured in two ways: gross assets (the total value of the assets someone owns) and net worth (the value of assets owned minus the amount of debt owed) (Gilbert 2003). Wealth is more stable within families and across generations than is income, occupation, or education (Conley 1999) and can be used to secure or produce wealth, enhancing one's **life chances**.

Life chances: Access provided by social position to goods and services

Table 2.1   Share of aggregate income received by each fifth, 2013

Fifth	Mean Income	Share
Top fifth	$185,206	51.0%
Second fifth	$83,519	23.0%
Third fifth	$52,322	14.4%
Fourth fifth	$30,509	8.4%
Lowest fifth	$11,651	3.2%

SOURCE: DeNavas-Walt and Proctor 2014.

As Melvin Oliver and Thomas Shapiro (1995) explain,

> Wealth is a particularly important indicator of individual and family access to life chances. Wealth is a special form of money not used to purchase milk and shoes and other life necessities. More often it is used to create opportunities, secure a desired stature and standard of living, or pass class status along to one's children. . . . The command over resources that wealth entails is more encompassing than income or education, and closer in meaning and theoretical significance to our traditional notions of economic well-being and access to life chances. (p. 2)

Wealth preserves the division between the wealthy and the nonwealthy, providing an important mechanism for the intergenerational transmission of inequality (Gilbert 2003). Scott Sernau (2001) tells us,

> Wealth begets wealth. . . . It ensures that those near the bottom will be called on to spend almost all of their incomes and that what wealth they might acquire, such as an aging automobile or an aging house in a vulnerable neighborhood, will more likely depreciate than increase in value, and the poor will get nowhere. (p. 69)

Data reveal that wealth is more unequally distributed and more concentrated than income. Since the early 1920s, the top 1% of wealth holders have owned an average of 30% of household wealth. During the late 1980s and 1990s, the top 1% of wealth owners owned more than 45% of all net worth and nearly 50% of all financial assets (Keister and Moller 2000; Wolff 2006). From 2007 to 2010, the proportion of families that reported they had saved money in the previous year fell from 56.4% to 52%. During the same period, median net worth decreased for all income groups except the top 10% (Bricker et al. 2012).

Richard Fry and Rakesh Kochhar (2014) reported how the wealth gap between upper-income and middle-income Americans reached its highest level on record in 2013. The median wealth of upper-income families ($639,400) was 6.6 times greater than the median wealth of middle-income families ($96,500). The wealth ratio is 70 times larger between upper-income and lower-income Americans ($9,300). Fry and Kochhar attribute the decline in middle-class and lower-class family wealth to the Great Recession of 2007–2009, describing these families as "financially stuck" and stating that "the economy recovery has yet to be felt for them."

. . . .

What Does It Mean to Me?

Consider your own income and wealth status. How would you define your social class based on your own income and wealth? Your family's income and wealth? Which reveals more about your life chances?

. . . .

 The Growing Wage Gap

WHAT DOES IT MEAN TO BE POOR?

The often-cited definition of poverty offered by the World Bank is an income of $1.25 per day. This represents "extreme poverty," the minimal amount necessary for a person to fulfill his or her basic needs. According to the organization (World Bank 2009),

> Poverty is hunger. Poverty is lack of shelter. Poverty is being sick and not being able to see a doctor. Poverty is not being able to go to school and not knowing how to read. Poverty is not having a job, is fear for the future, living one day at a time. Poverty is losing a child to illness brought about by unclean water. Poverty is powerlessness, lack of representation and freedom.

Due to significant improvements in education, gender equality, health care, environmental degradation, and hunger, there has been a decline in both the overall poverty rate and the number of poor according to the World Bank (2012). For 1981, a total of 1.94 billion people (or 52% of the population) in the developing world had consumption levels below $1.25. In 2008, the number had declined to 1.29 billion (or 22%), where it remains today.

Sociologists offer two definitions of poverty, absolute and relative poverty. **Absolute poverty** refers to a lack of basic necessities, such as food, shelter, and income. **Relative poverty** refers to a situation in which some people fail to achieve the average income or lifestyle enjoyed by the rest of society. Our mainstream standard of living defines the "average" American lifestyle. Individuals living in relative poverty may be able to afford basic necessities, but they cannot maintain a standard of living comparable to that of other members of society. Relative poverty emphasizes the inequality of income and the growing gap between the richest and poorest Americans. A definition reflecting the relative nature of income inequality was adopted by the European (EU) Council of Ministers: "The poor shall be taken to mean persons, families and groups of persons whose resources (material, cultural and societal) are so limited as to exclude them from the minimum acceptable way of life in the member state in which they live" (European Commission 1985).

[handwritten margin note: Millennials living with parents]

The Federal Definitions of Poverty

There are two federal policy measures of poverty: the poverty threshold and the poverty guidelines. These measures are important for statistical purposes and for determining eligibility for social service programs.

The **poverty threshold** is the original federal poverty measure developed by the Social Security Administration and updated each year by the U.S. Census Bureau. The threshold is used to estimate the number of people in poverty. Originally developed by Mollie Orshansky for the Social Security Administration in 1964, the original poverty threshold was based on the economy food plan, the least costly of four nutritionally adequate food plans designed by the U.S. Department of Agriculture

Absolute poverty: Lack of basic necessities

Relative poverty: Failure to achieve society's average income or lifestyle

Poverty threshold: The original federal poverty measure, based on the economy food plan

(USDA). Based on the 1955 Household Food Consumption Survey, the USDA determined that families of three or more people spent about one third of their after-tax income on food. The poverty threshold was set at three times the cost of the economy food plan. The definition of the poverty threshold was revised in 1969 and 1981. Since 1969, annual adjustments in the levels have been based on the consumer price index (CPI) instead of changes in the cost of foods in the economy food plan.

The poverty threshold considers money or cash income before taxes and excludes capital gains and noncash benefits (public housing, Medicaid, and the Supplemental Nutrition Assistance Program). The poverty threshold does not apply to people residing in military barracks or institutional group quarters or to unrelated individuals younger than age 15 (foster children). In addition, the definition of the poverty threshold does not vary geographically.

The **poverty guidelines**, issued each year by the U.S. Department of Health and Human Services, are used to determine family or individual eligibility for federal programs such as Head Start, the National School Lunch Program, or the Low Income Home Energy Assistance Program. The poverty guidelines are designated by the year in which they are issued. For example, the guidelines issued in January 2014 are designated as the 2014 poverty guidelines, but the guidelines reflect price changes through the calendar year 2013. There are separate poverty guidelines for Alaska and Hawaii. The current poverty threshold and guidelines are presented in Tables 2.2 and 2.3.

Poverty guidelines: Used to determine family or individual eligibility for relevant federal programs

Table 2.2 Poverty threshold in 2013 by size of family and number of related children under 18 years (in dollars)

Size of Family Unit	Related Children Under 18 Years								
	None	1	2	3	4	5	6	7	8+
One person under 65	12,119								
65 years or older	11,173								
Two people									
Householder under 65	15,600	16,057							
Householder 65 or older	14,081	15,996							
Three	18,222	18,751	18,769						
Four	24,028	24,421	23,624	23,707					
Five	28,977	29,398	28,498	27,801	27,376				
Six	33,329	33,461	32,771	32,110	31,128	30,545			
Seven	38,349	38,588	37,763	37,187	36,115	34,865	33,493		
Eight	42,890	43,269	42,490	41,807	40,839	39,610	38,331	38,006	
Nine or more	51,594	51,844	51,154	50,575	49,625	48,317	47,134	46,842	45,037

SOURCE: DeNavas-Walt and Proctor 2014.

Table 2.3 2014 federal poverty guidelines (in dollars)

Size of Family Unit	48 Contiguous States and District of Columbia	Alaska	Hawaii
1	11,670	14,580	13,420
2	15,730	19,660	18,090
3	19,790	24,740	22,760
4	23,850	29,820	27,430
5	27,910	34,900	32,100
6	31,970	39,800	36,770
7	36,030	45,060	41,440
8	40,090	50,140	46,110
For each additional person, add	4,060	5,080	4,670

SOURCE: U.S. Department of Health and Human Services 2014.

Who Are the Poor?

In 2011, the poverty rate was 14.5%, or 46.2 million, compared with the most recent low poverty rate of 11.3%, or 31.6 million, in 2000 (DeNavas-Walt, Proctor, and Smith 2007; DeNavas-Walt and Proctor 2014). This is the first decrease in the rate since 2006. (Refer to this chapter's Exploring Social Problems feature for a summary of poverty statistics for 2013.)

Based on 2013 U.S. poverty figures and redefined racial and ethnic categories, Whites (who reported being White and no other race category, along with Whites who reported being White plus another race category) compose the largest group of poor individuals in the United States. Though 41.5% of the U.S. poor are non-Hispanic Whites, the poverty rate for non-Hispanic Whites is the lowest, at 9.9%. Blacks continue to have the highest poverty rate, 27.2%, followed by Hispanics with a rate of 23.5% (DeNavas-Walt and Proctor 2014). Analysts predict that within a few years, Latinos will have a higher poverty rate than Blacks. Racial segregation and discrimination have contributed to the high rate of minority poverty in the United States. Minority groups are disadvantaged by their lower levels of education, lower levels of work experience, lower wages, and chronic health problems—all characteristics associated with higher poverty rates (Iceland 2003).

According to the National Center for Children in Poverty (2001), children are more likely to live in poverty than Americans in any other age group. Family economic conditions affect the material and social resources available to children. The quality of their education, the neighborhood environment, and exposure to environmental

Who Is Poor?

U.S. Data Map 2.1 Percentage of people in poverty by state, two-year average 2012–2013

20.1+
15.1–20.0
10.1–15.0
0–10.0
Overall: 14.7

SOURCE: DeNavas-Walt and Proctor 2014.

Figure 2.1 Percentage below poverty level by gender, 2013

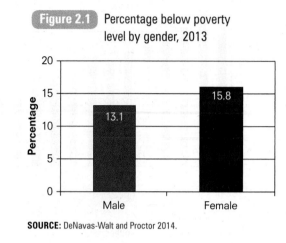

SOURCE: DeNavas-Walt and Proctor 2014.

Figure 2.2 Percentage below poverty by age, 2013

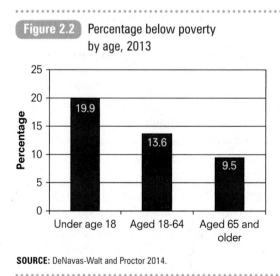

SOURCE: DeNavas-Walt and Proctor 2014.

Figure 2.3 Percentage below poverty by race and ethnicity, 2013

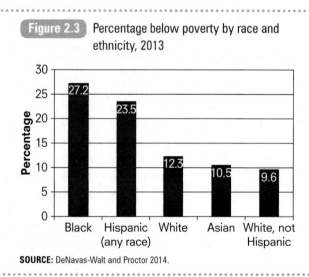

SOURCE: DeNavas-Walt and Proctor 2014.

WHAT DO YOU THINK?

In 2012–2013, the South had the highest poverty rate (16.1%), followed by the West (14.7%), the Midwest (12.9%), and the Northeast (12.7%) (DeNavas-Walt and Proctor 2014). The states with the highest two-year average poverty rates were Louisiana, New Mexico, and Mississippi. The variation in regional rates of poverty may be due to people-specific characteristics (percentage of racial/ethnic minorities, female heads of households) or characteristics based on place (labor market, cost of living).

As discussed in this chapter, your social position determines your life chances of being poor. Groups most likely to experience poverty in the United States are women (especially female householders with no husband present), children, or ethnic/racial minorities (refer to Figures 2.1 through 2.3).

Why are these groups more susceptible to poverty than other groups?

Figure 2.4 The percentage of children (aged 0 to 17) living in households with income below 50% of the national median income, 2013

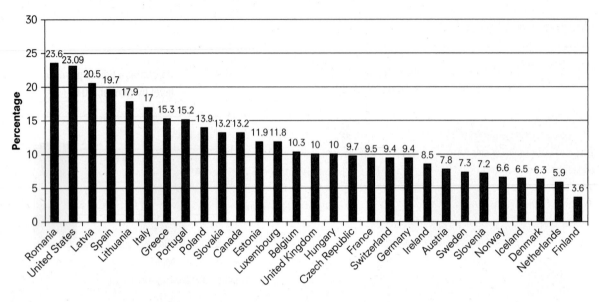

SOURCE: Adapted from UNICEF Office of Research 2013.

contaminants may reinforce and widen the gaps between poorer and more affluent children and adults (Holzer et al. 2008).

The poverty rate among children is higher in the United States than in most other major Western industrialized nations. In 2013, the United Nations Children's Fund (UNICEF) released its report on child well-being in rich countries, identifying the percentage of children living in relative poverty (in households with income below 50% of the national median income). Romania ranks highest at 23.6%, followed by the United States at 23.09%. (Refer to Figure 2.4 for additional data.) The lowest relative child poverty rate is in Finland (3.6%).

The poverty rate for U.S. children peaked in 1993 at 22.5%. In 2013, the poverty rate among children was 19.9% (DeNavas-Walt et al. 2007; DeNavas-Walt and Proctor 2014). The risk of being poor remains high among specific groups. In 2012, there were more poor Hispanic children (5.8 million) than poor Black (4.1 million) or poor White non-Hispanic children (5.2 million). More than two thirds of poor children lived in families with at least one working family member. There remains a wide variation in children's poverty rates among states; in 2012, rates ranged from 13.2% in North Dakota to 34.7% in Mississippi among children under age 18 (Children's Defense Fund 2014).

In 2013, families with a female householder and no spouse present were more likely to be poor than were families with a male householder and no spouse present, 30.6% versus 15.9%. In contrast, the poverty rate for married-couple families was 5.8% (DeNavas-Walt and Proctor 2014). Single-parent families are more vulnerable to poverty because there is only one adult income earner, and female heads of household are disadvantaged even further because women in general make less money than men do.

In their analysis of data from the Luxembourg Income Study, Lee Rainwater and Timothy Smeeding (2003) concluded that American single mothers' children fare worse than the majority of their global counterparts. The poverty rate among U.S. children living in single-mother families is close to 50%; the rate is slightly lower in Germany (48%) and Australia (46%). Countries with poverty rates below 20% include Sweden (7%), Finland (8%), Denmark (11%), Belgium (13%), and Norway (14%). Generous social wage (e.g., unemployment) and social welfare programs reduce the poverty rate in these Nordic countries. Rainwater and Smeeding note that, all combined, U.S. wage and welfare programs are much smaller than similar programs in other countries.

Poverty rates vary across geographic areas because of differences in person-specific and place-specific characteristics (Levernier, Partridge, and Rickman 2000). A region may have a higher rate of poverty because it contains disproportionately higher shares of demographic groups associated with greater poverty, such as racial/ethnic minority groups, female heads of household, and low-skilled workers. Area poverty is also related to place-specific factors, such as the region's economic performance, employment growth, industry structure, and cost of living.

There is an additional category of poverty—the working poor. These are men and women who have spent at least 27 weeks working or looking for work, but whose incomes have fallen below the official poverty level. For 2012, there were 10.6 million working poor (U.S. Bureau of Labor Statistics 2014). Black and Hispanic workers were more than twice as likely as White or Asian workers to be working poor. Individuals with less than a high school diploma were more likely to be classified as working poor than college graduates are. Service occupations accounted for one third of all those classified as working poor (U.S. Bureau of Labor Statistics 2014).

David Brady, Andrew Fullerton, and Jennifer Moren Cross (2010) compared the status of the working poor in the United States to that of 17 other affluent Western democracies. The rate of working poverty was highest in the United States (14.5% of the population). Belgium had the lowest rate of working poor at 2.23%. The sociologists documented how several demographic characteristics were related to the likelihood of being working poor—individuals from households with one income earner, with more children, or with a young household head with low educational attainment.

TAKING A WORLD VIEW

INCOME INEQUALITY IN CHINA

China's income inequality provides an interesting contrast with U.S. inequality. A 2012 survey conducted by Peking University's Chinese Family Panel Studies revealed that households in the top 5% of the income bracket earned 23% of China's total household income, while households in the lowest 5% earned 0.1% of the total income. Average annual income for a family was about $2,100 (converted into U.S. dollars). Average family income was higher for urban families ($2,600) compared to rural families ($1,600) (Wong 2013).

Shi Li, Hiroshi Sato, and Terry Sicular (2013) identify the role of strong structural forces that continue to shape China's income inequality. They describe two sources of inequality rooted in government practices and regulations.

One source is the persistent divide between urban and rural populations, regulated by China's household registration system, also known as the hukou system, established during the Maoist era in the late 1950s. The hukou system serves as an internal passport mechanism to control domestic population movements, limiting migration from rural to urban areas. Since the mid-1990s, as China has moved toward more democratic reforms, Community Party leaders have revised hukou to make it easier for rural migrants to move into urban areas and obtain higher-paying jobs. Yet there are still structural barriers—expensive housing, lack of public services, and lack of health care access—limiting the permanent relocation of rural workers. As a result, rural-to-urban migration is often temporary (Sicular 2013).

Another source of income inequality has been the creation of private property acquisition (Li, Sato, and Sicular 2013). During the Maoist era, private property ownership was prohibited. Laws in the 1990s allowed private property ownership, most of it in urban real estate markets. Complementary legislation also allowed private business ownership. While these policies have lifted many Chinese out of poverty, the privatization of property and business ownership fueled wealth accumulation among urban dwellers and an already privileged upper class (Sicular 2013). According to the Chinese Family Panel Studies, more than 87% of families owned or partially owned property in 2012 (Wong 2013). Recently, the Chinese government tightened banking and real estate policies in an effort to control a booming real estate market. In 2013, single-person households were banned from buying more than one residence in Beijing, the country's capital.

Summarize how structural forces continue to shape China's income inequality.

KIM KYUNG-HOON/REUTERS

Kim Kyung-Hoon/Reuters

Though most of China's citizens have increased their household income and standard of living, poverty still exists in the country. According to the United Nations, about 12 percent of the country lives on less than $1.25 per day.

SOCIOLOGICAL PERSPECTIVES ON SOCIAL CLASS AND POVERTY

Why do some prosper while others remain poor? Why does poverty persist in some families, but other families are able to improve their economic situation? In the next section, we will review the four sociological perspectives to understand the bases of class inequality.

Functionalist Perspective

Functionalists assume that not everyone in society can and should be equal. From this perspective, inequality is necessary for the social order, and it is equally important how each of us recognizes and accepts our status in the social structure. Erving Goffman (1951), an interactionist, offers a functional explanation of **social stratification**, defining it as a universal characteristic of social life. Goffman argues that as we interact with one another, accepting our status in society and acknowledging the status of others, we provide "harmony" to the social order. But "this kind of harmony requires that the occupant of each status act towards others in a manner which conveys the impression that his conception of himself and of them is the same as their conception of themselves and him" (Goffman 1951:294).

Functionalists contend that some individuals are more important to society because of their function to society. For example, society values the lifesaving work of a medical surgeon more than the retail function of a grocery store cashier. Based on the value of one's work or talent, society rewards individuals at the top of the social structure (surgeons) with more wealth, income, or power than those lower down in the social structure (grocery cashiers). According to this perspective, individuals are sorted according to their abilities or characteristics—their age, strength, intelligence, physical ability, or even sex—to play their particular role for society. Certain individuals are better suited for their positions in society than others. Our social institutions, especially education, sort everyone into their proper places and reward them accordingly. Because not all of us can (or should) become surgeons, the system ensures that only the most talented and qualified become surgeons. In many ways, the functionalist argument reinforces the belief that we are naturally different.

. . . .

What Does It Mean to Me?

The functionalist perspective is often criticized for its value argument. Does society accurately assess and reward a position for its value, for its function? For example, the average salary of a kindergarten and elementary school teacher in 2012 was $53,090, whereas the average salary of a National Football League (NFL) player in 2012 was $1.9 million. How does society determine the value of a professional football player? Of a public school teacher?

. . . .

Social stratification:
The ranking of individuals into social strata or groups

Functionalists observe that poverty is a product of our social structure. Specifically, rapid economic and technological changes have eliminated the need for low-skilled labor, creating a population of workers who are unskilled and untrained for this new economy. In many ways, theorists from this perspective expect this disparity among workers, arguing that only the most qualified should fill the important jobs in society and be rewarded for their talent.

Herbert Gans (1971) argued that poverty exists because it is functional for society. Gans explained that the poor uphold the legitimacy of dominant norms. The poor help reinforce cultural ideals of hard work and the notion that anyone can succeed if only he or she tries (so if you fail, it is your fault). Poverty helps preserve social boundaries. It separates the haves from the have-nots by their economics and according to their educational attainment, marriage, and residence. The poor also provide a low-wage labor pool to do the "dirty work" that no one else wants to do. Gans (1995) maintained that the positive functions of poverty should be considered in any antipoverty policy.

Our social welfare system, designed to address the problem of poverty, has been accused of being dysfunctional itself; critics suggest that the welfare bureaucracy is primarily concerned with its own survival. Poverty helps create jobs for the non-poor, particularly the social welfare system designed to assist the poor. As a result, the social welfare bureaucracy will develop programs and structures that will only ensure its survival and legitimacy. Based on personal experience working with and for the system, Theresa Funiciello (1993) observed, "Countless middle class people were making money, building careers, becoming powerful and otherwise benefiting from poverty. . . . The poverty industry once again substituted its own interests for that of poor people" (p. xix). We will discuss this further in the next perspective.

Conflict Perspective

Like the functionalist perspective, the conflict perspective argues that inequality is inevitable, but for different reasons. For a functionalist, inequality is necessary because of the different positions and roles needed in society. From a conflict perspective, inequality is systematically created and maintained by those trying to preserve their advantage over the system.

For Karl Marx, one's social class is solely determined by one's position in the economic system: You are either a worker or an owner of the means of production. Nancy Kreiger, David Williams, and Nancy Moss (1997) offer this explanation of class:

> Class, as such, is not an priori property of individual human beings, but is a social relationship created by societies. One additional and central component of class relations involves an asymmetry of economic exploitation, whereby owners of resources (e.g. capital) gain economically from the labor effort of non-owners who work for them. (p. 346)

Income: Money earned for one's work

Wealth: The value of one's personal assets

But social class, according to Max Weber, is multidimensional. Economic factors include **income**, the money earned for one's work, and **wealth**, the value of one's

 Race and the Wealth Gap

personal assets such as savings and property. A person's social class is also influenced by **prestige**, the amount of social respect or standing given to an individual based on occupation. We assign higher prestige to occupations that require specialized education or training, that provide some social good to society, or that make more money. A final component of class is **power**. Weber defined power as the ability to achieve one's goals despite the opposition of others. Power is the ability to do whatever you want because no one can stop you.

Power is not limited to individuals. People with similar interests (or with similar income, wealth, and prestige backgrounds) often collaborate to increase their advantage in society. C. Wright Mills ([1959] 2000) argued that the United States is ruled by what he called a **power elite**. According to Mills, this elite group is composed of business, political, and military leaders. This elite group has absolute power because of its ability to withhold resources and prevent others from realizing their interests. Mills identified how the power elite effectively make decisions regarding economic policy and national security—controlling the difference between a boom economy and a bust economy or peace and war abroad (Gilbert 2003). Refer to this chapter's In Focus feature for an in-depth look at the modern power elite.

Michael Harrington (1963) argues, "The real explanation of why the poor are where they are is that they made the mistake of being born to the wrong parents, in the wrong section of the country, in the wrong industry, or in the wrong racial or ethnic group" (p. 21). Inequalities built into our social structure create and perpetuate poverty. As Manning Marable (2000) states, capitalism is fraud. Although it promotes the idea that everyone has a fair and equal chance to succeed, advantages are given to members of particular groups based on their gender, race, or social class.

Conflict theorists assert that poverty exists because those in power want to maintain and expand their base of power and interests, with little left to share with others. Welfare bureaucracies—local, state, and national—represent important interest groups that influence the creation and implementation of welfare policies. A welfare policy reflects the political economy of the community in which it is implemented (Handler and Hasenfeld 1991).

Francis Fox Piven and Richard A. Cloward (1993) conclude that the principal function of welfare is to allow the capitalist class to maintain control over labor. Welfare policy has been used by the state to stifle protest and to enforce submissive work norms. During periods of economic crisis, the state expands welfare rolls to pacify the poor and reduce the likelihood of serious uprising. However, during economic growth or stability, the state attempts to reduce the number of people on welfare, forcing the poor or dislocated workers back into the expanding labor force. Those who remain on welfare are condemned and stigmatized for their dependence on the system. For example, in 2011, more than 36 states considered drug testing for Temporary Assistance for Needy Families (TANF) recipients (Sulzberger 2011).

Opponents of this policy argue that punitive testing policies perpetuate the stereotype that people on public assistance are morally corrupt and more likely to use drugs. It also distracts from the need for and access to drug treatment and

Prestige: Social respect or standing

Power: The ability to achieve one's goals despite resistance from others

Power elite: A select group possessing true power

Drug Testing

prevention. A 2012 assessment of the Florida welfare drug test law revealed that there were no direct savings for the state; contrary to the law's intent, it did not identify many drug users and had no effect on reducing the number of individuals applying for welfare assistance (Alvarez 2012). The Florida law was struck down by a federal appeals court in 2014; the court ruled that the state failed to demonstrate that drug abuse was more prevalent or unique among TANF clients than the general population.

Feminist Perspective

Feminist scholars define the welfare state as an arena of political struggle. The drive to maintain male dominance and the patriarchal family is assumed to be the principal force shaping the formation, implementation, and outcomes of U.S. welfare policy (Neubeck and Cazenave 2001).

Social welfare scholar Mimi Abramovitz (1996) notes that welfare has historically distinguished between the deserving poor (widows with children) and the undeserving poor (single and divorced mothers). In the 1970s and 1980s, media and politicians created the image of the "Cadillac driving, champagne sipping, penthouse living welfare queens" (Zucchino 1999:13), suggesting that women—specifically, single mothers—were abusing welfare assistance. Women were accused of having more children to avoid work and to increase their welfare benefits. Marriage, hard work, honesty, and abstinence were offered as solutions to their poverty. The negative stereotypes of poor women stigmatized these women and fueled support for punitive social policies (Abramovitz 1996), and they continue to be a part of welfare policies today.

The bias against women is reproduced systematically in our social institutions. Fraser (1989) argues that there are two types of welfare programs: masculine programs related to the labor market (social security, unemployment compensation) and feminine programs related to the family or household (Aid to Families with Dependent Children [AFDC], food stamps, and Medicaid). The welfare system is separate and unequal. Fraser believes that masculine programs are rational, generous, and nonintrusive, whereas feminine programs are inadequate, intrusive, and humiliating. The quintessential program for women, AFDC, institutionalized the feminization of poverty by failing to provide adequate support, training, and income to ensure self-sufficiency for women (Gordon 1994). The program operated from 1935 to 1996.

Our current welfare system, the Personal Responsibility and Work Opportunity Reconciliation Act (PRWORA) and its TANF program, have been criticized for its treatment of women and their families. PRWORA created a pool of disciplined low-wage laborers: women who must take any job that is available or find themselves and their families penalized by the government (Piven 2002). With its emphasis on work as the path to self-sufficiency, TANF forces women back to the same low-pay, low-skill jobs that may have led them to their poverty in the first place (Lafer 2002; Gilman 2012). The new program requirements, as Debra Henderson, Ann Tickamyer, and Barry Tadlock (2005) argue, also deny women the choice to be full-time mothers. Eligibility guidelines force poor women to work, making them choose

IN FOCUS

THE POWER OF POLITICAL ACTION COMMITTEES

G. William Domhoff (2002) argues that real power is **distributive power**, the power individuals or groups have over other individuals or groups. Power matters when a group has the ability to control strategic resources and opportunities to obtain such resources. Money, land, information, and skills are strategic resources when they are needed by individuals to do what they want to do (Hachen 2001). Domhoff argues that distributive power is limited to an elite group of individuals whose economic, political, and social relationships are closely interrelated. Control over four major social networks—economic, political, military, and religious—can be turned into a strong organizational base for wielding power (Mann 1986).

Political action committees (PACs) have been characterized as extensions of the influence of the power elite. While contributions to a candidate's campaign are limited to $2,500 per election from each individual donor, PACs, or super PACs as they are more often referred to, can collect unlimited amounts from individuals and corporations. In 1947, corporations were banned from using their profits to endorse or oppose political candidates; however, in 2010, the U.S. Supreme Court ruled the restriction unconstitutional and allowed corporations the same rights as individuals when it comes to political speech (the donation of money).

Campaign-finance reform activists predicted that the ruling would increase the influence of special interest groups, allowing what has been characterized as a corruption of our democracy or corporate electioneering. Though PACs cannot formally coordinate their activities or communicate exclusively with candidates, PACs are closely aligned with candidates and important sources for campaign money. For example, Sheldon and Miriam Adelson donated $10 million to Winning Our Future, the PAC that supported Newt Gingrich's 2012 presidential campaign. The Adelsons are longtime friends and supporters of Gingrich. Their contribution was described as leveling the political playing field between Gingrich and Governor Mitt Romney in critical primaries in Florida and South Carolina (Confessore 2012). The Adelsons supported Restore Our Future, Romney's PAC.

Another influential political coalition is the group of organizations known as the 527s, independent political groups named for a section of the Internal Revenue Service tax code that regulates the financial activities of all political groups. Like PACs, there are no restrictions on contributions to 527s. During the 2004 presidential election, Senator John Kerry was targeted by the 527 Swift Boat Veterans for Truth, who falsely attacked his Vietnam service record. The campaign was so memorable that the term *swift boating* has come to refer to an untrue or unfair political attack.

---

between the competing roles of good mother and good welfare recipient. The new policies fail to address the real barriers facing women: low job skills and educational attainment, racism and discrimination in the labor market, and the competing demands of work and caring for their children.

Distributive power: Power over other individuals or groups

Interactionist Perspective

An interactionist would draw attention to how class differences are communicated through symbols, how the meaning of these symbols is constructed or constrained

 Income Inequality by State

by social forces, and how these symbols reproduce **social inequality**. Our language reflects the quality of life that is associated with different amounts of economic resources. We distinguish the "very rich" from the "stinking rich" and someone who is "poor" from someone who is "dirt poor" (Rainwater and Smeeding 2003).

Some sociologists have suggested that poverty is based on a **culture of poverty**, a set of norms, values, and beliefs that encourage and perpetuate poverty. In this view, moral deficiencies of individuals or their families lead to a life of poverty. Oscar Lewis (1969), Edward Banfield (1974), and Myron Magnet ([1993] 2000) argue that the poor are socialized differently (e.g., living from moment to moment) and are likely to pass these values on to their children. Patterns of generational poverty—poor parents have poor children, who in turn become poor adults, and so on—seem to support this theory.

Yet the culture of poverty explanation has been widely criticized. Opponents argue that there is no evidence that the poor have a different set of values and beliefs. This perspective defines poverty as a persistent state; that is, once you are poor, your values prohibit you from ever getting out of poverty. In fact, poverty data reveal that for most individuals and families, continuous spells of poverty are likely to last less than two years (Harris 1993).

Interactionists also focus on the public's perception of welfare and of welfare recipients. Most Americans do not know any welfare recipients personally or have any direct contact with the welfare system. Their views on welfare are likely to be shaped by what they see on television and by what they read in newspapers and magazines (Weaver 2000). As a society, we have developed a sense of the "undeserving poor"; dependent mothers and fathers and nonworking recipients have become powerful negative symbols in society (Norris and Thompson 1995). Critics of social programs for the poor fear that the United States is becoming an entitlement society, creating a large segment of the population who would rather depend on government benefits than work (Sherman, Greenstein, and Ruffing 2012). During the 2012 presidential campaign, Governor Mitt Romney was secretly taped promoting this negative rhetoric of public assistance. In his comments, Romney referred to the 47% of Americans who were dependent on the government and who believed they were victims. Romney said his job was "not to worry about those people." His statements are at odds with welfare program facts: more than 90% of those on entitlement and mandatory programs are the elderly (people 65 and over), disabled, and members of working households (Sherman et al. 2012).

Martin Gilens (1999) explains that *welfare* has become a code word for *race*. Race and racism are important in understanding public and political support for antipoverty programs (Lieberman 1998; Neubeck and Cazenave 2001; Quadagno 1994). Gilens states that Americans perceive welfare as a Black phenomenon, believing that Blacks make up 50% of the poor population (compared with an actual 25%). This belief is exacerbated by the notion that Blacks are on welfare not because of blocked opportunities, but largely because of their lack of effort.

Gilens (1999) asserts that the news media are primarily responsible for building this image of Black poverty, that is, for the "racialization of poverty." During the

Social inequality:
Unequal distribution of resources, services, and positions

Culture of poverty: A set of norms, values, and beliefs that encourage and perpetuate poverty

War on Poverty in the early 1960s, the media focused on White rural America, but as the civil rights movement began to build in the mid-1960s, the media turned their attention to urban poverty, and the racial character of poverty coverage changed. Between 1965 and 1967, sensationalized portrayals of Black poverty were used to depict the waste, inefficiency, or abuse of the welfare system, whereas positive coverage of poverty was more likely to include pictures and portrayals of Whites. After 1967 and for most of the following three decades, larger proportions of Blacks appeared in news coverage of most poverty topics. "Black faces are unlikely to be found in media stories on the most sympathetic subgroups of the poor, just as they are comparatively absent from media coverage of poverty during times of heightened sympathy for the poor" (Gilens 1999:132). According to Gilens, this exaggerated link between Blacks and poverty is a serious obstacle to public support for antipoverty programs.

A review of all sociological perspectives is presented in Table 2.4.

Table 2.4 Summary of sociological perspectives: Inequalities based on social class

	Functionalist	**Conflict/Feminist**	**Interactionist**
Explanations of social class and poverty	Inequality is inevitable and emerges from the social structure. Poverty serves a social function.	Inequality is systematically maintained by those trying to preserve their class advantage. Class is based on multiple dimensions—income, wealth, prestige, and power. Welfare bureaucracies represent important interest groups that influence the creation and implementation of welfare policies.	Each social class has a specific set of norms, values, and beliefs. Poverty is a learned phenomenon based on a "culture of poverty" that encourages and perpetuates poverty. The public's perception of the welfare system and of welfare recipients is shaped by the media, political groups, and stereotypes.
Questions asked about social class and poverty	What are the functions and dysfunctions of inequality? What portions of society benefit from poverty?	What powerful interest groups determine class inequalities? How do our welfare policies reflect specific political, economic, and social interest groups?	Is poverty learned behavior? How are our perceptions of the poor determined by the media, news reports, and politicians? Has society created two images—the deserving versus the undeserving poor? Are these images accurate?

THE CONSEQUENCES OF POVERTY

The following section is not an exhaustive list of the consequences of poverty. Remaining chapters will also highlight the relationship between social class and the experience of a specific social problem (such as educational attainment or access to health care). Given the intersectionality of all the bases of inequality covered in this section of the book, there is a persistent overlap in the experience of social problems as a result of one's class, race, gender, sexual orientation, and age.

Food Insecurity and Hunger

About 15% of households, or 17.6 million American families, were food insecure for at least some time during 2011 to 2012 (Coleman-Jensen, Nord, and Singh 2013). Analysts attribute the increase to rising unemployment rates and food prices. **Food insecure** means that these families did not always have access to enough food for all members of the household to enjoy active and healthy lives. Fifty-nine percent of the food-insecure households said they had participated during the previous month in one or more federal food and nutrition assistance programs—the National School Lunch Program, the Supplemental Nutrition Assistance Program (described below), or the Special Supplemental Nutrition Program for Women, Infants and Children. The prevalence of food insecurity is higher for certain groups: single-female-headed households with children (35.4%), Black households (24.6%), Hispanic households (23.3%), and households with income below the poverty line (40.9%) (Coleman-Jensen et al. 2013). Food insecurity was more common in large cities and rural areas than in suburban areas and exurban areas around larger cities.

The USDA provided food assistance through one of 17 public food assistance programs. The U.S. food stamp program, now called the Supplemental Nutrition Assistance Program (SNAP), is the nation's largest nutrition program for low-income individuals and families. During 2013, the program served an average of 47 million low-income Americans each month. The average monthly benefit was $133 per person, $275 per household. Food stamps cannot be used to buy nonfood items (personal hygiene supplies, paper products), alcoholic beverages, vitamins and medicines, hot food products, or any food that will be eaten in the store. SNAP is described as a powerful tool in fighting poverty by the Center on Budget and Policy Priorities (2013a). Serving as a bridge program, SNAP provides temporary assistance to individuals and families during periods of unemployment or a crisis (Center on Budget and Policy Priorities 2013a). Although SNAP and other USDA programs have been shown to be effective in improving the purchasing power and nutritional

Food insecure: Lacking in access to sufficient food for all family members

Insecurity Persists
Despite Food Stamps

Food Insecurity
and Hunger

status of specific populations, a large segment of low-income Americans are not being adequately served or served at all by these programs. In 2012, only 67% of individuals who qualified for SNAP benefits participated in the program (Center on Budget and Policy Priorities 2013a).

For one week in 2007, Governor Theodore R. Kulongoski (D-OR) challenged fellow Oregonians to join him and his wife Mary in living on an average Oregon food stamp budget of $21 per week per person, or $3 a day. His efforts drew state, national, and global attention to food insecurity in his home state of Oregon, as well as the need for the federal government to preserve the current level of food stamp benefits. Before his challenge week, the governor and his wife had each spent an average of $51 per week on food, not including his meals while at work or during official functions; during his challenge week, their final food bill was $20.97 per person. Governor Kulongoski reported several challenges he and his wife experienced throughout the week—the demoralizing experience of not having enough to pay for all the food in their cart, having to make tough decisions on the quality and amount of food they could purchase, and experiencing hunger throughout the week as their food supply ran out (Kulongoski 2007). Since Kulongoski's challenge, there have been annual food stamp budget challenges sponsored by faith leaders, politicians, and news reporters, highlighting the difficulties of eating a healthy and sustainable diet on the standard food stamp allotments.

Republican congressional leaders supported deep cuts in the SNAP program in 2013, arguing that the program had grown too big and expensive and was another source of government dependency. Republicans advocated closing program loopholes and adding work requirements for recipients. When the 2014 Farm Bill was signed into law, it included $8.7 billion in cuts in the SNAP budget over 10 years, with some pilot work programs (Grovum 2014). Policy analysts predicted that the reduction would affect 850,000 recipients in 14 states and the District of Columbia, reducing their monthly benefit by an average of $90. However, most have been able to preserve their SNAP benefits by relying on a SNAP loophole, the "Heat and Eat" provision. Under the provision, a household is entitled to more food aid if it is enrolled in the federally funded Low Income Home Energy Assistance Program (LIHEAP). Previously, households would be eligible for LIHEAP if they received a minimum of $1.00 per year. Congress changed the law, increasing the minimum to $20 per year. In response, states increased their LIHEAP funding to support the new federal minimum, thus ensuring SNAP eligibility to more individuals and families (Grovum 2014).

As reported by Briefel et al. (2003), food pantries and emergency kitchens play an important role in the nutritional safety net for America's low-income and needy populations. These organizations are part of the Emergency Food Assistance System, a network of private organizations operating with some federal support. Almost one third of pantry client households and two fifths of kitchen client households are at or below 50% of the poverty line. The mean monthly income is $781 for pantry client households and $708 for kitchen client households. Food pantries considered by Briefel et al. were likely to serve families with children (45% of households included

Absolute Poverty

children), whereas emergency kitchens were likely to serve men living alone (38%) or single adults living with other adults (18%).

The U.S. Conference of Mayors (2014) reported that emergency food assistance had increased by an average of 7% in 25 surveyed cities. Unemployment was identified as the leading cause of hunger, followed by low wages, poverty, and high housing costs. Fifty-six percent of individuals requesting emergency food assistance were families. In 2013–2014, an average of 27% of the people needing emergency food assistance did not receive it.

Affordable Housing

Although most Americans still aspire to own a home, for many poor and working Americans, home ownership is just a dream (Freeman 2002). Despite the decline in home sales and values, housing affordability has declined (Savage 1999). The generally accepted definition of affordability is for a family to pay no more than 28% of its annual income on housing (30% for a rental unit). Nearly one in four working households (households where individuals work more than 20 hours per week and have a household income of no more than 120% of the median income in the area) spends more than half its income on housing costs (Williams 2012). Renters are more than twice as likely as homeowners to pay more than half their income for housing (Fischer and Sard 2013).

Lance Freeman (2002) explains that because housing is the single largest expenditure for most households, "housing affordability has the potential to affect all domains of life that are subject to cost constraints, including health" (p. 710). Most families pay their rent first, buying basic needs such as food, clothing, and health care with what they have left. The lack of public assistance, increasing prices, slow wage growth, and a limited inventory of affordable apartments and houses make it nearly impossible for some to find adequate housing (Pugh 2007).

The combination of low earnings and scarce housing assistance results in serious housing problems for the working poor. According to the National Low Income Housing Coalition (Arnold et al. 2014), there is no state where a full-time minimum-wage worker can afford a modest one- or two-bedroom unit. In 2014, it took, on average, 2.6 minimum-wage jobs to afford a modest two-bedroom unit. About 50% of all renters were using over 30% of their income for housing (Arnold et al. 2014). Increasing the minimum wage would not solve the affordable housing problem. Low-income households remain at higher risk for experiencing housing instability, eviction, poor housing conditions, and homelessness.

Consider the housing situation of Alice Greenwood and her 6-year-old son, Makalii (Magin 2006). When the home she had rented for 30 years for $300 a month was sold, she and her son joined some 1,000 people living in tents along the 13-mile stretch of beaches on the Waianae Coast of Oahu, Hawaii. In Waianae, homes that had rented for $200 to $300 per month a couple of years before now average more than $1,000 per month. For 2007, the median price of a home on

Robert Nickelsberg/Getty Images

Pictured here is a playground in the shadows of smoke and steam vapor stacks at the Bruce Mansfield Power Plant in Shippingport, Pennsylvania. The Bruce Mansfield Power Plant is one of 12 large coal plants in the U.S. emitting tons of carbon dioxide and particulate pollution annually. Fine particulate pollution has been associated with asthma attacks and heart and lung disease.

Oahu was $665,000. Most of Greenwood's tent neighbors are employed in service and construction sectors. The state's homeless shelter is not a viable option for Greenwood and other beach residents—it would take them away from their communities (it is about 10 miles from the beach park) and would make commuting difficult (it is located several miles from the nearest bus route).

Health

Regardless of the country where a person lives, social class is a major determinant of one's health and life expectancy (Braveman and Tarimo 2002); those lower on the socioeconomic ladder have worse health than those above them (Marmot 2004). The link between class and health has been confirmed in studies conducted in Australia, Canada, Great Britain, the United States, and Western Europe (Cockerman 2004). Although no factor has been singled out as the primary link between socioeconomic position and health, scholars have offered many factors—standard of living, work conditions, housing conditions, access to better-quality food, leisure activities, and the social and psychological connections with others at work, at home, or in the community—to explain the relationship (Krieger, Williams, and Moss 1997). According to Nancy Krieger and her colleagues (1997: 343) "poor living and working conditions impair health and shorten lives."

Rose Weitz (2001) offers several explanations for the unhealthy relationship between poverty and illness. The type of work available to poorly educated people can cause illness or death by exposing them to hazardous conditions. Poor and middle-class individuals who live in poor neighborhoods are exposed to air, noise, water, and chemical pollution that can increase rates of morbidity and mortality. Inadequate and unsafe housing contributes to infectious and chronic diseases, injuries, and illnesses, including lead poisoning when children eat peeling paint. The diet of the poor increases the risk of illness. The poor have little time or opportunity to practice healthy activities such as exercise, and because of life stresses, they may also be encouraged to adopt behaviors that might further endanger their health. Finally, poverty limits individual access to preventative and therapeutic health care.

The relationship between health and social class afflicts those most vulnerable, the young. Children in poor or near-poor families are two to three times more likely not to have a usual source of health care than are children in nonpoor families (Federal Interagency Forum on Child and Family Statistics 2007). Access to a regular doctor or care facility for physical examinations, preventative care, screening, and immunizations can facilitate the timely and appropriate use of pediatric services for youth. Even children on public insurance (which includes Medicaid and the State Children's Health Insurance Program) are more likely not to have a usual source of care than are children with private insurance. Children in families below the poverty level have lower rates of immunization and yearly dental checkups (both basic preventative care practices) than do children at or above the poverty level (Federal Interagency Forum on Child and Family Statistics 2007). Refer to Chapter 10, "Health and Medicine," for more on the impact of social class on health care access and quality.

RESPONDING TO CLASS INEQUALITIES

U.S. Welfare Policy

Throughout the 20th century, U.S. welfare policy has been caught between two values: the desire to help those who cannot help themselves and the concern that assistance could create dependency (Weil and Feingold 2002). The centerpiece of the social welfare system was established by the passage of the Social Security Act of 1935. The act endorsed a system of assistance programs that would provide for Americans who could not care for themselves: widows, the elderly, the unemployed, and the poor.

Under President Franklin D. Roosevelt's New Deal, assistance was provided in four categories: general relief, work relief, social insurance, and categorical assistance. General relief was given to those who were not able to work; most of the people receiving general relief were single men. Work relief programs gave government jobs to those who were unemployed through programs such as the Civilian Conservation Corps and the Works Progress Administration. Social insurance programs

President Lyndon Johnson's War on Poverty

included social security and unemployment compensation. Categorical assistance was given to poor families with dependent children, to the blind, and to the elderly. To serve this group, the original welfare assistance program, Aid to Dependent Children (later renamed AFDC), was created (Cammisa 1998).

Categorical programs became the most controversial, and the social insurance programs were the most popular. It was widely believed that social insurance paid people for working, whereas categorical programs paid people for not working. Shortly after these programs were implemented, officials became concerned that individuals might become dependent on government relief (Cammisa 1998). Even President Roosevelt (quoted in Patterson 1981) expressed his doubts about the system he helped create: "Continued dependence upon relief induces a spiritual and moral disintegration fundamentally destructive to the national fibre. To dole out relief in this way is to administer a narcotic, a subtle destroyer of the human spirit" (p. 60).

Soup kitchens emerged in the United States during the Great Depression, operated primarily by churches and local charities. Soup and bread meals were easy to to prepare and serve to the poor and unemployed.

The next great expansion of the welfare system occurred in the mid-1960s, when President Lyndon Johnson (1965) declared a War on Poverty and implemented his plan to create a Great Society. Rehabilitation of the poor was the cornerstone of Johnson's policies, and what followed was an explosion of social programs: Head Start, Upward Bound, Neighborhood Youth Corps, Job Corps, public housing, and affirmative action. Although poverty was not completely eliminated, defenders of the Great Society say that these programs alleviated poverty, reduced racial discrimination, reduced the stigma attached to being poor, and helped standardize government assistance to the poor. Conversely, opponents claim that these programs coddled the poor and created a generation that expected entitlements from the government (Cammisa 1998).

During the more than 50 years when the AFDC program operated, welfare rolls were increasing, and, even worse, recipients were staying on government assistance for longer periods. In a strange irony, welfare, the solution for the problem of poverty, became a problem itself (Norris and Thompson 1995). Between 1986 and 1996, many states began to experiment with welfare reforms. Wisconsin was the first state to implement such a reform with a program that included work requirements, benefit limits, and employment goals.

In 1996, PRWORA was passed with a new focus on helping clients achieve self-sufficiency through employment. PRWORA was a bipartisan welfare reform plan to reduce recipients' dependence on government assistance through strict work requirements and welfare time limits. Replacing AFDC, the new welfare program is called Temporary Assistance for Needy Families (TANF). Instead of treating assistance as an entitlement, as it was under AFDC, TANF declares that government help is temporary and has to be earned. Under TANF, there is a federal lifetime limit of 60 months (five years) of assistance, although states may put shorter limits on benefits. PRWORA also gave states primary responsibility for designing their assistance programs and for determining eligibility and benefits.

The act had an immediate effect on the number of poor. When PRWORA became law, the poverty rate was 13.7%; 36.5 million individuals were poor, by the government's definition. A year later, the rate had declined to 13.3%, and 35.6 million were poor. Rates declined to their lowest point in 2000, 11.3% or 31.6 million. According to the U.S. Census Bureau, the 2000 poverty rate was the lowest since 1979 (DeNavas-Walt et al. 2007).

PRWORA was reauthorized under the Deficit Reduction Act of 2005. The reauthorization requires states to engage more TANF clients in productive work activities leading to self-sufficiency. The five-year cumulative lifetime limit for TANF recipients remains unchanged. Funding was also provided for healthy marriage and responsible fatherhood initiatives (U.S. Department of Health and Human Services 2006).

During the 2007–2009 recession, there was increased concern that poverty was on the rise, straining the safety net of TANF and other government support programs. A depressed economy challenges everyone, but especially those already poor. According to Austin Nichols (2011), history shows that unemployment and poverty rates continue to rise after a recession ends. The effects of poverty deepen over time as individuals exhaust private resources and temporary benefits. The rate of deep poverty (incomes less than half the poverty level) increased from 6.3% in 2009 to 6.7% in 2010. Nichols (2011) advises, "Federal government initiatives are laudable, but cash-strapped families scarred by the labor market and housing market collapses will need more direct help, temporary or not" (p. 2).

Life After Welfare

A strong economy and increased aid to low-income working families contributed to the immediate decline in welfare caseloads after PRWORA (Besharov 2002). Welfare officials often point to how the first to leave welfare were those with the most employable skills. However, research indicates that the early employment success of welfare reform diminished as the economy faltered. According to the Urban Institute, 32% of welfare recipients were in paid jobs in 1999, but the number had fallen to 28% by 2002. Employment also declined for those who left welfare, from 50% in 1999 to 42% in 2002 (Zedlewski and Loprest 2003).

Under federal law, states are required to engage at least 50% of TANF families in work activities (e.g., employment or job search). The law limits the degree to which education and training count toward the work participation rate. According to the Center for Women Policy Studies (2002), after PRWORA, college enrollment among low-income women declined. Yet studies indicate that former TANF recipients with a college education are more likely to stay employed and less likely to return to welfare. For example, a study among former welfare recipients in Oregon found that only 52% of those with less than a high school diploma were employed after two years. In contrast, 90% of former TANF recipients with a bachelor's degree were still employed. Since 1996, 49 states—Oklahoma and the District of Columbia are exceptions—passed legislation to allow secondary education to count as activity under PRWORA.

Sandra Morgen, Joan Acker, and Jill Weigt (2010) examined the consequences of welfare reform among poor individuals and their families in Oregon from 1998 to 2002. Though more than half to three quarters of the TANF clients they followed were employed when they left the welfare rolls, they were working in low-wage occupations and earning wages so low that almost half had incomes below the official poverty line. Once off welfare, the majority of families continued to struggle to make ends meet and were forced to make tough decisions—for example, putting off medical care, skipping meals to stretch their food budget, or dealing with their utilities being turned off. Many continued to rely on benefits from Oregon's Adult and Family Services. The sociologists concluded that self-sufficiency was still elusive for many families. "Having to depend on low-wage work leaves millions of families facing a combination of job insecurity, inadequate household income, long hours of work, unsatisfactory child care arrangements, and lack of health insurance, sick leave or retirement benefits" (Morgen et al. 2010:148).

Though TANF evaluation studies reveal overall increases in employment, income, and earnings of families formerly on welfare, many families remained poor or near poor and struggled to maintain employment (Hennessy 2005) even before the 2007 recession. In their five-year study of TANF recipients in New Jersey, Robert Wood, Quinn Moore, and Anu Rangarajan (2008) found that recipients experienced economic progress and setbacks in the years after entering the program. On average, recipients' employment and income levels increased and poverty levels declined for recipients during the five-year period. However, their average income levels were low, about $20,000 per year, and almost half had incomes below the poverty line. Many recipients exited the labor market or returned to poverty sometime during the five years they were tracked. Most at risk were those without a high school degree, with limited work histories, and with work-limiting health conditions.

Eugenie Hildebrandt and Sheryl Kelber (2012) examined the experiences of women who were in different stages of TANF participation in a large Wisconsin urban county. Wisconsin was one of the first stages to experiment with work-based welfare and program limits. Their study included women who had exhausted their time limit. Hildebrandt and Kelber discovered that the women were unable to meet the needs of their families during or after being in the TANF program. They concluded, "TANF does not have the depth, breadth, or flexibility to adequately address multiple, complex barriers to work" (p. 138). "Barriers of limited education and work skills for well-paying jobs, chronic mental and physical health problems, and

VOICES IN THE COMMUNITY

MAURICIO LIM MILLER

Mauricio Lim Miller is the founder and CEO of the Family Independence Initiative (FII), a nontraditional antipoverty program. FII was launched as a research project by Lim Miller and then Oakland Mayor Jerry Brown in 2001. The program allows low-income families to find their own way to self-sufficiency, establishing their own initiatives and finding success. Instead of telling poor families what to do, FII provides a context in which families "can discover for themselves what's important to them and how they can best achieve those goals" (Burak 2001:27). According to Lim Miller (quoted in Bornstein 2011),

> when you come into a community that is vulnerable with professionals with power and preset ideas, it is overpowering to families and it can hold them back. Nobody wants to hear that because we are all good guys. But the focus on need undermines our ability to see their strengths—and their ability to see their own strengths.

The program promotes the importance of connections through social networks, greater choices, and the ability to create economic capital.

FII began with 25 families in three cohorts—8 African American families, 6 Salvadoran refugee families, and 11 Iu Mien families (Bornstein 2011). Family groups were asked to write down their goals (e.g., improving child's grades, starting business, buying a home), with FII promising to pay each family $30 for every success, a maximum of $200 per month. Families need to work on their plans together and report their progress to each other and to FII staff. The program structure builds a social network and social capital among the participating families (Burak 2011). The program is unstructured, but "the families have done well because we give them room to do whatever they feel they need to do to get ahead," says Lim (quoted in Fessler 2012).

Assessment data revealed that among the first group of 25 families, household incomes increased 25% after two years. Even after FII's payments stopped, incomes continued to increase, up to 40% higher than the baseline. Lim Miller also established his program in Hawaii and San Francisco. Client success was documented at these sites, with family incomes increasing by 23% and savings by 240% (Bornstein 2011).

In 2010, Lim Miller was invited to join President Obama's White House Council for Community Solutions, a group of individuals who have "dedicated their lives and careers to civic engagement and social innovation" (White House 2010).

As of 2014, the program had established six program sites.

---

personal and family challenges left them few options for escaping poverty" (p. 139). Among the women in the terminated group, the majority had chronic health problems (93%) and depressive symptoms (78%).

In 2012, the Obama administration gave states more control over how they administer their TANF program, instituting an experimental program for states to "test alternative and innovative strategies, policies and procedures that are designed to improve employment outcomes for needy families" (U.S. Department of Health and Human Services 2012).

Earned Income Tax Credit

Enacted in 1975, the Earned Income Tax Credit (EITC) program provides federal tax relief for low-income working families, especially those with children. The credit reduces the amount of federal tax owed and usually results in a tax refund for those who qualify. Similar programs are offered in the United Kingdom, Canada, France, and New Zealand. To qualify for the U.S. program, adults must be employed. A single parent with one child who had family income of less than $37,870 (or $43,210 for a married couple with one child) in 2013 could get a credit of as much as $3,250. The EITC can be claimed for children under age 19, or under age 24 if they are still in college.

Expansions of the program in the late 1980s and early 1990s made the credit more generous for families with two or more children. In 1994, a small credit was made available to low-income families without children (Freidman 2000). Receipt of the EITC does not affect receipt of other programs such as food stamp benefits, Medicaid, or housing subsidies. In 2009, the EITC was expanded to low-earning single and married workers without children, noncustodial parents, and parents with adult independent children.

Supporters of the EITC argue that the program strengthens family self-sufficiency, provides families with more disposable income, and encourages work among welfare recipients. The program acts as a short-term safety net during periods of shock to income (e.g., loss of job) or family structure (e.g., divorce) or as a long-term income support for multiple spells of income loss or poverty (Dowd and Horowitz 2011). Families use their credits to cover basic necessities, home repair, vehicle maintenance, or education expenses (Center on Budget and Policy Priorities 2012). Almost half of EITC recipients planned to save all or part of their refund (Smeeding, Ross, and O'Conner 1999). The program is credited with lifting more children out of poverty than any other government program (Llobrera and Zahradnik 2004).

In 2014, 25 states and the District of Columbia offered a state-level earned income credit for residents, usually a percentage of the federal credit.

. . . .

What Does It Mean to Me?

What do you think should be done to eliminate poverty? Will economic inequality ever be eliminated?

. . . .

Changing the Definition—Redefining Poverty

The calculation of the U.S. poverty measure has been described as outdated due to how consumption patterns and the types of family needs have changed. For example, the cost of housing now constitutes a larger proportion of household expenses than it did in the 1960s (Ruggles 1990). Due to the rising costs of goods and services other than food (the primary basis for the current poverty calculation),

SOCIOLOGY AT WORK

CRITICAL THINKING

Your college education involves more than just learning new things; it also includes developing the skills to apply your new knowledge. This skill is referred to as critical thinking. The American Association of Colleges and Universities (AAC&U 2013) defines critical thinking as "a habit of the mind characterized by the comprehensive exploration of issues, ideas, artifacts and events before accepting or formulating an opinion or conclusion." A good critical thinker is able to apply these habits in "various and changing situations encountered in all walks of life" (AAC&U 2013). What does critical thinking look like? Critical thinking does not consist of one specific activity or outcome; rather it involves the use of reason, logic, and evidence to solve a problem, to evaluate a claim or situation, or to investigate a new aspect of our social world.

Take, for example, the subject of this chapter: social class. Most sociological discussions about social class begin with a discussion on Karl Marx. A critical thinker would not simply accept Marx's theory as the only explanation about social class, but would also consider alternative perspectives and explanations, some that might even disagree with Marx. A critical thinker would look for evidence, considering whether historical data support or refute Marx's theory on the rise of the proletariat class. Critical thinking can also involve applying Marx's theory to the way that we work now. What would Marx think about our solutions for poverty?

Critical thinking is valued in the new workplace. According to a 2013 survey of business and nonprofit leaders, 75% of respondents said they wanted more educational emphasis on critical thinking, along with complex problem solving, written and oral communication, and applied knowledge in real-world settings (Hart Research Associates 2013).

How have you applied critical thinking in your sociology courses?

How could you use this skill in the workplace?

---

the poverty measure underestimates the income needed for all household necessities (Christopher 2005).

In 1995, a panel of the National Academy of Sciences (NAS) called for a new poverty measure to include the three basic categories of food, clothing, and shelter (and utilities) and a small amount to cover other needs such as household supplies, child care, personal care, and non-work-related transportation. Because the census measure does not show how taxes, noncash benefits, and work-related child care and medical expenses affect people's well-being, the NAS panel cautioned that the current poverty measure cannot reflect how policy changes in these areas affect the poor. In addition, the measure does not consider how the cost of basic goods (food and shelter) has changed since the 1960s. As we have already discussed, the federal poverty measurement assumes that costs are the same across most of the states, except Hawaii and Alaska. It does not make sense that a family of four in Manhattan, New York, is expected to spend the same amount of money for food, clothing, and shelter as a family of four in Manhattan, Kansas (Bhargava and Kuriansky 2002).

The U.S. Census Bureau has been calculating experimental measures of poverty since 1999. For 2001, in measuring the overall poverty rate, the experimental measures reported higher levels of poverty, especially when accounting for geographic differences in housing costs and for medical out-of-pocket expenses. Although the official rate was 11.7%, experimental measures varied between 12.3% and 12.9%. When looking at the poverty rate for specific groups, the experimental measures tend to present a poverty population that looks more like the total population in terms of its mix of people: the elderly, White non-Hispanic individuals, and Hispanics (Short 2001).

In 2011, the U.S. Census Bureau released the Supplemental Poverty Measure (SPM). Rebecca Blank (2011) explains that the SPM provides an alternative way to look at economic need among the lowest-income families. While adjusting for geographic differences, the measure considers the dollar amount spent on food, clothing, utilities and housing, medical needs, and work-related transportation. The measure also considers household income resources, including noncash government benefits such as SNAP and the earned-income tax credit. The official poverty statistics, according to Blank, are incomplete when it comes to reporting the effect of the government policy on the poor. For example, when SNAP benefits are counted as income, they lift almost 4 million people above the poverty line and reduce poverty for millions more (Center on Budget and Policy Priorities 2013b).

Though the SPM will not replace the official measure, it has led to a reexamination of the extent of poverty in the United States. Results showed higher SPM poverty rates than the official measure for most groups. For 2010, according to the official poverty measure, there were 46.6 million people (or 15.2% of the population) living in poverty. With the SPM calculation, the poverty estimate increased to 49.1 million (16%). The distribution of poverty also changes, with higher proportions of poor among adults aged 18–64 years and adults 65 and older, married-couple families and families with male householders, Whites, Asians, the foreign born, homeowners with mortgages, and those with private health insurance (Short 2011).

CHAPTER REVIEW

2.1 Explain the different definitions of poverty

Absolute poverty refers to a lack of basic necessities, such as food, shelter, and income. Relative poverty refers to a situation where people fail to achieve the average income or lifestyle enjoyed by the rest of society. Relative poverty emphasizes the inequality of income and the growing gap between the richest and poorest Americans. The poverty threshold is the original federal poverty measure developed by the Social Security Administration and is used for estimating the number of people in poverty annually by the Census Bureau. Poverty guidelines (issued each year by the U.S.

Department of Health and Human Services) are used for determining family or individual eligibility for federal programs.

2.2 Compare the four sociological perspectives on social class and poverty

Functionalists observe that class inequality is a product of our social structure. Lower wages and poverty are natural consequences of this system of stratification. Conflict theorists assert that poverty exists because those in power want to maintain and expand their base of power and interests, with little left to share with others. Welfare bureaucracies—local, state, and national—represent important interest groups that influence the creation and implementation of welfare policies. Feminist scholars argue that the welfare state is an arena of political struggle. The drive to maintain male dominance and the patriarchal family is assumed to be the principal force shaping the formation, implementation, and outcomes of U.S. welfare policy. Interactionists explain how poverty is a learned phenomenon. This perspective also focuses on the public's perceptions about poverty.

2.3 Identify two consequences of poverty

Food insecurity is defined as food insufficient for all family members to enjoy active and healthy lives for at least some time during the year. For a variety of reasons, poor families encounter higher food prices and a smaller selection of food than other families. Housing is another problem; the combination of low earnings and scarce housing assistance results in serious housing problems for the working poor.

2.4 Explain the evolution of U.S. welfare policy

The centerpiece of the social welfare system was established by the passage of the Social Security Act of 1935. The act endorsed a system of assistance programs that would provide for Americans who could not care for themselves: widows, the elderly, the unemployed, and the poor. Welfare policies and programs were expanded under Franklin D. Roosevelt's New Deal and Lyndon Johnson's Great Society reforms, yet policy makers grew concerned about increasing dependence on social welfare programming. A new era of social welfare began with the 1996 Personal Responsibility and Work Opportunity Reconciliation Act. PRWORA was a bipartisan welfare reform plan to reduce recipients' dependence on government assistance through strict work requirements and welfare time limits.

2.5 Assess whether life after welfare has improved since the passage of PRWORA

PRWORA had an immediate effect in reducing the number of people on welfare. However, although employment has increased among welfare recipients, many recipients have little education or work experience, have limited employment benefits, and continue to struggle to achieve self-sufficiency.

KEY TERMS

absolute poverty, 34	life chances, 32	prestige, 43
culture of poverty, 46	poverty guidelines, 35	relative poverty, 34
distributive power, 45	poverty threshold, 34	social inequality, 46
food insecure, 48	power, 43	social stratification, 41
income, 42	power elite, 43	wealth, 42

STUDY QUESTIONS

1. Examine the difference between income and wealth. Which do you think is the better measure of social class?

2. How would you describe a middle-class lifestyle? What are its characteristics—housing, vacations, cars, and lifestyle? Estimate what it takes to lead this middle-class life.

3. Review the different definitions of poverty (from sociologists and according to federal policy). What are the advantages and disadvantages of each?

4. Functionalists assume that not everyone in society can and should be equal. Do you agree with this statement? Why or why not?

5. How would Marx and Weber define your social status, that of Microsoft's Bill Gates, and that of your sociology professor?

6. How has the welfare system (past and present) discriminated against women?

7. The chapter reviews three consequences of poverty—health care, food insecurity, and housing. Which do you think is most serious and why? What other consequences of poverty can you identify?

$SAGE edge™

Sharpen your skills with SAGE edge at **edge.sagepub.com/leonguerrero5e**

SAGE edge provides a personalized approach to help you accomplish your coursework goals in an easy-to-use learning environment.

CHAPTER 3

Race and Ethnicity

LEARNING OBJECTIVES

3.1 Describe the difference between race and ethnic groups

3.2 Identify the different types of institutional discrimination

3.3 Summarize how the sociological perspectives explain problems related to race and ethnicity

3.4 Describe the impact of immigrant or illegal workers in the labor force

3.5 Explain how the college experience increases racial/ethnic diversity awareness

In 2014, the statue of civil rights figure James Meredith was vandalized on the campus of the University of Mississippi. Witnesses reported seeing three young men hanging a noose around the neck of the statue, along with an old Georgia flag with a Confederate battle emblem. Meredith had been the first African American student admitted to the then all-White university in 1962. A U.S. Supreme Court ruling granted Meredith's enrollment, which state and university officials resisted. Two people were killed and many injured during campus riots. President John Kennedy and Attorney General Robert Kennedy ordered hundreds of federal authorities to restore order and to escort Meredith onto campus.

Responding to the vandalism, university chancellor Dan Jones said, "These individuals chose our university's most visible symbol of unity and educational accessibility to express their disagreement with our values. Our response will be an even greater commitment to promoting the values that are engraved on the statue—courage, knowledge, opportunity and perseverance" (Ole Miss/University of Mississippi News 2014). As for Meredith, he believes Mississippi is still the "center of the universe" for the politics of race and income inequality; he said, "I think Mississippi is ready to do the right thing" (quoted in Dave 2014).

The United States is a diverse racial and ethnic society. The U.S. Census (U.S. Census Bureau 2012c) predicts that by 2043, non-Hispanic whites will no longer make up the majority of the U.S. population. Acting Census Bureau director Thomas L. Mesenbourg (U.S. Census Bureau 2012c) describes the United States as a "plurality nation, where the non-Hispanic white population remains the largest single group, but no

AP Photo/The Daily Mississippian, Thomas Graning

We Don't Want
your Cents, We
Unity
is is Our
NIVERSITY!
s Time For Action!
ASA
LUMNI:
JE the Students ARE THE
Symbolic Rac
is STILL Ra

In 2013, 19 million immigrants were naturalized U.S. citizens. In order to be eligible for citizenship, immigrants must meet requirements set by immigration laws. Eligibility includes age (at least 18 years of age or older) and residency (at least 3 or 5 years as a permanent resident), along with other requirements.

group is in the majority." The minority population (Hispanic, Black, Asian, American Indians, and Alaska Natives) is projected to account for 57% of the population by 2060 (U.S. Census Bureau 2012c).

Adding to the diversity of our population are increasing numbers of immigrants, their migration to the United States and throughout the world spurred by the global economy. In 2013, 69% of international migrants lived in high-income countries (nations with an average per capita income of $12,616 or more, such as the United States and Germany) compared with 57% in 1990 (Conner, Cohn, and Gonzalez-Barrera 2013). Population mobility since the middle of the 20th century has been characterized by unprecedented volume, speed, and geographical range (Collin and Lee 2003). At the end of 2013, 232 million people, or about 3% of the world's population, lived in a country other than their birth country (United Nations 2013). As Zygmunt Bauman (2000) said, "the world is on the move" (p. 77).

Regionally, Europe has the largest number of international migrants (about 72 million), followed by Asia (70.8 million) and the United States (53.1 million) (United Nations 2013) (refer to Table 3.1).

Table 3.1 Regional distribution of international migrants, 1960 versus 2013

	1960		2013	
	Total Immigrants (Millions)	Share of World Immigrants (%)	Total Immigrants (Millions)	Share of World Immigrants (%)
World by Region	74.1		231.3	
Africa	9.2	12.4	18.6	8
North America	13.6	18.4	53.1	23
Latin America and the Caribbean	6.2	8.3	8.5	3.7
Asia	28.5	38.4	70.8	30.6
Europe	14.5	19.6	72.4	31.3
Oceania*	2.1	2.9	7.9	3.4

*Oceania includes Micronesia, Melanesia, Polynesia, Australia, and New Zealand.

SOURCE: United Nations 2009, 2013.

Racial divisions remain a defining feature of our social lives (H. Brown 2013). Complete racial equality and harmony remain elusive in the United States. The high-profile deaths of Black people at the hands of police officers in Ferguson, Missouri; New York; and other U.S. cities have led to public protest and outrage, exposing sharp and uncomfortable divisions about race in our country. In this chapter, we explore how one's racial and ethnic status serves as a basis of inequality. Like social class, race or ethnicity alters one's life chances, and members of particular groups experience an increased likelihood of experiencing particular social problems. We begin first with understanding how race and ethnicity are defined.

DEFINING RACE AND ETHNICITY

From a biological perspective, a **race** can be defined as a group or population that shares a set of genetic characteristics and physical features. The term has been applied broadly to groups with similar physical features (the White race), religion (the Jewish race), or the entire human species (the human race) (Marger 2002). However, generations of migration, intermarriage, and adaptations to different physical environments have produced a mixture of races. There is no such thing as a "pure" race.

Social scientists reject the biological notions of race, instead favoring an approach that treats race as a social construct. In *Racial Formation in the United States: From the 1960s to the 1990s*, Michael Omi and Howard Winant (1994) explain how race is a "concept which signifies and symbolizes social conflicts and interests by referring to different types of human bodies" (p. 54). Instead of thinking of race as something "objective," the authors argued that we can imagine race as an "illusion," a subjective social, political, and cultural construct. In the United States, race tends to be a bipolar construct—White versus non-White. According to the authors, "the meaning of race is defined and contested throughout society, in both collective action and personal practice. In the process, racial categories themselves are formed, transformed, destroyed, and reformed" (Omi and Winant 1994:21). Robert Redfield (1958) says it simply: "Race is, so to speak, a human invention" (p. 67).

Race may be a social construction, but that does not make race any less powerful and controlling (Myers 2005). Omi and Winant (1994) argued that although particular stereotypes and meanings can change, "the presence of a system of racial meaning and stereotypes, of racial ideology, seems to be a permanent feature of U.S. culture" (p. 63).

Ethnic groups are set off to some degree from other groups by displaying a unique set of cultural traits, such as their language, religion, or diet. Members of an ethnic group perceive themselves as members of an ethnic community, sharing common historical roots and experiences. All of us, to one extent or another, have an ethnic identity. Increasingly, the terms *race* and *ethnicity* are presented as a single construct pointing to how both terms are being conflated (Budrys 2003).

Martin Marger (2002) explains how ethnicity serves as a basis of social ranking, ranking a person according to the status of his or her ethnic group. Although class and ethnicity are separate dimensions of stratification, they are closely related: "In

Race: Group or population sharing a set of genetic characteristics and physical features

Ethnic groups: Groups of people who are set off to some degree from other groups by displaying a unique set of cultural traits, such as their language, religion, or diet

virtually all multiethnic societies, people's ethnic classification becomes an important factor in the distribution of societal rewards and hence, their economic and political class positions. The ethnic and class hierarchies are largely parallel and interwoven" (Marger 2002:286).

The federal definition of ethnicity is based on the Office of Management and Budget's 1977 guideline (U.S. Census Bureau 2005), which defines ethnicity in terms of Hispanic/non-Hispanic status, contrary to the conventional social scientific definition as presented in the previous paragraphs. The U.S. Census treats Hispanic origin and race as separate and distinct concepts; as a result, Hispanics may be of any race. Since 2002, Hispanic Americans became the nation's largest ethnic minority group. The U.S. Census Bureau includes in this category women and men who are Mexican, Central and South American, Puerto Rican, Cuban, and other Hispanic. The 2013 ethnic and racial composition estimates of the United States are presented in Table 3.2.

In 2012, the U.S. Census reported that minority births were the majority—50.4% of children younger than age 1 year were Hispanic, Black, Asian, or of mixed race. Non-Hispanic Whites accounted for 49.6% of all births in a 12-month period (U.S. Census Bureau 2012b). Commenting on the report, demographer William Frey (quoted in Tavernise 2012:A1) said, "This is an important tipping point . . . [a] transformation from a mostly white baby boomer culture to a more globalized multiethnic country that we're becoming."

Native: Anyone born in the United States or a U.S. island area or born abroad of a U.S. citizen parent

Foreign born: Anyone who is not a U.S. citizen at birth

The U.S. Census distinguishes between native and foreign-born residents. **Native** refers to anyone born in the United States or a U.S. island area such as Puerto Rico or the Northern Mariana Islands or born abroad of a U.S. citizen parent; **foreign born** refers to anyone who is not a U.S. citizen at birth. Elizabeth Grieco (2010) writes, "The foreign born, through their own diverse origins, will contribute to the racial

Table 3.2   Annual estimates of the resident population by race and Hispanic origin, 2013

	Total
White, Alone	245,499,000
Black or African American, Alone	41,623,000
American Indian and Alaska Native, Alone	3,910,000
Asian, Alone	16,632,000
Native Hawaiian and Other Pacific Islander, Alone	722,000
Two or More Races	7,741,000

SOURCE: U.S. Census Bureau 2014a.

Figure 3.1 Country of birth for foreign-born population in the United States, 2012

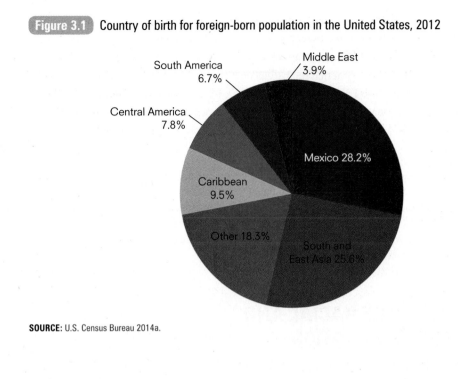

South America
6.7%

Middle East
3.9%

Central America
7.8%

Mexico 28.2%

Caribbean
9.5%

Other 18.3%

South and
East Asia 25.6%

SOURCE: U.S. Census Bureau 2014a.

What Does It Mean to Me?

There were 12 racial categories listed in the 1920 U.S. Census. The categories included four variations of White, Negro, Mulatto, Indian, Chinese, Japanese, Native, Foreign-born, and "All other." The number of racial categories was reduced to 8 in the 1960 Census and expanded again to 31 racial categories in the 2000 and 2010 Census. Based on the current definition, how would you identify your racial identity? From your perspective, are any racial categories missing from the list?

and ethnic diversity of the United States. How they translate their own backgrounds and report their adopted identities have important implications for the nation's racial and ethnic composition." In 2012, among the 40 million foreign born in the United States, most were from Latin America (42.7%, as displayed in Figure 3.1) Brown and Patten 2014a.

Refugees are defined by the Immigration and Nationality Act of 1980 as "aliens outside the United States who are unable or unwilling to return to his/her country of origin for persecution or fear of persecution on account of race, religion, nationality, membership in a particular social group, or political opinion." Data on the number of admitted refugees are collected annually by the U.S. Department of State. In 2013, 69,926 persons were admitted as refugees. Almost 65% of all admitted refugees were from three countries: Burma (24%), Iraq (28%), and Bhutan (13%) (U.S. Department of State 2014).

Refugees: Persons who are unable or unwilling to return to their country of origin due to persecution or fear of persecution on account of race, religion, nationality, membership in a particular social group, or political opinion

Tracy Ore (2003) acknowledges that externally created labels for some groups are not always accepted by those viewed as belonging to a particular group. For example, those of Latin American descent may not consider themselves to be "Hispanic." In this text, I've adopted Ore's practice regarding which racial and ethnic terms are used. In my own material, I use Latino to refer to those of Latin American descent, and Black and African American interchangeably. However, original terms used by authors or researchers (e.g., Hispanic as used by the U.S. Census Bureau) are not altered.

. . . .

What Does It Mean to Me?

You may not be able to tell from my last name (Leon-Guerrero), but I consider my ethnic identity to be Japanese. I am Japanese not only because of my middle name (Yuri) and because of my Japanese mother, but also because of the Japanese traditions I practice, the Japanese words I use, and even the Japanese foods I like to eat. Do you have an ethnic identity? If you do, how do you maintain it?

. . . .

PATTERNS OF RACIAL AND ETHNIC INTEGRATION

Ethnocentrism:
The belief that one's own group values and behaviors are right

Racism: The belief in the inferiority of certain racial or ethnic groups, often accompanied by discrimination

Individual discrimination:
Prejudiced actions against minority members by individuals; may include avoiding contact or physical or verbal attacks

Institutional discrimination:
Discrimination practiced by political or social institutions

Segregation: Physical and social separation of ethnic or racial groups

Sociologists explain that **ethnocentrism** is the belief that one's own group values and behaviors are right and even better than all others. Feeling positive about one's group is important for group solidarity and loyalty. However, it can lead groups and individuals to believe that certain racial or ethnic groups are inferior and that discriminatory practices against them are justified. This is called **racism**.

Though not all inequality can be attributed to racism, our nation's history reveals how particular groups have been singled out and subject to unfair treatment. Certain groups have been subject to **individual discrimination** and **institutional discrimination**. Individual discrimination includes actions against minority members by individuals. Actions may range from avoiding contact with minority group members to physical or verbal attacks against minority group members. Institutional discrimination is practiced by the government, social institutions, and organizations. Institutional discrimination may include segregation, exclusion, or expulsion.

Segregation refers to the physical and social separation of ethnic or racial groups. Although we consider explicit segregation to be illegal and a thing of the past, ethnic and racial segregation still occurs in neighborhoods, schools, and personal relationships. According to Debra Van Ausdale and Joe Feagin (2001),

racial discrimination and segregation are still central organizing factors in contemporary U.S. society. For the most part, Whites and Blacks do not live in the same neighborhoods, attend the same schools at all educational levels, enter into close friendships or other intimate relationships with one another, or share comparable opinions on a wide variety of political matters. The same is true, though sometimes to a lesser extent, for Whites and other Americans of color, such as most Latino, Native and Asian American groups. Despite progress since the 1960s, U.S. society remains intensely segregated across color lines. Generally speaking, Whites and people of color do not occupy the same social space or social status. (p. 29)

Exclusion refers to the practice of prohibiting or restricting the entry or participation of groups in society. In March 1882, U.S. Congressman Edward K. Valentine declared, "The [immigration] gate must be closed" (Gyory 1998:238). That year, Valentine, along with other congressional leaders, approved the Chinese Exclusion Act. From 1882 to 1943, the United States prohibited Chinese immigration because of concerns that Chinese laborers would compete with American workers. Through the 1940s, immigration was defined as a hindrance rather than a benefit to the United States.

Library of Congress, Prints & Photographs Division, FSA/OWI Collection, [LC-DIG-fsa-8a26761]

Jim Crow laws mandated the segregation of whites and blacks in public facilities, schools, and transportation in U.S. Southern states. The laws were enforced until 1954 when the U.S. Supreme Court ruled in *Brown v. Board of Education* that the racial segregation of public schools was unconstitutional. The Civil Rights Act of 1964, the Voting Rights Act of 1965, and the Fair Housing Act of 1968 further prohibited racial discrimination, ending Jim Crow laws once and for all.

Finally, **expulsion** is the removal of a group by direct force or intimidation. Native Americans in the United States were forcibly removed from their homelands by early settlers and the federal government before and after the American Revolutionary War. During the 1830s, members of the Cherokee and other nations were forcibly relocated to government-designated Indian territory (present-day Oklahoma). Their journey is known as the Trail of Tears, where thousands died along the way. In 2006, journalist Eliot Jaspin documented the extent of racial expulsion that occurred in towns from Central Texas through Georgia. After the Civil War through the 1920s, White residents expelled nearly all Black persons from their communities, usually using direct physical force. Thirteen countywide expulsions were documented in eight states between 1864 and 1923 in which 4,000 Blacks were driven out of their communities.

SOCIOLOGICAL PERSPECTIVES ON RACIAL AND ETHNIC INEQUALITIES

Functionalist Perspective

Theorists from the functionalist perspective believe that the differences between racial and ethnic groups are largely cultural. The solution is **assimilation**, a process where minority group members become part of the dominant group, losing their original distinct group identity. This process is consistent with America's image

Exclusion: The practice of prohibiting or restricting the entry or participation of groups in society

Expulsion: The removal of a group by direct force or intimidation

Assimilation: A process in which minority group members become part of the dominant group, losing their original group identity

as the "melting pot." Milton Gordon (1964) presents a seven-stage assimilation model that begins first with cultural assimilation (change of cultural patterns, e.g., learning the English language), followed by structural assimilation (interaction with members of the dominant group), marital assimilation (intermarriage), identification assimilation (developing a sense of national identity, e.g., identifying as an American, rather than as an Asian American), attitude receptional assimilation (absence of prejudiced thoughts among dominant and minority group members), behavioral receptional assimilation (absence of discrimination; e.g., lower wages for minorities would not exist), and finally civic assimilation (absence of value and power conflicts).

Assimilation is said to allow a society to maintain its equilibrium (a goal of the functionalist perspective) if all members of society, regardless of their racial or ethnic identity, adopt one dominant culture. This is often characterized as a voluntary process. Critics argue that this perspective assumes that social integration is a shared goal and that members of the minority group are willing to assume the dominant group's identity and culture, assuming that the dominant culture is the one and only preferred culture (Myers 2005). The perspective also assumes that assimilation is the same experience for all ethnic groups, ignoring the historical legacy of slavery and racial discrimination in our society.

Assimilation is not the only means to achieve racial/ethnic stability. Other countries maintain **pluralism**, where each ethnic or racial group maintains its own culture (cultural pluralism) or a separate set of social structures and institutions (structural pluralism). Cultural pluralism is also referred to as multiculturalism. Switzerland, which has a number of different nationalities and religions, is an example of a pluralistic society. The country, also referred to as the Swiss Confederation, has four official languages: German, French, Italian, and Romansh. Relationships between each ethnic group are described for the most part as harmonious because each of the ethnically diverse parts joined the confederation voluntarily seeking protection (Farley 2005). In his examination of pluralism in the United States, Min Zhou (2004) notes, "As America becomes increasingly multiethnic, and as ethnic Americans become integral in our society, it becomes more and more evident that there is no contradiction between an ethnic identity and an American identity" (p. 153).

Conflict Perspective

Pluralism: Each ethnic or racial group maintains its own culture (cultural pluralism or multiculturalism) or a separate set of social structures and institutions (structural pluralism)

According to sociologist W. E. B. Du Bois (1996), perhaps it is wrong "to speak of race at all as a concept, rather than as a group of contradictory forces, facts and tendencies" (p. 532). The problem of the 20th century, wrote Du Bois, is "the color line."

Conflict theorists focus on how the dynamics of racial and ethnic relations divide groups while maintaining a dominant group. The dominant group may be defined according to racial or ethnic categories, but it can also be defined according to social class. Instead of relationships being based on consensus (or assimilation), relationships are based on power, force, and coercion. Ethnocentrism and racism maintain the status quo by dividing individuals along racial and ethnic lines (Myers 2005).

Drawing upon Marx's class analysis, Du Bois was one of the first theorists to observe the connection between racism and capitalist-class oppression in the United States and throughout the world. He noted the link between racist ideas and actions to maintain a Eurocentric system of domination (Feagin and Batur 2004). Du Bois (1996) wrote,

> Throughout the world today organized groups of men by monopoly of economic and physical power, legal enactment and intellectual training are limiting with great determination and unflagging zeal the development of other groups; and that the concentration particularly on economic power today puts the majority of mankind into a slavery to the rest. (p. 532)

Marxist theorists argue that immigrants constitute a reserve army of workers, members of the working class performing jobs that native workers no longer perform. Michael Samers (2003) suggests that immigrants are a "quantitatively and qualitatively flexible labour force for capitalists which divides and weakens working class organization and drives down the value of labour power" (p. 557). Capitalist businesses profit from migrant workers because they are cheap and flexible—easily hired during times of economic growth and easily fired during economic recessions. In 2013, approximately 60,000 immigrants worked in the federal detention centers, working for 13 cents an hour. Immigrants held in local county jails also worked for free or in exchange for sodas or candy. Their work usually involves meal preparation or janitorial work. This labor practice, though voluntary and cost-saving (about $40 million per year for federal detention centers), has come under attack by detainees and immigrant advocates (Urbina 2014).

Hana Brown (2013) posits a racialized conflict theory regarding the development of welfare policies. Her use of the term *racialized* (versus *racial*) emphasizes the constructed nature of race. Racialized conflicts are "a series of events that draw boundaries based on racial difference, polarize political groups along racial lines and involve explicitly race-based claims" (p. 401). Brown predicts several effects of racialized conflict on the formation of welfare policy. First, Whites may feel threatened by a larger or growing minority population and may perceive that minorities are too reliant on public assistance. These beliefs become institutionalized in the political discourse, transforming welfare into a racialized issue. Finally, racialized conflict divides political groups along racial lines and encourages political leaders to exploit the existing racialized tensions in their favor.

Brown offers empirical support of her hypotheses based on Georgia's 1993–1994 welfare reform. Georgia's welfare legislation was preceded by a controversial proposal by Governor Zell Miller to remove the Confederate emblem from the state flag. Response to his proposal was racially divided, with the majority of Whites opposing and the majority of Blacks supporting the governor. The flag proposal never materialized, but it ignited racial tension and racialized the state's political discourse. Whites felt threatened by and resentful of Blacks, and this affected the welfare debate. According to H. Brown (2013), Miller's decision to shift his attention from the state flag to welfare reform "proved a politically convenient way to appeal to white resentment and threat, exploit the prevailing racial discourses, and resurrect his political career" (p. 421). Georgia passed one of the strictest and most punitive welfare programs emphasizing work and education.

Feminist Perspective

Feminist theory has attempted to account for and focus on the experiences of women and other marginalized groups in society. Feminist theory intersects with multiculturalism through the analysis of multiple systems of oppression, not just gender, but including categories of race, class, sexual orientation, nation of origin, language, culture, and ethnicity. Most notably, Patricia Hill Collins's (2000) Black feminist theory emerges from this perspective. Black feminists identify the value of a theoretical perspective that addresses the simultaneity of race, class, and gender oppression.

Black feminist scholars note the misguided application of traditional feminist perspectives of "the family," "patriarchy," and "reproduction" to understand the experience of Black women's lives. Black women do not lead parallel lives, but rather lead different lives. British scholar Hazel Carby (1985) argues that because Black women are subject to simultaneous oppression based on class, race, and patriarchy, the application of traditional (White) feminist perspectives is not appropriate and is actually misleading in attempts to comprehend the true experience of Black women. As an example, Carby (1985) analyzes an article on women in third-world manufacturing. Carby highlights how the photographs accompanying the article are of "anonymous Black women." She observes, "This anonymity and the tendency to generalize into meaninglessness, the oppression of an amorphous category called 'Third World Women,' are symptomatic of the ways in which the specificity of our experiences and oppression are subsumed under inapplicable concepts and theories" (Carby 1985:394).

Political scientist Maria Chávez (2011) documented how Latina attorneys experience workplace marginalization and discrimination due to the unique intersection of their racial, gender, and class identities. Latina attorneys, Chávez notes, experience a deep sense of professional isolation. Female attorneys lack social capital and earn less than their male counterparts. Female attorneys may face gender bias in the courts or experience sexual harassment in the workplace. She explains,

> Being the only Latina in a particular work environment in and of itself would not be so isolating if it were an accepting environment . . . . many times the professional and community environments in which they function are filled with sexist and/or racist people–filled with a negative culture that contributes to an increase in a Latina's sense of isolation. (p. 97)

Chávez reports that according to the American Bar Association, 100% of women of color quit practicing law or move into a different position after eight years of practice.

Interactionist Perspective

Sociologists believe that race is a social construct. We learn about racial and ethnic categories of White, Black, Latino, Asian, Native American, and immigrant through our social interaction. The meaning and values of these and other categories are provided by our social institutions, families, and friends (Ore 2003). Refer to page 75 for a discussion of children's literature as a source of racial and ethnic identity. As much as I and other social scientists inform our students about the unsubstantiated use of the term *race*, for most students, race is real. The term is loaded with social, cultural, and political baggage, making deconstructing it difficult to accomplish.

Social scientists have noted how people are raced, how race itself is not a category but a practice. Howard McGary (1999) defines the practice as "a commonly accepted course of action that may be over time habitual in nature; a course of action that specifies certain forms of behavior as permissible and others impermissible, with rewards and penalties assigned accordingly" (p. 83). In this way, racial categories and identities serve as intersections of social beliefs, perceptions, and activities that are reinforced by enduring systems of rewards and penalties (Shuford 2001). Racial practices are not uniform. For example, while in the United States we are accustomed to racial categorizations, for example, the Census Bureau's race measurement, France's census does not include measures for race, ethnicity, or religion.

Individuals are attempting to redefine racial boundaries by proposing the creation and acknowledgment of a new racial category: **multiracial**, or mixed race. This is different from other ethnic movements that work within the existing racial frameworks. For example, Latinos may challenge the meaning and use of the Census category Hispanic, but they are not trying to create a new racial identity (DaCosta 2007). Members of the multicultural movement advocate the formal acceptance of the multiracial category on U.S. Census and other governmental forms and have also worked on broader issues of racial and social justice (Bernstein and De la Cruz 2009).

Scholars have also observed the phenomenon of **ethnic attrition**, individuals choosing not to self-identify as a member of a particular ethnic group. Brian Duncan and Stephen Trejo (2011) found that about 30% of third-generation Mexican youth in their study failed to identify as Mexican, choosing instead to identify as White. These youth were more likely to have parents with higher levels of educational attainment and have more years of schooling themselves than youth who identified as Mexican. Scholars of race in Latin America have also confirmed patterns of intergenerational Whitening. Highly educated non-White Brazilians were found to be more likely to label their children White than less-educated non-White Brazilians (Schwartzman 2007).

A summary of all theoretical perspectives is provided in Table 3.3.

Multiracial: Mixed or multiple race

Ethnic attrition: Individuals choosing not to self-identify as a member of a particular ethnic group

Table 3.3 Summary of sociological perspectives: Inequalities based on race and ethnicity

	Functionalist	Conflict/Feminist	Interactionist
Explanations of racial and ethnic inequality	Assimilation into a dominant culture preserves the stability of society. Ethnic pluralism may also achieve stability.	Inequality is systematically maintained by those trying to preserve their advantaged positions. Class divisions overlap with racial and ethnic divisions. Feminist scholars advocate a theoretical perspective that simultaneously considers the intersection of race, class, and gender.	Race is a social construct. Racial and ethnic categories are also linked with positions of privilege or marginalization.
Questions asked about racial and ethnic inequality	How can minority groups be assimilated into mainstream society? Can cultural and structural pluralism be maintained?	What powerful interest groups determine racial and ethnic inequalities? How are these structures maintained?	How do we learn about race and ethnicity? How are some groups more privileged than others? How do our perceptions and beliefs perpetuate racial and ethnic inequalities?

THE CONSEQUENCES OF RACIAL AND ETHNIC INEQUALITIES

U.S. Immigration: Past and Present

Most U.S. families have an immigration history, whether it is based upon stories of relatives as long as four generations ago or as recent as the current generation. Immigration involves leaving one's country of origin to move to another. Though immigration has always been a part of U.S. history, the recent wave of immigration, particularly at the end of the 20th century and the beginning of the 21st, has led to the observation that we are in the "age of migration" (Castles and Miller 1998).

IN FOCUS

MULTICULTURAL CHILDREN'S LITERATURE

Children's literature is an important socializing agent about race. Research has confirmed how children prefer books with subject matter and characters relating to their personal experiences and characteristics (Purves and Beach 1972). Consider, for example, the main characters of J. K. Rowling's Harry Potter series. The U.S. cover for *Harry Potter and the Prisoner of Azkaban* features Harry and Hermione, two main White characters riding a hippogriff. But imagine for a moment if Harry were depicted as a Black teenager or Hermione as a Latina. What impact might that have for Black and Latino/a children? How would they respond to characters who look like them?

Educators have criticized the absence of racial and ethnic diversity and the promotion of Whiteness in children's literature. According to children's book author Walter Dean Myers (2014), the inclusion of racially diverse characters informs us about our own race and the race of others.

> Books transmit values. They explore our common humanity. What is the message when some children are not represented in those books? . . . Where are the future white loan officers and future politicians going to get their knowledge of people of color? Where are black children going to get a sense of who they are and what they can be? (p. 6)

Educator Violet Harris (1990: 552) warns, "If African American children do not see reflections of themselves in school texts or do not perceive any affirmation of their cultural heritage in those texts, then it is quite likely that they will not read or value school as much."

The Cooperative Children's Book Center at the University of Wisconsin–Madison compiles a list of children's books published in the United States that were created by and about people of color, including African Americans, American Indians, Asian Pacific

Table 3.4 Numbers and percentages of books created by or about specific ethnic groups, 2013 (based on 3,200 children's books)

	By	About
African/African Americans	68 (2%)	93 (2.9%)
American Indians	18 (.6%)	34 (0.1%)
Asian Pacifics/Asian Pacific Americans	90 (2.8%)	69 (2.1%)
Latinos	48 (1.5%)	57 (1.8%)

SOURCE: Cooperative Children's Book Center 2014.

Islanders, and Latinos. The center reviewed 3,200 children's books published in 2013 and reported the numbers (and percentages) of books created by or about specific racial/ethnic groups (refer to Table 3.4).

The center advocates **multicultural literature,** defined as literature that focuses on people of color, religious minorities, regional cultures, the disabled, or the aged (Harris 1996). According to the center (Cooperative Children Book's Center, 2014),

> the more [multicultural] books there are, especially books created by authors and illustrators of color, the more opportunities librarians, teachers, and parents and other adults have of finding outstanding books for young readers and listeners that reflect dimensions of their lives, and give a broader understanding of who we are as a nation.

Is the impact of children's literature on racial and ethnic construction overstated? Why or why not? How was race or ethnicity constructed in your favorite childhood books, movies, or television programs?

Multicultural literature: Literature that focuses on people of color, religious minorities, regional cultures, the disabled, or the aged

The regulation of immigration became a federal responsibility in 1875, and the Immigration Service was established in 1891. Before this, all immigrants were allowed to enter and become permanent residents. The Great Wave of immigration occurred from 1900 to 1920, when nearly 24 million immigrants, mostly European, arrived in the United States. Congress passed a national immigrant quota system in 1921, limiting the number of immigrants by national groups based on their representation in U.S. Census figures. The quota system, along with the Depression and World War II, slowed the flow of immigrants for several decades.

In 1965, Congress replaced the national quota system with a preference system designed to reunite immigrant families and attract skilled immigrants. Most of the immigrants who arrived after 1970 were from Latin America and Asia. Legislative reforms continued through the 1990s, targeting amnesty policies for illegal aliens (Center for Immigration Studies 2009). Despite the events of September 11, 2001, and a recent federal crackdown on illegal immigration, the United States still has the most open immigration policy in the world.

Most immigrants are motivated by the global economics of immigration—men and women will move from low-wage to high-wage countries in search of better incomes and standards of living. **Labor migration**, the movement from one country to another for employment, has been a part of U.S. history, beginning with Chinese male workers brought to build railroads in the 1800s. These men never brought their families or had any intention of staying after their work was completed.

In their analysis of migration trends, Gary Hytrek and Kristine Zentgraf (2007) note how an increasing number of highly skilled laborers are moving from less developed areas around the world to the United States and Europe. These migrants are more likely to return to their place of birth or move on to a third country. Migration tends to occur between geographically proximate countries—for example, Turkish and North African migration to Western Europe and Mexican and Central American migration to the United States.

In 2012, there were 40.8 million foreign-born individuals in the United States. This is the highest number of foreign born ever recorded in U.S. history. Steven Camarota (2007), reporting for the Center for Immigration Studies, notes that one of the striking patterns of recent immigration is the lack of diversity among immigrants themselves. Immigrants from Mexico and South and East Asia account for the majority of the foreign-born population. Refer to this chapter's Exploring Social Problems feature for an overview of the U.S. immigrant population.

The United Nations uses the analogy of multiple doors of a house to describe the different ways migrants enter a country. Migrants can enter a house through the front door (as permanent settlers), the side door (temporary visitors and workers), or the back door (irregular or illegal migrants). Back-door migrants have been the recent focus of political and economic debate.

The number of unauthorized or illegal immigrants peaked at 12 million in 2007. As of 2010, the number had declined to 11.2 million (Passel and Cohn 2012; Krogstad and Passel 2014). The majority of legal or illegal immigrants in the

Labor migration: The movement of people from one country to another for employment

The U.S. Immigrant Population

U.S. Data Map 3.1 Percentage of foreign-born population by state, 2012

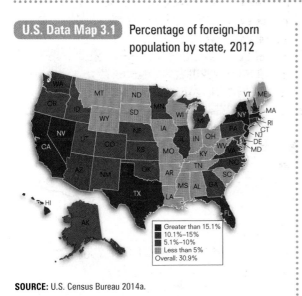

Greater than 15.1%
10.1%–15%
5.1%–10%
Less than 5%
Overall: 30.9%

SOURCE: U.S. Census Bureau 2014a.

Figure 3.2 Percentage distribution of foreign-born population by region of birth and date of arrival, 2012

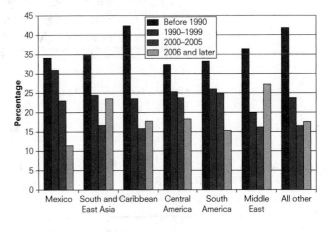

Before 1990
1990–1999
2000–2005
2006 and later

SOURCE: U.S. Census Bureau 2014b.

WHAT DO YOU THINK?

The U.S. immigrant population is concentrated in five states: California, New York, New Jersey, Nevada, and Hawaii. Though not shown here, California is home to the most undocumented immigrants, estimated at 2.5 million. Texas is the next largest with 1.7 million undocumented immigrants.

Figure 3.2 displays the percentage distribution of foreign born by their region of birth. The data reveal a decline in the percentage of Mexican, Caribbean, and South American immigrants over the four time periods. There has been a shift in where immigrants are coming from.

Which groups have shown an increase in the percentage of immigrants over the same time period?

United States are from Mexico. The number of unauthorized Mexican immigrants has been declining since 2007. According to Jens Manuel Krogstad and Jeffrey Passel (2014), as of 2012 there were 5.9 million unauthorized Mexican immigrants in the United States, compared with a peak of 7 million in 2007. They attribute this emigration decline to the Great Recession, declining job opportunities in the housing and construction industry, increasing border enforcement, a rise in deportations, and increasing dangers associated with border crossings.

The Immigrant Experience

While most immigrants come to the United States to pursue the promise of the freedom of choice, education, economic opportunity, and a better quality of life, their lives are often filled with challenges and problems.

The post-2000 wave of immigrants included men and women with lower educational attainment—34% have less than a high school education. Considering the population of illegal immigrants, the foreign-born population as a whole is much less educated than the native-born population. Camarota (2007) observes that these individuals' lower educational attainment has "enormous implications" for their economic and social integration. A larger proportion of immigrants than those who are native born have low incomes, lack health insurance, and rely on social assistance programs.

Data from the U.S. Census Current Population Survey reveals that 15.1% of immigrants lived in poverty in 2011. The higher incidence of poverty among immigrants as a group has increased the overall size of the population living in poverty. The lack of health insurance is also a significant problem for immigrants—34.1% of foreign-born individuals lack insurance compared with 13.8% of natives. Illegal immigrants are not eligible for Medicare, and legal immigrants must wait five years to qualify for the program. Camarota (2007) notes that immigrants' low rate of health insurance is associated with a lower level of education and their employment. Unskilled immigrants are likely to work at jobs that do not offer health insurance, and they are often unable to purchase insurance on their own.

John Moore/Getty Images

These Mexican farm workers are weeding a field in California's Imperial Valley. They are paid to work in the fields for about $9.00 an hour.

Immigrant labor is concentrated in construction, cleaning and maintenance, production, and farming occupations. Illegal immigrants are employed in similar areas: construction, building cleaning and maintenance, food preparation and service, transportation and moving, and agriculture. There are an estimated 8 million illegal immigrants in the labor force (Passel and Cohn 2012). Foreign-born workers are especially susceptible to abuse, stress, and unsafe working conditions due to their overrepresentation in dangerous industries, combined with their undocumented worker status, lack of training, and lack of English literacy (Migrant Clinicians Network 2009). As reported by the U.S. Bureau of Labor Statistics (2013), in 2012, Hispanics accounted for the largest proportion (39%) of foreign-born workers who died on the job. A total of 824 foreign-born workers died of fatal work injuries in 2012.

With the exception of the agricultural sector, the majority of workers in occupations where immigrants are concentrated are native-born workers (Camarota and Jensenius 2009). Yet, no single occupation is composed entirely of immigrant labor (Camarota 2009). Immigration has been found to have a negative effect on the wages of native-born Americans, primarily in low-paying, low-skilled occupations, reducing wages by an estimated 4% to 7% (Camarota 2009). As Camarota (2007) observes, "A central question for immigration policy is whether we should allow in so many people with little education—increasing job competition for the poorest American workers and the population needing assistance" (p. 39).

Carola Suárez-Orozco et al. (2011) report that there are an estimated 5.5 million children and adolescents living with illegal immigrant parents. Suárez-Orozco and her colleagues documented how the children of illegal immigrant parents lack access to quality educational (child care, preschool, school, and higher education) and employment opportunities. Despite having the same level of commitment to their children's education as authorized legal parents, illegal parents have fewer resources and skills (low social and educational capital) to help their children realize their educational goals. In addition, illegal parents' fear of deportation leads to lower levels of engagement with teachers or schools. Suárez-Orozco et al. conclude, "For millions of children and youth growing up in unauthorized families, the American Dream and the promise of a better tomorrow have become an elusive mirage" (p. 462).

As it has increased its immigration enforcement (including detainment and deportation), the Department of Homeland Security has been criticized for targeting immigrants with minor offenses, sometimes breaking up families in the process. Human Rights Watch (2009) reported that since stricter deportation laws were passed in 1996, most immigrants have been deported for minor offenses (such as marijuana possession or traffic offenses). The new laws disallowed judges to consider in deportation cases noncitizens' ties to the United States, including family, business or property ownership, and service in the U.S. armed forces. Among legal immigrants who were deported, over 70% had been convicted for nonviolent crimes. Many had lived in the United States for years and were separated from family members. Researchers from the Urban Institute documented short- and long-term effects on

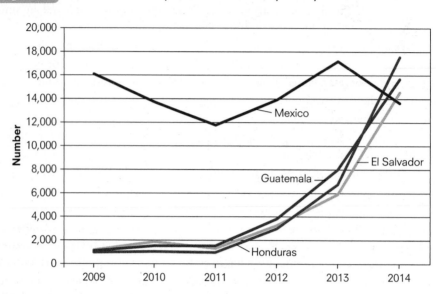

Figure 3.3 Number of unaccompanied alien children by fiscal years 2009–2013

SOURCE: U.S. Customs and Border Protection 2014.

children with deported or detained parents. These children experienced financial, food, and housing hardships in addition to behavioral changes such as changes in eating and sleeping habits and higher degrees of fear and anxiety (Chaudry et al. 2010). The Obama administration promised a more compassionate approach to enforcement that would focus on felony criminal offenders. In 2011, 396,906 immigrants were deported—the largest number in the history of Immigration and Customs Enforcement. Fifty-five percent were convicted of felonies or misdemeanors (U.S. Immigration and Customs Enforcement 2011).

During 2013–2014, there were an estimated 61,581 unaccompanied alien children entering the United States, an increase of more than 23,000 over the previous year (refer to Figure 3.3). The majority of children and families were from the Central American countries of Honduras, El Salvador, and Guatemala. Dan Restrepo and Ann Garcia (2014) attributed the increased flow of children to "the interrelated challenges" of regional violence and poverty that adversely affect residents of these countries. The surge of immigration by unaccompanied children was called a crisis, a humanitarian issue, and a threat to border security. U.S. House Republicans argued that the increase was due to the lack of border enforcement and to the Deferred Action for Childhood Arrivals (DACA) (refer to solutions discussion on p. 86). Restrepo and Garcia (2014) noted that the United States was not alone in experiencing the immigrant influx, as the immigrant surge also occurred in Mexico, Panama, Nicaragua, Costa Rica, and Belize. The flow of immigrants had been increasing since 2011.

TAKING A WORLD VIEW

GLOBAL IMMIGRATION

Migration has been elevated to a top international policy concern (Düvell 2005), largely because of the threat of terrorism and the challenge of global politics. Migrants now depart from and arrive in almost every country in the world. Politically and morally, migration pits two basic principles against each other. On one hand is the right of individuals to move freely across borders for economic or personal reasons, and on the other is the country's right to self-govern, to regulate its borders, and to determine the difference between a citizen and an alien (Benhabib 2012). Great Britain, Greece, France, Germany, Australia, and other countries have seen an increase in pro- and anti-immigration protests, as well as increased hate crime acts against immigrants.

Riots by immigrants took place in France in 2005 and in Italy during 2008–2010. In Italy, there are 4 million legal immigrants and estimates of more illegal immigrants residing in the country. Flavio Di Giacomo, a spokesman for the International Organization for Migration, described how immigrant workers live in semislavery. The riots, according to Di Giacomo, revealed how "many Italian economic realities are based on the exploitation of low-cost foreign labor, living in subhuman conditions, without human rights" (Donadio 2010a:A7). The African laborers were paid under the table, about $30 a day for picking fruit (Donadio 2010b). Asian and African immigrants in Greece have been the targets of violence and physical attacks since 2010. The violence has been fueled by public discontent over the economy and concern over job losses as well as demonization of immigrants in the press and in the political arena. From a social constructionist's perspective, immigrants were portrayed as the source of Greece's economic woes, defining them as a social problem and threat.

Migration flows are regarded as a threat to national and global stability, with some calling for an international migration policy (Düvell 2005). Globalization has intensified the need to coordinate and harmonize government policies. The United States, Canada, Great Britain, France, Germany, Belgium, Italy, Spain, and Japan have increased policy coordination regarding immigration, refugee admissions, and programs to integrate foreigners and their family members already present in each country (Lee 2006). Several countries have instituted immigration quotas and restrictions. In 2014, Swiss voters narrowly approved immigration quotas for European Union citizens. (Switzerland is not a member of the European Union.) Analysts describe the vote as a response to a growing concern that immigrants are eroding the Swiss life style and culture. According to the European Commission, the vote went against the principle of the free movement of people (Baghdjian and Schmieder 2014).

Would you support the closing of our borders to all new immigrants? Why or why not?

What Does It Mean to Me?

Immigration is part of a complex interdependent system, where native-born Americans depend on immigrants for their labor and immigrants depend on the economic opportunities that are available in our society. Is immigration a problem in your state? Who is affected and how? Is the 2010 Arizona law an effective solution to the problem of immigration?

Income and Wealth

"Race is so associated with class in the United States that it might not be direct discrimination, but it still matters indirectly," says sociologist Dalton Conley (Ohlemacher 2006:A6). Data reported by the U.S. Census reveal that Black households had the lowest median income in 2013 ($34,598), or 59% of the median income for non-Hispanic White households ($58,270). The median income for Hispanic households was $40,963, 70% of the median for non-Hispanic White households. Asian households had the highest median income ($67,065), 115% of the median for non-Hispanic White households (DeNavas-Walt and Proctor 2014).

Because of years of discrimination, low educational attainment, high unemployment, or underemployment, Blacks and Hispanics have not been able to achieve the same earnings or level of wealth as White Americans have. In 2011, the average household income for Whites was $67,175. Blacks earned, on average, about 59% of what White households earned, or $39,760. The amount was about the same for Hispanics ($40,007, or 60% of White average household income). The median household wealth of Black households was $6,446, less than one tenth the median net worth of White households ($91,405). Hispanic median net worth was also lower than that of White households at $7,843 (Pew Research Center 2014).

One measure of wealth is home ownership. Home ownership is one of the primary means to accumulate wealth (Williams, Nesiba, and Diaz McConnell 2005). It enables families to finance college and invest in their future. Historically, home ownership grew among White middle-class families after World War II, when veterans had access to government and credit programs that made home ownership more affordable. However, Blacks and other minority groups have been denied similar access because of structural barriers such as discrimination, low income, and lack of credit access. Feagin (1999) identifies how inequality in home ownership has contributed to inequality in other aspects of American life. Specifically, Blacks have been disadvantaged because of their lack of home ownership, particularly in their inability to provide their children with "the kind of education or other cultural advantages necessary for their children to compete equally or fairly with Whites" (Feagin 1999:86).

In 2004, U.S. home ownership reached a record high of 69.2%, with nearly 73.4 million Americans owning their own homes. However, racial gaps in home ownership persist. In 2011, 73.8% of White households owned their own homes, compared with 44.9% of Black and 46.9% of Hispanic households (U.S. Census Bureau 2012a).

Education

The U.S. Supreme Court's 1954 decision in *Brown v. Board of Education* ruled that racial segregation in public schools was illegal. Reaction to the ruling was

Table 3.5 Educational attainment by race and ethnicity (percentages reported), 2012

	Less Than 9th Grade	9th to 12th Grade	High School Graduate	Some College	College Graduate
Hispanic	21.1	14.7	26.6	23.5	13.9
Native born	7.3	12.3	29.0	33.3	18.0
Foreign born	32.3	16.7	24.7	24.7	10.6
White alone	2.6	5.9	28.7	28.7	32.6
Black alone	4.7	11.9	31.4	31.4	18.8
Asian alone	8.3	5.9	15.3	15.3	50.9
Other, not Hispanic	4.6	8.9	26.1	26.1	25.1
All	**5.7**	**7.9**	**28.0**	**29.2**	**29.2**

SOURCE: Brown and Patten 2014b.

mixed, with a strong response from the South. A major confrontation occurred in Arkansas, when Governor Orval Faubus used the state's National Guard to block the admission of nine Black students into Little Rock Central High School. The students persisted and successfully gained entry to the school the next day with 1,000 U.S. Army paratroopers at their side. The Little Rock incident has been identified as a catalyst for school integration throughout the South. Despite resistance to the Court's ruling, legally segregated education had disappeared by the mid-1970s.

However, a different type of segregation persists, called **de facto segregation**. De facto segregation refers to a subtler process of segregation that is the result of other processes, such as housing segregation, rather than an official policy (Farley 2005). Here, we clearly see the intersection of race and class. Schools have become economically segregated, with children of middle- and upper-class families attending predominantly White suburban schools and the children of poorer parents attending racially mixed urban schools (Gagné and Tewksbury 2003). Researchers, teachers, and policy makers have all observed a great disparity in the quality of education students receive in the United States (for more on social problems related to education, turn to Chapter 8). Educational systems reinforce patterns of social class inequality and, along with it, racial inequality (Farley 2005).

Though Latinos have the lowest educational achievement rates compared with all other major racial and ethnic groups in the United States (refer to Table 3.5), there

De facto segregation: A subtle process of segregation that is the result of other processes, such as housing segregation, rather than because of an official policy

has been a recent increase in rates of high school completion and college enrollment. Richard Fry and Paul Taylor (2013) reported that for the class of 2012, 69% of Hispanic high school graduates enrolled in college, compared with 67% of their White student peers. This percentage is an increase from what was reported for the class of 2000, when only 49% of Hispanic high school graduates enrolled in college. Fry and Taylor attribute the college enrollment increase to two structural factors: a tough and competitive job market and the importance Latino families place on a college education. Yet, Fry and Taylor also report that young Latinos are less likely than White students to complete a bachelor's degree. They cite U.S. Census Bureau data showing how only 11% of 22- to 24-year-old Latinos finish a four-year degree, compared to 22% of White students of the same age.

Much of the research on the achievement gap between Latinos and White students has focused on the characteristics of the students (family income, parents' level of education). However, according to the Pew Hispanic Center (Fry 2005), we need to also consider the social context of Hispanic students' learning, noting how educators and policy makers have more influence over the characteristics of their schools than over the characteristics of students. Based on their state and national assessment of the basic characteristics of public high schools for Hispanic and other students, the Pew Hispanic Center found that Latinos were more likely than Whites or Blacks to attend the largest public high schools (enrollment of at least 1,838 students). More than 56% of Hispanics attend large schools, compared with 32% of Blacks and 26% of Whites. Schools with larger enrollments are associated with lower student achievement and higher dropout rates. In addition, the center reported that Hispanics are more likely to be in high schools with lower instructional resources, including higher student-to-teacher ratios, which has been associated with lower academic performance. Nearly 37% of Hispanics are educated in public high schools with a student–teacher ratio greater than 22 to 1, compared with 14% of Blacks and 13% of White students (Fry 2005).

In June 2007, the U.S. Supreme Court, voting 5 to 4, invalidated the use of race to assign students to public schools, even if the goal was to achieve racial integration of a district's schools. The ruling addressed public school practices in Seattle, Washington (where 41% of all public school students are White), and Louisville, Kentucky (where two thirds of all public school students are White). Legal experts and educators were divided about whether the ruling affirmed or betrayed *Brown v. Board of Education*. Writing for the majority, Chief Justice John Roberts asserted, "Simply because the school districts may seek a worthy goal [racial integration] does not mean they are free to discriminate on the basis of race to achieve it." Though he voted with the majority, Justice Anthony M. Kennedy said in a separate statement that achieving racial diversity and addressing the problem of de facto segregation were issues that school districts could constitutionally pursue as long as the programs were "sufficiently 'narrowly tailored'" (Greenhouse 2007:A1).

Health

"Although race may be a social construct, it produces profound biological mani-festations through stress, decreased services, decreased medications, and decreased hospital procedures" (Gabard and Cooper 1998:346). Racial disparities in access to health care and outcomes are pervasive, according to Sara Rosenbaum and Joel Teitelbaum (2004). The issue is twofold: (1) access to health care and (2) the quality of care received once in the system.

First, the researchers point to this nation's approach to health insurance as a sys-tem that "significantly discriminates against racial and ethnic minorities" (Rosen-baum and Teitelbaum 2004:138). Data reveal how in a voluntary, employment-based health care system, racial and ethnic minority group members are more likely to be uninsured or publicly insured. In 2013, White non-Hispanics had the low-est uninsured rate (9.8%), compared with Blacks (15.9%), Asians (14.5%), and Hispanics (24.3%) (Smith and Medalia 2014). These disparities continue into old age—among those 65 years or older, non-Latino White seniors are more likely to have a private or employer-based supplemental health policy in addition to their Medicare coverage, whereas minority seniors are six to seven times more likely to have Medicaid (public assistance) in addition to Medicare. The Affordable Care Act Medicaid expansions or premium tax credits for exchange coverage (with full implementation in 2015) have the potential to increase insurance access for racial and ethnic minorities.

Second, the researchers observe that even after minority patients enter a partic-ular facility, they are less likely to receive the level of care provided to nonminority patients for the same condition, regardless of their insurance status. For example, Latino and African American patients with public insurance do not receive coro-nary artery bypass surgery at rates comparable to those of White, publicly insured patients. African American women with breast cancer receive lower-quality cancer care after diagnosis and are delayed in receiving treatments when compared with White women with breast cancer (Parker-Pope 2013). Medicaid-insured African American and Latino children use less primary care (depending usually on emer-gency treatment), experience higher rates of hospitalization, and die at significantly higher rates than do White children. Though the U.S. government has invested in community-based primary health centers and programs to address these health care gaps, Rosenbaum and Teitelbaum (2004) conclude that these programs can hardly overcome the immense and inaccessible system of specialized and extended health services.

W. Michael Byrd and Linda Clayton (2002) assert that the health crisis among African Americans and poor populations is fueled by a medical-social culture laden with ideological, intellectual and scientific, and discriminatory race and class prob-lems. They believe that America's health system is predicated on the belief that the poor and "unworthy" of our society do not deserve decent health. Consequently, health professionals, as well as research and educational systems, engage in what they describe as "self serving and elite behavior" that marginalizes and ignores the problems of health care for minority and disadvantaged groups. They caution that our failure to address, and eventually resolve, these race- and class-based health policy, structural, medical-social, and cultural problems plaguing the American health care system could potentially undermine any possibility of a level playing field in health and health care for African American and other poor populations—eroding at the front end the very foundations of American democracy (Byrd and Clayton 2002:572–73).

RESPONDING TO RACIAL AND ETHNIC INEQUALITIES

Immigration Policy

In 2006 and 2007, the George W. Bush administration proposed comprehensive immigration reforms (CIR). Illegal immigration became a primary concern for Americans, responding to the threat of terrorism and increasing competition in a struggling economy. While acknowledging the country's immigration heritage, the administration proposed strengthening security at our southern border with Mexico and establishing a temporary worker program without the benefit of amnesty. The plan was criticized for creating a class of workers who would never become fully integrated in U.S. society and for focusing specifically on Mexican workers, ignoring all other immigrant groups.

In 2009, similar to the Bush plan, Obama officials promoted the need for tougher enforcement laws against illegal immigrants and employers who hire them, a streamlined system for legal immigration, and a system for illegal immigrants to earn legal status (Preston 2009). However, the administration's continuing focus on punitive enforcement strategies has been criticized for failing to encourage and promote assimilation among immigrants and their children. Nationwide polls show broad support for tougher border and workplace enforcement, while also establishing an opportunity for citizenship.

After the U.S. Congress was unable to pass a bipartisan immigration bill, the states took matters into their own hands, debating similar immigration issues in their own state legislatures (Preston 2007). Between 2005 and 2011, more than 8,000 bills related to immigration were introduced throughout the country, and approximately 1,700 were signed into law (National Conference of State Legislatures 2011). These laws addressed a range of immigration issues—the use of unauthorized illegal workers, the use of false identification (e.g., Social Security), and the extension of education and health care benefits to legal immigrants. Arizona legislators passed SB 1070, the toughest immigration bill, in 2010, requiring local law enforcement agencies and officers to demand proof of citizenship from suspected illegal immigrants.

On International Workers Day, these Arizona marchers show their support for immigrants and immigration reform.

Failure to carry proper documentation, even if one is a legal immigrant, is defined as a misdemeanor.

In 2011, 31 states introduced legislation replicating all or part of SB 1070. Voters in five states—Alabama, Georgia, Indiana, South Carolina, and Utah—successfully passed immigration laws modeled after SB 1070. In 2012, the Supreme Court upheld part of Arizona's law, permitting the "show me your papers" provision, while ruling that the state could not pursue policies that undermined or conflicted with federal law, for example, by making it a crime under state law for immigrants to fail to register under a federal law, making it a state crime for illegal immigrants to work, and allowing police to arrest individuals without warrants (Liptak 2012). The decision will affect similar laws in the five other states. Civil rights groups and immigration advocates expressed concern that the justices' decision would encourage racial profiling. The Court suggested that it would be open to hearing new challenges based on any adverse impact its ruling might have on the civil rights of Arizona residents (Preston 2012a).

The impact of immigration especially for youth and young adults has been the focus of federal and state government debate. **Second generation** applies to those born in the United States to one or more foreign-born parents. Based on key measures of socioeconomic attainment (income, college graduation, homeownership, and poverty rates), most second-generation Americans are better off than first generation Americans. Their characteristics resemble the full U.S. adult population (Pew

Second generation:
Those born in the United States to one or more foreign-born parents

Research 2013). In contrast, the **1.5 generation** refers to individuals who immigrated to the United States as a child or an adolescent. The parents of the 1.5 generation are foreign born. Members of the 1.5 generation are described as living between two worlds; though they spend most of their life in the United States, they still are not legal citizens.

Through executive action, in 2012 the Obama administration blocked the deportation of more than 800,000 migrants who came to the United States before age 16 (Preston and Cushman 2012; White House 2012). The Deferred Action for Childhood Arrivals (DACA) allows those who have lived in the United States for at least five years and are currently enrolled in school, high school graduates, or military veterans in good standing to work legally and to obtain driver's licenses. An immigrant convicted of a felony, a serious misdemeanor, or three less serious misdemeanors would not be eligible. The Pew Hispanic Center estimated that as many as 1.4 million immigrants would be eligible for this measure (Preston and Cushman 2012), most of them (about 460,000) living in California (Preston 2012b).

As congressional gridlock on immigration continued in 2014, President Obama announced a series of executive actions that would grant up to 5 million unauthorized immigrants protection from deportation. His order created a deferred action program for parents of U.S. citizens. Undocumented immigrant parents would have to pass background checks, pay fees, and show that their child was born before the president's announcement. The president also announced the extension of DACA eligibility to men and women who entered the United States as children before January 2010, regardless of how old they are today. DACA relief will be extended to three years (White House 2014). In response, a group of 20 states filed a federal lawsuit, claiming that the president had overstepped his executive authority.

Affirmative Action

Since its inception 50 years ago, affirmative action has been a "contentious issue on national, state, and local levels" (Yee 2001:135). Affirmative action is a policy that has attempted to improve minority access to occupational and educational opportunities (Woodhouse 2002). No federal initiatives enforced affirmative action until 1961, when President John Kennedy signed Executive Order 10925. The order created the Committee on Equal Employment Opportunity and forbade employers with federal contracts from discriminating on the basis of race, color, national origin, or religion in their hiring practices. In 1964, President Lyndon Johnson signed into law the Civil Rights Act, which prohibits discrimination based on race, color, religion, or national origin by private employers, agencies, and educational institutions receiving federal funds (Swink 2003).

In June 1965, during a graduation speech at Howard University, President Johnson spoke for the first time about the importance of providing opportunities to minority groups, an important objective of affirmative action. According to Johnson (1965),

1.5 generation:
Individuals who immigrated to the United States as a child or an adolescent.

VOICES IN THE COMMUNITY

SOFIA CAMPOS

Sofia was 6 years old when she moved with her family from Peru to the United States. Sofia and her siblings quickly adjusted to their new lives in Los Angeles. It was not until she was accepted into UCLA that Sofia discovered that her family had immigrated illegally. Her mother revealed the secret when Sofia needed a Social Security number to apply for federal scholarships. Sofia explains, "I was angry at first that she hadn't told me. But I understand why they did that. It was to protect us for as long as they could, like any parent would do with their child" (quoted in Del Barco 2012).

Though she was able to pay in-state tuition (California is one of 13 states that allows undocumented students to pay in-state tuition), she could not receive any scholarships. Sophia worked her way through college and in five years, graduated with a double major in International Developmental Studies and Political Science.

Sofia began her activism while she was at UCLA. Inspired by her own experiences, her focus was on undocumented student rights. "That hateful language, you know, like 'illegal, alien, wetback leach'. People were talking about my brother, my sister, my mom, my dad. How can these people, who don't know me at all, who don't know the love that exists within my family, how can you be just so hateful?" (quoted in Del Barco 2012). She was a central figure in several UCLA student organizations, promoting the federal and California versions of the DREAM Act, also known as the Development, Relief, and Education for Alien Minors Act. Sofia currently serves as the board chair of United We Dream, the largest network of undocumented immigrant youth. In 2014, she was enrolled in a master's program at MIT (United We Stand 2014).

The DREAM Act was first introduced in the U.S. Congress in 2001. The DREAM Act would enact two major changes in the current law: (1) Certain immigrant students who have grown up in the United States would be permitted to apply for temporary legal status and to eventually obtain permanent legal status and qualify for U.S. citizenship if they went to college or served in the U.S. military, and (2) the federal provision that penalizes states that provide in-state tuition without regard to immigration status would be eliminated. Though the federal DREAM Act has not been passed, 15 states, including California, have passed their own versions of the act, extending in-state tuition and financial aid to undocumented college students.

Opponents of the DREAM Act argue that it is unfair to American-born and legal immigrant college students and their families. What do you think about the DREAM Act proposals? Has your state adopted a DREAM Act?

you do not take a person who, for years, has been hobbled by chains and liberate him, bring him to the starting line of a race and then say, "You are free to compete with all others" and still justly believe you have been completely fair. Thus it is not enough just to open the gates of opportunity. All our citizens must have the ability to walk through those gates. This is the next and the more profound stage of the battle for civil rights. We seek not just freedom but opportunity. (p. 366)

Employment

In September 1965, President Johnson signed Executive Order 11246, which required government contractors to "take affirmative action" toward prospective minority employees in all aspects of hiring and employment. Contractors are required to take specific proactive measures to ensure equality in hiring without regard to race, religion, and national origin. The order also established the Equal Employment Opportunity Commission (EEOC), charged with enforcing and monitoring compliance among federal contractors. In 1967, President Johnson amended the order to include discrimination based on gender (Swink 2003). In 1969, President Richard Nixon initiated the Philadelphia Plan, which required federal contractors to develop affirmative action plans by setting minimum levels of minority participation for federal construction projects in Philadelphia and three other cities (Idelson 1995). This was the first order that endorsed the use of specific goals for desegregating the workplace (Kotlowski 1998), but it did not include fixed quotas (Woodhouse 2002). India's affirmative action program relies on quotas in the public (government) sector. In Northern Ireland, affirmative action is practiced in public and private sectors, including government contractors, and does not rely on quotas (Muttarak et al. 2013).

According to Dawn Swink (2003), "While the initial efforts of affirmative action were directed primarily at federal government employment and private industry, affirmative action gradually extended into other areas, including admissions programs in higher education" (pp. 214–15). State and local governments followed the lead of the federal government and took formal steps to encourage employers to diversify their workforces.

Opponents of affirmative action believe that such policies encourage preferential treatment for minorities (Woodhouse 2002), giving women and ethnic minorities an unfair advantage over White males (Yee 2001). Affirmative action, say its critics, promotes "reverse discrimination," the hiring of unqualified minorities and women at the expense of qualified White males (Pincus 2003). Some believe affirmative action has not worked and ultimately results in the stigmatization of those who benefit from the policies (Heilman, Block, and Stahatos 1997; Herring and Collins 1995).

Proponents argue that only through affirmative action policies can we address the historical societal discrimination that minorities experienced in the past (Kaplan and Lee 1995). Although these policies have not created true equality, there have been important accomplishments (Tsang and Dietz 2001). As a result of affirmative action, women and people of color have gained increased access to forms of public employment and education that were once closed to them (Yee 2001). Yet, research indicates that ethnic minorities and women do not have an unfair advantage over White men. Women and ethnic minorities are not receiving equal compensation compared with White males with similar education and background (Tsang and Dietz 2001). Wage disparities and job segregation continue to exist in the workplace (G. L. A. Harris 2009).

G. L. A. Harris (2009) explains that although the record on affirmation action is mixed, there is evidence that without the policy and the use of gender, race, and/or other ethnicity as part of the employment hiring process, the employment status of women and underrepresented minorities would be worse. Affirmative action has been the "only comprehensive set of policies that has given women and people of color opportunities for better paying jobs and access to higher education that did not exist before" (Yee 2001:137). There is also evidence of how White employees benefit from the inclusion of these groups in the workplace; for example, companies with more than 100 employees with affirmation action programs have higher earnings for Whites, women, and minority employee groups (Pincus 2003).

Shawn Woodhouse (1999, 2002) argues that the differences in individual perceptions of affirmative action policy may be related to the differences of racial group histories and socialization experiences. She writes,

> Based upon these rationalizations, it is implicit that individuals interpret affirmative action through an ethnic specific lens. In other words, most individuals will assess their group condition when considering contentious legislation such as affirmative action because after all, a group's history impacts its view of American society. (Woodhouse 2002:158)

Education

Based on Title VI of the 1964 Civil Rights Act, affirmative action policies have been applied to student recruitment, admissions, and financial aid programs. Title VI permits the consideration of race, national origin, sex, or disability to provide opportunities to a class of disqualified people, such as minorities and women, who have been denied educational opportunities. Affirmative action policies have been supported as remedies for past discrimination as means to encourage diversity in higher education and as a tool for social justice. Such policies also have economic motivations, helping disadvantaged populations achieve economic self-sufficiency. Affirmative action practices were affirmed in the 1978 Supreme Court decision in the *Regents of the University of California v. Bakke*, suggesting that race-sensitive policies were necessary to create diverse campus environments (American Council on Education and American Association of University Professors 2000; Springer 2005).

Although affirmative action has been practiced since the Bakke decision, it has been under attack, particularly via challenges of the diversity argument in the Supreme Court's decision. The first challenge occurred in one of our most diverse states, California. In 1995, the California Board of Regents banned the use of affirmative action guidelines in admissions. In 1996, California voters followed and passed Proposition 209, the California Civil Rights Initiative, which effectively dismantled the state's affirmative action programs in education and employment. Also in 1996, a federal appeals court ruling struck down affirmative action in Texas. In the *Hopwood v. Texas* decision, the ruling referred to affirmative action policies as a form of discrimination against White students. State of Washington voters passed an initiative in 1998 that banned the use of race-conscious affirmative action in schools. In 1999, Florida governor Jeb Bush banned the use of affirmative action in admission to his state's schools.

The Hopwood ruling led to a decline in the number of minority students enrolling in Texas A&M and the University of Texas (Yardley 2002). California's state universities experienced a similar drop in minority student applications and enrollment after the Bakke decision and the California Civil Rights Initiative. In response, states have instituted other practices with the goal of increasing minority student recruitment. For example, California and Texas have initiated percentage solutions. In Texas, the top 10% of all graduating seniors are automatically admitted into the University of Texas system. (In 2009, the Texas Legislature voted to put limits on the program, setting enrollment caps on the number of students let in under the rule at 75% of the entering class.) California initiated a similar plan, covering only the top 4% of students, and Florida implemented the One Florida Initiative, allowing the top 20% of graduating high school seniors into the state's public colleges and universities (Schemo 2001). As of 2014, all three plans remain in effect.

For more than a decade, the University of Michigan's affirmation action program has been disputed. In 2000, a federal judge upheld the University of Michigan's program, ruling that "a racially and ethnically diverse student body produces significant educational benefits such that diversity, in the context of higher education, constitutes a compelling governmental interest" (Wilgoren 2000:A32). In 2003, the case was considered by the U.S. Supreme Court, and in a 5 to 4 vote, the Court upheld the University of Michigan's consideration of race for admission into its law school. Writing for the majority, Justice Sandra Day O'Connor stated, "In order to cultivate a set of leaders with legitimacy in the eyes of the citizenry, it is necessary that the path to leadership be visibly open to talented and qualified individuals of every race and ethnicity" (Greenhouse 2003:A1). In a separate decision, the U.S. Supreme Court voted 6 to 1, invalidating the university's affirmative action program for admission into its undergraduate program (Greenhouse 2003). In November 2006, Michigan voters approved Proposal 2, a state constitutional amendment banning consideration of race or gender in public university admissions or government hiring or contracting. Following the state's challenge to the amendment, in 2014, the U.S. Supreme Court upheld Proposal 2, ending race-based admissions at any Michigan state schools or at any other public university in states that have ended the practice. As of 2014, 10 states have outlawed the use of affirmative action in public schools. In most of these states, there has been a decrease in the enrollment of Black and Hispanic students in their most selective colleges and universities (Liptak 2014). To achieve diversity among their student body, colleges and universities will have to focus on student socioeconomic status rather than race.

Lucy Nicholson/Reuters

How ethnically and racially diverse is your community? What are the largest ethnic and racial groups?

Encouraging Diversity and Multiculturalism

Accelerated global migration and a resurgence of racial/ethnic conflicts characterized the close of the 20th century (Wittig and Grant-Thompson 1998) and certainly the beginning of the 21st. In an effort to reduce racial/ethnic conflict and to encourage multiculturalism, researchers, educators, political and community leaders, and community members have implemented programs targeting racism and prejudice. Acknowledging that both are complex phenomena with individual, cultural, and structural components, these strategies attempt to address some or most of the components.

Kathleen Korgen, J. Mahon, and Gabe Wang (2003) believe that colleges and universities have the potential to counter the effects of segregated neighborhoods and socialization in primary and secondary schools. Interaction among races thrust together on a college campus provides a unique opportunity for individuals to experience and discuss the aspects of racial/ethnic diversity in their lives, some for the first time (Odell, Korgen, and Wang 2005). Increased interaction with members of different groups should allow individuals an opportunity to learn from others, reducing hostility and prejudice (Shook and Fazio 2008). Interpersonal interactions with racially diverse peers also promote civic engagement, especially if the engagement is diversity related (Bowman 2011).

Gordon Allport (1954) argues that intergroup contact can have a positive effect in reducing interracial prejudice and increasing tolerance if four conditions are met: (1) there is cooperative interdependence among the groups, (2) the groups share a

SOCIOLOGY AT WORK

THE SCIENCE OF SOCIOLOGY: VALUES VS. FACTS

Almost everyone has an opinion about our country's immigration policy. Supporting amnesty for all undocumented immigrants is a value statement, as is expressing support for deporting every undocumented man, woman, and child. These opinions reflect our values, the way we think things should be (Day 2009). We demonstrate our values even in our language; for when we choose to use to refer to someone as "illegal" versus "undocumented," we are expressing a value statement.

But, as a student of sociology, you have learned how sociology and other social sciences require a separation of our values from the pursuit of knowledge. While values are subjective and feeling based, knowledge is objective and can be tested or validated empirically, based upon evidence (Levy 1973). The goal of science is to collect facts, to identify the way things are (Day 2009).

In Chapter 1, we considered how values influence what we choose to care about or research. A sociologist may study immigration policies because he was an immigrant himself or because he values a pluralistic society, yet the sociologist must collect and analyze his data objectively, not allowing his values or experiences to obscure the objective research process.

Throughout your college experience, you will encounter many contentious and divisive issues in the classroom, perhaps several in this social problems course. Your ability to distinguish values from facts and to separate objective versus subjective realities is important in your development as a social scientist, which we'll continue to examine in Chapter 4's Sociology at Work feature.

Identify the objective versus subjective realities of the immigration problem in the United States. Is it difficult to distinguish between values and facts? Why or why not?

common goal, (3) the groups are of equal status during contact, and (4) the groups have the support of authority figures.

Increasing numbers of colleges and universities are instituting course requirements that encourage students to examine diversity in the United States and globally. The Association of American Colleges and Universities (2000) reported that 62% of schools have a diversity course requirement or were in the process of developing one. This is quite an increase from 1990, when only 15% of colleges and universities had such a requirement. Cocurricular programming may also include cultural awareness workshops, identity-based student organizations, and multicultural events (Bowman 2011). Research is emerging on the effectiveness of diversity programming on college and university campuses. In one such study, D. A. Grinde (2001) found that more than 85% of University of Vermont students believed that diversity courses strengthened their understanding and appreciation of cultural diversity. In general, there appears to be an overall positive effect of curricular and cocurricular diversity activities in reducing the racial bias in college students. White students benefit more from these diversity activities than students of color (Denson 2009).

Educational programs are used most often to promote diversity in public and private workplaces. These programs attempt to eliminate incorrect stereotypes and unfounded prejudices by providing new information to participants (Farley 2005). Diversity training is thought to make managers aware of how their biases affect their actions in the workplace (Kalev, Dobbin, and Kelly 2006). Research indicates that such programs are effective when people are not made to feel defensive over past behavior but are participating in a learning process of new (vs. old) ideas. This has also been found to be effective in diversity simulation and experiential exercises (i.e., role-playing) (Farley 2005). These programs are designed to familiarize employees with antidiscrimination laws, to suggest behavioral changes that could address bias, and to increase cultural awareness and cross-cultural communication among employees (Bendick, Egan, and Lofhjelm 1998).

Business leaders are motivated to address diversity on principle and because they recognize how their company's productivity and success depend on it (Galagan 1993). General diversity and management programs have been established in companies such as Aetna, Ernst & Young, General Mills, and Hewlett-Packard. All programs note the importance of creating an "inclusive" workforce and work environment. In addition to diversity training or sensitivity programs, businesses have successfully implemented diversity management programs, targeting the development and advancement of women and people of color in their organizations.

. . . .

What Does It Mean to Me?

What diversity courses or programs are offered at your university? How have these experiences changed your perspective on racial and ethnic diversity?

. . . .

CHAPTER REVIEW
. . . .

3.1 Describe the difference between race and ethnic groups

From a biological perspective, a race can be defined as a group or population that shares a set of genetic characteristics and physical features. Social scientists reject the biological notion of race, instead treating race as a social construct. Ethnic groups are set off to some degree from other groups by displaying a unique set of cultural traits, such as their language, religion, or diet.

3.2 Identify the different types of institutional discrimination

Institutional discrimination may include segregation, exclusion, or expulsion. Segregation refers to the physical and social separation of ethnic or racial groups. Exclusion refers to the practice of prohibiting or restricting the entry or participation of groups in society. Expulsion is the removal of a group by using direct force or intimidation.

3.3 Summarize how the sociological perspectives explain problems related to race and ethnicity

Functionalists believe that the differences between racial and ethnic groups are largely cultural. The solution is assimilation, a process where minority group members become part of the dominant group, losing their original distinct group identity. Conflict theorists focus on how the dynamics of racial and ethnic relations divide groups while maintaining a dominant group. Ethnocentrism and racism maintain the status quo by dividing individuals along racial and ethnic lines. Feminist theory intersects with multiculturalism through the analysis of multiple systems of oppression, including categories of race, class, sexual orientation, nation of origin, language, culture, and ethnicity. From an interactionist perspective, race is a social construct. Social scientists have noted how people are raced, how race itself is not a category but a practice.

3.4 Describe the impact of immigrant or illegal workers in the labor force

No single occupation is composed entirely of immigrant labor. Immigration has been found to have a negative effect on the wages of native-born Americans, primarily in low-paying, low-skilled occupations.

3.5 Explain how the college experience increases racial/ethnic diversity awareness

Interaction among races thrust together on a college campus provides a unique opportunity for individuals to experience and discuss the aspects of racial/ethnic diversity in their lives, and to learn from others, reducing hostility and prejudice.

KEY TERMS

1.5 generation, 88

assimilation, 69

de facto segregation, 83

ethnic attrition, 73

ethnic groups, 65

ethnocentrism, 68

exclusion, 69

expulsion, 69

foreign-born, 67

individual discrimination, 68

institutional discrimination, 68

labor migration, 76

multicultural literature, 75

multiracial, 73

native, 67

pluralism, 70

race, 65

racism, 68

refugees, 67

second generation, 87

segregation, 68

transnational, 96

STUDY QUESTIONS

1. How are race and ethnicity socially constructed? Why do you think racial distinctions persist?

2. Distinguish between assimilation and pluralism (or multiculturalism). What are the advantages and disadvantages of each? Which model best describes racial and ethnic relations in the United States?

3. The term **transnational** has been used to describe the immigrants who "maintain familial, economic,

cultural, and political ties across international borders, in effect making the home and host society a single arena for social action" (Foner 2000:170). In effect, transnationals have two homes. Is this functional for society? Is it functional for the life of an immigrant?

4. The interactionist perspective argues that certain races or ethnicities are bestowed power and privilege not given to other groups. Do you agree with this statement? What examples of privilege can you think of, and what are their consequences?

5. Identify and explain the two types of racial disparities in health care.

6. What are the consequences of a less-educated, lower-skilled immigrant population? How is this associated with employment, economic inequality, and health care access?

7. Which sociological perspective best explains the problem of immigration in our society? Explain.

8. Explain how having contact and interaction with other racial or ethnic groups (at school or at work) reduces interracial prejudice.

$\circledS$ SAGE edge™

Sharpen your skills with SAGE edge at **edge.sagepub.com/leonguerrero5e**

SAGE edge provides a personalized approach to help you accomplish your coursework goals in an easy-to-use learning environment.

Sex: Physiological distinctions between male and female

Gender: Social construction of masculine and feminine attitudes and behaviors

In 2012, an all-male panel testified on Capitol Hill on the Blunt Amendment, a proposed federal policy exception that would have allowed religious groups and employers to opt out of providing any kind of health care service, including contraception, for religious reasons. The photo of the panel was widely distributed in the media, often accompanied by the headline "What is wrong with this picture?" The exclusion of a female voice on a panel on contraception stirred up a firestorm. Two female House representatives walked out of the hearing. House representatives followed with their own hearing featuring one female witness, Georgetown student Sandra Fluke, who had been turned away from the original hearing. Democrats argued that Republicans were turning back the clock on women's rights (Pear 2012).

There is no society where men and women perform identical functions, nor are they ranked or treated equally. Regardless of their level of technological development or the complexity of their social structure, all societies have some form of gender inequality (Marger 2008). Some may argue that there are fundamental differences between males and females based on fixed physiological differences or our **sex**. Yes, there are biological differences—our sexual organs, our hormones, and other physiological aspects—that are relatively fixed at birth (Marger 2008), but more than that makes us unequal.

Sociologists focus on the differences determined by our society and our culture, our **gender**. Although we are born male and female, we must understand and learn masculine or feminine behaviors. Gender legitimates certain activities and ways of thinking over others; it grants privilege to

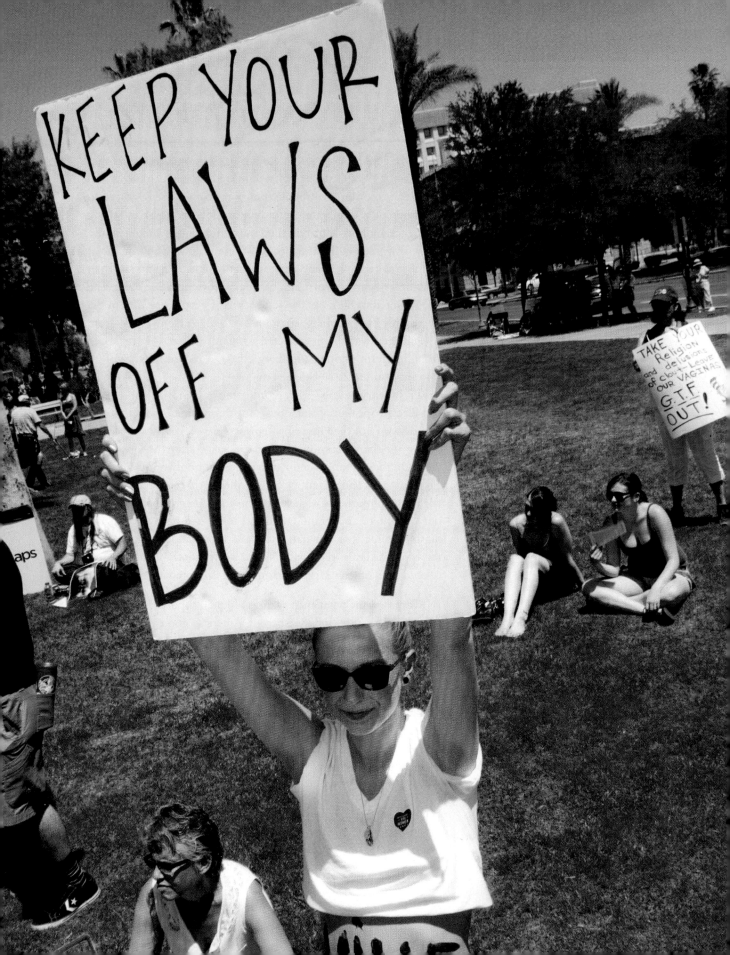

one group over another (Tickner 2002). **Sexism** refers to prejudice or discrimination based solely on someone's sex or gender. Although sexism has come to refer to negative beliefs and actions directed toward women, men can also be subject to sexism.

Social scientists believe that gender differences are not caused by biological differences; rather, they are a product of socialization, prejudice, discrimination, and other forms of social control (Bem 1993). For example, religious ideologies can define and regulate gender differences. According to Islamic tradition, women are relegated to home and family life, while men dominate everything outside the home. A strong patriarchal system is enforced among Mormon fundamentalists in the United States.

Consider the history of women in the U.S. Senate. There is nothing automatic at birth that makes men more suited to become senators than women. The first woman senator was Rebecca Latimer Felton, sworn into office on November 21, 1922. The Georgia senator was appointed to fill a vacancy and served for only one day. In the early 1990s, there were only two women senators. In 1992, Patty Murray, from my home state of Washington, was the first elected woman senator to have young children at home during her term in office (Stolberg 2003). A record number of 20 women were elected to serve in the 2013 U.S. Senate.

Sexism: Prejudice or discrimination based solely on someone's sex

On January 4, 2007, U.S. representative Nancy Pelosi (D-CA) was elected Speaker of the House, the first woman to fill this role in the history of the House of Representatives. Pelosi was second in line for the succession of the presidency, after the vice president. On the day of her induction, Pelosi not only noted how her election was an important victory for her party but also acknowledged the importance of her election for women. She said, "For our daughters and granddaughters, today we have broken the marble ceiling. For our daughters and our granddaughters now, the sky is the limit" (Pelosi 2007). Yet a few months later, as Pelosi celebrated Women's History Month, she is quoted as saying,

> Women want what men want: an equal opportunity to succeed, a safe and prosperous America, good paying jobs, better access to health care, and the best possible education for our children. . . . Yet in terms of policies to assist women, we are lagging behind. Paychecks for women have dropped three years in [a] row by almost $1,000. On average, working women earn only 77 cents for every dollar working men earn, and over the last five years, the number of women living in poverty has grown by almost 3 million. (Pelosi 2007)

Despite the record number of women serving in Congress, the United States is behind other countries in female representation in national parliament or congress. Refer to Table 4.1 for more information.

Table 4.1 Ten countries with the highest percentage of seats in national parliaments held by women, August 2014

Country	Percentage of Women
Rwanda	63.8
Andorra	50.0
Cuba	48.9
Sweden	45.0
Seychelles	43.8
Senegal	43.3
Finland	42.5
Nicaragua	42.4
Ecuador	41.6
South Africa	40.8

SOURCE: Adapted from Inter-Parliamentary Union 2014.

NOTE: In the list compiled by the Inter-Parliamentary Union (2014), the United States ranks 72nd; 19.4% of seats are held by women.

 Changing Gender Roles

....

What Does It Mean to Me?

In 2011, the U.S. Coast Guard Academy named Rear Admiral Sandra Stosz its first female superintendent. She is the first woman to lead a U.S. service academy. Examine the academic leadership in your university. How many top positions are held by men? By women? Is leadership gendered at your university?

....

SOCIOLOGICAL PERSPECTIVES ON GENDER INEQUALITY

Functionalist Perspective

Functionalists argue that gender inequality is inevitable because of the **gendered division of labor** in the household. According to Émile Durkheim, social evolution led to the exaggeration of sex differences in personalities and abilities. In the most basic of social institutions, the family, it became necessary for men and women to establish role differentiation as well as functional interdependence. In other words, men and women would have complementary but different roles in the household.

Durkheim (2007) wrote of the biological differences between men and women, claiming that women had smaller brain capacity than males: "Woman retired from warfare and public affairs and consecrated her entire life to her family" (p. 43). As a result, women led completely different lives than men. This division of labor applied both in and out of the home—women were charged with familial roles, taking care of their children and their home, while men were charged with public work roles, assuming their primary role as family breadwinner. Although this division of labor may have been practical in preindustrial society, these roles remain gender specific in modern society (Marger 2008). Though women have transitioned from a housekeeper role to a dual role of earner and caregiver, men's involvement in domestic work remains low.

The principle that women and men are suited for different roles extends to the workplace. Women dominate service and caring professions (e.g., teaching, health care, sales, and administrative support), while men are overrepresented in instrumental work (e.g., construction, heavy labor, and mechanics). Even in the same professions, men and women are on different professional tracks. Among medical students, women choose primary care specialties, while a higher percentage of men choose surgical specialties. Women place a greater emphasis on the physician–patient relationship than men (McFarland and Rhoades 1998). For more on occupational segregation, refer to the section of this chapter titled "The Consequences of Gender Inequality."

This gendered division of labor and gender roles is held as the standard for society. Gender inequality is defined not as a product of differential power but rather as a functional necessity (Marger 2008). Yet women who assert their rights for social and economic equality are seen as attacking the structure of society (Bonvillian

Gendered division of labor: Assignment of different tasks to men and women

 Tough Guise

2006). Theorists from this perspective note that as increasing numbers of women have entered the workforce, the number of divorces and the frequency of nonmarital childbearing have also increased. They suggest that children are more likely to suffer from divorce, more likely to become delinquent without adequate parental supervision, and more likely to be disadvantaged economically and socially if born to a single mother (Bonvillian 2006; Farley 2005). According to a 2013 Pew Research Center survey, most Americans believe that the increase in the number of working women has made it harder for parents to raise children and harder for marriages to succeed (Wang, Parker, and Taylor 2013). From this perspective, a change in gender roles (among women in particular) undermines the stability of the family (Farley 2005) and, ultimately, society.

Conflict and Feminist Perspectives

Gender inequality exists because it benefits a group in power and with power to shape society—men. Theorists from both perspectives argue that women will remain in their subordinate position as long as men maintain their social, economic, and cultural advantage in society. A system where men are dominant over women is referred to as a patriarchy, as defined earlier in Chapter 1.

Women's subordinate position in society is linked to their relationship to the means of production. As the next section of this chapter describes, compared with women, men are rewarded in our capitalist economy with higher wages, more prestige, and greater authority in the workplace (Bonvillian 2006). At home, men are treated with deference by their wives and children.

Bonvillian (2006) explains the interrelationship between patriarchal social relations and capitalist economies. As capitalistic economies developed, they incorporated preexisting patriarchal relations. Capitalism benefits from women's subordinate position at home. Women are willing to work in different types of jobs and for different wages than men because they define themselves according to their familial relationships as supporters rather than as breadwinners.

Capitalism also takes advantage of men's adherence to patriarchal values, subordinating men to their employers just as patriarchal relations subordinate women to men. Men are duty bound to their jobs because of a sense of self-worth and obligation tied to their ability to provide for their families (Bonvillian 2006). As men are limited to their prescribed positions in the economy and production, their inner emotional states are devalued in society. According to Böhnisch (2003), this limits the development of their full human potential (much like Marx cautioned), also contributing to a range of male problems (e.g., health and chronic illnesses, risk-taking, and violence).

Early feminist scholars treated gender as an individual attribute, as a property of individuals or as part of the role that was acquired through socialization. However, contemporary feminist theorists define gender as a system of social practices that creates and maintains gender distinctions and inequalities (Ridgeway and Smith-Lovin 1999).

 Ambition and the Gender Pay Gap

VOICES IN THE COMMUNITY

SANDRA FLUKE

Sandra Fluke gained national celebrity status after she testified before Congress in 2012 about the importance of contraceptive coverage in health insurance. Her comments were mostly about how her university, Georgetown University, refused to include contraceptive coverage in student insurance plans because it was a religiously affiliated (Catholic) school. Before this day, Fluke had a long history as an advocate for women's reproductive rights; Fluke is past president of the Georgetown Law Students for Reproductive Justice group.

Fluke explained that she wanted to tell the stories of women who did not have birth control:

> I wanted to be able to share their stories. My testimony would have been about women who have been affected by their policy, who have medical needs and suffered dire consequences . . . The committee did not get to hear real stories I had to share, about actual women who have been dramatically affected by this policy. (Quoted in Kliff 2012)

Fluke spoke about a gay friend who had an ovary removed because her insurance company wouldn't cover the prescription for birth control that she needed to control the growth of her cysts. "When you let university administrators or other employers, rather than women and their doctors, dictate whose medical needs are legitimate and whose are not, a woman's health takes a back seat to a bureaucracy focused on policing her body" (Fluke 2012).

Vicious attacks from conservative radio talk show host Rush Limbaugh continued to keep Fluke in the media spotlight after her testimony. Fluke wrote on her Tumblr site,

> No woman deserves to be disrespected in this manner. This language is an attack on all women, and has been used throughout history to silence

AP Photo/Nick Ut

Sandra Fluke gained national status after she testified before Congress in 2012 about the importance of contraceptive coverage in health insurance. Even before her testimony, Fluke had a long history as an advocate for women's reproductive rights.

> our voices. The millions of American women who have and will continue to speak out in support of women's health care and access to contraception prove that we will not be silenced. (Quoted in May 2012)

Limbaugh eventually apologized for his comments, but did not back down from his central argument that taxpayers' money should not be used to pay for contraception.

After graduating from Georgetown, in 2014, Fluke unsuccessfully ran for office in the California State Senate.

From an interactionist perspective, what effect, if any, did Limbaugh's comments have on Fluke's testimony or public image?

Gender is referred to as a process, where gender is continually produced and reproduced. Not only is this an individual characteristic, but also it exists within patterns of social interaction and social institutions (Wharton 2004).

Gender inequality is a product of a complex set of social forces: "These may include the actions of individuals, but they are also found in expectations that guide social interaction, the composition of social groups, and the structures and practices of the institutions" (Wharton 2004:157). Sexism may be an individual act, but it can also become institutionalized in our organizations or through laws and common practices.

True gender equality is possible only if women are able to assume positions of power in the economy and political system (Marger 2008) and redefine the structures and practices that oppress them. Though gender issues have been defined primarily as women's issues, the call for integrating men's issues into the discussion of gender inequality has become louder (Scambor and Scambor 2008). Structural inequalities between men and women don't just discriminate against women. From this perspective, tackling gender inequality means questioning gendered structures at various levels (labor, child care, socialization, family) and addressing the experience of men and women equally.

Interactionist Perspective

As interactionists explain, many social values and meanings are expressed in our language. Language, write Stephanie Wildman and Adrienne Davis (2000), "contributes to the invisibility and regeneration of privilege" (p. 50). These scholars argue that we need to sort individuals into categories such as race and gender. Upon hearing that someone has a new baby, why is it important to ask if it's a girl or a boy? This type of social categorization is important because it sets into motion the production of gender difference and inequality. Norms, values, and beliefs about the differences between boys and girls and men and women are reinforced through the gender socialization process. We won't know how to relate to this child without knowing its gender, and children won't understand what it means to be male or female in our society unless they are socialized accordingly. People respond to others based on what they believe is expected of them and assume that others will do the same (Wharton 2004).

Wildman and Davis note that characteristics of those who are privileged become societal norms—the standard of what is good, correct, and normal versus bad, incorrect, and aberrant. In terms of gender, men are privileged and serve as the standard. Wildman and Davis (2000) refer to Catharine MacKinnon's observation that, among many things, "men's physiology defines most sports, their health needs largely define insurance coverage . . . their perspectives and concerns define quality in scholarship, their experiences and obsessions define merit, . . . their image defines god, and their genitals define sex" (p. 54).

 Gender at the Toy Store

Male privilege defines many aspects of American culture from a distinctly male point of view. For example, the use of *he* is accepted as an all-inclusive pronoun, but a generic *she* is not permitted; some actually get upset if you try to use it (if you have any doubt, try referring to God as *she*). The response, according to Wildman and Davis, is not about incorrect grammar; rather, it is about challenging the system of male privilege.

A summary of the sociological perspectives is presented in Table 4.2.

Table 4.2 Summary of sociological perspectives: Inequalities based on gender

	Functionalist	Conflict/Feminist	Interactionist
Explanations of gender inequality	Gender inequality is a functional necessity. A gendered division of labor and gender roles is needed to ensure the stability of society.	Women will remain in their subordinate position as long as men maintain their social, economic, and cultural advantage. Conflict theorists identify how women's subordinate position is linked to their relationship to the means of production. Feminist theorists refer to gender as a process, a system of social practices that creates and maintains gender distinctions and inequalities.	Social values and meanings are expressed in our language. Our language reflects the privileged position granted to men.
Questions asked about gender inequality	What societal values are supported by our (traditional) gender roles? Can gender roles be changed without jeopardizing the stability of society?	How is gender inequality created and maintained? How can gender inequality structures and practices be altered? Can they be eliminated?	How does our use of language identify the privileged position of men in society? Can language be changed to reflect gender equality?

What Does It Mean to Me?

The Disney Channel's *Doc McStuffins* features an African American girl in pigtails who runs a home clinic for her stuffed animals and dolls. Her mom is a doctor, and her dad stays at home. *Doc McStuffins* has been praised for being a positive and inspirational role model for African American girls. According to the American Medical Association, in 2012, there were 18,533 Black female physicians, 2% of all U.S. doctors (Elber 2012). What role do the media play in shaping gender identity? In shaping occupational choices for boys and girls?

THE CONSEQUENCES OF GENDER INEQUALITY

Gender inequality is a persistent feature of all modern societies. In this section, we will review the consequences of inequality in women's employment and income. Additional discussions on gender inequality are presented in Chapter 8, "Education," and Chapter 9, "Work and the Economy." The section ends with an examination of violence against women.

Occupational Sex Segregation

Sex segregation in the workplace remains a historical and contemporary fact. Despite educational and occupational gains made by women, women continue to dominate traditionally female occupations, which is referred to as **occupational sex segregation**. These occupations include preschool and kindergarten teachers (98%), child care workers (95%), and receptionists (92%) (U.S. Department of Labor, Women's Bureau 2014). For the top five occupations of employed U.S. women, refer to Table 4.3. Researchers confirm that working in an occupation with a large proportion of female workers leads to lower wages, lower prestige, worse working conditions, and slower career mobility for both men and women (Perales 2013).

AP Photo/Elaine Thompson

The U.S. labor force continues to be segregated along gender lines. Although a small percentage of women, 25% or less, are employed in traditionally male blue-collar occupations (such as construction, truck driving, and manufacturing), women continue to dominate administrative (clerical) and service occupations, constituting more than 80% of employees in these occupations (U.S. Department of Labor, Women's Bureau 2014).

Occupational sex segregation: The degree to which men and women are concentrated in occupations that predominantly employ workers of one sex

Horizontal segregation: The separation of men and women into different industries and occupations

Vertical segregation: The separation of men and women in workplace hierarchies; lower-ranking positions are dominated by women, while management ranks are dominated by men

Social scientists examine two types of sex segregation in the workplace—horizontal and vertical. **Horizontal segregation** represents the separation of women into nonmanual labor and men into manual labor sectors. **Vertical segregation** identifies the elevation of men into the best-paid and most desirable occupations in nonmanual and manual labor sectors, whereas women remain in lower-paid positions with no job mobility.

Maria Charles and David Grusky (2004) identify several social factors that promote and reproduce horizontal segregation. Employer and institutional discrimination help maintain the separation of women and men in the workplace, for example, by excluding women intentionally or unintentionally from physically strenuous jobs. The process of child socialization encourages girls and boys to internalize sex-typed expectations of others, which in turn shapes their occupational aspirations and preferences. Sociologists have examined how girls and boys are subject to differential gender socialization from birth. Traditional gender role stereotypes are reinforced through the family, school, peers, and the media with images of what is appropriate behavior for girls and boys. This includes defining appropriate occupations for women versus men.

Table 4.3 Five leading occupations for employed women, 2013 (annual averages)

Occupation	Women (%)	Women's Median Weekly Earnings	Men's Median Weekly Earnings
Elementary and middle school teachers	81%	$937	$1,025
Secretaries and administrative assistants	94%	$677	$772
Registered nurses	90%	$1,086	$1,236
Nursing, psychiatric, and home health aides	89%	$450	$499
Customer service representatives	66%	$616	$639

SOURCE: U.S. Department of Labor, Women's Bureau 2014.

Internalization of sex-typed expectations also leads workers to believe that if they transgress norms about gender-appropriate labor, they will be subject to sanctions (from disapproval from their parents to harassment from fellow workers). Years of horizontal segregation have given the advantage to men who have a disproportionate number of peers and network ties in the manual sector.

Vertical segregation is based on deeply rooted and widely shared cultural beliefs that men are more competent than women and are better suited than women for positions of power. According to Charles and Grusky (2004), vertical segregation is reproduced because it is consistent with the value of "male primacy." In her analysis of vertical segregation among men and women on Wall Street, Louise Marie Roth (2006) discovered how the gendered division of labor in the family spilled over into the workplace. Wall Street's workaholic culture assumes that the ideal employee has no external (family) obligations, setting work as the primary priority. Since child care is defined as women's responsibility, Wall Street women were routinely penalized for having families—women were expected to quit once they had children and were often treated differently after the birth of children. On the other hand, male Wall Street professionals were perceived as more committed and stable when they were married and had children. Roth concludes that males with traditional stay-at-home wives were able to maintain their ideal employee role.

What Does It Mean to Me?

What are your beliefs about who should be responsible for child care? When you become a parent, how will you manage your parental and workplace roles?

Occupational sex segregation is a worldwide phenomenon. Many studies have examined segregation cross-nationally and have found that though it is a feature of all industrial societies, the degree to which it exists varies. In her analysis of vertical and horizontal segregation in 10 countries including the United States, Charles (2003) found that women were underrepresented in the manual sector and that within the manual and nonmanual sectors, women's occupations were of lower average status. She reports the highest levels of horizontal segregation in Sweden and France, where women are about 30 times more likely to work in white-collar than in blue-collar sectors. The likelihood is lower in the United States—women are 14 times more likely to work in white-collar sectors. The highest levels of vertical segregation were found in France and in the United Kingdom. Vertical segregation for the United States was third lowest among the 10 countries Charles examined. The countries with the lowest levels of horizontal and vertical segregation were Portugal and Italy, which Charles attributed to the countries' development of two main occupational groups—professionals and craft-operations workers.

Jane Elliot's (2005) research revealed that there was greater occupational segregation between men and women and between full-time and part-time working women in the United Kingdom than in the United States. She characterizes employed women in the United Kingdom as having a "returner" pattern of labor participation (periodic employment vs. continual employment as in the United States) and notes that UK women are primarily concentrated in occupational groups that rely on part-time labor. UK labor laws encourage the hiring of part-time employees versus full-time employees, which encourages women's employment patterns. Elliot suggests that UK women may be less attached to their employment than U.S. women are because national health services are available regardless of employment. In the United States, one's employer usually provides health insurance.

Income Inequality

According to the National Committee on Pay Equity (2014), in 2013, for every dollar earned by a man, a woman made 78.3 cents (refer to Table 4.4 for wage gap data from 1960 to 2013). U.S. Data Map 4.1 reports the wage gap between women and men by state. Another way to measure the earning difference is to examine wage ratios, comparing the annual earnings of women and women who work full-time all year—what is the difference in men's and women's lifetime earnings? Stephen Rose and Heidi Hartmann (2004) examined data for 1983 to 1998 and concluded that women workers in their prime earning years make 38% of what men make. During the 15-year period, an average prime-age working woman earned only $273,592 compared with $722,693 earned by the average working man (in 1999 dollars). (For information regarding the gap between college men and women graduates, turn to this chapter's In Focus feature.)

Why do men earn more? Social scientists have attempted to answer the question, offering different explanations for the earning gap. Some have emphasized the

 Examining the Pay Gap

Table 4.4 Gender wage gap, 1960–2012

Year	Women's Earnings	Men's Earnings	Women's Earnings as a Percentage of Men's Earnings
1960	$16,144	$26,608	60.7%
1970	$20,567	$34,642	59.4%
1980	$22,279	$37,033	60.2%
1990	$25,451	$35,538	71.6%
2000	$27,355	$37,339	73.3%
2005	$31,858	$41,386	77.0%
2010	$36,931	$47,715	77.4%
2013	$39,157	$50,033	78.3%

SOURCE: National Committee on Pay Equity 2014.

role of **human capital**, the knowledge and skills workers acquire through education, training, and work experience. **Human capital theory** suggests that women earn less than men do because of differences in the kind and amount of human capital they acquire (Wharton 2004). Because their labor force participation is assumed to be interrupted by marriage and child-rearing responsibilities, most women will invest less in their job-related human capital or will choose occupations that provide flexible hours or lesser penalties after reentry (e.g., teaching). In the United States, women do have less continuous work experience than men do; their labor is interrupted by childbirth and child rearing. Yet, research indicates that even among women with continuous work experience, their earnings are less than men's (England 2001).

Another explanation offered by social scientists focuses on the **devaluation of women's work**. A higher societal value is placed on men than on women, and this is reproduced within the workplace. Caring or emotional labor is undervalued and defined as women's work, while professional or corporate skills are valued and defined as men's work. The relative worth of men's and women's economic activities is assessed within this value system, with men and masculine activities being valued more highly than women and feminine activities (Wharton 2004). According to Maume (1999), a higher value is granted to male occupations or job skills, permitting discrimination against the type of jobs women do, but not against women themselves.

In 2007, the Supreme Court limited workers' ability to challenge wage discrimination in court. The Supreme Court ruled that employees could not challenge ongoing compensation discrimination if the employer's original discriminatory act or decision occurred more than 180 days earlier. Prior to this decision, each discriminatory

Human capital: Job-related skills acquired through education and work experience

Human capital theory: Theory that attributes gender income differences to differences in the kind and amount of human capital men and women acquire

Devaluation of women's work: When the higher societal value placed on men than on women is reproduced within the workplace

EXPLORING social problems

The Wage Gap

Gender wage gap by state as ratio of median earnings for women and men working full-time, year-round, 2012

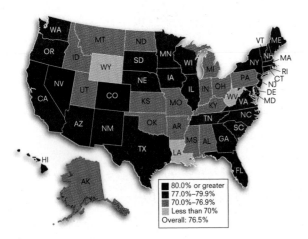

SOURCE: National Women's Law Center 2013.

Figure 4.1 Ratio of median earnings for minority women working full-time, year-round, 2013

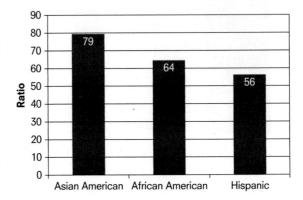

SOURCE: National Women's Law Center 2014a.

Figure 4.2 Ratio of median earnings for women and men working full-time, year-round, 1960–2013

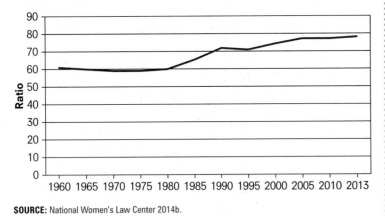

SOURCE: National Women's Law Center 2014b.

WHAT DO YOU THINK?

The wage gap is largest in Wyoming (63.8), Louisiana (66.9), and West Virginia (66.9). The states with the smallest wage gaps are Maryland (85.3), Nevada (85.3), and New York (83.9). Where does your state rank?

Overall, the wage gap is 78 cents. However, the wage gap is larger for African American and Hispanic women (refer to Figure 4.1). As presented in Figure 4.2, progress on the wage gap has been slow. The lowest ratio was recorded in the 1970s. A woman working full-time, year-round made 59 cents for every dollar paid to her male counterpart.

Which sociological theories offer the best explanation for why the gender wage gap still exists?

Whitehouse.gov

At the signing of the Lilly Ledbetter Fair Pay Act of 2009, President Obama stated that the issue of fair pay isn't just a women's issue. According to Obama, the bill ensures that all Americans are able to make a living and provide for their families. The law's namesake was at the president's side at the signing of the act (she is shown standing behind him, just to his right, in this photo).

paycheck was treated as a separate discriminatory act and reset the 180-day clock allowed for filing a claim. In the original case, Lilly Ledbetter, an area manager at Goodyear Tire and Rubber Company, charged that she was paid less than her 15 male counterparts. Ledbetter was paid $3,727 per month, and the lowest-paid male manager received $4,286 per month. Though a jury awarded Ledbetter $3.3 million in damages, the court of appeals reversed the verdict, stating that her case was filed too late.

The Lilly Ledbetter Fair Pay Act was signed into law by President Barack Obama in January 2009. The act reinstated the prior law that allowed pay discrimination claims on the basis of sex, race, national origin, age, religion, and disability to accrue whenever an employee received a discriminatory paycheck. At the signing of the bill, Ledbetter acknowledged that she would not receive any money as a result of the law named after her. "Goodyear will never have to pay me what it cheated me out of . . . . But with the president's signature today I have an even richer reward" (quoted in Stolberg 2009).

INTIMATE PARTNER VIOLENCE AND SEXUAL ASSAULT

A global review of scientific data on the prevalence and effects of intimate partner violence and sexual violence by someone other than a partner was cosponsored

IN FOCUS

THE PAY GAP BETWEEN COLLEGE-EDUCATED MEN AND WOMEN

In 2012, women working full-time still earned just 75.6% of what men earned. In separate analyses of data from the U.S. Department of Labor and the U.S. Department of Education, the Economic Policy Institute (a nonprofit nonpartisan think tank) and the American Association of University Women (AAUW) Educational Foundation revealed surprising earning disparities between men and women college graduates. Though the wages of college-educated women had grown rapidly since 1979, in 2009 a female college graduate earned 82% of what a male college graduate made (AAUP 2013; Mishel, Bernstein, and Allegretto 2007). One year out of college, women working full-time earn only 80% as much as their male peers. Ten years after graduation, women's earnings drop to 69% of men's. Despite controlling for hours of work, occupational type, and family status, college-educated women still earn less than college-educated men (Dey and Hill 2007).

A 2012 report by the U.S. Census Bureau also documented the persistent wage gap between college-educated men and women (refer to Table 4.5). Women earned less per month than men at every degree level and in all fields of training. Stephanie Ewert (2012) highlighted the progress made by women in the natural sciences. In this field, men's and women's median monthly earnings did not significantly differ at the bachelor's degree levels (and associate's degree, not shown here), but women still earned significantly less than men at the advanced degree level.

Though men and women pay the same amount for their college education, since they do not reap the same pay rewards after graduation, women's debt burden is greater than it is for men (AAUP 2013).

How can we resolve the gender pay gap? At the individual level? At the employer level?

Table 4.5 Median monthly earnings by educational attainment, sex, and field of training among the population aged 18 and older, 2009

	Median Earnings	
	Men	**Women**
Bachelor's Degree	5,117	3,750*
Business	5,000	4,000*
Computers	5,833	4,900
Engineering	6,250	(B)
Liberal Arts	4,600	3,599*
Social Science	4,314	3,417
Natural Science	4,583	4,200
Education	3,984	3,333*
Other	5,000	4,000*
Advanced Degree	6,667	5,000*
Business	7,250	5,833*
Computers	8,333	(B)
Engineering	7,794	(B)
Liberal Arts	5,000	4,500
Social Science	7,416	5,400*
Natural Science	8,334	5,724*
Education	5,167	4,642*
Other	6,250	5,000*

SOURCE: Ewert 2012.

NOTES: (B) denotes base < 200,000; * significant difference at the .10 level.

by the World Health Organization, the London School of Hygiene and Tropical Medicine, and the South African Medical Research Council. Results of the collaborative review were released in 2013, documenting the continuing violence against women and recommending how health agencies and programs should respond (World Health Organization 2013).

Based upon selected published literature since 2008 and multi-country surveys, the researchers estimated that 35% of women worldwide suffer physical or sexual violence, with the most common form of abuse being physical violence inflicted by an intimate partner. Globally, only 7% of women have been sexually assaulted by someone other than a partner. The systematic killing of women, **femicide**, is different from the murder of men and often involves sexual violence. As many as 38% of all murders of women are committed by a husband or boyfriend.

In 2006, the United Nations attributed violence against women to historically unequal power relations between men and women and pervasive discrimination against women. Violence, said the United Nations, "is one of the key means through which male control over women's agency and sexuality are maintained" (United Nations 2006:1). Violence against women is not confined to one nation, culture, or region; however, a woman's personal experience of violence is likely to be shaped by her ethnicity, class, age, sexual orientation, disability, nationality, and/or religion.

The 2013 World Health joint report identifies intimate partner violence as a major contributor to women's problems related to mental health, sexual and productive health, maternal health, and neonatal health. For example, women who experience partner violence are more than twice as likely to experience depression and in some areas are 1.5 times more likely to acquire HIV than women who do not suffer partner violence. The authors concluded,

> The findings underpin the need for the health sector to take intimate partner violence and sexual violence against women more seriously. All health-care providers should be trained to understand the relationship between violence and women's ill health and to be able to respond appropriately. . . . This evidence highlights the need to address the economic and sociocultural factors that foster a culture of violence against women. (World Health Organization 2013:35–36)

RESPONDING TO GENDER INEQUALITIES

Feminist Movements and Social Policies

Historians mark the beginning of the feminist movement in the United States and throughout the world in the 19th century. The U.S. feminist movement began in 1848 with the first Women's Rights Convention. A group of women, led by Elizabeth Cady Stanton and Lucretia Mott, adopted a declaration of sentiments demanding, among other things, women's right to vote. During the same time, the women's suffrage

Femicide: The killing of women; the term is used in contrast to the literal meaning of homicide as the killing of men

TAKING A WORLD VIEW

LEAVING NO GIRL BEHIND

Malala Yousafzai was shot in the face at point-blank range by a masked Taliban gunman on her way to school. This 15-year-old girl was targeted for advocating girls' education in Pakistan. As an 11-year-old, she had faced the media and criticized the Taliban for taking away her basic right to education. She said into the camera, "You may stop me from going to school, but you will not stop me from learning." The assassination attempt transformed Malala into a global ambassador and advocate.

Despite overall progress in girls' educational access and achievement, a generation of young women has been left behind. This is the conclusion that has been made by the United Nations Girls Education Initiative (UNGEI) (2013a). In 2011, there were 31 million girls out of school; 55% are expected never to enroll. The UNGEI estimates that women account for almost two thirds of the world's illiterate population.

UNGEI attributes the lack of girls' educational participation to structural factors, namely, values and norms that discriminate against girls, preventing them from attending and remaining in schools. Even in areas where they enroll in equal numbers in primary education, girls are likely to drop out before reaching secondary education due to child marriage, early pregnancy, gender-based violence in schools and at home, and the burden of domestic labor (UNGEI 2013b).

Research has demonstrated how education improves women's economic security in the world's poorest countries "and makes it more likely [for women] not

Malala Yousufzai was honored with the Nobel Peace Prize in 2014. At 17 years of age, Yousufzai is the youngest Nobel recipient.

just to be employed, but also to hold jobs that are more secure and provide good working conditions and decent pay" (UNGEI 2013a:20). Public health workers have also observed how education improves the health of children. Educated women ensure that their children are vaccinated and are likely to practice preventative health measures, thus reducing infant and child mortality due to pneumonia or diarrhea.

After surviving her injuries, Malala and her family relocated permanently to the United Kingdom. Her father, Ziauddin, was named an adviser on global education by Prime Minister Gordon Brown. Malala established her own organization, Malala Fund, and continues to serve as an advocate for girls' education. Malala was honored with the 2014 Nobel Peace Prize.

How else does education improve the quality of life for girls and young women?

movement began in Great Britain, with increasing demands for women's political and economic equality. The Nineteenth Amendment in 1920 affirmed for U.S. women the right to vote. In Great Britain, women were given the right to vote in 1918.

The feminist movement has been defined in "waves," the first beginning in the 19th century, followed by the second during the 20th century. Politically, the second wave focused on expanding legal rights for women. During this period, Title VII of the Civil Rights Act of 1964 was passed, prohibiting sexual harassment in the workplace and providing equal workplace opportunities for women and minorities (refer to Chapter 3, "Race and Ethnicity," for a discussion on affirmative action in employment and education), and Title IX of the Education Amendments was passed in 1972 (refer to the next section). Still, the movement was unsuccessful in passing the Twenty-Seventh Amendment to the U.S. Constitution, the Equal Rights Amendment (ERA), which proposed, "Equality of rights under law shall not be denied or abridged by the United States, or by any state, on account of sex." Though passed by the U.S. Congress in 1972, it was not ratified by the required 38 states to become a constitutional amendment. In 1977, Indiana became the 35th state to ratify the amendment. ERA ratification bills have been introduced in the remaining states without any success.

The third wave of feminism began in the 1990s. Though second-wave feminists are credited with achieving greater gender equality, they are criticized for assuming the universalization of the White woman's experience and for focusing exclusively on oppression based solely on sex. The third wave of feminism attempts to address multiple sources of oppression—acknowledging oppression based on race and ethnicity, social class, and sexual orientation in addition to sex. Instead of focusing on gender equality within one country or nation, the focus has expanded to a goal of global equality. Some third-wave activists even distance themselves from the use of the term *feminist*, believing the term is too confining or negative.

A fourth wave of feminism has been noted in scholarly and popular literature. The wave is defined in various ways. Brazilian sociologists Solange Simões and Marlise Matos (2009) define the term as a process of gendered democratic institutionalization and policy making, which includes a "revitalization of a classic feminist rights agenda under the influence of transnational feminism and the globalization of local women's agendas" (p. 95). The fourth wave synthesizes the second wave's emphasis on equality and the third wave's focus on global inequality. Fourth-wave feminism has also been described as a movement without one cohesive cause, leader, or platform. Younger women, to whom equality and rights have always been granted, seek new ways to remain politically and socially engaged (e.g., the Internet).

The European Union, since the late 1990s, has embraced **gender mainstreaming** as its main strategy to address inequalities between men and women. It is defined as the integration of the gender perspective into every stage of the policy process (design, implementation, monitoring, and evaluation). Before this, gender equality policies focused primarily on the experience of women. In contrast, gender mainstreaming explicitly addresses the experiences of men, such as parental leave as a jurisdictional claim for men or labor policies for men in female-dominated

Gender mainstreaming: The integration of the gender perspective into every stage of the policy process (design, implementation, monitoring, and evaluation)

occupations (e.g., nursing) (Scambor and Scambor 2008). Gender mainstreaming can also apply to health care, equally promoting women's and men's health care needs (Kuhlmann and Annandale 2012). In many countries, coronary heart disease is defined through a masculine lens, influencing all areas of medical care from prevention to rehabilitation. Though this leads to overlooking women's cardiac needs, it also may negatively impact men who do not seem to fit the model of hegemonic masculinity (Riska 2010).

. . . .

What Does It Mean to Me?

Do you identify as a feminist? Why or why not? What does being a feminist mean to you?

. . . .

Title IX

Among the achievements of the second wave of feminism was the passage of Title IX of the Education Amendments of 1972. Title IX of the Education Amendments prohibits the exclusion of any person from participation in an educational program or the denial of benefits based on one's sex (Woodhouse 2002). The preamble to Title IX states, "No person in the United States shall, on the basis of sex, be excluded from participation in, be denied the benefits of, or be subject to discrimination under any educational programs or activity receiving federal financial assistance."

© Tim Clayton/30154666A/Corbis

In 2013–2014, an estimated 3.2 million girls participated in high school sports programs. The top three sports were track and field, basketball, and volleyball. Title IX is credited with increasing girls' participation in high school sports.

 Funding Sports Fairly

In particular, the law requires that members of both sexes have equal opportunities to participate in sports and enjoy the benefits of competitive athletics (National Women's Law Center 2002b). According to Title IX, schools receiving federal aid are required to offer women and men equal opportunities to participate in athletics. This can be done in one of three ways: schools demonstrate that the percentage of men and women athletes is about the same as the percentage of men and women students enrolled (also referred to as the "proportionality rule"), or the school has a history and a continuing practice of expanding opportunities for women students, or the school is fully and effectively meeting its women students' interests and abilities to participate in sports. In addition, schools must equitably allocate athletic scholarships. The overall share of financial aid going to women athletes should be the same as the percentage of women athletes participating in the athletic program. Finally, schools must treat men and women equally in all aspects of sports programming. This requirement applies to supplies and equipment, the scheduling of games and practices, financial support for travel, and the assignment and compensation of coaches (National Women's Law Center 2002a).

The law has been widely credited with increasing women's participation in high school and collegiate sports and for women's achievement in education. For instance, in the 1971–1972 season, 294,015 girls participated in high school athletics (comprising 7% of all high school athletes); by 2010–2011, the number had grown to nearly 3 million (41% of all high school athletes). In 1971–1972, 29,977 females participated in collegiate athletics (15% of all college athletes); by 2010–2011, the number exceeded 190,000 (44% of all college athletes) (National Coalition for Women and Girls in Education 2012). The representation of women in athletic leadership has also increased. In 2008, almost 15,000 women were employed in intercollegiate athletics, as athletic directors, coaches, or trainers. One out of five athletic directors is a woman, the highest representation since the mid-1970s (Acosta and Carpenter 2009). Regarding college enrollment, in 1973, 41% of women high school graduates were enrolled in college; in 2010 the percentage increased to 74% (U.S. Bureau of Labor Statistics 2011).

After more than 35 years, the controversy regarding Title IX continues. Many blame Title IX for the demise of collegiate men's programs. To achieve proportionality between the number of men and women athletes, schools have reduced the number of men athletes in minor sports programs such as wrestling, gymnastics, golf, and tennis (Garber 2002). However, according to the National Coalition for Women and Girls in Education (2012), between the 1988–1989 and 2010–2011 school years, NCAA institutions added 3,727 men's sports teams and dropped 2,748, for a net gain of nearly 1,000 teams. During the same period, 4,641 women's teams were added and 1,943 were eliminated. Women made greater gains because they started with a deficit in the number of athletic teams. Evidence also indicates that not all colleges and universities are complying with the law. Although women in Division I colleges represent more than half the student body, women's sports receive only 42% of athletic scholarships, 31% of recruiting funds, and 28% of operating budgets (National Women's Law Center 2012).

SOCIOLOGY AT WORK

SOCIOLOGY AS A SCIENCE: THEORY AND DATA

Your Sociology major requirements will likely include coursework in research methods and statistics. In your methods course, you'll learn different ways to collect qualitative and quantitative data. You will use a data software program such as SPSS, SAS, or R to analyze your data. But the important skill that you'll acquire is the ability to make sense of data, to analyze it, and to apply it.

One of my favorite sociology quotes comes from Peter Berger's (1963) classic *Invitation to Sociology: A Humanistic Perspective*: "Statistical data by themselves do not make sociology. They become sociology when they are sociologically interpreted, put within a theoretical frame of reference that is sociological" (p. 11). Although data are important in answering sociological questions, the data themselves do not constitute sociology (Berger 1963); it is you (the sociologist) that makes the data sociological.

For example, in this chapter we've reviewed the gender wage gap. In Table 4.4, wage gap data for 1960 to 2012 are presented. The data in the table are just numbers. Human capital theory, the devaluation of women's work, or theories on vertical or horizontal segregation help us better understand the persistent wage gap between women and men. These theories identify how cultural beliefs, such as the belief that women will invest less in their employment due to marriage and childbearing responsibilities, are replicated in the workplace and reinforce gender income inequality.

Sociologists Kathleen Korgen, Jonathan White, and Shelley White (2011) explain the power of sociological research methods and their connection to sociological theory.

In order to make society better, we must first have a firm understanding of how and why it functions in the ways it does. Following the basic steps of scientific research helps us to see and measure patterns in society, so that we can better understand how it operates. Once we have done so, we can then begin to understand why it operates that way (through critical, sociological analysis and theories). (p. 39)

How is analyzing and understanding data an important work place skill?

On the 38th anniversary of Title IX in 2010, in addition to noting the progress made in women's athletics, U.S. secretary of education Arne Duncan identified the need to ensure safe learning environments free from sexual violence and assault. Colleges and universities receiving federal funding are required under Title IX to respond promptly and effectively to sexual violence against students. This includes schools' efforts to prevent sexual violence, the creation of enforcement strategies, and the implementation of investigation procedures. In 2014, President Barack Obama created the White House Task Force to Protect Students from Sexual Assault, maintaining the administration's commitment to ending sexual violence on college campuses. Later that year, the U.S. Department of Education released a list of 55 colleges and universities under investigation for possible violations over the handling of sexual violence and harassment complaints (U.S. Department of Education 2014).

CHAPTER REVIEW

4.1 Explain the difference between sex and gender

Sex is based upon fixed physiological or biological differences, while gender refers to our masculine and feminine behaviors determined by our society or culture.

4.2 Describe how the different sociological perspectives explain problems related to sex and gender

According to functionalists, gender inequality is defined not as a product of differential power but rather as a functional necessity. Theorists from both conflict and feminist perspectives argue that women will remain in their subordinate position as long as men maintain their social, economic, and cultural advantage in society. From a conflict perspective, women's subordinate position in society is linked to their relationship to the means of production. Contemporary feminist theorists refer to gender as a process, a system of social practices that creates and maintains gender distinctions and inequalities. From an interactionist's perspective, language defines and maintains privilege in society; regarding gender, men are privileged and set many standards.

4.3 Distinguish the two types of occupational segregation

Horizontal segregation represents the separating of women into nonmanual labor and men into manual labor sectors. Vertical segregation identifies the elevation of men into the best-paid and most desirable occupations in nonmanual and manual labor sectors, whereas women remain in lower-paid positions with no job mobility.

4.4 Explain human capital theory

Human capital theory suggests that women earn less than men do because of differences in the kind and amount of human capital they acquire. The assumption is that women will invest less in their job-related capital due to marriage and child-rearing responsibilities.

4.5 Compare the four feminist waves

The first wave began in the 19th century, with women's suffrage as its primary goal. The second wave began in the 20th century, with increased political focus on ensuring legal rights for women. The third wave of feminism began in the 1990s, attempting to address multiple sources of oppression and acknowledging oppression based on race and ethnicity, social class, sexual orientation, and sex. The emerging fourth wave synthesizes the second wave's emphasis on equality and the third wave's focus on global inequality. Fourth-wave feminism has also been described as a movement without one cohesive cause, leader, or platform.

KEY TERMS

devaluation of women's work, 109

femicide, 113

gender, 98

gender mainstreaming, 115

gendered division of labor, 101

horizontal segregation, 106

human capital, 109

human capital theory, 109

occupational sex segregation, 106

sex, 98

sexism, 100

vertical segregation, 106

STUDY QUESTIONS

1. What is the difference between sex and gender? How is gender socially constructed?

2. Define sexism. Identify one example of institutional sexism.

3. Examine occupational segregation from the functionalist and conflict perspectives.

4. From an interactionist perspective, Wildman and Davis (2000) offer several examples of how our language privileges men over women. Can you identify cases of female privilege over men?

5. The gender role socialization process reinforces our beliefs about the differences between men and women. Is it possible to raise boys and girls the same way, to be gender neutral in the socialization process? Why or why not?

6. How do sociologists explain the wage gap between men and women? Do you think it is possible to reduce or eliminate the gap?

7. Explain the importance of the four waves of feminism.

8. We take special note of female firsts—the first woman secretary of state (Madeleine Albright), the first woman Speaker of the House (Nancy Pelosi), the first woman president of Harvard University (Drew Gilpin Faust), and the first woman to lead General Motors (Mary Barra). All these events occurred during the late 20th and early 21st centuries, two centuries after the beginning of the feminist movement. In your opinion, has the feminist movement been successful? What remains to be achieved? Would you describe yourself as a feminist? Why or why not?

$SAGE edge™

Sharpen your skills with SAGE edge at **edge.sagepub.com/leonguerrero5e**

SAGE edge provides a personalized approach to help you accomplish your coursework goals in an easy-to-use learning environment.

CHAPTER 5

Sexual Orientation

Sexual orientation: The classification of individuals according to their preference for emotional-sexual relationships and lifestyle

Homosexuality: Sexual orientation toward the same sex

Heterosexuality: Sexual orientation toward the opposite sex

In a 2009 announcement that led to worldwide condemnation, lawmakers in Uganda considered adopting an antihomosexuality law, proposing the death penalty for certain homosexual acts (e.g., with a minor, if the perpetrator was HIV positive, or for serial offenders) (Gettleman 2010). David Kato was one of the leading voices against the legislation. Despite threats of violence and harm, Kato, an openly gay man, maintained, "If we keep on hiding, they will say we are not here." Kato cofounded the advocacy group Sexual Minorities Uganda (SMUG). In 2011, Kato was murdered several weeks after winning a court decision over a Ugandan tabloid that called for the killing of homosexuals. Uganda's antihomosexuality bill was passed in 2013, substituting the death penalty clause for life imprisonment. SMUG reported an increase in the cases of intimidation and violence against Uganda's homosexual population after the passage of the bill. In 2014, Uganda's constitutional court overturned the law. The gay and lesbian community celebrated the ruling with its first gay pride rally.

One's sexual orientation serves as a basis of inequality. **Sexual orientation** is defined as the classification of individuals according to their preference for emotional-sexual relationships and lifestyle with persons of the same sex (**homosexuality**) or persons of the opposite sex (**heterosexuality**). **Bisexuality** refers to emotional and sexual attractions to persons of either sex. The term **transgender** does not refer to a specific sexual orientation; rather, it refers to individuals whose gender identity is different from the one assigned to them at birth. The term **LGBT** is often used to refer to lesbians, gays, bisexuals, and transgender individuals as a group.

There is no definitive study on the number of individuals who identify as homosexual or bisexual. The study that is most often cited was conducted in 1994 by Robert Michael and his colleagues. Based on a random survey of 3,432 U.S. adults ages 18 to 59 years, Michael et al. found that 2.8% of men and 1.4% of women thought of themselves as homosexual or bisexual. About 5% of surveyed men and 4% of women said they had had sex with someone of the same gender after they turned 18. About 6% of men and 4% of women reported that they were sexually attracted to someone of the same gender.

When the Gallup Organization conducted a national survey of more than 120,000 Americans in 2012, 3.4% of respondents identified as lesbian, gay, bisexual, or transgender (Gates and Newport 2012). In 2014, the Centers for Disease Control and Prevention reported that less than 3% of the U.S. population identify as gay. Based on the CDC's National Health Interview Survey, 1.6% of adults self-identify as gay or lesbian and 0.7% as bisexual (Ward et al. 2014).

Gay rights have progressed in the United States and globally. In 1996, South Africa became the first country to establish a constitutional ban against discrimination based on sexual orientation. In 2000, Vermont was the first U.S. state to recognize civil unions between same-sex partners; in 2004, Massachusetts was the first state to legalize same-sex marriage. Though national polls indicate increased support of gay and lesbian individuals, as a group they are still not immune to the experience of social problems. Based on their sexual orientation, LGBT individuals continue to experience prejudice, discrimination, harassment, and violence. Their struggle for equal protection and opportunities continues.

SOCIOLOGICAL PERSPECTIVES ON SEXUAL ORIENTATION AND INEQUALITY

Our understanding of sexual orientation is based upon research from biology, psychology, and sociology. Each examines the causes and consequences of sexual orientation from its unique and sometimes controversial point of view.

Researchers exploring the biological basis of sexual orientation have considered two theoretical approaches. The first is neurohormonal theory, arguing that homosexuality is caused by atypical sex hormone levels in utero. Human studies have suggested that specific centers in the brain are related to sexual orientation and sexual behavior. The second approach is based upon behavioral genetics, identifying the source and magnitude of genetic influences on sexual orientation. This line of research was first motivated by the idea that gay men are genetically female, a hypothesis that was eventually discredited.

Confirmation of the genetic link to sexual orientation has been found through comparative studies of identical twins (twins who have nearly identical genetic makeup) and fraternal twins (twins who share some similar genetic makeup). Bailey and Pillard (1991) and Bailey and Bell (1993) found it more likely that identical

Bisexuality: Sexual orientation toward either sex

Transgender: Individuals whose gender identity is different from that assigned to them at birth

LGBT: Term used to refer to lesbians, gays, bisexuals, and transgender individuals as a group

Gay Lifestyle Myth

twins will both be gay (if one is gay) than is the case for fraternal twins. In their assessment of biological research on sexual orientation, Brian Mustanski, Meredith Chivers, and Michael Bailey (2002) concluded that sexual orientation is influenced by biological factors to some degree. They say that the questions that remain to be answered are how and when these biological factors act and to what degree these factors influence sexual orientation in women and men.

Early psychological studies treated homosexuality as a pathology, as a mental illness. This perspective was not universal among psychologists. Havelock Ellis argued that homosexuality was inborn, and therefore could not be considered a disease (Robinson 1976). Sigmund Freud believed that all humans were innately bisexual and that homosexuality and heterosexuality were the result of social and personal experiences. Both agreed that homosexuality was not an illness.

However, homosexuality was explicitly defined as a mental illness by the American Psychiatric Association in its *Diagnostic and Statistical Manual of Mental Disorders* until 1973; a diagnosis for ego-dystonic homosexuality was introduced in 1980 but removed entirely in 1986. The World Health Organization removed a similar classification from its *International Classification of Diseases and Related Health Problems* in 1992. The declassification of homosexuality as a mental illness was in response to empirical research but also to more favorable cultural and social norms pertaining to homosexuality.

Shifting away from homosexuality as an illness, psychologists currently examine the impact of a homosexual identity. Rates of mental health problems (e.g., depression, anxiety, substance abuse, and suicidality) are higher among homosexual men and women due in part to the social discrimination and cultural stigmatization they experience. Researchers in this field also examine the causes of attitudes toward homosexuality, particularly homophobia. A socially determined prejudice, **homophobia** is an irrational fear or intolerance of homosexuals (Lehne 1995). Homophobia is particularly directed at gay men.

In contrast to these biological and psychological perspectives, the sociological perspective examines the social and structural factors that affect sexual orientation.

Functionalist Perspective

Theorists in this perspective examine how society maintains our social order. Émile Durkheim argued that our social order depends on how well society can control individual behavior. Our most basic human behavior—our sexuality—is controlled by society's norms and values. Functionalists identify how society upholds heterosexuality and a marital union between a man and a woman as ideal normative behavior. This is also referred to as **institutionalized heterosexuality**, the set of ideas, institutions, and relationships that define the heterosexual family as the societal norm (Lind 2004).

Our legal, political, and social structures work in harmony to support these ideals (the conflict perspective of this is presented in the next section). Section 3 of

Homophobia:
An irrational fear or intolerance of homosexuals

Institutionalized heterosexuality: The set of ideas, institutions, and relationships that define the heterosexual family as the societal norm

the 1996 Defense of Marriage Act (DOMA) denied federal recognition of same-sex unions, defining marriage as a legal union only between a man and a woman. This legislation served as a declaration about how the heterosexual family is valued and how all other family forms are not. Society grants legitimate kinship and familial obligations only through the heterosexual family. Consequently, society defines all other forms of sexuality and families that do not fit this ideal image as problematic. These forms are considered deviant or unnatural because they do not fit society's ideal.

Nonetheless, during the past decades, the gay rights movement has effectively influenced family rights, employment, and discrimination policies throughout the world. The movement has been successful largely because of its ability to affect institutional (macro) level changes—the focus of the functionalist perspective.

Conflict and Feminist Perspectives

Gore Vidal (1988) observed the following:

> In order for a ruling class to rule, there must be arbitrary prohibitions. Of all prohibitions, sexual taboo is the most useful because sex involves everyone. . . . We have allowed our governors to divide the population into two teams. One team is good, godly, straight; the other is evil, sick and vicious.

Vidal's statement addresses the focus of both these perspectives, how conflict in our society is based on sexual orientation, with heterosexuals having been given the advantage. This reaffirmation of heterosexuality as the moral standard is the basis of the culture wars, the struggle over creating and regulating codes of personal, social, and sexual behavior for every American. Contemporary culture wars have also concerned issues of race, ethnicity, and immigration, but the majority of culture wars revolve around issues of sexuality and gender (Bronski 1998).

Sociologists recognize that heterosexuals are granted a privileged place in our society. **Heterosexism** assumes that heterosexuality is the norm, encouraging discrimination in favor of heterosexuals and against homosexuals. Heterosexual privilege is defined as the set of privileges or advantages granted to some people because of their heterosexuality.

From a conflict perspective, Amy Lind (2004) identifies how DOMA helped institutionalize heterosexism because it blocked future proactive and protective legislation for gays and lesbians. She focuses specifically on heterosexual biases in social welfare policy, identifying its impact in three ways: through policies that explicitly target LGBT individuals as abnormal or deviant, through federal definitions that assume that all families are heterosexual, and through policies that overlook LGBT poverty and social needs because of stereotypes about affluence among LGBT families.

Evidence of the first type of heterosexual bias can be found in federal legislation such as DOMA and policy initiatives such as the healthy marriage promotion

Heterosexism:
The privileging of heterosexuality over homosexuality

and fatherhood programs promoted by President George W. Bush. Current legislation funds abstinence only through marriage education programs in schools. Lind (2004) explains that gay, lesbian, and bisexual adolescents have no access to sexual education that pertains to their sexual experience. In an effort to preserve the traditional heterosexual family, these programs deny LGBT people their rights and needs.

The second type of heterosexual bias concerns how the U.S. Census defines the family and household. Lind (2004:28) refers to the 2003 definitions used by the U.S. Census. Family is defined as "a group of two or more (one of whom is the householder) related by birth, marriage, or adoption and residing together." A household "consists of all people who occupy a housing unit" and is distinguished by family versus nonfamily households. Family households are defined as "a household maintained by a householder who is in a family (as defined above) and includes any unrelated people who may be residing there," whereas a nonfamily household is "a householder living alone or where the householder shares a home exclusively with people to whom he/she is not related." Lind argues that these definitions privilege marital unions over domestic partnerships and the status of heterosexual families over other types of families. Beginning with the 2010 Census, same-sex couples can select between two options to indicate their relationship status: "husband and wife" and "unmarried partners."

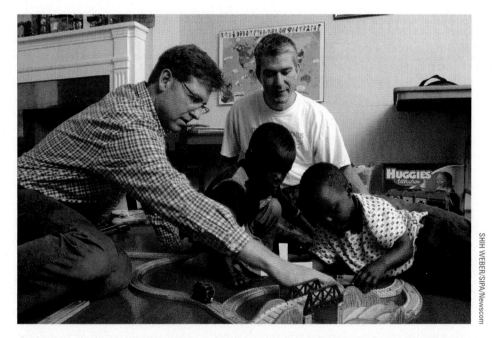

Families like Oliver du Wulf (L) and Steven Boulliane's (R) help expand our definition of a "family." Public polls reveal increasing support for same-sex marriage. As of 2015, more than 50% of surveyed Americans were in favor of the legal recognition of same-sex marriage.

Finally, the third type of heterosexual bias is based on stereotypes of lesbian, gay, and bisexual (LGB) individuals and families as affluent, despite evidence that LGB families are as economically diverse and stratified as heterosexual families. Lesbians, gays, and bisexuals remain invisible in poverty studies or policies because they are assumed to be childless, have fewer family responsibilities, and thus have higher overall incomes than heterosexual households. The Movement Advancement Project, the Family Equality Council, and the Center for American Progress (2012) report that contrary to the stereotype, children raised by same-sex couples are twice as likely to live in poverty than children raised by heterosexual couples. With the exception of HIV/AIDS, it is assumed that LGB individuals do not need any economic, social, or health-related services.

· ·

What Does It Mean to Me?

What other examples of heterosexual bias can you identify? Is heterosexuality still valued as the norm?

· ·

From a feminist perspective, the question about gay marriage rights is bound to the ongoing critique of marriage as an institution (Bevacqua 2004). Scholars have argued that lesbian and gay marriages will positively disrupt the gendered definitions of marriage and the assumption that marriage is a prescribed hierarchy (Hunter 1995). However, just as feminists have criticized traditional marriage as an oppressive and dominating institution against women, feminists have also supported sexual freedom. Thus, supporting gay marriages would mean supporting the very institution that perpetuates women's inequality.

Ann Ferguson (2007) explains that there are two main sides of the feminist argument: radical feminists who reject marriage outright on the basis of marriage as an oppressive institution versus liberal reform feminists who support the choice to marry on the understanding that men and women (or same-sex couples) can conduct their marriages in nontraditional ways. While she does not oppose long-term relationships or partnerships, radical feminist Claudia Card (1996) objects to the origins and consequences of marriage. Marriage, according to Card, has its roots not in love but in property and power, which may include the power of men over women and children. Ultimately the state, an authority external to the relationship, legitimates marriage and its subsequent benefits (i.e., federal, state, and legal benefits extended to heterosexual couples). Card states that since the institution of marriage is flawed in its origin and practice, gays and lesbians should focus their efforts on other institutional changes, such as a national health care policy that provides everyone with health coverage and access. On the other hand, Ferguson (2007) supports the liberal reform side, arguing, "We should not simply reject marriage and hope it withers away, but instead should attempt to reform it as a better way to achieve these feminist goals [equality, freedom, and care]" (p. 52). On the topic of gay marriage, however, she concludes that some gay persons should not marry, not because it is a risky institution for women, but because the right to form one's family should not be tied to one's marital status. "We should defend gay marriage as the formal right to access a basic citizen right" (Ferguson 2007:54).

Interactionist Perspective

In our society, no one gets "outed" for being straight. There is little controversy in identifying someone as heterosexual. Socially, culturally, and legally, the heterosexual lifestyle is promoted and praised. Although homosexuality has existed in most societies, it has usually been attached to a negative label—*abnormal*, *sinful*, or *inappropriate*. A homosexual identity also becomes a **master status**, an identity that determines how others view individuals and how individuals view themselves.

Interactionists examine how sexual orientation is constructed within a social context. We tend to think of heterosexuality as unchanging and universal; however, Jonathan Katz (2003) explains how the term is a social invention that "designates a word and concept, a norm and role, an individual and group identity, a behavior and a feeling, and a peculiar sexual-political institution particular to the late nineteenth and twentieth centuries" (p. 145). Though heterosexuality existed before it was actually named in the early nineteenth century, "The titling and envisioning of heterosexuality did play an important role in consolidating the construction of the heterosexual's social existence" (Katz 2003:145). He argues that acknowledging heterosexuality as a social invention—time bound and culturally specific—challenges the power of the heterosexual ideal.

Interactionists also examine the process of how individuals identify themselves as homosexual, what scholars describe as part of the development of a gay identity. Coming out (being gay and disclosing it to others) has come to symbolize the pursuit of individual rights and self-identification (Chou 2001). Coming out implies not just the disclosure of a gay identity but also the individual's positive attitude toward and commitment to that identity (Dubé 2000). The disclosure of a gay identity merges a private sexual identity with a public social identity (Cass 1979). To come out successfully, a gay individual needs social and institutional support, in the form of support from family and friends, legal protection from discrimination and violence, cultural acceptance, financial equality, and access to health services (D'Augelli 1998).

The process of coming out to family members is particularly stressful for LGB youth. Fear of parental reactions has been identified as a major reason that LGB youth do not come out to their families (D'Augelli, Hershberger, and Pilkington 1998). Following disclosure, youth report verbal abuse and even physical attacks by family members. Youth who lived with their families and disclosed their sexual orientation were victimized by their families more often than were youth who had not disclosed their orientation (D'Augelli et al. 1998).

Master status:
An identity that determines how others view individuals and how individuals view themselves

To avoid negative response from others, young lesbians and gay men hide their sexual orientation from family and friends (Rivers and Carragher 2003). Gay and lesbian youth may use one or more of the following concealment strategies: inhibiting behaviors and interests associated with homosexuality, limiting exposure to the opposite sex, avoiding exposure to information about homosexuality, assuming antigay positions, establishing heterosexual relationships, and avoiding homoerotic feelings through substance abuse (Radkowsky and Siegel 1997). Research is inconclusive about how effective such concealment strategies are in reducing anxiety among lesbian and gay youth.

. . . .

What Does It Mean to Me?

Is your sexual orientation or sexual identity a master status? Why or why not?

. . . .

A summary of sociological theories regarding sexual orientation and inequality is presented in Table 5.1.

Table 5.1   Summary of sociological perspectives: Inequalities based on sexual orientation

	Functionalist	**Conflict/Feminist**	**Interactionist**
Explanations of sexual orientation and inequality	The heterosexual family is the way in which society identifies legitimate kinship and familial obligations. Society defines all other forms of sexuality and families that do not fit this ideal image as problematic in society.	Inequality is based on one's sexual orientation. Heterosexuality is privileged in our society. Debate about same-sex marriage is bound to the feminist critique about the oppressive nature of marriage.	Sexual orientation is a social construct—time bound and culturally specific. The development of a gay identity also depends on the support and reactions of others.
Questions asked about sexual orientation and inequality	How do our social structures endorse the heterosexual family? Is it possible to change the structures, to allow inclusiveness of other family forms and other sexual orientations?	In what ways do our social structures maintain heterosexism? What other forms of oppression exist for the LGBT community? Will same-sex marriage challenge the gendered definitions of marriage?	Who or what shapes our definitions of sexual orientation? How are LGBT individuals affected by inaccurate stereotypes or labels? How can negative stereotypes or labels be changed? What social support is necessary for someone to develop a positive gay identity?

SEXUAL ORIENTATION AND INEQUALITY

U.S. Legislation on Homosexuality

Bisexual or homosexual men, women, and their families are subject to social inequalities through practices of discrimination and prejudice, many of them surprisingly institutionalized in formal law.

For example, sodomy laws criminalize oral and anal sex between two adults. Although the laws may apply to homosexuals and heterosexuals, sodomy laws are more vigorously applied against same-sex partners. Twelve U.S. states still had state sodomy laws in 2014 (in 1960, sodomy was outlawed in every state).

In 1998, John Lawrence and Tyron Garner were fined $200 and spent a night in jail for violating a Texas statute that prohibited "deviate sexual intercourse" between two people of the same sex. The Texas statute did not apply to heterosexual couples. Their case was heard before the U.S. Supreme Court in March 2003. Attorneys for Lawrence and Garner argued that the Texas law was an invasion of their privacy and violated the equal protection clause of the Fourteenth Amendment because it unfairly targeted same-sex couples. Attorneys for the state argued that Texas had the right to set moral standards for its residents. In June 2003, the court voted 6 to 3 to overrule the Texas law and all other remaining sodomy laws. Writing for the decision, Justice Anthony Kennedy said, "The state cannot demean their [homosexuals'] existence or control their destiny by making their private sexual conduct a crime" (Greenhouse 2003:A17). According to Kevin Cathcart, executive director of Lambda Legal (2003), "this ruling starts an entirely new chapter in our fight for equality for lesbian, gay, bisexual, and transgendered people."

In 2009, the U.S. Congress passed legislation to grant gay individuals protection under hate-crime laws. The legislation was in response to the brutal deaths of James Byrd Jr., an African American who was dragged to death in Texas, and Matthew Shepard, a gay college student who was beaten and left to die in Wyoming. The federal hate-crime law, enacted in 1968, had been limited to crimes based on race, color, religion, and national origin. Though supported by civil rights and law enforcement groups, some conservative and religious groups opposed the legislation, saying that the bill would create special classes of federally protected crime victims. The 2009 legislation also extended protections for disabled individuals. At the signing of the bill, President Barack Obama promised that people would be protected from violence based on "what they look like, who they love, how they pray or who they are" (Feller 2009).

The U.S. Supreme Court upheld the first-of-its-kind California law that bans psychological counseling aimed at changing the sexual orientations of gay and lesbian minors. Conversion or reparative therapy refers to counseling and psychotherapy to eliminate sexual desires for members of one's own sex (American Psychological Association 2008). Under the 2012 California law, reparative therapy is prohibited for patients under the age of 18. Governor Jerry Brown and gay rights advocates

 Matthew Shepard's Murder

supported the law, arguing that these therapies have no medical or scientific bases. The American Psychiatric Association determined that reparative therapy poses a risk of depression, anxiety, self-hatred, and self-destructive behavior for patients (Levs 2012). New Jersey was the second state to ban sexual orientation conversion therapy. As of 2014, bans were also being considered in Massachusetts and New York.

The Rights and Recognition of Same-Sex Couples

Before 2013, DOMA permitted states to ban all recognition of same-sex marriages. According to the law, the federal government would not accept marriage licenses granted to same-sex couples, regardless of whether a state provides equal license privileges to all types of partnerships. DOMA denied these couples the same federal benefits that are available to or required for married opposite-sex couples. Gay and lesbian families were denied common legal protections that non-gay families take for granted, such as adoption, custody, guardianship, social security, and inheritance.

The legal recognition of same-sex couples began incrementally at the federal level. In June 2002, President George W. Bush signed into law the Mychal Judge Act, which allows federal death benefits to be paid to the same-sex partners of firefighters and police officers who die in the line of duty (Bumiller 2002). In 2006, the federal Pension Protection Act became law, containing two key provisions that extend financial protections to same-sex couples and Americans who leave their retirement savings to non-spouse beneficiaries. Under the law, an individual's retirement plan benefit can be transferred to a domestic partner or other non-spouse beneficiary. The second provision allows gay couples and others with non-spouse beneficiaries to draw on their retirement funds in the case of a medical or financial emergency. And in 2010, President Barack Obama instructed the secretary of the Department of Health and Human Services to draft rules requiring hospitals that receive Medicare and Medicaid payments (which includes most of the nation's medical facilities) to grant all patients the right to say who has visitation rights and who can help make medical decisions. These rules would allow full recognition of advanced health directives among gay and lesbian couples.

In 2011, President Obama directed the U.S. Justice Department to stop defending DOMA in court after concluding that the law was unconstitutional (Savage and Stolberg 2011). In 2012, President Obama expressed his support for marriage of same-sex couples. Governor Mitt Romney, the 2012 Republican presidential nominee, continued to advocate marriage as a relationship between one man and one woman. In 2013, the U.S. Supreme Court ruled that DOMA was unconstitutional.

For more on same-sex marriage legislation, refer to the discussion on family legislation in the last section of this chapter.

 Same-Sex Marriage and the Supreme Court

. . . .

What Does It Mean to Me?

What is your opinion on the rights of same-sex couples? Who or what has influenced your beliefs?

. . . .

Employment

The need to "manage a disreputable sexual identity at the workplace" has been called the most persistent problem facing lesbians and gay men (Schneider 1986:464). Between 16% and 46% of gays, lesbians, and bisexuals have experienced workplace discrimination based on sexual orientation (Katz and LaVan 2004). Title VII of the Civil Rights Act prohibits discrimination because of sex. Sex has been interpreted to mean gender, which means that protection for homosexuals based on sexual orientation is not covered.

M. V. Badgett and Mary King (1997) note that, unlike discrimination based on easily observable characteristics such as skin color or gender, discrimination against gays and lesbians must be based on knowledge or suspicion of someone's sexual orientation. Lesbians and gay men who reveal their sexual orientation risk loss of income and lower chances at career advancement. A review of existing studies on workplace discrimination reveals that somewhere between one quarter and two thirds of LGB people report losing their jobs or missing promotions because of their sexual orientation.

Protections against public and private workplace discrimination because of one's sexual orientation exist in 21 states, the District of Columbia, and several hundred U.S. cities and counties. Eighty-eight percent of all Fortune 500 companies have anti-discrimination policies that include sexual orientation, and 57% have policies that include gender identity (Human Rights Campaign 2013). Currently there is no federal law that protects LGBT individuals from employment discrimination. In 2009, the Employment Non-Discrimination Act (ENDA) was introduced in the U.S. Congress. If passed, the act would provide basic protections against workplace discrimination on the basis of sexual orientation or gender identity.

Professional competitive sports have been referred to as the "last closet." "Sports associate boys and men with masculine dominance by constructing their identities and sculpting their bodies to align with hegemonic perspectives of masculinist embodiment and expression" (Anderson 2011). Since 2012, several professional and collegiate players have revealed their sexual orientation: Jason Collins (NBA), Brittney Griner (WNBA), and Michael Sam (NFL). Nearly all professional sport leagues ban discrimination based on sexual orientation, along with race, religion, and ethnicity. Yet, Cyd Zeigler, editor of *Outsports*, an online publication covering LGBT men and women in sports, says,

> I think homophobia for decades has been more entrenched in sports than it has in most other areas in our culture . . . It starts when these kids are young.

Employment Discrimination

And they're five years old and 10 years old and playing sports and the coach calls them a faggot and tells them not to be a sissy and this idea that being a faggot is less than being a man. (Quoted in Chibbaro 2013)

Upon his retirement from the NBA, Collins (2014) said,

When we get to the point where a gay pro athlete is no longer forced to live in fear that he'll be shunned by teammates or outed by tabloids, when we get to the point where he plays while his significant other waits in the family room, when we get to the point where he's not compelled to hide his true self and is able to live an authentic life, then coming out won't be such a big deal. But we're not there yet.

· ·

What Does It Mean to Me?

Lambda Legal is a national organization committed to achieving full recognition of the civil rights of lesbians, gay men, transgender individuals, and people with HIV/AIDS. The organization identifies each state that prohibits sexual orientation discrimination in employment. Investigate your state's discrimination laws by logging on to Lambda Legal's website. If your state does include such laws, a brief summary of the legislation is included.

· ·

RESPONDING TO SEXUAL ORIENTATION INEQUALITIES

In this section, we'll review the progress on marriage equality and military service. Despite the progress in these two areas, it is important to note how LGBT individuals still lack basic legal protections. According to the Human Rights Campaign (2014d), "the patchwork nature of current LGBT civil rights protections protects millions of people, but leaves millions more subject to uncertainty and potential discrimination that impacts their safety, their family and their very way of life." As of December 2014, the Employment Non-Discrimination Act had yet to be passed in the U.S. Congress. There are no explicit protections prohibiting the denial of credit (including housing loans) based on sexual orientation or gender identity, no consistent federal protections for students based on sexual orientation or gender identity, and no federal protections that prohibit discrimination against LGBT people in public spaces, such as hotels or restaurants (Human Rights Campaign 2014a).

Family Legislation

In May 2004, Massachusetts became the first state in the nation to legalize same-sex marriage. As of May 2015 in addition to Massachusetts, 36 other states—Alaska, Alabama, Arizona, California, Colorado, Connecticut, Delaware, Florida, Hawaii,

IN FOCUS

GAY-FRIENDLY CAMPUSES

"What campuses do you consider to be LGBT-friendly?" This question was posed by the editors of the *Advocate College Guide for LGBT Students*. In 2006, the editors collected nominations from current LGBT college students as well as additional information from interviews with students and faculty or staff members from the nominated schools.

The editors based their final selections on 10 criteria, as reported in the guide. According to editor Bruce Steele, the editors intended to assess "the effort that's being put forth by the colleges themselves to make their LGBT students comfortable" (Rosenbloom 2006:S2). The 10 criteria are as follows:

1. Active LGBT student organization(s) on campus. Prospective LGBT students are looking for a sense of community with their peers and organizations that can offer social, educational, and leadership opportunities on campus.

2. Out LGBT students. Prospective students look for other LGBT students to be visible and active in academic and campus life settings.

3. Out LGBT faculty and staff. LGBT faculty and staff can serve as advisers and visible role models for LGBT students.

4. LGBT-inclusive policies. Supportive campuses should have policies that include "sexual orientation" in their discrimination policy or have policies supporting same-sex domestic partner benefits.

5. Visible signs of pride. The prominent presence of rainbow flags and pink triangles can create a sense of openness, safety, and inclusion.

6. Out LGBT allies from the top down. Support from college administrators and alumni is essential to LGBT students.

7. LGBT-inclusive housing and gender-neutral bathrooms. Campuses may have options for LGBT-themed housing to foster a living and learning atmosphere for students.

8. Established LGBT campus center. What committed campus resources are available for LGBT students and organizations?

9. LGBT/Queer Studies academic major or minor. Students are looking for classes where they can learn about LGBT identity, politics, and history.

10. Liberal attitude and vibrant LGBT social scene. LGBT students want to be accepted fully. Students may want to live on a campus or in a city that offers queer entertainment.

Based on these criteria, would your school qualify as a LGBT-friendly campus? How does your campus support LGBT students?

Idaho, Illinois, Indiana, Iowa, Kansas, Maine, Maryland, Minnesota, Montana, Nevada, New Hampshire, New Jersey, New Mexico, New York, North Carolina, Oklahoma, Oregon, Pennsylvania, Rhode Island, South Carolina, Utah, Vermont, Virginia, Washington, West Virginia, Wisconsin, and Wyoming—had legalized gay marriage. (Refer to this chapter's Exploring Social Problems feature to understand the increasing support for marriage equality.)

In 2004, Del Martin (left) and Phyllis Lyon were the first legally married, same-sex couple in California, after San Francisco Mayor Gavin Newsom (center) allowed marriage licenses to be issued to same-sex couples. Within a few months, their marriage license, along with several thousand other licenses, was declared invalid. They were married again in 2008, after the California Supreme Court ruled that same-sex marriage was legal.

Data on same-sex marriages were first released by the U.S. Census Bureau in 2009. Previously the bureau argued that DOMA prevented the federal government from recognizing these marriages, and as a result, it would not include them in any census reporting. Same-sex marriages, unions, and partnerships were counted for the first time in the 2010 Census. The 2010 U.S. Census estimated that there were 131,729 same-sex married-couple households and 514,735 same-sex unmarried-partner households (O'Connell and Feliz 2011). The cities with the highest rates of same-sex couples were Provincetown, Massachusetts; Wilton Manors, Florida; and Palm Springs, California (Tavernise 2011). It is estimated that 2 million children are being raised in LGBT families (Movement Advancement Project et al. 2012).

Denmark was the first European country to recognize same-sex unions, in 1989. In 2006, South Africa passed its Civil Union Act, extending the legal rights of marriage to same-sex unions. The act is based on South Africa's constitution, which was the first in the world to prohibit discrimination based on sexual orientation. Marriages legal in these and other countries may not be recognized by other countries. (Refer to Table 5.2 for a complete list of same-sex marriage and partnership recognition throughout the world.)

The laws governing the rights and responsibilities of gay parents still vary from state to state. Every state allows an individual to petition to adopt a child. (Until

2010, Florida was the only state that explicitly forbade adoption by unmarried gay, lesbian, or bisexual individuals. First enacted in 1977, the Florida law was ruled unconstitutional by a state court of appeals.) At the end of 2014, 23 states and the District of Columbia allowed same-sex couples to petition jointly to adopt; 8 states restricted or banned these adoptions (Human Rights Campaign 2014b). Second-parent or stepparent adoptions options are available in 24 states and the District of Columbia (Human Rights Campaign 2014c).

Academic research has consistently indicated that gay parents and their children do not differ significantly from heterosexual parents and their children (Schumm 2006). There is little or no evidence that the children of gay or lesbian parents are disadvantaged in any important way in comparison with children of heterosexual parents (Patterson and Redding 1996); children raised by gay or lesbian parents have no increased gender-identity problems and are just as socially well adjusted as children raised by heterosexual couples (Schumm 2006; Redding 2008).

For their classic 2001 research, Judith Stacey and Timothy Biblarz examined the findings of 21 studies that explored how parental sexual orientation affects children. Based on the evidence, they concluded that there are no significant differences between children of lesbian mothers and children of heterosexual mothers on measures of social and psychological adjustment, such as self-esteem, anxiety, and depression. Across studies, there was no relationship between parental sexual orientation and measures of children's cognitive ability. Also, levels of closeness and the quality of parent–child relationships did not vary significantly by parental sexual orientation. Stacey and Biblarz (2001) concluded,

> We propose that homophobia and discrimination are the chief reasons why parental sexual orientation matters at all. Because lesbigay parents do not enjoy the same rights, respect and recognition as heterosexual parents, their children contend with the burdens of vicarious sexual stigma. (p. 177)

In their 2012 report, the Movement Advancement Project et al. documented how difficult it was for same-sex couples to establish legal ties to each other and to their

Table 5.2 Countries where same-sex marriage is legal nationwide, as of May 2015

Country	Year First Recognized
The Netherlands	2001
Belgium	2003
Canada	2005
Spain	2005
South Africa	2006
Norway	2008
Sweden	2009
Argentina	2010
Iceland	2010
Portugal	2010
Denmark	2012
France	2013
Brazil	2013
Uruguay	2013
New Zealand	2013
United Kingdom	2013
Finland	2014
Ireland	2015

NOTE: Countries that offer most or all spousal rights to same-sex and couples, but stop short of marriage, include the following: Germany, and Italy. Countries that offer some spousal rights to same-sex couples include the following: Croatia, Hungary, Israel, and Switzerland.

Support for Same-Sex Marriage

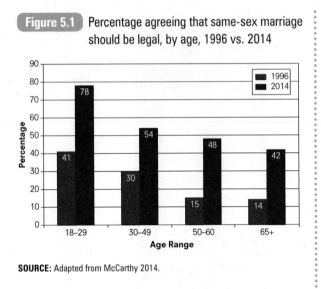

Figure 5.1 Percentage agreeing that same-sex marriage should be legal, by age, 1996 vs. 2014

SOURCE: Adapted from McCarthy 2014.

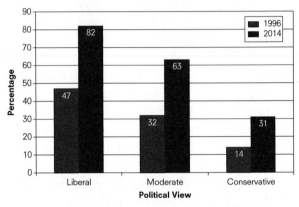

Figure 5.2 Percentage agreeing that same-sex marriage should be legal, by political views, 1996 vs. 2014

SOURCE: Adapted from McCarthy 2014.

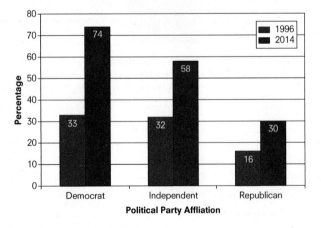

Figure 5.3 Percentage agreeing that same-sex marriage should be legal, by political party affiliation, 1996 vs. 2014

SOURCE: Adapted from McCarthy 2014.

WHAT DO YOU THINK?

The majority of Americans support laws recognizing same-sex marriage.

According to a 2014 Gallup poll, 55% of those surveyed considered same-sex marriages legally valid, with the same rights as traditional marriage (McCarthy 2014).

Support for same-sex marriage varies by demographic characteristics, such as age (Figure 5.1), political views (Figure 5.2), and political party affiliation (Figure 5.3), and has changed over time.

Based on these graphs, what patterns in support can you identify?

Social scientists hypothesize that support for same-sex marriage increases as more individuals have contact or relationships with LGBT individuals. Sociologically speaking, why do you think contact with LGBT individuals increases support for same-sex marriage?

VOICES IN THE COMMUNITY

DAN SAVAGE

After hearing the news of the suicide of Billy Lucas, a 15-year-old gay teen who reportedly endured bullying at school, Dan Savage and his husband, Terry Miller, posted a video about their lives—their family, their friends, and experiences they say they would have missed if they had killed themselves when they were bullied as teens.

Explaining how gay teenagers do not have access to positive gay role models, information, or resources, Savage wrote, "I wish I could have talked to this kid for five minutes. I wish I could have told Billy that it gets better. I wish I could have told him that, however bad things were, however isolated and alone he was, it gets better" (Savage 2010). Savage invited others to tell gay, lesbian, bisexual, or transgender teens how "it gets better" and submit their video to his YouTube channel. Savage (quoted in Chen 2012) explains,

The goal is to build and maintain these videos and all the support in them for LGBT kids who are growing up right now: 13-, 14-, and 15-year-olds; people who are nine years old right now but who will see these videos in five to six years. We want to make sure

Cliff DesPeaux/REUTERS

Dan Savage (l) is pictured here with his husband Terry Miller (r). The couple married in 2012 afer Washington voters passed a ballot initiative extending marriage rights to same-sex couples.

that videos are still being made and that LGBT kids know how to find these videos, how to find us.

As described on its website, the It Gets Better Project has become a worldwide movement, with more than 50,000 personal videos reminding LGBT teens that they are not alone and that it will get better. Celebrities, politicians, professional athletes, and activists have posted their submissions.

Visit the website at www.itgetsbetter.org.

children. Due to outdated state family laws that do not recognize or support contemporary family structures, children living in LGBT families are more likely to have legal ties to only one parent than children living with heterosexual married parents. As a result, LGBT families bear a variety of financial, legal, and emotional costs. For example, only one parent may have the authority to make routine or emergency decisions for the child, or the child may not be eligible to receive medical coverage through the employer of the nonbiological or nonlegal parent. If the biological or legal parent were to die, the child would be placed with a distant relative or in foster care instead of being placed with the nonlegal parent. The report concludes with recommendations for legislative solutions focusing on the best interests of the children, establishing legal ties to both parents, and eliminating the potential for bias and discrimination against LGBT families.

 Bullying Statistics   It Gets Better Project

Military Service

During his first presidential campaign, Bill Clinton promised to extend full civil rights to gays and lesbians, including those in military service (Belkin 2003). The military policy at that time banned gay and lesbian individuals from the armed forces, stating that homosexuality was incompatible with military service. (For information on gay military service in other countries, refer to this chapter's Taking a World View feature.) In 1993, President Clinton suspended the policy, and the National Defense Authorization Act became law.

Part of the law is the infamous "Don't Ask, Don't Tell" (DADT) policy, a political compromise criticized since its inception. According to the policy, known homosexuals were not allowed to serve in the U.S. military, but the military was banned from asking enlistees questions about their sexual orientation. In addition, significant restrictions were placed on commanders wanting to investigate whether a soldier was gay (the complete policy is actually "Don't Ask, Don't Tell, Don't Pursue, Don't Harass"). Service members who disclosed that they were homosexual were still subject to military discharge. Between the inception of DADT and the end of 2009, more than 13,000 service members were discharged (Servicemembers Legal Defense Network 2007); from World War II to the repeal of DADT, an estimated 114,000 military personnel were discharged because of their sexual orientation (Burke 2013). It is not known how many gay and lesbian service members did not reenlist because of the policy without revealing their homosexuality.

In 2007, John Shalikashvili, retired Army general and former chairman of the Joint Chiefs of Staff, declared his support for the repeal of the DADT policy. Shalikashvili (2007) described how his conversations with gay soldiers and marines, some with Iraq combat experience, "showed me how much the military has changed, and that gays and lesbians can be accepted by their peers" (p. A19). He also cited evidence from a recent poll of 500 service members returning from service in Afghanistan and Iraq, indicating that 75% of those surveyed were comfortable interacting with gay people. In the same year, the Pentagon revealed that 58 Arabic-language experts had been discharged from military service since the inception of the policy because they were gay. U.S. House representatives were critical of the Pentagon, believing that the policy and its actions were homophobic rather than focused on the country's national security needs.

A congressional bill to repeal DADT was enacted in December 2010. In 2011, a ruling from a federal appeals court barred further enforcement of DADT. DADT ended on September 20, 2011. In their assessment of the repeal of DADT, Aaron Belkin and his colleagues (2012) concluded that the repeal "has had no overall negative impact on military readiness or its component dimensions, including cohesion, recruitment, retention, assaults, harassment, or morale. . . . [G]reater openness and honesty resulting from the repeal seem to have promoted increased understanding, respect and acceptance" (p. 4). It is estimated that gay, lesbian, and bisexual service members make up at least 2% of the U.S. military's active duty and reserve forces (Bumiller 2012). In 2013, the Defense Department announced that it would provide spousal and family benefits to the same-sex spouses of military personnel and other employees.

 Repeal Don't Ask, Don't Tell

TAKING A WORLD VIEW

GAY MILITARY SERVICE POLICIES

In addition to the United States, the NATO (North Atlantic Treaty Organization) and non-NATO countries whose militaries have lifted their bans on gay military service are Australia, Austria, Belgium, Canada, the Czech Republic, Denmark, Estonia, Finland, France, Germany, Greece, Hungary, Ireland, Israel, Italy, Lithuania, Luxembourg, the Netherlands, New Zealand, Norway, Poland, Portugal, Slovenia, South Africa, Spain, Sweden, Switzerland, and the United Kingdom (Belkin 2003). Turkey is the only NATO country that does not permit gays and lesbians to serve openly in the military.

Aaron Belkin (2003) examined the early experiences of four countries that lifted their bans on homosexual military personnel. In each country—Australia, Canada, Israel, and Great Britain—the bans were lifted with opposition from the military services.

Belkin explains that each country lifted its ban for different reasons. In Canada, the ban was lifted in 1992, after federal courts ruled that the military policy violated the Canadian Charter of Rights and Freedoms. The ban was also lifted in 1992 in Australia, when Prime Minister Paul Keating argued that the ban was not consistent with his country's integration of several international human rights conventions into its domestic laws and codes. Israel's military ban was lifted in 1993 after public response to Knesset hearings on the matter. In 1999, the European Court of Human Rights ruled that Great Britain's gay ban violated the right to privacy guaranteed in the European Convention on Human Rights.

All military personnel, academics, veterans, politicians, and nongovernmental observers interviewed for Belkin's research did not believe that lifting the gay bans undermined "military performance, readiness, or cohesion, lead [*sic*] to increased difficulties in recruiting or retention or increased the rate of HIV infection among the troops" (Belkin 2003:110). Grim predictions and anxiety about how military personnel would refuse to work with or share showers, undress, or sleep in the same room with

In 2012, the U.S. Department of Defense allowed gay soldiers to march in their uniforms in a gay pride parade for the first time in U.S. history.

AP Photo/Gregory Bull

gay soldiers were not substantiated in these countries. Many interviewed described the policy change as a "nonevent" or "not that big a deal for us" and said that the change was "accepted in 'true military tradition'" (Belkin 2003:110–11).

Interviewed military leaders stressed how all soldiers were held to the same standard of professional conduct regardless of sexual orientation or personal beliefs about homosexuality. Belkin (2003) states that none of the four militaries attempted to force military personnel to accept homosexuality. Data from the four countries confirm that soldiers refrained from the abuse and harassment of homosexual military personnel, though gay bashing and sexual harassment cases were documented in two of the countries (Australia and Israel).

During the war with Iraq, before the repeal of "Don't Ask, Don't Tell," U.S. forces served side by side with allied forces from nine countries that allowed gays and lesbians to serve openly. In some cases, these forces worked together in integrated units (Servicemembers Legal Defense Network 2007).

From a social constructionist perspective, how was the repeal of gay military service bans (not just in the United States) framed by supporters and opponents? What was the social problem both sides were trying to address?

SOCIOLOGY AT WORK

INTERNSHIPS AND SERVICE LEARNING

Experiential learning allows students to learn from direct experience. It is the process of learning by doing, also referred to as active learning. There are two types of experiential learning opportunities that can help you learn more about yourself and help refine your professional goals.

An internship is described as a pre-professional experience. A student is employed in an organization to learn job or career skills specific to an organization (social service office) or occupation (social worker). Internships may be paid or unpaid, full-time or part-time, completed with or without academic credit. Through your internship, you gain on-the-job experience to include on your resume.

Service learning is defined as "an educational experience involving an organized service activity with structured reflection to guide students' learning" (Bringle and Hatcher 1999). Usually partnering with a community organization or program, students provide a range of services such as painting, cleaning, food service, or working with individuals or families. According to Sam Marullo (1996), service learning "bridges theory and practice, offering a crucible for learning that enables students to test theories with life experiences, and forces upon them an evaluation of their knowledge and understanding grounded in their service experience."

Internships or service learning should not be confused with volunteer community service. If you are a weekend volunteer at your local soup kitchen, no one will expect you to write a paper about your experiences. Experiential learning includes an academic component or expectation. As part of your experience, you may be assigned readings and required to write a final project, paper, or reflection journal.

Investigate your department or school's experiential learning options. Some departments manage their own list of internship placements or may coordinate with an internship or service learning office. Consider the experience you will gain and the work skills you can develop. Marullo (1996) says that through these experiential learning experiences,

critical thinking skills are enhanced because students are forced to confront simplistic and individualistic explanations of social problems with the complex realities they see in their volunteer work. Real world problems and constraints help students to develop their problem solving skills. Students' conflict resolution skills are developed because the situations in which they serve are rife with conflict.

What type of internship or service learning experience would you like to explore?

CHAPTER REVIEW

5.1 Define sexual orientation

Sexual orientation is defined as the classification of individuals according to their preference for emotional-sexual relationships and lifestyle with persons of the same sex (homosexuality) or persons of the opposite sex (heterosexuality). Bisexuality refers to emotional and sexual attractions to persons of either sex.

5.2 Describe how each sociological perspective addresses sexual orientation and inequality

Functionalists identify how society upholds heterosexuality and a marital union between a man and a woman as ideal normative behavior. This is also referred to as institutionalized heterosexuality, the set of ideas, institutions, and relationships that define the heterosexual family as the societal norm. From a conflict perspective, heterosexuals are granted a privileged place in our society. Heterosexual privilege is defined as the set of privileges or advantages granted to some people because of their heterosexuality. Feminist scholars have argued that lesbian and gay marriages will positively disrupt the gendered definitions of marriage. Interactionists examine how sexual orientation is constructed within a social context. The development of a gay identity

has familial, social, legal, financial, religious, and health implications.

5.3 Explain the expansion of the rights and recognition of same-sex couples in the United States

The legal recognition of same-sex couples began incrementally at the federal level. In the 2010 Census, same-sex marriages, unions, and partnerships were counted for the first time. Legalization of same-sex marriage has been recognized in more than 20 states, along with expansion of adoptions, second-parent adoptions, and stepparent adoptions for same-sex couples.

5.4 Examine whether children raised by gay or lesbian parents have different life outcomes compared to children raised by heterosexual parents

According to academic research, there is little or no evidence that the children of gay or lesbian parents are disadvantaged in any important way in comparison with children of heterosexual parents. Children raised by gay or lesbian parents have no increased gender-identity problems and are just as well socially adjusted as children raised by heterosexual couples.

KEY TERMS

bisexuality, 124

heterosexism, 126

heterosexuality, 122

homophobia, 125

homosexuality, 122

institutionalized heterosexuality, 125

LGBT, 124

master status, 129

sexual orientation, 122

transgender, 124

STUDY QUESTIONS

1. Compare and contrast the biological, psychological, and sociological perspectives on sexual orientation.

2. Examine how heterosexuality is privileged in society.

3. How, from a sociological perspective, is our sexuality defined/controlled by our norms, values, and language?

4. Explain the role of power and privilege in understanding sexual orientation.

5. How has repeal of the military policy of "Don't Ask, Don't Tell" affected military service by gays and lesbians?

6. Explain how gays and lesbians are discriminated against in the workplace and in the military.

$SAGE edge™

Sharpen your skills with SAGE edge at **edge.sagepub.com/leonguerrero5e**

SAGE edge provides a personalized approach to help you accomplish your coursework goals in an easy-to-use learning environment.

Age and Aging

More than 500 retired scientists and researchers volunteered as first responders to the nuclear plant accident at the Fukushima Daiichi power plant in 2011. The Skilled Veterans Corps volunteers ranged in age from 60 to 78 years. According to Yasuteru Yamada (pictured to the right), a retired physicist, "young workers who may reproduce a younger generation and are themselves more susceptible to the effects of radiation should not be engaged in such work. This job is a call for senior citizens like me" (quoted in Glionna 2011a). The story of Yamada and his colleagues was characterized as "a lesson about growing old gracefully, about demonstrating the sheer willfulness in an aging body" (Glionna 2011b). Yamada maintains that he is nobody's hero. Despite their expertise and their willingness to help, the volunteers were not permitted to assist with the cleanup.

Age is both a biological and a social classification (McConatha et al. 2003). There are social dictates regarding age—socially and culturally defined expectations about the meaning of age, our understanding of it, and our responses to it (Calasanti and Slevin 2001). We make a fuss over the 77-year-old Ironman triathlete and the 13-year-old college student because they are unexpected or deemed unusual for people of their age. Age distinguishes acceptable behavior for different social groups. Voting, the legal consumption of alcohol, military enlistment, and the ability to hold certain elected offices (you can't be president of the United States until you are at least 35 years old) are examples of formal age norms. Informal age norms also demonstrate how a society defines what is considered appropriate by age (Calasanti and Slevin 2001).

Melanie Stetson Freeman/The Christian Science Monitor/Getty Images

Age is both a biological and a social classification. Active seniors expand our beliefs and expectations of elderly behavior and roles.

Life course perspective: A theoretical perspective that considers the entire course of human life (from childhood, adolescence, and adulthood to old age) as social constructions that reflect the broader structural conditions of society

Gerontology: The study of aging and the elderly

Population aging: The increase in the number or proportion of older individuals in the population

Demography: The study of the size, composition, and distribution of human populations

Sociologists examine age and the process of aging through a **life course perspective**. This perspective examines the entire course of human life from childhood, adolescence, and adulthood to old age. The life course perspective tends to view "stages of life" as social constructions that reflect the broader structural conditions of society (Moody 2006). Aging occurs within a social context: one's social class, education, occupation, gender, and race will determine how one experiences adolescence or old age. However, there is also room for individuals to make their own choices in interpreting or embracing age-related roles (Moody 2006). **Gerontology** is the specific study of aging and the elderly, the primary focus of this chapter.

OUR AGING WORLD

Much has been written about the graying or aging of America, a change in our demographic structure referred to as **population aging** (Clark et al. 2004). One way to confirm population aging is to look at the median age of the U.S. population. (The median age is the age where half the population is older and the other half is younger.) The median age was 17 years in 1820 and 23 years in 1900, and by 2000 it had increased to 35 years. By 2030, the median age is predicted to increase to 42 years.

Demography is the study of the size, composition, and distribution of populations, and demographers have identified several reasons for population aging. First, population aging is caused by a decline in birthrates (Moody 2006). With a smaller

 Age and Society

number of children, the average age of the population increases. In 1900, America was a relatively young population, with children and teenagers making up 40% of the population. By 1990, however, the proportion of youth had dropped to 24%.

Population aging can also occur because of improvements in life expectancy as a result of medical and technological advances (Moody 2006), improved access to health care, healthier lifestyles, and better health before 65 years of age (National Center for Health Statistics 2009). As people live longer, the average age of the population increases. In 1900, life expectancy at birth was 47 years; according to the Centers for Disease Control and Prevention, the life expectancy for a child born in 2011 is 78.7 years (National Center for Health Statistics 2009; Hoyert and Xu 2012).

Longer life expectancy has also made it necessary to redefine what it means to be old or elderly. Gerontology scholars and researchers now make the distinction between the young-old (aged 65 to 75), the old-old (aged 75 to 84), and the oldest-old (aged 85 or older) (Moody 2006). Unless noted otherwise, the use of the term *elderly* in this chapter will refer to those aged 65 years or older.

Finally, the process of population aging can be influenced because of birth cohorts (Moody 2006). A cohort is a group of people born during a particular period who experience common life events during the same historical period. For example, the Depression of the 1930s produced a small birth cohort that had a minimal impact on the average age of the population. However, the baby boom cohort after World War II is a very large cohort, and its middle-age baby boomers will contribute to the aging of the U.S. population. When Kathleen Casey-Kirschling, our nation's first baby boomer, born January 1, 1946, applied for her Social Security benefits in 2007, Social Security commissioner Michael Astrue said it signaled "America's silver tsunami" (Ohlemacher 2007:A1). An estimated 10,000 people a day will become eligible for Social Security benefits during the next two decades (Ohlemacher 2007). Graphically, the aging of the United States is displayed in Table 6.1. Data from the U.S. Census Bureau dramatically show the effect of the baby boom generation on the overall age structure.

Demographers predict that the number of Americans aged 65 years or older will increase over several decades. To provide a context for aging in the United States, it is helpful to examine trends in the rest of the world (He et al. 2005). Populations are aging in all countries, though the level and pace vary by geographic region. Fertility decline, improved health and longevity, and increasing urbanization have contributed to the unprecedented growth of older populations throughout the world. In 2008, 506 million people (7%) in the world were 65 years old or older; by 2040, the number is projected to increase to 1.3 billion (14%). By 2020, for the first time, people aged 65 or over are expected to outnumber children under age 5.

Figure 6.1 reports the percentage of elderly in the population from 2010 and projected through 2030 and 2050. Europe and

Table 6.1 Percentage aged 65 and older of the total U.S. population: 2000–2050, projected

Year	Percentage
2000	12.4
2010	13.0
2020	16.8
2030	20.3
2040	21.0
2050	20.9

SOURCE: West et al. 2014.

NOTE: The reference population for these data is the resident population.

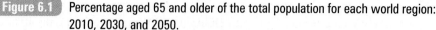

Figure 6.1 Percentage aged 65 and older of the total population for each world region: 2010, 2030, and 2050.

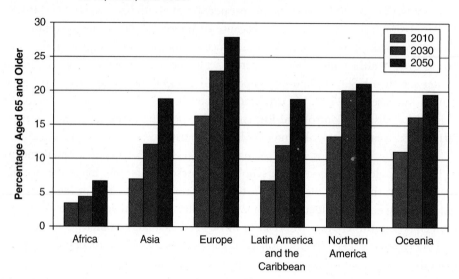

SOURCE: West et al. 2014.

Northern America will continue to have the highest percentage of elderly in the world. The percentage of elderly in Asia and Latin America and the Caribbean are predicted to more than double due to high fertility and low mortality rates. In less developed countries, though the proportion of the elderly is low, the number of elderly is large due to the size of their populations. In India, there were 63 million older people, representing only 5.3% of the population (West et al. 2014).

Gerontologist Harry Moody (2006) warns, "Population aging is a long-range trend that will characterize our society as we continue into the 21st century. It is a force we all will cope with for the rest of our lives" (p. xxiii). Population aging means an increase in the number or proportion of elderly and signals the need for changes in health care, employment status, living arrangements, and social welfare for the elderly and the rest of society.

The aging of U.S. society is likely to transform state, regional, city, and sub-urban populations. A 2007 Brookings Institution report (Frey 2007) predicts the emergence of two major senior populations, each with a set of specific needs and geographic impacts. "Yuppie senior" affluent populations are expected to emerge in the South and West (in cities such as Las Vegas, Denver, Dallas, and Atlanta), increasing their demands for new types of community cultural amenities. Their affluence will continue to support and encourage the economic and civic growth of their geographic areas. Conversely, cities in the Northeast and Midwest are predicted to have a disproportionately higher population of "mature seniors"—less financially stable or physically able than yuppie seniors. Mature seniors are likely to

 United States Population Pyramid

TAKING A WORLD VIEW

AGING IN CHINA

The growth of the older population in China is expected to accelerate in the next 50 years, surpassing the aging population in many Western European countries and the United States. Charles Kincannon, Wan He, and Loraine West (2005) report that more than a half century ago, 1 in 25 Chinese people was aged 65 years or older, but by the beginning of the 21st century, 1 in every 14 Chinese was an older person.

According to population projections by the U.S. Census Bureau's International Programs center, China's older population will quadruple. Given China's total population of over 1.2 billion in 2000, this accelerated aging process will involve huge numbers of people. By 2050, it is projected that there will be 349.0 million people 65 years old or older in China, almost one fourth more than the total population of the United States in 2000 (Kincannon et al. 2005:245). (In contrast, the 2050 projection for the number of elderly in the United States is 33.7 million.)

Elderly Chinese rely on a variety of sources for financial support. In 2000, just over half the Chinese men aged 65 years or over who were no longer working relied primarily on their family for financial support, while 4 in 10 received primary support from a retirement pension. Older women were far more likely to be dependent on their families for support—82%—and much less likely to rely on a retirement pension—13% (Kincannon et al. 2005:250).

Reliance on family support is greatest among the oldest-old Chinese population, largely because they are not eligible to receive benefits under China's pension system (first established in the 1950s and limited to those with at least 20 years of employment) or, if they do qualify, because pension benefits are insufficient to use as the primary source of financial support.

The researchers predict that as China expands its system of social insurance programs, reliance on family support is likely to decline. Since the 1990s, China's government policies have expanded community social services for the elderly. Community-based in-home care has gained popularity in urban areas. In this model of care, the elderly receive supplemental or respite care at home if their children work and are unable to care for them or if their children do not live with them (Xu and Chow 2011).

The progressive aging of its older population is a serious issue for China. Better medical care and health conditions in China have led to longer lives for older people in the country. As Kincannon et al. (2005) observe,

> over time, a nation's older population may grow older on average as a larger proportion survives to 80 years and beyond (the oldest old). The oldest old and the young old have very different economic, demographic, and health statuses, thus they also have very different needs for health services, old-age care, residential arrangements, or assistance with the requirements of daily life. The oldest old are more likely to be widowed (especially the oldest-old women), to be frail or sick, and to be unemployed and lack financial resources. Their needs may put tremendous pressures on their families as well as on society. The oldest old, therefore, are a group within the older population that warrants special attention. (p. 245)

require more social and public support programs, along with affordable private and institutional housing and accessible health care providers (Frey 2007), ultimately leading to competition over resource allocation such as funding for schools versus senior services.

SOCIOLOGICAL PERSPECTIVES ON AGE, AGING, AND INEQUALITY

Functionalist Perspective

Age helps maintain the stability of society by providing a set of roles and expectations for each particular age group or for a particular life stage. These roles are reinforced by our major social institutions—education, the economy, and family. We assume that children, 18 years old or younger, should be in school. After high school graduation, young adults have the choice of entering the workforce or continuing their education (where their student role continues), whereas adulthood is a time set aside to build one's career and to begin a family. Retirement is another important age-related stage, with societal roles and expectations for a retired person.

· ·

What Does It Mean to Me?

The term **boomerangers** refers to young adults who leave home for college but return after graduation because of economic constraints or personal choice. Surveys of recent college graduates conducted in the early 2000s noted that nearly half of those surveyed expected to live with their families for some period. According to Jeffrey Jones (2014), 14% of adults 24 to 34 years old are living with their parents. Is boomeranging a viable transitional stage for recent college graduates? For you?

· ·

Boomerangers: Young adults who leave home for college, but return after graduation because of either economic constraints (they may be unemployed or underemployed) or personal choice

Disengagement theory: Theoretical perspective that defines aging as a natural process of withdrawal from active participation in social life

Consider how each age group has its own function or role—the young attend school preparing for their adult lives, adults are employed and building their lives, and the elderly retire. **Disengagement theory** defines aging as a natural process of withdrawal from active participation in social life. Older people disengage from society (from their work and certain parts of their lives), and in turn, society disengages from them (Turner 1996). The theory contends that people enter and exit a set of roles throughout their lives. These transitions are natural and functional for society (Mabry and Bengston 2005; Moody 2006).

This process is portrayed as orderly, timely, and necessary for the well-being of the entire society. For example, in the workplace, older workers must relinquish their

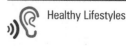
Healthy Lifestyles

jobs to make room for younger workers in the labor market. This process is socially supported through retirement plans, pensions, and Medicare (Mabry and Bengston 2005). Disengagement is portrayed as positive for the elderly because it enables them to participate in activities and a lifestyle that earlier would not have been possible (they may become more fully engaged in community, family, or leisure activities). The final form of disengagement is death.

However, this perspective fails to acknowledge how vulnerable and powerless adults are in their older years. Is this disengagement natural or forced by society? The next perspective answers this question.

Conflict Perspective

The **modernization theory of aging** suggests that the role and status of the elderly declines with industrialization. Specifically, their power, wealth, and prestige are linked with their labor contribution or relationship to the means of production. In hunting and gathering societies, the elderly had a low status because they were unable to contribute to the primary means of production. However, their status increased during the time of stable agricultural societies, when older people controlled land ownership. In modern industrial society, life experience is surpassed by technological expertise; thus, the status of the elderly declines.

From a conflict perspective, the two groups at odds with one another are the young and the old. As Donald Cowgill (1974) explains, society systematically advantages the young, supported by what he calls the "cult of youth"—a value system that glorifies youth "as a symbol of beauty, vigor and progress and discriminates in favor of youth in employment and in the allocation of community resources" (pp. 15–16).

Cowgill (1974) identifies how four aspects of modernization lower the status of older people. The first is health technology. Modern health advances improve the population's overall health and longevity. This creates an older and healthier workforce, willing and able to stay in the labor force a bit longer: "As the lives of workers are prolonged, death no longer creates openings in the labor force as it once did" (Cowgill 1974:12). Society then creates a new opening through retirement, forcing people out of their most valued and senior roles in the labor force. Elderly workers are reduced to retirement status with less income and influence.

The next two aspects, education and economic technology, are related to one another. In a modern society, the young have more opportunities to acquire education and training. The status of younger members of society is elevated because they become more literate than their parents. Society relies on their

> **Modernization theory of aging:** Theoretical perspective that links the role and status of the elderly with their labor contribution or their relationship to the means of production

The modernization theory of aging suggests that the declining status of the elderly is associated with their decreasing economic and labor contribution. What status do we attribute to the position of store greeter? High or low?

J.D. Pooley/Getty Images

increased literacy in the workplace, creating new information- and technology-based occupations. The people most qualified for these positions are the younger, more literate workers. Older workers perform more traditional jobs, some that are less valued or that eventually become obsolete.

The final aspect is urbanization. A modern society is more urban, characterized by increased social mobility and migration. Cowgill (1974) argues that the young migrate more than the old do. The migration produces a physical and emotional separation between a child and the family of origin, tearing down the bonds of the extended family. Yet it also promotes the cultural image of the young moving to something better, while the old are left behind.

Researchers have challenged the assumption that modernization and economic conditions automatically lead to the status decline of the elderly. Sociologists and anthropologists have documented how the status of older persons varies by race and ethnicity, gender, culture, and social class. Among Hispanics and Asians, where multigenerational households are common, the elderly are respected and honored.

Feminist Perspective

Women constitute the majority in the U.S. older population. In 2010, there were 23 million women aged 65 years or older, compared with 17 million men (U.S. Census Bureau 2012). Women outnumber men in the older population at every single year of age from 65 to 100 years and over (Werner 2011). The standards of our culture create more problems for women than for men as they transition into their middle and later years. Women seem more vulnerable to societal pressure to retain their youth and, consequently, face more questions about their self-worth, which may lead to serious problems ranging from low self-esteem to depression (Saucier 2004). Questions about self-worth and value are also raised in the workplace, where researchers have documented how women experience greater age discrimination during all ages than do men (Duncan and Loretto 2004). In many ways, aging is socially constructed through a gendered lens.

Susan Sontag (1979) notes how society is much more permissive about aging in men. She writes about the **double standard of aging**—men are judged in our culture according to what they can do (their competence, power, and control), but women are judged according to their appearance and beauty. Women's identity is more closely associated with their physical appearance than is the identity of men. As a result, society considers men distinguished in their old age, but women must disguise the fact that they are aging. Sontag argues that because women are unable to maintain their youthful looks as they age, they are pressured to defend themselves against aging at all costs.

Feminist scholars argue that the cosmetic industry focuses on a male and youth standard. Though cosmetic products are advertised for women's use (ever notice that there are no male cosmetics counters at your department store?), feminists assert that the industry is responding to the male-defined standard of female beauty. In addition,

Double standard of aging: Separate standards of aging for men and women; men are judged in our culture according to what they can do (their competence, power, and control), but women are judged according to their appearance and beauty

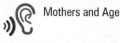 Mothers and Age

the industry is responding to the image of unattainable youthful beauty upheld by society (Calasanti, Slevin, and King 2006). When Laura Hurd Clarke (2000) interviewed women aged 61 to 92, she discovered that while older women say that their overall health is more important to them than physical attractiveness, they still exhibit an internalization of ageist beauty norms. As Sontag (quoted in Freedman 1986:200) says, "women are trained to want to continue looking like girls forever."

This perspective also examines how ageism and sexism are reflected in the media. Though older adults are underrepresented in U.S. film, television programs, and advertisements in comparison with younger adults, older women are less likely to be featured than older men (Peterson and Ross 1997; Sanders 2002). When older women are portrayed, their characters represent negative stereotypes and are often shown as less successful compared with older men. Similar patterns were also documented in German media (Kessler, Rakoczy, and Staudinger 2004).

Interactionist Perspective

Interactionists reveal how our age-related roles are socially defined and expected. Age is tied to a system of matching people and roles (Hagestad and Uhlenberg 2005). What does it mean to be middle aged? Middle age is not just measured according to years, but is also associated with a set of role expectations. We share a definition of what it means to be middle aged, and there is an expectation that we need to assume a particular role once we are middle aged.

....

What Does It Mean to Me?
Who or what defines aging in our society? How are these definitions perpetuated, and how can they be altered?

....

These role expectations stigmatize particular age groups. **Stigma**, coined by Erving Goffman ([1963] 1986), is defined as a discrediting attribute. Older adults are discredited in society, stereotyped as less capable, fragile, weak, and frail. **Ageism** or the stereotyping of (or discrimination against) older adults can damage the self-concepts of the elderly (Miller, Leyell, and Mazachek 2004) and represents a self-perpetuating cycle of fears that old and younger adults have toward aging in general, disability, death, competition for resources, and the perceived inferiority of particular individuals (Yang and Levkoff 2005). These images may increase social isolation, dependency, and elder abuse and may become a self-fulfilling prophecy for others (Thornton 2002). However, researchers have found that older adults from cultures with more positive attitudes toward aging than mainstream society may be able to avoid exposure to or internalization of the negative stereotypes of old age (Levy and Langer 1994).

Interactionists examine how the problems associated with aging have been defined and by whom. Society relies on trained experts such as gerontologists,

Stigma: A discrediting attribute

Ageism: Prejudice or discrimination based on someone's age

 Extreme Longevity

physicians, nurses, and social workers to identify and respond to the problems of aging. Yet research indicates that this group of professionals is just as likely to be prejudiced against older people as other groups are. A. J. Levenson (1981) argues, "Medical students' attitudes have reflected a prejudice against older persons surpassed only by their racial prejudice" (p. 61). He points to medical schools as part of the problem, putting little value on geriatrics as a specialty. Doctors often think that because aging cannot be stopped, illnesses associated with old age are not that important.

The medical industry has not ignored aging completely. Though controversial, the medical and cosmetic industries actively promote antiaging vitamins, hormones, surgeries, and pharmaceutical drugs, encouraging wellness to patients and clients while sending a message that they can "beat back old age" (Wilson 2007:BU1). Americans spend nearly $50 billion per year on antiaging vitamins, treatments, hormones, and pharmaceutical drugs (Wilson 2007). Are we responding to a genuine problem or one carefully manufactured by the medical and cosmetic industries?

A summary of all sociological perspectives is presented in Table 6.2.

Table 6.2   Summary of sociological perspectives: Inequalities based on age and aging

	Functional	Conflict/Feminist	Interactionist
Explanations of age and inequality	As we age, we enter and exit age-specific roles and statuses. Each status helps maintain social stability. Elderly disengagement is a normal and necessary process.	Inequality is based on one's relationship to the labor force—with the elderly having the least amount of power in society. Women are disadvantaged in the aging process more than men are.	Our age-related roles are socially defined and expected.
Questions asked about age and inequality	How do our age-related roles and statuses contribute to the stability of society? Is there a way to successfully disengage the elderly from society?	How does modernization contribute to lowering the status of the elderly? What can be done to improve the status of the elderly? How and why does society have two standards for aging—one for men, the other for women? What can be done to reduce the negative impact of the aging standard for women?	How do we learn our age-related roles? In what ways do our perceptions and beliefs perpetuate ageism?

THE CONSEQUENCES OF AGE INEQUALITY

Ageism

Ageism is defined by Robert Butler (1969) as the "systematic stereotyping of and discrimination against people because they are old, just as racism and sexism accomplish this with skin color and gender" (p. 243). Todd Nelson (2005) described ageism as "prejudice against our feared self." He suggests that age prejudice is one of the most socially condoned and institutionalized forms of prejudice. For example, a standard message in birthday greeting cards is how unfortunate one is to be a year older. In 2012, researcher Ye Luo and his colleagues reported that 63% of older adults reported at least one type of everyday discrimination (e.g., being treated with less courtesy, receiving poorer service, being threatened or harassed). Among older adults, Blacks; separated, widowed, or divorced individuals; and those with lower household assets have higher levels of discrimination than Whites, married individuals, and those with more assets (Luo et al. 2012).

Ageism marks a sharp distinction between "us" and "them." William Bytheway (1995) explains it this way: "The issues of these pronouns creates a conceptual map on which groups of people are variously included and excluded. In particular, the old who are discriminated against occupy a different territory on these us/them maps from 'us'" (p. 117).

Older adults tend to be marginalized, institutionalized, and stripped of their responsibility, dignity, and power (Nelson 2002). Dependency is one of the most negative attributes of being identified as "old" in our society (Calasanti and Slevin 2001). Stereotypes about the capacities, activities, and interests of older people reinforce the view that they are incapable of caring for themselves (Pampel 1998). Older adults are not generally disliked, but they are likely to be victims of paternalistic prejudice, which stereotypes them as likable but incompetent (Packer and Chasteen 2006). There is widespread acceptance of negative stereotypes about the elderly regarding their intellectual decline, conservatism, sexual decline, and lack of productivity (Levin and Levin 1980).

In a comparative study of young adults in the United States and Germany, German young adults tended to view aging more negatively than did Americans in the sample (McConatha et al. 2003). Germans were more likely to be pessimistic about the likelihood of finding contentment in old age and did not expect to feel good about life when they were older. The study attributed the differences in aging attitudes to Germany's more prevalent negative stereotypes of older people, a response to the increasing costs of providing extension pension and health benefits to the elderly in Germany. On the other hand, in the United States, effective political advocacy groups, increasingly healthy and influential older adults, and educational aging programs may account for a reduction of ageism. The study also revealed that American and German women were more concerned about age-related physical changes than were men.

....

What Does It Mean to Me?

Jasim McConatha and her colleagues (2003) asked young adult Germans and Americans what age they considered "old." The average age that Germans reported was 64 years for men and 60 for women; the U.S. sample reported younger ages—53 years for men and 48 for women. What age do you consider old? What expectations do you have about growing older?

....

Age and Social Class

The most economically vulnerable in our society are very young or old. As discussed in Chapter 2, the rate of child poverty in the United States is one of the highest among Western industrialized countries. According to the U.S. Census, the poverty rate for children was 19.9%, or 14.7 million, in 2013 (DeNavas-Walt and Proctor 2014). For a more extensive discussion on children and poverty, refer to Chapter 2, "Social Class and Poverty."

Though most of us envision a retirement filled with leisure activities, travel, and good living, there is another possibility—that one's retirement will be a time of serious economic hardship. In 2013, 4.2 million elderly (or 9.5%) were living in poverty in the United States (DeNavas-Walt and Proctor 2014). Retirement represents a precipitous income drop for most elderly (DeNavas-Walt, Proctor, and Smith 2012). The median income by age of householder was highest, at $67,141, for those aged 45 to 54 years for 2013 (DeNavas-Walt and Proctor 2014). Median income begins to decline with the next age group, those aged 55 to 64, to $57,538. Finally, for those aged 65 or older, the reported median income was $35,611 (DeNavas-Walt and Proctor 2014). For 2012, poor older adults relied on Social Security benefits more than higher-income older adults (refer to this chapter's Exploring Social Problems feature for more information).

The economic recession depleted the incomes and savings of many older workers, leading some to admit that they are unable or afraid to retire. For example, 58-year-old Barbara Petrucci, a hospital employee from Atlanta, Georgia, set aside her dreams for an early retirement. After family savings were depleted by the declining stock market, Petrucci admits that retirement is "an elusive dream" (Rampell and Saltmarsh 2009).

As we have discussed in earlier chapters, the inequalities based on race/ethnicity and gender will also determine one's economic status. Poverty rates among the elderly vary by race/ethnicity and gender. Older women have higher rates of poverty than older men do, 10.7% versus 6.6% (Issa and Zedlewski 2011). Women are especially susceptible to economic insecurity because of a number of factors. Women have longer life expectancies and are more likely to be widowed and live alone in old age. Because of gender differences in employment and salaries, women are likely to have less retirement income than men do. During 1999, women aged 65 or older received, on average, $8,000 annually as pension income, whereas men received

Elderly Income

Social Security is funded through the Old-Age, Survivors, and Disability Insurance program. The earliest age that workers can receive benefits is 62, though benefits are about 25% lower than they would be at full retirement age. Though full retirement is often associated with 65 years of age, your actual retirement age will depend on your birth year. For those born in 1937 or earlier, retirement is 65 years. With each year from 1939, the retirement age is extended by monthly increments. For example, for someone born in 1941, his or her retirement age is 65 and 8 months. Currently the highest retirement age is 67 for those born in 1960 or later.

Figure 6.2 Income sources for the population aged 65 and over, lowest quintile, percentages reported, 2010

Earnings 2.4%
Pensions and Retirement Savings 2.9%
Assets 1.8%
Other 1.6%
Government Transfers 7%
Social Security 84.3%

SOURCE: West et al. 2014.

Figure 6.3 Income sources for the population aged 65 and over, highest quintile, percentages reported, 2010

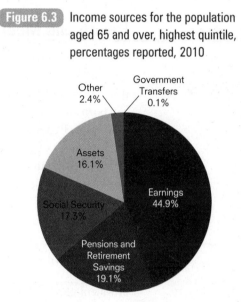

Other 2.4%
Government Transfers 0.1%
Assets 16.1%
Social Security 17.3%
Earnings 44.9%
Pensions and Retirement Savings 19.1%

SOURCE: West et al. 2014.

Figure 6.4 Workers aged 55 and over who are very confident about retirement finances, 2000 and 2010

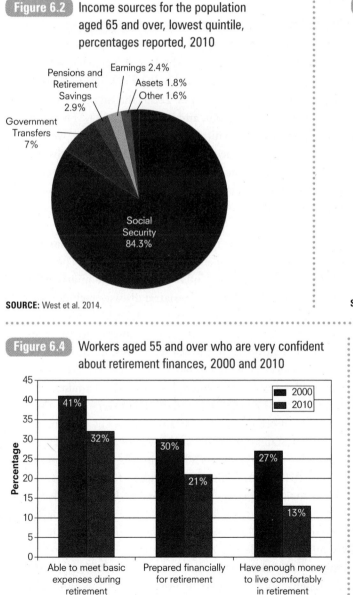

- 2000
- 2010

	Able to meet basic expenses during retirement	Prepared financially for retirement	Have enough money to live comfortably in retirement
2000	41%	30%	27%
2010	32%	21%	13%

Percentage

SOURCE: West et al. 2014.

WHAT DO YOU THINK?

For those 65 years of age or older, Social Security payments accounted for the largest share of income, 36.7%, in 2010. The second largest share was from earnings at 30.2% (West et al. 2014). Figures 6.2 and 6.3 report income shares for the lowest and highest income quintiles.

Describe the difference in the income sources between these two quintiles.

In an annual survey, workers aged 55 and over were asked how confident they were about their retirement finances. The percentages of those who were very confident are reported in Figure 6.4. Results are presented for 2000 and 2010.

The data reported in Figure 6.4 combines responses from males and females. Hypothesize how gender might affect the level of confidence in retirement finances. Would men be more confident than women in their ability to meet their basic expenses during retirement? Why or why not?

$14,000 annually (He et al. 2005). Non-Hispanic White elderly have lower poverty rates than other reported racial groups. Blacks have the highest rate (19.3%), followed by Latinos (19.0%) and Whites (7.4%) (Rhee 2012).

In the European Union (EU25), about one in six elderly persons is at risk for living in poverty. In 14 of all EU25 countries, the elderly populations are at higher risk of being poor compared with working-age populations. The risk of poverty is highest in Cyprus, Ireland, and Slovenia. Rates are lowest among the elderly residing in the Czech Republic, Slovakia, Lithuania, Latvia, the Netherlands, and Luxembourg (Zaidi 2006).

Health and Medical Care

Much as they are more economically vulnerable, the young and the old experience the highest health risks among all age groups. We think of death as something that happens in one's old age, yet the age group with the highest risk of mortality is newborns and infants within their first year of life. For 2009, the infant mortality rate was 6.39 deaths per 1,000 births (Murphy, Xu, and Kochanek 2012). The three leading causes of death among infants are congenital birth defects, low birth weight, and sudden infant death syndrome. Among the elderly, the majority of deaths are caused by heart disease, cancer, and stroke. The elderly also experience chronic conditions such as hypertension (high blood pressure) and heart disease that may contribute to fatal disorders. The elderly are more likely to experience chronic illnesses than younger age groups do, 46% versus 12% (Moody 2006).

Geriatrics is a medical specialty that focuses on diseases of the elderly; some are chronic, not all are life threatening, and others will eventually lead to death. The most prevalent chronic disease of the elderly is arthritis, inflammation of the joints and a leading cause of disability in the United States. Other geriatric diseases include osteoporosis (deterioration of bone tissue, prevalent among women), Parkinson's disease (a degenerative neurological disorder), and dementia and Alzheimer's disease (progressive loss of mental abilities and functions). For the last set of diseases, it should be noted that most older adults experience no mental impairment at all (Moody 2006). (A discussion of caregiving and elder abuse is presented in Chapter 7, "Families.")

American elderly, who constitute 13% of our population, consume more than 35% of total health expenditures—more than four times what is spent on younger people (Moody 2006). The United States spends about 17.4% of its gross domestic product (GDP) on health care—the largest expenditure in this category among industrialized countries. During 2010, total health care spending reached $2.6 trillion, with an average of $8,086 spent per person (Centers for Medicare and Medicaid Services 2012).

According to the Centers for Disease Control and Prevention (Robinson 2007), older women face distinctly different challenges to maintain their health compared with older men. The financing and availability of health care is particularly important for older women. Because women make up a higher proportion of the older and frailer population, are less likely to have a spouse to assist them, and need more help with personal care and routine needs, older women use more health care and long-term care services than men do. Most older adults are covered by Medicare, but because older women rely on long-term care (not covered under Medicare), they make higher out-of-pocket payments or rely on Medicaid more often than older men do. Women rely on informal (unpaid) caregivers (adult children, family members, or friends), community-based services (senior centers and convenient transportation), and formal (paid) care services (home health care and nursing home care).

Ageism in the Workplace

In some businesses, age discrimination has an acronym, TFO, "too f___ing old" (Fisher 2004:46). Although much attention has been given to the marginalization of Black, Latino, or female workers, members of another labor force group—older workers—have experienced their own set of unique problems. In 2011, 22.1 million Americans aged 55 to 64 years were employed (U.S. Census Bureau 2011).

Helen Dennis and Kathryn Thomas (2007) document how ageism continues to affect the hiring and promotion of older workers and workplace attitudes toward them. For example, most interview research indicates that older job interviewees whose qualifications are equal to those of younger candidates are less likely to be hired. Ageism restricts job opportunities for mature workers, as they are not offered the same promotion opportunities, training, or compensation as younger workers. Managers have mixed perceptions about older workers. Although older workers are valued for their work habits, skills, and performance, negative perceptions also exist. Older workers are perceived as inflexible, unwilling to adapt to technology, and more expensive (due to health insurance costs) when compared with younger workers.

In the United States, older workers are protected under the Age Discrimination in Employment Act of 1967. The act prohibits employers from discriminating based on age against people 40 to 64 years old. However, in 2008 the U.S. Supreme Court created a tougher burden of proof for plaintiffs in age bias cases. An employee would have to prove that age was the decisive factor (as opposed to a motivating factor) in an adverse employment decision. All EU countries have legislation banning age discrimination in employment, though in the United Kingdom 65 years old is considered the default mandatory retirement age.

In their study of older women's employment agency placements in Auckland, New Zealand, Jocelyn Handy and Doreen Davy (2007) identified gendered age-ism as a key barrier to permanent full-time employment for older women. Tracking women applicants in their mid-40s to early 60s, Handy and Davy documented how these women, despite their skills and qualifications, faced negative stereotypes concerning their appearance (looking their age) and a lack of "team fit." One job seeker explained how a placement consultant told her that she was not suited for a position because she would remind the manager of his mother. Consultants valued physical presentation (beauty and youth) and also acknowledged how younger managers

Employment Rate Doubles for Older Women

IN FOCUS

THE POLITICAL INFLUENCE OF YOUNG AND OLDER VOTERS

The enactment of Social Security, Medicare, and other old-age–related policies has created a political constituency of older beneficiaries (Campbell 2003) and, along with it, the perception of political might. A form of ageism, the stereotype of "greedy" older voters willing to put their needs (Social Security and Medicare) ahead of the needs of other age groups, is accepted in many social, political, and media circles (Street and Crossman 2006).

Robert Binstock (2005, 2006) reveals some truths and myths about this perception of senior power. He explains that the senior political power model builds on the fact that older people represent a significant proportion of the electorate. Age is associated with voter registration and actual voting, which is also related to the length of residence in one's home, along with one's level of knowledge about political and social issues. Older persons are likely to have resided in their homes longer than have younger persons, and older people tend to be more knowledgeable about politics and news issues than

Older Americans have higher rates of voter registration than younger Americans. In addition, older men and women are more likely to contribute to a political campaign and contact their elected representatives regarding issues that matter to them.

younger people are. Studies indicate that older persons' high level of interest in politics does not decline even as they reach advanced old age.

In addition to their higher rates of voting participation, the elderly have higher rates of participation in other political areas. The elderly make campaign contributions at higher rates than do younger people—about 28% of all contributions to the 2000 presidential campaign came

would perceive older workers as a threat. The older job seekers were often placed in low-paid, low-skilled temporary positions. The researchers concluded, "The gendered ageism affecting mature female clerical workers will not be solved simply by countering common stereotypes concerning older workers' skills and necessitates greater attention to combating prejudices surrounding inter-age dynamics within the workplace" (pp. 95–96).

RESPONDING TO AGE INEQUALITIES

Social Security and Medicare are social insurance programs designed to protect citizens against a specific set of risks. In the case of Social Security, the risk is that one might have insufficient resources at retirement and that one's resources might

from older persons. Older voters are twice as likely to contact their state and federal representatives about issues that matter to them as younger voters are.

So, what impact does the voting participation by elderly Americans have on elections? One noticeable impact is on how it shapes candidate behavior—candidates actively court the senior vote. Recent presidential candidates have made key appearances at senior centers or promoted their proposals on Social Security and Medicare to selected senior audiences. But Binstock (2006) argues that the senior vote does not have a "distinctive impact on the outcome of elections" (p. 26). He explains that older Americans do not vote cohesively or as a bloc. Their votes are as diverse as those of any other age group, divided along partisan, class, gender, and racial lines. Age is just one characteristic among many that influence voting patterns.

For example, in the 2004 presidential election, the 65-or-older votes were distributed in approximately the same proportions—52% for President George W. Bush and 47% for Senator John Kerry—as were the votes of the general electorate—51% for Bush and 48% for Kerry. In the 2012 presidential election, older voters went against the popular vote—56% supported Governor Romney versus 44% who supported President Obama.

According to Scott Keeter, Juliana Horowitz, and Alec Tyson (2008), young voters have emerged as a key voting bloc for the Democratic Party. Since 2004, the majority of those under the age of 30 years have voted for a Democratic candidate in the general election. In 2008, 66% of voters 18 to 29 years of age voted for Barack Obama compared to 53% of all voters. This is the largest measured difference since exit polling began in 1972. Young voters are more ethnically and racially diverse and are less likely to be affiliated with a religious tradition than voters age 30 years or older. Additionally, voters 18 to 29 years of age expressed liberal views on the role of government (to solve problems) and were more likely to disapprove of the Iraq war than older voters. Though younger voters were less likely to contribute money to a campaign, the 18- to 29-year-old voter group had a rate of campaign event participation in battleground states higher than that of any other age group (Keeter et al. 2008). In 2012, President Obama received 60% of the youth vote in his campaign for reelection (Center for Information and Research on Civic Learning and Engagement 2012).

not last one's lifetime. How much health care will we need, and for how long are the risks addressed by Medicare? Both are proven, effective antipoverty programs, supporting elderly financial independence and enabling the elderly to live better and healthier lives (Feder and Friedland 2005). Since their inception, however, both programs have been the subjects of much debate.

Social Security

Social Security was first enacted with the Social Security Act of 1935. A year before, President Franklin D. Roosevelt convened an executive committee to examine economic insecurity, responding to the nation's Great Depression. The committee's recommendation was to create a program to address the long-range problem of economic security for the aged and poor, focusing not on providing social assistance

 A Secure Social Security

(such as welfare assistance) but rather on a social insurance plan against an uncertain future (Social Security and Medicare Boards of Trustees 2007). We tend to think of Social Security only as the monthly payments one receives after retiring, but the program also supports unemployment insurance, aid to dependent children, and state grants to provide medical care.

Demographic shifts have led to new ways to think about aging and economic security throughout the globe. The current public pension system in the United States and in most of Europe is a pay-as-you-go system—current workers support current beneficiaries of the program (Curl and Hokenstad 2006), or today's workers pay for today's retirees (Moody 2006). Angela Curl and M. C. Hokenstad (2006) compared the U.S. Social Security system with public pension systems in Sweden and Canada. In Sweden, pensions are based on average life expectancy at the time of retirement. Workers can retire any time after 61 years of age, but the later they retire, the higher their payments will be. Because of the availability of part-time jobs and the flexible work environment, the program allows Swedes to draw a partial pension for partial retirement. The elderly can mix their employment income with their pension funds. The system is funded by an 18.5% payroll tax (the United States collects 12.4%). Unlike the U.S. system, Sweden's system is partially privatized. Individuals can invest the money from their pension account, or the government invests on their behalf.

The Canadian public pension system is described as combining "income protection for older adults with policies that promote flexibility" (Curl and Hokenstad 2006:95). The Canadian system has three parts: the Old Age Security program, the Canada Pension Plan, and private pensions and savings. The minimum age of eligibility for early retirement benefits is 60 years. Canada collects a 9.9% payroll tax to support the program. As in the United States, both Canada and Sweden have residency requirements (persons must have lived for a certain number of years in the country) and a universal guaranteed monthly minimum benefit. The researchers praised both countries for promoting flexibility in retirement through gradual or partial retirement programs.

In the United States, policy analysts have long warned about the danger of having few workers paying for the benefits for a growing number of retirees. At the time the Social Security system was established, the elderly constituted 5% of the population (Moody 2006), and the average life expectancy was about 50 years of age (Curl and Hokenstad 2006). The proportion of the elderly in 2000 grew to 12%, and is projected to increase to 21% by 2050 (He et al. 2005). For 2014, the U.S. Social Security Administration paid benefits of $863 billion to nearly 59 million beneficiaries. On average, Social Security benefits represent about 38% of elderly income; 34% of workers have no retirement savings at all (Social Security Administration 2014a).

The Social Security and Medicare Boards of Trustees (2007), a nonpartisan panel responsible for reporting on the financial status of the Social Security Trust Funds, projects that tax revenues will fall below actual program costs in 2017. This is the year when the program will spend more than it receives through payroll deductions.

 Attitudes About Aging Populations

VOICES IN THE COMMUNITY

BARBARA YOUNG

Encore.org is a nonprofit organization supporting older individuals as they pursue jobs in the nonprofit or public sector during the second half of their lives. The organization honors outstanding older employees with the annual Purpose Prize (Encore.org 2014). Barbara Young was a 2013 prize honoree (Encore.org 2013).

At the age of 63, Young joined the staff of the National Domestic Workers Alliance (NDWA) as a national organizer. Since arriving to the United States from Barbados in 1993 with her five children, Young had worked as a bus conductor and then as a full-time nanny.

In 2001, Young enrolled in a nanny course for CPS and first-aid training, but the course also exposed Young to the history and labor abuses of domestic work. Young describes this as a pivotal moment, helping her decide to change the way nannies and other domestic workers define themselves and their work. "If the work you

are doing is lifting up and enhancing the life of another person, then that work has value. This is the work that domestic workers do, day in and day out" (quoted in Encore.org 2013). Young worked first with the local Domestic Workers United before joining the national staff of NDWA.

In describing her work as a union organizer, Young says, "The goal was to let people know they matter, they are important, the job they were doing was important. And if I could get them to come and be a part of this organization [Domestic Workers United]—for me, it was building power, lifting up voices and building power" (quoted in Raab 2013). "And I want every domestic worker to see themselves as professionals, and to really know within themselves that they are a great big help and support in this economy" (quoted in Raab 2013).

Young was instrumental in the 2010 passage of New York State's Domestic Workers' Bill of Rights, which requires payment at minimum wage, higher overtime pay, and paid time off.

The trustees predict that the trust funds will be exhausted in 2041 (OASDI Trustees 2007). Any worker born after 1975 will reach full retirement age after the trust fund is depleted. At the release of their 2007 report, the Social Security and Medicare Boards of Trustees warned, "The longer we wait to address these challenges, the more limited will be the options available, the greater will be the required adjustments, and the more severe the potential detrimental economic impact on our nation."

Medicare

The nation's largest health insurance program, Medicare, covers about 54 million elderly or disabled Americans. Medicare has two parts: Part A (hospital insurance) helps pay for care received as an inpatient in critical access hospitals or skilled nursing facilities, as well as some home health care; Part B (physician and outpatient coverage) pays for medically necessary services and supplies that are not covered under Part A. Each part is financed under a different structure. Part A is offered as an automatic premium because most recipients (or their spouses) paid Medicare

SOCIOLOGY AT WORK

SOCIAL WORK

Kacie Blanchard – Class of 2006

Undergraduate Major: Sociology

Undergraduate Minor: Communications

In a survey of BA Sociology graduates, the American Sociological Association (Spalter-Roth and Van Vooren 2008) reported that that largest category of alums working full time, 27%, were employed in social service and counseling occupations. Social work is the primary occupational field in the social services. Preparing for a career as a social worker can be ambiguous, as positions vary widely, from caseworker to mental health assistant to clinical social worker. To enter the field of social work, a bachelor's degree is the most common requirement; however, a clinical position may require a master's degree and up to two years of experience.

After completing her Sociology BA, Kacie Blanchard earned a Master of Social Work degree in a two-year accredited program. She credits her internship experience with helping her identify her career path. "I was unsure what direction my degree would take me until I had the experience of working with child protective services. Once I had this opportunity, I knew I wanted to attend graduate school and become a social worker. I then saw social work as putting sociology into action."

In her current position as a medical social worker, Kacie works with clients to assess their need for placement and home safety following changes in their health and medical needs. She also conducts mental health assessments, identifying psychosocial needs to assist patients upon their return from the hospital to maintain their health and safety. Kacie also works as a crisis intervention therapist on a mobile outreach crisis team. In Kacie's occupation, interpersonal skills are important because of the specific nature of the work—helping clients from diverse populations during some of the most difficult times in their lives.

When asked how she applies sociology in her social work practice, Kacie replied,

Knowledge of social systems and the entire picture of each individual with the understanding of psycho-social history assists me each day to direct my interventions and predict outcomes. Sociology is the foundation of my social work practice. Sociology ignited my passion and is the root of my daily interactions as a social worker. I continue to engage my sociological imagination by remembering this foundation and applying it to my career as a social worker.

For current Sociology majors, Kacie recommends

focusing on an aspect of sociology that is most interesting to them, whether that be criminal studies, child welfare, family systems, and use that as a starting point for a career. For me, my introduction into child welfare started my career path that continues to grow. Keep your connections with sociology classmates and professors for networking and support.

taxes while they were working. Part A is financed through a payroll tax paid equally by employers and workers. Three fourths of the financing for Medicare Part B is received from general tax revenues, and the remaining quarter is financed directly through paid premiums, $104.90 (for those with individual incomes of $85,000 or less) or $146.90 or higher (for those with individual incomes higher than $85,000) in 2012.

Since the program's inception, some have been concerned that Medicare spending, especially for Part A, will outpace its revenue sources (Moon 1999). Medicare has been referred to as a pay-as-you-go system; every payroll tax dollar that is contributed into the fund is immediately spent by those currently enrolled (Goodman 1998). Since 2008, the trust has been spending more on benefits than it has been receiving through payroll taxes. In a 2014 report, the trustees warned that the Medicare fund would be depleted by 2030 (Social Security Administration 2014b).

Political rhetoric continues to swirl around how to preserve the system while trying to expand its services to an ever-increasing population of elderly. In 2003, the U.S. Congress passed the Medicare reform law, which included a prescription drug benefit for the first time in the program's history. The bill provides for a prescription drug benefit for older and disabled Americans, offered and managed by private insurers and health plans under contract with the federal government. Critics attacked the plan for its coverage gap, arguing that the bill failed to provide seniors with substantial relief for the cost of prescription drugs. Seniors with low incomes will qualify for extra assistance under the bill. The cost of the bill is estimated at more than $900 billion over 10 years. Analysts predict that the reform bill will have little effect on slowing down the increasing costs of prescription drugs and medical services for the elderly.

The traditional nursing home care model is no longer considered financially viable or medically justified. There has been an increase in the utilization of older adult managed care at home, at day care centers, and in visits to specialists (Berger 2012). Similar programs have been adopted in Canada, like the Comprehensive Home Option for Integrated Care of the Elderly (CHOICE). CHOICE has been credited with keeping elderly men and women healthier longer and out of long-term care homes because medical workers are able to more closely monitor their patients' health (Howell 2011). Medicare and other medical service organizations have encouraged the use of older volunteers as health coaches, advocates, and aides to help individuals and families navigate through the health care system. For example, the Rose Community Foundation in Denver trains older adults as community health workers (Pope 2012).

For more on increasing medical costs and alternative models of care, refer to Chapter 10, "Health and Medicine."

CHAPTER REVIEW

6.1 Explain how age is both a biological and a social classification

Our age is measured biologically, by how old we are, and we have socially and culturally defined expectations about the meaning of age, our understanding of it, and our responses to it. Age distinguishes acceptable behavior for different social groups.

6.2 Identify the causes of population aging

Demographers study the size, composition, and distribution of human populations. Population aging is caused by a decline in the birthrate. Aging can also occur because of an improvement in life expectancy as a result of medical and technological advances. Finally, the process of population aging can be influenced by characteristics of birth cohorts.

6.3 Describe how the sociological perspectives address age, aging, and inequality

Functionalists rely on disengagement theory to explain aging as a natural process of withdrawal from active participation in social life; people enter and exit a set of roles throughout their lives. Conflict theorists offer the modernization theory of aging to explain how the role and status of the elderly decline with industrialization. The power, wealth, and prestige of the elderly are linked with their labor contribution or their relationship to the means of production. According to the feminist perspective, the standards of our culture create more problems for women than for men as they transition into their middle and later years. Interactionists reveal how our age-related roles are socially defined and expected.

6.4 Explain how age serves as a basis for prejudice or discrimination

Ageism is the systematic stereotyping of and discrimination against people, primarily the elderly. Age distinguishes acceptable behavior for different social groups.

6.5 Examine the characteristics of young and older voters

Though age is related to voter registration, actual voting, and political participation, older Americans do not vote cohesively or as a bloc. Their votes are as diverse as those of any other age group. Younger voters were a key voting bloc in recent presidential elections. Young voters are more ethnically and racially diverse and less likely to be religiously affiliated.

KEY TERMS

ageism, 155

boomerangers, 152

demography, 148

disengagement theory, 152

double standard of aging, 154

gerontology, 148

life course perspective, 148

modernization theory of aging, 153

population aging, 148

stigma, 155

STUDY QUESTIONS

1. How do social norms—formal or informal—shape our definition of age?

2. Identify the societal consequences of population aging.

3. Disengagement theory defines aging as a natural process of withdrawal from active social participation. Do you think this disengagement is a natural process or brought on by social factors? Explain.

4. From an interactionist's perspective, how can we improve the status of the elderly?

5. In what ways are elderly women disadvantaged in society in comparison with elderly men?

6. Compare and contrast the U.S. Social Security system with the pension systems in Sweden and Canada.

$SAGE edge™

Sharpen your skills with SAGE edge at **edge.sagepub.com/leonguerrero5e**

SAGE edge provides a personalized approach to help you accomplish your coursework goals in an easy-to-use learning environment.

PART II

Our Social Institutions

Émile Durkheim first described the importance of our social institutions. He likened them to organs in a human body. Each organ does one specific thing—a heart is responsible for the circulatory system, a brain is the key to the nervous system, and a pair of lungs regulates the respiratory system. If something happens to the heart, its functions cannot be assumed by other organs, and as a result, the body as a whole becomes compromised.

Social institutions are defined as a stable set of statuses, roles, groups, and organizations that provides a foundation for addressing fundamental societal needs (Newman 2006), each with a specific role in society. As discussed in Chapter 1, Durkheim believed that an essential set of institutions is necessary for society to function. For our discussion, we focus on five institutions—family, education, work and the economy, health and medicine, and the media.

If you've taken an Introduction to Sociology course, these institutions may have been presented as the basis for socialization—what do we need to learn to make us human, and how do we learn through each of these institutions? However, in the chapters that follow, our focus is on the social problems affecting each institution. You will learn how the bases of inequality we reviewed in Part I are intricately related to the social problems based in each institution. Each chapter concludes with a discussion about the policies and community efforts that are being made to address these social problems.

Social institutions: A stable set of statuses, roles, groups, and organizations that provides a foundation for addressing fundamental societal needs; an example of a social institution is the family

Do you recall the first "crew" you ever hung out with? You know the one—all its members know each other, speak the same language, laugh at the same jokes, dress alike, and maybe even look alike. Sound familiar? These are the people with whom you slept, ate, and lived in your own home: your family.

You may not always think of it this way, but your family is part of the larger **social institution** of "the family." Consider for a moment that your family was among the 115 million family groups counted by the U.S. Census in 2010 (U.S. Census Bureau 2013). What does your family have in common with the other family groups? Your first response might be that your family has nothing in common with the others. No other family has the unique arrangement or history of individuals related through blood or by choice. From this position, any problem experienced by your family, such as a divorce, would be defined as a personal trouble. A divorce is a private family matter kept among immediate family members. It would be none of anyone else's business.

If we use our sociological imagination, however, we can uncover the links between our personal family experiences and our social world. Divorce is not just a family matter but also a public issue. Looking at the recent divorce rate of 3.6 divorces per 1,000 people, divorce occurs not in just one household but in millions of U.S. households. It affects the economic and social well-being of millions of women, men, and children. Divorce challenges the fundamental values of home and love and the value of the family itself. Divorce could be everyone's business.

In this chapter, our goal is to explore this private, yet public, world of the family. For our discussion, we define the family as a construct of meaning and relationships both emotional and economic. The **family** is a social unit based on kinship relations—relations based on blood, and those created by choice, marriage, partnership, or adoption. A **household** is defined as an economic and residential unit. These definitions allow for the diversity of families that we discuss in this chapter, while not presenting one configuration as the standard. As you'll see, the family as we think we know it may not exist at all.

What Does It Mean to Me?

In January 2007, two abducted boys were discovered in St. Louis, Missouri. Michael Devlin was charged with the felony of kidnapping of the boys. The older boy, Shawn Hornbeck, lived with Devlin for more than four years in the apartment complex where he, along with William Ownby, was finally discovered. Neighbors reported that they assumed Hornbeck and Devlin were family and had no reason to interfere, despite occasionally hearing violent noises coming from their apartment. This incident highlights how family life is considered private by society and how, in this case, a child kidnapper went unsuspected for many years. What would you have done if you were a neighbor? Should problems in the family be considered private troubles or public issues?

MYTHS OF THE FAMILY

The **nuclear family**—two parents and their biological children living together—is exalted as the ideal family. Yet families are much more diverse than this. First, the percentage of families composed of married couples with children declined from 40.3% in 1970 to 19.6% in 2010 (Vespa, Lewis, and Kreider 2013). Take note—the traditional family form, married with children, is less than a quarter of all U.S. households. The largest family form is married couples without children (29.1%).

Public attitudes are shifting away from traditional ideals of marriage and child-bearing in Western industrialized societies such as the United States, Austria, (West) Germany, Great Britain, Ireland, and the Netherlands. Zoya Gubernskaya (2010) found that female, never-married, better-educated, employed, and secularized individuals had less traditional views about marriage and children. Support for the statement that "people who want children ought to get married" declined in these countries from 1988 to 2002. Gubernskaya attributes the increasing nontraditionalism to a rise in secularization, a shift toward individualism, and an increasing focus on education and employment achievement that are at odds with traditional family formation.

Second, the only increase in family groups during this period came in the category of "other family households." Other family households include families with other relatives residing, what we also refer to as **extended families**. When President Obama moved into 1600 Pennsylvania Avenue, much attention was paid to the

Family: Social unit based on kinship relations, a construct of meaning and relationships both emotional and economic

Household: An economic and residential unit

Nuclear family: Family consisting of parents and their children

Extended families: Two or more adult generations, related by blood, who live together in a single household

 Who's at Home?

Table 7.1 Households by type: 1970 and 2012 (percentage)

	1970	2012
Total number of households	63 million	119 million
Nonfamily households		
Men living alone	5.6	12.3
Women living alone	11.5	15.2
Family households		
Married couples with children	40.3	19.6
Married couples without children	30.3	29.1
Other family households	10.6	17.8

SOURCE: Kreider and Elliot 2009, Figure 1; Vespa, Lewis, and Kreider 2013.

NOTE: Columns may not add to 100% due to rounding.

fact that his mother-in-law, Marian Robinson, would also be a resident. The last time a mother-in-law had been a full-time White House resident was during Harry Truman's presidency. Other family households made up 17.8% of all U.S. households, increasing from 10.6% in 1970. Included in this category are 8.2 million single-parent families, 6 million headed by mothers and 2.2 million headed by fathers. Finally, there has been an increase in the percentage of nonfamily households (refer to Table 7.1).

In 2007, U.S. Census data revealed that for the first time, more American women were living without a husband than with one. Based on 2005 data, 51% of women were living without a spouse, an increase from 35% in 1950 and 49% in 2000. In contrast, 47% of men reported living without a spouse in 2005. The pattern varies by race, with 30% of Black women, 49% of Hispanic women, 55% of non-Hispanic White women, and 60% of Asian women reporting that they were living with a spouse. Analysts reported that several factors contributed to the increase in the number of single women: late marriage for women, women living longer as widows or after a divorce, and women being more likely than men to delay remarriage (Roberts 2007).

In addition to the false image of the nuclear family, we also embrace other myths about the family. We tend to believe that the families of the past were better and happier than modern families are. We believe that families should be safe havens, protecting their members from harm and danger. And a final myth relates to the topic of this book: we also assume that the family and its failings lead to many of our social problems.

There is a persistent belief that nontraditional families, such as divorced, fatherless, or working-mother families, threaten and erode the integrity of the family as an institution. These "pathological" family forms are blamed for drug abuse, delinquency, illiteracy, and crime. As a group, female-headed households were condemned in the Personal Responsibility and Work Opportunity Reconciliation Act of 1996, also known as the Welfare Reform Act, for their dependency on the public welfare system.

SOCIOLOGICAL PERSPECTIVES ON THE FAMILY

Functionalist Perspective

From a functionalist perspective, the family serves many important functions in society. Some functionalists claim that the family is the most vital social institution. The family serves as a child's primary group, the first group membership we claim. We inherit not only the color of our hair or eyes but also our family's social position. The family confers social status and class. The family helps define who we are and how we find our place in society. And, without the family, who would provide for the essential needs of the child: affection, socialization, economic support, and protection?

Social problems emerge as the family struggles to adapt to a modern society. Functionalists have noted how many of the family's original functions have been taken over by organized religion, education, work, and the government in modern society (Lenski and Lenski 1987), but still, the family is expected to provide its remaining functions of raising children and providing affection and companionship for its members (Popenoe 1993). From a functionalist perspective, the family is inextricably linked to the rest of society. The family does not work alone; rather, it functions in concert with the other institutions. Changes in other institutions, such as the economy, politics, or law, contribute to changes and problems in the family.

Consider the education of children. Before the establishment of mandatory public school systems, the family educated its own children. As a formal system, education has become its own institution, taking primary responsibility for educating and socializing everyone's children. Functionalists examine how the institutions of the family and education effectively work together. To what extent should parents participate in their children's education, and to what extent is the educational system responsible for raising our children?

Because of this perspective's emphasis on the family and its social and emotional functions, when the family fails—as in the case of divorce or domestic violence—functionalists take these problems seriously. These problems afflict the family and, according to functionalists, can lead to additional problems in society, such as crime, poverty, or delinquency.

Conflict and Feminist Perspectives

For the conflict theorist, the family is a system of inequality where conflict is normal. Conflict can derive from economic or power inequalities between spouses or family members. From a feminist perspective, inequality emerges from the patriarchal family system, where men control decision-making in the family. Persistent social ideals that view the woman as homemaker and the man as breadwinner are problematic from both perspectives. Men's social and economic status increases as their work outside the home is more visible and rewarded, whereas women's work inside the home remains invisible and uncompensated.

The family structure, as our society has come to define it, upholds a system of male social and economic domination. Theorist Friedrich Engels argued that the family was the chief source of female enslavement. Within the family, Engels believed, the husband represented the bourgeois, whereas his wife represented the proletariat (Engels 1902). Among the middle class, where property is the primary consideration, marriage was a respectable form of prostitution. Just as members of the proletariat were oppressed in the economy, women were oppressed at home. Freedom for women, wrote Engels, would come with their economic independence and participation in the workplace (activities based outside the home).

Feminist theory also examines power within the family. According to this perspective, men can maintain their position of power in the family through violence or the threat of violence against women. Feminists argue that domestic violence cannot be solely explained by men's individual attitudes and behavior. Rather, violence against women is linked to larger social structures of male dominance, such as political, economic, and other social institutions like the family. Theorists have encouraged the integration of feminist analyses of gender and power to better comprehend the mechanisms leading to violence, arguing that to stop such violence, structures of gender inequality must change (Brownmiller 1975).

Feminist theorists have also acknowledged how the cultural differences of domestic violence have not been fully recognized. According to Tricia Bent-Goodley (2005), "research has largely focused on White and poor women, despite the fact that domestic violence crosses race, ethnicity, socioeconomic status, religion and sexual orientation" (p. 197). She notes that this narrow research focus has encouraged the perception that women of color, middle- and upper-class women, and women in same-sex relationships do not experience domestic violence, despite evidence to the contrary. And though data indicate that disabled women experience a greater risk of abuse and violence in comparison with the general population, studies on the nature of the oppression and consequences of domestic abuse against women with disabilities still remain largely ignored (Mays 2006).

Families are also subject to powerful economic and political interest groups that control family social programs and policies. Conflict arises when the needs of particular family forms are promoted while others are ignored. As discussed in Chapter 1, the Defense of Marriage Act systematically devalued nonheterosexual

John Ewing/Portland Press Herald via Getty Images

Does the family pictured here align with your image of what a family is? From an interactionist perspective, how do we learn about different family forms?

unions or couples. To resolve social problems in the family, both perspectives suggest the need for structural change.

Interactionist Perspective

Through social interaction, we create and maintain our definition of a family. As we do this, it affects our larger social definition of what everyone's family should be like and how we envision the family that we create for ourselves.

Within our own families, our interaction through words, symbols, and meanings defines our expectation of what the family should be like. How many children are in the family? Who does the housecleaning? Who gets to carve the holiday turkey? What does it mean to be a wife, a husband, a partner? As a family, we collectively create and maintain a family definition on which members agree. Problems arise when there is conflict about how the family is defined. A couple starting their own family must negotiate their own way of doing things. Two partners may carry definitions and expectations from their families of origin, but together, they create a new family reality.

Problems may also occur when partners' expectations of family or marriage do not match their real lives. In our culture, romantic love is idealized, misleading individuals to believe that they are destined for a fulfilling emotional partnership with one perfect mate. After the realities of life set in, including the first fight, the notion of romantic love is shattered. Couples recognize that it may take more than romantic love to make a relationship work.

Conflict also arises when a family arrangement is different from societal norms and expectations. Blended families, gay or lesbian families, or single-parent families become social problems based only on how they deviate from the definition of a "normal" family. Society assigns meaning to particular family groups or relations. More than half a century ago, when a child was born to unmarried parents, it was assumed that the child was unwanted and that the child's future would be less than promising. There was a major social stigma with being referred to as a bastard child. But because currently one in three births involves parents who are not legally married, and most births are wanted or planned, the use of the term *bastard* has disappeared, as has the stigma attached to such a birth (Rutter and Tienda 2005).

But definitions vary by culture. In South Korea, there is still a strong negative stigma regarding unwed motherhood. In 2007, 2% of all births in South Korea were to unmarried women, compared with 40% of all U.S. births. The Korean discussion on unmarried motherhood has focused on how to eradicate the "evil" of unmarried motherhood as it threatens the patriarchal social structure (Kim and Davis 2003). Journalist Choe Sang-Hun (2009) reports how "social pressure drives thousands of unmarried women to choose between abortion, which is illegal but rampant, and adoption, which is considered socially shameful but is encouraged by the government" (p. A6). Unmarried women who decide to raise a child risk a life of poverty and disgrace, even being ostracized by family members. Lee Mee-Kyong, whose family disowned her after the birth of her son, says, "Once you become an unwed mom, you're branded as immoral and a failure. You fall to the bottom rung of society" (quoted in Sang-Hun 2009:A6).

Putting all our separate definitions of the family together, we create a portrait of what the family should be like. But as some political and religious forces uphold and encourage a heteronormative conception of the nuclear family as the norm, by default, other family forms are considered deviant against some set of moral codes, or not families at all (Smith 1993). **Heteronormativity** refers to the promotion of heterosexual, married, monogamous, White, and upper-middle-class norms (Branzel 2005).

However, in 2010, sociologists Brian Powell, Catherine Bolzendahl, Claudia Geist, and Lara Carr Steelman reported how our definition of the family was expanding. In the 2003 Constructing the Family Survey, respondents were asked about which living arrangements constituted a family. Each survey respondent indicated that an arrangement with a husband, a wife, and children constituted a family. However, the majority also defined the following as a family: single mothers (94%) or single fathers (94.2%) with children and married couples with no children (93.1%). According to the researchers, "the most-agreed-upon family forms tend to rely on at least one of two prerequisites: the presence in the home of a child, and a legal heterosexual relationship—or, more precisely, a relationship that is not a same-sex

Heteronormativity: The promotion of heterosexual, married, monogamous, White, and upper-middle-class norms

\

relationship or a cohabitating heterosexual one" (Powell et al. 2010:20). There was less agreement that an unmarried cohabitating couple with children could be defined as a family (78.7%). For arrangements with same-sex couples, couples with children were more likely to be defined as a family than couples without children (e.g., 55% of the sample defined two women with children as a family compared with 26.8% who defined two women with no children as a family) (Powell et al. 2010).

Refer to Table 7.2 for a summary of all sociological perspectives on the family.

. . . .

What Does It Mean to Me?

In 2012, it was reported that more than half of births to American women under 30 years old occurred outside marriage. The fastest growth in nonmarital births is among White women in their 20s with some college education. Women with college degrees are still more likely to marry before having children (DeParle and Tavernise 2012). Is there a social stigma related to nonmarital birth? Why is there an increasing number of nonmarital births?

. . . .

Table 7.2   Summary of sociological perspectives: The family

	Functional	**Conflict/Feminist**	**Interactionist**
Explanation of the family and its social problems	Functionalists examine how the family interacts with other social institutions. Functionalists believe that social problems emerge as the family struggles to adapt to a modern society. Functionalists also examine the manifest and latent functions of the family.	Problems emerge from conflict inherent in the family structure. Conflict can derive from economic or power inequalities between family members. From a feminist perspective, the family is a patriarchal system, where men dominate social and economic spheres.	An interactionist focuses on the social meaning and expectations of the "family." Interactionists will also focus on how family members define their own families.
Questions asked about the family	What functions does the family serve? How is the family affected by other social institutions? How does the problem reflect changes between the family and other social institutions?	What is the basis of conflict within the family? How does conflict affect family members and their relationships?	How do we define the "family"? What social forces influence our definition of the family? What are the consequences of these definitions?

PROBLEMS IN THE FAMILY

Divorce

If you do an Internet search on divorce, you might be surprised at your search results. In addition to divorce facts and access to support groups, you'll find handy guides to complete your own divorce paperwork. Looking to save time, money, and pain? Please try our services. Looking for a divorce lawyer? Why not search for one online? And if you'd like to send a divorce greeting card that says, "Happy to be without you," you can find one of those online, too.

Divorce was a rare occurrence until the 1970s. In the 1950s and 1960s, the divorce rate was about 2.2 to 2.6 per 1,000 individuals (U.S. Census Bureau 1999). With the introduction of no-fault divorce laws in the 1970s, the divorce rate began to climb, reaching a high of 5.3 in 1979 and 1981 (U.S. Census Bureau 1999). The increase in divorce rates has been attributed to other factors: the increasing economic independence of women, the transition from extended to nuclear family forms, and the increasing geographic and occupational mobility of families. Furthermore, as our societal and cultural norms about divorce have changed, the stigma attached to divorce has decreased.

In recent years, the divorce rate has remained stable around 3.5 divorces per 1,000 individuals in the total U.S. population. The rate was 4.0 in 2000, declining to 3.6 in 2011 (Centers for Disease Control and Prevention 2013). The U.S. marital rate declined during the same period: from 8.2 for 2000 to 6.8 for 2011 (Centers for Disease Control and Prevention 2013). When compared with European Union (EU) countries, the United States has the higher divorce rate. In 2008, the estimated divorce rate for the EU was 2.0 per 1,000 (Eurostat 2009). EU marital rates were also lower for 2008, at 4.87 per 1,000 (Eurostat 2009).

Recent Census data on divorce indicate that certain groups are more susceptible to divorce than others. Based on 2001 Census data, Rose Kreider (2005) reported that although one in five U.S. adults had been divorced, the percentage of those having been divorced was highest among men and women 50 to 59 years of age (41% and 39%, respectively). The majority of separated and divorced men and women were between 25 and 44 years of age. The median age of divorce from first marriage was 29.4 years for women and 31.4 years for men. Divorce rates are higher among couples married before 20 years of age, living at 200% of the poverty level, with a high school degree or some college, or working full-time (Kreider and Fields 2002).

Sociologists have paid particular attention to immediate and long-term effects of divorce on children. In general, the research indicates that children with divorced parents have moderately poorer life and educational outcomes (emotional well-being, academic achievement, labor force participation, divorce, and teenage child-bearing) than do children living with both parents (Amato 2000; Hetherington and Kelly 2002). For example, boys living with a divorced mother are four times more likely to display severe delinquency or to engage in early sexual intercourse than are

Marriage and Divorce Today

those living in two-parent households (Simons 1996). Some of these effects carry into adolescence and young adulthood (Amato and Keith 1991; Cherlin, Kiernan, and Chase-Lansdale 1995), with more negative outcomes for adult females than for adult males, such as a greater incidence of relationship conflict or difficulty with intimate relationships. Children of divorce have less commitment to the idea of lifelong marriage than children from intact families (Amato and DeBoer 2001) and have a higher likelihood of instability in their own marriages (Wolfinger 2005).

Conversely, research also suggests that marital separation is beneficial to the well-being of children (Videon 2002). Favorable outcomes have included increased maturity, enhanced self-esteem, and increased empathy among children from divorced families (Brooks Conway, Christensen, and Herlihy 2003). Parental divorce may shift children from traditional sex-role beliefs and behavior toward more androgynous attitudes and behavior (MacKinnon, Stoneman, and Brody 1984). Parent–child relations are important influences on children's well-being, even mediating the effects of marital dissolution (Videon 2002). Divorce is less disruptive if both parents maintain a positive relationship with the child, if parental conflict decreases after separation or divorce, and if the level of socioeconomic resources for the child is not reduced (Amato and Keith 1991).

Research consistently indicates that although men experience minimal economic declines after divorce, most women experience a substantial decline in household income and increased dependence on social welfare (Smock 1994). Data from the 2001 U.S. Census show that although only 15% of recently divorced men lived in households where they (or someone they lived with) received noncash public assistance, more than twice as many recently divorced women (or someone they lived with) received noncash public assistance (34%) (Kreider 2005). As first reported in Chapter 2, the poverty rate among female-headed households (no male present) is 30.6%, compared with 15.9% among male-headed households (no female present).

In his analysis of 14 countries in the EU, Wilfred Uunk (2004) documented a 24% decline in women's median household income after divorce—comparable, he says, to the income change experienced by U.S. women after divorce. Uunk's research revealed how median income declines were lower among divorced women from southern European countries (Greece, Italy, Spain, and Portugal) and Scandinavian countries (Demark and Finland), but higher among women from Austria, France, Luxembourg, and the United Kingdom.

Declines in economic well-being also occur among women from previously cohabiting couples (Avellar and Smock 2005). Cohabiting couples have more precarious financial circumstances, experiencing lower personal and household incomes than married couples. After the dissolution of a relationship, the level of household income for cohabiting men declines 10%, but it declines 33% for cohabiting women. After the dissolution of a cohabiting relationship, women have a higher level of poverty than men, 30% versus 20%. Hispanic and African American women are more vulnerable than White women to experiencing economic decline. Cohabiting relationships may also include children affected by the same economic decline. These children are even more vulnerable, because cohabiting mothers have less access to their former partner's income than divorced mothers do.

Violence and Neglect in the Family

Intimate Partner Violence

One of the myths mentioned at the beginning of this chapter is that the family provides a safe place for its members. This myth ignores the incidence of violence and abuse in families. Family violence is unique because the aggressor and the victim(s) are part of the same relational unit, with emotional bonds, attachments, and particular power dynamics (Breines and Gordon 1983).

In the United States, nearly 25% of surveyed women and 8% of surveyed men reported that they had been raped or physically assaulted by a current or former intimate partner in their lifetime. Based on these estimates, approximately 1.5 million women and 835,000 men are raped or physically assaulted by an intimate partner annually in the United States (Tjaden and Thoennes 2000). (Refer to Table 7.3 for Bureau of Justice Statistics data from 1994 to 2010.) Data confirm that violence by an intimate partner is a common experience worldwide. A review of more than 50 population-based studies in 35 countries revealed that between 10% and 52% of women reported that they had been physically abused by an intimate partner at some point in their lives (Garcia-Moreno et al. 2006).

Research has consistently linked specific social factors to family violence: low socioeconomic status, social and structural stress, and social isolation (Gelles and Maynard 1987). Feminist researchers argue that domestic violence is rooted in gender and represents men's attempts to maintain dominance and control over women (Anderson 1997). Comparative data reveal how the severity and pattern of violence against women is higher in countries with high societal violence and low empowerment of women (Garcia-Moreno et al. 2006).

Studies have also documented how domestic violence is a significant predictor in maternal parenting behavior. Intimate partner violence involving a female victim often occurs in a household where a child is present (refer to Figure 7.1). According to Alytia Levendosky and Sandra Graham-Bermann (2000), psychological abuse, rather

Table 7.3 Intimate partner violence, 1993–2010

	Rate per 1,000 persons age 12 or older			
Sex	**1994**	**2000**	**2005**	**2010**
Female	16.1	8.4	5.8	5.9
Male	3.0	1.6	1.7	1.1

SOURCE: Adapted from Catalano 2012.

Domestic Violence
Victim Speaks

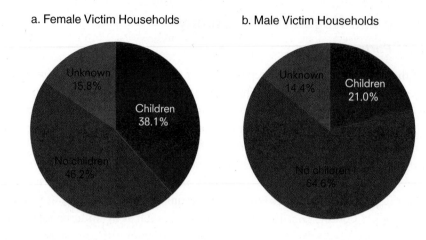

Figure 7.1 Percentage of households experiencing nonfatal intimate partner violence where children under age 12 resided, by gender of victim, 2001–2005

a. Female Victim Households

Unknown 15.8%
Children 38.1%
No children 46.2%

b. Male Victim Households

Unknown 14.4%
Children 21.0%
No children 64.6%

SOURCE: U.S. Bureau of Justice Statistics 2012.

than physical abuse, is more likely to negatively affect a mother's parenting, which in turn is related to children's behaviors. The researchers report that a mother's experience with psychological abuse is significantly related to a child's antisocial behavior. Children in middle childhood begin to identify with the aggressor and act in emotionally aggressive ways toward their mothers. Yet female victims identify positive and negative impacts on their parenting from domestic violence (Levendosky, Lynch, and Graham-Bermann 2000). Battered women report that their emotional feelings or concerns make parenting difficult, noting the reduced amount of quality time or emotional energy they can devote to their children. But these women also report increased empathy and caring toward their children. Researchers suggest that battered women actively work to protect their children from the effects of violence in their household.

Child Abuse and Neglect

Some children are subject to abuse and neglect in their families. While physical, sexual, and emotional abuses are often identified, cases of neglect often go unnoticed. **Physical abuse** is defined as nonaccidental physical injury, from bruising to death; on the other hand, **neglect** is characterized by a failure to provide for a child's basic needs (e.g., healthy regular meals), and it can be physical, educational (failure to enroll a school-age child in school, allowing chronic truancy), or emotional (spousal abuse in the child's presence, permitting drug or alcohol use by the child, inattention to a child's needs for affection) in nature (Child Welfare Information Gateway 2007).

Physical abuse: Nonaccidental physical injury, from bruising to death

Neglect: Failure to provide for a child's basic needs

  Perfect Parenting?

The immediate emotional and behavioral effects of abuse and neglect—isolation, fear, low academic achievement, delinquency—may lead to lifelong consequences, including low self-esteem, depression, criminal behavior, and adult abusive behavior (Child Welfare Information Gateway 2006). In 2012, 686,000 children were victims of maltreatment. Most child victims, about 78%, suffered from neglect. The highest rates of victimization (per 1,000 children) were among ethnic minorities: African Americans (14.2%), American Indians or Alaska Natives (12.4%), and children of multiple races (10.3%). Tragically, about 1,640 children died as a result of abuse or neglect in 2012 (U.S. Department of Health and Human Services; Administration for Children and Families; Administration on Children, Youth and Families; Children's Bureau 2013).

Multiple factors related to the child, the parent or caregiver, the family structure, and the environment have been identified as contributing to child maltreatment. Though children are not responsible for being victims of maltreatment, certain factors make some children more vulnerable than others. For example, children with physical, cognitive, and emotional disabilities are at higher risk for maltreatment than other children. Infants and young children are vulnerable to particular forms of maltreatment, such as shaken baby syndrome. Teenagers are at greater risk for sexual abuse. Evidence indicates that abusing parents were victims of abuse and neglect themselves as children. Marital conflict, domestic violence, single parenthood, unemployment, and financial stress may increase the likelihood of maltreatment (Goldman et al. 2003). Poverty is consistently identified as a risk factor for child abuse. It is not clear whether the relationship exists because of the stresses associated with poverty or if reporting is higher because of the constant scrutiny of poor families by social agencies. Poor health care, lack of social and familial support, and fragmented social services have been linked with both poverty and child abuse (Bethea 1999).

Elder Abuse and Neglect

The elderly are also victims of abuse, usually when in the care of their older children and their families. Elder abuse can also occur within a nursing home or hospital setting. Federal definitions of elder abuse, neglect, and exploitation first appeared in the 1987 Amendments to the Older Americans Act (National Center on Elder Abuse 2002a). Elder abuse can consist of physical, sexual, or psychological abuse, neglect or abandonment, or financial exploitation. Domestic elder abuse refers to any form of maltreatment of an older person by someone who has a special relationship with the elder (a spouse, child, friend, or caregiver); institutional elder abuse refers to forms of abuse that occur in residential facilities for older people.

The number of U.S. adults aged 60 years or older is projected to increase from 35 million in 2000 to more than 72 million by 2030 (He et al. 2005). As the population ages, there will be an increased need for long-term care of the elderly, with spouses and adult children assuming the role of caretaker. An estimated 15 million individuals provide informal care to relatives and friends (Navaie-Waliser et al. 2002).

 Elder Abuse

Although caregiving can positively affect the physical and psychological well-being of care recipients, the added burden of elder care may strain the family's and the caregiver's emotional and financial resources.

The National Elder Mistreatment Study estimates that about 11% of older surveyed men and women reported experiencing at least one form of mistreatment (U.S. Department of Justice 2011). Elder abuse, particularly with family perpetrators, has been attributed to social isolation, personal problems such as mental illness or abuse of alcohol or drugs, and domestic violence (spouses make up a large percentage of elder abusers) (National Center on Elder Abuse 2002a). A major risk factor is dependency: abusers tend to be more dependent on the elderly person for housing, money, and transportation than are relatives who do not abuse (Lang 1993).

Teen Pregnancy and Newborn Abandonment

The U.S. teen birthrate is the highest in the developed world. The birthrate for teenagers (aged 15 to 19 years) declined from 1991 through 2012, falling from 62 live births per 1,000 teenagers in 1991 to 29.4 in 2012 (Martin et al. 2013). Despite the overall decline, birthrates for Black (47.3) and Hispanic (49.6) teens remain higher than for any other ethnic/racial group. The lowest rate was reported for Asian or Pacific Islander teens at 10.2 live births per 1,000 women (Martin et al. 2013). The U.S. teen birthrate has been attributed to a range of factors, from inadequate sexuality education to declining morals (Somers and Fahlman 2001). Research suggests that earlier or more frequent sexual activity among U.S. teens is not the cause of the higher birthrates; rather, sexually active American teens are less likely to use contraceptives than are their European peers (Card 1999; Kirby 2007). Jessica Silk and Diana Romero (2013, p. 1356) argue that cultural norms in the United States are "less open and supportive about sexual behavior among adolescents." Though comprehensive sex education has been shown to be effective in reducing sexual risk-taking and negative social and health outcomes, it is denied to American youth for cultural reasons (Kirby 2007). The popular discourse on family values and framing sex education as a family matter has prevented health and human service providers and sexuality educators from delivering sex and health education to youth (Silk and Romero 2013). Refer to this chapter's Exploring Social Problems feature for more information on teen birthrates.

Heather Weaver, Gary Smith, and Susan Kippax (2005) noted that the number of births per 1,000 U.S. adolescents between the ages of 15 and 17 years was 8.5 times greater than in the Netherlands, 5.5 times greater than in France, and 3 times greater than in Australia. In contrast, the rate of contraceptive use at first intercourse was highest among Dutch (85%) and Australian (90% for males and 95% for females) teens, followed by French (74% and 77%) and U.S. (a minimum of 65%) youth. School-based sex education programs are mandatory in the Netherlands, France, and Australia. There are no federal laws in the United States that require sexual health education in schools.

 Teen Pregnancy

EXPLORING **social problems**

Teen Birthrates

Birthrates for teenagers aged 15–19, 2012 (per 1,000)

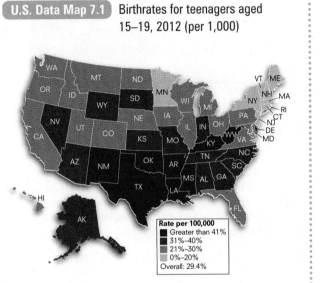

SOURCE: Martin et al. 2013.

Rate per 100,000
- Greater than 41%
- 31%–40%
- 21%–30%
- 0%–20%
- Overall: 29.4%

Birthrates per 1,000 females aged 15–19 by race/ethnicity, 1990–2012

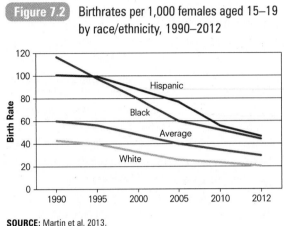

SOURCE: Martin et al. 2013.

WHAT DO YOU THINK?

There is much geographic variation in teen birthrates. Overall, the lowest teen birthrates were in the Northeast, while rates were highest in the South. How does your state compare?

Historically, birthrates are higher among Black and Hispanic adolescent females than among White adolescent females (Figure 7.2). Although they have the highest teen birthrates, the rates for Black and Hispanic teens have had the most dramatic decline in recent years. After 2007, Blacks had the highest reduction, 41%, followed by Hispanics, with a 39% decline. The birthrate for White teens declined the least at 25%.

What social factors may have contributed to the decline in teen birthrates for each of these groups?

Teen mothers, in comparison with their childless peers, are more likely to be poorer and less educated, less likely to be married, and more likely to come from families with lower incomes (Hoffman 1998). Their children often lag behind in standards of early development (Hoffman 1998); are less likely to receive proper nutrition, health care, and cognitive stimulation (Annie E. Casey Foundation 1998); and are at greater risk of social behavioral problems and lower intellectual and

IN FOCUS

TEEN PARENTING AND EDUCATION

Pregnant teens and teen parents were routinely expelled from school until Title IX prohibited public schools from discriminating against them. High school graduation rates and college enrollment are lower for teen mothers than for those bearing children later in life, though some longitudinal research reveals that most teen mothers improve their education, income, and employment over time (Furstenberg 2007). Frank F. Furstenberg, Jeanne Brooks-Gunn, and S. Phillip Morgan (1987) found that teen mothers with the best life outcomes are those who have higher educational aspirations and better-educated and financially stable families.

In her longitudinal study, Lee SmithBattle (2007) examined the impact of parenting on 19 teen mothers' educational goals and school progress. Contrary to popular belief, she observed the teens' renewed commitment to their education. However, based on the accounts of the teen mothers, she discovered that "schools exacerbated their difficulties by failing to provide educational options or by enforcing policies that disregard their complex realities" (SmithBattle 2007:366). She writes,

> In addition to work demands, family responsibilities, and transportation difficulties, school policies and practices created additional barriers that undermined teens' aspirations and hindered their school progress . . . continuing or remaining in school was complicated by cumbersome enrollment processes, stringent attendance policies, lack of educational options, and bureaucratic mismanagement.

© John Raoux /AP/Corbis

Kali Gonzalez is pictured here with her daughter Kiah. Kali is a student at St. Johns State College. Researchers have found that teen mothers with the best life outcomes are those who had higher educational aspirations and better-educated and financially stable families.

> Kate's schooling was interrupted for a full year as a result of enrollment difficulties and limited-schooling options. When morning sickness led to many school absences early in her pregnancy, she was referred to the pregnancy school in her urban district. Because home tutoring was not offered as an option, she was forced to withdraw when enrolling in the pregnancy school proved insurmountable. . . .
>
> Kate's mother added that "we just gave up" when Kate's home school failed to transfer her transcript to the pregnancy school in a timely manner. Jenna was also referred to the pregnancy program but refused to be transferred because of its poor academic reputation. She dropped out near the end of her pregnancy for a full year because homeschooling

academic achievement (Hoffman 2006). Early childbearing also affects teen fathers. Teen fathers are more likely to engage in delinquent behaviors such as alcohol abuse or drug dealing. In addition, they complete fewer years of school and earn less per year (Annie E. Casey Foundation 1998).

was not offered. As she said, "When I was 7 or 8 months pregnant, I stopped going to school. When the new semester started, I withdrew, because after the baby, I would have had to wait a certain amount of weeks to go back and then I'd end up failing. So it was no use." . . .

[A] cascade of negative events, including inflexible school policies and disciplinary practices, landed Dawn, a suburban student, in educational limbo. After being homeschooled for several months, she returned to her senior year expecting to graduate with her class. She was eventually notified that she would not graduate because she had not completed assignments for one course, presumably because the teacher of that course had not relayed them to her homeschooling teacher. Deeply disappointed, Dawn resolved to return to school the following fall and take the few credits she needed to graduate. At the beginning of the fall semester, Dawn was driving her son to day care, going on to school, and leaving midmorning for work. Her plan to graduate at the end of the fall semester crumbled when the school principal revoked her parking privileges for a declining grade point average after a car accident led to the lack of transportation and several absences. Without a parking pass, Dawn could not drive her son to day care or go to work after school. She was thoroughly discouraged and lacked the skills and family support to appeal to the school board. Her student status was further complicated when she was kicked out of her home and moved in with her grandmother who resided in a different school district.

"I'm tryin' to get into a school here in the city. But they're tellin' me that I have to go two semesters in order to graduate from this new school, when I only would have had to go one semester to graduate from my school. It's just a mess . . . I actually want to go to school and they won't let me because of something stupid."

At her last interview, she was considering reenrolling in her suburban school so that she could complete the few credits she needed to graduate. Her plans seemed unrealistic because of the lengthy driving time involved (at least 30 to 40 minutes one way) and the complex scheduling that would be required with day care and an employer. (SmithBattle 2007:360–63)

SmithBattle (2007) concludes,

The gap between teen mothers' aspirations and the support to achieve them suggests that educators and other professionals are missing a critical opportunity to promote teen mothers' school-progress and their long-term educational attainment and success. Schools that cultivate teen mothers' educational ambitions may ultimately contribute to positive chain reactions and the reduction of teen mothers' prior adversity. (p. 369)

Explain how C. Wright Mills would define Kate's experiences. Is she experiencing a private trouble or a public issue?

SOURCE: Reprinted with permission from SmithBattle 2007.

Significant public costs are also associated with adolescent childbearing. For 2004, the estimated annual cost to taxpayers of births to young mothers was $9 billion, taking into consideration lost tax revenue, public assistance, health care for children, child welfare, and the criminal justice system (Hoffman 2006). Costs related to births to women 17 years old or younger were higher per birth than for those 18 to 19 years of age.

Although teenage childbirth has always been considered a social problem, reports of abandoned babies found in trash bins, restrooms, parks, and public buildings captures the public's attention. The first case that caught national attention was "Prom Mom" Melissa Drexler. While attending her senior prom in 1997, Drexler gave birth to a full-term baby boy in a bathroom stall. She wrapped her baby in several plastic bags, left him in a garbage can, and returned to her prom. She pleaded guilty to manslaughter. There is no comprehensive national reporting system for abandoned babies.

The Problems of Time and Money

According to Beck (1992:89), "families . . . become the scene of continuous juggling of diverging multiple ambitions among occupational necessities, educational constraints, parental duties and the monotony of housework." In a survey conducted by the Radcliffe Public Policy Center (2000), nearly all respondents reported feeling pressed for time in their lives, wanting to spend more time with their families, have more flexible work options, and even just have more time to sleep. In an analysis of couples in the eight EU countries, Tanja van der Lippe, Annet Jager, and Yvonne Kops (2006) concluded that work-home pressure was highest among couples from Sweden, the United Kingdom, and the Netherlands. Even in Sweden with its family-friendly policies, couples felt the pressure to successfully combine paid work and family life, especially when negotiating long working hours and overtime.

Families with children must determine how best to provide financial support, while making sure their children have parental time. Suzanne Bianchi, John Robinson, and Melissa Milkie (2006) reported that in about 30% of families with children, both parents work full-time. Compared with their counterparts in other countries, a higher percentage of American dual-worker couples work long weeks (80 or more hours combined), leaving less family time during the week. Mothers still spend more time with children, an average of 13 hours per week compared with 7 hours per week for fathers. Mothers do most of the routine care (custodial daily care) of children, whereas fathers spend their time with children doing interactive activities (enrichment activities such as talking or reading to them) (Bianchi et al. 2006).

According to Lillian Rubin (1995), economic realities make it especially difficult for working-class parents to maintain their juggling act. In her book *Families on the Fault Line*, Rubin documented how structural changes in the economy undermine the quality of life among working-class families. This is a functional argument: Because the family is part of our larger social system, what happens at an economic level will inevitably affect the family. The reality of long workdays and workweeks does take its toll on families: the loss of intimacy between couples, the lack of time for couples and their children, tense renegotiations over household work, and juggling child care arrangements are just some of the issues that working families face.

REUTERS/Shannon Stapleton

Military family members outnumber military personnel by 1.4 to 1. In 2011, 726,500 spouses and more than 1.2 million dependent children lived in active-duty families (U. S. Department of Defense 2012).

Rubin's study shed some light on the condition of working-class families, but often overlooked is the plight of lower-income families—too rich to be classified as living in poverty, but still too poor to be working class. In a two-year study, Lisa Dodson, Tiffany Manuel, and Ellen Bravo (2002) studied lower-income families in Milwaukee, Wisconsin; Denver, Colorado; and Boston, Massachusetts. The researchers concluded that lower-income families deal with basic problems on a daily basis: managing the safety, health, and education of their children while staying employed. Lower-income parents are not "bad" parents; it's just that their parenting may require more time and resources than they have. Among low-income families, there is a higher prevalence of children with chronic health issues or special learning needs; at least two thirds of the families in the Dodson et al. study reported having a child with special needs. These children require much more time and patience from their parents, sometimes jeopardizing parents' ability to maintain employment and earnings. To support lower-income parents, the authors recommend comprehensive and flexible child care, along with workplace flexibility (taking time off work, adjusting their work schedule) (Dodson et al. 2002).

The Iraq and Afghanistan wars heightened our awareness of the difficulties associated with families separated by war. An estimated 1.2 million children live with military families, and approximately 700,000 of them have at least one parent deployed (Johnson et al. 2007). Research on the adjustment of children and adolescents of

 Military Families Cope With the Stress of War

deployed military personnel indicates that the separation experience is stressful. Parental deployment has been linked with several negative youth outcomes, including depression (Jensen, Martin, and Watanabe 1996), behavioral problems (Levai et al. 1994), and poor academic performance (Hiew 1992). Boys suffer more effects of disruption than girls (Johnson et al. 2007). And as they are more aware of the risks involved in deployment, school-aged children experience anxiety and concern about the safety of the absent parent compared to younger children (Andres and Moelker 2011). More than 100,000 female soldiers who have served in the Iraq and Afghanistan wars have been mothers. As reported by Lizette Alvarez (2009), the majority of deployed women are primary caregivers, and a third are single mothers like Army Specialist Jaymie Holschlag. While she was deployed in Iraq, Holschlag's 10-year-old son and 4-year-old daughter lived with their grandparents. Concerned about the effects of her deployment on herself and her children, Holschlag requested a transfer when she returned home.

COMMUNITY, POLICY, AND SOCIAL ACTION

The Family and Medical Leave Act of 1993

The Family and Medical Leave Act (FMLA) of 1993 was envisioned as a way to help employees balance the demands of the workplace with the needs of their families. The act provides employees with as many as 12 weeks of unpaid, job-protected leave per year. It also provides for group health benefits during the employee's leave. The FMLA applies to all public agencies and all private employers with 50 or more workers. To be eligible, employees must work at least 1,250 hours per year. In 2008, the FMLA was expanded to include families of wounded military personnel.

As of 2014, 11 states and the District of Columbia have enacted their own family and medical leave laws, extending the coverage provided by the FMLA or extending coverage to those not eligible under FMLA guidelines. In 2004, California became the first state to enact a law that provides paid family care leave. The California Family Rights Act allows employees to take paid leave to care for a child, spouse, parent, or domestic partner who has a serious health condition or to bond with a new child. Paid leave was extended to workers to care for a parent-in-law, grandparent, grandchild, or sibling in 2013. Employees who take such leave can receive 55% of their pay up to $1,067 per week for a maximum of six weeks. The California law applies to all employers, not just those with 50 or more employees (State of California, Economic Development Department 2014).

Although there is strong support for the FMLA and its stated goals, the act has also been criticized since its enactment. Almost 50% of workers are not covered by the FMLA because they work for private employers not covered under the law or small businesses employing fewer than 50 people. Though it has been used an estimated 100 million times, nearly two thirds of eligible workers have not taken advantage of the FMLA because they can't afford the lost wages (National Partnership for Women and Families 2009).

TAKING A WORLD VIEW

PARENTAL LEAVE POLICIES

Rebecca Ray, Janet Gornick, and John Schmitt (2010) examined the generosity and the gendered structure of parental leave policies in 21 high-income countries. The researchers argue that the duration and benefit levels of parental leave policies are important because the policies

> can shape the time that employed parents have to care for family members at home. In addition, leave policies can strengthen or weaken women's labour market attachment, depending, to a large degree, on their design. Likewise, leave policies can influence men's share in family caregiving, as policy rules affect the availability of leave for men and shape their incentives for take-up. (Ray et al. 2010:199)

Ray et al.'s analysis reveals a range of leave policies for two-parent families, from 14 weeks in Switzerland to over 300 weeks in Spain and France (refer to Figure 7.3). The United States ranks 20th with 24 weeks. Switzerland ranks last, but provides 80% of a mother's usual earnings during the parental leave period.

A second key dimension of parental leave is whether it is paid and, if so, how generously. For many low- and middle-income families, unpaid leave is not particularly helpful because families cannot afford the time away from work. The United States provides a striking example. According to a 2000 U.S. Department of Labor survey, for example, over a 22-month period in 1999 and 2000, 3.5 million people in the United States needed leave for family or medical reasons but did not take it; almost 80% of those who did not take the leave said they could not afford to do so.

Most countries provide between three months and one year of FTE (full time equivalent) paid leave. Denmark falls right at the middle of the paid-leave scale, guaranteeing about 20 weeks of FTE paid leave. No country provides more than one year of FTE paid leave, but Sweden and Germany each offer 47 weeks. Five other countries offer at least six months of FTE paid leave: Norway (44 weeks), Greece (34 weeks), Finland (32 weeks), Canada (29 weeks) and Japan (26 weeks). (Ray et al. 2010:203)

The researchers also note that Australia and the United States offer no paid leave to two-parent families.

What does the extent of parental leave coverage reveal about the social and familial values of each country?

Figure 7.3 Total and full-time-equivalent (FTE) paid parental leave for two-parent families, in weeks

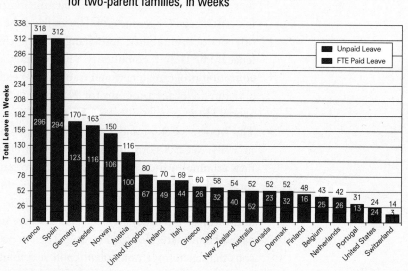

SOURCE: Ray et al. 2010:203.

Community Responses to Domestic Violence and Neglect

Responses to domestic violence can be characterized as having a distinct community approach. In the area of child abuse, the U.S. Office of Juvenile Justice and Delinquency Prevention established community-based children's advocacy centers to provide coordinated support for victims in the investigation, treatment, prosecution, and prevention of child abuse in all 50 states. Programs at each center are uniquely designed by community professionals and volunteers to best meet their community's needs. One such center is Project Harmony, based in Omaha, Nebraska. Project Harmony provides medical exams, assessment, and referrals. Project Harmony serves children who are victims of abuse and their nonabusing family members. By placing project staff and representatives from child protective services and law enforcement in the same facility, Project Harmony attempts to improve communication and coordination among all professionals involved in a child's case. Refer to this chapter's Voices in the Community feature to learn more about a rural support program based in Vermont.

Since its inception in 1995, the Office on Violence Against Women (VAW) has handled the U.S. Department of Justice's legal and policy issues regarding violence against women. The office offers a series of program and policy technical papers for individuals, leaders, and communities to support their efforts to end violence against women. These papers highlight some of the best program models and practices and were produced by the Promising Practices Initiative of the STOP Violence Against Women Grants Technical Assistance Project (Little, Malefyt, and Walker 1998). Two featured programs, still operating in 2014, are the following:

- The Minnesota Domestic Abuse Intervention Project (DAIP) was developed in 1980 and serves as a national and international program model. It was the first program of its kind to coordinate the intervention activities of each criminal justice agency in one city. The goals of the program include victim safety, offender accountability, and changes in the climate of tolerance toward violence in the Duluth community. The program also offers a men's nonviolence education program, a national training and technical assistance program, and a victim advocacy program for Native Americans through the Mending the Sacred Hoop project.

- The Women's Center and Shelter (WC&S) of Greater Pittsburgh was founded in 1974. WC&S coordinates its program efforts with the medical community, criminal justice agencies, and other organizations. The programs focus on the ability of women to take control of their own lives. WC&S provides comprehensive victim services, which include parenting education and legal and medical advocacy. WC&S has also created a school-based curriculum called Hands Are Not for Hurting. The curriculum uses age-appropriate lessons that encourage nonviolent conflict resolution and teach youth that they are responsible for the choices they make.

VOICES IN THE COMMUNITY

WYNONA WARD

Wynona Ward thought she had left her violent childhood behind her. But in 1991, when her sisters called to inform her that their brother Richard had raped a child in the family, she was not surprised. The child had also been raped by her grandfather—Ward's father—years earlier. Ward describes Richard as "living up to his father's expectations. He was expected to grow up to be a child abuser" (quoted in Jetter 2000). Ward, her mother, and her siblings were subjected to years of sexual and physical abuse by her father. She and other family members supported the victim during her brother's trial and subsequent incarceration. The experience motivated Ward to enroll in law school, and after graduating from Vermont Law School, Ward established Have Justice Will Travel, a mobile law office serving battered women in Vermont.

Driving more than 30,000 miles a year, Ward is able to reach victims who otherwise would not have access to legal or social services. With her mobile office (her truck is equipped with a radio, scanner, computer, and printer), Ward brings support and hope to women who have none. The group also provides transportation to and from court hearings and free legal representation. Ward says, "[We] work with these women so they can become strong and independent and self-reliant and be able to support themselves and their children" (as quoted in Brown 2010).

Since 1998, Have Justice Will Travel has assisted 10,000 victims with legal and social services. From its humble start at Ward's kitchen table, the program has expanded to three locations with the assistance of staff and student volunteers from Ward's alma mater, Dartmouth College, and other local colleges. Ward divides her time on the road between working with clients and writing grant proposals to support the program. Growing her program to serve more women and their families continues to be her goal.

> Everyday [sic] in this country, we have more and more women that are working in social services, more women that are entering the legal field, more people that can have empathy for victims. . . . Different donors have asked me, "well, how are you going to expand Have Justice?" There's only one Wynona. But I say to them, "no, you're wrong. There are many Wynonas out there." (Ward 2002)

How effective is Have Justice Will Travel? Does the program address the problem at an individual or structural level?

The National Center on Elder Abuse (NCEA) believes that community education and outreach are important in combating the problem of elder abuse and neglect. The NCEA supports community "sentinel" programs, which train and educate professionals and volunteers to identify and refer potential victims of abuse, neglect, or exploitation. In 1999, the NCEA established partnerships with the Humane Society of the United States (HSUS), the Meals on Wheels Association of America (MOWAA), and the National Association of Retired and Senior Volunteer Program Directors. These organizations were selected because of their unique access to isolated elders in their homes. The NCEA funded six coalition projects in Arizona, California, New York, North Carolina, and Utah. The program trained more than

1,000 professionals and volunteers to serve as sentinels; as a result, there was an increase in the number of abuse referrals in communities where sentinels were used. Administrators also noticed an increase in the level of satisfaction among volunteers, who as a result of the project were able to assist individuals who they believed might be victims or potential victims (National Center on Elder Abuse 2002b).

Teen Pregnancy and Infant Abandonment

From an interactionist perspective, sex education has been framed as a private, family issue. There are no U.S. federal laws that require sexual health education in schools. According to health professionals and educators, this framework has denied young men and women access to basic sex education information and services (Silk and Romero 2013). As a result, sexual health education has been defined as the responsibility of social and health service programmers. In the 1980s, these programmers defined prevention as an effective way to address the problems of teen pregnancy and parenthood (Card 1999). In the 1990s, several new prevention approaches emerged, particularly after the passage of the Welfare Reform Act of 1996. Under Section 905 of the act, the U.S. Department of Health and Human Services (HHS) was mandated to ensure that at least 25% of all U.S. communities had teen pregnancy prevention programs in place. Most states identified target goals related to teen birthrates.

Curriculum-based sexual health education programs are categorized into two groups (Kirby 2007). The most prominent form, abstinence-only programs, promotes abstinence from sex and not condom or other contraceptive use. Comprehensive programs promote abstinence along with condom and other contraceptive use. Programming in both groups may vary. For example, some abstinence programs emphasize abstinence until marriage, while others do not. Some comprehensive programs feature only an educational component, while others include contraceptive services.

In his review of abstinence-only program evaluations, Douglas Kirby (2007) noted that only a small number of abstinence programs have been evaluated. He concluded, based on the limited research, that there was little evidence to suggest that any particular abstinence program delays the initiation of sex. Kirby found that comprehensive programs were more likely to have a positive impact on teen sexual behavior—at least 40% of the programs resulted in increased condom and contraceptive use. Researchers also documented increased abstinence, reduced numbers of sexual partners, and delayed initiation of sex among students participating in comprehensive programs.

In response to newborn and infant abandonment, since 1999 all states have passed laws that offer safe and confidential means to relinquish unwanted newborns without the threat of prosecution for child abandonment. State laws vary according to the child's age (72 hours to 1 year old) and the personnel or places authorized to accept the infant (hospital personnel, emergency rooms, church, and police).

It is unclear how effective these safe-surrender or safe-haven laws have been in reducing infant abandonment or death. New Jersey, home of the first infant abandonment case that gained national attention, passed a safe-haven law in August 2000, modeled after Texas 1999 legislation. Between August 2000 and November 2003, New Jersey officials assisted 17 babies. These children were adopted, placed in foster care, or returned to their mothers (New Jersey Safe Haven Protection Act 2007). In 2006, however, six dead newborns were found abandoned in New York, despite the state's safe-haven laws. Critics argue that the state's safe-haven laws were poorly advertised, with most residents not knowing about the laws' provisions. In Illinois, a discussion of the safe-haven law is included in the high school health curriculum, possibly ensuring more awareness among high-risk youth (Buckley 2007).

In 2007, a mother abandoned her 3-month-old baby boy at a neonatal clinic in Rome, Italy. She was the first to use Casilino Polyclinic's modern foundling wheel. The original foundling wheel, used in the Middle Ages, was a revolving wooden barrel built into the church's exterior wall; the mother could deposit her baby and turn the wheel, and the baby would be safely protected inside the church. The Rome clinic uses a small modern structure equipped with a heated cradle and a respirator. Also available at other Italian hospitals and churches, these structures are equipped with an alarm to alert medical or church staff when a child is deposited. Foundling wheels or designated drop-off locations for unwanted newborns are used in other countries such as Germany, Switzerland, and the Czech Republic (Povoledo 2007).

. . . .

What Does It Mean to Me?

Investigate your state's safe-haven law. What are the features of the law? What protections does it offer the mother? How many children have been protected under the law? How well do you think the law has been promoted?

. . . .

Supporting Different Family Forms

According to sociologist David Popenoe (1993), there has been a serious decline in the structure and function of the family since the 1960s. Families are not meeting society's needs as they once did and have lost most of their "functions, social power and authority over their members" (Popenoe 1993:527–28). He attributes the weakening of family function to high divorce rates, declining family size, and the growing absence of fathers and mothers in their children's lives. Data reviewed at the beginning of this chapter—the declining percentage of nuclear families, along with the increase in single-parent families and nonfamily households—lend support to his observation.

But critics of Popenoe's position argue that the family-in-decline hypothesis relies too heavily on the definition of family in its nuclear form (Bengston 2001). Sociologist Judith Stacey (1996) agrees that the "family" as defined by a nuclear

Non-Traditional Families

form of mom, dad, and children is in decline. This family system has been replaced by what Stacey calls a postmodern family condition, one characterized by diverse family patterns and forms, where no single family form is dominant. There have been significant changes in the traditional family's structure and functions (Bengston 2001); modern families are best characterized by their diversity (Hanson and Lynch 1992). Indeed, "a single, all-encompassing definition of 'family' may be impossible to achieve" (Erera 2002, p. 3).

The proportion of nuclear families is decreasing and being replaced with family structures that include single-parent, blended, adoptive, foster, grandparent, and same-sex-partner households (Copeland and White 1991). The increasing diversity of American families requires that we broaden our research and policy agendas beyond traditional family forms (Demo 1992). Perhaps one solution to the "problem" of families is to appreciate and embrace other family forms. Let's examine two family forms: cohabitation and grandparents as primary caregivers to grandchildren.

Cohabitation

Larry Bumpass (1998) argues that the increase in cohabitation reflects and reinforces the declining significance of marriage as a life course marker in our society. He reports that almost half of the young adults in the United States have lived in a cohabiting union at some point in their lives, a trend reflected in most Western societies. **Cohabiting** is defined as sexual partners not married to each other but residing in the same household.

There were nearly 7.5 million cohabiting (opposite-sex) couples in 2010 (Kreider 2010). A quarter of unmarried women aged 25 to 39 are currently living with a partner, and an additional quarter have lived with a partner sometime in the past. According to the National Marriage Project (2009), cohabitation is more likely to occur among those of lower educational and income levels and among those who are less religious than their peers and who experienced parental divorce or high levels of marital discord during childhood. The pattern is particularly true for Black, Hispanic, and mainland Puerto Rican women compared with White women (Bumpass and Lu 2000). Cohabitation rates have increased among Black and White adults; higher increases have been observed among Whites. Larry Bumpass and Hsien-Hen Lu (2000) report that for women aged 19 to 44 years, 59% of high school dropouts have cohabited compared with 37% of high school graduates.

Data on the proportion of households cohabiting for selected countries are presented in Figure 7.4. In 11 European countries, cohabiting partners have the possibility of entering a civil union (via registration) other than marriage. In other countries, cohabiting couples who have not registered their union, but have lived together for a specific period of time, are considered to have the same legal rights and obligations as married couples or partners who have formalized their relationships. For example, in Australia and New Zealand, couples living together for a specific period of time are legally considered to be in a partnership with status equal to marriage (Organisation for Economic Co-operation and Development 2010). Many countries

Cohabiting: Sexual partners, not married to each other, but residing in the same household

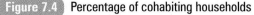

Figure 7.4 Percentage of cohabiting households

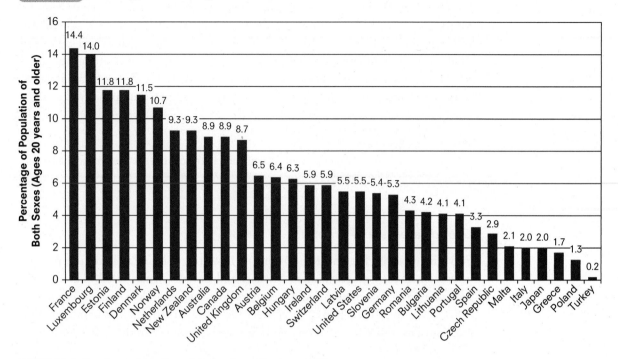

SOURCE: Adapted from Organisation for Economic Co-operation and Development 2009.

have responded to the increasing number of cohabiting couples by expanding their rights and legal recognition.

Researchers acknowledge that not all cohabitations will eventually lead to marriage and may instead serve as alternative forms of marriage (Manning and Smock 2002), though marriage still represents the cultural ideal, signaling a higher level of commitment. For many, cohabitation is considered a pathway to marriage. The percentage of marriages that began as cohabiting relationships rose from 41% in the early 1980s to 65% of marriages between 1995 and 2002 (Manning and Jones 2006).

Dafoe Whitehead and Popenoe (2005) cite a study that concluded that premarital cohabitation, when limited to a woman's future husband, was not associated with an elevated risk of divorce. Conversely, they observe, "No evidence has yet been found that those who cohabit before marriage have stronger marriages than those who do not." For data collected in 2002, the probability of a woman's marriage lasting 10 years if she had cohabitated before marriage was lower than the probability of a woman's marriage lasting the same amount of time if she did not cohabit before marriage, 61% versus 66% (Goodwin, Mosher, and Chandra 2010). However, the difference between the two groups is not significant. If a couple were engaged when they began cohabiting, the probability that the woman's marriage would survive 10 years was similar (65%) to the probability for couples who did not cohabit at all (66%) (Goodwin et al. 2010).

The increase of cohabitation has coincided with the increase in unmarried child-bearing—more than 40% of cohabiting couple households contain children (National Marriage Project 2013). Though data indicate that about two fifths of all children will live with their mother and a cohabiting partner and that about a third of the time children spend with unmarried mothers is spent in a cohabiting relationship, family scholars acknowledge that more needs to be known about the impact of cohabitation on the family experiences and life outcomes of these children (Bumpass and Lu 2000).

What Does It Mean to Me?

Does cohabitation threaten the institution of marriage? How does it redefine or challenge our definition of the "family"?

Grandparents as Parents

Fifty-nine-year-old Pat and Ken Owens of Lewistown, Maryland, are the primary caretakers of their grandchildren, Michael and Brandi (Armas 2002). Pat and Ken are among the 2.7 million grandparents raising their grandchildren. According to U.S. Census, in 2012, White children were more likely than children of other ethnic/racial groups to live in a grandparent's household with or without a parent present (Ellis and Simmons 2014). The role of grandparents as primary guardians to grand-children has not been addressed in many other countries. In the United Kingdom, a study of 870 grandparents revealed that only 0.5% had custodial care of their grandchildren, while 61% were their grandchild's regular day care provider (Clarke and Roberts 2004).

Grandparents may assume caretaking responsibilities when parents are unable to live with or care for their children because of death, illness, divorce, incarceration, substance abuse, or child abuse or neglect. The HIV/AIDS epidemic has been identi-fied as a significant contributor to African American grandparents assuming primary parenting roles (Crewe 2012). Pat and Ken Owens have not heard from Michael and Brandi's mother in the past two years and only recently began receiving financial support from Michael's father. The alternative for their grandchildren would have been foster care, something that Pat Owens did not want to happen: "I don't want to make it sound like it's easy because there are some tough, tense times. But I'm very proud of the fact that all the grandchildren still play together and go to school together" (Armas 2002:A6).

Research identifies how grandparents who care for their grandchildren are at high risk for emotional and physical distress. This distress is related to a deficit of social resources, such as marital status, social support, economic resources, and the demands of the caregiving role itself. Grandparent caregivers are more likely to experience depression and suffer from fair to poor physical health and activity limitations than are grandparents in more traditional roles (Chase Goodman and Silverstein 2006). Counseling and the use of school programs (tutoring and special

SOCIOLOGY AT WORK

PARALEGALS AND LEGAL ASSISTANTS

Carlos Sandoval—Class of 2013

Undergraduate Major: Sociology
Undergraduate Minor(s):
Philosophy, Religion

Paralegals and legal assistants do a variety of tasks to support lawyers in law firms, corporate legal departments, and government agencies. Many law firms utilize paralegals and legal assistants in an attempt to lower their expenses and billing costs to clients and to increase the efficiency of their legal services (U.S. Bureau of Labor Statistics 2014). Though Carlos Sandoval initially wanted to work for a police department or correctional facility, after graduating he was hired as a legal assistant for a county prosecutor's office. He is currently assigned to the Family Support Division doing mostly clerical work, interacting with clients, organizing files and documents, scheduling hearings, and mailing out notices for court dates.

There are many ways to become a paralegal or legal assistant. Some community colleges offer an associate's degree in paralegal studies, though law firms hire college graduates with a bachelor's degree (U.S. Bureau of Labor Statistics 2014). Previous work experience is preferred, but not necessary. During Carlos's job interview, sociology helped him address his lack of job experience:

> Having minimal work experience, it is hard to talk about what skills you have or how you can apply your previous experience to this new job. That being said, as soon as I walked into the interview, I tried to apply sociology to every question I was asked. This allowed me to continue talking about any particular subject with confidence. For example, one of the questions asked was "How do you feel with working

with minority groups and groups from lower income families?" I began by explaining what I know about groups in poverty and minority groups and how they may be less fortunate than others and not have all the resources they may need. I don't remember much from the interview, but I do remember having used sociology in each of my answers.

Carlos credits his internship experiences at a juvenile detention center and at a child protective services office with helping him develop work experiences with clients and confidential cases. He says,

> Although they may have not been related to my job now, my previous employers gave excellent references for my work ethic and skills. At the end of the day, all an employer wants is a good worker and someone they can see themselves working with. I believe it was my interview and references that gave me this job.

Carlos offers the following career and job search advice for undergraduates:

> The first advice I would give is to do as many internships and volunteer positions as you can for the field you are trying to work in. Even if the job is not directly relatable, the reference you will receive from doing good work is truly invaluable. This also allows you to experience different fields and find out which is right for you. Next I would say apply for as many jobs as possible. Many employers take a long time to hire someone. Even though it feels like everyone is rejecting you, employers will begin to call back all at the same time. Also, visit any and all preparedness workshops, if they are available. Especially for government jobs with standardized tests, there are workshops and practice tests that are available; people often fail for simply not studying.

education) provide grandparents and grandchildren some emotional and academic support (Trail Ross and Aday 2006; Kelch-Oliver 2011). Despite the negative consequences, grandparents also report satisfaction and rewards related to caring for their grandchildren.

The sudden responsibility for children leaves many grandparents on fixed incomes with unexpected financial burdens. In one study, children living in a grandparent's household without a parent present were twice as likely to be living below the poverty level as were children living with both grandparents and a parent. Children who lived with just their grandparents were also at risk of not being covered by health insurance (Fields 2003). If eligible, grandparents can get assistance through HHS Temporary Assistance for Needy Families (TANF). Some states, such as Illinois, Pennsylvania, and Wisconsin, offer guardianship or kinship care subsidy programs for grandparents.

Emotional and social support is available for grandparent-headed households. Local grandparent support groups are listed by organizations such as AARP, Generations United, and GrandsPlace. These organizations also provide fact sheets, community links, and suggestions for clothing and school supplies, recipes, and travel and activity guides for grandparents and their grandchildren. AARP (2002) has recognized several model support programs such as the Kinship Support Network in San Francisco, California; Project Healthy Grandparents in Atlanta, Georgia; and Grandma's Kids Kinship Support Program in Philadelphia, Pennsylvania.

CHAPTER REVIEW

7.1 Describe how the sociological perspectives explain social problems related to the family

From a functionalist perspective, social problems emerge as the family struggles to adapt to a modern society. From the conflict theorist, the family is a system of inequality where conflict is normal. Conflict can derive from economic or power inequalities between spouses or family members. From a feminist perspective, inequality emerges from the patriarchal family system, where men control decision-making in the family. According to an interactionist, we create and maintain our definition of a family through social interaction. This process affects our larger social definition of what everyone's family should be like and the kind of family that we create for ourselves.

7.2 Summarize the effects of divorce on children

In general, the research indicates that children with divorced parents have moderately poorer life and educational outcomes (emotional well-being, academic achievement, labor force participation, divorce, and teenage childbearing) than do children living with both parents. Research also suggests that marital separation is beneficial to the well-being of children. Divorce is less disruptive if both parents maintain a positive relationship with the child, if parental conflict decreases after separation or divorce, and if the level of socioeconomic resources for the child is not reduced.

7.3 Identify why the U.S. teen pregnancy rate is the highest in the developed world

Teen pregnancy has been attributed to many factors, including the lack of sex education in school and low contraception use among teens. The "family values" discourse has been blamed for blocking comprehensive sex education to American youth, thus increasing risky sexual behavior (low contraceptive use) and teen pregnancy rates.

7.4 Explain the difference between physical abuse and neglect

Neglect is characterized by a failure to provide for a child's basic needs. It can be physical, educational, or emotional in nature. Physical abuse is nonaccidental physical injury, causing bodily harm to a child.

7.5 Explain the relationship between cohabitation and marriage

Cohabitation is often considered a precursor to marriage. Yet researchers acknowledge that not all cohabitations will eventually lead to marriage and may instead serve as an alternative form of marriage.

KEY TERMS

cohabiting, 198

extended families, 174

family, 174

heteronormativity, 179

household, 174

neglect, 184

nuclear family, 174

physical abuse, 184

social institutions, 172

STUDY QUESTIONS

1. Compare and contrast the myths and realities of the American family.

2. Even though the nuclear family is not the statistical majority in our society, its image as the "perfect" family persists. Why do you think this is the case? How could the "perfect" family be redefined?

3. How does capitalism influence family structure and relationships? Do you agree with this perspective? Why or why not?

4. How does society's definition of the "family" lead to social problems, prejudice, and discrimination?

5. Identify the effects of divorce on children and adults.

6. What is the relationship between teen parenthood and educational attainment? What can be done to support the academic success of teen parents?

7. Explain the difference between abstinence-only and comprehensive sexual health education programs.

8. Compare the United States with other countries on the following family demographics (as reported in this chapter): marriage, divorce, teen pregnancy, and cohabitation.

$SAGE edge™

Sharpen your skills with SAGE edge at **edge.sagepub.com/leonguerrero5e**

SAGE edge provides a personalized approach to help you accomplish your coursework goals in an easy-to-use learning environment.

Education is assumed to be the great equalizer in our society. There are inspirational stories of women and men who, after a tough childhood or adulthood, complete their education, become successful members of society, and are held as role models. Education is presented as an essential part of their success, serving as a cure for personal or situational short-comings. If you are poor, education can make you rich. If your childhood was less than perfect, a college degree can make up for it. On the occasion of launching the Head Start program in 1965, President Lyndon Johnson is quoted as saying, "If it weren't for education, I'd still be looking at the southern end of a northbound mule" (Zigler and Muenchow 1992).

Yet along with these images of success, we are bombarded with images of failure. Media coverage and political rhetoric highlight problems with our educational system, particularly with our public schools. In recent state and national political campaigns, the quality of teaching and the preparation of teachers were scrutinized, and school districts with low scores on standardized exams were criticized. U.S. students are said to be falling behind the accelerated pace of higher education internationally. Though 43% of 25- to 64-year-old Americans have earned an associate's degree or higher, there are several industrial countries with higher rates of college attainment (refer to Figure 8.1). Additionally, the increase in the proportion of the population with a college degree is lower in the United States (a 7% increase between 2000 and 2012) in comparison with other industrialized countries (an average of 11% over the same time period) (Organisation for Economic Co-operation and Development 2014).

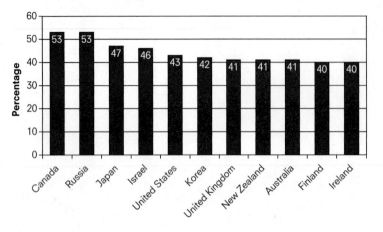

Figure 8.1 Percentage of adults 25–64 years of age with an associate's degree or higher, 2012 (only countries 40% or higher reported)

SOURCE: Organisation for Economic Co-operation and Development 2014.

In 2006, a panel of education, labor, and public policy experts, including two former education secretaries, warned that if the United States does not keep pace with the educational gains made in other countries, our standard of living will be seriously compromised. During his first year in office, President Barack Obama set a goal for the United States to have the highest proportion of college students in the world.

So which is it: is education a key to individual success or an institutional failure? In this chapter, we'll first examine this question by reviewing our educational system from different sociological perspectives. Then we'll explore current social problems in education, along with policy and program responses.

THE NEW EDUCATIONAL STANDARD

We tend to define a high school degree as the educational standard of the past, now replaced with a bachelor's degree. Actually, data from the U.S. Census Bureau confirm that the United States is acquiring an increasingly more educated population (see Table 8.1 and U.S. Data Map 8.1).

For 2013, the U.S. Census Bureau (2014) reported that 88.2% of adults (25 years and older) had completed at least a high school degree, and more than 31% of all adults had attained at least a bachelor's degree. Educational attainment levels of adults will continue to rise as younger, more educated age groups replace older, less educated ones.

Table 8.1 Educational attainment of the population 25 years and older, 2013

Characteristics	High School Graduate or More	Bachelor's Degree or More
25 years and over	88.2	31.0
25–29 years old	89.9	33.6

SOURCE: U.S. Census Bureau 2014.

 International Student Acheivement

 College Education Race

EXPLORING **social problems**

Educational Attainment in the United States

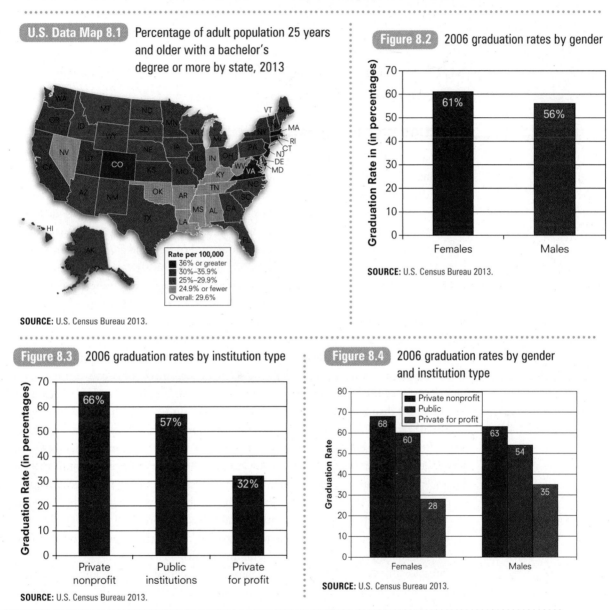

WHAT DO YOU THINK?

The 1990 Student Right-to-Know and Campus Security Act requires all schools to publish their graduate rates—the percentage of students that complete their program within 150% of the normal time for completion, which is six years for students enrolled in four-year bachelor's degree program. Students who transfer and complete their degree in another school are not counted as completers in these data.

Populations in the Northeast had the highest proportions with a bachelor's degree or higher. The state with the highest proportion was Massachusetts (40.3%). West Virginia had the lowest proportion (18.9%). What is the proportion for your state?

Graduation rates vary by gender (Figure 8.2) and type of institution (Figure 8.3). Females have higher graduation rates than males in public and private nonprofit institutions (Figure 8.4).

Contact your institutional research office about your school's graduation rates since 2000. How does your school compare with other schools in your state?

. . . .

What Does It Mean to Me?

Compare the educational attainment of three generations of your family: yourself, your parents, and your grandparents. Are younger generations more educated than older generations in your family? Why or why not?

. . . .

SOCIOLOGICAL PERSPECTIVES ON EDUCATION

Functionalist Perspective

The institution of education has a set of manifest and latent functions. **Manifest functions** are intended goals or consequences of the activities within an institution. Education's primary manifest function should come as no surprise: it is to educate! The other manifest functions include socialization, personal development, and employment. Our educational system ensures that each of us will be appropriately socialized and adequately educated to become a contributing member of society (and the labor force). As Nicola Ansell (2008) writes, "Educational systems view children as 'human becomings' that they are explicitly preparing for work" (p. 808). We learn skills and knowledge, as well as about society's norms, values, and beliefs, which are necessary for our survival and, ultimately, the society's survival.

Education's **latent functions** may be less obvious. One unintended function that education serves is as a public babysitter. No other institution can claim such a monopoly over the total number of hours, months, and years of a child's life. From kindergarten through high school, parents can rely on teachers, administrators, and counselors for their child's education and for supervision, socialization, and discipline. In addition, education controls the entry of young women and men into the labor force and the timing of that entry. Consider the surge in employment rates after high school and college graduation. There is always a rush to get a job each summer; employers rely on the temporary labor of high school and college students during busy summer months. Finally, education establishes and protects social networks by ensuring that individuals with similar backgrounds, education, and interests are able to form friendships, partnerships, or romantic bonds.

Manifest functions: Intended and recognized consequences

Latent functions: Unintended and often hidden consequences

Functionalists argue that education has been assigned so many additional tasks that it struggles in its primary task to educate the young. In addition to its own main functions, our educational system has taken over functions of other institutions. For example, the educational system provides services to students with family problems, emotional needs, or physical challenges. Schools also provide services for parents in the form of adult education or parenting classes.

Conflict Perspective

Conflict theorists do not see education as an equalizer; rather, they consider education a "divider"—dividing the haves from the have-nots in our society. Conflict theorists focus on the social and economic inequalities inherent in our educational system and on how the system perpetuates these inequalities.

Conflict theorists highlight the socialization function of education as part of the indoctrination of Western bureaucratic ideology. The popular posters and books on "what I learned in kindergarten" could serve as the official list of adult life rules: share everything, play fair, and put things back where you found them. Never mind kindergarten—the indoctrination can begin as early as nursery school. Rosabeth Moss Kanter (1972) describes a child's experience in nursery school as an "organizational experience" creating an **organizational child**. Carefully instructed and supervised by their teachers, students are guided through their day in ordered agendas; they are rewarded for conformity, and any signs of individuality are discouraged. The organizational child is sufficiently prepared for the demands and constraints of a bureaucratic adult world.

Although we consider education the primary method of achieving equality and mobility in our society, conflict theorists argue that it actually sustains the structure of inequality. As Martin Marger (2008) explains, the relationship between education and socioeconomic status operates in a cycle perpetuated from one generation to the next. It begins with high-income and high-status parents who can ensure a greater amount and greater quality of education for their children. Pierre Bourdieu (1977) argues that children from upper- and middle-class families are advantaged in our educational system due to their possession of **cultural capital**, linguistic and cultural competence, and familiarity with culture that is passed on by their parents and their social position. Children whose parents introduce them to a culture consistent with the class-based assumptions of education are more likely to succeed than those whose parents do not (Lareau 2003).

But there is another form of capital to consider. **Social capital** refers to investments in social relationships and networks (Lin 2011) and is also distributed unequally by social class. Young children who are more engaged in extracurricular activities and have increased opportunities to build personal relationships with adults outside their immediate family demonstrate greater academic progress than children who lack access to these activities or opportunities (Freeman and Condron 2011).

Jonathan Kozol, in his classic studies *Savage Inequalities: Children in America's Schools* (1991) and *The Shame of the Nation: The Restoration of Apartheid Schooling in America* (2005), presents a discouraging portrait of student learning in inner-city schools that are understaffed, undersupplied, and in disrepair. This educational inequality is created by public school systems that rely on property taxes to finance school staffing and operations. As a result, a caste system has emerged in our educational system. Despite the U.S. Supreme Court's 1954 *Brown v. Board of Education*

Organizational child: A child prepared by education for a bureaucratic adult world

Cultural capital: Cultural skills and knowledge passed on to youth by their parents and through their social and economic position

Social capital: Investments in social relationships and networks distributed unequally by social class

Growing Segregation

From a conflict perspective, we do not invest the same amount of public spending, political interest, or public attention in the educational achievement of students from lower social classes compared to students from middle or upper classes.

ruling, de facto school segregation still exists. Income and residential segregation have led to greater differentiation in school quality and opportunities between rich and poor neighborhoods (Reardon 2011).

The gap between the haves and the have-nots is so wide it seems impossible to attain educational equity. As Kozol (1991) observes,

> children in one set of schools are educated to be governors; children in another set of schools are trained to be governed. The former are given the imaginative range to mobilize ideas for economic growth; the latter are provided with the discipline to do the narrow tasks the first group will prescribe. (p. 176)

Kozol introduces us to 8-year-old Alliyah. At the time, the New York City Board of Education spent $8,000 for her education in a public school in the Bronx. She would have received a public education worth $12,000 had she been educated in a typical White suburb of New York, and $18,000 if she had resided in a wealthy White suburb. According to Kozol (2005), what society chooses to spend on lower-class neighborhoods and schools "surely tells us something about what we think these kids are worth to us in human terms and in the contributions they may someday make to our society" (p. 44).

Feminist Perspective

Inequalities are based not just on social class but also on gender. Research reveals the persistent replication of gender relations in schools, evidenced by the privileging of males, their voices, and their activities in the classroom, on the playground, and in hallways (D. E. Smith 2000).

One of my favorite illustrations of the privilege given to a male voice comes from my own discipline. In sociology, there is a concept called the "definition of the situation," which refers to the phrase "If men define situations as real, they are real in their consequences" (Thomas and Thomas 1928:572). The concept is an important one to the symbolic interactionist perspective and is often attributed solely to sociologist W. I. Thomas. However, the correct attribution is to Thomas and his wife, Dorothy Swaine Thomas. R. S. Smith (1995) investigated the citation in more than 244 introductory sociology textbooks and found that most attributed the concept solely to W. I. Thomas. One reason for the omission of Swaine Thomas is that she may not have contributed to the phrase (although there is no documented evidence to support this), but R. S. Smith (1995) suggests that the omission is because of a professional and structural ideology that historically represented sociology as a "male" domain. Smith notes that the citations began to include Swaine Thomas after the mid-1970s, a time when sociology and introductory texts began to respond to and to reflect the changes brought about by a growing women's movement and increasing numbers of female sociologists.

Gender bias and gender stereotypes work to exclude and alienate girls early in their educational experience (American Association of University Women 1992; Sadker and Sadker 1994; Sadker and Zittleman 2009). Males have favored status in education, particularly in their interactions with their teachers. In the classroom, girls are invisible, often treated as second-class educational citizens. This is how Myra and David Sadker (1994) explained the subtle yet consequential gender bias in the classrooms they visited. After observing teachers and their interactions with girls and boys in more than 100 elementary classrooms, the Sadkers found that teachers were more responsive to boys and were more likely to teach them actively. Overall, girls received less attention, whereas boys got a double dose, both negative and positive. Boys received more praise, corrections, and feedback, whereas girls received a cursory "OK" response from their teachers. Sadker and Sadker concluded that over time, the unequal distribution of teacher time and attention may take its toll on girls' self-esteem, achievement rates, test scores, and ultimately careers. In a 2009 follow-up study, David Sadker and Karen Zittleman confirmed a reduction of classroom gender bias, but recommended that much more work needed to be done to eliminate gender bias.

For example, Sian Beilock and her colleagues examined the effects of teacher math anxiety on student math anxiety in an elementary school setting (quoted in Schmid 2010). They found that students tend to model themselves after adults of the same sex. A female teacher who is anxious about math may pass on the same concerns to her female students, reinforcing the belief that boys are better at math than girls. Though student math anxiety was not related to teacher math anxiety at the beginning of the school year, by the end of the year, the more anxious teachers were about their math skills, the more likely it was that their female students agreed that boys are good at math and girls are good at reading. Girls who agreed with this statement scored lower on math tests than boys and girls who had not developed this belief (Schmid 2010).

Structural factors along with interpersonal dynamics also contribute to the creation and maintenance of gender inequality on college and university campuses (Stombler and Yancey Martin 1994). Men and women experience college differently and have markedly different outcomes (Jacobs 1996). College women are subjected to male domination through their peer relations (Stombler and Yancey Martin 1994) in the classroom, in romantic involvements (Holland and Eisenhart 1990), and in organized activities. Even activities such as fraternity "little sister" programs, which Mindy Stombler and Patricia Yancey Martin (1994) studied, provide the structural and interpersonal dynamics necessary to create an atmosphere conducive to women's subordination.

Interactionist Perspective

Sadker and Sadker's 1994 study identified the differential effects of teacher communication on female and male students. The interaction between teachers and students daily reinforces the structure and inequalities of the classroom and the educational system. From this micro perspective, sociologists focus on how classroom dynamics and practices educate the perfect students and at the same time create the not-so-perfect ones. In what ways does classroom interaction educate and create?

Assessment and testing are standard practices in education. Students are routinely graded and evaluated based on their work and ability. Interactionists would argue that along with assessment comes unintended consequences. Based on test results, students may be placed in different ability or occupational tracks. In the practice called **tracking**, advanced learners are separated from regular learners; students are identified as college bound versus work bound.

Advocates of tracking argue that the practice increases educational effectiveness by allowing teachers to target students at their ability level (Hallinan 1994). Yet placing students in tracks has been controversial because of the presumed negative effects on some students. Opponents argue that labels such as an *upper* versus *lower* track or *"special"* or *slow learners* are used systematically to deny a group of students access to education (Ansalone 2004). In addition to creating unequal learning opportunities (Hallinan 2003), tracking may encourage teachers, parents, and others to view students differently according to their track, and as a result, their true potential may be hindered (Adams and Evans 1996). African Americans, Latinos, and students from lower socioeconomic backgrounds are less likely to enroll in advanced placement or honors courses (Mickelson and Everett 2008). Countries that practice ability tracking have greater educational inequity than countries who do not track their students (Schofield 2010). Although tracking is intended to aid students, it may lead to a self-fulfilling prophecy: Students will fail because they are expected to do so.

Despite the documented negative consequences of tracking, the practice continues in approximately 60% of all elementary schools and 80% of all secondary schools (Ansalone 2001). Although interactionists do not assess the appropriateness of the label, they would address how the label affects students' identity and educational outcomes. Issues of inequality must also be addressed if the data suggest that students of particular gender or ethnic/racial categories are targeted for tracking.

A summary of all sociological perspectives on education is presented in Table 8.2.

PROBLEMS AND CHALLENGES IN EDUCATION

Tracking: Designation of academic courses for students based on presumed aptitude

The idea that there is a public education crisis is not a new one. A 1918 government report referred to the "erosion of family life, disappearing fathers, working mothers, the decline of religious institutions, changes in the workplace, and the millions of

Table 8.2 Summary of sociological perspectives: Education

	Functional	Conflict/Feminist	Interactionist
Explanation of education	Using a macro perspective, functionalists examine the functions of the educational system. The educational system is strained from performing multiple functions.	Conflict and feminist theorists address how the educational system perpetuates economic, ethnic, and gender inequalities. Students, depending on their social backgrounds, are differentially treated by the educational system.	Using a micro perspective, an interactionist focuses on how the educational experience is created through interaction and shared meanings in the classroom.
Questions asked about education and its social problems	What manifest or latent functions does education serve? How is education affected by other social institutions?	How does education perpetuate social inequalities? Is one group more disadvantaged than another?	How do classroom dynamics determine the educational success of a student? What is the relationship between teacher–student interaction and student success? How does student tracking or labeling impact student achievement?

newly arrived immigrants" as potential sources of the public education crisis (Meier 1995:9). At the time, the government's response was the creation of the modern school system with two tracks, one for terminal high school degrees and the other for college-bound students (Meier 1995).

The current call for educational reform was initiated during President Ronald Reagan's administration. In 1983, the National Commission on Excellence in Education released its report, *A Nation at Risk: The Imperatives for Educational Reform*, a scathing indictment of the education system. The commission was created by Secretary of Education T. H. Bell to respond to what he called the "widespread public perception that something is seriously remiss in our educational system" (National Commission on Excellence in Education 1983:7). Claiming that we are raising a scientifically and technologically illiterate generation, the commission noted the relatively poor performance of American students in comparison with their international peers, declining standardized test scores, the weaknesses of our school programs and educators, and the lack of a skilled American workforce (National Commission on Excellence in Education 1983).

The educational reform movement marches on, gaining momentum with each elected president. At one time or another, each president after Reagan has referred to himself as the "Education President," declaring an educational crisis and calling for change. Educators and reformers agree that this is an exciting time for American education (Ravitch and Viteritti 1997). Under George H. W. Bush's administration, Congress passed America 2000, which was followed by the Goals 2000: Educate America Act in 1994 during Bill Clinton's administration. Congress passed the No Child Left Behind (NCLB) Act of 2001 under George W. Bush's administration. All congressional acts call for coordinated improvements and sweeping reform of our educational system.

David Berliner and Bruce Biddle (1995) contend that the crisis in public education is a manufactured one, constructed by well-meaning or not-so-well–meaning politicians, educational experts, and business leaders. Berliner and Biddle don't believe that public schools are problem free; rather, by focusing on the manufactured crisis, they believe we're not addressing the real problems facing our schools, those based in social and economic inequalities. What is the evidence regarding these problems and challenges to our educational system? Let's first examine the basis of education: literacy.

The Problem of Basic Literacy

The United Nations Educational, Scientific and Cultural Organization (UNESCO 2013) estimates that there are more than 781 million illiterate adults and 126 million illiterate youth in the world. Most live in South and West Asia, East Asia, and sub-Saharan Africa. Multiple barriers restrict the achievement of widespread literacy: insufficient access to quality education, weak support for youth exiting the educational system, poorly funded and fragmented educational programs, and limited opportunities for adult learning. Literacy disparities are associated with gender, poverty, place of residence, ethnicity, language, and disabilities. Gender disparities are particularly pronounced in developing countries. Women account for 75% (UNESCO 2013) of adults worldwide who cannot read and write (refer to Table 8.3).

According to the Literacy Volunteers of America (2002), very few U.S. adults are truly illiterate, yet the United States is not a literacy superpower (ProLiteracy Worldwide 2006). What continues to be of concern is the number of adults with low literacy skills who are unable to find and retain employment, support their children's education, and participate in their communities. Basic literacy skills, such as understanding and using information in texts (newspapers, books, a warranty form) or instructional documents (maps, job applications) or completing mathematical operations (filling out an order form, balancing a checkbook), are related to social, educational, and economic outcomes (Sum, Kirsch, and Taggart 2002).

Data from the 2003 National Assessment of Adult Literacy (ProLiteracy Worldwide 2006) reveal that 30 million U.S. adults demonstrated skills at the "below basic" level (from being nonliterate in English to being able to follow written directions to fill out a form). About 63 million adults demonstrated skills at the basic level (having basic literacy skills to read and understand information in short, simple

Toppling Adult Illiteracy

TAKING A WORLD VIEW

EDUCATIONAL TRACKING AND TESTING IN JAPAN

After World War II, Japan adopted a 6-3-3-4 model of education that includes six years of elementary school (*shogakko*), three years of junior high school (*chugakko*), three years of high school (*kotogakko*), and four years of university study. Tracking does not occur in Japanese elementary and junior high schools; instead, their educational system emphasizes effort and hard work, discounting differences in ability. No effort is made to identify below- or above-average children in the classroom. All elementary and junior high schools offer the same curriculum, regulated by the national Ministry of Education, Culture, Sports, Science and Technology (MEXT; Ansalone 2004).

However, a highly competitive form of tracking (*ruikei*) begins at the high school level, separating students into two distinct tracks: general high schools leading to college and vocational high schools leading to jobs. Educational leaders argue that this system is able to accommodate students' different interests and talents and improves students' overall performance on national entrance exams (Ansalone 2004). Entrance examinations, also known as *jyuken higoku* (examination hell), serve as the major sorting mechanism for Japan's high schools and colleges (Bjork and Tsuneyoshi 2005).

Unintentionally, this tracking system has created a two-tier system of schools. Vocational high schools are students' second choice (Ono 2001). In his analysis of vocational high schools in the city of Kobe, Thomas Rohlen (1983) reports that one vocational high school draws students from the lower third of graduating ninth graders in the city. When asked if they had had a choice, 80% of the students said they would rather have attended a general high school. Vocational high schools have developed a negative reputation for school violence, smoking, and drug abuse, and their students are considered second-class citizens (Rohlen 1983). In his comparative analysis of educational systems in Japan and the United States, George Ansalone (2004) concluded that tracking "promotes differentiation of the curricula, teacher expectations, school misconduct, race, class, gender bias, and the development of separate friendship patterns. When tracking is employed, upper-track students receive a higher quantity and quality of instruction from more qualified instructors who utilize a greater variety of instructional techniques" (p. 150).

During the last two decades of the 20th century, several significant changes have occurred in the Japanese educational system. First, government leaders and educational scholars asserted that the emphasis on entrance examinations combined with the demands on students to learn large volumes of content had actually dulled students' interest in learning (Bjork and Tsuneyoshi 2005). Educational reforms began in the 1970s, reducing the amount of material covered by teachers, incorporating more student-centered and integrated learning in the classroom, and reducing the intensity of student learning and testing. MEXT referred to these reform policies as *yutori kyoiku* or reduced-intensity reforms. Response to the reforms has been mixed, with some applauding the new student-centered emphasis of the curriculum but others worrying about the impact of a "watered down" curriculum (Bjork and Tsuneyoshi 2005).

Second, admissions into Japan's universities have become less competitive. As its population of 18-year-olds has decreased by more than half a million since 1992, Japan's universities have had trouble recruiting students. According to Rie Mori (2002), entrance examinations were expected to identify the best students for university education, but this is no longer necessary because there are more universities to accept students who do not score well on the exams. The universalization of higher education in Japan has led to a greater number of students entering universities who are not as high achieving as students of the past. Japanese higher education must figure out how to educate students with a broader range of learning styles and abilities (Mori 2002).

How has tracking been part of your educational experience? Does tracking take place in your college?

Table 8.3 Estimated number of illiterate adults (age 15+) and percentage who are female, 2005–2014

Country	Total Number (in Thousands)	Female (%)
Sub-Saharan Africa	181,950	61.2
Arab States	47,603	66.2
Central Asia	290	62.7
East Asia and the Pacific	89,478	70.5
South and West Asia	407,021	63.8
Latin America and the Caribbean	35,614	55.1
Central and Eastern Europe	4,919	77.5

SOURCE: United Nations Educational, Scientific and Cultural Organization 2013.

documents). A total of 43% of all Americans are estimated to be at these two levels. In contrast, 57% of Americans were categorized at the higher levels—intermediate (able to complete moderately challenging literacy tasks, e.g., refer to a reference document for information) and proficient (able to read and integrate various materials) (ProLiteracy Worldwide 2006).

The U.S. Department of Education reports that individuals at higher levels of literacy are more likely to be employed, to work more weeks per year, and to earn higher wages than are individuals with lower levels of literacy (Kirsch et al. 2002). Education increases an individual's literacy skills, which determine educational success. Basic academic skills influence such educational outcomes as high school completion, college enrollment, persistence in college, field of study, and type of degree obtained (Sum et al. 2002).

Although the United States spends more per capita on education than other high-income countries, our literacy scores are below average in a world comparison. In 2013, the Organization for Economic Cooperation and Development (OECD) compared literacy scores for native-born U.S. adults and residents in 22 other OECD member countries. OECD measured a set of necessary work skills related to information and communication technologies, which it labeled technology-rich environments. The literacy scores of U.S. adults ranked 16th out of 23 countries in literacy proficiency (decoding written words, interpreting and evaluating complex texts), 21st in numeracy proficiency (solving math problems), and 14th in problem solving (solving personal or work problems using a computer). The nations that scored higher were Japan, Finland, Netherlands, and Sweden. The report revealed that socioeconomic background had a stronger effect on proficiency levels in the U.S. than in other OECD countries.

Inequality in Educational Access and Achievement

Social Class and Education

Socioeconomic status is one of the most powerful predictors of student achievement (College Entrance Examination Board 1999). The likelihood of dropping out of high school is five times higher among students from lower-income families than among their peers in high-income families (Laird et al. 2006). Dropping out of high school is related to negative economic outcomes. For example, the 2010 median income of persons who had not completed a high school degree was $20,241. In contrast, the median income of persons who had completed at least a high school credential (e.g., general equivalency diploma) was $30,627 (U.S. Census Bureau 2012).

Students from lower-income homes or who have parents with little formal education score lower on average than students from families earning more than $100,000 per year or who have parents with a bachelor's degree or higher. In 2013, the average critical reading SAT score was 434 for a student with a family income below $20,000 versus 522 for a student with a family income of $100,000 to $120,000. The highest average score was 565 for students with a family income greater than $200,000. For students with parental education less than a high school diploma, the average critical reading score was 423. In contrast, students with parental education of at least a bachelor's degree had an average score of 523. For students with parental education of a graduate degree, the average critical reading score was 560 (College Board 2013).

High-income families can invest more time and resources into their children's cognitive development than lower-income families; high-income families have greater socioeconomic and social resources that benefit their children than lower-income families; and, according to Douglas Downey, Paul von Hippel, and Beckett Broh (2004), the primary source of inequality between children of high and low socioeconomic status lies in the children's disparate nonschool (home and neighborhood) environments. High-income families can invest more time and resources into their children's cognitive development than lower-income families; high-income families have greater socioeconomic and social resources that benefit their children than lower-income families (Reardon 2011).

Research suggests that spending time in novel environments (not at home or at school and not being cared for by a parent or day care provider) and in particular activities (interactive play) has educational benefits. When Meredith Phillips (2011) examined the socioeconomic differences in how parents spend their time with children, she found that high-income children spend about 1,300 more hours in novel places between birth and six years of age than low-income children. For example, high-income infants and toddlers spend an additional four and a half hours per week in indoor and outdoor recreation facilities, at church, or at businesses when compared with infants and toddlers from low-income families. After children begin school, the time in novel contexts continues as high-income children and children with college-educated mothers spend three more hours per week in

Remedying the Achievement Gap

IN FOCUS

CONTROLLING THE COST OF HIGHER EDUCATION

A college education is still part of the American Dream. Sallie Mae, a financial service company specializing in education, annually releases a national report on how college tuition is managed by parents and their students. In the 2012 report, Sallie Mae and Ipsos (an independent marketing research company) found that 83% of college students and parents strongly agreed that higher education is an investment in the future, college is needed now more than ever (70%), and college is the path to earning more money (69%).

But the truth is that most young adults do not attend a four-year college. According to Paul Taylor and his colleagues (2011), the main barrier to higher education is financial. Among individuals 18 to 34 years old who are not in school and do not have a bachelor's degree, about two thirds report that they are not continuing their education in order to support a family; more than half say they prefer to work and make money (Taylor et al. 2011).

In his 2012 State of the Union speech, Barack Obama called on the federal government, states, colleges, and universities to promote access and affordability in higher education. Obama proposed educational and legislative reforms tying federal campus aid to responsible tuition policies. Aiming primarily at state colleges and universities, Obama outlined financial incentives for schools to contain their tuition, enhance teaching and learning, and increase affordability and graduation rates (White House 2012).

The president's announcement received a mixture of praise and caution from educational leaders and college groups (Field 2012). David Warren (2012), director of the National Association of Independent Colleges and Universities, said,

> The collective challenge facing the nation is to make college more affordable, without losing our position of having the best higher education system in the world. . . . The answer is not going to come from more federal controls on colleges or states, by telling families to judge the value of an education by the amount young graduates earn in the first few years after they graduate.

Warren, along with other academic leaders, warned about the unintended consequences of Obama's proposals—reducing educational quality, cutting back essential student services, and disproportionately harming schools that serve larger numbers of at-risk students (Field 2012).

Sallie Mae and Ipsos (2012) report that, in 2012, families adjusted how they paid for college in three ways. First, parents cut their contributions from income and savings. For 2012, parents spent an average of $5,955 from their income and savings, down from $6,664 in 2011. Second, fewer families utilized scholarships—35% in 2012 compared with 45% in 2011. Some of this decline is attributed to colleges reducing the amount of scholarships that they are able to offer. Finally, students paid more out of pocket through their savings and income and borrowing more in 2012 than in previous years. In 2012, students contributed 18% of the total cost of college through borrowing compared with 15% the previous year and 14% in 2008–2010.

Are finances the only barrier to higher education? What other barriers can you identify?

novel places than low-income children or children in less-educated families. Phillips hypothesizes that exposure to novel contexts is directly related to income, as families with higher incomes have more money to spend on novel-context activities and settings.

What Does It Mean to Me?

What other reasons might explain someone dropping out of school? Is dropping out of school a personal trouble or a public issue?

In research conducted by the Public Agenda organization (Johnson et al. 2009), the number-one reason students gave for leaving college is that they had to simultaneously balance work and school. College dropouts were less likely to report being bored or not enjoying their classes as the reason why they quit. More than half of those who left school identified the "need to work and make money" and the stress related to juggling both. Most students did not receive financial assistance from their families or from their schools. Public Agenda researchers suggest that today's college students are not leading the stereotypical college life of balancing classes and weekend parties; instead, they are balancing classes with working to pay rent.

What Does It Mean to Me?

Peter Sacks (2009) observes how our educational system, despite the promise of equal opportunity, is profoundly stratified. There is a growing concentration of lower- and working-class students in community colleges, while middle- and upper-class students are more likely to attend four-year colleges and universities. How would you describe the class composition of your school? Does it recruit or cater to a particular social class? How does this compare with other colleges or universities in your area?

Gender and Education

In the fall of 2013, 11.7 million women and 8.9 million men enrolled in undergraduate programs. In postbaccalaureate programs, there were 1.7 million females and 1.2 million males (U.S. Department of Education, National Center for Education Statistics 2014). Women represent a 57% majority in higher education (college or university) enrollment. In all measures—percentage of high school graduates completing college preparatory curriculum, percentage of high school graduates immediately enrolling in college, and total higher education enrollment—women rank higher than men. The American Council on Education (ACE; King 2006) attributes the increasing enrollment and degree attainment figures for women to the rising share of young women taking college preparatory courses during the 1990s and 2000s. Yet ACE concludes that there is "no consensus on the causes of the gender gap and little comprehensive empirical research upon which to base firm conclusions" (King 2006:20). That other industrialized countries are experiencing similar educational gains for women suggests that this phenomenon is not just an American one.

However, there is still some traditional gender segregation by major (refer to Figure 8.5). Men receive most bachelor's degrees in Math, Computer Science, and Engineering (78.6%), while the percentage of women graduates is highest in the health professions (85.1%) and education (79.5%).

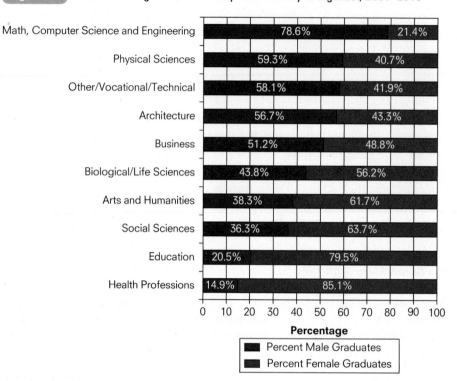

Figure 8.5 Bachelor's degrees conferred by field of study and gender, 2009–2010

SOURCE: American Council on Education 2012.

The continued domination of men in the science, technology, engineering, and mathematics (STEM) fields remains a concern. Though gender differences in advanced-level math and science course enrollment have disappeared (Riegle-Crumb, Farkas, and Muller 2006) and girls are earning slightly higher grades in math and science classes than boys (U.S. Department of Education 2007), fewer women than men pursue these majors in college (Hill, Corbett, and St. Rose 2010).

A study by Linda K. Silverman (1986) suggests that females will eventually achieve less than males because they are gradually conditioned by "powerful environmental influences" such as the educational system, peers, and parents to believe that they are less capable than males. A "hidden curriculum" perpetuates gender inequalities in math and science courses. This curriculum takes the form of differential treatment in the classroom, where boys tend to dominate class discussion and monopolize their instructors' time and attention, whereas girls are silenced and their insecurities reinforced (Linn and Kessel 1996). Research suggests that girls, especially gifted ones, fail to achieve their potential because of lower expectations of success, the attribution of any success to chance, and the belief that success will lead to negative social consequences (Silverman 1986).

Catherine Hill, Christianne Corbett, and Andresse St. Rose (2010) confirmed the effects of the social structure and the social environment on girls' achievements and interests in science and math. The researchers identified how girls and women face persistent messages that STEM studies and successes are incompatible with traditional gender roles and expectations. Two negative stereotypes—girls are not as good as boys in math, and scientific work is better suited to boys and men— affect women's and girls' performance and aspirations in math and science. Hill and her colleagues recommend exposing girls to successful female role models to help counter these negative stereotypes.

Ethnicity/Race and Education

About 3.4 million students entered kindergarten in U.S. public schools last fall and already . . . researchers foresee widely different futures for them. Whether they are White, Black, Hispanic, Native American or Asian American will, to a large extent, predict their success in school. (Johnson and Viadero 2000:1)

In the mid-1990s, underrepresented minorities received less than 13% of all the bachelor's degrees awarded (College Entrance Examination Board 1999). The College Entrance Examination Board noted that in the latter half of the 1990s, only

Mario Tama/Getty Images

The 2012 graduation rate for first-time full-time undergraduate students who were first enrolled in fall 2006 was 59% (U.S. Deparment of Education, National Center for Education Statistics 2014). Graduation rates were highest for Asian (70.6%) students, followed by White (62.5%), Hispanic (51.9%), and Black (40.2%) students.

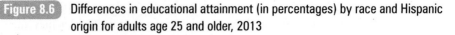

Figure 8.6 Differences in educational attainment (in percentages) by race and Hispanic origin for adults age 25 and older, 2013

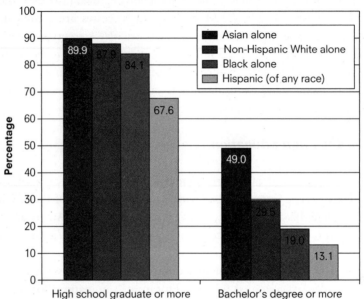

SOURCE: U.S. Census Bureau 2014.

small percentages of Black, Hispanic, and Native American high school seniors in the National Assessment of Educational Progress test samples had scores "typical" of students who are well prepared for college. Few students in these groups had scores indicating academic skills required for the most selective colleges or universities.

Persistent academic achievement gaps remain between Black, Hispanic, and Native American students and their White and Asian peers (refer to Figure 8.6 for differences in educational attainment). For example, among the 2013 college-bound students, White and Asian students had the highest average SAT critical reading score: 527 for Whites and 521 for Asians (College Board 2013). Lower critical reading scores were reported for Black students (431), Mexican or Mexican American students (449), and other Hispanic or Latino students (450). The same pattern exists for SAT mathematics and writing scores.

By 2015, there will be large increases in the number of Latino and Asian American youth, a substantial growth in the number of African American students, and a slight drop in the number of White students. The challenges to our educational system will only increase if demographic predictions hold true. Current educational gaps among racial and ethnic categories have the potential to grow into larger sources of inequality and social conflict.

Ethnicity/race, along with poverty, defines major sources of disadvantage in educational outcomes (Maruyama 2003). For example, among Latino families, poverty produces significant educational disadvantages: Parents may work multiple jobs, may not have the time to spend reading or going over homework with their children, and may not have the skills to read to their children. Economics also plays a role in dropout decisions. To support their families, Latino/a teens may leave school for a paying job. The power of parental and peer influence on Latino/a educational attainment has also been recognized. Parents may have expectations for their children that conflict with school expectations or requirements (American Association of University Women 2001).

According to Claude Steele and Joshua Aronson (1995), the pressure to conform to an image or a stereotype is so strong that it can actually impair intellectual performance. Steele and his colleagues tested the effects of a stereotype threat among African American (Steele 1997; Steele and Aronson 1995) and female college students (Spencer, Steele, and Quinn 1999). The **stereotype threat** is the risk of confirming in oneself a characteristic that is part of a negative stereotype about one's group. The threat is situational, present only when a person can be judged, be treated in terms of the group, or self-fulfill negative stereotypes about the group (and the self) (Spencer et al. 1999). In their studies, Steele and his colleagues investigated the effect of the stereotype that African Americans and women have lower academic abilities than do White or male students.

It doesn't matter if the individual actually believes the stereotype; if the stereotype demeans something of importance, such as one's intellectual ability, the threat can be disrupting enough to impair intellectual performance (Steele and Aronson 1995). Subjects were compared in test-taking situations using Graduate Record Examinations (GRE), Scholastic Assessment Test (SAT), or American College Test (ACT) sample questions. In all study conditions where the tests were represented as affected by gender or race, African American and female students underperformed their comparison group. In situations where the stereotype threat was moderated (where subjects were not told that the tests produced gender differences or where subjects were not asked to report their race on the examination form), African American and female students performed as well as White or male students.

Violence and Harassment in Schools

School violence can be characterized on a continuum that includes aggressive behavior, harassment, property crimes, threats, and physical assault (Flannery 1997). Despite the public concern over school homicides, the percentage of youth homicides occurring at school is less than 2% of the total number of youth homicides. Victims of school violence may include students, teachers, and staff members. For the 2010–2011 school year, there were 1,336 homicides of youth ages 5 to 18 years. Eleven of those homicides occurred at school; the remaining 1,325 deaths occurred away from school. There were a total of 31 student, staff, and non-student school-associated violent deaths for the same year (Robers et al. 2014).

The deadliest U.S. incident took place in April 2007 at Virginia Polytechnic Institute and State University, where 33 students and faculty were killed by a student.

Stereotype threat:
The risk of confirming in oneself a characteristic that is a negative stereotype

Preventing Violence

© ZUMA Press, Inc / Alamy

According to Hill and Kearl (2011) 48% of all students experience some sort of sexual harassment during their school lives.

The deadliest international incident occurred in 1996 when a gunman killed 16 primary school students and one teacher, as well as himself, in Scotland. Though schools have been characterized as "battlegrounds" where both teachers and students fear for their safety (Kingery et al. 1993), they remain a safe place for students, the risk of a violent death being less than 1 in 2 million (Dinkes et al. 2009).

The 2013 national school-based Youth Risk Behavior Surveillance System (YRBSS) survey conducted annually by the Centers for Disease Control and Prevention (CDC) found that nationwide about 7.1% of students had missed more than one day of school because they felt unsafe at school or on their way to or from school (CDC 2014). Among all students, 5.2% said they carried a weapon (a gun, knife, or club) on the school campus. About 6.9% of all students reported being threatened or injured with a weapon on school property, and about 8.1% of students had been in a physical fight on school property (CDC 2014).

Lesbian, gay, bisexual, and transgender (LGBT) youth are subject to verbal and physical harassment in high schools and middle schools. As reported by the Gay, Lesbian and Straight Education Network's 2011 National School Climate Survey, 63.5% of LGBT youth reported feeling unsafe in school because of their sexual orientation (Kosciw et al. 2012). About 40% had experienced some form of physical harassment because of their sexual orientation; 18.3% had been

Sexual Assault on Campus

physically assaulted for the same reason. Almost 82% of the surveyed students reported being verbally harassed in school the past year. The majority of students who had been harassed or assaulted did not report the incident to school staff or administrators. LGBT students' experience with harassment negatively affected their school attendance, their academic performance, and, ultimately, their college aspirations. Students who experienced more frequent harassment, either verbal or physical, were more likely to indicate that they were not planning to go on to college than were students who did not experience the same type of harassment (Kosciw et al. 2012).

The extent of sexual harassment in schools has been documented by the Educational Foundation of the American Association of University Women (AAUW) (Hill and Kearl 2011). According to its 2010–2011 report, 48% of students experience some form of sexual harassment during their school lives. Girls are more likely than boys to experience sexual harassment. How is sexual harassment defined in schools? The definition offered by the Equal Employment Opportunity Commission (2001) under Title VII of the Civil Rights Act of 1964 reads,

> Unwanted sexual advances, requests for sexual favors, and other verbal or physical conduct of a sexual nature constitutes sexual harassment when submission or rejection of this conduct explicitly or implicitly affects an individual's employment, unreasonably interferes with an individual's work performance or creates an intimidating, hostile or offensive work environment.

In schools, sexual harassment can include such behaviors as sexual messages written on walls or in locker rooms, sexual rumors, being flashed or mooned, being brushed up against in a sexual way, or being shown sexual pictures or material of sexual content (Fineran 2002) and includes online harassment (e.g., receiving unwelcome comments or photos through texts, being the subject of sexual rumors or information) (Hill and Kearl 2011). Sexual harassment of students has serious consequences, including mental health symptoms (such as loss of appetite, disturbances in sleep, feelings of isolation, and sadness) and school performance difficulties (Fineran 2002).

COMMUNITY, POLICY, AND SOCIAL ACTION

As a nation, we support the principle of educational excellence and, along with it, the assumption of educational opportunity for all, but in reality, we have an educational system that embraces these ideas yet fails to achieve them (Ravitch 1997). The educational experiences of poor and minority students fundamentally conflict with the principles of public education, namely, that public schools should provide these children with opportunities so that all children can succeed as a result of hard work and talent (Maruyama 2003). Reformers argue that school choice, standardized testing, and school vouchers are improving our educational system. Critics argue that these strategies threaten to erode an already-weak public school structure. There is a deepening chasm between what the American public deems important in education (safety, skills, discipline) and the goals of the reform movement (access, standardization, multiculturalism) (Finn 1997). Although we have not completely abandoned our public educational system, we still have not found a way to agree on what is appropriate or essential to save it.

Policy Responses—The Basis for Educational Reform
The Educate America Act of 1994 and NCLB

Providing fuel to the reform movement have been congressional acts passed in 1994 and 2001. Although they were adopted under presidents from different political parties, both congressional acts provide strong support for school reform and, along with it, changes to our educational system.

The Goals 2000: Educate America Act introduced the notion of "standards-based reform" at the state and community levels. This 1994 act, signed into law by President Clinton, provided the grounds for sweeping reform at all levels and from all angles: curriculum and instruction, professional development, assessment and accountability, school and leadership organization, and parental and community involvement. However, school reform hinged on the use of student performance standards and the creation of the National Education Standards and Improvement Council. A summary of the act reported, "Performance standards clearly define what student work should look like [at] different stages of academic progress and for diverse learners" ("Goals 2000" 1998:14). The act established performance and content standards in math, English, science, and social studies, and it encouraged participation from the entire community—local officials, educators, parents, and community leaders—in raising academic standards and achievement.

When George W. Bush signed the NCLB Act, he approved a plan that increased federal pressure on states to pursue a standards-based reform agenda. Under NCLB, states are required to institute a system of standardized testing for all public school students in Grades 3 to 8 and high school, about 45 million tests annually. Each state must have a plan for adequate yearly progress (AYP) toward the goal of academic proficiency for all students, a 100% rate regardless of economic status, ethnicity/race, gender, or disability, by 2014.

The more controversial elements of the act signed by George W. Bush included the provision for public school choice and charter schools. The act provided support to permit children in chronically failing public schools to transfer to other schools with better academic records. The bill also provided for annual testing of students in reading and math in the third to eighth grades, which would establish academic records for comparison. If there were no improvements in test results in two years, parents would have the option to move their children to another school. In such an event, the school district would be required to pay for the child's transportation to a better school, and the failing school would lose the per-pupil payment. Critics argued that such school choice provisions would work only if there were schools to choose from within a district and if there was room in these schools. The law does not provide school leaders with the means to create new slots for students (Schemo 2002).

Although expressing commitment to the basic intent of NCLB, many state leaders and educators expressed frustration in implementing the act's requirements and achieving its goals. In particular, school administrators and educators were critical of a key feature of NCLB: the one-size-fits-all accountability standard that assumes that all schools, districts, and groups of students will demonstrate progress according to the standardized measures. The standards, said critics, seriously compromise the abilities of schools to address the unique educational needs of special education students, low-income and minority students, and students with limited English proficiency.

In their 2010 proposal to reauthorize NCLB, the Obama administration set a new educational goal: "Every student should graduate from high school ready for college or a career regardless of their income, race, ethnic or language background, or disability status" by 2020 (U.S. Department of Education 2010:3). The proposal identified four policy and programming areas: improving teaching and principal effectiveness, providing information to families to evaluate and improve their children's schools and to educators to help improve student learning, implementing college- and career-ready standards and assessments, and improving student learning and achievement in the lowest-performing schools by providing support and effective interventions. In 2012, the Obama administration granted NCLB waivers to 24 states, in exchange for adopting the administration's educational standards and a new focus on accountability and teacher effectiveness. These states will need to set new performance targets for students and schools but will not be sanctioned as they were under the old law for schools failing or for not making adequate progress. More states will seek a waiver under the new plan (Hu 2012). Many characterized this as the beginning of the end of the NCLB era.

Since 2010, 43 states have voluntarily adopted a set of college and career-ready standards for English language arts/literacy and math for all kindergarten through 12th-grade students. The Common Core State Standards (CCSS) propose clear and consistent standards for what a child should know and be able to do at each grade level, allowing school districts to design their own curricula and teachers to implement their own teaching methods. CCSS encourages students to demonstrate and learn critical thinking skills, moving away from memorization to a deeper understanding of material. However, critics argue that the standards do not consider the diversity of the U.S. student population and fail to consider the differences in student learning. As of December 2014, several states that adopted CCSS have opted out.

National polls suggest that parents, teachers, and students have grown tired and suspicious of high-stakes standardized testing (Kirp 2014).

Promoting Educational Opportunities— Head Start and Prekindergarten

Called the most popular and most romantic of the War on Poverty efforts (Traub 2000), Head Start remains the largest early childhood program. More than 30 million poor and at-risk preschoolers have been served under Head Start since 1965. Head Start began with a simple model of service: organized preschool centers. At these centers, programs focused on the "whole child," examining and encouraging physical and mental health. Integrating strong parental involvement, Head Start provided a unique program targeting child development and school preparedness. Over the years, the Head Start program expanded to serve school-age children, high school students, pregnant women, and Head Start parents. In 1994, amendments to the Head Start Act established Early Head Start (EHS) services targeting economically disadvantaged families with children 3 years old or younger. EHS serves both children and their families through a comprehensive service plan that promotes child development and family self-sufficiency (Wall et al. 2000).

The effectiveness of Head Start programming, particularly the educational component, has been the focus of public and government debate (Washington and Oyemade Bailey 1995). Early program research and evaluation efforts were spotty, with the major findings pointing to short-term or "fade out" gains in student learning and testing (Washington and Oyemade Bailey 1995). In its 2005 impact study report, HHS compared the performance of Head Start children with non–Head Start children from fall 2002 through summer 2005. For Head Start children in both age groups, small to moderate positive effects were found in prereading, prewriting, and vocabulary skills. Both groups also had significantly better access to health care; in addition, the 3-year-olds reported significantly better overall health than did the non–Head Start group. Positive parenting practices (e.g., reading to one's child) were also documented for children in both Head Start age groups (U.S. Department of Health and Human Services 2005). Head Start was reauthorized in 2007 with increased funding for Migrant and Seasonal Head Start and the Indian Head Start programs. The reauthorization also increased educational requirements for Head Start teachers.

As of 2013, there were 53 state-funded preschool programs in 40 states and in the District of Columbia (Barnett et al. 2013). These programs are funded, controlled, and administered by the state, serving children ages 3 and 4. About 1.3 million children attended state-funded pre-K in 2013. Pre-K programs have gained popularity as an alternative to Head Start, promising a preschool experience for all children, regardless of economic need. Research indicates that effective, high-quality pre-K programming can improve the academic and social-emotional outcomes for students, with some effects lasting into middle and high school.

The first universal prekindergarten (or pre-K) program was established in Georgia in 1996. The program is open to all 4-year-olds regardless of household income. In their comparison between Head Start and Georgia pre-K students, Gary Henry, Craig Gordon, and Dana Rickman (2006) concluded that economically disadvantaged pre-K students were better prepared for kindergarten than children who attended Head Start. Pre-K students performed significantly higher in picture-word vocabulary, recognition of letters and words, and oral and written skills at the beginning of kindergarten than their Head Start peers.

Mentoring, Supporting, and Valuing Networks

Women and Girls

In its 1992 report, the AAUW called on local communities and schools to promote programs that encourage and support girls studying science, technology, engineering, and mathematics (STEM). Studies indicate that most girls and women learn best in cooperative, rather than competitive, learning activities. With seed money from the W. K. Kellogg Foundation, the AAUW Educational Foundation initiated the Girls Can! Community Coalitions Project in 1996. The project funded 10 community-based projects that encouraged schools and community groups to improve girls' educational opportunities.

AAUW continues its support of STEM projects through the National Girls Collaborative Project established in 2005. The National Girls Collaborative Project goals include maximizing access to shared resources within projects and with public and private organizations interested in expanding girls' STEM participation, strengthening the capacity of existing and evolving projects by sharing promising research and program models, and using the collaboration of individual girl-serving STEM programs to create the tipping point for gender equity in STEM (National Girls Collaborative Project 2014).

Fourteen regional collaborative sites operate in California, Florida, Massachusetts, the mid-Atlantic, and the Northwest. Small mini-grants help fund tutoring, career days, field trips, and special events to expose girls and boys to STEM education and careers. One such grant helped fund California State Summer School for Mathematics and Science (COSMOS), a month-long residential academic experience for top California high school students in science and mathematics. Students reside at one of four University of California campuses—Davis, Irvine, San Diego, or Santa Cruz—while taking COSMOS classes in their areas of interest.

Mentoring can also begin in one's own community and among friends. In 1996, Michele Deane noticed that a number of girls in her Boyle Heights (Los Angeles, California) neighborhood did not have anything to do after school. She created a youth organization for local Mexican American and Latin American girls and

VOICES IN THE COMMUNITY

WENDY KOPP

Wendy Kopp's vision for Teach for America began as her senior undergraduate thesis. This Princeton graduate is the youngest and only female to receive the university's Woodrow Wilson Award, the highest honor bestowed to alumni. In the following excerpt from her book *One Day, All Children: The Unlikely Triumph of Teach for America and What I Learned Along the Way*, Kopp (2001) explains how Teach for America began with an idea:

Princeton University was not the most likely place to become concerned about what's wrong in education, but it made me aware of students' unequal access to the kind of educational excellence I had previously taken for granted. I got to know students who had attended public schools in urban areas—thoughtful, smart people—as well as students who attended the East Coast prep schools. I saw the first group struggle to meet the academic demands of Princeton and the second group refer to it as a "cake walk." Clearly at Princeton I could not glimpse the depths of educational inequity in our country, but the disparities I did see got me thinking. It's really not fair, I thought, that where you're born in our country plays a role in determining your educational prospects.

BRIAN SNYDER/REUTERS/Newscom

Wendy Kopp was the first to receive the John F. Kennedy New Frontier Award, an honor presented to Americans under the age of 40 for their commitment to public service.

In an effort to figure out what could be done about this problem, I organized a conference about the issue. At this time I led an organization called the Foundation for Student Communication. . . . So in November of my senior year, my colleagues and I gathered together fifty students and business leaders from across the country to propose action plans for improving our educational system. . . .

women, beginning with a group of her friends, that now serves more than 200 girls and women each year. According to Deane, her organization, Girls Today, Women Tomorrow, created a state of consciousness for thinking "bigger":

What do I want to do? Who can I become with the support of everyone around me? It's a state of consciousness coming from the world around you instead of seeing only the obstacles. Once they saw other people doing it, they started doing it for their friends, for the younger kids growing up. (Quoted in Wiland and Bell 2006:187)

 Teach for America

At one point during a discussion group, after hearing yet another student express interest in teaching, I had a sudden idea: Why didn't this country have a national teacher corps of top recent college graduates who would commit to teach in urban and rural public schools? A teacher corps would provide another option to the two-year corporate training programs and grad schools. It would speak to all college seniors who were searching for something meaningful to do with our lives. . . .

The more I thought about it, the more convinced I became that this simple idea was potentially very powerful. If top recent college graduates devoted two years to teaching in public schools, they could have a real impact on the lives of disadvantaged kids. Because of their energy and commitment, they would be relentless in their efforts to ensure their students achieved. They would throw themselves into their jobs, working investment-banking hours in classrooms instead of skyscrapers on Wall Street. They would question the way things are and fight to do what was right for children.

Beyond influencing children's lives directly, a national teacher corps could produce a change in the very consciousness of our country. . . .

In the end, I produced "A Plan and Argument for the Creation of a National Teacher Corps," which looked at the educational needs in urban and rural areas, the growing idealism and spirit of service among college students, and the interest of the philanthropic sector in improving education. The thesis presented an ambitious plan: In our first year, the corps would inspire thoughts of graduating college students to apply. We would then select, train, and place five hundred of them as teachers in five or six urban and rural areas across the country. (pp. 5–6, 10)

In its first year, Teach for America received 2,500 applications, of which, as Kopp planned, 500 were selected and trained for two years of teaching. Since then, more than 37,000 teachers have been placed or are currently placed in more than 50 urban and rural sites throughout the United States. Corps members' salaries and health benefits are paid directly by the school districts they are placed in.

Kopp adapted the Teach for America model to a global model, cofounding Teach for All in 2007.

What social problem does Teach for America address? What evidence is necessary to determine if it is an effective strategy?

SOURCE: Kopp 2001:5–6, 10. Published by PublicAffairs, a member of Perseus Books Group.

The volunteer program includes fitness activities, a computer lab, video shooting and editing classes, and a community garden. The garden serves as a connection to the environment and the girls' Latin culture and raises their awareness about the kind and quality of food they consume. Program graduates return to the program and serve as mentors and volunteers. Ginette Sanchez credits the program for her academic and life successes: "I always thought that I wouldn't have a future. Now that I have positive role models, I'm going to college and I'm being positive by thinking that I'm going to be someone in life as well" (quoted in Wiland and Bell 2006:189).

. . . .

What Does It Mean to Me?

What type of learning experiences or opportunities supported your learning in middle school or high school? How did these experiences lead you to college?

. . . .

LGBT Students

The best estimate of the number of LGBT students is about 5% to 6% of the total student population (Human Rights Watch 2001). LGBT youth have been a driving force behind creating change in their schools and communities. Support groups and organized student activities have emerged in states such as California, Illinois, and Washington, providing valuable support to LGBT teens and their friends and families (Bohan and Russell 1999; Human Rights Watch 2001).

One such student group is the Gay–Straight Alliance (GSA) in East High School in Salt Lake City, Utah. As Janis Bohan and Glenda M. Russell (1999) chronicle, a group of students proposed creating a student alliance to provide a support network for LGBT students and their heterosexual friends in October 1995. In response to the students' proposal, the school board and the state legislature banned all noncurricular clubs rather than allow the GSA. The club continued to meet, paying rental and insurance fees for the use of school facilities. According to Bohan and Russell, students indicated how the club had a positive impact on their lives. The alliance served as a safe refuge, decreasing their feelings of isolation and vulnerability, students said, and they reported decreases in substance abuse, depression, suicidal impulses, truancy, and conflict with parents. The straight student members also reported positive effects. In September 2000, Utah's Salt Lake City School District Board of Education voted to permit noncurricular student groups to meet on school grounds, reversing its 1995 decision against the GSA (Human Rights Watch 2001). According to the Gay, Lesbian and Straight Education Network, there are more than 4,000 registered clubs for LGBT students and their friends throughout the United States.

Schools are allowing students to participate in the national Day of Silence in April. A vow of silence for the day symbolizes the silencing effect of antigay harassment and bullying. The event was founded in 1996 by students at the University of Virginia. In 2012, the day was observed in 9,000 schools in over 70 countries. Although some religious and parent groups object to what they consider "promotion" of homosexuality, most agree that it is important to create and promote a safe school environment for LGBT youth.

Antiviolence and Antibullying Programs in Schools

As awareness of school violence has increased, so have the calls for effective means of prevention (Aber, Brown, and Henrich 1999). The current focus is less on reacting to school violence and more on promoting school safety through prevention, planning, and preparation (Shaw 2001).

The largest and longest-running school program focusing on conflict resolution and intergroup relations is the Resolving Conflict Creatively Program (RCCP). Initiated in 1985 in New York City by the local chapter of Educators for Social Responsibility, the program is a research-based K–12 school program in social and emotional learning. RCCP is in 400 schools nationwide, serving 6,000 teachers and more than 175,000 students. RCCP begins with the assumption that aggression and violent behavior are learned and therefore can be reduced through education. The program teaches children conflict resolution skills, promotes intercultural understanding, and provides models and opportunities for positive ways of dealing with conflict and differences. For kindergarten students, puppets and other objects are used to illustrate how conflict can be resolved by talking rather than hitting. RCCP includes training for teachers, parents, administrators, and school staff.

An evaluation of the New York City programs indicated that students who received RCCP instruction developed more positively than did students without any RCCP exposure. RCCP students were more prosocial, perceived their world in a less hostile way, saw violence as unacceptable, and chose nonviolent ways to resolve conflict. Reading and math scores were higher for RCCP students, especially those who had 25 RCCP lessons over the school year. Evaluators concluded that the RCCP-intensive children were more able to focus on academics when there was less conflict with peers (Shaw 2001).

The Safe Schools Improvement Act and the Student Non-Discrimination Act were introduced in Congress in 2011 in an effort to support safe schools and enrich the learning environment. Both bills would require schools that accept federal funding to track, create policy regarding, and demonstrate reduction in bullying and harassment incidents. Bullying and harassment data would be reported biennially. While ensuring the safety and well-being of all students, the bills were applauded for their focus on students with disabilities and LGBT students.

With the increase in school violence, more attention has been given to school safety through security screening or police–school liaison projects. Schools are more aware of the links between safety and violence and other student behaviors such as dropout rates, academic failures, bullying, and suicide (Shaw 2001). Violence prevention programs have become common throughout the country with the primary focus on early education. In addition to the RCCP, national initiatives include the Office of Safe and Healthy Students and the Safe Schools/Healthy Students Initiative. Regional initiatives include the PeaceBuilders elementary program and Students Against Violence Everywhere. U.S. and international approaches focus more on school safety and less on school violence, use programs to serve students and the entire school population, develop school–community partnerships, and use evaluated program models (Shaw 2001). The most effective school-based violence prevention programs are those that include parental involvement and support, with parents backing school limits and consequences at home (Flannery 1997). Antiviolence programs have also been established on college and university campuses. As noted in Chapter 4, "Gender," schools receiving federal funding under Title IX are required to respond promptly and effectively to sexual violence against students.

Does Having a Choice Improve Education?

There is a new term now, *public school choice*. Data issued by the National Center for Education Statistics reveal that more parents are turning away from local public schools to private schools or charter schools (Zernike 2010). As of the 2011–2012 school year, 42 states and the District of Columbia have passed charter school legislation. There were 5,696 charter schools in operation from 2011 to 2012, with 2.1 million students enrolled (U.S. Department of Education, National Center for Education Statistics 2014). In the 2011–2012 school year, California enrolled the largest number of students in charter schools (413,000 students), followed by the District of Columbia (29,000 students).

Parents and children have two additional options within the public education system: magnet schools and charter schools. Magnet schools offer specialized educational programs from elementary school through high school. These schools are organized around a theme such as performing arts, science, technology, or business or around different instructional designs such as free (where students can direct their own education) or open schools (with informal classroom designs). Often, magnet schools are placed in racially isolated schools or neighborhoods to encourage students of other races to enroll. Magnet schools have been criticized for creating a two-tier system of education (Kahlenberg 2002).

Charter schools are nonsectarian public schools of choice that operate free from most state laws and local school board policies that apply to traditional public schools. Charter schools are funded with public funds, like public schools. A charter contract establishes the school's operation, usually limited to three to five years, detailing the school's mission and instructional goals, student population, educational outcomes, and assessment methods, along with a management and financial plan. These schools have grown in popularity since 1991, when Minnesota became the first state to pass an outcome-based school law. Charter schools are characterized by innovative teaching practices and accountability to students and families. If a school fails to meet its goals, it cannot be renewed under its charter.

School choice has become an even hotter topic with the idea of school vouchers. Simply stated, school vouchers allow the transfer of public school funds to support a student's transfer to a private school, which may include religious institutions. Supporters of school vouchers argue that the system would give parents more choice and freedom in school selection and would create incentives for school improvement (Good and Braden 2000; Kennedy 2001).

Opponents argue that vouchers would siphon money away from public schools, removing any ability to resolve the schools' problems, thus only increasing problems. Others argue that schooling is a public good and must be provided by the

SOCIOLOGY AT WORK

AFTERSCHOOL EDUCATION

Sergio Beltran—Class of 2010

Undergraduate Major: Sociology
Undergraduate Minor: Anthropology

Afterschool programs (ASPs) provide safe structured learning environments for students outside their regular school day. Typically, these programs operate for two to three hours following the end of the school day. ASPs may address one or many areas of student development: academic (tutoring, homework), enrichment (sports, art), service (volunteering), or vocational or college preparation. Approximately 20% to 30% of U.S. youth spend three to five afternoons a week in organized afterschool programs (Halpern 2003). ASPs are run by teachers or paraeducators (teaching assistants). Each state has its own educational and qualifying requirements to become a teacher or paraeducator.

Sergio is an afterschool tutoring and resource center coordinator in a local nonprofit organization. His work has many elements: coordinating homework tutoring, running structured programs for student groups, and forming and maintaining community partnerships with principals and counselors. The latest program he's implemented involves the exploration of social justice through heroes and "sheroes" (their word for woman heroes) from cultures that represent the center's community (e.g., Somali, Ethiopia, Southeast Asia, Latin America).

Sociology gave Sergio a new perspective, especially as a man of color:

I try to help my students think about how they fit into the world. Sociology is embodied in the work I do; for example, last year my staff and I focused on the content that we provide to our youth. Many of our families are immigrant and refugee families who live in a public/subsidized housing community. Our focus lately has been encouraging our youth to learn more about their racial identity and the empowerment of their culture. Last year we did a project on

Sergio Beltran

immigration and life experiences via story telling. The goal was to give our youth a safe and welcoming environment to share their life struggles, success, and concerns about coming to the United States.

Sergio offers several recommendations to current students:

[A mentor] helped me remain organized (in my final years) and understand careers I could pursue post graduation. I also think networking with colleagues on a regular basis would be an excellent idea. I wish I would have done this while still in school, rather than after. You can get a better understanding of where your colleagues are interning or maybe even working. You will have the opportunity to meet other people in the field as well and explore different options. Lastly, remain active in your community. I believe that being a big part of your communities opens doors for you later in life.

government to all children (Good and Braden 2000) equally and fairly. In June 2002, the U.S. Supreme Court ruled that school voucher programs did not violate any church-versus-state separation and upheld the constitutionality of using public funds to support private school systems (Bumiller 2002). Charter schools have been criticized for increasing income and racial school segregation. David Garcia (2008) documented how charter elementary school choosers enter charter schools that are more racially segregated than the schools they exited. High school choosers enter charter schools that are as racially segregated as or more integrated than the school districts they exited.

A number of education and social science researchers have noted the paradox of charter school reform: Although these schools provide parents and educators with an opportunity to more actively participate in the content, organization, and governance of public schools, charter schools often benefit people who are able to gather private resources (Stambach and Crow Becker 2006). According to researchers Salvatore Saporito and Annette Lareau (1999), if there is one consistent finding on school choice, it is that students from poorer families or with less educated parents are less likely to apply to or participate in public choice programs than are those from middle-class families. In addition, the researchers raise questions about the school selection process for White and African American families. Although school choice advocates suggest that promoting racial equality is one of the by-products of school choice, Saporito and Lareau found that White families as a group are more likely to avoid schools with higher percentages of Black students, whereas African American families show no such sensitivity to race. African American families in their study were likely to select schools with lower poverty rates. The researchers concluded that race was a persistent factor in the choice process. Their findings have been confirmed by other researchers, suggesting the need to examine the social and political processes by which race and class stratification are perpetuated (Stambach and Crow Becker 2006).

On the effectiveness of voucher programs and charter or magnet schools, the research remains mixed. The same issues concerning charter schools and voucher systems continue to be the subject of inquiry and debate: defining clear systems of accountability, establishing comparable performance standards, and ensuring the racial and economic integration of students.

Research conducted by the Center for Research on Education Outcomes (2013) at Stanford University concluded that charter school students in 26 states had greater learning gains in reading than their student peers in traditional public schools. In the National Charter School Study 2013, Center researchers also reported that there was no difference in learning gains in mathematics between charter school and traditional public school students. Charter school enrollment increased among poor, Black, and Hispanic students. The study concludes with the recommendation for policy makers to raise performance and accountability standards for charter schools and to hold these schools to higher standards.

CHAPTER REVIEW

8.1 Compare how the sociological perspectives examine the social problems related to education

Education's primary manifest function is to educate. The other manifest functions include personal development, proper socialization, and employment. Conflict theorists focus on the social and economic inequalities inherent in our educational system and how the system perpetuates these inequalities. Inequalities are based not just on social class but also on gender. Research reveals the persistent replication of gender relations in schools. From an interactionist perspective, the interaction between teachers and students reinforces the structure and inequalities of the classroom and the educational system.

8.2 Explain the process of educational tracking

Based on test results, students may be placed in different ability or occupational tracks. In the practice called tracking, advanced learners are separated from regular learners; students are identified as college bound versus work bound. Advocates of tracking argue that the practice increases educational effectiveness by allowing teachers to target students at their ability level; yet placing students in tracks has been controversial because of the presumed negative effects on some students.

8.3 Describe the educational inequalities related to social class, gender, and race and ethnicity

Socioeconomic status is one of the most powerful predictors of student achievement.

The likelihood of dropping out of high school is higher among students from lower-income families. Census data indicate slight differences in educational attainment for men and women. A hidden curriculum perpetuates gender inequalities in math and science courses. Persistent academic achievement gaps remain between Black, Hispanic, and Native American students and their White and Asian peers. Latino/a students are at greater risk of not finishing school than any other ethnic/racial group.

8.4 Summarize the history of U.S. educational reform

The focus on standards-based reform characterizes the modern educational reform movement. During their terms in office, Presidents Clinton, Bush, and Obama advocated educational policies that linked educational success with student test results. President Obama implemented performance standards related to career and college readiness.

8.5 Assess whether school choice has improved educational outcomes

The research is mixed on the effectiveness of school choice, as educators, scholars, and policy analysts debate the importance of defining clear systems of accountability, establishing comparable performance standards, and ensuring the racial and economic integration of students in any comparative analysis. Researchers have consistently identified how families with social and economic capital are able to take advantage of school options for their children.

KEY TERMS

cultural capital, 209

latent functions, 208

manifest functions, 208

organizational child, 209

social capital, 209

stereotype threat, 223

tracking, 212

STUDY QUESTIONS

1. Explain the shift in the educational standard from high school degree to college degree.

2. How does the educational system socialize children for adulthood and employment? Which theoretical perspectives support this argument?

3. Do you think tracking is a necessary educational practice? In your answer, consider evidence from Japan's tracking system.

4. Explain how social class, gender, and race/ethnicity contribute to educational inequality in the United States.

5. How effective are U.S. policies, including NCLB, in improving educational achievement?

6. Is public school choice a viable educational alternative? Why or why not?

$SAGE edge™

Sharpen your skills with SAGE edge at **edge.sagepub.com/leonguerrero5e**

SAGE edge provides a personalized approach to help you accomplish your coursework goals in an easy-to-use learning environment.

CHAPTER 6

Work and the Economy

News headlines in our country often refer to unemployment as a social problem. Between 2008 and 2009, the United States lost 8.4 million jobs, or about 6.1% of all payroll employment, the largest job loss since the Great Depression (Economic Policy Institute 2012). The Great Recession of 2007–2009 was referred to as "one of the most difficult financial and economic episodes in modern history" by former U.S. Federal Reserve chairman Ben Bernanke (2009).

Unemployment was no longer limited to people of color, immigrants, or the undereducated. Unique to the recession was its impact on the educated and the (formerly) middle class. Many more people, across different demographic groups, experienced the hardships of unemployment. For September 2014, the U.S. Bureau of Labor Statistics (2014a) reported that 9.3 million women and men were unemployed, an overall rate of 5.9%. This is the lowest unemployment rate since 2008. More than 146 million women and men were employed in the United States, about 63% of the population aged 16 years or older (U.S. Bureau of Labor Statistics 2014a).

After the recession ended, unemployment rates declined in Asia, in India, and throughout the European Union (EU). In the EU, the unemployment rate was 11.5% in August 2014, with rates being highest in Greece and Spain (Eurostat 2014). The 2013 U.S. median household income was estimated at $51,759 (DeNavas-Walt and Proctor 2014). The 2013 real household income was 8.0% lower than in 2007 ($54,489), the year before the recession.

 What Was the Great Recession?

AP Photo/The Flint Journal, Jake May

Though political and economic attention has shifted to job creation, economic stimulus packages, and unemployment, these aren't the only problems facing workers. For some, work remains a dangerous place, leading to injury or death. Others are victims of discrimination or harassment in the workplace. And for many men and women, even though they are employed, their paychecks do not provide a livable wage.

Beginning in 2012, hundreds of fast-food workers staged sit-ins or one-day work strikes around the country. Workers and protestors even appeared at McDonald's corporate headquarters in Illinois just in time for the 2014 annual shareholder meeting. Holding signs that read, "Low pay is not okay" and "We are worth more," workers and protest organizers were demanding a $15-per-hour wage and the right to unionize. On average, a McDonald's employee makes $8.25 per hour before taxes.

Work isn't just what we do; work is a basic and important social institution. It fuels our economy and provides economic support for individuals and families. Work is also important for our social and psychological well-being. Individuals find a sense of fulfillment and happiness, and for most, work provides a self-identity. Much of our social status is conferred through our occupation or the type of work we do. Because of the importance of work, problems related to work become categorized as social problems, as everyone's problem. In this chapter, we examine the work that we do, the social organization of work itself, and the social problems associated with our work and economy. We begin first with a review of the changing nature of work.

What Does It Mean to Me?

How did the recession affect you or any members of your family? Did it affect your spending? Your college plans? Your decision for your major?

THE CHANGING NATURE OF WORK

During the late 18th and early 19th centuries, the means of production shifted from agricultural to industrial. In agrarian societies, economic production was very simple, based primarily on family agriculture and hunting or gathering activities. Each family provided its own food, shelter, and clothing. This changed during the **Industrial Revolution**, an economic shift in how people worked and how they earned a living. Family production was replaced with market production, in which capitalist owners paid workers wages to produce goods (Reskin and Padavic 1994).

As a whole, we don't produce goods anymore; we provide services. Since the late 1960s, the U.S. economy has shifted from a manufacturing to a service-based economy (Brady and Wallace 2001). In 1950, manufacturing accounted for 33.7% of all nonfarm jobs; by 2000, manufacturing's share had dropped to 14% (Pollina 2003). The **service revolution** is an economy dominated by service and information occupations. Examine Table 9.1, which lists the 10 fastest-growing projected occupations between 2012 and 2022. Only one category involves manufacturing (brick and stonemasons), while the rest involve jobs in health care and service.

Industrial Revolution: Economic shift from family to market production

Service revolution: Economic shift toward service and information occupations

 What Was the Industrial Revolution?

Table 9.1 Ten occupations with the largest projected job growth (in thousands), 2012–2022

Industry Description	2012	2022
Personal care aides	1,190.6	1,771.4
Home health aides	875.1	1,299.3
Interpreters and translators	63.6	92.9
Diagnostic medical sonographers	58.8	85.9
Occupational therapy assistants	30.3	43.2
Insulation workers, mechanical	28.9	42.4
Helpers—brickmasons, blockmasons, stonemasons, and tile and marble setters	24.4	34.9
Physical therapist assistants	7.14	100.7
Genetic counselors	2.1	3.0
Industrial-organizational psychologists	1.6	2.5

SOURCE: U.S. Bureau of Labor Statistics 2013.

This shift has been referred to as **deindustrialization,** a widespread, systematic disinvestment in our nation's manufacturing and production capacities (Bluestone and Harrison 1982). Less manufacturing takes place in the United States because most jobs and plants have been transferred to other countries. The expansion of industrialization in other regions such as Asia, the Caribbean, Eastern Europe, and Africa has encouraged managers to reduce their manufacturing costs by exporting manufacturing jobs there (T. Sullivan 2004). In addition, U.S. factories have closed as a result of mergers or acquisitions as well as poor business. And thanks to technological advances, it takes fewer people to produce the same amount of goods.

U.S. manufacturing lost 5.7 million or about 33% of manufacturing jobs in the 2000s. Affected areas have experienced devastating social and economic losses, turning some into ghost towns (Brady and Wallace 2001) or leading cities into deep debt or bankruptcy—the plight of Cleveland, Ohio, and Detroit, Michigan. The phenomenon was also observed in Great Britain in the 1970s and 1980s in cities such as Birmingham and Manchester (Carley 2000). Lost manufacturing jobs are often replaced with unstable, low-paying service jobs or no jobs at all. As a result, cities may experience a significant loss of revenue to support basic public services such as police, fire protection, and schools (Bluestone and Harrison 1982).

In addition to the transformation in the type of work we do, there has been a transformation in who is doing the work. The first significant workforce change began in World War II with the entry of record numbers of women into the workplace. In

Deindustrialization: Systematic disinvestment in manufacturing and production capacities

1940, the majority of 11.5 million employed women were working as blue-collar, domestic, or service workers out of economic necessity (Gluck 1987). White and Black women's entry into defense jobs signaled a major breakthrough. One fourth of all White women and nearly 40% of Black women were wage earners who had previously worked in lower-paid clerical, service, or manufacturing jobs.

By 1944, 16% of working women held jobs in war industries. At the height of wartime production, the number of married women in the workplace outnumbered single working women for the first time in U.S. labor history. Almost one in three women defense workers were former full-time homemakers. In Los Angeles, women made up 40% of the aircraft production workforce.

These heavy industry jobs may have paid better, but the jobs held an important symbolic value: these jobs were men's jobs. After the war, although the proportion of women workers in durable manufacturing increased in many cities, many women were forced back into low-paying, female-dominated occupations (Gluck 1987) or back to their homes.

Labor force participation rates have steadily increased for White, Black, and Hispanic women since World War II (see Table 9.2). In 2012, 72.6 million or 58% of women aged 16 years or older were labor force participants (working or looking for work) (U.S. Bureau of Labor Statistics 2014b). Women dominated financial (53%),

Table 9.2 Civilian labor force participation rates (%) for White, Black, and Hispanic women, 1930–2020

	All Women	White Women	Black Women	Hispanic Women
1930	24.3	n.a.	n.a.	n.a.
1940	25.4	n.a.	n.a.	n.a.
1950	31.4	n.a.	n.a.	n.a.
1960	37.1	36.2	n.a.	n.a.
1970	41.6	42.6	49.5	n.a.
1980	51.5	51.2	53.1	47.4
1990	57.5	57.4	58.3	53.1
2000	59.9	59.5	63.1	57.5
2010	58.6	58.5	59.9	56.5
2020 Projected	57.1	56.9	57.9	56.1

SOURCE: U.S. Bureau of Labor Statistics 2012; U.S. Census Bureau 1951, 1960, 1966.

NOTE: n.a. = not available.

education and health services (75%), and leisure and hospitality (51%) occupations during that year (U.S. Bureau of Labor Statistics 2014b). In 2010, for the first time in U.S. history, women outnumbered men in the workplace (nonfarm jobs)—50.3% versus 49.7%. Legislation ensuring gender equality, along with increasing higher education enrollment among women, has improved women's value and participation in the labor market (*Economist* 2009).

···

What Does It Mean to Me?

Just for one week, count the number of times you hand cash, a credit card, or a check to someone for payment. How many times do you hand it to a woman? Mary Frank Fox and Sharlene Hesse-Biber (1984) offered the following description of the typical working woman—a working mother who attended high school and has little or no college experience, working in a retail, clerical, or service occupation. View the current list of the 20 leading occupations for employed women at the U.S. Department of Labor's Women's Bureau website. Has "women's work" changed? Why or why not?

···

The second workforce change has been the record numbers of elderly Americans returning to work. Since the mid-1980s, the labor force participation rates of older Americans have consistently increased (Toossi 2005). In 2013, 31 million Americans aged 55 or older were employed in the labor force, reflecting a 38% participation rate (U.S. Bureau of Labor Statistics 2014a). The percentage of Americans aged 55 years or older staying employed or going back to work after retirement is projected to increase by 2020, more than for any other age group (refer to Figure 9.1).

Although Americans are working longer partly because they are living longer, additional factors contribute to the increase in 55-plus employment. Government policies have eliminated mandatory retirements and outlawed age discrimination in the workplace. In 2000, older Americans were also encouraged to go back to work with the removal of age restrictions and taxes on their earned wages (Toossi 2005). Stung by the economic recession, older Americans are still delaying their retirement, deciding that they should work longer.

Immigration is the source of the last workforce shift, affecting the numbers and diversity of labor force participants. The number of foreign-born workers rose from a low of 4.3 million in 1970, to 11.6 million in 1990, to 17.3 million in 2000. For 2013, there were 25.3 million foreign workers in the United States, about 16% of the labor force (Newburger and

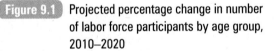

Figure 9.1 Projected percentage change in number of labor force participants by age group, 2010–2020

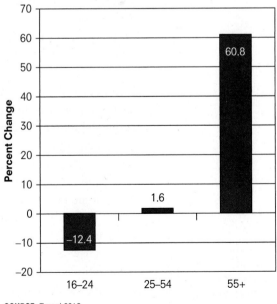

SOURCE: Toossi 2012.

Gryn 2009; U.S. Bureau of Labor Statistics 2014c). Foreign-born workers are more likely to be male, less educated, and younger (in their late 20s and early 30s) than native-born workers. Ronald Pollina (2003) predicted that, as our native population continues to age, the U.S. workforce will become increasingly dependent on foreign-born workers.

For 2013, foreign-born workers were more likely than native-born workers to be employed in service occupations and less likely to be employed in management, professional, and sales and office occupations. About 40% of foreign workers lived in the West and the Northeast (U.S. Bureau of Labor Statistics 2014c). Immigrants settle in regions with perceived economic opportunities, seeking established ethnic enclaves providing interpersonal and job support (Mosisa 2002). The median weekly earnings of full-time foreign-born workers was $643, about 80% of the earnings of full-time native-born workers ($805).

SOCIOLOGICAL PERSPECTIVES ON WORK

Functionalist Perspective

According to the functionalist perspective, work serves specific functions in society. Our work provides us with some predictability about our life experiences. We can expect to begin paid employment around the age of 18 years or after high school graduation (or we could delay it for four or five more years by attending college and graduate school). Your work may determine when you get married, when you have your first child, and when you purchase your home. Work serves as an important social structure as we become stratified according to our occupations and our income. Finally, even for the most independent among us, the way we live depends on the work of thousands—for our food, clothing, safety, education, and health. Our lives are bound to the products and activities of the labor force (Hall 1994).

Recall that from this perspective, work can also produce a set of dysfunctions that can lead to social problems (or that may be problems themselves). Employers encourage workers to become involved with their work, hoping to increase their productivity as well as their quality of work (a function). However, getting too involved in one's work may lead to job stress, overwork, and job dissatisfaction for workers (all are dysfunctional). Although technology improves the speed and quality of work for some (a function), as machines replace human laborers, technology can also lead to job and wage losses (dysfunctions).

As some researchers have focused on the functions and dysfunctions of work, others have tried to understand the nature of work itself. Frederick W. Taylor, a mechanical engineer, offered an analysis that revolutionized 19th- and 20th-century industrial work. Using what he called **scientific management**, Taylor broke down the functional elements of work, identifying the most efficient, fastest, best way to complete a task. In one of his first research projects, Taylor determined the best shovel design for shoveling coal. He believed that with the right tools and the perfect

Scientific management: Analysis and implementation of the best way to complete a task

system, any worker could improve his or her work productivity, all for the benefit of the company. In his book *The Principles of Scientific Management*, Taylor (1911) wrote, "In the past the man has been first; in the future the system must be first" (p. 5).

Although scientific management in its pure form has rarely been implemented, Taylor's principles continue to serve as the foundation for modern management ideology and technologies of work organization (Bahnisch 2000). Beyond simply changing how work was organized, Taylor offered his ideas about the organization of work: the need for defining a clear authority structure, separating planning from operational groups, providing bonuses for workers, and insisting on task specialization. In contrast, Max Weber ([1925] 1978) warned that in exchange for the efficiency and predictability of bureaucracy, workers would lose their individual freedom, ultimately dehumanizing their labor. Indeed, Taylor's model shifted power to management, forcing skilled workers to give up control of their own work (Hirschhorn 1984), which was a cause for concern expressed by theorists from the next theoretical perspective.

From a conflict perspective, capitalism produces a unequal social structure. Owners of the means of production occupy the highest position, while laborers occupy the lowest.

Conflict Perspective

Power, explained Karl Marx, is determined according to one's relationship to the means of production. Owners of the means of production possess all the power in the system, he believed, with little (probably nothing) left for workers. As workers labor only to make products and profits for owners, workers' energies are consumed in the production of things over which they have no real power, control, or ownership (Zeitlin 1997). According to Marx, man's labor becomes a means to an end; we work only to earn money. Marx predicted that eventually we would become alienated or separated from our labor, from what we produce, from our fellow workers, and from our human potential. Instead of work providing a transformation and fulfillment of our human potential, work would become the place where we felt least human (Ritzer 2000).

Modern systems of work continue to erode workers' power over their labor. In an extreme case, 17 young Chinese men and women committed suicide at Foxconn Technology, a computer hardware company that makes products for Apple,

 Deskilling: The Perils of Automation

Dell, and HP. The 2010 suicides and suicide attempts involved workers aged 18 to 24, recently hired by the company. Ma Xiangqian, a 19-year-old worker, leapt to his death from his dormitory floor. Company records revealed that Xiangqian had worked 286 hours in the month before he died, including 112 hours of overtime (three times the legal labor limit). He earned about $1.00 per hour, even with extra pay for overtime. Thousands of Foxconn factory workers resigned from their jobs (Barboza 2010).

Deskilling refers to the systematic reconstruction of jobs so that they require fewer skills and, ultimately, management can have more control over workers (Hall 1994). Although Taylor (1911) proposed scientific management as a means to improve production, sociologist Harry Braverman (1974) argued that by altering production systems, capitalists and management increase their control over workers. Once dependent on the workers' abilities, the nature of work shifts to managerial and organizational priorities. Management, according to Braverman (1974), "controls each step of the labor process and its mode of execution" (p. 119). This heightened level of control and routinization increases worker alienation and hinders creativity and flexibility among workers. Deskilling may also limit job prospects for the employee, as job tasks and specialization become company specific, not transferrable to another (Jagoda 2013).

Although Marx predicted that capitalism would disappear, capitalism has grown stronger, and at the same time, the social and economic inequalities in U.S. society have increased. Capitalism has become more than just an economic system; it is an entire political, cultural, and social order (Parenti 1988). Modern capitalism includes the rise and domination of corporations, large business enterprises with U.S. and global interests. Conflict theorists argue that capitalist and corporate leaders maintain their power and economic advantage at the expense of their workers and the general public.

Feminist Perspective

From a feminist perspective, work is a gendered institution. Through the actions, beliefs, and interactions of workers and their employers, as well as the policies and practices of the workplace (Reskin and Padavic 1994), men's and women's identities as workers are created, reproduced, and then solidified in the everyday routines of informal work groups and formal workers' organizations (Brenner 1998). We already discussed the importance of World War II for women's employment; but recall that after the war, there was pressure on women to resume their roles as housewives or to assume more appropriate occupations. As a gendered institution, work defined the roles appropriate for World War II women and defines them for women today. The workplace does not treat women and men equally. Women are concentrated in different—and lower-ranking—occupations than men, and women are paid less than men (Reskin and Padavic 1994).

A fundamental feature of work is the gendered division of labor, the assignment of different tasks and work to men and women. This division of labor leads to a devaluing of female workers and their work, providing some justification for the differential compensation between men and women (Reskin and Padavic 1994). In the United States, as in most other countries, women earn less than men (England and Browne 1992). There is no country in the world where women make the same as or more than men (refer to Figure 9.2). In the early 1960s, U.S. women earned about 59 cents for every dollar earned by men (Armas 2004). By 2013, for every dollar a man earned, a woman made 78.3 cents (National Committee on Pay Equity 2014). (Refer to Table 9.3 for a comparison of women's median weekly earnings by race, for 2013.)

In pay, compared with men, women are disadvantaged because they are in lower-paying feminized jobs or because they are paid less for the same work (Budig 2002). Sociologists and feminist scholars insist that no natural differences between men and women would lead to this. Instead, these researchers offer several structural explanations for the differences: differential socialization (women are socialized to pursue careers that traditionally pay less or are lower in status), differential training (men are better educated, so should be rewarded with higher pay), and workplace discrimination (Reskin and Padavic 1994). For additional discussion of these perspectives, refer to Chapter 4, "Gender."

Figure 9.2 Women's earnings as a percentage of men's earnings, in U.S. dollars, 2003

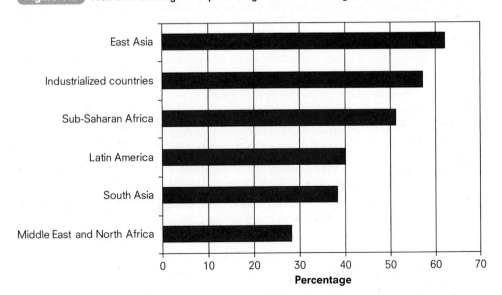

SOURCE: UNICEF 2012.

Table 9.3 Median weekly earnings for all full-time wage and salary workers in the United States, 2013

	Median Weekly Earnings
All women	$706
All men	$860
White women	$722
White men	$884
Hispanic women	$541
Hispanic men	$594
Black women	$606
Black men	$664
Asian women	$819
Asian men	$1,059

SOURCE: U.S. Department of Labor, Women's Bureau 2014.

A problem feminist advocates and scholars have addressed is workplace discrimination based on pregnancy or motherhood. In a 2006 study of women in the United Kingdom, one in six women identified revealing their pregnancy to their employer as one of the most challenging experiences of their work career (Phillips 2006). The U.S. federal government has enacted several laws protecting mothers against discrimination. The Family and Medical Leave Act of 1993 (FMLA) allows both men and women to take 12 weeks of unpaid leave for the birth or adoption of a child. Feminist scholars argue that FMLA assumes that women can afford to take leave, perpetuating stereotypes that women are dependent on men as providers and that women, not men, are the primary caregivers and less dedicated employees (Reuter 2005).

What Does It Mean to Me?

In 1996, there was only one female CEO of a Fortune 500 company. In 2014, there were 24 female CEOs, 4.8% of all Fortune 500 CEOs. From a sociological perspective, why aren't there more women CEOs? Are women less qualified to lead a major corporation? What would it take to increase the number of female CEOs?

Interactionist Perspective

The sociologies of work and symbolic interaction were developed side by side in the 1920s and 1930s at the University of Chicago. There are strong similarities between the two sociological perspectives: in the same way that symbolic interactionists are interested in how individuals negotiate their social order, the sociologists of work are interested in the negotiated order of work (Ritzer 1989). Interactionists address norms in the workplace, how workers interact with their peers, how workers deal with stress, and how workers find meaning in the work they do. This perspective allows us to understand the process by which individuals understand, interpret, and create their work.

For example, Geraldine Byrne and Robert Heyman (1997) interviewed nurses in the United Kingdom, investigating the relationship between their perceptions of work and patients and how it influenced their communication with patients. The researchers noted how nurses distinguished their work with "major trauma" and "minor" patients. They defined their work as more valuable and satisfying in trauma cases, giving them an opportunity to feel technically expert and rewardingly useful. Their time with minor patients was described as boring or repetitive and a small part of their daily work. Although nurses felt that all patients experience some anxiety in the hospital, they felt that those with more serious illnesses or injuries would be more anxious than others. As a result, they spent more time with the seriously ill or

The American Dream in Crisis

injured patients, but they made sure to "pop in" with all patients as a way of demonstrating that they had not forgotten about them and providing some nursing contact.

According to symbolic interactionists, we attach labels and meanings to an individual's work (and major). If you meet a fellow student for the first time, one of the first questions you may ask is "What's your major?" Why ask about a major? Think of it as a shortcut for who you are. Based simply on whether you are a Sociology major or a Physics major, people make assumptions about how much you study or your academic quality. This is no different from asking someone what he or she does for a living. These social constructs create an order to our work and our lives, but they can also create social problems.

Problems arise when these social constructs serve as the basis of job discrimination. A study by researchers from the University of Chicago and Massachusetts Institute of Technology revealed discrimination in the recruiting process based only on what was perceived about someone's first name (Bertrand and Mullainathan 2003). Researchers sent 5,000 résumés in response to job advertisements in the *Boston Globe* and *Chicago Tribune*. First names were selected based on a review of local birth certificates. Fictional applicants with "White" first names—Neil, Brett, Emily, and Jill—received one callback for every 10 résumés mailed out. In contrast, equivalent "Black" applicants—with names such as Aisha, Rasheed, Kareem, and Tamika—received one response for every 15 résumés sent. Other aspects of discrimination were revealed in the study. If the résumé indicated that the applicant lived in a wealthier, more educated, or more-White neighborhood, the rate of callbacks increased. This effect did not vary by race.

Though employers report positive attitudes toward people with disabilities, actual hiring rates reveal an opposite trend. Since 1986, the jobless rate of people with disabilities has been around 66%. Researchers have attributed the persistence of stigma regarding the disabled and the negative impact on hiring them to a variety of reasons. For many, disability is associated with low or no ability, poor performance, or unsafe work behavior (Rubin and Roessler 2008). Employers are also concerned about the perceived costs of accommodations and the possibility of other workers demanding special consideration themselves (Schur, Kruse, and Blanck 2005). The stigma attached to disability is compounded by other personal characteristics such as age, race or ethnicity, or gender; these individuals are doubly disadvantaged in the workplace (McMahon et al. 2008).

See Table 9.4 for a summary of all perspectives.

PROBLEMS IN WORK AND THE ECONOMY

Unemployment and Underemployment

According to the U.S. Bureau of Labor Statistics (2014a), about 146.6 million Americans were employed and 9.3 million were unemployed in September 2014. Compared with the (seasonally adjusted) unemployment rate of Whites, 5.1%, the

Table 9.4   Summary of sociological perspectives: Work and the economy

	Functional	Conflict/Feminist	Interactionist
Explanation of work and the economy and its social problems	Sociologists use this perspective to examine the functions and dysfunctions of work and employment. Functionalists also analyze the functional elements of work itself.	Conflict or feminist theorists focus on how economic, ethnic, and gender inequalities are perpetuated in the economy and the workplace.	From this perspective, sociologists investigate how our work experiences are created through interaction and shared meanings. Social problems emerge from the meanings we associate with our work.
Questions asked about work and the economy	How does the institution of work help preserve the social order? How is economic and social stability maintained by the institution of work? How do other institutions affect our work or our economy?	What social inequalities are present in the institution of work? How do we become alienated from our work?	How is our work and workplace socially defined? How do we behave based on our meaning of work? Are there positive and negative meanings of work?

rate was 11.0% for African Americans and 6.9% for Hispanics. Nearly 3.2 million individuals were long-term unemployed or unemployed for 27 weeks or more (U.S. Bureau of Labor Statistics 2014a).

The recent recession has been characterized as a man's recession or a "man-cession." In 2008–2009, the U.S. unemployment rate for men increased more steeply than the rate for women, due largely to layoffs in manufacturing and construction, where men made up roughly 70% and 85% of the workforce, respectively (Cook 2009). On the other hand, women are concentrated in occupations that are more resistant to the economic decline, such as health, education, and public service. Health care employment has been among the strongest in this recession (Rampell 2010). Post-recession, as of September 2014, 5.9% of men aged 16 or older were unemployed, compared with 6.0% of women in the same age group (U.S. Bureau of Labor Statistics 2014a).

During and after the Great Recession, the unemployment rate for young adults has been a concern in the United States and globally. In the United States, the unemployment for all four-year college graduates is 4.5%; however, the unemployment rate for recent four-year graduates is higher at 6.8% and for recent high school graduates is nearly 24% (Carnevale, Jayasundera, and Cheah 2012). A college degree has been described as "the best umbrella in this historic economic storm and the best preparation for the economy that is emerging in recovery" (Carnevale et al. 2012:1). For Europeans 15 to 24 years of age (level of education not identified), the rate of unemployment was 21.6% in 2011 (Eurostat 2012).

In addition to unemployment, we should be aware of another rate, underemployment. **Underemployment** is defined as the number of employed individuals who are working in a job that underpays them, is not equal to their skill level, or involves fewer working hours than they would prefer (taking a part-time job when a full-time job is not available). In September 2014, the number of people working part-time because of cutbacks or because they were unable to find a full-time job was 7.1 million (U.S. Bureau of Labor Statistics 2014a).

There is significant variation in unemployment and underemployment rates. People who are young, non-college-educated, and members of ethnic/racial minorities have higher underemployment rates (Bernstein 1997). Minority group underemployment is significantly higher than underemployment among non-Hispanic Whites. Min Zhou (1993) reports that at least 40% of the members of each minority group he analyzed (Puerto Ricans, Blacks, Mexicans, Cubans, Chinese, and Japanese) were underemployed. In particular, Blacks and Puerto Ricans have the highest rates of labor force nonparticipation (were not in the labor force and had not worked in the last two years) and joblessness. Joblessness includes subemployment (individuals who were not in the labor force but worked within the last two years) and underemployment rates (based on either low wage or occupational mismatch). Recent immigrants, a large portion of the Asian and Hispanic minority groups, may have difficulty in securing employment because of lack of job skills or language proficiency and, as a result, are more likely underemployed than are native-born and non-Hispanic White workers (DeJong and Madamba 2001).

Scholars have documented the destructive effects of joblessness on overall health (Rodriguez 2001) and emotional well-being (Darity 2003). Unemployment has been consistently linked with higher levels of alienation, anxiety, and depression (Rodriguez 2001) and a lower sense of overall health (Darity 2003). Cross-national data reveal how long periods of unemployment are related to increased rates of suicide and spousal abuse (Darity 2003). Among Blacks and non-Hispanic Whites, long-term exposure to unemployment produces a "scarred worker effect." The experience of unemployment undermines the worker's will to perform, leading that person to become less productive and less employable in the future (Rodriguez 2001).

The Problem of Globalization

Globalization, introduced in Chapter 1, is a process whereby goods, information, people, communication, and forms of culture move across national boundaries. Though we tend to think of globalization as an economic phenomenon, we should not lose sight of its political, social, and cultural implications (Eitzen and Baca Zinn 2006).

Globalization has transformed the nature of economic activity (Eitzen and Baca Zinn 2006). It has been credited with bringing the world together—creating a world market where all businesses, employers, and employees must

Underemployment: Employment under less-than-optimal conditions regarding pay, skill, or working hours

 How to Stop Outsourcing Jobs

Characteristics of Minimum-Wage Workers

Figure 9.3 Percentage of workers earning minimum wage or below, by gender and age, 2013

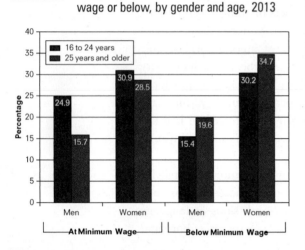

SOURCE: U.S. Bureau of Labor Statistics 2014d.

NOTE: Due to rounding, these percentages do not add up to 100%.

Figure 9.4 Percentage of workers earning minimum wage or below, by occupation, 2013

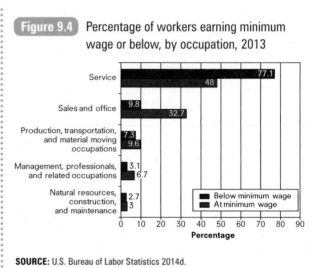

SOURCE: U.S. Bureau of Labor Statistics 2014d.

Figure 9.5 Percentage of workers earning minimum wage or below, by educational attainment, 2013

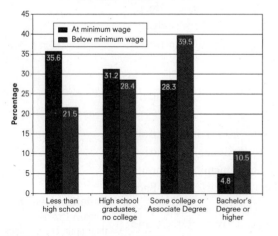

SOURCE: U.S. Bureau of Labor Statistics 2014d.

WHAT DO YOU THINK?

For 2013, 3.3 million workers earned wages at or below the federal minimum wage of $7.25 per hour.

The probability of earning minimum wage or lower varies by your social characteristics. Figures 9.3 to 9.5 present data on the percentage of minimum wage workers by gender, occupation, and educational attainment.

Review the data presented in Figure 9.3. Overall, a higher percentage of women work at or below the minimum wage than men. Those 25 years or older are more likely to work at or below the minimum wage level than those 16 to 24 years of age.

Based on the data presented in Figure 9.4, which occupation has the highest rate of workers earning at or below minimum wage? Which jobs within this occupation would earn below minimum wage?

Does having some college education or a college degree decrease the likelihood of earning below minimum wage? What evidence from Figure 9.5 supports your answer?

Explain how the gendered division of labor might contribute to the minimum wage patterns presented in Figures 9.3 and 9.4.

compete. This competition keeps corporations focused on innovation, quality, and production. Increasing productivity and output creates more jobs and stimulates economic growth (Weidenbaum 2006), creating a new middle class and reducing poverty in many countries (Yergin 2006). The United States has benefited from globalization, having experienced a doubling in foreign trade during the 1990s, which led to the creation of more than 17 million new jobs (Yergin 2006).

Yet, globalization has its dark side (Weidenbaum 2006). Foremost, worker security has declined everywhere, including in the United States. Skilled workers are threatened by the unfair competition of low-cost sweatshops, of cheaper labor to be found in other nations. More than 3 million U.S. manufacturing jobs were lost from 2001 to 2004 (Dobbs 2004). These high-paying jobs ($16 per hour) migrated to other countries, in a process characterized as the "race to the bottom." Corporations are moving to lower-wage economies, shifting their production from the United States to Mexico to China (where the average manufacturing wage is 61 cents per hour) (Eitzen and Baca Zinn 2006).

There are conflicting assessments on the relationship between globalization and poverty. Some highlight how progress in poverty reduction has been limited and geographically isolated (Weller and Hersh 2006). Others conclude that globalization has reduced global poverty (pointing to the overall reduction of the number of poor according to the World Bank standard, discussed in Chapter 2), while also warning about the threat from the persistent inequality between rich and poor countries. Developed (rich) countries are able to reap more economic benefits from less developed (poor) countries through the system of globalization (Shin 2009).

Women are particularly vulnerable in the new global economy. The global assembly line is filled with girls and women engaged in work that is low-wage, temporary, part-time, or home-based and usually performed under unsafe working conditions. More than half the world's legal and illegal immigrants are women—third-world women moving to postindustrial societies for jobs as nannies, maids, and sex workers (Eitzen and Baca Zinn 2006).

Minimum Wage

One way the United States addresses economic inequality is through the federal minimum wage. A three-step wage increase was passed by Congress in 2007, when the minimum hourly wage was $5.15. The current federal minimum wage is $7.25. However, when adjusted for inflation, the current federal minimum is still less than the minimum wage from 1961 to 1981 (Filion 2009). Most states have a minimum wage above the federal minimum.

While the minimum wage raises the wages of low-income workers in general, many low-income families continue to move in and out of poverty. Data indicate that low-wage or poverty-level workers are likely to be minority, female, non-college-educated, and nonunion, working in low-end sales and service occupations

(Bernstein 1997; Bernstein, Hartmann, and Schmitt 1999; Mishel, Bernstein, and Shierholz 2009; U.S. Department of Labor 2002).

In her 2001 book *Nickel and Dimed: On (Not) Getting By in America*, Barbara Ehrenreich explored life and work on minimum wage in three states: Florida, Maine, and Minnesota. Working as a hotel maid, a nursing home aide, a sales clerk, a waitress, and a cleaning woman, Ehrenreich rated her work performance as a B or maybe even a B+. In each new job, Ehrenreich had to master new terms, new skills, and new tools (and not as quickly as she thought she would be able to master them). How did Ehrenreich survive on minimum wage? She discovered that she needed to work two jobs or seven days a week to achieve a "decent fit" between her income and her expenses. She describes getting her meals down to a "science": chopped meat, beans, cheese, and noodles when she had a kitchen in which to cook; if not, fast food at about $9 per day. For housing, she shuffled between motel rooms and apartments, moving to a trailer park at one point. Ehrenreich (2001) concluded,

> Something is wrong, very wrong, when a single person in good health, a person who in addition possesses a working car, can barely support herself by the sweat of her brow. You don't need a degree in economics to see that wages are too low and rents too high. (p. 199)

A Hazardous and Stressful Workplace

According to the U.S. Bureau of Labor Statistics (2014e), there were 4,405 fatal work injuries in 2013. The majority of fatalities occurred in men, mostly caused by the type of work they do. The private construction industry had the highest number of fatal occupational injuries, about 18% in 2013. Highway or transportation incidents are the most common cause of fatal work injuries (about 40%). Workplace violence—including assaults and suicides—accounted for 17% of all work-related fatal occupational injuries in 2013.

In the same year, a total of 3.0 million nonfatal injuries and illnesses were reported in private industry workplaces, a rate of about 3.4 cases per 100 full-time workers (U.S. Bureau of Labor Statistics 2013b). Approximately 2.8 million were injuries, the most occurring in the service-providing industries (trade, transportation, and utilities). The goods-producing industries had the largest share of occupational illnesses, about 34.3%. The U.S. Department of Labor monitors illnesses such as skin diseases, respiratory conditions, and poisonings. New reported workplace illnesses were related directly to work activity, such as contact dermatitis or carpal tunnel syndrome. Some conditions, such as long-term illnesses related to exposure to carcinogens, are usually underreported and not adequately recognized (U.S. Bureau of Labor Statistics 2009).

The 2010 explosions at the Upper Big Branch Mine in West Virginia and the Deepwater Horizon oil platform in the Mississippi River Delta heightened concerns about the safety of industrial workers. In West Virginia, 29 were killed in

The 2010 Deepwater Horizon explosion resulted in the deaths of 11 workers and led to the largest marine oil spill in U.S. history.

an explosion in the country's worst mine disaster in 40 years. These incidents led to an ongoing reevaluation of mine regulation, employee training, and safety and the development of emergency response teams, along with improvements in underground communications technology. Coal mining is an inherently dangerous occupation, with deaths and injuries having been documented worldwide. China and Russia have the largest number of coal mine fatalities annually. The Deepwater Horizon explosion resulted in the deaths of 11 operators and is the largest marine oil spill in U.S. history.

The National Institute for Occupational Safety and Health (NIOSH) (2003) defines job stress as the harmful emotional or physical response that occurs when a job's characteristics do not match the capabilities, resources, or needs of the worker. Certain job conditions are likely to lead to job stress: a heavy workload, little sense of worker control, a poor social environment, uncertain job expectations, or job insecurity. Eventually, job stress can lead to illness, injury, or job failure. Studies have analyzed the impact of stress on our physical health, noting the relationship of stress to sleep disturbances, ulcers, headaches, or strained relationships with family or friends. Recent evidence suggests that stress also plays a role in chronic diseases such as cardiovascular disease, musculoskeletal disorders, and psychological disorders (NIOSH 2003).

MEXICO'S MAQUILADORAS

Maquiladoras are textile, electronics, furniture, chemical, processed food, or machinery assembly factories where workers assemble imported materials for export (Abell 1999; Lindquist 2001). The maquiladora program allows imported U.S. materials to enter Mexico without tariffs; when the finished goods are sent back to the United States, the shipper pays duties only on the value added by the manufacturer in Mexico (Abell 1999; Gruben 2001). The program began in 1965 as an employment alternative for Mexican agricultural workers. Drawn to Mexico because of its proximity to U.S. borders and by low labor costs, nearly every large U.S. manufacturer has a maquiladora location. Several Asian and European companies including Sony, Sanyo, Samsung, Hitachi, and Philips also have maquiladora locations (Lindquist 2001). There are an estimated 5,000 export manufacturers along Mexico's border with the United States, employing over 1.3 million workers (Bacon 2011). The maquiladora program has been described as the engine of growth in Mexico (Mollick and Ibarra-Salazar 2013).

The maquiladora program became controversial as soon as it appeared (Gruben 2001). Supporters of the maquiladora program argue that if these plants had not located in Mexico, they would have gone to other low-wage countries. Opponents argue that the program helped U.S. firms and others take advantage of the low-wage Mexican labor force. The maquiladoras have been criticized for their treatment of female workers, dangerous work conditions, and impact on the physical and social environment of border towns.

Most maquiladora workers are women. Yolanda is a worker from Piedras Negras.

As the sun rises, Yolanda is already awake and working—carrying water from a nearby well, cooking breakfast over an open fire, and cleaning the one-room home that she and her husband built out of cardboard, wood, and tin. She puts on her blue company jacket and boards the school bus that will take her and her neighbors across Piedras Negras to a large assembly plant. Yolanda and 800 coworkers each earn US$25 to US$35 a week for 48 hours' work, sewing clothing for a New York–based corporation that subcontracts for Eddie Bauer, Joe Boxer, and other U.S. brands. These wages will buy less than half of their families' basic needs (Abell 1999:595).

Yolanda's job provides a wage, but it is not adequate to support her or her family. The daily salary for maquiladora women is about $4.67, described not as a standard of living but, rather, as a standard for survival (Moffatt 2005). According to Elizabeth Fussell (2000), early maquiladora factories attracted the "elite" of the Mexican female labor force: young, childless, educated women. Current maquiladora laborers are likely to be the least-skilled Mexican women: slightly older, poorly educated women with young children (Fussell 2000).

Yolanda's town of Piedras Negras is no different from other maquiladora towns such as Tijuana and Matamoros. Once-quaint border towns have been transformed by maquiladora activity. Despite their profits, companies do not invest in the physical and social infrastructure of these border towns. As a result, most factory neighborhoods lack basic health and public services such as clean drinking water or sewage systems, electricity, schools, health facilities, and adequate housing (Abell 1999).

Sexual harassment is often used as a method of intimidation in the maquiladora. Supervisors taunt female workers and proposition them by offering lighter workloads in exchange for dates and sexual favors. Supervisors have also sexually assaulted female workers. Women, on and off their jobs, are subject to intimidation and violence (Moffatt 2005). As noted by Joanna Swanger (2007), female factory workers are subject to a deep and violent sexism, a culture that regards them as little more than prostitutes.

Under the 1994 North American Free Trade Agreement (NAFTA), tariff breaks formerly limited to all imported parts, supplies, and equipment used by Mexican maquiladoras now also apply to manufacturers in Canada and the United States (Lindquist 2001). During the recent national debate about immigration, NAFTA and the maquiladora program were blamed for failing to improve Mexico's economic and business infrastructure and thus failing to reduce illegal immigration in the United States.

IN FOCUS

SWEATSHOP LABOR

According to Sweatshop Watch (2003), there is no legal definition of a "sweatshop." The General Accounting Office (1994) defines a *sweatshop* as a workplace that violates more than one federal or state labor law. The term has come to include exploitation of workers, for example, with no livable wages or benefits, poor and hazardous working conditions, and possible verbal or physical abuse (Sweatshop Watch 2003); employers who fail to treat workers with dignity and violate basic human rights (Co-op America 2003); and businesses that violate wage or child labor laws and safety or health regulations (Foo 1994). The term *sweatshop* was first used in the 19th century to describe a subcontracting system in which the contractors earned profits from the margin between the amount they received for a contract and the amount paid to their workers. The margin was "sweated" from the workers because they received minimal wages for long hours in unsafe working conditions (Sweatshop Watch 2003).

Jill Esbenshade (2008) describes the networks of production that promote sweatshops and labor exploitation. She identifies how a single company, like Gap or Levi's, relies on manufacturing in dozens of countries on four or five continents supported by an extensive competitive network of agents, factories, and small subcontractors. This type of production arrangement severs the legal liability of the brand-name companies from the workers who make their products. For example, in 2012, Apple was scrutinized for poor working conditions among iPad production workers in China. Esbenshade (2008) explains, "For garment workers this means they have little leverage in the production system,

© EdStock/iStock

Though there is no legal definiton of a sweatshop, the term has come to refer to the exploitation of workers with no livable wages or benefits, working in poor or hazardous working conditions.

and in general have not been able to successfully organize to change their conditions. Garment factories, with little capital investment, close down and move on when confronted with an organized and demanding labor force" (p. 457). Clothing and other lightly manufactured products sold in the United States are made in more than 100 countries (International Labor Rights Forum 2011).

All U.S. manufacturers must follow the Fair Labor Standards Act (FLSA), which establishes federal minimum wage, overtime, child labor, and industrial homework standards. The Department of Labor's Wage and Hour Division makes routine enforcement sweeps in major garment centers, fining businesses that are in violation of the FLSA. Globally, antisweatshop activists have increased regulatory and monitoring systems in producing countries and have pressured contractors to improve working conditions and to recognize unions (Esbenshade 2008).

COMMUNITY, POLICY, AND SOCIAL ACTION

Federal Policies

When President William Howard Taft signed Public Law 426-62 in March 1913, he created the U.S. Department of Labor. From the beginning, the department was

 Trendy Clothes Are Cheaper Than Ever. Why?

intended to foster and promote the welfare of U.S. wage earners, to improve working conditions, and to advance opportunities for profitable employment. In its current mission statement, the department includes improving working conditions, advancing opportunities for profitable employment, protecting retirement and health care benefits, helping employers find workers, and strengthening collective bargaining as part of its charge. The department administers and enforces more than 180 federal laws that regulate workplace activities for about 10 million employers and 125 million workers.

In addition to the FLSA, the Department of Labor enforces several statutes applicable to most workplaces. It regulates the Employee Retirement Income Security Act (pension and welfare benefit plans), the Occupational Safety and Health Act (ensuring work and a workplace free from serious hazards), the Family and Medical Leave Act (granting eligible employees as many as 12 weeks of unpaid leave for family care or medical leave), and several acts that cover workers' compensation for illness, disability, or death resulting from work performance.

There have been two legislative responses to the labor market and income consequences of the recent recession. In 2009, the American Recovery and Reinvestment Act (ARRA) was signed into law. ARRA was a stimulus package that allowed for benefit increases and tax cuts for households, along with federal investments in infrastructure and technology. A second stimulus package, the Tax Relief, Unemployment Insurance Reauthorization, and Job Creation Act, was signed into law in 2010. This package extended temporary income and payroll tax cuts and provided additional funding for emergency unemployment compensation. The nation's long-term recovery after the recession was a primary focus of the 2012 presidential election.

Two labor issues continue to be debated in Congress. The first is raising the minimum wage. In 2001, Senator Ted Kennedy of Massachusetts and Representative David Bonior of Michigan, both Democrats, introduced legislation that proposed a $1.50 raise in the minimum wage over three years. Efforts to increase the minimum wage are supported by unions and poverty organizations, which argue that doing so will help the nation's working poor and low-income families. Opponents, who include members of the business community and the U.S. Chamber of Commerce, argue that increasing the minimum wage would put an unnecessary stress on medium-size and small businesses but would not decrease poverty. Some predict that businesses would be forced to eliminate jobs, reduce work hours, or close altogether. Results from policy analyses and academic research have not provided conclusive evidence for either argument (Information for Decision Making 2000). In 2007, the U.S. Congress passed legislation that would increase the minimum wage to $7.25 over two years.

The second issue involves protection against workplace discrimination based on sexual orientation. The Equal Employment Opportunity Commission (EEOC) was established in 1964 by Title VII of the Civil Rights Act. The EEOC monitors and enforces several federal statutes regarding employment discrimination based on Title VII of the Civil Rights Act of 1964 (race, color, gender, national origin, or religion), the Age Discrimination in Employment Act (1967), the Vocational Rehabilitation Act (1973), and the Americans With Disabilities Act (1990). The EEOC (2013) has

Sweatshop:
A workplace that violates more than one federal or state labor law; the term has come to include exploitation of workers, for example, in workplaces with no livable wages or benefits, poor and hazardous working conditions, and possible verbal or physical abuse

Job Market Relief in 2014

received between 95,000 and 99,000 charges of employment discrimination annually since 2008.

The Employment Non-Discrimination Act, which prohibits employment discrimination based on sexual orientation, has been introduced in every Congress (except the 109th) since 1994. The bill has yet to pass. Twenty-nine states and the District of Columbia have passed laws prohibiting employment discrimination based on sexual orientation, and 32 states and Washington, DC, also prohibit discrimination based on gender identity (Human Rights Campaign 2015). In 2015, President Obama's executive order prohibiting workplace discrimination on the basis of sexual orientation and gender identity by all federal contractors went into effect.

The Living Wage Movement

The term "living wage" was first used in the 1800s, as labor activists argued that employers should pay employees wages high enough to support themselves and a family. More recently, living wages have been promoted as a policy tool to address economic and social inequality (Luce 2012). Maryland became the first state to require a living wage, effective October 2007. For 2011, Maryland employers with state contracts were required to pay workers a minimum of $12.49 an hour in the Baltimore-Washington areas and $9.39 an hour in rural counties (Maryland Department of Labor, Licensing and Regulation 2011). States, unwilling to wait for congressional action on a federal minimum wage increase, have passed higher minimum wage laws during the past decade (Uchitelle 2006). Between 2004 and 2006, 25 states increased their minimum wage. City and county governments have done the same. Seattle residents voted to increase the city's minimum wage to $15 per hour by 2018. Mayors in Los Angeles, New York, and San Francisco were also promoting higher minimum wages for their residents. Currently there are living wage ordinances in over 140 cities, counties, and universities.

Though opponents claim that higher living wages will hurt the local economy, research has not confirmed these negative consequences. Based on scholarly research and city program evaluation, there is no evidence of increased costs for city contracts (and higher taxes for city residents) or a decrease in the number of firms bidding on contracts as a result of living wage ordinances. Additionally, none of the existing studies documented employment loss (Luce 2012).

What has been consistently noted is how the living wage increases worker's wages. Based on a study of Boston workers, the living wage ordinance raised earnings by $6,950 per year, from $21,770 to $28,720, for workers who stayed with the same employer before and after the ordinance. Stephanie Luce (2012:19) argues,

> The ordinances are not always enough to raise workers out of poverty, and still do not reach enough workers. They are difficult to enforce and, in fact, have been repealed or blocked in some cities. Where implementation is more successful, it requires constant effort by workers or worker organizations to monitor employers and the city.

VOICES IN THE COMMUNITY

JUDY WICKS

Businesses have also found a way to give back to their communities, to combine their work with their social activism. Judy Wicks accomplished this as the owner of Philadelphia's White Dog Café between 1983 and 2009. In an interview with Maryann Gorman (2001), Wicks examined how her business and activist philosophies merged at the White Dog:

> A person could go to the White Dog Café just to eat. Many customers do—at least for the first time. . . . But many of the diners who come just for the food end up staying for the activism. Wicks tells of a salesman who sold the restaurant its insurance, then attended a Table Talk on the School of the Americas and became a regular at the annual protests held at the School. Wicks jokes, "I use food to lure innocent customers into social activism."

The Dog offers diners an array of learning experiences in lecture or hands-on formats as well as field trips to other countries. There are Table Talks on a variety of topics: the American war on drugs, the Supreme Court's decision in the 2000 election, racism. And the White Dog often organizes rides to rallies and

Judy Wicks successfully combined her business, the White Dog Café, with her social and political activism.

marches, like the demonstrations against Clinton's impeachment that Jesse Jackson called for, the Million Mom March, Stand for Children and more. . . .

Wicks' White Dog venture began when she sensed the dissonance between her profession and her activism. Her energies drained by splitting her values into the commercial and nonprofit worlds, she sought a simpler solution, which first led her to managing someone else's restaurant. "I realized with the

---

In his 2014 State of the Union address, President Obama endorsed a $10.10 national minimum wage. He later signed an executive order to raise the minimum wage for individuals working on new federal service contracts to $10.10 per hour. There are living wage campaigns in the United Kingdom, Canada, and Japan.

Worker-Friendly Businesses—Conducting Business a Different Way

Each year *Fortune* magazine releases a list of the "100 Best Companies to Work For." For 2007, the magazine wrote,

nonprofit and the for-profit that in order to really be effective, I needed to focus on one organization," Wicks says. "So I eventually abandoned the publishing work and focused on the restaurant. But it wasn't all my restaurant, and when I started experimenting with bringing my values to work, like having a breakfast for Salvadoran refugees, I had to part ways with my partner there. This idea of compartmentalizing your life, and having certain values in one area and other values in another, has never worked for me."

The first step, Wicks says, was simply to change her life so that she lived where she worked. "I think that society teach[es] us, 'Separate work from home; don't mix them together. That'll be too stressful.' And I've always worked against that." So the White Dog, located in a block of row houses near the University of Pennsylvania, became both her home and her business. "I'm kind of a holistic person," she says. "I live where I work. I live 'above the shop,' in the old-fashioned way of doing business." . . .

Not only does she not have to commute, . . . but she doesn't have to go food shopping or do the dishes.

"But it's more than that," she says, "It's about energy and focus. And relationships. Being able to foster all these relationships."

The relationships she speaks of are those with her staff. One of the White Dog's missions is "Service to Each Other," an in-house goal of creating a tolerant and fair workplace. . . . Moving past standard business boundaries in this way has informed Wicks' creative development of the White Dog's missions. From encouraging her employees to re-create their job descriptions to fostering a sense of community among other Philadelphia restaurants, Wicks has shown that profitable businesses don't have to be stark-raving competitive.

In 2009, Wicks sold the White Dog Café to allow her to focus full-time on her social and humanitarian efforts. In 2001, Wicks cofounded the national organization Business Alliance for Local Living Economies. The organization brings together more than 22,000 independent U.S. and Canadian businesses to build economies that are community-based, green, and fair (Business Alliance for Local Living Economies 2012).

SOURCE: Gorman, Maryann. 2001. "The White Dog's Tale" *YES! Magazine,* Spring 2001. Reprinted from *YES! Magazine,* Bainbridge Island, WA 98110. Subscriptions: 800/937-4451. Web: www.yesmagazine.org

Ten years ago, when we began compiling this list, the idea that your employer would deliver your groceries (a new perk at Microsoft) or allow you to do your laundry at work (Google) might have seemed crazy. . . . Indeed, much has changed in the American workplace over the past decade. (Levering and Moskowitz 2007:94)

No. 1 on Fortune's 2014 list was Google. This employer features 30 free gourmet cafeterias in its Mountain View, California, headquarters. But Google was named number one for more than its food. This business rewards its 46,000 employees with benefits that include competitive salaries and stock options, on-site laundry and dry-cleaning, outdoor and indoor recreational facilities, a community-supported fishery program, and a generous parental leave program (22 weeks for new mothers and 12 weeks for new fathers).

There is no big secret to creating worker-friendly organizations, although some organizations are slow to learn their values. Beyond the standard employee benefit package of vacations, health care, retirement plans, and life insurance, innovative employers have used dependent care, flexible work options, expanded leave time, and enhanced traditional benefits to attract and retain employees. As a result, these employers have reduced employee turnover, increased employee satisfaction, and improved worker productivity (Schmidt and Duenas 2002).

Flexible work hours help facilitate an employee's work–life balance, especially for women (C. Sullivan and Lewis 2001). Female employees can change their schedules to take children to school, be home when children return from school, or attend special school events (McDonald et al. 2005). Flexible work hours also permit employees to manage other personal matters. Employees who choose to work nonstandard hours or to work remotely may increase their production due to less distractions or creating an environment that optimizes their creativity and work flow (Shockley and Allen 2012).

. . . .

What Does It Mean to Me?

What work benefits inspires you to be more productive or to enjoy your work more? How can work be structured to make you a happier worker?

. . . .

Organized and Fighting Back

Historically, labor unions have served as bargaining agents for workers, fighting for fair wages, safe work environments, and benefits from employers. Many of the worker benefits advocated by early labor unions are now mandated through federal, state, or local labor laws. In our changing and global economy, unions cannot sustain themselves by simply negotiating pay, benefits, and working rights. To remain vital and relevant, unions need to develop multilevel strategies and use new skills (Lazes and Savage 2000). In 1983, the first year when union membership data were available, the rate of membership was 20.1%, accounting for 17.7 million union members. For 2012, the rate of membership was 11.2%, with a total of 14.5 million members (U.S. Bureau of Labor Statistics 2014f).

Following years of declining membership, U.S. unions shifted their membership strategy (Fantasia and Voss 2004). Changing their focus from the declining U.S. manufacturing sector, union organizers began to successfully rebuild their membership in the service and public sectors dominated by female, immigrant, and minority workers. During 2012, membership in the manufacturing industries was 10.5%, while employees in the utilities industry had the highest rate of membership, 25.6%

 Voices of Young Workers

SOCIOLOGY AT WORK

LAW

Stacey Stone Semmler—Class of 2006

*Undergraduate Majors: Sociology,
Political Science*

*U.S. Supreme Court Justice Sonia Sotomayor says
that being a lawyer is one of the best jobs in the world,
because "every lawyer, no matter whom they represent,
is trying to help someone. . . . To me, lawyering is the
height of service" (quoted in Campos 2013).*

Earning a juris doctor (JD) degree usually takes
seven years of full-time study—completing an
undergraduate degree followed by three years of
law school. Most states require practicing lawyers
to earn their degree at an American Bar Association
(ABA) accredited program. There are more than 200
accredited law schools in the United States; the
majority of schools require applicants to take the
Law School Admission Test (LSAT). In the second
and third year of law school, students can customize
their coursework for a particular area of law practice.
There are many major areas of law practice, including
bankruptcy, business, civil rights, criminal, environment,
family, labor and tax law. In order to practice, one must
successfully complete licensure, also referred to as a
state bar exam.

Stacey Stone Semmler practices civil litigation in a
variety of fields, including insurance defense, commercial
debt collection, election and campaign finance law,
and construction and workers' compensation defense.
Her undergraduate internship at Girl Scouts Beyond
Bars inspired her career and served as an important
experience:

> That opportunity demonstrated to me that the law
> has power. It truly motivated me to attend law
> school. I gained so much experience in interacting
> with a variety of people and personalities from a
> variety of ethnic backgrounds and social classes.
> My current job is not necessarily directly related

Stacey Stone Semmler

Courtesy of Stacey Stone Semmler

> to my work with Girl Scouts; however, each time I
> interviewed for a job, that experience was discussed.

Sociology is still part of her work, especially during a trial.

> In my field we often have to consider the perception,
> especially when representing a corporation. If we
> have multiple lawyers, will it look bad? If we have too
> much technology, does it look like the poor opposing
> party is just being outspent? There are numerous
> things to consider. It also is beneficial when picking
> a jury. You have to consider your client and how he/
> she will be judged by the person who sits before you
> on a panel based on things such as their race, social
> class, job position, relationships, and community
> involvement.

(U.S. Bureau of Labor Statistics 2014f). Unions are presented as organizational vehicles of social solidarity, "emphasizing direct [worker] action as an important source of collective power" (Fantasia and Voss 2004:128). In addition, these unions have a strong orientation toward social justice that appeals to their new members, connecting the labor movement with the movement for social citizenship and universal civil rights (Fantasia and Voss 2004) and encouraging broad-based movement building and worker self-organization (Avendaño and Hiatt 2012).

In recent years, innovative collaborations have been forged. Unions have collaborated with other types of social movements to better support workers and their families. Nonunion social movements include worker advocacy groups representing women, immigrants, racial and ethnic groups, and working families. Living-wage campaigns and worker centers have also been part of the effort to increase worker power (Kalleberg 2011).

One example of union innovation is the Union of Needletrades, Industrial, and Textile Employees (UNITE). In 1996, it launched a "Stop Sweatshops" campaign linking union, consumer, student, civil rights, and women's groups in the fight against sweatshops. UNITE helped form United Students Against Sweatshops (USAS) in 1997, bringing together a coalition of student groups to raise awareness about the problem of sweatshop labor in the manufacturing of collegiate clothing (caps, shirts, and sweatshirts sold in campus stores). In March 1998, Duke University adopted the nation's first code of conduct for university trademark licensees. Under the code, any clothing with the Duke logo would be subject to labor and human rights standards. The student group Duke Students Against Sweatshops played a key role in shaping the antisweatshop code (Sweatshop Watch 2000). In 2004, UNITE announced that it was merging with the Hotel Employees and Restaurant Employees International Union. The new union, called UNITE HERE (2012), represents workers in the hotel, gaming, food service, manufacturing, textile, distribution, laundry, and airport industries.

Also working with USAS is the Student Labor Action Project (SLAP). This campus-based coalition supports the growing economic justice movement among college students by "making links between campus and community organizing, providing skills training to build lasting student organizations, and developing campaigns that win concrete victories for working families" (Student Labor Action Project 2007). The organization sponsors a national student labor week of action each year, highlighting issues such as the DREAM Act, fair contracts for campus employees, environmental and workforce sustainability, and living wages. In recent years, SLAP has also organized against educational cuts in state budgets and increasing tuition.

CHAPTER REVIEW

9.1 Describe the transition from agricultural to industrial production

During the late eighteenth century and early nineteenth century, the means of production shifted from agricultural to industrial. In agrarian societies, economic production was very simple, based primarily on family agriculture and hunting or gathering activities. During the Industrial Revolution, an economic shift occurred in how people worked and how they earned a living. Family production was replaced with market production, in which capitalist owners paid workers wages to produce goods.

9.2 Compare how the sociological perspectives explain social problems related to work

According to the functionalist perspective, work serves specific functions in society. Our work provides us with some predictability about our life experiences. Conflict theorists argue that capitalist and corporate leaders maintain their power and economic advantage at the expense of their workers and the general public. From a feminist perspective, work is a gendered institution. Men's and women's identities as workers are created, reproduced, and then solidified in the everyday routines of informal work groups and formal workers' organizations. According to symbolic interactionists, we attach labels and meanings to an individual's work. These social constructs create an order to our work and our lives but can also create social problems.

9.3 Explain the difference between unemployment and underemployment

While unemployment is defined as the number of individuals who are looking for a job, underemployment is the number of employed individuals who are working in a job that underpays them, is not equal to their skill level, or involves fewer working hours than they would prefer. Both are measured by the U.S. Department of Labor.

9.4 Identify which forms of discrimination workers are protected against

U.S. workers are protected against discrimination based on race, color, gender, national origin, religion, age, and disabilities. Though states have passed laws prohibiting employment discrimination based on sexual orientation, there is no federal law in place.

9.5 Identify how labor unions have changed their membership strategy

Union organizers have rebuilt their membership in the service and public sectors dominated by female, immigrant, and minority workers. These unions have a strong orientation toward social justice that appeals to new members, connecting the labor movement with the movement for social citizenship and universal civil rights and encouraging broad-based movement building and worker self-organization. Student groups have provided strong support for unions and living wage organizations on college campuses.

KEY TERMS

deindustrialization, 243

scientific management, 246

sweatshop, 260

Industrial Revolution, 242

service revolution, 242

underemployment, 253

STUDY QUESTIONS

1. Which population of workers has changed the U.S. workplace the most—women or foreign-born workers? Explain the reason for your answer.

2. Using a coffee barista as an example, identify and explain Karl Marx's theory of worker alienation.

3. Why and how are women disadvantaged in the workforce—in both the types of jobs they occupy and their salary level?

4. Identify the positive and negative consequences of globalization.

5. From a functionalist and conflict perspective, examine the role of a contingent workforce in the U.S. economy.

6. Why have labor unions declined in membership? How can labor unions expand their appeal and membership to workers, and how can they do this during the economic recession?

7. Human trafficking includes the involuntary movement of individuals within one country or from one country to another for exploitation. Exploitation may include physical labor or sexual exploitation (United Nations Office on Drugs and Crime, Anti–Human Trafficking Unit 2006). In 2012, the United Nations reported that 2.4 million people are victims of human trafficking at any one time, with the majority being exploited as sexual slaves (Lederer 2012). The United States is reported to be a frequent destination country where victims are brought to be exploited, yet not much is discussed about our country's role in human trafficking. Is trafficking a U.S. social problem? Why or why not?

$SAGE edge™

10

Health and Medicine

If you are thinking that this is going to be a discussion about human physiology and theories about germs and viruses, full of medical terms, you're wrong. Although medicine can identify the biological pathways to disease (Wilkinson 1996), we will need a sociological perspective to address the social determinants of health. "Health is a result of an individual's genetic makeup, income and educational status, health behaviors, communities in which the individual lives, and the environments to which he or she is exposed" (Lurie and Dubowitz 2007: 1119). To better understand the connection between our social structure and health, we must investigate how our political economy, our corporate structure, and the distribution of resources and power influence health and illness (Conrad 2001a).

Consider the gross inequalities in health between and within countries. Life expectancy at birth is highest for a child born in Japan (81.9 years) and lowest for one born in Sierra Leone (34 years). Within the United States, there is a 20-year gap in life expectancy between the most and least advantaged populations (Marmot 2005). There is no biological reason why life expectancy should be 48 years longer in Japan than in Sierra Leone or why there is a gap in life expectancy between the rich and the poor in the United States. In *Health, United States, 2013* (National Center for Health Statistics 2014), the CDC reported that life expectancy had reached 78.7 years (see Table 10.1). Although Americans are living longer, life expectancy gains have lagged behind other Organisation for

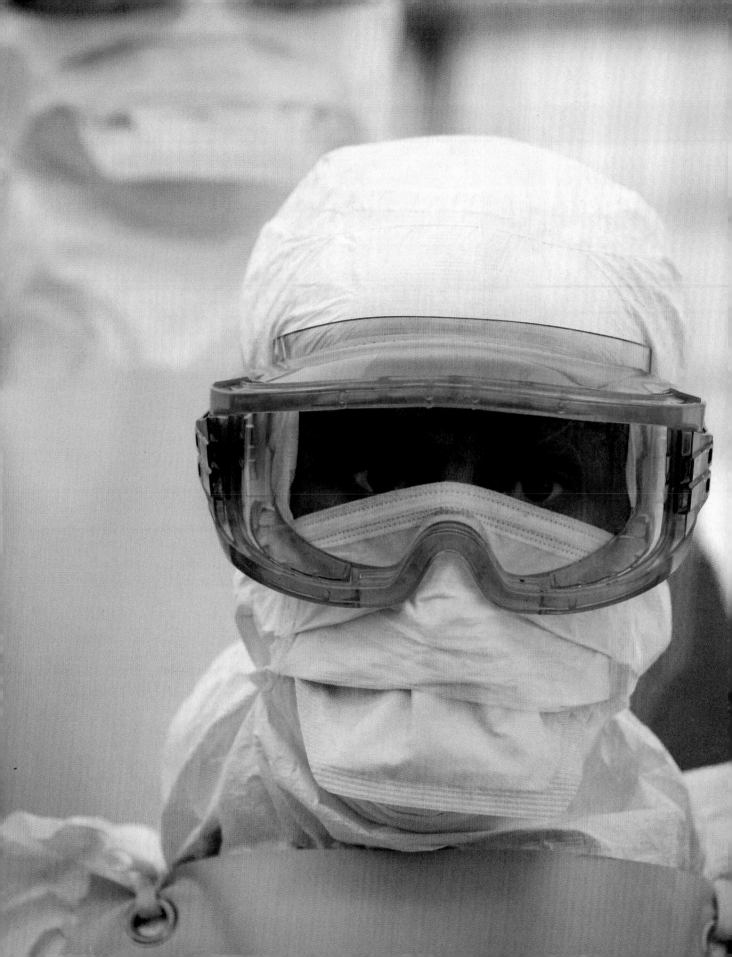

Table 10.1   Life expectancy at birth in years according to race and sex in the United States, selected years

	All Races		White		Black	
	Male	**Female**	**Male**	**Female**	**Male**	**Female**
1900	46.3	48.3	46.6	48.7	32.5	33.5
1950	65.6	71.1	66.5	72.2	59.1	62.9
1960	66.6	73.1	67.4	74.1	61.1	66.3
1970	67.1	74.7	70.7	78.1	60.0	68.3
1980	70.0	77.4	70.7	78.1	63.8	72.5
1990	71.8	78.8	72.7	79.4	64.5	73.6
2000	74.3	79.7	74.9	80.1	68.3	75.2
2010	76.2	81.0	76.5	81.3	71.8	78.0

SOURCE: National Center for Health Statistics 2014.

Economic Co-operation and Development (OECD) countries (Institute for Health Metrics and Evaluation 2013).

When two U.S. aid workers contracted the Ebola virus while working in West Africa in 2014, they were flown back to the states and treated with an experimental drug. There is no vaccine for this hemorrhagic virus. News of the experimental and special treatment of the doctor and nurse raised criticism, most notably why ZMapp was not made available in West Africa but was made available in the United States to two White aid workers. As of the end of 2014, Ebola had infected 15,145 people and killed 5,420 in Liberia, Sierra Leone, Guinea, and Nigeria. Between 60% and 90% of those infected had died from the disease. The aid workers were declared fully recovered, though it is unclear whether the drug, ZMapp, contributed to their recovery.

Finally, consider how politics and the law serve as agents of health system change. Before the Patient Protection and Affordable Care Act of 2010 (also referred to as the Affordable Care Act, ACA, or Obamacare), 44 million Americans did not have health insurance. President Barack Obama said he was signing the bill on behalf of his mother, along with others who struggled to find affordable and comprehensive health coverage. The signing of the bill enshrined "the core principle that everybody should have some basic security when it comes to their health care" (Obama 2010). Under the law, health insurance coverage was expanded through private insurance or Medicare or Medicaid plans.

SOCIOLOGICAL PERSPECTIVES ON HEALTH, ILLNESS, AND MEDICINE

The sociology of health and illness includes the field of epidemiology. **Epidemiology** is the study of the patterns in the distribution and frequency of sickness, injury, and death and the social factors that shape them. Epidemiologists are like detectives, investigating how and why groups of individuals become sick or injured (Cockerman and Glasser 2001). They don't focus on individuals; rather, epidemiologists focus on communities and populations, addressing how health and illness experiences are based on social factors such as gender, age, race, social class, or behavior (Cockerman and Glasser 2001). Epidemiology has successfully increased public awareness about the risk factors associated with disease and illness, leading many to quit smoking, to participate in more physical exercise, and to eat healthier diets (Link and Phelan 2001).

For example, type 2 diabetes, the most common form of the disease, occurs when the body does not produce enough insulin or when the cells ignore the insulin. An estimated 25.8 million Americans have type 2 diabetes (diagnosed or undiagnosed). However, the disease can be effectively managed with healthy behaviors such as meal planning, exercise, and weight management (American Diabetes Association 2012). Modernization, fast foods, and physical inactivity have led to significant increases in the number of type 2 diabetes cases in countries such as Brazil and India. Indian public health officials estimate that by 2035 there will be 109 million diabetic patients ages 20 to 79 (Lipska 2014). A disease that usually affects the old is affecting the younger Indian population, primarily because they have adopted a modern lifestyle and diet (Kleinfield 2006). Similar dire predictions are made for China; by 2035 it is expected that there will be 142.7 million Chinese with diabetes (Lipska 2014).

. . . .

What Does It Mean to Me?

All of us practice healthy behaviors we believe or were told can prevent or cure illness or disease. Brushing our teeth is one practice that we routinely do without really remembering why we do it. What other healthy behaviors do you practice? Why do you do them? Where did you learn them?

. . . .

Epidemiologists use three primary measures of health status: fertility, mortality, and morbidity. These data are routinely collected by the National Center for Health Statistics, CDC. **Fertility** is the level of childbearing for an individual or a population. The basic measure of fertility is the crude birthrate, the number of live births per 1,000 women ages 15 to 44 in a population. The U.S. crude birthrate for 2012 was 12.6 births per 1,000 women (Martin et al. 2013). Related to this is the measure of **fecundity**, the maximum number of children that could be born (based on the number of women of childbearing age in the population).

Epidemiology: Study of patterns in the distribution and frequency of sickness, injury, and death and the social factors that shape them

Fertility: The level of childbearing for an individual or a population

Fecundity: The maximum number of children that could be born, based on the number of women of childbearing age in a population

 Population Clock

 Population Growth and Health Care

In the early 1900s, a woman could expect to give birth to about four children, whereas a woman during the Great Depression of the 1930s could expect to have only two (U.S. Census Bureau 2002). The lowest number of births per woman was 1.8 children in the mid-1970s. Since then, the rate has averaged around two births per woman. Fertility is determined by a set of biological factors, such as the health and nutrition of childbearing women. But innovations in medicine, in the form of infertility treatments, have also made childbirth possible for women who once considered it impossible. Social factors, such as our social values and definitions of the role of women, the ideal family size, and the timing of childbirth, can influence fertility. Fertility rates have also been determined by the ethnic and foreign-born composition of the population. Demographer Kenneth Johnson explains, "You could shut off immigration tomorrow and the impact of the foreign born on U.S. demographic trends would still be a powerful force" (quoted in Roberts 2010:A13). Hispanics are not only the largest minority group in the United States but also the youngest. One in four newborns is Hispanic (Pew Hispanic Center 2009).

Mortality is the incidence of death in a population. The basic measure of mortality is the crude death rate, the number of deaths per 100,000 people in a population in a given year. For 2011, the U.S. death rate was 807.3 deaths per 100,000 people (Hoyert and Xu 2012). In the United States, it is unlikely that we'll die from acute infectious diseases, such as an intestinal infection or measles. Rather, the leading causes of death are chronic conditions such as coronary heart disease, cancer, stroke, and chronic lower respiratory disease, all of which have been linked to heredity, diet, stress, and exercise. The leading causes of death vary considerably by age. The leading cause of death of college-age Americans is unintentional injuries, followed by homicide and suicide. Among the elderly, mortality caused by chronic diseases (heart disease, cancer, chronic bronchitis, diabetes) is more prevalent.

Infant mortality is the rate of infant death per 1,000 live births. For 2010, the infant mortality rate was 6.1 deaths per 1,000 live births (MacDorman et al. 2014). The three leading causes of death among U.S. infants were congenital birth defects, low birth weight, and sudden infant death syndrome. Infant mortality is considered a basic indicator of the well-being of a population, reflecting the social, economic, health, and environmental conditions in which children and their mothers live. Though infant mortality rates in the United States have declined, rates are disproportionately higher for minority children. In 2010, the highest rate, 11.61 deaths per 1,000 live births, for infants of non-Hispanic Black mothers, was more than double the death rate of infants born to White mothers (5.19) (Murphy, Xu, and Kochanek 2012).

The infant mortality rate is historically higher in the U.S. than in other developed countries. (Refer to Figure 10.1 for a comparison of 2010 infant mortality rates.) When comparing U.S. infant mortality rates with the rates of other countries, researchers note that maternal health care is more widely and uniformly available in countries with national health care programs (UNICEF 2012).

Mortality: Incidence of death in a population

Infant mortality: Rate of infant deaths per 1,000 live births

Figure 10.1 Infant mortality rates: Selected Organisation for Economic Co-operation and Development Countries, 2010

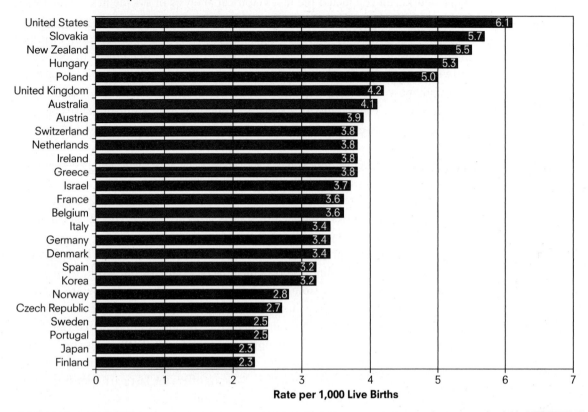

Rate per 1,000 Live Births

SOURCE: MacDorman et al. 2014.

Morbidity is the study of illnesses and disease. Illness refers to the social experience and consequences of having a disease, whereas disease refers to a biological or physiological problem that affects the human body (Weitz 2001). Epidemiologists track the **incidence rate**, the number of new cases within a population during a specific period, along with the **prevalence rate**, the total number of cases involving a specific health problem during a specific period (Weitz 2001). For example, the 2013 incidence rate for diabetes was 1.7 million people age 20 years or older; the prevalence rate was 29.1 million or 9.3% of the population (American Diabetes Association 2014). Incidence rates help measure the spread of **acute illnesses**, which strike suddenly and disappear quickly, such as chicken pox or the flu. The prevalence rate measures the frequency of long-term or chronic illnesses, such as diabetes, asthma, or HIV (Weitz 2001). The National Center for Health Statistics publishes the *Morbidity and Mortality Weekly Report*, a weekly summary of surveillance information on reported diseases and deaths.

In addition to epidemiological analyses, sociologists have applied theoretical perspectives to better explain the social problems of health and illness.

Morbidity: Study of illnesses and disease

Incidence rate: The number of new cases of disease within a population during a specific period

Prevalence rate: Total number of cases involving a specific health problem during a specific period

Acute illnesses: Illnesses that strike suddenly and disappear quickly

Functionalist Perspective

Émile Durkheim conducted the first empirical analysis of suicide in the late 1800s. Before Durkheim's work, scientists attributed suicide primarily to psychological or individual factors. However, Durkheim treated suicide as a social fact and identified the relationship between suicide and the level of social attachment or regulation between an individual and society. His research is the first true epidemiological analysis, and, most important, it revealed the relationship between illness and the larger social structure. The stability of society is paramount from a functionalist's perspective. Consider for a moment what happens when you become sick. When are you sick enough not to attend class? How do others begin to treat you? According to the functionalist perspective, illness has a legitimate place in society. The first sociological theory of illness was offered by Talcott Parsons (1951); the theory addresses how individuals are expected to act and to be treated while sick (Weitz 2001), a set of rights and responsibilities condoned by society (Barclay 2012). This set of behaviors is part of Parsons's theory of the sick role.

The **sick role** has four parts. In the first, sick people are excused from fulfilling their normal social role. Illness allows them to be excused from work, from chores around the house, or even from attending class! Second, sick people are not held responsible for the illness. The flu that's going around is no one's fault, so you aren't personally blamed if you catch it (although your roommates may blame you if they catch what you have). Third, sick people must try to get well. Illness is considered a temporary condition, and sick people are expected to take care of themselves with appropriate measures. In relation to this, Parsons offers the last part, that sick people are expected to visit medical authorities and to follow their advice.

Although Parsons legitimized the social role of illness, he also identified a critical source of the problem in health care today. In the fourth element, Parsons identified the authority and control of the physician. Even though you're the one who is sick, the doctor has the ultimate power to diagnose your condition and to tell you that you're "really" sick.

Doctors play a prominent role in managing our illnesses, but they don't do it alone. Doctors, along with nurses, pharmaceutical corporations, hospitals, and health insurers, form a powerful medical industry. The medical industry has served us well with its technological and scientific advances, offering a wider array of medical services and treatment options. However, this industry has also created a set of problems, or dysfunctions, as functionalists like to refer to them. Medicine has shifted from a general practitioner model (a family doctor who took care of all your needs) to a specialist model (where one doctor treats you for a specific ailment). You are receiving quality care, but at a price (and you are paying to be treated by many different doctors, instead of just one). As a result, health care costs have become less affordable, leaving many without adequate coverage and care. The system intended to heal us does not treat everyone fairly. We will explore this further in the next perspective.

Sick role: Set of behaviors regarding actions and treatment of ill persons

What Does It Mean to Me?
The last time you were sick, did you comply with the sick role? Did you see your physician or visit your school's health clinic? How did you play your sick role?

Conflict Perspective

According to conflict theorists, patterns of health and illness are not accidental or solely the result of an individual's actions. Conflict theorists identify how these patterns are related to systematic inequalities based on ethnicity/race or gender and on differences in power, values, and interests.

Conflict theorists may take a traditional Marxist position and argue that our medical industry is based on a capitalist system, founded not on the value of human life, but on a pure profit motive. A conflict theorist argues that instead of defining health care as a right, our capitalistic system treats health care as a valuable commodity dispensed to the highest bidder. Studies consistently find that those in upper social classes have better health, health insurance, and medical access than men and women of lower socioeconomic status. The alternative would be a dramatic change in the medical system, ensuring that health care is provided to all regardless of their race, class, or gender.

According to this perspective, what we have in place is a medical system driven by economics. In their investigation of pharmaceutical companies in the United States and Latin America, Rebeca Jasso-Aquilar and Howard Waitzkin (2011) documented how the government, transnational corporations, and international governance bodies such as the World Health Organization (WHO) are favorable partners with pharmaceutical companies. WHO, while it has promoted various initiatives and funding for mental health in low- and middle-income countries (Saraceno and Saxena 2004), also "contributed to the expansion of the market for pharmaceutical products and health insurance companies, while generally disregarding culturally-based ways of healing and patient–healer interaction" (Jasso-Aquilar and Waitzkin 2001, p. 249). The researchers warn about the increasing reliance of poor countries on a Western model of disease and treatment.

The medical system itself ensures that those already in charge maintain power. In health care, no other group has greater power than medical physicians and their professional organization, the American Medical Association (AMA), established in 1847. On its website, the AMA identifies itself as "the nation's most influential medical organization." In his book *The Social Transformation of American Medicine*, Paul Starr (1982) explains how the AMA's authority over the medical profession and education was secured in the early 1900s, with a series of events that culminated with the Flexner Report. The 1910 report was written by Abraham Flexner and was commissioned by the Carnegie Foundation and supported by the AMA. Through the report, Flexner and the AMA were able to pass judgment on the quality of each medical school, based on an assessment of its curriculum, facilities,

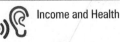 Income and Health

faculty, admission requirements, and state licensing record. This report eventually led to strict licensing criteria for all medical schools, which led to the closure of schools that could not meet the new standards. Starr reveals that although the increased standards and school closures may have improved the quality of medical training and care, they also increased the homogeneity and cohesiveness of the profession. From 162 schools in 1906, the number of medical schools dropped to 81 by 1922. Some of the closed schools were exclusively for African Americans and women. According to Rose Weitz (2001), with the increasing cost of education and higher educational prerequisites, fewer minorities, women, immigrants, and poor students could meet the requirements. As a result,

> fewer doctors were available who would practice in minority communities and who understood the special concerns of minority or female patients. At the same time, simply because doctors were now more homogenously White, male, and upper class, their status grew, encouraging more hierarchical relationships between doctors and patients. (Weitz 2001:327)

The legacy of the Flexner Report—higher medical standards and more limited access to medical education and care—continues to this day. Examinations of the social and economic backgrounds of medical students in the United States, Canada, and Great Britain confirm that medical students tend to be recruited from families with higher socioeconomic standing and with medical professionals among their members (Magnus and Mick 2000; Mathers and Parry 2009). African Americans, Hispanics, and Native Americans are the most underrepresented minority groups in the medical profession. Though together they make 25% of the U.S. population, only 6% of practicing doctors come from these groups (Association of American Medical Colleges 2010).

. . . .

What Does It Mean to Me?

The consumer movement has shifted some of the power in the doctor–patient relationship to the patient. Drug ads, previously reserved for professional medical journals, are now commonly featured in popular magazines and in television advertisements. Pharmaceutical companies routinely take two or three full-page ads, featuring drug warnings, side effects, and precautions, along with a description of their drug and its benefits. It sometimes is difficult to figure out what the drug is for. How do you think this popular diffusion of pharmaceutical information has redefined the relationship between doctor and patient? Between your doctor and you?

. . . .

Feminist Perspective

According to Peter Conrad (2001b), illness and how we treat it can reflect cultural assumptions and biases about a particular group. Take, for example, the case of women and their medical care. Conrad explains that throughout history, there are examples of medical and scientific explanations for women's health and illnesses that reflect dominant and often negative conceptions of women. Since the 1930s, women's natural physical conditions and experiences, such as childbirth, menopause, premenstrual syndrome, and menstruation, have been medicalized. **Medicalization** refers to the process through which a condition or behavior becomes defined as a medical problem (Weitz 2001). Although the medicalization of these conditions may have been effective in treating women, various feminist theorists see it as an extension of medicine's control of women (Conrad 2001b), specifically normal female experiences linked with the female reproductive system (Markens 1996), inappropriately emphasizing the psychological, biomedical, or sociocultural origins (Hamilton 1994). Once a condition is defined as a medical problem, medicine, rather than the woman herself, gains control of its diagnosis and treatment.

Menopause, a natural physiological event for women, was defined in the medical community as a "deficiency disease" in the 1960s when commercial production of estrogen replacement therapy became available (Conrad 2001b; Lock 1993). Although a few medical writers refer to menopause as a natural process, many continue to describe it as a "hormonal imbalance" that leads to a "menopausal syndrome" (Lock 1993). Though estrogen replacement treatment has been presented as a means for women to retain their femininity and to maintain good health, feminists argue that menopause is not an illness; actually, estrogen therapy may not be necessary and may be dangerous (Conrad 2001b) and may do little to improve the quality of older women's lives (Haney 2003).

Studies have suggested that the meanings and experiences of menopause may also be bound by cultural definitions. In North America, where women are defined by their youth and beauty, aging women are set up as a target for medicalization. In Japan, however, public attention focuses on a woman's life course experience. For a middle-aged Japanese woman, what matters is how well she fulfills her social and familial duties, especially the care of elderly family members, rather than her physical or medical experiences. The Japanese medical community has a different perspective on menopause than its American colleagues do: most doctors in Japan define menopause as natural and an inevitable part of the aging process (Lock 1993). Asian American midlife women also report lower rates of physical and psychological symptoms related to menopause compared with midlife women from other ethnic groups (Sievert et al. 2007).

The gender pay gap we discussed in Chapters 4 and 9 also exists among physicians. Historically, female physicians earn less than male physicians, the difference previously attributed to specialty choice (women selecting general practice, while men choose specialty fields) and hours worked (women working less hours than men). However research has confirmed that salary differences continue to exist, even after controlling for specialty, practice type, and hours worked. Seth Seabury, Amitabh Chandra, and Anupam Jena (2013) reported that the 1987–1990 earnings of male physicians were higher than those of female physicians by $33,480. Though they also controlled for differences in hours worked and years of experience,

Medicalization:
Process through which a condition or behavior becomes defined as a medical problem

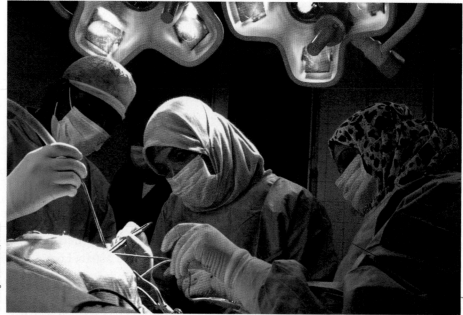

© George Steinmetz/Corbis

Gender salary inequality exists in the medical profession. Overall, female physicians earn less than male physicians, even after controlling for specialty, practice type, and hours worked (Seabury et al 2013).

the gender gap in physician earnings continued to increase over time: $34,620 in 1996–2000 and $56,019 in 2006–2010.

Interactionist Perspective

From the interactionist perspective, health, illness, and medical responses are socially constructed and maintained. In the previous sections, we discussed how health issues are defined by powerful interest or political groups. We just reviewed how the medicalization of women's conditions reflects our cultural assumptions or biases about women. Each example demonstrates how social, political, and cultural meanings affect our definition and response to health and illness.

A patient's experience with the medical system can be disempowering (Goffman 1961), but the experience can be mediated by social meaning and interpretations (Lambert et al. 1997). According to Suni Peterson, Martin Heesacker, and Robert C. Schwartz (2001), when people contract a disease, they define their illness according to a socially constructed definition of the disease, which includes a set of images, beliefs, and perceptions. Patients use these definitions to create a personal meaning for their diagnosis and to determine their subsequent behavior. The authors argue that these social constructs have a greater influence on the patient's actions and decisions about his or her health than recommendations from health professionals do.

Sociologists also examine how the relationship between doctors and their patients is created and maintained through interaction. In particular, sociologists focus on how medical professionals use their expertise and knowledge to maintain control over patients. Research indicates that doctors' power depends on their cultural authority, their economic independence, cultural differences between patients and doctors, and doctors' assumed superiority to patients (Weitz 2001). Studies consistently demonstrate the systematic differences in the level of information provided by physicians to their patients. Although differences might be attributed to the doctor responding to a patient's particular communication style, researchers argue that information varies according to the doctor's impressions of a patient (e.g., intelligence), subjective judgments about what information the patient needs (Street 1991), and status differentials between doctor and patient (male vs. female or White vs. non-White) (Peck and Conner 2011). Educated and younger patients tend to receive more diagnostic information, as do patients who ask more questions and express more concerns; doctors are likely to communicate as equals with their educated, older male patients (Street 1991). African Americans, Asian Americans, and Hispanics are more likely than Whites to experience difficulties in communicating with their doctors. The difficulties include not understanding their doctors, not feeling that their doctors are listening to them, and having questions for their doctors that they did not ask (Collins et al. 2002).

Interactionists and social constructionists also investigate how a disease is socially constructed. This doesn't mean that disease and illness do not exist. Rather, the focus is on how illness is created and sustained according to a set of shared social beliefs or definitions. In his essay "The Myth of Mental Illness," Thomas Szasz (1960) argues that mental disorders are not actually illnesses. He considers mental illness a convenient myth to cover up the "everyday fact that life for most people is a continuous struggle" (Szasz 1960:118). The disease of mental illness is constructed and maintained through a set of medical, legal, and social definitions. The social construction of disease has also been applied to infertility (Greil, McQuillan, and Slauson-Blevins 2011), attention-deficit disorder (Mather 2012), and HIV/AIDS.

For a summary of sociological perspectives on health and medicine, see Table 10.2.

HEALTH INEQUALITIES AND PROBLEMS

Gender

As noted in Table 10.1, women live about five years longer than men. The three leading causes of death for males and females are identical: heart disease, cancer, and stroke. Although women live longer than men, women experience higher rates of nonfatal chronic conditions (Waldron 2001; Weitz 2001). Men experience higher rates of fatal illness, dying more quickly than women when illness occurs (Waldron 2001; Weitz 2001).

Table 10.2   Summary of sociological perspectives: Health and medicine

	Functional	Conflict/Feminist	Interactionist
Explanation of the social problems of health and medicine	Although illness may threaten the social order, it does have a legitimate place in society. This perspective also addresses the functions and dysfunctions of the medical industry.	Patterns of health and illness reflect systematic inequalities based on ethnicity/race or gender, and on differences in power, values, and interests. Conflict theorists examine the power of the medical industry and its consequences. Feminist theorists examine medicine's control of women, specifically of normal female experiences linked with the female reproductive system.	This perspective acknowledges how illness is created and sustained according to a set of shared social beliefs or definitions. Theorists in this perspective address how social, political, and cultural meanings affect our definition and response to health and illness.
Questions asked about health and medicine	What is the role of illness in our society? What functions and dysfunctions does the medical industry provide?	How does the medical industry exert control over its patients? Is everyone treated fairly and equally by the medical system?	Who or what defines what it means to be "sick" in our society? How do our definitions of disease and illness shape our beliefs and behaviors?

These differences in mortality have been attributed to three factors: genetics, risk taking, and health care (Waldron 2001). Biological differences seem to favor women; more females than males survive at every age (Weitz 2001). Because of differences in gender roles, men are more likely to engage in risk-taking behaviors or potentially dangerous activities: driving too fast or incautiously, using legal or illegal drugs, or participating in dangerous sports (Waldron 2001). The workplace offers more dangers for men. More men than women are employed, and men's jobs tend to be more hazardous (Waldron 2001); about 9 of every 10 fatal workplace accidents occur to men (U.S. Bureau of Labor Statistics 2014a). Finally, because women obtain more routine health examinations than men do, their health problems are identified early enough for effective intervention (Weitz 2001). Typically, women eat healthier diets and smoke and drink less alcohol than men do (Calnan 1987).

According to the Men's Health Network (2002), "no effective program exists which is devoted to awareness and prevention of the leading killers of men." Although men die of cancer at twice the rate of women by the age of 75, there is little education for men in cancer self-detection and prevention. Whereas there is a popular national campaign for breast cancer, there is no national educational campaign teaching men how to self-examine for testicular cancer, a leading killer of men from 15 to 40 years of age. In addition, there are no quality educational programs regarding prostate cancer. Prostate cancer is the second most common cancer among men, after skin cancer.

Education

A similar relationship has been documented between education and health—the higher your education, the better your health (no matter how it is measured—mortality, morbidity, or other general health measures). Education might be a more important correlate to good health than is one's occupation or income (Grossman and Kaestner 1997), as it serves as a pathway to health because it is a resource itself (Mirowsky and Ross 2005).

Recent studies on the effects of compulsory education in Sweden, Denmark, England, and Wales consistently identify that a longer educational experience leads to better health (Kolata 2007). Michael Murphy and his colleagues (2006) identified mortality trends by educational level for Russian men and women between 1980 and 2001. Murphy et al. concluded that better-educated men and women had a significant mortality advantage over less-educated men and women. In 1980, life expectancy at age 20 for university-educated men was three years greater than for men with only an elementary education. By 2001, however, the gap between university- and elementary-educated men had increased to 11 years. Similar differentials were also noted among Russian women.

Researchers suggest that education helps individuals choose and practice a healthier lifestyle regarding diet, exercise, and other health choices. Highly educated men and women are likely to visit their primary physicians more often and regularly and may be more willing to use new medical technologies or medicines. Knowledge about the health consequences of smoking and drinking has been shown to decrease smoking and excessive alcohol consumption. Educated parents will also transmit their healthier lifestyle to their children (Grossman and Kaestner 1997). Education represents both the long-term influence of early life circumstances and the influence of adult circumstances on adult health (Beckles and Truman 2011).

Researchers have demonstrated the link between education and future orientation. Future-oriented individuals attend school for longer periods. Educated individuals are able to link their current actions to their future, not only for their education but also for preventative health care practices. For example, a future-oriented person will say, "I'm going to college now so that I can have a good job when I graduate." Applied to health behaviors, the same person will say, "I won't start smoking because I know there are long-term health consequences of smoking." Studies have shown that men and women who discount the future are more likely to become addicted to alcohol or other drugs (Becker and Mulligan 1994).

For more information about what other demographic characteristics are related to health care utilization, refer to this chapter's Exploring Social Problems feature.

. . . .

What Does It Mean to Me?
How has your education influenced your health and lifestyle choices?

. . . .

Inactivity and Health

Health Care Utilization

Figure 10.2 Percentage of Americans who had doctor, emergency department, or home visits four to nine times in the past 12 months, by gender

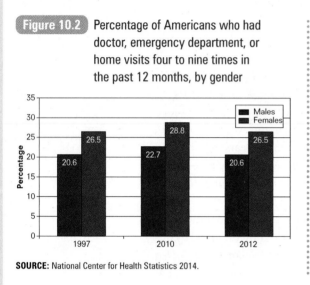

SOURCE: National Center for Health Statistics 2014.

Figure 10.3 Percentage of Americans who had doctor, emergency department, or home visits four to nine times in the past 12 months, by ethnicity

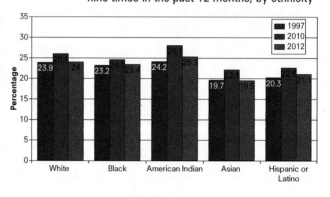

SOURCE: National Center for Health Statistics 2014.

Figure 10.4 Percentage of Americans who had doctor, emergency department, or home visits four to nine times in the past 12 months, by age

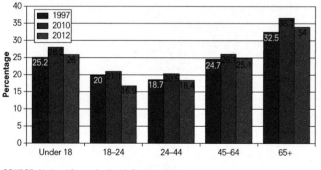

SOURCE: National Center for Health Statistics 2014.

WHAT DO YOU THINK?

Multiple social factors determine how much health care people use, the types of health care they access, and the timing of that care. Gender, race and ethnicity, and age are just some of the demographic characteristics tracked by medical and public health researchers.

Health care utilization for 1997 through 2012 is presented in Figures 10.2 through 10.4. Health care utilization is defined as accessing a doctor, visiting an emergency department, or having a home visit four to nine times in the last year and is reported by percentages for each group.

Review each figure and identify the group or groups with the lower percentages of utilization.

What types of educational or outreach programs would increase the number of health care visits?

Immigrant Health Care Use

Figure 10.5 Total health expenditures per capita, United States and selected countries, 2012 (or nearest year)

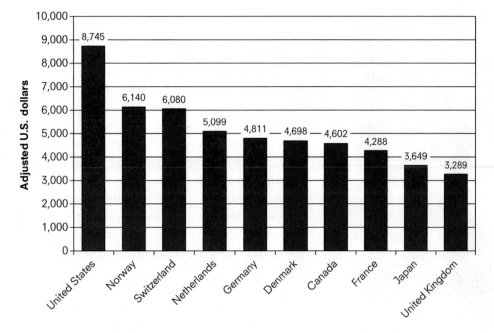

SOURCE: Organisation for Economic Co-operation and Development 2014.

The Cost of Health Care

The United States spends about 17% of its gross domestic product (GDP) on health care—the largest expenditure in this category among industrialized countries. (A per capita spending comparison with other countries is presented in Figure 10.5.) In 2012, total health care spending reached $2.8 trillion, with an average of $8,915 spent per person in health expenses (Centers for Medicare and Medicaid Services 2014a). U.S. national health care spending had grown more slowly after 2010, attributed to the Great Recession and to a sluggish economy. More Americans delayed visits to their doctors or hospitals, reduced their prescription drug purchases (Pear 2012), or lost their insurance coverage along with their jobs (Lowrey 2012). Changes in Medicare's payment policies, growth in patient cost-sharing, and state efforts to contain Medicaid costs have also been identified as contributing to the decline in health spending (Holahan and McMorrow 2013).

Even though the U.S. health system is the most expensive in the world, "comparative analyses consistently show the United States underperforms relative to other countries on most dimensions of [health] performance" (Davis et al. 2007:viii). In their pre–Affordable Care Act analyses of health care systems and outcomes in Australia, Canada, Germany, New Zealand, the United Kingdom, and the United States, Karen Davis and her colleagues (2007) concluded that the

 Rising Medical Costs Analysis

The fastest-growing sector of medical care is prescription drug spending. In 2012, $263.3 billion was spent on prescription drugs. The cost of drugs remains a significant burden for elderly Americans.

United States failed to achieve better health outcomes and scored last on the dimensions of access, quality, efficiency, and equity despite spending the most per capita on health care.

Given our lack of universal health care coverage, when compared with these other nations, more Americans are uninsured or underinsured and are more unlikely to seek necessary care because of costs. Davis and her colleagues (2007) identify how

> other nations ensure the accessibility of care through universal health insurance systems and through better ties between patients and the physician practices that serve as their long term "medical home." . . . It is also apparent that the U.S. is lagging in adoption of information technology and national policies that promote quality improvement. (p. viii)

(Information systems in countries such as Germany, New Zealand, and the United Kingdom enhance the ability of physicians to monitor patients' chronic conditions and medication use. These countries also routinely use nonphysician clinicians to assist with patients with chronic diseases.) Germany ranked first on access to health care (the ability of patients to obtain affordable care in a timely manner), and the United Kingdom ranked first for health care quality (safe, coordinated, and patient-centered health care), efficiency (maximizing the quality of care and outcomes given the system's resources), and equity (providing care that does not vary in quality because of personal characteristics, such as gender, ethnicity, and socioeconomic status). The United States ranked last on both measures.

The cost of medical care, particularly out-of-pocket expenses, is a financial burden even to those with health insurance. Harvard researchers concluded that illness or medical bills contributed to 62% of all bankruptcies in 2007 (Sack 2010). More than three fourths of those with medical debt had medical insurance (Sack 2010). Though spending on prescription drugs in the United States is the highest in the world, economic hard times caused some patients to alter their spending or their dosage of prescription drugs (Saul 2008). Through the first eight months of 2008, the number of all dispensed prescriptions was lower than in the same period of time in 2007 (Saul 2008). The decrease was attributed to individual cost-cutting measures, causing concern among physicians about the health and well-being of their patients. Patients reduced their medications (cutting their pills in half or taking medications every other day) or, among those who could no longer afford their medications, stopped taking their medicine altogether without consulting their physician (Saul 2008).

Policy makers and consumers have been keeping an eye on the cost of prescription drugs, one of the fastest-growing sectors of medical care. Increases in drug costs are expected to outstrip the overall growth in health care spending for the next 10 years. Spending for prescription drugs in 2012 totaled $263.3 billion. Out of this total, about $47 billion was out-of-pocket expenses (Centers for Medicare and Medicaid Services 2014b).

The Uninsured Population

A year before the full implementation of the ACA insurance mandate, surveyed Americans reported the primary reason for not being insured was the affordability of coverage, followed by loss of employment (Kaiser Family Foundation 2014). (Refer to the In Focus discussion for a summary of health insurance plans.) Data from the U.S. Census Bureau reveal that 42.0 million Americans or 13.4% of the U.S. population had no health insurance at any time during 2013 (Smith and Medalia 2014). As reported by the Kaiser Family Foundation (2014), almost a third of uninsured adults went without medical care due to cost. Most uninsured were in low-income working families; nearly 8 in 10 were in a family with a worker. Adults were more likely to be uninsured than children. People of color were at a higher risk of being uninsured than non-Hispanic Whites.

The Kaiser Family Foundation (2014) tracked ACA enrollment data for most of 2014, confirming that the U.S. uninsured rate is falling. The data reveal that over 8 million selected plans through the federal or state Marketplaces, though the 2013 online enrollment was plagued by serious technological glitches. Data also show that Medicaid enrollment grew by 8 million, highest among states that chose to expand Medicaid eligibility under ACA.

Expanding health care coverage has many benefits. In 2008, Oregon's Medicaid agency realized that it had enough funds to provide health insurance to an additional 10,000 adults (Oregon Health Study 2012). The agency decided to distribute the extra funds via a lottery system, drawing names to determine who would receive the Medicaid coverage. As part of the implementation, the Oregon Health Study was initiated to track the social, economic, and health outcomes among those enrolled in Medicaid and those who were not. Results of the study will provide policy makers with data on the effects of expanding health insurance at both individual and system levels. After a year of tracking the two study groups, Amy Finkelstein and her colleagues (2011) concluded that enrollment in Medicaid increased access to and use of health care (including preventative care and regular office or clinic visits), increased financial security (decreasing the probability of having an unpaid medical bill sent to a collection agency), and improved health and well-being (reporting to be in good to excellent health, increased probability of not screening positive for depression) compared to those who were not enrolled in the Oregon Medicaid program.

IN FOCUS

U.S. HEALTH INSURANCE AND HEALTH CARE DELIVERY SYSTEMS

The U.S. health care system is often referred to as a private health care system, but in reality, it is a mixed system of public and private insurance (Oberlander 2002). Refer to the Taking a World View section of this chapter for more information. Most Americans receive health insurance from their employers. This type of insurance is referred to as group insurance or as employment-based private insurance. Employers buy into a health insurance program, paying for part or all of the cost of the insurance premiums. A premium is a monthly fee to maintain your health coverage.

Under the Affordable Care Act, health insurance coverage was expanded through three avenues: subsiding insurance premiums for lower-income individuals and families, expanding the coverage of Medicare and Medicaid, and legally requiring everyone to sign up for a policy.

That handy insurance card in your wallet identifies your insurance provider, the amount of your deductible (payment due at the time of service), and the amount of coverage for prescription drugs or emergency services. There are many different types of group insurance programs:

Fee-for-service plan. Under this plan, also known as an indemnity health plan, insurance companies pay fees for services provided to the people covered by the policy. This type of program emphasizes patient choice and immediate patient care.

Health maintenance organization (HMO). These organizations operate as prepaid health plans. For your premium, the HMO provides you and your family comprehensive care. This plan is also known as managed health care, a plan that controls costs by controlling access to care. You'll be assigned to a primary care provider, who will provide most of your medical care, but if necessary, that doctor will refer you to specialists within the HMO practice or to providers contracted by the HMO. Under the plan, there is limited coverage for any treatment outside the HMO network.

Preferred provider organization (PPO). A PPO is a combination of the fee-for-service and HMO plan. With a PPO, you can manage your own health care needs by selecting your own doctors. These specialists will be on a preferred provider list supported by the PPO plan. If you use a provider outside your plan, you may have to pay a larger percentage of your health care expenses.

Federal health plans. Medicare is available to Americans 65 years or older or those with disabilities, whereas Medicaid pays for medical and long-term care for the poor; low-income children, pregnant women, and elderly; the medically needy; and people requiring institutional care.

The Kaiser Family Foundation (2014) report concludes,

Even with the availability of new coverage options, millions remain uninsured. Previous analyses show that many poor adults in states that do not expand Medicaid will continue to be at risk to be uninsured. People of color, people living in the South, and individuals living in rural areas are especially at risk to be left out of ACA coverage expansions.

The program's second enrollment period began in the fall of 2014. National surveys reveal that the majority of Americans (56%) disapprove of the law, while 37% approve (McCarthy 2014).

COMMUNITY, POLICY, AND SOCIAL ACTION

Health Care Reform

During his first administration, President Bill Clinton said problems connected with the U.S. health care system were the most pressing in the United States. In 1993, Clinton pushed for passage of the Health Security Act, an attempt at comprehensive health care reform. The act would have required all employers to provide health insurance to their employees and would have given small businesses and unemployed Americans subsidies to purchase insurance. After Congress rejected Clinton's health care plan, Americans looked to the private market to restrain health care costs and to enhance patient care and choice. U.S. medicine moved aggressively toward managed care arrangements, HMOs, and for-profit health plans (Oberlander 2002).

Sixteen years later, with Democratic majorities in the U.S. House of Representatives and the Senate, President Barack Obama declared "a season for action. . . . Now is the time to deliver on health care" (Obama 2009). After months of contentious and politically charged debate, Congress passed a compromise health reform bill in March 2010. Obama signed the Patient Protection and Affordable Care Act, along with the Health Care and Education Reconciliation Act of 2010, into law. Several ACA elements went into immediate effect: young adults up to age 26 remain covered by their parents' health insurance, plans were available for those with preexisting conditions, and lifetime limits on coverage were eliminated.

The full implementation of the law was challenged in the country's highest court. In 2012, the U.S. Supreme Court upheld the constitutionality of the ACA, examining specifically the individual health insurance mandate and the portion of the law that will require states to expand their Medicaid rolls by 2014. The majority of justices likened the penalty for not obtaining health insurance to a tax. "Because the Constitution permits such a tax, it is not our role to forbid it, or to pass upon its wisdom or fairness," wrote Chief Justice John G. Roberts Jr. (quoted in Liptak 2012:A1). The Medicaid expansion was upheld by the Court, but states would be permitted to keep their current federal money for Medicaid while refusing to expand the program. The Court ruled that states could decide whether to go along with the expansion without penalties to their existing Medicaid payments (Liptak 2012).

The expansion of Medicaid has been controversial, not only for the increased cost to states but also because of claims that the program is ineffectual and may also be associated with worse health (Belluck 2012). More than a dozen Republican governors announced that their states would not comply with the Medicaid expansion. However, most governors from both parties responded to the ruling with caution, stating that they would need to study the impact of Medicaid expansion

Passing the Affordable Care Act

on their state's budget and on their uninsured population (Cooper 2012). The Congressional Budget Office (2012b) estimated that the Supreme Court's decision would lead to about 6 million fewer people being covered by the federal Medicaid program, yet half of them should gain private insurance coverage through health insurance exchanges established by ACA. The other half, a predicted 3 million, would be uninsured.

By 2014, all citizens and legal residents had to purchase health insurance or face an annual fine. Additionally, states are required to expand Medicaid coverage to those with incomes at 133% of the federal poverty line. Another feature of the law is elimination of gender rating, using gender as a factor in setting health insurance rates. It is estimated that by 2016, the ACA will increase the number of nonelderly people with health insurance by 30 to 33 million (Congressional Budget Office 2012a).

State Health Care Reforms

Several states aggressively moved forward on health reform, and several—Florida, Hawaii, Massachusetts, Minnesota, Oregon, and Washington—expressed commitment to providing health coverage for all their citizens. It is unclear how implementation of the ACA will impact these state plans. Following are summaries of three state plans.

Hawaii was one of the first states to act on health care reform. In 1974, the state passed the Hawaii Prepaid Health Care Act, requiring employers to provide health insurance for all employees working more than 20 hours per week and to pay at least 50% of the cost. Hawaii is the only state that requires employer payments to medical insurance under a congressional exemption of the Employee Retirement Income Security Act (ERISA). ERISA bars states from requiring all employers to offer health insurance, from regulating or taxing self-insured plans, and from mandating the specific benefits to be covered by employer health plans (Beatrice 1996). Hawaii's plan also limits employees' share of the insurance premium expenses to no more than 1.5% of their income. Recently, there has been a call to repeal or at least revise the Prepaid Health Care Act because of increasing health care costs. The percentage of uninsured Hawaiians is 7.8% (DeNavas-Walt, Proctor, and Smith 2012).

Massachusetts became the first state to provide universal health care coverage to all its residents in 2006. The plan reduced the number of uninsured in the state to 3.7% (Smith and Medalia 2014), the lowest in any state. The plan allows the state to provide sliding-scale coverage, low-cost coverage, and free insurance coverage to uninsured residents depending on their income, age, or employment status. Individuals who can afford health insurance will be penalized on their state income taxes if they do not purchase it. There were modest provisions included in the plan to control costs, but not enough. Massachusetts spends 23% more per person on health care ($9,000) than the national average ($8,000). While spending continues to be a concern, analysts have noted how health care reform has led to gains in access to and use of health care in the state (Long, Stockley, and Dahlen 2012). Massachusetts government and health industry officials agreed that universal coverage would not be sustainable if they did not address the growth of health care spending (Sack 2009). In 2012, the state legislature passed a bill that would not allow health care spending to grow any faster than the state's economy through 2017 (Goodnough 2012).

MinnesotaCare became law in Minnesota in 1992. Also known as the Health Right Act, the legislation included a variety of laws aimed at reducing costs and expanding access to health care for the uninsured (Beatrice 1996). MinnesotaCare is funded through a tax on health care providers and through enrollee premiums (based on family size, number of people covered, and income) (Sacks, Kutyla, and Silow-Carroll 2002). The act set price controls for health care spending (repealed in 1997), set statewide managed care guidelines, initially mandated that all non-HMO physicians follow a state fee structure (repealed in 1995), placed all HMOs under the regulation of the Commission of Health, and mandated that HMOs be nonprofit (Citizens Council on Health Care 2003). The act also subsidized health insurance for low- and middle-income uninsured families and individuals. Minnesota placed all MinnesotaCare recipients into HMOs (Beatrice 1996; Citizens Council on Health Care 2003). A small number of Minnesotans, about 9.2%, are uninsured (DeNavas-Walt et al. 2012).

Children's Health Insurance Program

The Children's Health Insurance Program (CHIP) was adopted in 1997 as an amendment to the Social Security Act, Title XXI. The program is administered under the Centers for Medicare and Medicaid Services (CMS). CHIP enables states to implement their own children's health insurance programs for uninsured low-income children 18 years old or younger and targets the children of working parents or grandparents. For example, a family of four that earns as much as $44,700 a year (in 2011) is eligible. The insurance plan pays for regular checkups, immunizations, prescription medicines, and hospitalizations. CHIP uses comprehensive outreach materials and educational programs to recruit eligible children and their families, especially through elementary and secondary schools. In many states, as CHIP enrollments began, so did Medicaid enrollments. In 2011, the number of children enrolled in CHIP had reached a record high of more than 7.7 million.

Based on his concern that CHIP expansion would be too costly and would be a step toward universal health coverage, in fall 2007, George W. Bush vetoed a House bill that proposed coverage for more than 10 million children as well as expansion of coverage to include dental services, mental illness, and pregnant women with low incomes. The expansion bill was supported by many state governors whose states were running out of federal funds to support the program (Pear 2007). CHIP advocates accused the president and his congressional supporters of placing their concerns for socialized medicine over the necessary expansion of health coverage for

TAKING A WORLD VIEW

NOT-SO-FOREIGN MODELS OF HEALTH CARE

Opponents of health care reform equated Obama's plan to "socialized medicine," believing that increasing government control of health care is intrusive and restrictive. Journalist T. R. Reid (2009) describes the term as a powerful political weapon, first used in 1947 to disparage President Truman's national health care proposal. But, as Reid explains, the argument against socialized medicine is flawed. First, most national health care systems are not socialized. Many countries provide universal health care using private doctors, hospitals, and insurance plans. In fact, there is no single health care system in the world that is exclusively government owned and operated. Second, the United States already has socialized medicine, government-run medicine, in the form of the Department of Veterans Affairs and the Medicare system.

As Reid (2009) explains, "We're like no other country, because the United States maintains so many separate systems for separate classes of people" (p. 21). In his 2009 book *The Healing of America: A Global Quest for Better, Cheaper, and Fairer Health Care*, Reid identifies the four separate systems of health care in our country:

1. *Bismarck model.* For most working Americans under 65 years of age, health care coverage is similar to the health systems in Germany, France, and Japan. Under this model, the worker and the employer share the cost of health insurance premiums.

2. *Beveridge model.* Native Americans, military personnel, and veterans are covered under health care systems much like Great Britain and Cuba. Care is provided by doctors who are government employees working in government-owned clinics and hospitals. Patients who use this system never receive a medical bill.

3. *National health insurance model.* Americans over the age of 65 are covered under Medicare, a system similar to the Canadian health system. Most health care providers are private, but the payer is a single government-run insurance program that every citizen pays into.

4. *Out-of-pocket model.* Americans without a health insurance policy are no different from citizens from poor countries such as Cambodia or parts of rural China or India. If medical care is available, individuals will have to pay the bill out of their own pocket. Care is often available from emergency rooms or community-based free clinics.

In his analysis of these different models of care, Reid (2009) concludes that no system is perfect. Health care reform debates are taking place in other countries.

children. With the House unable to override the president's veto, the administration promised to work with Congress on a bill compromise.

In 2009, Obama signed the CHIP expansion bill. The measure provided coverage to an additional 4 million uninsured children over the next five years, raising the total number of uninsured children covered by the program to 11 million. Obama praised the program for providing access to quality affordable health care and emphasized the program's importance during a time when families had lost their

VOICES IN THE COMMUNITY

VICTORIA HALE

In 2005, Victoria Hale was named by *Esquire* magazine as its businesswoman of the year. She is the director and founder of OneWorld Health, the first nonprofit pharmaceutical company in the United States.

Hale was working as an analyst for the U.S. Food and Drug Administration's Center for Drug Evaluation and Research and then at Genentech (a biotechnology firm) when she first envisioned her company. Her position in the pharmaceutical industry allowed her to see how drugs were being set aside simply because they were not making enough money. The industry dedicates less than 10% of its total research and development budget to eradicating diseases of the developing world, which account for 90% of the world's total infections (Heffernan 2005). Of the more than 1,500 drugs marketed worldwide between 1974 and 2004, only 21, or 1.3%, were used to treat diseases of the developing world (Buse 2006).

She established OneWorld Health to accomplish what she believed the industry should be doing—investing in the development and distribution of drugs that could be used to eradicate diseases in the developing world. Says Hale, "We deliberately chose neglected diseases that others were not working on. . . . There has been little research done on these diseases, and limited money for research or development. We don't choose projects because money is available, we choose projects and then we go find funding" (Roth 2006:2). OneWorld Health is funded by charitable contributions.

Hale's strategy was simple. She searched for drugs whose patents had expired or were not being used because of low profit margins. The first drug OneWorld Health invested in was paromomycin, an antibiotic that cures a parasitic disease called visceral leishmaniasis, also known as black fever or kala-azar. The disease afflicts half a million people annually worldwide, particularly in Bangladesh, Brazil, India, Nepal, and Sudan. Hale discovered that the development of paromomycin had been shelved before its clinical trials were completed. After continuing and completing clinical trials with the drug, Hale found a company, Gland Pharma, based in Hyderabad, India, that agreed to produce paromomycin and sell it for $10 per full course of treatment, affordable for the poor people of India.

Victoria Hale combined her pharmaceutical background with a mission to reduce health inequities. She currently leads Medicines360.

The use of paromomycin was approved in India in late 2006. The government publicly announced its goal of eradicating the disease by 2010. Eradication dates have also been set in Bangladesh and Nepal for 2015. After dealing with the initial skepticism of the pharmaceutical industry and its executives, Hale's OneWorld Health has been heralded as an innovative, socially minded organization. Hale's work will continue: "You can't take care of all two billion of the world's poorest poor at one time. But you can go disease by disease and determine which one you can succeed with" (Roth 2006:2). OneWorld Health is working on three additional drugs—for malaria (the most severe parasitic disease), diarrhea (the number-two killer of children in the developing world), and soil-transmitted hookworm infection (nearly 2 billion people have active infections).

In 2009, Hale founded Medicines360. The organization's mission is to "address unmet needs of women by developing innovative, affordable, and sustainable medical solutions," beginning with access to birth control (Medicines360 2014).

Eradicating Black Fever

SOCIOLOGY AT WORK

MEDICINE

Matthew Peters – Class of 2013

Undergraduate Major: Sociology

Undergraduate Minors: Biology, Chemistry

All U.S. physicians complete four years of undergraduate school, four years of medical school, and three to eight years in an internship or residency program depending on their specialty. While no specific undergraduate major is required, all students must complete prerequisite coursework in biology, chemistry, physics, English, mathematics, and the social sciences (sociology) and humanities. Applicants must also submit letters of recommendation, Medical College Admission Test scores, and evidence of volunteer or service experience in a health care setting (U.S. Bureau of Labor Statistics 2014b).

When he started his undergraduate program, Matthew Peters knew that he wanted to be a doctor, but didn't know anything about sociology. But after taking two sociology courses, Matthew decided to become a Sociology major while remaining on his prerequisite track

Courtesy of Matthew Peters

Matthew Peters

for medical school. He is currently in medical school and admits,

jobs and health insurance. The bill was passed with partisan support from House and Senate Democrats. The expansion was financed with a 62-cent-per-pack increase in the federal tax on cigarettes.

The Affordable Care Act of 2010 maintains CHIP eligibility standards through 2019 and provided funding to promote Medicaid and CHIP enrollment.

State Prescription Drug Plans

In an effort to control drug costs for their residents, several states have offered innovative cost-control models. Pennsylvania is second to Florida in the proportion of its population that is 65 years or older (Pear 2002). More than 300,000 people in Pennsylvania are enrolled in the Pharmaceutical Assistance Contract for the Elderly (PACE) or PACENET. For PACE, men and women 65 years or older can enroll in

Sociology in many ways is what brought me to medicine. To my knowledge, there are not many physician-sociologists, but I believe that is beginning to change, primarily because our country is currently engaged in big conversations about the future of healthcare in our country, from the social determinants of health to health equity. On the patient-care side of things, I believe that my sociological imagination makes me a more aware, sensitive, and thoughtful physician. Although it is easy to become caught up in the science of medicine, my "soci-brain" (as my wife puts it) has a tendency to make me pull back, think about a patient's social context, then use that perspective to shape the encounter and care of the patient.

Through his Sociology program, Matthew completed a summer internship at a federally funded community health center. The experience was invaluable:

Although my tasks as an intern were not always traditional sociological work, the position really

opened my eyes to the experiences of various disadvantaged populations as I began to see the disparities they face to receive fair and equal care. Working with large homeless, immigrant, and recently released convict populations challenged me to rethink my idealistic views of medicine in our country, while also realizing that my draw to medicine isn't simply a fascination or interest; it's a vocation and a mission.

"Do what excites you—even if you do not immediately see how it connects to sociology. Sure, there are 'traditional' sociology careers that are great for some, but do not let yourself feel locked into something that you are not enthusiastic about," says Matthew. "That is one of the best things about sociology—it helps us to be aware of the boxes that contain us in everyday life and step outside of them. Sociology is more than a skill set; it is a way of thinking that I believe can make you more successful in any field."

the program if they have annual incomes less than $23,500 for an individual or $31,500 per couple. The program is financed largely from state lottery proceeds. The program requires the use of low-cost generic drugs, which account for about 45% of all filled prescriptions. PACE was established in 1984 with strong bipartisan support, but with the rising cost of drugs and the increasing number of patients, lawmakers are looking for more cost-cutting strategies (Pear 2002). Pennsylvania also supports PACENET, an assistance program available for elderly individuals with household incomes between $14,500 and $23,500, or between $17,700 and $31,500 per couple. PACE and PACENET members pay a $6 or $8 copay for generic prescription drugs.

U.S. laws prohibit the importation of drugs from other countries into the United States, unless their safety is certified by the U.S. Department of Health and Human Services. The Health and Human Services Task Force on Drug Importation concluded that savings on foreign drugs were not as much as consumers would expect and warned about significant risks to consumers purchasing imported drugs. The report questioned the safety and effectiveness of foreign-made drugs.

At the release of the report, consumer and health advocates weighed in, criticizing the task force for failing to address the fundamental problem of providing affordable prescription drugs to those who cannot afford them. Unlike other countries, in the United States drug prices are set according to market demands. Critics often remark how U.S. patients subsidize the rest of the world's drug supply. The U.S. constitutes less than 5% of the world's population, but buys more than 50% of its prescription drugs (Werth 2013).

Despite the federal restrictions, several states and cities permit their residents to buy prescription drugs from other countries. Maine is the first state to allow residents to buy mail-order drugs from accredited pharmacies in Canada, the United Kingdom, New Zealand, and Australia. The FDA and Pharmaceutical Research and Manufacturers of America objected to the legislation, arguing that access to the foreign drugs would jeopardize patient safety. Supporters of the law argued that Maine residents would have access to affordable medication.

Community-Based Health Centers

Community health centers (CHCs) were based on neighborhood health clinics first established during the War on Poverty in the 1960s. CHCs are operated by a variety of nonprofit organizations, health departments, religious and faith-based organizations, medical organizations, and schools. Costs are covered through a variety of sources, ranging from private insurance to government contracts or grants. These centers have been called the most effective tool to reduce health disparities and can increase access to health care to the poor, racial and ethnic minorities, and other underserved populations (Hargreaves, Arnold, and Blot 2006).

The U.S. Health Resources and Services Administration (HRSA) administers the network of nearly 1,300 nonprofit centers, sometimes also referred to as Federally Qualified Health Centers. These centers provide comprehensive, culturally competent, quality primary health care to medically underserved communities and vulnerable populations. Health centers are located in every state, the District of Columbia, Puerto Rico, the U.S. Virgin Islands, and the Pacific Basin. These centers served more than 21 million people in 2013. It is estimated that one of out every 15 people relies on a HRSA-funded clinic for primary care (HRSA 2014a, 2014b).

With a clinic motto of "Trust.Heal.Care.," the Erie Family Health Center, based in Chicago, Illinois, serves more than 50,000 medical patients each year (Erie Family Health Center 2014). The clinic was established in 1957 by volunteer physicians with a mission of health care as a right, not a privilege. The clinic serves patients at 13 sites across the city, including several large primary care facilities and school-based health centers and a freestanding teen health provider.

Almost 80% of its patients are Hispanics, 54% are served in Spanish, and 68% are female. Eighty-three percent come from households with incomes below the federal poverty line.

Under the ACA, a five-year $11 billion fund was established for the operation, expansion, and construction of 300 new health centers and the renovation of 600 clinics.

CHAPTER REVIEW

10.1 Describe the social determinants of health

A sociological perspective addresses the social determinants of health. Research continues to demonstrate the relationship between the individual and society and the structural effects on health: how our health is affected by our social position, work, families, education, and wealth and poverty.

10.2 Explain the three measures of epidemiology

Epidemiology is the study of the patterns in the distribution and frequency of sickness, injury, and death and the social factors that shape them. Epidemiologists focus on communities and populations, addressing how health and illness experiences are based on social factors such as gender, age, race, social class, and behavior.

10.3 Describe how the different sociological perspectives address problems related to health and medicine

According to the functionalist perspective, illness has a legitimate place in society. Conflict theorists believe that patterns of health and illness reflect systematic inequalities based on ethnicity/race or gender and differences in power, values, and interests. Although the medicalization of such conditions as premenstrual syndrome and menopause may have been effective in treating women, various feminist theorists see this trend as an extension of medicine's control of women. From an interactionist's perspective, health, illness, and medical responses are socially constructed and maintained.

10.4 Identify the relationship between education and health

Researchers suggest that education helps individuals choose and practice a healthier lifestyle regarding diet, exercise, and other health choices. Highly educated men and women are likely to visit their primary physicians more often and regularly and may be more willing to use new medical technologies or medicines. Educated parents will transmit their healthier lifestyle to their children.

10.5 Summarize the different models of health care in the United States

There are four models of health care: (1) the Bismark model, in which the worker and the employer share the cost of health insurance premiums; (2) the Beveridge model, in which care is provided by doctors who are government employees in government-owned clinics and hospitals; (3) the national health insurance model, in which every citizen pays into a single government-run insurance program; and (4) the out-of-pocket model, in which patients pay for their care out of their own pocket.

KEY TERMS

acute illnesses, 275

epidemiology, 273

fecundity, 273

fertility, 273

incidence rate, 275

infant mortality, 274

medicalization, 279

morbidity, 275

mortality, 274

prevalence rate, 275

sick role, 276

STUDY QUESTIONS

1. How is health examined from a sociological perspective?

2. How is illness functional in society? What behavior is expected from someone who is sick?

3. Explain from a conflict perspective how health inequalities are shaped by conflict and competing interests between groups.

4. Using eating disorders as the basis for your answer, examine how illness and disease are socially constructed.

5. Review the inequalities of health and health care access by gender, race/ethnicity, and social class.

6. Why is the United States the last industrial country to adopt a national health care program? Which sociological perspective(s) best explains

why public and political support for health care reform has been difficult to achieve?

7. Do you know what a "mommy job" is? Featured in print and television advertisements, a mommy job is a cosmetic surgical procedure that may include a breast lift, a tummy tuck, and liposuction to reduce the stretch marks, slackened skin, and excess fat that result from pregnancy and childbirth. Targeting women of childbearing age, the marketing of mommy makeovers has been described as an attempt to "pathologize the postpartum body, characterizing pregnancy and child birth as maladies with disfiguring aftereffects that can be repaired with the help of scalpels" (Singer 2007:E3). From a sociological perspective, is a mommy job a surgical necessity or an invention? What do you think?

$\circledS$ SAGE edge™

Sharpen your skills with SAGE edge at **edge.sagepub.com/leonguerrero5e**

SAGE edge provides a personalized approach to help you accomplish your coursework goals in an easy-to-use learning environment.

CHAPTER 11

The Media

Media: Technological processes that facilitate communication

Imagine that you wake up tomorrow in a sort of "Twilight Zone" parallel society where everything is the same except that media do not exist: no television, no movies, no radio, no recorded music, no computers, no Internet, no books or magazines or newspapers.

—Croteau and Hoynes (2000:5)

What would your life be like without the media? Without communication, and the media to communicate with, there would be no society. The term *media* is the plural of *medium*, derived from the Latin word *medius*, which means middle. A *medium* is a method of communication—television, telephone, cable, Internet, radio, or print—between (or in the middle of) a sender and a receiver. But taken all together, the **media**, as defined by David Croteau and William Hoynes (2000), are the "different technological processes that facilitate communication between the sender of the message and the receiver of that message" (p. 7).

Communication is a basic social activity (Seymour-Ure 1974). It is impossible not to communicate and not to come in contact with the media. Today's college students are described as "digital natives" who are technology dependent and capable of accessing information instantly and using many technological devices for everyday living and communication (Black 2010). Take a moment and inventory the number of devices you own—cell phone, laptop, desktop, e-reader, iPod, digital camera?

It is estimated that by the age of 21, Millennials have averaged 10,000 hours playing video games, 2,000 hours watching television, 10,000 hours on the cell phone, and have sent or read 200,000 emails (Barnes, Marateo, and Ferris 2007).

What Does It Mean to Me?

For at least a week, monitor your own media usage. How many hours of television do you watch? How many hours are you on the Internet and on your phone? Would it be possible for you to live a day without media?

The media reflect "the evolution of a nation that has increasingly seized on the need and desire for more leisure time" (Alexander and Hanson 1995:i). Technological developments have increased our range of media choices, from the growing number of broadcast and cable channels to the ever-increasing number of Internet websites. New technologies have also increased our viewing control of and access to the media. For example, technology allows us to choose where and when we want to see a recent film. Are you taking a long road trip? You can download your favorite movie to your notebook or your phone and watch it on the road. Need to access your e-mail? You can check e-mail with a wireless connection in your classroom or with your phone from nearly any location. In fact, u cn comnC8 w/yr F W txt msgN A3 (translation: You can communicate with your friends with text messaging anytime, anywhere, anyplace). As Croteau and Hoynes (2001) observed, "We navigate through a vast mass media environment unprecedented in human history" (p. 3).

Yet, the media have been blamed for creating and promoting social problems and accused of being a problem themselves. Media critics have expressed concern about the highly controlled process by which the images that we see are conceived, produced, and disseminated by media conglomerates. Social researchers and policy makers have identified the unequal advantage some social groups have over others in our increasingly high-tech media environment. Are we losing our individual rights and privacy for the sake of increasing connectivity? Before we review the media and their related social problems, we first examine the media from a sociological perspective.

What Does It Mean to Me?

The digital equivalent of hanging out can be found on social networking sites such as Facebook and Twitter. Also referred to as **social media**, these sites provide teens and adults opportunities for personal expression and connection. How do these sites provide a way to connect with others? If you have your own page, how does it work for you? Are there any dysfunctions related to these social networking sites? Are you concerned about your privacy when using these sites?

Social media: Media that are based on conversation and interaction with individuals online

SOCIOLOGICAL PERSPECTIVES ON THE MEDIA

Functionalist Perspective

Functionalists examine the structural relationship between the media and other social institutions. Even before the content is created, political, economic, and social realities set the stage for media content. The media are shaped by the social and economic conditions of American life and by society's beliefs about the nature of men and women and the nature of society (Peterson 1981). The first American printing press arrived in Boston along with a group of Puritans fleeing England in 1638. The press became an instrument of religion and government, used to print a freeman's oath that presented the conditions of citizenship in this new country, as well as an almanac and a book of hymns (Peterson 1981).

Through electronic and print messages, the media continue to frame our understandings about our lives, our nation, and our world. The media serve as a link between individuals, communities, and nations. They help create a collective consciousness, a term used by Émile Durkheim to describe the set of shared norms and beliefs in a society. The mass media provide people with a sense of connection that few other institutions can offer. Live media events, such as the Olympics, the Super Bowl, or the Oscars, are set off from other media programs. People gather in groups to watch, they talk about what they see, and they share the sense that they are watching something special (Schudson 1986). News events captured by the media, such as the 2012 Summer Olympic games, the 2013 Boston Marathon bombing, or the 2014 demonstrations in Ferguson, Missouri, connect a nation and even the world.

. . . .

What Does It Mean to Me?

How does the mass media provide a sense of connection for you—for instance, how did the media do so for the 2011 royal wedding of Prince William and Kate or the 2012 presidential election?

. . . .

In particular, television has contributed to a corresponding nationalization of politics and issues, taking local or regional events and turning them into national debates. Socially and politically, the media make our world smaller. Thanks to various forms of social media, the world watched as millions of Egyptians converged on Tahrir Square in 2011 demanding the overthrow of the regime of President Hosni Mubarak. Mubarak resigned after 18 days of demonstrations. Facebook and Twitter are credited with unifying protestors and ultimately shaping the political debate.

An estimated 18.6 million U.S. households watched television coverage of the 2011 royal wedding of Prince William and Kate Middleton. In addition to network and cable television programming, the ceremony was streamed live online via Facebook, Yahoo, and Hulu. iPad and iPhone apps also allowed fans to follow the royal nuptials.

Samir Hussein / Getty Images

Social media platforms such as Facebook and Twitter were credited with helping organize Egyptian protestors during the 2011 Arab Spring.

The media have been accused of creating serious dysfunctions and social problems in society. Research has documented the link between viewing of media violence and the development of aggression, particularly among children who watch dramatic violence on television and film. Television has been called the "other parent" or the "black box," accused of draining the life and intelligence out of its young viewers. Popular media culture has been accused of undermining our educational system and subverting traditional literacy (Postman 1989). Public health studies have documented the link between television viewing and poor physical health among children and adults. The one thing television viewers seem to do while watching television is eat, and the danger is in what they choose to eat and drink—unhealthy snack foods or high-calorie drinks (Van den Bulck 2000).

Conflict Perspective

The media, says Noam Chomsky (1989), are like any other businesses. The fundamental principle in American media is to attract an audience to sell to advertisers. Yes, you read that correctly. Commercial television and radio programming depend on advertising revenue, and in turn, the networks promise that you, the consumer audience, will buy the advertisers' products. "The market model of the media is based on the ability of a network to deliver audiences to these advertisers" (Croteau and Hoynes 2001:6).

In the United States, media organizations are likely to be part of larger conglomerates where profit making is the most important goal (Ball-Rokeach and Cantor 1986). Since the very beginning of mass communications, ideas, information, and profit have mixed. The first books printed in the colonies may have been devoted to religion, but the printers made money (Porter 1981). The media, according to conflict theorists, can only be fully understood when we learn who controls them.

One of the clearest, and some say most problematic, trends in the media is the increasing consolidation of ownership. The corporate media play a major role in managing consumer demand, producing messages that support corporate capitalism, and creating a sense of political events and social issues (Kellner 1995). In 1984, more than 50 corporations controlled most of our newspapers, magazines, broadcasting, books, and movies. By 1997, Ben Bagdikian reported that there were 10 media giants. The top five entertainment multinational conglomerates controlling the media for 2011 are listed in Table 11.1. These companies are truly multimedia corporations, producing movies, books, magazines, newspapers, television programming, music, videos, toys, and theme parks in the global marketplace. Under this increasing media consolidation, women- and minority-owned broadcasting has

 Who Owns the Media?

declined. People of color own only 3% of commercial television stations (Wade 2008).

Miller (2002) warned that the most corrosive influence of the 10 media conglomerates cited by Bagdikian (1997) was their impact on journalism. Journalism has traditionally been referred to as the fourth estate, an independent institutional source of political and social power that monitors the actions of other powerful institutions such as politics, economics, and religion. However, conflict theorists remind us that someone is in charge of the fourth estate. Those who control the media are able to manipulate what we see, read, and hear. The media, serving the interest of interlocking state and corporate powers, frame messages in a way that supports the ruling elite and limits the variety of messages that we read, see, and hear (Chomsky 1989).

Edward Jay Epstein (1981) reveals that what we consider news is not the product of chance events; "it is the result of decisions made within a news organization" (p. 119). He explains that the crucial decisions on what constitutes news—what will and won't be covered—are made not by the journalists but by executives of the news organization. Although the public expects news reporters to act like independent fair-minded professionals, reporters are employees of corporations that control their hiring, firing, and daily management (Bagdikian 1997). News executives are in control of the selection and deployment of specific reporters, the expenditure of time and resources for gathering the news, and the allocation of space for the presentation of news (Epstein 1981). And because they are economically motivated, news organizations are mindful of their audiences' preferences and try to cater to those preferences as much as possible (Baron 2006).

Regina Branton and Johanna Dunaway concluded that audience preferences and newspaper profit motives result in differences between English and Spanish news coverage of immigration in the United States. In their 2008 study, Spanish-language news outlets generated a larger volume of immigration coverage than English-language outlets. On the other hand, English-language news media were more likely to focus on negative aspects of immigration than Spanish-language media outlets. Both patterns, according to the researchers, are motivated by profit and the desire to satisfy their different target audiences. Branton and Dunaway suggest that conflicting media coverage may even contribute to the differences in immigration attitudes between Anglos and Latinos.

Feminist Perspective

Douglas Kellner (1995) says that the media represent "a contested terrain, reproducing on the cultural level the fundamental conflicts within society" (p. 101). Feminist theorists attempt to understand how the media represent and devalue women and

Table 11.1	Five largest entertainment companies

Rank	Company
1	Walt Disney (United States)
2	News Corporation Ltd. (Australia)
3	Time Warner Inc. (United States)
4	CBS (United States)
5	Viacom (United States)

SOURCE: CNN Money 2011.

NOTE: For more information about these media companies, visit the website "Who Owns What," sponsored by the *Columbia Journalism Review*. Log on to the SAGE edge select companion site, Chapter 11, at http://edge.sagepub.com/leonguerrero5e for a link.

Body Evolution

minorities. This perspective examines how the media either use stereotypes disparaging women and minorities or completely exclude them from media images (Eschholz, Bufkin, and Long 2002).

One of the most important lessons young children learn is expected gender roles, learning masculine versus feminine behaviors. Although these lessons are taught by parents and teachers, a significant source of cultural gendered messages is television programs (Powell and Abels 2002). Regular exposure to television's stereotypical gender roles has been associated with young children having more stereotypical beliefs about masculine and feminine characteristics and activities (Signorielli and Lears 1992). In his analysis of children's programming, Mark Barner (1999) found that women are typically portrayed in passive roles as housewives, waitresses, and secretaries, whereas men are seen in active roles as construction workers or doctors. Rivadeneyra and Ward (2005: 454) argue, "If women are seldom portrayed as problem solvers, heroines, and working mothers, and if men are rarely depicted as nurturant and sensitive, viewers' own self-conceptions, aspirations and gender ideologies may become equally constrained."

Feminist scholarship demonstrates how the media undermine women, particularly those who challenge traditional gender roles (Gibson 2009). In 2006, Katie Couric made history when she debuted as the first woman to solo anchor a major network newscast. Her debut and performance, according to Katie Gibson (2009), was critiqued in the media through a sexualized frame. By focusing primarily on her body and her appearance (her hair style, legs, and fashion), the media objectified Couric and undermined her as a legitimate news professional.

Researchers have identified how female political candidates receive different attention from their male counterparts. News reports focus on political women's physical appearance, lifestyle, and family life rather than on campaign issues and how women are the targets of negative coverage regarding their lack of experience and knowledge (Wasburn and Wasburn 2011). Coverage about a female candidate's political positions will feature women's topics such as abortion, child care, or education as opposed to men's issues such as the economy or national security. Philo Wasburn and Mara Wasburn (2011), in their analysis of media coverage of Governor Sarah Palin's vice presidential campaign, concluded that "with respect to the coverage of political women, the political culture of America's commercial media remained largely unchanged through decades of election cycles" (p. 1039). Though there was more coverage of Palin than Joe Biden, the Democratic vice presidential candidate, Palin was objectified by the media and treated as a sex object through references to her beauty queen background, her

During the 2008 U.S. presidential campaign, media reports addressed Governor Sarah Palin's lack of political experience, but also focused on her appearance and her beauty pageant background.

appearance, and her wardrobe. There was frequent mention of her lack of national and global political experience, and policy coverage was focused on her take on women's issues.

Interactionist Perspective

In what they tell us and what they choose not to tell us, the media define our social world (McNair 1998). The interactionist perspective focuses on the symbols and messages of the media and how the media come to define our "reality." It might be best to view the media, as Michael Gurevitch and Mark Levy (1985) suggest, as "a site on which various social groups, institutions, and ideologies struggle over the definition and construction of social reality" (p. 9).

The mass media become the authority at any given moment for "what is true and what is false, what is reality and what is fantasy, what is important and what is trivial" (Bagdikian 1997:xliv). The mass media define what events are newsworthy. The first criterion is proximity; events happening close are more newsworthy than those happening at a greater distance. Second, deviation is an important criterion. Events that can be reported as disruptions (natural disasters, unexpected deaths, murders), deviations from cultural or social norms of behavior (especially sexual, e.g., philandering clergy or politicians), and lifestyle deviance (alternative lifestyle reports) make the news (Galtung and Ruge 1973).

Sociologist Herbert Gans (1979) explained that the news isn't about just anyone; it is usually about "knowns." Women and men identified by their position in government or their fame and fortune are automatically newsworthy. Knowns are elites in all walks of life, but especially from politics, the entertainment industry, and sports. Incumbent presidents appear in the news most often. The president is the only individual whose routine activities are noteworthy. (When was the last time that a news crew followed your every move?) In recent years, "celebutantes" (daughters from wealthy or famous families), such as the Kardashian sisters, have been deemed newsworthy by the media, with their every move and fumble chronicled.

One of the biggest news stories of the late 20th century was the death of Princess Diana. The facts and circumstances of her 1997 death and the fairy-tale life that preceded it conformed to all the criteria of newsworthiness. Although it occurred in France, her death involved cultural proximity: Princess Diana was a worldwide celebrity. The nonstop coverage of her life and death began as a story of celebrity fascination but ended as an international tragedy (McNair 1998). Shortly after Princess Diana's death, Mother Teresa, a renowned humanitarian, died. Although Mother Teresa's death was a news story, it never got the same attention and coverage as the death of Princess Diana did. As journalist Daniel Schorr (1998) said, the difference between the two women's lives was "the difference between a noble life well lived and a media image well cultivated. . . . Mother Teresa was celebrated, but was not a celebrity" (p. 15).

 Growing Up Online

The mass media play a large role in shaping public agendas by influencing what people think about (Shaw and McCombs 1997) and, ultimately, what people consider a social problem (Altheide 1997). David Altheide (1997) describes the news media as part of the "problem-generating machine" produced by an entertainment-oriented media industry. The news informs the public, but its message is also intended to serve as entertainment, an opportunity for voyeurism, and a "quick fix" rather than providing an understanding of the underlying social causes of the problem.

Altheide (1997) argues that the fear pervasive in American society is mostly produced through messages presented by the news media. The disproportionate coverage of crime and violence in the news media affects readers and viewers (Glassner 1997). Despite evidence that Americans have a comparative advantage in regard to diseases, accidents, nutrition, medical care, and life expectancy, American women and men perceive themselves to be at greater risk than do their counterparts elsewhere and express fears about this (Altheide 1997). In a national poll, respondents were asked why they believe the country has a serious crime problem. About 76% said they had seen serious crime in the media, whereas only 22% said they had had a personal experience with crime (Glassner 1997). In a study of 56 local news programs, crime was the most prominently featured subject, accounting for more than 75% of all news coverage in some cities (Klite, Bardwell, and Salzman 1997).

For a summary of sociological perspectives, see Table 11.2.

Table 11.2 Summary of sociological perspectives: The media

	Functional	Conflict/Feminist	Interactionist
Explanation of the media and social problems	Functionalists examine the structural relationship between the media and other social institutions. Sociologists using this perspective also examine the functions and dysfunctions of the media.	Conflict theorists focus on the media and how their messages are controlled by an elite group. Feminist theorists address how the media use stereotypes disparaging women and minorities or completely exclude them from media images.	From this perspective, sociologists investigate how the media define our social reality.
Questions asked about the media	How do other institutions affect the media and their content? What functions do the media serve in society? What are their dysfunctions?	Who owns the media? How are the media's messages manipulated? What images of women and minorities are presented by the media?	How do the media define what is newsworthy? How do the media define the public agenda? How do the media define what we believe is a social problem?

TAKING A WORLD VIEW

WOMEN'S FEATURE SERVICE, NEW DELHI, INDIA

Established in 1978, the Women's Feature Service (WFS) began as an effort to include gender analyses and views in the media. The international news service is directed and staffed by women, syndicating 250 to 300 articles a year in print and electronic media. By gathering and providing access to these stories about women's lives, WFS seeks to build awareness about women's lives, rights, and concerns (Women's Feature Service 2014).

> WFS exists because of the felt need for a gender balance in news coverage and because of dissatisfaction about the ways in which news organizations—in India and elsewhere—treat news coverage about women. Often, the media either ignore important stories altogether, relegate reporting to obscure places in the newspaper, or sensationalize incidents without examining the underlying context or causes. The media tend to focus on women only when it comes to "women's issues," forgetting that women also have an equal stake in so-called "male concerns" such as the budget, economy, globalization, agriculture, and conflict resolution. (Parekh 2001)

Women occupy about 36% of all reporting jobs based on an international survey of 59 nations (International Women's Media Foundation 2010).

Pamela Phillopose served as WFS editor until 2014. As a journalist, she advocates the importance of telling people-centric stories.

> In a country like India, where the well-being of an increasing number of people is being threatened, directly and indirectly, by reversals of all kinds, ranging from the food and environmental crises to global recessions, there is space for a more people-centric definition of journalism. We need more than ever media practitioners who travel beyond the confines of privileged enclaves, leaving behind the "big spenders" of metropolitan India, to tell their stories. We need media practitioners who have the knowledge, capacity and technological ability to communicate on the real issues of our times and speak truth to power in compelling ways. (Phillopose, quoted in Neupane 2014)

The news organization also sponsors international conferences on women-related issues and media workshops for journalists. WFS is based in New Delhi, India (Women's Feature Service 2014).

From an interactionist's perspective, how does the media define what is newsworthy? Is there a way to alter the media's influence?

THE MEDIA AND SOCIAL PROBLEMS

Loss of Privacy

Erving Goffman (1959) theorized that individuals practice **impression management,** creating a favorable impression of themselves to others. He argued that we maintain a distinction between a public self (performing on a front stage for the benefit of

Impression management: Creating a favorable impression of oneself to others

 What Corporations Know

others) and a more private self (more natural and comfortable on the backstage). However the advent of social media has increasingly blurred the lines between public and private. "Before our children can walk or talk, we teach them to share. So it is no wonder that we have flocked to social media, a platform based on sharing, to share everything from our birth dates to films of our child's birth," said Julie Brill, commissioner of the Federal Trade Commission (FTC) (quoted in Naoum 2012).

And in some cases you do not have a choice in what information you share. Documents leaked by former National Security Agency subcontractor Edward Snowden in 2013 confirmed how for years the agency was intercepting phone calls and online communications of American citizens. Under its PRISM program, the agency was gathering data on non-U.S. citizens through its access of Apple, Facebook, Google, Skype, and Yahoo servers. Though the agency was accused of violating the U.S. Constitution and several federal privacy laws, General Keith Alexander (NSA's Chief) defended the program citing the Patriot Act. According to Alexander, the agency's phone and Internet surveillance programs were essential to preventing terrorist acts around the world (Bash and Cohen 2013). In 2014, a British court ruled that electronic mass surveillance under programs like PRISM were legal and had enough safeguards to protect individuals' online privacy (Scott 2014).

Websites routinely track your personal information and online activities (Nguyen 2011). Websites and online applications use cookies to track information about users. Cookies allow website operators to see your browsing history, store your log-in information, and help personalize sites by remembering your preferences and searches from previous visits. Though many Internet users have learned how to disable cookies through control panels, most Internet users do not do so. Facebook and other social media networks also maintain and track personal data about their users, including where the users live and users' personal interests and activities. Many Facebook applications (including Zynga, the creator of the online game FarmVille) were transmitting Facebook user IDs to advertisers and Internet tracking firms. Facebook and Zynga both pledge not to share personally identifiable information with third parties (Nguyen 2011).

Google's and Facebook's privacy policies have been scrutinized by media watch groups, politicians, and consumers. In 2011, Facebook settled FTC charges that it deceived users by telling them that it would keep their Facebook information private, though it was sharing users' personal data with others. According to its settlement, Facebook must not make any deceptive privacy claims, is required to get consumers' approval before making changes in data sharing, and is required to obtain assessments of its privacy practices by independent, third-party auditors through 2031 (FTC 2011). In 2012, Google announced plans to unify data collections across all its services, including its search engine, YouTube, and Gmail. Consumer privacy groups expressed concern that the data consolidation would reveal information about a person's location, religion, sexual orientation, health status, and personal interests. Google claims that it maintains a priority on user security, transparency, and control.

IN FOCUS

THE BOUNDARY-LESS WORKPLACE

Wendy Boswell and Julie Olson-Buchanan (2007) describe how communication technology (CT) has changed the media we use to communicate with each other in the workplace, but also how it has significantly changed our connection to work. CT allows for greater flexibility in managing one's work, but it may give employees little opportunity to disengage from work. We don't think much about responding to a voice message after dinner or checking e-mail messages while on vacation. Though employees may not be officially on the job, CT has "enabled an anytime-anywhere connectedness of employees to their work" (Fenner and Renn 2004:184).

Teresa Sullivan (2014) cautions against the merging of work versus non-work time. Referring to Lewis Coser's (1974) concept of greedy institutions, she highlights how different institutions compete for the limited energies and time commitments of individuals. The workplace has become our primary greedy institution via CT. "Continuous connectivity allows employers to reach into the after hours of their employees' lives, extending the workday beyond its traditional limits. And globalization, which extends a firm's reach across many time zones, requires more workers to be alert and responsive for more hours of the day" (Sullivan 2014:4).

CT use during non-work time has been positively correlated to an employee's workload and career ambitions. Remaining connected is viewed as a convenient means to keep up with one's work and as a way to get ahead in one's organization or occupation (Boswell and Olson-Buchanan 2007). This high level of connectivity could be described as an expectation of our work. At the same time, CT use during non-working hours has been linked to higher employee stress levels, job burnout, and lower job satisfaction (Fonner and Roloff 2010; Leonardi, Treem, and Jackson 2010). In their 2014 study, Kevin Wright and his colleagues discovered that as the number of outside-of-work hours increased via CT, perceptions of work versus life conflict increased. Individuals noted how their personal life suffered or their personal needs were neglected because of checking in on their work online.

In 2014, Daimler, the German automobile corporation, announced that their employees can take advantage of a Mail on Holiday program. The program automatically deletes all incoming email while an employee is on vacation. The sender is notified that the email has not been received and then is asked to contact a substitute. How does this program alter expectations of the employee?

The Digital Haves and Have-Nots

The term **digital divide** was first used in the mid-1990s by policy leaders and social scientists concerned about the emerging split between those with and those without access to computers and the Internet. The term refers to the gap separating individuals who have access to new forms of technology from those who do not. In addition, others have identified a gap between those who can effectively use new information and communication tools and those who cannot (Gunkel 2003). Despite the increasing diffusion of computers and an overall increase in Internet use, a deep divide remains "between those who possess the resources, education and skills to reap the benefits from the technology and those who do not" (Servon 2002:4). President

Digital divide: The gap separating individuals who have access to and understanding of new forms of technology from those who do not

 Social Media's Growing Influence

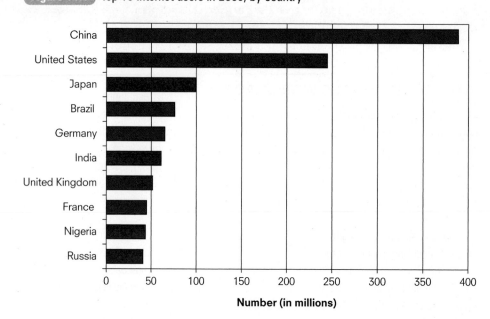

Figure 11.1 Top 10 Internet users in 2009, by country

Number (in millions)

SOURCE: Central Intelligence Agency 2012.

Obama has pledged to make high-speed Internet service available to most Americans, raising access to 90% in the coming decade.

The divide is also a global phenomenon. Less than 10% of the world's population uses the Internet (Guillén and Suárez 2005). According to data collected by the Central Intelligence Agency (2012), China and the United States rank the highest with Internet users—each has more than 200 million users (refer to Figure 11.1). Developing non-Western countries such as those in Africa, South America, and South Asia have fewer than a million Internet users.

The Internet has been described as both empowering and discriminating, enabling residents in some countries to pursue a better life while others are left behind (Guillén and Suárez 2005). Cross-national research has linked the diffusion of Internet technology with developed service sector economies, an educated population, economic development, and significant research and development investment. Users in less-developed countries have basic access problems: economic (cost of basic necessities vs. cost of Internet access), technological (varying ability of local networks), and geographical (limited access outside urban areas) aspects (Vartanova 2002). Mainly because of income differentials, the Internet is beyond the reach of global citizens. For example, in countries with low human development, the average annual income is about $1,200 (in U.S. dollars); the cost of owning a cheap personal computer would take more than half of that income, about $700 (Drori 2004; United Nations Development Programme 2001). On the other hand, pay-as-you-go plans have made cellular phones more affordable. Nearly 40% of all adults living in

    Reducing the Digital Divide

poverty are cellular-only users compared with 21% of adults with higher incomes (Blumberg et al. 2011). Some states also provide cellular phone subsidies for low-income residents.

The digital divide implies a chain of causality. Access and ability to use computers and Internet technology help improve one's social and economic well-being; lack of access to computers and the Internet harms one's life chances. But it is also true that those who are already marginalized in society will have fewer opportunities to access and use computers and the Internet (Warschauer 2003). Among persons with incomes of $30,000 or less, only 52% have broadband access compared with 91% of individuals with incomes more than $75,000. Data also indicate that rates of broadband usage are higher among individuals with a bachelor's degree or more (90%) than among those with a high school degree (58%) (Pew Research Internet Project 2013). The U.S. Census Bureau (2010) projected that the average consumer would spend almost $1,000 for media usage (e.g., television, Internet, cell phone, and radio) in 2010. In contrast, in 2004, the average consumer spent $770.

The digital divide is a symptom of a larger social problem in the United States: social inequality based on income, educational attainment, and ethnicity/race. Data from the Pew Internet & American Life Project (2012) reveal how Internet use is divided along demographic and socioeconomic lines. Internet use is higher among Whites and Blacks than among Hispanics. Higher Internet use is positively associated with higher incomes and educational attainment. (Refer to this chapter's Exploring Social Problems feature for more information about the digital divide.) However, as digital access has improved, researchers have noted an overall increase in the use of media for time wasting among youth and continuing disparities. As reported by the Kaiser Family Foundation (Rideout, Foehr, and Roberts 2010), youth whose parents attained a high school degree or less spend more time per day exposed to media (television, music, video games, and movies) than youth whose parents have a college degree.

Internet access is not the only issue facing underserved communities. Wendy Lazarus and Francisco Mora (2000) identified four online content barriers. The greatest barrier is the lack of locally relevant information. They discovered that low-income users seek practical and relevant information that affects their daily lives, on topics such as education (adult high school degree programs), family (low-cost child care), finances (news on public benefits, consumer information), health (local clinics, low-cost insurance resources), and personal enrichment (foreign-language newspapers). In some instances, information may be available in printed documents, but these may be difficult to locate or obtain. General information may exist online, but it might not be suitable to low-income audiences. For example, online housing services might list high-end rental units rather than lower-rent housing.

The second barrier identified by Lazarus and Mora (2000) was the lack of information at a basic literacy level. According to the authors, a number of online tutorials that review computer program and Internet skills are written at a higher level of literacy. The third barrier was the need for content for non-English speakers. There

Internet Access

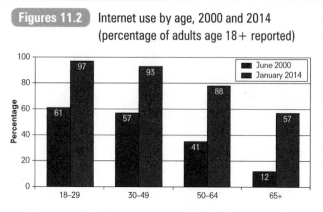

Figures 11.2 Internet use by age, 2000 and 2014 (percentage of adults age 18+ reported)

June 2000
January 2014

SOURCE: Fox and Rainie 2014.

Figure 11.3 Internet use by educational attainment, 2000 and 2014 (percentage of adults age 18+ reported)

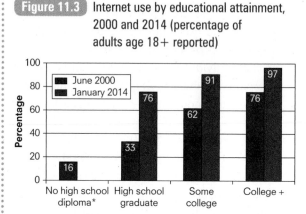

June 2000
January 2014

SOURCE: Fox and Rainie 2014.

NOTE: For 2014, high school graduate and no high school diploma categories were combined.

Figure 11.4 Internet use by income level, 2000 and 2014 (percentage of adults age 18+ reported)

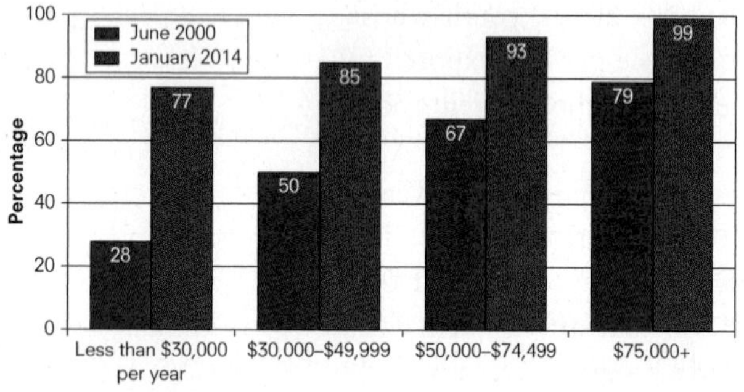

June 2000
January 2014

SOURCE: Fox and Rainie 2014.

Figure 11.5 Internet use by race, 2000 and 2014 (percentage of adults age 18+ reported)

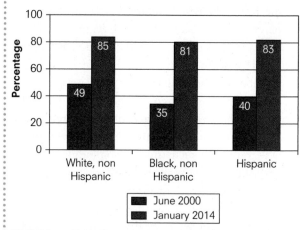

June 2000
January 2014

SOURCE: Fox and Rainie 2014.

WHAT DO YOU THINK?

In 1995, only 14% of U.S. adults had Internet access, mostly through dial-up modem connections, according to the Pew Research Center. Forty-two percent had never heard of the Internet. Two decades later, 87% of U.S. adults use the Internet for either work or personal use (Fox and Rainie 2014).

Figures 11.2 through 11.5 present 2000 and 2014 U.S. data on Internet use based on four demographic variables—age, education, income, and race.

How would you describe the change in Internet use between the two reported years? Which demographic characteristic has had the most increase in level of use?

Fifty-three percent of Internet users say it would be very hard to give up the Internet (Fox and Rainie 2014). Could you give up Internet access in some or all parts of your life?

is little government material (e.g., on voting, Medicare, or taxes) translated into Spanish. Last, there is a need for more websites that reflect diverse cultural heritages and practices.

....

What Does It Mean to Me?

Is there a digital divide among students at your school? What advantages are there for students who own and use laptops and/or smartphones? What do you think is the minimum equipment requirement for staying digitally connected or for being technologically literate?

....

The Death of the Newspaper?

As the fourth estate, journalism serves as a watchdog for government activities. Independent reporters, especially through print media, keep the public informed about political issues and activities. According to Robert McChesney and John Nichols (2010), citizens should have "media that regard the state secret as an assault to popular governance, that watch the politically and economically powerful with a suspicious eye, that recognize as their duty the informing and enlightening of citizens" (p. 2).

Yet, in our increasingly digital age, newspaper readership has declined while the use of online news sources has increased. In 2010, 37% of Americans said they read a paper yesterday (compared with 43% in 2006), while the number who said they read news online yesterday was 34% (compared with 29% in 2006) (Project for Excellence in Journalism 2011).

This transition has caused concern among those in the newspaper industry: owners and employees. According to the Newspaper Association of America (2012), in 2000, there were 1,468 daily papers. By 2011, the number of daily papers had declined to 1,382. Nearly every large paper has fewer pages and fewer articles; some have eliminated entire sections (Pérez-Peña 2009). In 2012, 2,600 full-time newsroom jobs were cut. While some argue that news is more accessible via the Internet, the quality and content of the news is changing. According to the Pew Research Center's Project for Excellence in Journalism (2012), the decline in print newspapers will mean "less coverage of government in suburbs or remote cities, pulling back on state government coverage, the decimation of specialty beats like science or religion, fewer feature stories and elimination of many weekday feature sections."

So what will take the place of your local newspaper? Several online companies have created hyperlocal news sites that allow readers to create their own neighborhood-focused news site—with stories, information, and advertising catering to their specific interests and needs. But some think that online news services are not the same. In a 2009 Senate hearing on journalism, Senator Benjamin Cardin (D-MD) testified, "As local newspapers disappear, we lose an important check on local governments, state governments, the federal government, elected officials, corporations, school districts, businesses, individuals and more. Newspapers and

Newspaper Readership Then, Now and in the Future

the investigative journalism they provide are essential in a free, democratic society and must be preserved" (quoted in Tucker 2009:8). According to Gary Kebbel, journalism program director for the Knight Foundation, the news business "is in a difficult time period right now, between what was and what will be" (quoted in Miller and Stone 2009:B1).

Driving Distracted

In 2007, a 53-year-old male driver was checking his e-mail while driving and caused a five-car pileup on Interstate 5 outside of Seattle, Washington. Driving while texting (DWT) is part of the growing phenomenon of distracted driving. Texting, along with the use of cell phones while driving, has been attributed to at least 1.3 million traffic accidents. Cell phone use causes more crashes than texting—1.3 million versus 200,000. According to the National Safety Council (2010), 28% of all traffic accidents involve talking and texting on cell phones. Drivers who use a cell phone—handheld or hands-free—are four times more likely to be involved in an accident.

The Seattle incident led to the passage of two laws, the first of their kind in the nation. One law prohibits driving while texting, and the second prohibits the use of a handheld phone while driving. Both laws are secondary enforcement laws, which means a driver will be ticketed for the offense only if pulled over for another driving violation. Public support for laws banning cell phone use while driving is gaining momentum (National Safety Council 2010). Since 2009, 44 states have enacted bans

© sshepard/iStock

Texting, along with the general use of cell phones while driving, has been attributed to at least 1.3 million traffic accidents.

on texting while driving, and 38 states have enacted total cell phone bans for young drivers. Fourteen states ban the use of handheld devices while driving (Governors Highway Safety Association 2014).

In an executive order signed by President Obama, federal employees are not allowed to text while driving. The federal government also plans to ban texting by interstate bus drivers and truckers. The use of cell phones may be limited to emergency situations.

Do You Trust the News Media?

Whether we are watching CNN, ABC, NBC, CBS, or Fox, we rely on reporters for most if not all our information about our community and our world. According to the Project for Excellence in Journalism (2004), public attitudes about the press have been growing less positive for about 20 years. In its report, *The State of the News Media 2004*, the Project for Excellence in Journalism identified the disconnection between the public and the news media over motive as the fundamental reason for the decline in public support. Whereas journalists believe they are working in the public interest, the public believes that news organizations are working primarily for profit and that journalists are motivated by professional ambition. In 2011, reporters from the *News of the World*, a tabloid newspaper in Great Britain, were exposed for phone hacking practices used to gather information about celebrities, politicians, and other people in the news.

The public debate about whether U.S. media are liberal or conservative also sensitizes the public to how the media could be manipulative or subjective in content. In addition, people are increasingly distrustful of the large multinational corporations that own and control most of the news media (Project for Excellence in Journalism 2004). These findings are confirmed by the Pew Research Center (2011). Eighty percent of the public feel that news organizations are influenced by powerful people and organizations rather than being independent. Approximately 60% of Americans consider news organizations politically biased. In addition, more than 75% believe news organizations tend to favor one side rather than treat all sides fairly.

In addition, the Pew Research Center examined how Americans regard their news organizations over time. In 1985, 55% of those surveyed felt that the news media usually get their facts straight, while 34% believed that news organizations usually provide inaccurate reports. In 2011, the percentages have switched: 25% of those surveyed felt that the news media get the facts straight and 66% believed their stories are often inaccurate (Pew Research Center 2011). The 2011 survey found that most Americans prefer news with no political viewpoint.

During the early months of the 2008 presidential campaign, a news report claimed that Democratic candidate Senator Barack Obama had attended a madrassa (a Muslim religious school) while living in Indonesia. The allegation was first raised in *Insight*, a conservative Internet magazine owned by the *Washington Times*, and it was repeated by other news services. The magazine alleged that Obama had been raised as a Muslim and that the sources of its information were researchers close to rival Senator Hillary Rodham Clinton's campaign. The deputy headmaster of the school Obama attended stated that the school is a public one that does not focus on religion. Obama's campaign staff maintained that the story was "completely ludicrous" and identified the candidate as a committed Christian. Clinton's staff claimed that they had nothing to do with the story.

COMMUNITY, POLICY, AND SOCIAL ACTION

Federal Communications Commission and the Telecommunications Act of 1996

The Federal Communications Commission (FCC) was established by the Communications Act of 1934 and is charged with regulating interstate and international communications by radio, television, wire, satellite, and cable. As an independent agency, the FCC oversees violations of federal law and policies and reports directly to the U.S. Congress (FCC 2004). Under current FCC rules, radio stations and broadcast television channels cannot air indecent language or material that shows or describes sexual or excretory functions between 6 a.m. and 10 p.m., when children may be watching. In response to a violation, the FCC may issue a warning, revoke a station's license, or impose a monetary fine. In the entire history of the FCC, the commission has fined two television stations for indecency (K. Kelly, Clark, and Kulman 2004).

Introduced a week before the Super Bowl in 2004, the Broadcast Decency Enforcement Act was designed to amend the Communications Act of 1934. The bipartisan bill increased penalties to $500,000 for violating FCC regulations. Broadcasters could also lose their license if they violated indecency standards three times. The act would not apply to cable television programming. In the case of the 2004 Super Bowl halftime show, each CBS station that aired the program could have been fined as much as $27,500. After the 2004 Super Bowl halftime show (and Janet Jackson's wardrobe malfunction), television broadcasters began to police their programming more closely.

Through the FCC, the public can file complaints on a range of issues: billing disputes, wireless questions, telephone company advertising practices, telephone slamming (switching a consumer's telephone service without permission), unsolicited telephone marketing calls, and indecency and obscenity complaints. Along with the FTC, the FCC is enforcing the National Do Not Call Registry, which went into effect in October 2002. The FCC and FTC report that more than 55 million people have signed up for the registry.

The first major overhaul of the original 1934 act, the Telecommunications Act of 1996, was seen as a way to encourage competition in the communications industry.

The law specified how local telephone carriers may compete, how and under what circumstances local exchange carriers can provide long-distance services, and ways to deregulate cable television rates. Also included in the act were provisions to make telecommunications more accessible to disabled Americans. A Decency Act makes it a crime to knowingly convey pornography over the Internet on a website accessible to children.

Although the act was presented as an opportunity to encourage competition and break down media monopolies, industry watchers noted that the 1996 law swept away the minimal consumer and diversity protections of the original 1934 act. The 1996 act reduced competition and allowed more cooperation between media giants. Data we reviewed in an earlier section of this chapter seem to support this. The new law permitted some of the largest industries—those not active in creating media content, such as telephone companies—to enter the television, radio, and cable industry. New industries joined older media companies to form interlocking partnerships, rather than become independent competitors as the act had predicted. For example, U.S. West, one of the largest telephone companies in the country, acquired Continental Cablevision, the third-largest cable system. Sprint, the long-distance telephone company, formed a joint venture with TCI, a cable company. The merger between Disney, ABC Broadcasting, and Capital Cities was made possible only through the passage of the 1996 law (Bagdikian 1997).

Who Is Watching the Media?

Numerous organizations have emerged as watch groups monitoring media accuracy and content. Groups such as Accuracy in Media (AIM) and the Center for Media and Public Affairs (CMPA) are nonprofit, grassroots organizations that attempt to expose biased and inaccurate news coverage while encouraging members of the media to report the news fairly and objectively. AIM publishes a newsletter and weekly newspaper column, broadcasts a daily radio commentary, and promotes a speaker's bureau to expose faulty reporting. On its website, current news stories are posted, along with AIM's analysis of the story's accuracy. CMPA conducts scientific research of the news and entertainment events, such as coverage of the presidential elections, the current presidential administration, international media, science and health, and religion (Center for Media and Public Affairs 2012).

Several organizations attempt to improve and protect the integrity of journalists in print, electronic, and Internet media. The Project for Excellence in Journalism (2004) began as an initiative by journalists to clarify and raise the standards of American journalism. The project serves as a research organization, conducting an annual review of local television news, producing a series of content studies on press performance, and offering educational programs for journalists. The project also provides information to the public about what to expect from the press, how to write a letter to the editor, and how to talk to the news media. Another organization, the Committee to Protect Journalists, is an independent, nonprofit

VOICES IN THE COMMUNITY

GEENA DAVIS

Responding to the lack of female characters in television and motion picture programming, Geena Davis founded the See Jane program to promote and advance gender balance in media for children 11 years of age or younger. Davis (2006) explains that after she gave birth to her daughter and began to watch preschool programs, she did a study of her own, examining the characters in her daughter's videos, and she realized that the programs were dominated by male characters. The See Jane program was renamed the Geena Davis Institute on Gender in Media.

Where the Girls Aren't was the first research project sponsored by the program, using content analysis to examine 101 top-grossing G-rated animated and live action films from 1990 to 2004 (Kelly and Smith 2006). In these films, researcher Stacy Smith found that there were three male characters for every one female character. Twenty-three percent of speaking characters were female, and more than 80% of film narrators were male. This gender imbalance can affect children's gender development, reinforcing children's stereotypical attitudes and beliefs about gender. According to Davis, "by making it common for our youngest children to see everywhere a balance of active and complex male and female characters, girls and boys will grow up to empathize with and care more about each other's stories" (quoted in Kelly and Smith 2006:9–10).

In the institute's 2014 study, Stacy Smith, Marc Choueiti, and Katherine Pieper examined female characters in the most popular films released between January 2010 and May 2013 in 11 countries. Their study confirms the continuing absence of women and girls on screen. Based on a total of 5,799 speaking or named characters on screen, only 31% were female, a gender ratio of 2.24 males to every one female. Only 23.3% of the films had a girl or woman as the lead or co-lead in the story. When females were shown, they were more than two times likely to be shown in sexually revealing clothing (24.8% vs. 9.4%), thin (38.5% vs. 15.7%), or partially or fully naked (24.2% vs. 11.5%) than males (Smith, Choueiti, and Pieper

Geena Davis visits a class of second graders to promote lessons on gender stereotypes in the media. Davis leads the Geena Davis Institute on Gender in Media, advocating for more girls and women in television and films, in front of and behind the camera.

2014). Smith and her colleagues highlight the important relationship between filmmaker gender and character gender—films with at least one female director or writer have a higher percentage of girls/women on the screen than those without—and conclude that the industry needs more female directors and writers to improve the number of female lead characters.

Certainly Davis's experience on the film *Thelma and Louise* helped her recognize the impact of a strong female character on women and men. She acknowledges the effect of media images on adults, but her concern is on the impact on children. "We know that kids learn their value by seeing themselves reflected in the culture. They say, 'I see myself! I must matter. I must count.'" Her goal is for media portrayals to be "normal and natural for children to see worlds and characters—be they Martians or dinosaurs or talking toaster ovens—that are roughly half female and male. Just like the real world that our kids live in" (Davis 2006).

In addition to ongoing research, the institute continues to educate parents and child professionals about the importance of gender equity in the media. The program's goal is to see females constituting half of all characters in media made for young children.

organization promoting press freedom worldwide by defending the rights of journalists to report the news without fear of reprisal. The organization documents attacks on the press worldwide, including the number of journalists killed, missing, or imprisoned. For 2014, the committee reported that 60 journalists were killed; international journalists covering conflict and dangerous situations in the Middle East, Ukraine, and Afghanistan were at higher risk (Committee to Protect Journalists 2014).

Media Literacy and Digital Literacy

There are ongoing efforts among scholars, policy makers, and educators to promote **media literacy**, the ability to understand, analyze, and critique media content. It is about shifting from the role of a passive receiver of media to an active critical receiver and includes asking several questions: For whom is this media message intended? Who wants to reach this audience, and why? From whose perspective is this story being told? Whose voices are being heard, and whose are absent? (Media Awareness Network 2004). This type of literacy develops one's abilities to examine the social and commercial context of media messages as well as the consequences of those messages (Considine, Horton, and Moorman 2009). Media literacy is important for the development of democracy and active citizenship, lifelong learning, and economic and labor competitiveness (Livingston, Van Couvering, and Thumin 2004).

Recently, the definition of literacy has expanded to include digital media. **Digital literacy** refers to an individual's ability to appropriately use digital tools and skills to identify, manage, evaluate, analyze, and synthesize digital sources; to construct new knowledge; and to communicate with others (Martin 2006). Elizabeth Thoman and Tessa Jolls (2004) observed how "teens today have no memory of life without television; kindergarteners know only a world with cell phones, laptops, instant messaging, and movies on DVD. To ignore the media-rich environment they bring with them to school is to shortchange them for life."

Since 2007, the European Commission has promoted a set of guiding principles and initiatives promoting media literacy, with a focus on digital media and technology, claiming,

> The rapid rise of digital technology and its increasing use in business, education and cultural activities has offered new challenges as well as new opportunities. With the nature of media changing and the volume of information increasing, it is important to ensure that individuals have the necessary skills to be able to use and make informed decisions about media and digital technologies. (European Commission 2014)

There is no U.S. federal initiative regarding media literacy.

Media literacy: The ability to assess and analyze media messages

Digital literacy: An individual's ability to appropriately use digital tools and skills to identify, manage, evaluate, analyze, and synthesize digital sources; to construct new knowledge; and to communicate with others

 Media Effects

SOCIOLOGY AT WORK

SOFTWARE DEVELOPMENT

Jenny Grinblo – Class of 2011
Undergraduate Major: Sociology
Undergraduate Minor: Global Citizenship

Software developers write the hidden codes for your word processing program or for your favorite app on your phone. The U.S. Bureau of Labor Statistics (2014) describes software developers as the "creative minds" behind computer programming. To enter this occupational field, you will need a bachelor's degree, usually in a related area like Computer Science. You should also have strong computer programming skills. There are two types of software developers: applications software developers, who design computer applications such as games, and systems software developers, who create operating systems for computers (U.S. Bureau of Labor Statistics 2014).

Since graduating in 2011, Sociology alum Jenny Grinblo has worked in a mobile app agency in London, where she leads the User Experience and Design Team. She describes her job as an intersection of her internship (as a graphic designer in a local theatre) and her Sociology degree. Jenny helps "build digital products which balance client business needs and end-user needs well, and are useful, easy to use, and provide a positive experience."

A large part of my work is being able to ignite empathy among our team and clients, so that they can "walk in the shoes" of our apps' end users. I frequently employ ethnographic interviewing, surveys, and do the equivalent of literature reviews of relevant resources. I've also given talks and run workshops to teach people how to employ qualitative research methods in order to uncover people's needs and find patterns in individual stories.

Jenny received the majority of her career advice from networking (in person and via Twitter) and online resources (job postings, LinkedIn, and blogs). To current majors considering their future employment, Jenny says,

I would advise Sociology majors to look beyond their immediate academic activities and make a list of the skills and interests they possess, for example: writing, understanding people, gathering a lot of information and making sense of it, etc., and look for intersections between those interests and skills, rather than trying to apply a portion of them due to a perceived lack of options. I was lucky to meet a mentor who suggested that the combination of my skills could be applied in the User Experience field, but there might be other fields out there that can allow Sociology majors to build on their core skills and interests in a similar way.

CHAPTER REVIEW

11.1 Define media

Media are the technological processes facilitating communication between a sender and a receiver.

11.2 Explain how the different sociological perspectives examine social problems related to the media

Functionalists examine the structural relationship between the media and other social institutions that affect content, including the social and economic conditions of American life and society's beliefs about the nature of men, women, and society. Conflict theorists believe that the media can be fully understood only when we learn who controls them. The media frame messages in a way that supports the ruling elite and limits the variety of messages that we read, see, and hear. Feminist theorists attempt to understand how the media represent and devalue women and minorities. They examine how the media either use stereotypes disparaging women and minorities or completely exclude them. The interactionist perspective focuses on the symbols and messages of the media and how the media come to define our social reality.

11.3 Review the importance of the digital divide

The term *digital divide* refers to the gap separating individuals who have access to and understanding of new forms of technology from those who do not. This divide is a symptom of a larger social problem: social inequality based on income, educational attainment, and ethnicity/race.

11.4 Explain the relationship between media technology and a boundary-less workplace

E-mail and smartphones may help employees manage their work better, but these technologies also give employees little opportunity to disengage from their work. Their work becomes boundary-less as their work continues online or on the phone after work hours or at home.

11.5 Identify the importance of media literacy

Evidence shows that media education can help mitigate the harmful effects of the media. Parents can provide the most effective intervention to reduce the effects of media violence on children, and school-based intervention also seems to help. The goal is media literacy, shifting the viewer from the role of passive receiver to that of active critical receiver.

KEY TERMS

digital divide, 311

digital literacy, 321

impression management, 309

media, 300

media literacy, 321

social media, 302

STUDY QUESTIONS

1. Explain how the media serve to unite and divide members of society.

2. How is control over the content of the media (according to conflict and feminist perspectives) problematic? What groups are in conflict?

3. From an interactionist perspective, examine how Michael Jackson's death met the three criteria for newsworthiness.

4. How is one's access to media and technology related to one's life chances?

5. Which sociological perspective could best explain how trust is earned by new agencies and outlets? Do you trust the news media? Why or why not?

6. Define what is meant by media literacy. How does media literacy mitigate the harmful effects of the media?

$SAGE edge™

Sharpen your skills with SAGE edge at **edge.sagepub.com/leonguerrero5e**

SAGE edge provides a personalized approach to help you accomplish your coursework goals in an easy-to-use learning environment.

PART III

Our Social and Physical Worlds

Drug abuse and criminal behavior are usually perceived as personal troubles. Both are considered deviant behavior, deviating from the normal expectation of not abusing drugs or engaging in criminal activity. We tend to believe that someone turns to drug use or criminal activity because of some personal defect, individual failure, or weakness. Yet both can be defined as public issues, emerging from the social structure and threatening the quality of human life.

Drug abuse and crime are the subject and focus of extensive scholarly research attempting to understand the extent and origins of both. Both problems also receive global attention, including from governments and public agencies monitoring and combating drug abuse and crime in their part of the world. These problems will be discussed in Chapters 12 and 13.

In the last three chapters of Part III, we will review social problems that affect our physical and natural worlds—problems related to urbanization (Chapter 14), the environment (Chapter 15), and war and terrorism (Chapter 16).

Though these issues involve our physical and natural worlds, both have definite human connections—humans cause these problems or experience consequences as a result of them. Environmentalist Paul Hawken (1993) explains, "Human activity *is* part of the natural world, in the largest sense, but human activity ignores the means-and-ends, give-and-take factors that are inherent in any maturing ecosystem" (p. 26). "Starting a war is a very bad idea, " writes *New York Times* columnist Paul Krugman (2014), "but it keeps happening anyway."

CHAPTER 12

Alcohol and Drug Abuse

LEARNING OBJECTIVES

12.1 Explain how the different sociological perspectives explain alcohol and drug problems

12.2 Describe how the social structure regulates drinking

12.3 Identify the correlates of Ecstasy use among college students

12.4 Assess the theory that college students mature out of heavy or binge drinking

12.5 Examine the pros and cons of the drug legalization movement

President Richard Nixon first declared the War on Drugs in 1971. Some refer to it as a war with "no rules, no boundaries, no end" (PBS 2000). Since the mid-1980s, the United States has adopted a series of aggressive law enforcement strategies and criminal justice policies aimed at reducing and punishing drug abuse (Fellner 2000). Changes in federal law require all sentenced federal offenders to serve at least 87% of their court-imposed sentences. Many drug offenders are subject to mandatory minimum sentences based on the type and quantity of drugs involved in their arrest (Scalia 2001). According to the most recent Uniform Crime Report (Federal Bureau of Investigation 2013), 1,552,432 drug arrests were made in 2012. Although some consider the large number of drug arrests a good sign, critics charge that mandatory sentencing denies drug users what they really need: access to treatment. Tougher sentencing has failed to decrease the availability of drugs and has failed to reduce illicit drug use. And some say that the war's greatest legacy is the increase in the prison population; since 1980, the number of drug offenders in federal prison has increased by 21 times (*Washington Post* 2014).

There seems to be no argument about the seriousness of the drug problem in the United States and worldwide. According to the 2013 National Survey on Drug Use and Health, 24.6 million Americans (or 9.4%) age 12 or older reportedly were current users of illicit drugs other than marijuana (Substance Abuse and Mental Health Services Administration [SAMHSA] 2014). (Refer to Figure 12.1 for illicit drug use among persons aged 12 years or older.) Nearly 17 million American adults abuse

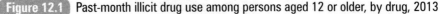

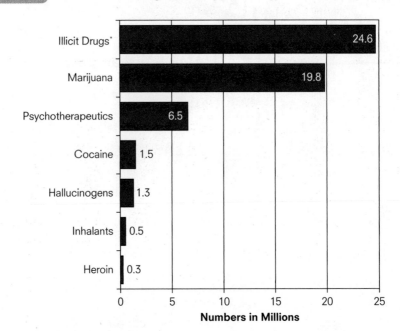

Figure 12.1 Past-month illicit drug use among persons aged 12 or older, by drug, 2013

SOURCE: Substance Abuse and Mental Health Services Administration 2014.

NOTE: Includes marijuana, cocaine, heroin, hallucinogens, inhalants, or prescription-type psychotherapeutics.

alcohol or are alcoholics (National Institute on Alcohol Abuse and Alcoholism [NIAAA] 2014). Globally, more than 76 million individuals have diagnosable drinking problems (World Health Organization 2004), and between 15 and 39 million are problem drug users (United Nations Office on Drugs and Crime [UNODC] 2012b). The most widely produced and consumed illicit drug is cannabis, or marijuana. Refer to Figure 12.2 for more information.

Although we might focus first on one drug user and his or her personal trouble with drugs, it doesn't take long to recognize how drug use affects the user's family and friends, workplace or school, and neighbors and community. Throughout this chapter, we will examine the social problem of drug abuse, reviewing its extent, its social consequences, and our solutions. We begin first with a look at how the sociological perspectives address the problem of drug abuse.

SOCIOLOGICAL PERSPECTIVES ON DRUG ABUSE

Biological and psychological theories attempt to explain how drug abuse is based on the individual. Both perspectives assume that there is little a person can do to escape from his or her abuse: a person's abuse is genetic or inherited. Abuse may emerge from a biological or chemical predisposition or from a personality or behavioral disorder. Such explanations also have consequences for treatment. Programs

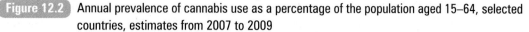

Figure 12.2 Annual prevalence of cannabis use as a percentage of the population aged 15–64, selected countries, estimates from 2007 to 2009

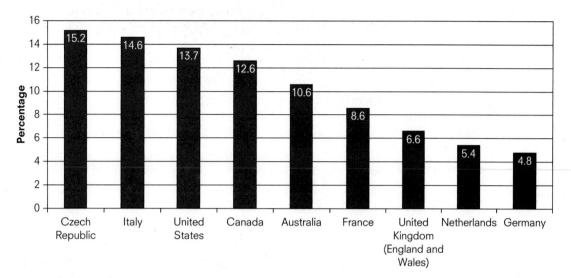

SOURCE: United Nations Office on Drugs and Crime 2012b.

focus on the individual, arguing that the abuser needs to be "fixed." Although both perspectives have been important in shaping our understanding of drug abuse, these perspectives cannot explain the social or structural determinants of drug abuse. In this next section, we will examine how sociological perspectives address the problems of drug abuse.

Functionalist Perspective

Functionalists argue that society provides us with norms or guidelines on drug use. Cross-cultural studies reveal that there is variation in the way people expect to behave when they drink. For example, violent behavior is associated with alcohol consumption in the United States, Great Britain, and Australia; yet drinking behavior is described as "peaceful and harmonious" in Mediterranean and South African countries (Social Issues Research Center 1998).

A set of social norms identifies the appropriate use of drugs and alcohol. The use of prescription drugs, as directed by a physician, is considered acceptable behavior. Prescription drugs alleviate pain, reduce fevers, and curb infections. Alcohol in moderation may be routinely consumed with meals, for celebration, or for health benefits. One glass of red wine a day has been shown to reduce one's risk of heart disease.

Yet society also provides norms regarding the excessive use of drugs. For example, college students share the perception that excessive college drinking is a cultural norm (Butler 1993); this perception is enforced by the media and advertisers (Lederman et al. 2003). Aaron Brower (2002) argues that binge drinking is determined by and is a product of the college environment. For example, because of particular organization norms that support binge drinking, members of Greek social organizations have higher rates of binge drinking when compared to other college students (Chauvin 2012). According to Brower (2002), unlike alcoholics, college students are able to turn their willingness to binge drink on and off depending on their circumstances (e.g., whether they have to study for an exam).

To explain drug abuse, functionalists identify a culture or the social structure as the cause. In examining substance abuse among adolescents, researchers contend that peers may be the most influential (Allen et al. 2003). Howard Kaplan, Steven Martin, and Cynthia Robbins (1984) write, "The use of illicit drugs persists as part of ongoing peer subculture(s) which may endorse, if not require, use of illicit drugs" (p. 271). Peer influence may be direct or indirect: peers provide social opportunities to engage in substance abuse, and peers shape attitudes toward substance abuse (Leventhal and Cleary 1980; Prinstein and Wang 2005).

Émile Durkheim believed that under conditions of rapid cultural change, there would be an absence of common social norms and controls, a state he called anomie. If people lack norms to control their behavior, they are likely to pursue self-destructive behaviors such as alcohol abuse (Caetano, Clark, and Tam 1998). During periods when individuals are socially isolated (such as moving to a new neighborhood, experiencing a divorce, or starting a new school year), they may experience high levels of stress or anxiety, which may lead to deviant behaviors, including drug abuse. Society can also be the source of **role strain**—when an individual has insufficient resources to deal with demanding social situations or circumstances. The strain occurs when the demands of one's role exceed one's ability and resources to fulfill that role (Wheaton 1990). Illicit drug use or self-medication can be perceived as an adaptive coping response to stress—people turn to drug use to reduce their level of stress (Crutchfield and Gove 1984). For example, Shelly McGrath, Catherine Marcum, and Heith Copes (2012) documented how drug use was used as a coping strategy among adult prisoners experiencing a sense of danger or stress during their incarceration.

Conflict Perspective

Although many drugs can be abused, conflict theorists argue that intentional decisions have been made over which drugs are illegal and which ones are not. Powerful political and business interest groups are able to manipulate our images of drugs and their users.

Role strain: Strain experienced when the demands of one's role exceed one's ability and resources to fulfill that role

Economist Arthur Benavie (2009) explains how the War on Drugs in this country is defined by subjective social, religious, and political positions. For example, drugs are classified by five schedules, categories that define their susceptibility to abuse and medical application. Criminal penalties are applied to the drugs in Schedules I and II, dangerous drugs with a high potential for abuse. Benavie highlights how the

Why Fight Drugs?

classification of these drugs is determined by the U.S. Drug Enforcement Administration (DEA) of the U.S. Department of Justice (DOJ) rather than the Food and Drug Administration (FDA) or the Surgeon General.

Our history of drug laws, concludes Benavie (2009), has little to do with objective information about the effects or dangers of illicit drugs. Drug policy has been fueled by racial, ethnic, and economic antagonisms. For example, heroin, opium, and marijuana were considered legal substances in the late 18th and early 19th centuries, but public opinion and law changed when their use was linked to

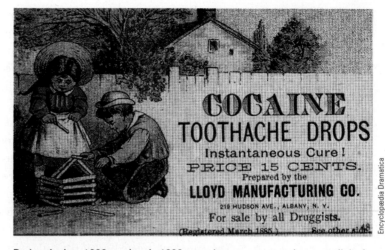

During the late 1800s and early 1900s cocaine was promoted as a medicinal ingredient to treat pain or coughing. Heroin and opium were also used in over the counter treatments.

ethnic minorities and crime. Opium smoking, most associated with Chinese immigrants brought here to work on the railroads, became the subject of intense antidrug efforts after completion of the railroad system. At the same time, the oral consumption of opium, more widespread among Whites, was never considered problematic (Reinarman and Levine 1997).

According to Benavie (2009), the War on Drugs is a crusade, fueled by a fear of social disorder and disease, a perceived threat to our capitalistic economic structure, and a religious crusade against sin and vice.

Feminist Perspective

Theorists and practitioners in the field of alcohol and drug abuse have ignored the experiences unique to women, ethnic groups, gay and lesbian populations, and other marginalized groups. Women face unique social stigmatization as a result of their drug use and may also experience discrimination as they attempt to receive treatment (Drug Policy Alliance 2003).

The scientific literature did not address women's addiction until the 1970s. Specifically, there has been a lack of sensitivity to the range of drug abuse experiences beyond the male or White perspective. Early prevention and treatment models treated female abusers no differently than men were treated, failing to provide comprehensive services for women such as prenatal and gynecologic care, contraceptive counseling, job training, and abuse counseling (Roberts 1991). However, there is increasing recognition of the importance of gender-specific and gender-sensitive treatment models, including the development of separate women's treatment programs. Female users have a variety of different treatment and psychosocial needs, influenced by their backgrounds, experiences, and drug problems. Most outpatient clinics do not provide child care, and many residential programs do not admit children (Roberts 1991). And single, career-oriented women without children will have different treatment needs and priorities than will single mothers or married mothers (National Clearinghouse for Alcohol and Drug Information [NCADI] 2003a).

Data suggest that the dramatic increase in women's imprisonment (refer to Chapter 13) is due primarily to the prosecution of drug offenses, leading some researchers to characterize the War on Drugs as the war on women (Bush-Baskette 1998). Katherine Beckett (1995) and Dorothy Roberts (1991) describe how women of color were unfairly targeted in the War on Drugs in the 1980s. As crack cocaine use spread throughout the inner cities, prosecutors shifted their attention to drug use among pregnant women, making drug and alcohol abuse during pregnancy a crime. The approach treated pregnant drug users as criminals and was "aimed at punishing rather than empowering women who use drugs during their pregnancy" (Beckett 1995:589). As Beckett (1995) explains, "Prosecutions of women for prenatal conduct thus create a gender specific system of punishment and obscure the fact that male behavior, socio-economic conditions, and environmental pollutants may also affect fetal health" (p. 588). Roberts (1991) argues that poor Black women are the primary targets for prosecutors. Research indicates that African American women are about 10 times more likely than are other women to be reported to civil authorities for drug use.

In the 1990s, federal drug legislation shifted to methamphetamine offenses, making some of the penalties similar to crack cocaine offenses. Though methamphetamine convictions were last among the five types of drugs women were convicted for in 1996 (10.3%), Stephanie Bush-Baskette and Vivian Smith (2012) report that by 2006, the number of methamphetamine convictions had doubled (23%). There was a 300% increase in the number of women convicted and sentenced for methamphetamine offenses between 1996 and 2006. White women represented the largest percentages of women incarcerated for methamphetamine. The majority of those women had little or no prior criminal record.

Interactionist Perspective

Sociologists Edwin Sutherland and Howard Becker argue that deviant behavior, such as drug abuse, is learned through others. Sutherland (1939) proposed the theory of **differential association** to explain how we learn specific behaviors and norms from the groups we have contact with. Deviance, explained Sutherland, is learned from people who engage in deviant behavior. In his classic study "Becoming a Marijuana User," Becker (1963) demonstrated how a novice user is introduced to smoking marijuana by more experienced users. Learning is the key in his study:

Differential association: The learning of behaviors and norms from the groups we have contact with

No one becomes a user without (1) learning to smoke the drug in a way which will produce real effects; (2) learning to recognize the effects and connect them with drug use . . . ; and (3) learning to enjoy the sensations he perceives. (Becker 1963:58)

This perspective also addresses how individuals or groups are labeled *abusers* and how society responds to them. For example, consider alcohol abuse among the Native American population. Alcohol abuse and alcoholism are leading causes of mortality among Native Americans, and there are disproportionately higher rates of alcohol-related crimes among Native Americans. Yet Malcolm Holmes and Judith Antell (2001) argue that alcohol abuse and its related problems are not entirely objective phenomena; they also involve interpretation and stigmatization of deviant behavior. One persistent societal myth maintains that as a group, Native Americans have problems handling alcohol. However, research indicates that factors such as demography (a young population) and geography (rural Western environment) may explain high rates of alcohol-related problems in Native American populations.

The authors highlight the considerable variation in drinking patterns within and between tribal communities; there is a large segment of the Native population that do not drink or are non-problem drinkers (Hawkins and La Marr 2012). The social construction of the "drunken Indian" stereotype links alcohol abuse to the perceived "weaker" cultural and individual characteristics of Native Americans. Holmes and Antell (2001) explain, "The persistence of such myths in the symbolic-moral universe of the dominant White culture, despite evidence to the contrary, suggests that alcohol use by Native Americans still documents allegations of weak will and moral degeneracy" (p. 154).

For a summary of these four sociological perspectives, see Table 12.1.

WHAT IS DRUG ABUSE?

Drug abuse is the use of any drug or medication for a reason other than the one it was intended to serve or in a manner or in quantities other than directed, which can lead to clinically significant impairment or distress. **Drug addiction** refers to physical or psychological dependence on the drug or medication. Although many drugs can be abused, three drugs will be reviewed in the following section—alcohol, nicotine, and marijuana—along with rave or club drugs. Marijuana and club drugs are considered illicit (illegal) drugs. Most of the information presented in this section is based on data from the National Institute on Drug Abuse (NIDA) and the Office of National Drug Control Policy (ONDCP). For more information, log on to the SAGE edge select companion site, Chapter 12, at http://edge.sagepub.com/leonguerrero5e.

Drug abuse: The use of any drug or medication for unintended purposes, which can lead to clinically significant impairment or distress

Drug addiction: Physical or psychological dependence on a drug or medication

Table 12.1   Summary of sociological perspectives: Alcohol and drug abuse

	Functional	**Conflict/Feminist**	**Interactionist**
Explanation of drug abuse	Drug abuse is likely to occur when society is unable to control or regulate our behavior.	Powerful groups decide which drugs are illegal. Certain social groups are singled out for their drug abuse. There has been a lack of sensitivity to the range of drug abuse experiences.	Drug abuse is learned through interaction with others. The perspective also focuses on society's reaction to drug abuse, noting that certain individuals are more likely to be labeled as drug users than others.
Questions asked about drug abuse	What rules exist to control or encourage drug abuse? Are some groups or individuals more vulnerable to drug abuse than others?	What groups are able to enforce their definitions of the legality or illegality of drug use? How are they able to enforce their definitions? How are the experiences of women and minority drug users different from those of White males?	How is drug abuse learned through interaction? How are drug users labeled by society? Why are specific groups targeted?

Alcohol

Alcohol is the most abused drug in the United States. Although the consumption of alcohol by itself is not a social problem, the continuous and excessive use of alcohol can become problematic. Four symptoms are associated with alcohol dependence or **alcoholism**: craving (a strong need to drink), loss of control (not being able to stop drinking once drinking begins), physical dependence (experiencing withdrawal symptoms), and tolerance (the need to drink greater amounts of alcohol to get "high") (NIAAA 2003b). Alcohol use is related to a wide range of adverse health and social consequences, both acute (traffic deaths or other injuries) and chronic (stroke, alcohol dependence, liver damage) (NIAAA 2005).

National surveys reveal the differences in alcohol consumption by individual attributes, cultural factors, and structural factors. For example, in 2013, current drinking (12 or more drinks in the past year) among adults was highest for Whites and persons reporting two or more races. Heavy alcohol use (five drinks on a single day at least once a month for adults) was highest among Native Hawaiians or other Pacific Islanders and Whites. Overall, alcohol consumption was lowest among Asian, Hispanic, and Black adults and Asian and Black college students (SAMHSA 2014).

Alcoholism:
Alcohol dependence, characterized by the symptoms of craving, loss of control, physical dependence, and tolerance

World Health Organization: Alcohol Abuse

Studies suggest that ethnic/racial groups have different sets of norms and values regulating drinking. While some groups exhibit low rates of problem drinking because their culture associates the use of alcohol primarily with eating, social occasions, or rituals (Herd and Grube 1996), other ethnic/racial groups may consider drinking as an activity separate from eating or ritual celebrations, leading to higher rates of problem drinking. In an examination between first- and second-generation Asian American adults, second-generation adults are at higher risk for alcohol use or abuse. Some researchers attribute this higher risk to the process of acculturation—when individuals from different cultures come together, practices and behaviors that are different from one's own group may be adopted or learned. Due to acculturation, second-generation Asian Americans begin to develop drinking behaviors similar to their non-Asian peers (Iwamoto, Takamatsu, and Castellanos 2012).

Although social class, occupational and social roles, and family history of alcohol use all play a role in determining the drinking patterns of people in general, specific factors put women particularly at risk (Collins and McNair 2003). Research indicates that a woman's risk for drinking increases with the experience of negative affective states, such as depression (Hesselbrock and Hesselbrock 1997) or loneliness, and negative life events, such as physical or sexual abuse during childhood or adulthood (Wilsnack et al. 1997). Other factors decrease women's chances of developing alcohol problems. Traditionally, women are socialized to abstain from alcohol use or to drink less than men (Filmore et al. 1997). Women who do not participate in the labor force may have less access to alcohol than men do (Wilsnack and Wilsnack 1992), and women's roles as wife and mother may also discourage alcohol intake (Leonard and Rothbard 1999).

. . . .

What Does It Mean to Me?

How would you describe the drinking culture on your campus? Is alcohol consumption an acceptable and normal part of college life? Why or why not?

. . . .

Tobacco and Nicotine

Tobacco is the world's number-one problem drug, killing more people than all other drugs combined (Goode 2004). According to the World Health Organization (2014), if current smoking patterns continued, by 2030 8 million people per year worldwide would die of diseases caused by cigarette smoking. Cigarette smoking is the most prevalent form of nicotine addiction, and tobacco is the most frequently used addictive drug in the United States (NCADI 2003b). Nicotine is both a stimulant and a sedative to the central nervous system. An average cigarette contains about 10 milligrams of nicotine. Through inhaling the cigarette smoke, the smoker takes in

1 to 2 milligrams of nicotine per cigarette. In 2013, 66.9 million Americans (or 26%) reported current use of a tobacco product (SAMHSA 2014).

In the United States, the prevalence of smoking is highest among Native Americans and Alaska Natives (40.1%), followed by persons who reported two or more races (31.2%), Whites (29.5%), Blacks (27.3%), and Hispanics (21.9%) (SAMHSA 2014). Thirty-seven percent of young adults aged 18 to 25 years were current smokers (SAMHSA 2014).

Cigarette smoking is the most important preventable cause of cancer in the United States. It has been linked to most cases of lung cancer in Europe and in the United States (Crispo et al. 2004). Smoking has also been linked to other lung diseases, such as chronic bronchitis and emphysema, and to cancers of the mouth, stomach, kidney, bladder, cervix, pancreas, and larynx. The overall death rates from cancer are twice as high among smokers as nonsmokers (NIDA 1998). It is estimated that more than 400,000 annual deaths are attributable to cigarette smoking in the United States (American Lung Association 2006).

Passive or secondhand smoke is a major source of indoor air contaminants. Nonsmokers exposed to secondhand smoke at home or work increase their risk of developing heart disease by 25% to 30% and lung cancer by 20% to 30% (NIDA 2006). Secondhand smoke is estimated to cause about 3,000 lung cancer deaths per year and may contribute to as many as 34,000 deaths related to cardiovascular disease in the United States (Centers for Disease Control and Prevention [CDC] 2014a; NIDA 1998). More than 79,000 adults die each year as a result of passive smoking in the European Union countries (European Lung Association 2006).

Despite the persistent public health message that smoking is bad for your health, smoking among teenagers has been on the rise since 1991 (Lewinsohn et al. 2000). In a study comparing adolescent smokers with nonsmokers, adolescent smokers were found to have more stressful environments, more academic problems, and poorer coping skills than nonsmokers have. Adolescent smoking has also been associated with a number of environmental factors, such as disruptive home environment, parental and peer smoking, low social support from family and friends, conflict with parents, and stressful life events (Lewinsohn et al. 2000). About three out of four teen smokers will become adult smokers (CDC 2014b).

E-cigarettes arrived on the U.S. market in 2007. The cigarettes are battery operated, turning nicotine and other chemicals into a vapor. Smoking the cigarettes is also referred to as vaping. As of November 2014, the U.S. Food and Drug Administration had not reviewed clinical studies about the safety of e-cigarettes. The FDA had not approved any e-cigarette product for therapeutic uses or as a cessation aid. Concerns have been raised about the appeal of the e-cigarettes to the teen market. In 2014, the National Institute on Drug Abuse report found that e-cigarette use surpassed traditional cigarette use among 8th-, 10th-, and 12th-grade teens (Tavernise 2014). According to the CDC (2014b), more than 260,000 youth who had never smoked a cigarette used an e-cigarette in 2013, representing a three-fold increase from 79,000 teen e-cigarette users in 2011.

Marijuana

Marijuana is the most commonly used illicit drug, widely used by adolescents and young adults (NIDA 2002). An estimated 125 and 203 million (between 2.8% and 4.5%) of the world population used cannabis at least once during the past year (UNODC 2012a). It is a favorite drug among youth and adolescents, with use (at least once in a lifetime) estimated as high as 37% in some countries (UNODC 2006). The major active chemical in marijuana is THC or delta-9-tetrahydrocannabinol, which causes the mind-altering effects of the drug. THC is also the main active ingredient in oral medications used to treat nausea in chemotherapy patients and to stimulate appetite in AIDS patients (ONDCP 2006).

According to the Centers for Disease Control and Prevention, 38.4% of surveyed high school students and 49% of college students reported lifetime use of marijuana. Longitudinal data show increases in marijuana use during the 1960s and 1970s, declines in the 1980s, and increasing use since the 1990s (NIDA 2002). In 2010, there were a reported 19.8 million current (past-month) users of the drug, or 7.5% of the population (SAMHSA 2014).

Acute marijuana use can impair short-term memory, judgment, and other cognitive functions, as well as a person's coordination and balance, and it can increase heart rate. Chronic abuse of the drug can lead to addiction, as well as increased risk of chronic cough, bronchitis, or emphysema. Addictive use of the drug may interfere with family, school, or work activities. Smoking marijuana increases the risk of lung cancer and cancer in other parts of the respiratory tract more than smoking tobacco does (NIDA 2002). Marijuana smoke contains 50% to 70% more carcinogenic hydrocarbons than tobacco smoke does (ONDCP 2006). Because marijuana users inhale more deeply and hold their breath longer than cigarette smokers do, they are exposed to more carcinogenic smoke than cigarette smokers are.

. . . .

What Does It Mean to Me?

As of 2014, 23 states and the District of Columbia have laws legalizing marijuana in some form. Opponents of these laws argue that marijuana is not a safe or benign substance, characterizing it as a gateway drug to other more serious drug abuse. What do you think? Is marijuana a safe drug or not?

. . . .

Club or Rave Drugs

Raves began in the 1990s as illegal underground all-night dance parties. Though raves are advertised as safe and/or alcohol-free parties, they remain a popular venue for the distribution of club drugs such as MDMA (an amphetamine-based hallucinogenic), GHB (a nervous system depressant), methamphetamine (a central nervous stimulant), ketamine (a hallucinogenic), and Rohypnol (a sedative, also

 Electronic Music and Ecstasy   Colorado Drug Legislation

TAKING A WORLD VIEW

THE MARIJUANA LEGALIZATION MOVEMENT

The 2012 legalization of marijuana in Colorado and Washington has been credited with encouraging legalization efforts in other states and in other countries. The small South American country of Uruguay was the first in the world to legally regulate the production, sale, and consumption of marijuana for adults. Beginning in 2014, Uruguayans over the age of 18 have had legal access to marijuana through home cultivation of up to 6 plants per household, membership clubs where 15 to 45 members can collectively grow up to 99 plants, or sales of up to 10 grams per week through licensed pharmacies. The system is regulated through the Institute for Regulation and Control of Cannabis (IRCCA) and includes educational and health programming for residents (Hetzer 2014).

As reported by the United Nations Office of Drug and Crime (2014), between 125 million and 227 million people (or between 2.7% and 4.9%) between the ages of 15 to 64 years were estimated to have used marijuana in 2012. Globally, countries with the highest rate of use are Western and Central Europe and North America.

Marijuana is grown in almost every country in the world, ranging from personal home cultivation to large-scale farm and warehouse operations. In 2012, more than 5 tons of cannabis were seized. The largest quantity was seized in the United States, which accounts for over 60% of the seizures worldwide. The area with the second highest amount of seizers was Central and South America and the Caribbean (UNODC 2014).

In its 2014 report, the UNODC expresses concern regarding cannabis legalization in Washington and Colorado. The organization warns, "While it is not yet clear how the market will change, the commercialization of cannabis may also significantly affect drug-use behaviors. Commercialization implies motivated selling, which can lead to directed advertisements that promote and encourage consumption" (p. 43).

Jamaica, Mexico, Morocco, and other countries have expressed interest in changing their marijuana laws, moving to some form of legalization. Economics is often cited as the motivation for legalization.

Do you agree with the UNODC's concern about the commercialization of marijuana? Why or why not?

---

referred to as the date rape drug). Today, rave parties are larger organized festivals featuring different types of electronic dance music. Drugs remain a key part of the rave experience.

Antidrug organizations have heightened their concern regarding the risks and health consequences associated with MDMA use. Ecstasy is the pill form of the drug, while Molly is the powder or crystal form of MDMA. Even when they are not fatal, Ecstasy or Molly are not harmless. MDMA produces an intense release of serotonin in a user's brain, which can cause irreparable damage to the brain and memory functions. Research indicates that long-term brain damage, especially to the parts of the brain critical to thought and memory, may result from its use. Users may also experience psychological difficulties (such as confusion, depression, and sleeping problems)

The Legalization of Marijuana in Colorado: The Impact

while using the drug and sometimes for weeks after. As a result of using the drug, individuals can also experience increases in heart rate and blood pressure and physical symptoms such as nausea, blurred vision, or faintness (NIDA 2003a). When users overdose, they can experience rapid heartbeat, high blood pressure, faintness, panic attacks, and even loss of consciousness (Vaughn 2002).

In a study of undergraduates at a large midwestern university, Carol Boyd, Sean E. McCabe, and Hannah d'Arcy (2003) found that men and women were equally likely to have used Ecstasy, and that several factors predicted its use. White students were more likely to report lifetime Ecstasy use than

Though advertised as drug free zones, raves continue to be a venue for the distribution and use of club drugs like MDMA and GHB.

were African American or Asian students. According to the researchers, sexual orientation was also related to Ecstasy use: those who identified themselves as gay, lesbian, or bisexual were more likely to report lifetime, annual, or past-month Ecstasy use than were heterosexual students. Students with a grade point average (GPA) of 3.5 or higher were consistently less likely to have used Ecstasy in the past year or their lifetime than were students with GPAs below 2.5. Students who reported binge drinking within the past two weeks were also more likely to report past-month Ecstasy use. In a separate study, Kira Levy et al. (2005) confirmed the role of social pressure in the experimentation with and use of Ecstasy among college students. When sober and surrounded by Ecstasy-using friends, students described the urge to experience the drug's effect with others.

Though deaths associated with the drug remain rare, overdoses and emergency room visits have increased in recent years. In 2013, two rave concertgoers died from Molly overdoses. Ecstasy-related emergency room visits increased from 10,200 in 2004 to 17,865 visits in 2008, an increase of 75% (ONDCP 2014). Canada is the primary source of MDMA smuggled into the United States.

THE PROBLEMS OF DRUG ABUSE

Drug Use in the Workplace

Employers have always been concerned about the impact of substance abuse on their workers and their businesses because drug use may undermine employee productivity, safety, and health (Frone 2004). It is estimated that 14 million U.S. workers meet the diagnostic criteria for substance dependence (Jacobson and Sacco 2012).

Drug abuse cost American businesses $120 billion in lost productivity, due mainly to labor participation costs, participation in drug abuse treatment, incarceration, and premature death (ONDCP 2014).

In their examination of occupational risk factors for drug abuse, Scott MacDonald, Samantha Wells, and T. Cameron Wild (1999) found that problem drinking or drug use was linked to the quality and organization of work, drinking subcultures at work, and the safety of the workplace. Respondents reporting alcohol problems were more likely to have jobs involving repetitive tasks and dangerous working conditions. Respondents with alcohol problems were also more likely to drink with coworkers and experience some social pressure to drink. The same pattern was true for workers with drug problems: They considered their jobs "boring" or repetitive, they identified their job as dangerous, they experienced stress at work, or they were likely to be part of a drinking subculture at work. Among all factors they identified, the presence of a drinking subculture at work was the strongest risk factor for alcohol and drug abuse.

By occupation, the highest rates of current illicit drug use and heavy drinking were reported by construction workers (15%), sales personnel (11.4%), and food preparation, wait staff, and bartenders (11.2%) (U.S. Department of Labor 2014). Among employed adults, White, non-Hispanic males between the ages of 18 and 25 who have less than a high school education are likely to report the highest rates of heavy drinking and illicit drug use (U.S. Department of Labor 2003).

Problem Drinking Among Teens and Young Adults

For 2013, the National Survey on Drug Use and Health (NSDUH) reported that the highest prevalence of binge drinking (drinking five or more drinks within a few hours or within one sitting) was for young adults aged 21 to 25 (43.3%), followed by 26- to 29-year-olds (40%). Heavy drinking (five or more drinks on the same occasion on at least five different days in the past 30 days) was reported by 13.1% of those 21 to 25 years of age (SAMHSA 2014). See Figure 12.3 for a summary of heavy alcohol use among persons ages 12 and older for 2013.

An international comparative study on drinking trends among 15- and 16-year-olds revealed that teens in the United Kingdom were among those most likely to drink heavily and to experience intoxication. In 2003, 52% of boys and 56% of girls reported binge drinking in the past 30 days (Plant, Miller, and Plant 2005). From 1995 to 2003, although there was no significant increase in the proportion of boys engaging in binge drinking, researchers observed a sharp increase in the proportion of girls binge drinking since 1999. The rise in binge drinking among girls is consistent with recent reports documenting the increase in heavy episodic or binge drinking among young women in Britain. The majority of surveyed teens, 75%, reported that they had at some time "been drunk" in 2003. Researchers concluded that U.K. teenagers drink in ways that are potentially harmful and that binge drinking among U.K. teens is a matter of real concern (Plant et al. 2005).

 Teen Substance Abuse

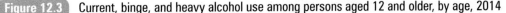

Figure 12.3 Current, binge, and heavy alcohol use among persons aged 12 and older, by age, 2014

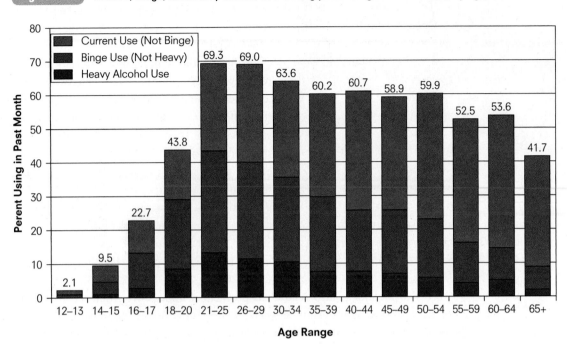

SOURCE: Substance Abuse and Mental Health Services Administration 2014.

By the time they reach the eighth grade, nearly 50% of U.S. adolescents report having had at least one drink, and more than 20% report having been drunk (NIAAA 2003b). Underage drinkers account for nearly 20% of the alcohol consumed in the United States (Tanner 2003). In 2013, 16- to 17-year-olds had the highest rate of currently alcohol use (23%), followed by persons aged 14 or 15 (10%) and persons aged 12 or 13 (2%) (SAMHSA 2014).

Binge drinking among college students has been called a major U.S. public health concern (Clapp, Shillington, and Segars 2000). (Refer to Figure 12.4 for a comparison of heavy drinking among those enrolled full-time in college and those who are not. Drinking rates are consistently higher for those enrolled full-time.) Henry Wechsler (1996) reported results from the 1996 Harvard School of Public Health College Alcohol Study, highlighting how binge drinking had become widespread among college students. In the Wechsler study, binge drinking was defined as five or more drinks in a row one or more times during a two-week period for men and four or more drinks in a row one or more times during a two-week period for women. The author explains that men, students younger than 24, fraternity and sorority residents, Whites, students in athletics, and students who socialize more are most likely to binge drink. On average, students who engaged in high-risk behaviors such as illicit drug use, unsafe sexual activity, and cigarette smoking were more likely

REUTERS/Gerardo Garcia

Binge drinking among college students has been called a major U.S. public health concern. According to the 2013 National Institute for Drug Use and Health, 43.3% of 21-25-year-olds reported binge drinking during the year (SAMSHA 2014).

to be binge drinkers. In contrast, students who were involved in community service, the arts, or studying were less likely to be binge drinkers (Wechsler 1996).

Although the demographic and social correlates of college drinking have been consistently identified in many studies, attempts to explain the behavior through various sociological perspectives have been limited. Most prevalent in the literature are theories that identify drinking as part of the social learning process: addressing the role of peer groups, students' attitudes, and perceptions as well as the social construction of drinking norms related to alcohol consumption. Similar social learning theories have also been linked to substance abuse (Durkin, Wolfe, and Clark 2005).

Access to alcohol is also related to problem drinking. Weitzman et al. (2003) reported a positive relationship between alcohol outlet density (number of bars and liquor stores near campus) and frequent drinking (drinking on 10 or more occasions in the past 30 days), heavy drinking (five or more drinks at an off-campus party), and drinking problems (self-reported).

The Task Force of the National Advisory Council on Alcohol Abuse and Alcoholism (2010) concluded that 1,825 college students between the ages of 18 and 24 die each year from alcohol-related unintentional injuries, including motor vehicle crashes. About half a million students between the ages of 18 and 24 are unintentionally injured while under the influence of alcohol, and more than 600,000 students are assaulted by another student who has been drinking. In addition, the task force reports that 25% of college students report academic consequences (poor grades, poor performance, missing classes) as a result of their drinking, and more than 150,000 develop an alcohol-related health problem. Based on self-reports about their drinking, 31% of college students meet the criteria for alcohol abuse, and 6% meet the criteria for alcohol dependence (Task Force of the National Advisory Council on Alcohol Abuse and Alcoholism 2010).

Brower (2002) explains that there is no evidence that drinking in college leads to later-life alcoholism or long-term alcohol abuse. He writes, "Real life is a strong disincentive for the kind of binge drinking that college students do" (Brower 2002:255). He suggests using the term **episodic high-risk drinking** to describe more accurately how college students drink: infrequently drinking a large quantity of alcohol in a short period. Brower and other researchers describe a "maturing out" of college drinking, shifting to moderate alcohol consumption with no associated alcohol use problems. The maturing-out process usually coincides with life changes such as employment, marriage, or a general shift to a conventional life style.

Episodic high-risk drinking: Infrequently drinking a large quantity of alcohol in a short period

Figure 12.4 Heavy alcohol use among adults aged 18 to 22, by college enrollment: 2002 to 2013

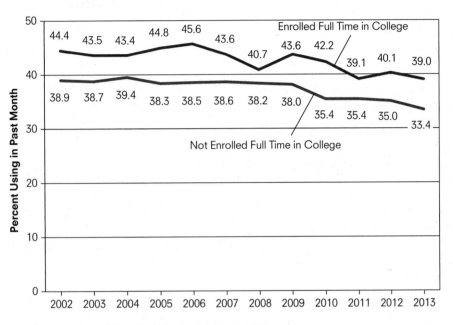

SOURCE: Substance Abuse and Mental Health Services Administration 2014.

. . . .

What Does It Mean to Me?

What is the drinking policy on your campus? Does your campus culture promote safe drinking? What educational or service programs are provided for students who abuse alcohol?

. . . .

Punishment or Treatment?

Stricter federal policies have increased the number of men and women serving jail or prison time for drug-related offenses. As conflict and symbolic interaction theories suggest, drug laws are not enforced equally, with certain groups being singled out. Although most illicit drug users are White, Blacks constitute about 80% to 90% of all people sent to prison on drug charges (Fellner 2000). Nationwide, Black men are sent to state prison on drug charges at 13 times the rate of White men (Fellner 2000). Most women in prison are untreated substance abusers incarcerated for nonviolent offenses (Alleyne 2007). Drug enforcement usually targets urban and poor neighborhoods while ignoring drug use among middle- or upper-class people. Whereas our society treats middle- or upper-class drug use as a personal crisis, lower-class drug use is defined as criminal. Consider, for example, how the media reported the drug treatment of celebrities Lindsay Lohan and Britney Spears—was either referred to as a criminal?

Federal Drug Laws and Criminal Sentencing

IN FOCUS

ALCOPOPS

Flavored alcoholic beverages, sugary fruit-flavored alcoholic beverages such as Mike's Hard Lemonade and Bacardi Silver, have become popular with young drinkers. Though the alcohol content must be included in the packaging, some packaging makes these beverages appear more like nonalcoholic soft drinks or energy drinks than an alcoholic beverage containing 5% to 7% alcohol per volume. State lawmakers and parents have increasingly grown concerned about the popularity of these drinks, believing that these beverages contribute to underage drinking (Marshall 2007) and referring to them as "gateway" drugs (leading youth to more traditional alcoholic beverages).

A 2001 national poll revealed that 41% of all teens ages 14 to 18 had tried an alcopop, with twice as many 14- to 16-year-olds preferring them to beer or mixed drinks. When asked why they would choose these beverages over beer, wine, or liquor, teens reported that they liked the sweet taste of the drinks and the disguised taste of alcohol. Most surveyed teens believed the products were marketed to their age group (Alcohol Policies Project 2001).

However, there appears to be more concern about the growing consumption of these beverages among young girls. The American Medical Association released 2004 poll results that indicated that a third of all teen girls older than age 12 have tried alcopops. As part of an effort to urge then-governor Arnold Schwarzenegger to reclassify these beverages as hard liquor, Cinthya Luis, a high school senior and member of the San Diego Youth Council, explained, "Kids all over the state and the nation call these products 'cheerleader beer' and 'girlie beer' because they are so popular with underage girls—their sweet taste is designed to appeal to young drinkers." Though Schwarzenegger vetoed the bill in 2005, the California State Board of Equalization voted to reclassify alcopops as distilled spirits (taxable at $3.30 per gallon) rather than beer (taxable at $0.20 per gallon). Prevention and youth advocates applauded the decision, hoping the higher cost would discourage underage consumption.

In addition to California, several other states, such as Arkansas, Illinois, and Nebraska, have considered reclassifying these beverages as hard liquor. Critics argue that these beverages are no different from beer, which contains 4% to 6% alcohol per volume. Maine and Utah have already reclassified these beverages as hard liquor.

Sasha Abramsky (2003) explains that with tougher drug laws, the U.S. drug war was taken away from public health and medical officials and placed into the hands of law enforcement and the courts. The notion that drug abuse is a disease was replaced with the idea that drug abuse is a crime. A punishment model has also been adopted in China, where its rehabilitation centers serve as forced labor camps punishing, not treating, addicts (Jacobs 2010). In contrast, the Netherlands defines drug abuse as a public health issue and has implemented harm reduction strategies, placing the priority on drug education and treatment rather than on punishment.

However, as overall crime rates began to decline, public support for the get-tough-on-drugs policy began to wane. Research conducted by the Pew Research

Center revealed how 63% of Americans favored rolling back mandatory minimum sentences for nonviolent drug offenders and 67% believed drug use should be treated as a disease rather than as a crime (Desilver 2014).

Abramsky (2003) identified key legislative changes in several states. Arizona and California passed legislation that diverted thousands of drug offenders into treatment programs instead of prisons. In 1998, Michigan repealed its mandatory life sentence law for those caught in the possession of more than 650 grams of certain narcotics. In 2002, Michigan governor John Engler signed legislation that rolled back the state's tough mandatory-minimum drug sentences. The Kansas Sentencing Commission proposed reforms of the state's mandatory sentencing codes, along with expansion of treatment programs. The reforms were accepted in March 2003. Though California's 2010 ballot initiative to legalize marijuana did not pass, that same year Governor Arnold Schwarzenegger signed into law a bill that reduced the penalty for marijuana possession from a misdemeanor to a nonarrestable infraction (e.g., a traffic ticket).

At the federal level, the Obama administration, through the ONDCP, has focused on addiction as a disease and has called for increases in drug prevention and treatment programs for all who need them, including drug-involved offenders. In 2010, President Obama signed the Fair Sentencing Act into law, reducing the disparity in the amounts of powder cocaine and crack cocaine required for the imposition of mandatory minimum sentences. In 2011, the U.S. Sentencing Commission voted to retroactively apply the new guidelines to individuals sentenced before the federal law was enacted. In 2014, Governor Jerry Brown signed the California Fair Sentencing Act, reducing the same sentencing disparity in crack versus powder cocaine offenses.

COMMUNITY, POLICY, AND SOCIAL ACTION

Federal Programs

Throughout the first part of this chapter, I have already referred to three U.S. offices: NIDA, the ONDCP, and the NIAAA. All three programs are federally funded.

The NIAAA was established after the passage of the Comprehensive Alcohol Abuse and Alcoholism Prevention, Treatment, and Rehabilitation Act of 1970. Signed into law by President Richard Nixon, the legislation acknowledged alcohol abuse and alcoholism as major public health concerns. The law instructed the NIAAA to "develop and conduct comprehensive health, education, research, and planning programs for the prevention and treatment of alcohol abuse and alcoholism and for the rehabilitation of alcohol abusers and alcoholics" (NIAAA 2003a). Since then, the NIAAA's mission has been revised to include support and implementation of biomedical and behavioral research, policy studies, and research in a range of scientific areas to address the causes, consequences, treatment, and prevention of alcoholism and alcohol-related problems (NIAAA 2003b).

NIDA was established in 1974 as the federal office for research, treatment, prevention, training services, and data collection on the nature and extent of drug abuse. Like the NIAAA, NIDA is part of the National Institutes of Health, the federal biomedical and behavioral research agency. NIDA's stated mission is to bring "the power of science to bear on drug abuse and addiction" (NIDA 2003b). NIDA supports more than 85% of the world's research on the health aspects of drug abuse and addiction.

The ONDCP is the newest federal drug program, operated through the White House. Established in 1988 through the Anti-Drug Abuse Act, the ONDCP's mission was to set national priorities, design comprehensive research-based strategies, and certify federal drug control budgets. According to the act, the purpose of the office was to prevent young people from using illegal drugs, reduce the number of drug users, and decrease the availability of drugs (ONDCP 2003). Ten years later, the ONDCP's mission was expanded under the Reauthorization Act of 1998. Some of the legislative requirements included a commitment to a five-year national drug control program budget, the establishment of a parents' advisory council on drug abuse, development of a long-term national drug strategy, and increased reporting to Congress on drug control activities (ONDCP 2003). The act also provided support for the High Intensity Drug Trafficking Areas (HIDTA) program, coordinating local, state, and federal law enforcement drug control efforts.

Use of illegal drugs continues despite the efforts of these three lead agencies. And the War on Drugs comes with huge economic costs, with the Obama administration having requested $25.4 billion for prevention and treatment programs and law enforcement and incarceration for 2015.

Drug Legalization

The contemporary debate about the legalization of drugs emerged in 1988 during a meeting of the U.S. Conference of Mayors. Baltimore's Kurt L. Schmoke called for a national debate on drug control policies and the potential benefits of legalizing marijuana and other illicit substances (Inciardi 1999). Proponents present several arguments for the legalization of drugs: current drug laws and law enforcement initiatives have failed to eradicate the drug problem, arresting and incarcerating individuals for drug offenses does nothing to alleviate the drug problem, drug crimes are actually victimless crimes, legalization will lead to a reduction in drug-related crimes and violence and improve the quality of life in inner cities, and legalization will also eliminate serious health risks by providing clean and high-quality substances (Cussen and Block 2000; Silbering 2001). Many supporters of legalization argue that drugs should be legalized based on the libertarian legal code (Trevino and Richard 2002), namely that the legalization of drugs would give a basic civil liberty back to citizens by granting them control over their own bodies (Cussen and Block 2000).

The term *legalization* is often used interchangeably with another term, *decriminalization*. The terms vary in the extent to which the law can regulate the distribution and consumption of drugs. In general, **decriminalization** means keeping criminal penalties but reducing their severity or removing some kinds of behavior from inclusion under the law (e.g., eliminating bans on the use of drug paraphernalia). Some would support regulating drugs in the same way alcohol and tobacco are regulated, whereas others would argue for no restrictions at all. **Legalization** suggests removing drugs from the control of the law entirely (Weisheit and Johnson 1992).

Several European countries including Portugal, the United Kingdom, and Switzerland have moved toward drug legalization or decriminalization in some form. The country most identified with liberal drug policies is the Netherlands. Since the mid-1970s, Netherlands coffee shops have been allowed to sell marijuana products. Though possession and sale of marijuana are not legal, in practice sales through these shops are not prosecuted, and buyers (18 years of age or older) are not prosecuted for possession of small (personal use) amounts.

In the United States, drug legalization is generally opposed by the medical and public health community (Trevino and Richard 2002). The American Medical Association has consistently opposed the legalization of all illegal drugs, arguing that most research shows drugs, particularly cocaine, heroin, and methamphetamines, to be harmful to an individual's health. Opponents charge that drug use is a significant factor in the spread of sexually transmitted diseases such as HIV, and drug users are more likely to engage in risky behaviors and in criminal activity (Trevino and Richard 2002). The DEA has also been clear about its opposition to drug legalization, citing concerns about potential increases in drug use and addiction, drug-related crimes, and costs related to drug treatment and criminal justice.

In the 1990s, the drug debate began to change, with legalization proponents advocating a "harm reduction" approach. Many opposed to legalization began to accept aspects of the harm reduction approach. Harm reduction is a principle suggesting that "managing drug misuse is more appropriate than attempting to stop it all together" (Inciardi 1999:3). Proponents acknowledge that current drug policies are not working, but they are still not in favor of full decriminalization (McBride, Terry, and Inciardi 1999). The harm reduction approach emphasizes treatment, rehabilitation, and education (McBride et al. 1999), including advocacy for changes in drug policies (such as legalization), HIV/AIDS-related interventions, broader drug treatment options, counseling and clinical case management for those who want to continue using drugs, and ancillary interventions (housing, healing centers, advocacy groups) (Inciardi 1999). Refer to this chapter's Exploring Social Problems feature for a discussion on the legalization of marijuana.

Decriminalization: Reduction of the kinds of behavior included under the law

Legalization: Removal from control of the law

. . . .

What Does It Mean to Me?

What is your position on the legalization of drugs? What are the intended and unintended consequences of drug legalization?

. . . .

Support of the Legalization of Marijuana

Figure 12.5 Percentage who support legalization of marijuana, 2003, 2010, and 2014

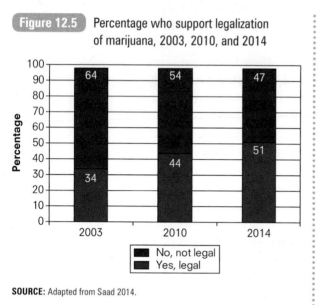

No, not legal
Yes, legal

SOURCE: Adapted from Saad 2014.

Figure 12.6 Percentage who support legalization of marijuana, by political views, 2010, 2012, and 2014

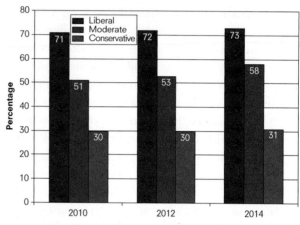

Liberal
Moderate
Conservative

SOURCE: Adapted from Saad 2014.

Figure 12.7 Percentage who support legalization of marijuana by age cohort, 2014

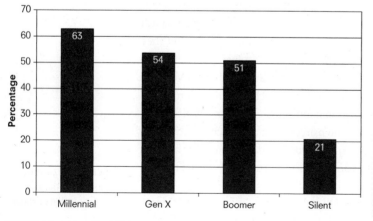

SOURCE: Adapted from Motel 2014.

WHAT DO YOU THINK?

Though general support for the legalization of marijuana has shifted in recent years (refer to Figure 12.5), there is still some variation by social groups (refer to Figures 12.6 and 12.7).

Based on Figure 12.6, compare the differences in legalization support for the three groups presented. Which group's level of support changed the most? Which group's level of support changed the least?

How would you describe the difference in legalization support by generational group (Millennials born 1981–1998, Gen X born 1966–1980, Boomers born 1948–1964, and Silent born 1928–1945) as reported in Figure 12.7? How does age affect level of support?

From a sociological perspective, how are attitudes about marijuana legalization dependent upon social or structural factors?

Drug Treatment and Prevention Programs

Individual Approaches

Drug addiction is a "treatable disorder" (NIDA 2003b). Traditional treatment programs focus on treating the individual and his or her addiction. The ultimate goal of treatment is to enable users to achieve lasting abstinence from the drug, but the immediate treatment goals are to reduce drug use, improve users' ability to function, and minimize their medical and social complications from drug use.

Treatment may come in two forms: behavioral treatment includes counseling, support groups, family therapy, or psychotherapy; medication therapy, such as maintenance treatment for heroin addicts, may be used to suppress drug withdrawal symptoms and craving. Short-term treatment programs can include residential treatment, medication therapy, or drug-free outpatient therapy. Long-term programs (longer than six months) may include highly structured residential therapeutic community treatment or, in the case of heroin users, methadone maintenance outpatient treatment. Research conducted during the past 25 years indicates that treatment does work to reduce drug intake and drug-related crimes. Patients who stay in treatment longer than three months have better outcomes than do people who undergo shorter treatments (NIDA 2003b).

Workplace Strategies

Certain employers, such as employers in the transportation industry and organizations with federal contracts in excess of $100,000, are required by law to have drug-free workplace programs. The federal government, through the Drug Free Workplace Program, also encourages private employers to implement such programs in an effort to reduce and eliminate the negative effects of alcohol and drug use in the workplace (SAMHSA 2003b). It is estimated that more than 80% of employers implement drug testing at the workplace. After implementing a drug-free workplace program, employers, unions, and employees are likely to see a decrease in administrative work losses (sick leave abuse, health insurance claims, disability payments, and accident costs), hidden losses (poor performance, material waste, turnover, and premature death), legal losses (grievances, threat to public safety, work site security), and costs of health and mental health care services (SAMHSA 2003a).

Drug-testing programs have been subject to lawsuits during the past decade for challenging the employees' right to privacy and their constitutional freedom from unreasonable searches by the government (SAMHSA 2003b). There have also been challenges to the accuracy of drug tests. Critics have asserted a positive test does not always correlate with poor job performance, a criterion for assessing the adverse effects of drugs (Klingner, Roberts, and Patterson 1998). Consistent with conflict theories on drug use, some have argued that drug testing promotes various political agendas and reflects the manipulation of interest groups that market and sell drug testing and security services (Klingner et al. 1998). Yet many U.S. companies consider drug-testing programs part of an effective policy against

 The New Heroin Addicts

substance abuse among workers (Hoffman and Larison 1999). Drug testing is also part of a preventative strategy, as the U.S. Department of Labor (2007) reports that between 10% and 20% of workers who die on the job test positive for alcohol or other drugs.

Paul Roman and Terry Blum (2002) report that employee assistance programs (EAPs) are the most common intervention used in the workplace to prevent and treat alcohol and other drug abuse among employees. The primary goal for many of these programs is to ensure that employees maintain their employment, productivity, and careers. These EAPs usually include health promotion, education, and referral to abuse treatment as needed. Most of these programs do not target the general workplace population; rather, services are directed to those already affected by a problem or in the early stages of their abuse. There is some evidence of the effectiveness of these programs, returning substantial proportions of employees with alcohol problems to their jobs (Roman and Blum 2002). In their 2012 study, Jodi Jacobson and Paul Sacco noted how EAPs are in a prime position to reach out to working adults and engage them in education and treatment for alcohol and drug abuse problems earlier than traditional community-based substance abuse programs. They also stated how EAPs could better target racial or ethnically diverse worker groups.

Campus Programs

The U.S. Supreme Court ruled that drug testing in schools is legal for student athletes (1993) and for students in other extracurricular activities (2002). In both rulings, the Court stated that drug screenings play an important role in deterring student drug use.

However, a national study of 76,000 high school students reported no significant difference in drug use among students in schools with testing versus students in schools without testing. Researchers Ryoko Yamaguchi, Lloyd Johnston, and Patrick O'Malley (2003) reported that 37% of 12th graders in schools that test for drugs said that they had smoked marijuana in the previous year, compared with 36% of 12th graders in schools that did not test. In addition, 21% of 12th graders in schools with testing reported that they had used illicit drugs (cocaine or heroin) in the previous year compared with 19% of 12th graders in schools without drug screenings. The study found that only 18% of schools did any kind of drug screening between 1998 and 2001. Large schools (22.6%) reported more testing than did smaller schools (14.2%). Most drug tests were conducted in high schools. The study did not compare schools that conducted intensive regular screenings with those that occasionally tested for drugs. The study indicated that education, rather than testing, may be the most effective weapon against abuse (Winter 2003).

Colleges and universities play critical roles in the prevention and early intervention of drug use, as they are able to implement large-scale prevention and educational programming to reach young adult students. In their review of 94 college drug prevention programs, Andris Ziemelis, Ronald Buckman, and Abdulaziz Elfessi (2002) identified three prevention models that produced the most favorable outcomes of drug use prevention efforts. The first model includes student participation and involvement, such as volunteer services, advisory boards, or task forces, to discourage alcohol or other drug use or abuse. The researchers documented how these activities reinforce students' beliefs that they are in control of the outcomes in their lives and that their efforts and contributions are valued. This model encourages student ownership and development of the program. The second model includes educational and informational processes, such as instruction in classes, bulletin boards and displays, and resource centers. The most effective informational strategies were those that avoided coercive approaches but instead encouraged interactive communication between students and professionals on campus. The last model includes efforts directed at the larger structural environment, changing the campus regulatory environment and developing free alternative programming, such as providing alcohol-free residence halls or mandatory alcohol and drug abuse classes as part of campus intervention. In general, models that discouraged or deglamorized alcohol and drug use were associated with better outcomes than were those that merely banned or restricted substance use (Ziemelis et al. 2002).

Community Approaches

In 1997, the Drug-Free Communities Act became law. The act was intended to increase community participation in substance abuse reduction among youth. The program is currently directed by the White House's ONDCP. The program supports more than 700 coalitions of youth; parents; law enforcement; schools; state, local, and tribal agencies; health care professionals; faith-based organizations; and other community representatives. The coalitions, such as Project Northland, rely on mentoring, parental involvement, community education, and school-based programs for drug prevention and intervention.

Based in northern Minnesota, Project Northland was the largest community trial in the United States to address the prevention of alcohol use and alcohol-related problems among adolescents (Williams and Perry 1998). Adopting a holistic approach, the project assumed that prevention efforts should be directed at adolescents and their immediate social environment (family, peers, friends) and should include larger peer groups (teachers, coaches, religious advisers) as well as the broader community of businesses and political leaders. The project was recognized for its programming by SAMHSA, the U.S. Department of Health and Human Services, and the U.S. Department of Education.

Project Northland included youth participation and leadership, parental involvement and education, community organizing and task forces, media campaigns, and school curriculum as part of its strategies for alcohol use prevention. The program included two phases. Phase 1 focused on strategies to encourage adolescents not to use alcohol. Phase 2 emphasized changing community norms about alcohol use, reducing the availability of alcohol among high school students, and adopting a functionalist approach in reinforcing community norms and boundaries. Community strategies included making compliance checks of age-of-sale laws (coordinated through local police departments), holding training sessions for responsible beverage servers at retail outlets and bars, and encouraging businesses to adopt "gold card"

VOICES IN THE COMMUNITY

SHILO MURPHY

Syringe or needle exchange programs emerged at the height of the AIDS epidemic to reduce the spread of HIV/AIDS and other blood-borne diseases. The programs also facilitate access to drug treatment and health care services. The first needle exchange program was introduced in Amsterdam, Holland, to reduce the risk of hepatitis B and HIV among injecting drug users. These programs also serve a public health function, reducing accidental needle-stick incidents among the general public.

In 1997, Shilo Murphy was a homeless addict when he found the University District Needle Exchange in Seattle, Washington. He says he began volunteering for the program to change the life conditions of his friends and family. Murphy currently serves as the program's executive director.

The needle exchange was renamed the People's Harm Reduction Alliance (PHRA) in 1999. PHRA, according to Murphy, is "a user-run organization, so active drug users make all of our decisions. . . . We're a living, breathing organization in that we constantly change our policies by the needs of people we serve and our bosses are the people we serve" (quoted in Gunawan 2014). The alliance distributes approximately 3 million needles each year and is supported by more than 100 volunteers in three Western Washington counties.

Murphy explains,

> I think [needle exchanges are] important so that a new generation of drug users don't have to go through the pain and suffering when we had to bury so many people who overdosed, so many people who committed suicide because society hated them so much . . . I wanted another generation to have the opportunity to have a better life. (quoted in Gunawan 2014)

Murphy describes his clients as members of a community, members of his family, and individuals who are precious and worthy of love. "[Exchange volunteers] will always follow our hearts and we always take the knowledge and experience of the drug users we serve to give their lives just a little better place" (Murphy 2014).

As of 2013, it was estimated that there were needle exchange sites in 30 U.S. states and the District of Columbia.

Identify other functions or benefits of needle exchange programs.

---

programs where discounts are provided to students who pledge to remain free of alcohol. At the end of Phase 2, significant differences between the intervention and comparison groups were observed. The rates of increase in underage drinking were lower among the intervention students (Perry et al. 2002). In 2002, Project Northland was implemented internationally. First-year program data from primary and secondary schools in Croatia reveal that Project Northland was effective in increasing dialogue between Croatian students, parents, and teachers about students' actual use of alcohol (Abatemarco et al. 2004).

The Community Anti-Drug Coalitions of America (CADCA) is a nonprofit organization that provides technical assistance and training to community-based coalitions. The organization was established in 1992 by Jim Burke and Alvah Chapman

SOCIOLOGY AT WORK

PUBLIC HEALTH

Erika Meyer—Class of 2011

Undergraduate Majors:
Sociology, Global Studies

Public health is "the science of protecting and improving the health of families and communities through promotion of healthy lifestyles, research for disease and injury prevention and detection and control of infectious diseases" (CDC Foundation 2014). Unlike doctors and nurses who treat the sick or injured, public health professionals also address disease prevention through educational programs, research, and public policy.

Educational requirements for employment in the public health sector vary. A bachelor's degree is the minimum requirement to become a health educator or community worker; but to work as an epidemiologist (studying the patterns and causes of disease and injury in humans), you will need at least a master's degree (U.S Bureau of Labor Statistics 2014).

After earning her bachelor's degree in Sociology and her master's in Public Health, Erika Meyer now works as a program associate at Training Programs in Epidemiology and Public Health Interventions Network (TEPHINET). A partner with the Centers of Disease Control and Prevention, TEPHINET manages and provides resources to 59 field epidemiology training programs (FETPs) in over 80 countries. Erika's primary work involves coordinating the accreditation process for the FETPs. She also serves as a project manager for several other projects, including working with CDC's Infection Disease Surveillance and Response Team to build an online disease detection and reporting course for community health workers in Africa.

Erika says that she engages her sociological imagination most when she's designing training and programs for field epidemiologists in countries and cultures very different from her own.

For example, in response to the Ebola epidemic, CDC and TEPHINET are putting together basic surveillance trainings for frontline staff—nurses, community healthcare workers, labor and delivery staff—to teach them about disease reporting. They not only need to know what kinds of symptoms to look for (including Ebola, but also influenza, polio, cholera, etc.), but who to tell that information to and what the data feedback loop should look like. We have to work with the Ministries of Health in the 10 countries to make sure this is a culturally relevant and sensitive training, and that there is the administrative capacity to handle what we are hoping will be an upswing in reporting of outbreaks. We have to carefully navigate the political and social structures that hold decision-making power and sway. The Ebola epidemic provides a salient case study of a "public issue," and my project has to respect the post-colonial scars affecting each country as they response to a crisis of this magnitude.

If your school does not have any courses or programs in a field you're interested in, Erika suggests doing the research on your own as she did.

I sought out summer and school-year internship opportunities that fit my academic and professional interests, and also had the opportunity to spend a semester abroad studying global public health, which afforded me incredible personal and academic growth. I found this to be a great way for me to "try on" the discipline academically, and it really piqued my interest to continue this work in graduate school and as a career.

and currently serves more than 5,000 antidrug coalitions in 18 countries. The program provides community groups with lobbying handbooks, alerts on drug-related legislation, funding information, and coalition training on various drug abuse topics. One CADCA affiliate is California's Ashland Cherryland Together. Through community data collection, the coalition recognized how prescription drugs were being improperly used or shared or resold on the illegal market. The coalition identified the need for a permanent, policy change that would provide access to and awareness of convenient disposal of unused medication. The community partners supported the adoption of the Safe Medication Disposal Ordinance in July 2012. The first law of its kind, it brings together government, medical, environmental, and community organizations in a comprehensive campaign around the effects of prescription drug misuse. There are more than 30 drug disposal locations throughout the community (CADCA 2014).

CHAPTER REVIEW

12.1 Explain how the different sociological perspectives explain alcohol and drug problems

Functionalists argue that society provides us with norms or guidelines on alcohol and drug use. A set of social norms identifies the appropriate use of drugs and alcohol. Conflict theorists address how powerful political and business interest groups have made intentional decisions about which drugs are illegal. Feminists argue that theorists and practitioners in the field of alcohol and drug abuse have ignored experiences unique to women and other marginalized groups. The interactionist perspective examines how drug abuse is learned from others; it also addresses how individuals or groups are labeled abusers and how society responds to them.

12.2 Describe how the social structure regulates drinking

Studies suggest that ethnic/racial groups have different sets of norms and values regulating drinking, such as encouraging moderate alcohol consumption on social events or celebrations.

The consumption of alcohol among women is also moderated by social norms. Women's roles of wife and mother may discourage alcohol intake.

12.3 Identify the correlates of Ecstasy use among college students

Some of the correlates identified in Boyd et al.'s 2003 study include: White students were more likely to report lifetime Ecstasy use than were African American or Asian students. Those who identified themselves as gay, lesbian, or bisexual were more likely to report lifetime, annual, or past-month Ecstasy use than were heterosexual students. Students with a grade point average (GPA) of 3.5 or higher were consistently less likely to have used Ecstasy in the past year or their lifetime than were students with GPAs below 2.5.

12.4 Assess the theory that college students mature out of heavy or binge drinking

According to researchers, maturing-out is a natural process related to a general shift toward a conventional life style, employment, and/or marriage.

12.5 Examine the pros and cons of the drug legalization movement

Opponents charge that drug use is a significant factor in the spread of sexually transmitted diseases such as HIV, and that drug users are more likely to engage in risky behaviors and in criminal activity. There are also expressed concerns about drug-related crimes and costs related to drug treatment and criminal justice. Proponents acknowledge that current drug policies are not working, emphasizing a harm reduction approach that focuses on treatment, rehabilitation, and education.

KEY TERMS

alcoholism, 334

decriminalization, 347

differential association, 332

drug abuse, 333

drug addiction, 333

episodic high-risk drinking, 342

legalization, 347

role strain, 330

STUDY QUESTIONS

1. How are sociological explanations of drug abuse different from biological or psychological approaches?

2. From a functionalist perspective, explain how the social structure contributes to drug use.

3. Explain how stereotypes of drug use and abusers influence how specific individuals and groups are labeled *abusers* and how society responds to them.

4. Define drug abuse and drug addiction.

5. Is drinking a problem among teens and young adults? Why or why not?

6. Define drug legalization. Would it be effective in reducing the amount of drug use? Why or why not?

7. What treatment programs are available to drug users? What type of prevention programs?

⑤SAGE edge™

Sharpen your skills with SAGE edge at **edge.sagepub.com/leonguerrero5e**

SAGE edge provides a personalized approach to help you accomplish your coursework goals in an easy-to-use learning environment.

13

Crime and Criminal Justice

LEARNING OBJECTIVES

13.1 Explain the difference between biological, psychological, and sociological theories of crime

13.2 Identify how the different sociological perspectives examine crime

13.3 Summarize the different types of crime

13.4 Explain how race/ethnicity is an important predictor of offender or victim status

13.5 Describe the transformation of American policing

13.6 Explain whether private prisons are more effective than public prisons

Felonies: Crimes that are serious offenses, punishable by more than one year's imprisonment or death

Misdemeanors: Crimes that are minor offenses, punishable by a fine or less than one year's imprisonment

Think of a crime, any crime. Picture the first "crime" that comes into your mind. What do you see? The odds are you are not imagining a mining company executive sitting at his desk, calculating the costs of proper safety precautions and deciding not to invest in them. Probably what you see with your mind's eye is one person physically attacking another or robbing something from another via the threat of a physical attack.

—Reiman (1998:57)

When we think of crime, we imagine violent or life-threatening acts, not white-collar crimes committed by men and women using accounting ledgers and calculators as deadly weapons. Yet, an act does not have to be violent or bloody to be considered criminal. For our discussion, a crime is any behavior that violates criminal law and is punishable by fine, jail, or other negative sanctions. Crime is divided into two legal categories. **Felonies** are serious offenses, including murder, rape, robbery, and aggravated assault; these crimes are punishable by more than a year's imprisonment or death. **Misdemeanors** are minor offenses, such as traffic violations, that are punishable by a fine or less than a year in jail. In this chapter, we examine crimes as a social problem. We consider a full range of crimes, not just violent events that make the headlines on your evening news. Before we review the specifics about crimes, let's review sociological explanations of why people commit crime.

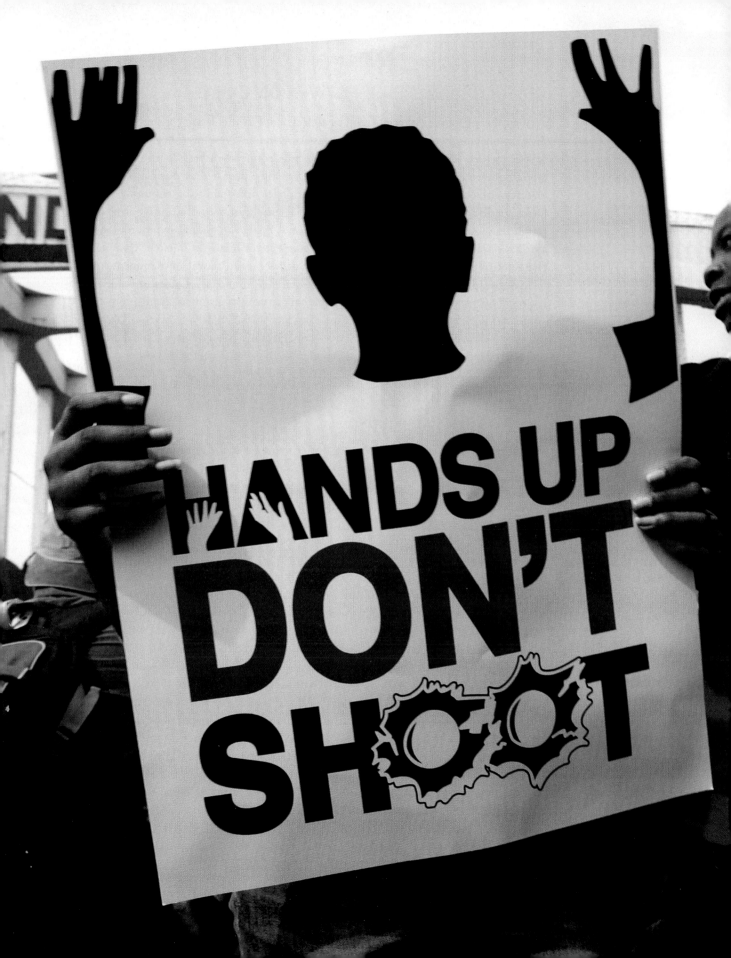

SOCIOLOGICAL PERSPECTIVES ON CRIME

Biological explanations of crime tend to address how criminals are "born that way." Early explanations were intended to classify criminal types by appearance and genetic factors, such as Cesare Lombroso's 19th-century theory of "born criminal" types. Lombroso argued that criminals could be easily identified by distinct physical features: a huge forehead, a large jaw, and a longer arm span. Contemporary biological explanations focus on biochemical (diet and hormones) and neurophysical (brain lesions, brain dysfunctions) characteristics related to violence and criminality. Like biological theories, psychological perspectives focus on inherent criminal characteristics. Researchers link personality development, moral development, or mental disorders to criminal behaviors. Both biological and psychological theories address how crime is determined by individual characteristics or predispositions to crime, but they fail to explain why crime rates vary between urban and rural areas, different neighborhoods, or social or economic groups (Adler, Mueller, and Laufer 1991). Sociological theories attempt to address the reasons for these differences, highlighting how larger social forces contribute to crime.

Functionalist Perspective

Functionalists offer several explanations for criminal behavior. For the first explanation, we return to one of the first sociologists, Émile Durkheim. Criminal behavior, according to Durkheim, is normal and inevitable. Criminal behavior is functional because it separates acceptable from unacceptable behavior in society. Though not a criminologist, Durkheim provided the field with one of its most enduring concepts—anomie (Walsh and Ellis 2007). Recall from our discussion in Chapter 1 that Durkheim argued that society and its rules are what make people human; without any social regulation, people are able to pursue their own desires (even criminal ones). He defined anomie as a state of normlessness, a structural condition where there is no or little regulation of behavior, which leads to deviant or criminal behavior.

Robert K. Merton applied Durkheim's theory of anomie to develop the strain theory of criminal behavior. He argued that we are socialized to attain traditional material and social goals: a good job, a nice home, or a great-looking car. We assume that society is set up in such a way that everyone has the same opportunity or resources to attain these goals. Merton explains that society isn't that fair; some experience blocked opportunities or resources because of discrimination, social position, or talent. People feel strained when they are exposed to these goals but do not have the access or resources to achieve them. This disjunction between cultural goals and structural impediments is anomic, and this is where crime is bred (Walsh and Ellis 2007).

This anomie creates an opportunity to establish new norms or break the old ones to attain these goals. Merton's **strain theory** explains how people adapt to life in this anomic situation. Merton presents five ways in which people adapt to society's goals and means, as presented in Table 13.1. Most individuals fit under the first category,

Strain theory: Robert K. Merton's theory that predicts that criminal behavior is likely to occur when individuals are unable to achieve social and material goals because of insufficient access or resources

Table 13.1 Robert Merton's strain theory

Mode of Adaptation	Agrees With Cultural Goals	Follows Institutional Means	Method of Adaptation
Conformity	+	+	Nondeviant Agrees with cultural goals and institutional means to achieve them
Innovation	+	−	Criminal Agrees with cultural goals, adopts nontraditional means to achieve them
Ritualism	−	+	Deviant, noncriminal Rejects cultural goals but continues to conform to institutional means
Retreatism	−	−	Deviant, could be criminal Rejects cultural goals and the approved means to achieve them
Rebellion	−/+	−/+	Deviant Challenges cultural goals and the approved means to achieve them; offers alternative goals and means

conformity. Conformers accept the traditional goals and have the traditional means to achieve them. Attending college is part of the traditional means to attain a job, an income, and a home. Criminal behavior comes under the innovation category. Innovators accept society's goals, but they don't have the legitimate means to achieve them. They are under a great strain or pressure to achieve these positively valued goals and thus innovate by stealing from their boss, cheating on their taxes, or robbing a local store to achieve them.

Working from Merton's assumptions, scholars argue that criminal activity would decline if economic conditions improved. Solutions to crime would target strained groups, providing access to traditional methods and resources to attain goals. Several studies have confirmed that when anomie is reduced among the poor, lower crime rates may result. Factors usually associated with anomie—the prevalence of female-headed families, the percentage of the population that is African American, and family poverty rates—are more weakly related to crime in areas with higher levels of welfare support (Hannon and Defronzo 1998). But in general, there has been a lack of empirical support for Merton's theory.

Robert Agnew (1992) expanded upon Merton's strain theory to consider multiple individual and structural sources of strain, asserting that negative experiences and relationships motivate and promote criminal behavior (Kaufman et al. 2008). In his general strain theory, Agnew identified three types of social-psychological sources of strain: the failure to achieve positively valued outcomes (not only due to blocked opportunities as explained by Merton, but also because of individual inadequacies due to ability or skill), the removal of positive or desired stimuli from the individual (e.g., the loss of something or someone of great worth), and the confrontation with negative action (or stimuli) by others (e.g., child abuse, adverse school experiences) (Akers and Sellers 2009). Agnew's theory is able to explain criminal offending differences by gender, class, race/ethnicity, communities, and those that occur over the life course, as well as situational variations in crime (Akers and Sellers 2009).

The second functionalist explanation links social control (or the lack of it) to criminal behavior. Whereas Merton's and Agnew's theories ask why someone commits a crime, social control theorists ask why someone *doesn't* commit crime. Society functions best when everyone behaves. Durkheim identified how well society provides us with a set of norms and laws to regulate our behavior. According to sociologist Travis Hirschi (1969), society controls our behavior through four elements: attachments, our personal relationships with others; commitment, our acceptance of conventional goals and means; involvement, our participation in conventional activities; and beliefs, our acceptance of conventional values and norms. Delbert Elliot, Suzanne Ageton, and Rachelle Canter (1979) redefined Hirschi's elements as integration (involvement with and emotional ties to external bonds) and commitment (expectations linked with conventional activities and beliefs). They believe that when all these elements are strong, criminal behavior is unlikely to occur.

Conflict Perspective

Sociologist Austin Turk (1969) explains that criminality is not a biological, psychological, or behavioral phenomenon; rather, it is a way to define a person's social status according to how that person is perceived and treated by law enforcement. An act is not inherently criminal; society defines it that way. Theorists from this perspective argue that criminal laws do not exist for our own good; rather, they exist to preserve the interests and power of specific groups.

In this view, criminal justice decisions are discriminatory and designed to sanction offenders based on their minority or subordinate group membership (race, class, age, or gender) (Akers and Sellers 2009). Turk (1969, 1976) states that criminal status is defined by members of the dominant class. Criminal status is imposed on members of the subordinate class, regardless of whether a crime has actually been committed. Francis Cullen and Robert Agnew (2011, p. 271) explain,

> In general, the injurious acts of the poor and powerless are defined as crime, but the injurious acts of the rich and powerful—such as the corporations selling defective products or the affluent allowing disadvantaged children to go without health care—are not brought into the reach of the criminal law.

Laws serve as a means for those in power to promote their ideas and interests against others. Law enforcement agents protect the interests and power of the dominant class at the expense of subjects. Police may use force, sometimes excessive; "when economic inequality is extreme, elites and polity as a whole may see a need for show of violent force to discourage civil disturbances" (Liska 1992:13). Excessive police force in Brazil is featured in this chapter's "Taking a World View" section.

From this perspective, problems emerge when particular groups are disadvantaged by the criminal justice system. Although the powerful are able to resist criminal labels, the labels seem to stick to minority power groups—the poor, youth, and ethnic minorities. Minority power groups' interests are on the margins of mainstream society, so most of their activities can be criminalized by dominant authorities (Walsh and Ellis 2007). Conflict theorists argue that the criminal justice system is intentionally unequal and serves as the vehicle for conflicts between opposing groups. The solution is the creation of a more equitable and just society (Cullen and Agnew 2011).

Feminist Perspective

For a long time, criminology ignored the experiences of women, choosing to apply theories and models of male criminality to women. Feminist researchers have been credited with making female offenders visible (Naffine 1996) and with documenting

© Scott Houston/Corbis

Female inmates wait to be chained together before being transported for "burial duty," where they will bury dead homeless and indigents at White Tanks Cemetery, 40 miles west of Estrella Jail in Phoenix, Arizona. Approximately 4 feet of chain separates each inmate, and there are four or five inmates to a group. Estrella Jail, in Maricopa County, is home to the only female chain gang in America.

Incarcerated Women

the experiences of women as the victims or survivors of violent men and as victims of the criminal justice system (Chesney-Lind and Pasko 2004). Feminist scholarship has attempted to understand how women's criminal experiences are different from those of men and how experiences of women differ from each other based on race, ethnicity, class, age, and sexual orientation (Chesney-Lind and Pasko 2004; Flavin 2001).

Freda Adler (1975) was one of the first to explain that women were "liberated" to commit crime when they were no longer restrained by traditional ideals of feminine behavior and could take on more masculine traits, including criminal behavior. Called the liberation approach, the logic of the argument is that as gender equality increases, women are more likely to commit crime. Although the approach was met with wide public acceptance, it has been discredited because of lack of empirical evidence (Chesney-Lind and Pasko 2004).

Recently, gender inequality theories have been presented as explanations of female crime. According to Darrell Steffensmeier and Emilie Allan (1996), patriarchal power relations shape gender differences in crime, pushing women into criminal behavior through role entrapment, economic marginalization, and victimization or as a survival response. The authors point out, "Nowhere is the gender ratio more skewed than in the great disparity of males as offenders and females as victims of sexual and domestic abuse" (p. 470). The logic of the inequality argument is that female crime increases as gender inequality increases.

Women are more likely to kill intimate partners, family members, or acquaintances than men are, "so the connection between women's overall homicide offending rates and gender inequality lies largely in the connection between gender stratification and women's domestic lives," explains Vicki Jensen (2001:8). Jensen describes gender inequality as being composed of economic, political-legal, and social inequalities experienced by women. Lower gender equality can negatively affect women's freedom and opportunities; these situations can push women into situations in which lethal violence seems to be the only way out. In the case of women killing abusive intimate partners, low levels of economic security limit women's opportunities to escape abusive situations. Low levels of gender equality can increase the emphasis on traditional gender norms, placing the responsibility on women to please men and requiring that women must be submissive and accept whatever their partner does (including violence). Jensen explains that most women who kill an intimate partner do so in response to abuse situations, in imminent self-defense, or when all other strategies have failed.

Research indicates that the surge in women's incarceration has little to do with any major change in women's criminal behavior. In comparison to men's, women's crime participation rates have remained stable over time (Becker and McCorkel 2011). Since 1995, the annual rate of growth in the number of U.S. female prisoners averaged 5%, higher than the 3% for male prisoners (refer to Table 13.2). The public's "get tough with crime" approach, along with a legal system that encourages treating women equally to men, has resulted in the greater use of imprisonment as punishment for female criminal behavior (Chesney-Lind and Pasko 2004).

Sarah Becker and Jill McCorkel (2011) examined how gender affects access to criminal opportunities, specifically looking at the types of crime committed by men and women and considering how the presence of a male co-offender alters women's crime participation. They found that most men and women co-offend with men; all-female offender groups are rare. Their analysis of national crime data revealed how women are more likely to be involved in gender-atypical offenses like drug trafficking, homicide, gambling, kidnapping, and weapons offenses when they have at least one male co-offender compared to when they work alone or in a same-sex group. The range of women's crime participation increases with the presence of a male co-offender.

During 2013, 111,300 females were in prison, accounting for 7% of all U.S. prisoners (Glaze and Kaeble 2014). The International Centre for Prison Studies analyzed data on the number of incarcerated women worldwide at the beginning of 2012. Based on data from 212 prison systems in countries and dependent territories, the center reported that more than 625,000 women and girls were currently being held in penal institutions as pretrial detainees or having been convicted and sentenced. The highest numbers of female detainees or prisoners were in the United States (201,200), China (84,600), the Russian Federation (59,002), and Brazil (35,596) (Walmsley 2012).

The increase in the number of women inmates has caused prison officials to reconsider custody procedures for women, especially specific programs and services available to women. Also, there are major differences between male and female prisoners, which have implications for women's confinement and release (Galbraith 2004). In particular, women are more likely (a) to be serving their first sentence, (b) to be the primary caregiver of their children, (c) to be victims of sexual abuse and trauma (Morash, Byrum, and Koons 1998), and (d) to suffer from depression. Parenting has become a focus of many programs.

Table 13.2 Number of prisoners under the jurisdiction of state or federal correctional authorities and incarceration rate by gender, 2000, 2010, and 2013

	Males	Females
All inmates		
2000	1,298,027	93,234
2010	1,499,573	112,822
2013	1,412,745	104,134
Incarceration Rate*		
2000	904	59
2010	943	67
2013	904	65

*The number of persons with a sentence of more than one year per 100,000 U.S. residents.

SOURCE: Guerino, Harrison, and Sabol 2011; Sabol, West, and Cooper 2009; Carson 2014.

Interactionist Perspective

Interactionists examine the process that defines certain individuals and acts as criminal. The theory is called **labeling theory**, highlighting that what's important isn't the criminals or their acts, but rather the audience that labels the persons or their acts as criminal. As Kai Erickson (1964) explains, "deviance is not a property inherent in certain forms of behavior; it is a property conferred upon these forms by audiences which directly or indirectly witness them" (p. 11). The theory also considers how definitions of crime or deviance can change over time.

Labeling theory: Theory stating that individuals and acts are defined or labeled as criminal

 The Psychology of Evil

The basic elements of labeling theory were presented by sociologist Edwin Lemert (1967), who believed that everyone is involved in behavior that could be labeled delinquent or criminal, yet only a few are actually labeled. Lemert's theory identifies the consequences of being labeled and treated as a criminal. He explained that deviance is a process, beginning with primary deviation, which arises from a variety of social, cultural, psychological, and physiological factors. Although most primary acts of deviance go unnoticed, they may lead to a social response in the form of an arrest, punishment, or stigmatization. Secondary deviation includes more serious deviant acts, which follow the social response to the primary deviance. Once a criminal label is attached to a person, a criminal career is set in motion.

John Braithwaite (1989) observed that nations with low crime rates are those where shaming has great social power. Braithwaite defined shaming as all processes of "expressing disapproval which have the intention or effect of invoking remorse in the person being shamed and/or condemnation by others who become aware of the shaming" (p. 9). Braithwaite agreed with Lemert that shaming could be "stigmatizing" (increasing the distance between the offender and society) and lead to additional criminal acts. However, he proposed that shaming should be "reintegrative" (restoring the link between the offender and society) and lead to less crime.

. . . .

What Does It Mean to Me?

What are your perceptions of a typical victim or perpetrator? What roles do the media—news, television, and movies—play in creating these perceptions? From what other sources are these perceptions learned?

. . . .

Interactionists also attempt to explain how deviant or criminal behavior is learned through association with others. Edwin Sutherland's (1949) theory of differential association states that individuals are likely to commit deviant acts if they associate with others who are deviants. This criticism is often raised about our jail and prison systems; instead of rehabilitation, prisoners are able to learn more criminal activity and behavior while serving their sentences. Psychologists Craig Haney and Philip Zimbardo (1998) noted how "department of corrections data show that about a fourth of those initially imprisoned for nonviolent crimes are sentenced a second time for committing a violent offense. Whatever else it reflects, this pattern highlights the possibility that prison serves to transmit violent habits and values rather than to reduce them" (p. 721). Sutherland's theory does not address how the first criminal learned criminal behavior, but he does highlight how criminal behavior emerges from interaction, association, and socialization.

For a summary of sociological perspectives, see Table 13.3.

Table 13.3   Summary of sociological perspectives: Crime and criminal justice

	Functional	Conflict/Feminist	Interactionist
Explanation of crime and criminal justice	Crime emerges from the social order. People experience "strain" when they are exposed to cultural goals but do not have the access or resources to achieve them. Individuals are likely to make some new rules (or break the old ones) to attain these goals. Society also controls criminal behavior through four elements: attachments, commitment, involvement, and beliefs.	Criminal justice decisions are discriminatory and designed to sanction offenders based on their minority or subordinate group membership (race, class, age, or gender). Problems emerge when particular groups are disadvantaged more than others by the criminal justice system.	Interactionists examine the process that defines certain individuals and acts as criminal. Interactionists also examine how criminal or deviant behavior is learned through association with others.
Questions asked about crime and criminal behavior	How/why are individuals denied access to resources to achieve their goals? What social controls are in place to reduce criminal behavior?	How do our criminal justice policies reflect political, economic, and social interests? Why/how are particular groups targeted as "criminals"? How do women's experiences as crime victims and offenders differ from men's?	Is criminal behavior the result of being labeled a "criminal"? Is criminal behavior learned? How are our perceptions of criminals and victims socially created?

SOURCES OF CRIME STATISTICS

We rely on three sources of data to estimate the nature and extent of crime in the United States. The primary source is annual data collected by the Federal Bureau of Investigation (FBI). Since 1930, the FBI has published the Uniform Crime Report (UCR), data supplied by 17,000 federal, state, and local law enforcement agencies. The UCR reports two categories of crimes: index crimes and nonindex crimes. **Index crimes** include murder, rape, robbery, assault, burglary, motor vehicle theft, arson, and larceny (theft of property worth $50 or more). All other crimes except traffic violations are categorized as nonindex crimes. The UCR provides law enforcement officers and agencies with useful data about serious rates across states, counties, and cities, as well as trend and longitudinal data since its inception. The second source of crime data emerged in 1982, when the FBI began to use the National Incident-Based

Index crimes: Crimes including murder, rape, robbery, assault, burglary, motor vehicle theft, arson, and larceny

Reporting System (NIBRS), which adds detailed offender and victim information to the UCR data. Currently, 31 states provide NIBRS information.

However, the often-cited problem with the UCR and the NIBRS is that the data reflect only reported crimes. The FBI cannot collect information on crimes that have not been reported, but it is estimated that only 3% to 4% of crimes are actually discovered by police (Kappeler, Blumberg, and Potter 2000). Also, being reported doesn't mean that a crime has actually occurred. The FBI does not require that a suspect has been arrested or that a crime is investigated and found to have actually occurred; it only needs to be reported (Kappeler et al. 2000).

In addition to the UCR, the FBI releases the Crime Clock, a graphic display of how often specific offenses are committed. Although it may make for good newspaper copy or give law enforcement and political officials clout (Chambliss 1988), the Crime Clock has been accused of exaggerating the amount of crime, leaving the public with the impression that they are in imminent danger of being victims of violence (Kappeler et al. 2000).

The third data source about crime is the National Crime Victimization Survey (NCVS or NCS), which has been published by the Bureau of Justice Statistics since 1972. The survey is based on victimization surveys first conducted in Denmark (in 1720) and Norway (in the late 1940s). Twice a year, the U.S. Census Bureau interviews members of about 77,200 households regarding their experience with crime.

The NCVS identifies crime victims whether or not the crime was reported. The survey includes information about victims and crimes but covers only six offenses (compared with the eight index crimes reported by the UCR). Also included is information on the experiences of victims with the criminal justice system, self-protective measures used by victims, and possible substance abuse by offenders. NCVS crime victim data for 2013 are presented in Table 13.4.

The results of the NCVS are often compared with the UCR to indicate that the number of crimes committed is actually higher than the number of crimes reported, suggesting that the UCR may not be an adequate measure of violent crime. However, "a more thoughtful interpretation of the inconsistency between these statistical reports concludes that while neither the UCR nor the NCVS is by itself an adequate measure of violence, each is an estimate of the scope and nature of violent crime" (Brownstein 2001:8–9).

Table 13.4 Number of crime victims and prevalence rate for selected personal and property crimes, 2013

Type of Crime	Number of Incidents	Prevalence Rate
Violent crimes	3,041,170	1.2%
-Rape/sexual assault	173,610	0.1%
-Robbery	369,070	0.1%
-Assault	2,600,920	1.0%
Property crimes	11,531,420	9.0%
-Household burglary	2,458,360	1.9%
-Motor vehicle theft	555,660	0.4%
-Theft	9,070,680	7.1%

SOURCE: Truman and Langton 2014.

NOTE: Prevalence rate calculated by percentage of persons aged 12 or older who had experienced at least one victimization during the year for violent crime, and the percentage of households that had experienced one victimization during the year for property crime.

TYPES OF CRIME

Violent Crime

Violent crime is defined as actions that involve force or the threat of force against others and includes aggravated assault, murder, rape, and robbery. The victimization rate for crimes of violence in 2013 was 23.2 victimizations per 1,000 people age 12 or older, declining from 26.1 in 2012 (Truman and Langton 2014).

In 2013, males and females had similar rates of violent victimization—23.7 per 1,000 males and 22.7 per 1,000 females (Truman and Langton 2014). Male homicide victimization rates are higher than female rates worldwide. Comparing homicide victimization rates from 1950 to 2001, the countries with the highest male homicide victimization rates were Mexico, 35.13 per 100,000, followed by Puerto Rico, 24.64. For female homicide, the highest victimization rate was in Puerto Rico, 3.53 per 100,000; Mexico was second at 3.40. For the same period, rates for the United States were reported at 11.88 for males and 3.37 for females (LaFree and Hunnicutt 2006). For 2010, the victimization rate for U.S. males (11.6 per 100,000) was three times higher than the rate for females (3.4 per 100,000) (Cooper and Smith 2011).

Males are more likely to be victimized by a stranger, whereas women are more likely to be violently victimized by a friend, an acquaintance, or an intimate partner (U.S. Bureau of Justice Statistics 2003a). For rape and sexual assault victimization tracked for 1994–2010, most victims (about 75%) knew their offender. For 2005–2010, 34% of all rape or sexual assault victimizations were committed by an intimate partner (former or current spouse, girlfriend or boyfriend), 6% by a relative or family member, and 38% by a friend or acquaintance (Planty et al. 2013). In 2012, the federal government expanded the definition of forcible rape to include male victims and the types of sexual assault that would be counted by the FBI's Uniform Crime Report. The revised definition includes forcible oral or anal penetration, along with nonconsensual sex (Savage 2012).

Intimate violence (violence at the hands of someone known to the victim) is primarily committed against women in both the developed and developing worlds. The World Health Organization (WHO) (2005), in its study of women from 10 different countries, revealed that violence by an intimate partner is "common, widespread, and far-reaching in its impact" (WHO 2005:viii). WHO reports that the proportion of ever-partnered women who had experienced physical or sexual violence or both by an intimate partner ranged from 29% to 62% in most studied countries. Women in Japan were the least likely to experience either type of violence, and the greatest amount of violence was reported by women living in provincial rural areas of Bangladesh, Ethiopia, Peru, and the United Republic of Tanzania (WHO 2005). In 2010, U.S. women experienced 407,700 rape, sexual assault, robbery, aggravated assault, and simple assault victimizations at the hands of an intimate partner; among men, 101,530 were victims of violent crimes by an intimate partner (Truman 2011).

Violent crime: Criminal acts that involve force or the threat of force against others and include aggravated assault, murder, rape, and robbery

EXPLORING **social problems**

Violent Crime Victimization

Figure 13.1 Victimization rate per 1,000 persons aged 12 or older, by gender, 2013

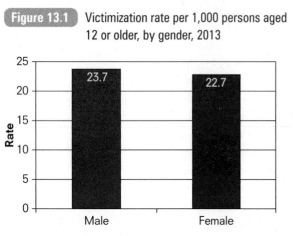

SOURCE: Adapted from Truman and Langton 2014.

Figure 13.2 Victimization rate per 1,000 persons aged 12 or older, by race/ethnicity, 2013

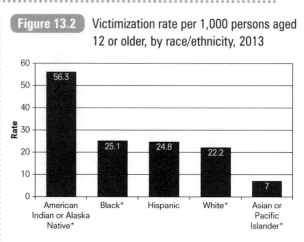

SOURCE: Adapted from Truman and Langton 2014.

NOTE: *Excludes persons of Hispanic Origin

Figure 13.3 Victimization rate per 1,000 persons aged 12 or older, by age, 2013

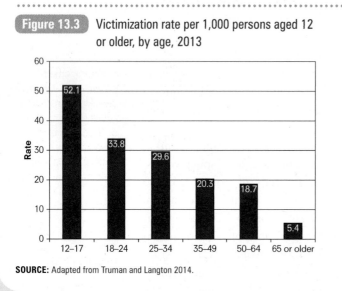

SOURCE: Adapted from Truman and Langton 2014.

WHAT DO YOU THINK?

Figure 13.1 to 13.3 present the rate of victimization for violent crimes per 1,000 persons age 12 or older by gender, race/ethnicity, and age. The discussion in the previous section reviews data trends presented in these figures.

From a sociological perspective, explain why some groups are more likely to be victims of violent crime than others. For example, what makes the 12- to 17-year-old age group more than twice as likely to experience violent crime than the group of 35- to 49-year-olds?

Since 1973, Blacks have had the highest violent crime victimization rates. In 2013, 25.1 of 1,000 Black people experienced a violent crime versus 22.2 out of 1,000 Whites and 24.8 out of 1,000 Hispanics (Truman and Langton 2014). Research by William Julius Wilson (1996) and Robert Sampson and Wilson (1995) revealed that structural disadvantages, rather than race, contribute to higher levels of crime and victimization in Black communities (Ackerman 1998). The structural factors include neighborhood poverty, unemployment, social isolation, and economic disadvantage.

Data collected for 2008 reveal that disabled persons are more likely to experience higher rates of violence (40 crimes per 1,000 persons age 12 or older) than those without a disability (2% or 20 crimes per 1,000 persons). The violent crime rate was approximately 86% for youth ages 16 to 19 with disabilities versus 34% for youth without. Females with a disability had a higher victimization rate than males with a disability (Harrell and Rand 2010). Refer to this chapter's Exploring Social Problems feature for a summary of violent crime victimization by selected social characteristics.

Property Crime

Property crime consists of taking money or property from another without force or the threat of force against the victims. Burglary, larceny, theft, motor vehicle theft, and arson are examples of property crimes. Property crimes make up about three fourths of all crime in the United States. In 2013, there were an estimated 16.8 million property crimes, including 3.3 million household burglaries and 661,250 motor vehicle thefts (Truman and Langton 2014).

Juvenile Delinquency

The term **juvenile delinquent** often refers to a youth who is in trouble with the law. Technically, a **juvenile status offender** is a juvenile who has violated a law that applies only to minors 7 to 17 years old, such as cutting school or buying and consuming alcohol (Sanders 1981). In certain cases, minors can be tried as adults. Crimes committed by juveniles are more likely to be cleared by law enforcement than crimes committed by adults.

The Office of Juvenile Justice and Delinquency Prevention monitors data on rates of **juvenile crime**. For 2011, the total number of juvenile arrests was 1.47 million. Females accounted for 29% of juvenile arrests. Almost half of all juvenile arrests involved larceny-theft, simple assault, drug abuse violations, disorderly conduct, or liquor law violations. Only 5% of all violent crimes involved offenders younger than age 18 (Puzzanchera 2013). Unlike the United States, many countries do not collect systematic data on delinquency, and among the countries that do, their data are described as "incomplete because of faulty record keeping" (Stafford 2004:486).

For 2011, the racial composition of the U.S. juvenile population was 76% White (Hispanics are also classified as White), 17% Black, 5% Asian/Pacific Islander, and 2% American Indian. Although Black youth accounted for 17% of the youth population between the ages of 10 and 17, they were involved in 51% of the arrests for violent crimes and 35% of property crimes (Puzzanchera 2013).

Delinquency is often explained by the absence of strong bonds to society or the lack of social controls. In studies of serious adolescent crime, research indicates that

Property crime: Criminal acts that involve the taking of money or property from another without force or the threat of force against the victims; burglary, larceny, theft, motor vehicle theft, and arson are examples of property crimes

Juvenile delinquent: A youth who engages in criminal behavior

Juvenile status offender: A juvenile who has violated a law applying only to minors

Juvenile crime: Criminal acts performed by juveniles

 Inside Juvenile Prison

the economic isolation of inner-city neighborhoods, along with the concentration of poverty and unemployment, leads to an erosion of the formal and informal controls that inhibit delinquent behavior (Laub 1983). Juveniles without any or much social control are likely to engage in illegal behavior when they live in any environment that offers opportunities for illegal activities. Youth who are strongly bonded to conventional role models and institutions (parents, teachers, school, community leaders, and law-abiding peers) are least likely to engage in delinquent behaviors.

White-Collar Crime

The term **white-collar crime** was first used by Sutherland in 1949. He used the term to refer to "a crime committed by a person of respectability and high social status in the course of his occupation" (Sutherland 1949:9). Since then, the term has come to include three categories of offense: crimes committed by an offender (someone of high social status and respectability as described by Sutherland), crimes committed for financial or economic gain, and crimes taking place in a particular organization or business (Barnett n.d.).

The FBI (1989) has defined white-collar crime by the type of crime:

[White-collar crime includes] illegal acts which are characterized by deceit, concealment, or violation of trust and which are not dependent upon the application or threat of physical force or violence. Individuals or organizations commit these acts to obtain money, property or services; to avoid payment or loss of money or services; or to secure personal and business advantage. (p. 3)

Such acts include credit card fraud, insurance fraud, mail fraud, tax evasion, money laundering, embezzlement, and theft of trade secrets. Corporate crime may also include illegal acts committed by corporate employees on behalf of the corporation and with its support. Corporate fraud has been identified as the highest priority of the FBI's Financial Crimes Section. As of the end of fiscal year 2011, the FBI had pursued 726 cases, several which involved losses to public investors that individually exceeded $1 billion (FBI 2011). White-collar crimes cost taxpayers more than all other types of crime.

One of the most widespread forms of white-collar crime is Internet fraud and abuse, also known as **cybercrime**. The Internet Crime Complaint Center (IC3) is a joint partnership between the FBI and National White Collar Crime Center. IC3 handles complaints and crimes that include identity theft, online credit card fraud schemes, theft of trade secrets, sales of counterfeit software, and computer intrusions (a hacker breaking into a system). Years ago, when computer systems were relatively self-contained, there was no concern about cybercrime. Committing cybercrime is easier with the growth of the Internet, increasing computer connectivity, and the availability of break-in programs and information. As computer-controlled infrastructure and networks have expanded, many systems—power

White-collar crime: Crimes committed by someone of high social status, for financial gain, or in a particular organization

Cybercrime: A form of white-collar crime that involves Internet fraud and abuse

 Cybercrime Infographic

grids, airports, rail systems, hospitals—have become vulnerable (Wolf 2000). In response to Internet crimes, the FBI and the Department of Justice have established computer crime teams or offices. Some states, such as Massachusetts and New York, have created high-technology crime units.

What Does It Mean to Me?

Crime rates have dropped significantly in most large cities since the 1990s. Consider the homicide rate. The rate peaked in 1980 at 10.2 homicides per 100,000 people (Blumstein and Rosenfeld 1998). For 2011, the homicide rate was 4.7 homicides per 100,000 people (Smith and Cooper 2013). There is less violent crime, but do we still live in fear? Which type of crime do you fear the most? Why?

Table 13.5 Percentage of prisoners under state or federal jurisdiction by gender and race, based on inmates with sentences of more than one year, December 2013

	Males	Females
White	32.1	49.4
Black	37.2	22.2
Hispanic	22.3	16.9
Other*	8.3	11.4

*OTHER includes American Indians, Asians, Native Hawaiians, other Pacific Islanders, and persons identifying two or more races.

SOURCE: Adapted from Guerino, Harrison, and Sabol 2011.

What Does It Mean to Me?

Dharun Ravi, a former Rutgers University student, was convicted in 2012 of using a webcam to spy on his roommate kissing another man. Using Twitter and text messages, he encouraged others to watch the video. His roommate, Tyler Clementi, committed suicide after learning of the video. Because Ravi had targeted Clementi, a gay man, his crime was classified as a hate crime. Ravi was sentenced to 30 days in jail, along with three years of probation and 300 hours of community service. Ravi served a total of 20 days, having earned early release for good behavior and his work in jail. Does this punishment fit his crime? Why or why not?

THE INEQUALITIES OF CRIME— OFFENDERS AND VICTIMS

Offenders

Reports consistently reveal that African American males are overrepresented in incarceration statistics. Most jail or prison inmates are male and African American (refer to Table 13.5). On December 31, 2013, almost 3% of the Black male U.S. population of all ages were imprisoned, compared to 1% of Hispanic males and 0.5% of White males. On the same day, Black females were imprisoned at more than twice the rate of White females (Carson 2014). That a category of people is overrepresented among violent offenders does not necessarily mean that this group is responsible for more violent acts (Brownstein 2001). Keep in mind that these statistics are based only on those who were caught by the criminal justice system.

 Mass Incarceration: Locked out of the American Dream

A number of studies confirm that regardless of the seriousness of the crime, racial and ethnic minorities, particularly African Americans and Hispanics, are more likely to be arrested or incarcerated than are their White counterparts. Though Latinos make up only 13% of the U.S. adult population, they account for 40% of federal prison inmates, due in part to tougher enforcement of immigration laws (Lopez and Light 2009). This is also true for minority juvenile delinquents. Minority youth are overrepresented at every stage in the juvenile justice system; they are arrested more often, detained more often, overrepresented in referrals to juvenile court, and institutionalized at a disproportionate rate compared with White youth (Joseph 2000). In its analysis of contacts between police and the public for 2008, the U.S. Bureau of Justice Statistics reported that Black (12.3%) and Hispanic (5.8%) motorists were more likely to be searched during a traffic stop than White drivers (3.9%) (Eith and Durose 2011). Blacks and Hispanics were more likely than Whites to report being involved in an incident where police force was used (Eith and Durose 2011).

An early criminological explanation was offered by Marvin Wolfgang and Franco Ferracuti (1967), who argued that Blacks have adopted violent subcultural values, creating a "subculture of violence." Although this is an often-cited theory, there is insufficient empirical evidence to support the idea that Blacks are more likely to embrace a violent value system. Actually, studies have indicated that White males are more likely to express violent beliefs or attitudes than Black males (Cao, Adams, and Jensen 2000).

Family structure, specifically the presence of female-headed households in African American communities, has also been identified as a potential source for racial crime disparities. Yet, criminological research has not articulated how family structure or family processes are related to crime (Morenoff 2005). Does the structure of the family itself increase the likelihood of crime? Is the incidence of crime related to the amount of parental supervision, the level of parental effectiveness, or the nature of the parent–child relationship? These questions remain the focus of researchers.

Criminologists and sociologists have examined patterns of racial bias or discrimination in the law enforcement and criminal justice system. **Racial profiling** is the use of race or ethnicity by law enforcement, consciously or unconsciously, as a basis of judgment for criminal suspicion. Racial profiling is supported by some in law enforcement as a rational and efficient strategy, targeting those most likely to commit crime. Yet most agree that profiling is dysfunctional, creating "racial inequities by denying people of color privacy, identity, place, security, and control over their daily life" (Cross 2001:5). President Obama, responding to the acquittal of George Zimmerman in the shooting death of Trayvon Martin, said, "Trayvon Martin could have been me 35 years ago . . . There are very few African-American men in this country who have not had the experience of being followed when they are shopping at a department store. That includes me" (White House 2013).

Racial profiling: The use of race or ethnicity by law enforcement consciously or unconsciously as a basis of judgment for criminal suspicion

Michelle Alexander (2010) characterizes mass incarceration as a caste system, much like the Jim Crow laws (1876–1965) that defined permanent second-class status for Black Americans. Specifically, the War on Drugs served as a form of legalized discrimination, entrapping African Americans in the criminal justice system. The harm to individuals and families only intensifies when prisoners are released. She explains,

> They enter a separate society, a world hidden from public view, governed by a set of oppressive and discriminatory rules and laws that do not apply to everyone else. They become members of an undercaste—an enormous population of predominately black and brown people who, because of the drug war, are denied basic rights and privileges of American citizenship and are permanently relegated to an inferior status. (Alexander 2010:181–82)

New racial profiling rules were released by the Obama administration after nationwide protests over the decisions in New York and Ferguson, Missouri, not to prosecute White officers for the deaths of unarmed Black men (Apuzzo and Schmidt 2014). Citing the need for "even-handed law enforcement," the categories of racial profiling were expanded to include religion, national origin, gender, sexual orientation, and gender identity. Under the new rules, law enforcement officials cannot consider any of those factors in making routine or spontaneous law enforcement decisions. Agencies whose officers make traffic stops may not use any of these categories as a reason to pull someone over. The new guidelines apply to federal law enforcement officers and to local police assigned to federal task forces, but not to local police agencies (Apuzzo and Schmidt 2014; U.S. Department of Justice 2014).

Victims

Early studies on crime victims tended to perpetuate the image that the victim was simply at the "wrong place at the wrong time" (Davis, Taylor, and Titus 1997). Following that reasoning, not being a victim of crime could be explained simply as good luck. However, research indicates that some individuals, by virtue of their social group or social behavior, are more prone than others to become victims (Davis et al. 1997). What people do, where they go, and with whom they associate affect their likelihood of victimization (Laub 1997).

Victimization is distributed across key demographic dimensions (Laub 1997). Victimization rates are substantially higher for the poor, the young, males, Blacks, single people, renters, and central city

For most individuals, their interaction with police officers is limited to traffic violation stops. Police departments are incorporating new methods of policing based on community and problem-solving approaches, hoping to increase the interaction between officers and citizens.

© Douglas Kirkland/Corbis

residents (Davis et al. 1997). The likelihood of being injured because of a violent crime is higher among the young, the poor, urban dwellers, Blacks, Hispanics, and American Indians (Simon, Mercy, and Perkins 2001). Injury rates are lower for the elderly, for people with a higher income or higher educational attainment, and for people who are married or widowed (Simon et al. 2001).

Black males have the highest rate of violent victimization, and White females have the lowest (Laub 1997). Blacks also have the highest rate of overall household victimization. Although rates of violent crimes declined during the 1990s, mortality from homicide among minority groups is still high. Homicide is the leading cause of death among Black males between the ages of 15 and 24, and it is the second leading cause of death for Latino males in the same age group (Rich and Ro 2002). People who have been victims once are at an elevated risk of becoming victims again. Repeat victimization is likely to occur in poor, predominantly Black areas (Davis et al. 1997).

· ·

What Does It Mean to Me?

Crime rates have dropped significantly in most large cities since the 1990s. There is less reported violent crime, but do we still live in fear? Why or why not?

· ·

OUR CURRENT RESPONSE TO CRIME

The Police

For 2011, there were more than a million full-time law enforcement employees. About 70% were sworn officers. Local police departments were the largest employer (60% of all employees) (FBI 2014a). We rely on the police force to serve as the first line of defense against crime, and some officers lose their lives in the line of duty. In 2013, 27 law enforcement officers were feloniously killed in the line of duty, and 49 were killed in accidents (FBI 2014b).

American policing has gone through substantial changes during the past several decades (MacDonald 2002). Traditional models of policing emphasized high visibility and the use of force and arrests as deterrents to crime. Policing under these models relies on three tactics: police patrols, rapid response to service calls, and retrospective investigations (M. Moore 1999). These models reinforce an "us" versus "them" division, sometimes pitting the police against the public they were sworn to protect. High-profile incidents of police brutality and violence, such as the cases that involved Rodney King in Los Angeles and Amadou Diallo in New York City, increased public distrust and tainted the image of policing.

Studies indicate that "net of all other factors, race and personal experience with racial profiling are among the strongest and most consistent predictors of attitudes toward the police" (Weitzer and Tuch 2002:445). Whites trust police more and have more positive interactions with them than do Blacks; Hispanics fall between these two groups (Norris et al. 1992). Black youth tend to have the most negative or hostile feelings toward police (Norris et al. 1992). Residents from poor or disadvantaged areas have a much lower regard for the police than does the general public. However, research has also indicated that when citizens believe they are treated fairly, they tend to grant police more legitimacy and are more likely to comply with police (Stoutland 2001).

Police departments are now incorporating new methods of policing based on the community and problem-solving approaches (Goldstein 1990; MacDonald 2002). The community policing approach refers to efforts to increase the interaction between officers and citizens, including the use of foot patrols, community substations, and neighborhood watches (Beckett and Sasson 2000). By 2000, two thirds of all local police departments and 62% of sheriff's offices had full-time sworn personnel engaged in community policing activities (U.S. Bureau of Justice Statistics 2003b). We learn more about community policing in the section titled "Community, Policy, and Social Action."

Prisons

Despite the decline in crime rates, prison populations are increasing (Anderson 2003), though the rate of new admissions has declined in recent years (Sabol, West, and Cooper 2009). At the end of 2013, the federal and state inmate population was more than 1.6 million. Though the United States represents 5% of the world's population, the number of incarcerated in our country represents nearly 25% of the world's prison population (Rosen 2010). Data reveal that the United States has the highest prison population rate in the world (refer to Figure 13.4).

Figure 13.4 Highest prison population rates in the world, 2013

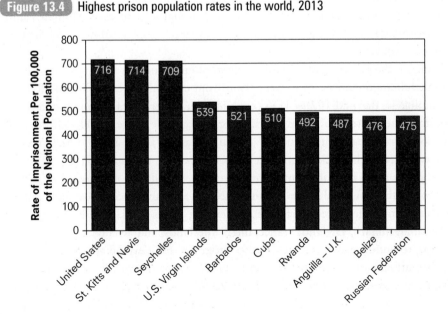

SOURCE: Adapted from Walmsley 2014.

Mandatory sentencing, especially for nonviolent drug offenders, is a key reason why inmate populations have increased for the past 30 years. Drug offenders now make up more than half of all federal prisoners (Anderson 2003). The United States incarcerates more people for drug offenses than any other country (Justice Policy Institute 2008). The majority of men and women sentenced under these laws are nonviolent, low-level drug offenders—couriers, street dealers, bystanders, or drug addicts—convicted for possession or sales of small amounts of drugs (Human Rights Watch 1999, 2000).

Additionally, probation and parole revocations are a growing source of prison admissions. Among prisoners released in 2005 who returned to prison, 49.7% had a parole or probation violation or an arrest for a new offense within three years that led to imprisonment, and 55.1% had a parole or probation violation or an arrest that led to imprisonment within five years (Durose, Cooper, and Snyder 2014).

Along with the increase in the number of prisoners comes an increase in prison budgets. In 2010, the average state inmate cost about $31,286 per year (Henrichson and Delaney 2012). Average operating costs per inmate varied by state, indicating differences in costs of living, wage rates, and other related factors. The three states with the highest annual operating costs per inmate were New York ($60,076), New Jersey ($54,865), and Connecticut ($50,262).

Human Rights Watch (2012) documented the aging of the U.S. prison population, reporting that the number of prisoners age 65 or older increased by 63% between 2007 and 2010. For 2012, there were 26,200 prisoners in this age group. Providing medical care to older prison populations suffering from chronic, disabling, and terminal illnesses will be expensive, no different from the level of care and spending required for an older nonprison population. While no systematic data are available regarding the annual cost of care, Human Rights Watch (2012) reported a range of state expenses from $4,000 to $8,500 per elderly prisoner per year.

What is the purpose of the prison system? Some argue that the system is intended to rehabilitate offenders, to prevent them from committing crime again. However, beginning in the mid-1970s, U.S. rehabilitation programs and community-based programs began to lose funding. Probation and parole offices redefined their core missions from treatment to control and surveillance (Tonry 2004). Other Western governments, such as Germany, the Netherlands, and the Scandinavian countries, continue to make large investments in treatment and educational programs in comparison with the United States (Albrecht 2001), with evidence revealing that some programs are able to reduce future reoffending (Gaes et al. 1999). For example, Belgium, Denmark, England, France, the Netherlands, and Sweden have established crime prevention agencies that develop programs for developmental, community, and situational crime prevention (Tonry and Farrington 1995); there are no comparable agencies in the United States (Tonry 2004).

TAKING A WORLD VIEW

POLICING IN BRAZIL

Policing in Brazil has a dark and ugly history. The death squads of Brazil began in 1958, when Army General Amaury Kruel, chief of the police forces in Rio de Janeiro, handpicked a group of special policemen to combat rising theft and robberies in the city. These "bandit hunters" were given permission to hunt and kill these criminals. In other states and cities, teams of police hunters were formed to pursue *pistoleiros* (armed criminals), undesirables, and gangsters. Each new death squad, whether targeting economic or political criminals, became more distant from the formal criminal justice system (Huggins 1997). Through several political regimes, Brazilian police have never abandoned their practices of violent enforcement and vigilantism.

After 21 years of military dictatorship (1964–1985), the civilian government (inaugurated in 1985) set out to reform Brazil's authoritarian practices. In 1988, armed with a new constitution, the democratic leadership lifted the barriers to political participation and attempted to restore the legal premises of universal citizenship rights (Mitchell and Wood 1999). In 1996, President Fernando Henrique Cardoso released the National Human Rights Plan, a comprehensive set of measures to address human rights violations in Brazil, including cases of police abuses (Human Rights Watch 1997).

Yet, police violence and human rights violations all increased dramatically under democratic rule (Caldeira and Holston 1999). Police are some of the primary agents of violence in Brazil. According to organizations such as Amnesty International and Human Rights Watch, many citizens continue to suffer systematic abuse and violations at the hands of their own police force. Police in Rio de Janeiro and São Paulo have killed more than 11,000 people since 2003 (Human Rights Watch 2009). For 2012, 1,890 people died during police operations in Brazil, an average of five people per day (Human Rights Watch 2014).

Although Brazilian law endorses due process, criminal proceedings and police methods subvert this principle (Mitchell and Wood 1999), supporting extralegal conduct in the majority of cases (Huggins 1997; Mitchell and Wood 1999). Government leaders also offer their support of extralegal activities. Three days after state civil police officers killed 13 suspected drug traffickers, Marcello Alencar, governor of Rio de Janeiro, was quoted as saying, "These violent criminals have become animals. They are animals. They can't be understood any other way. These people don't have to be treated in a civilized way. They have to be treated like animals" (Human Rights Watch 1997).

According to Martha Huggins (1997), police violence in Brazil comes in two forms: on-duty police violence and death squads. Highly organized, elite police units carry out extralegal killings while on duty. The police violence is usually deliberately planned and conducted during routine street sweeps and dragnets, actions justified by the state's war on drugs and crime. There is also death squad violence conducted by a group of murderers, usually off-duty police, who are paid by local businesses or politicians for their services. Huggins calls them privatized security guards serving commercial or political interests.

In 1985, Brazil implemented women's police stations, *Delegacias de Policia dos Direitos da Mulher* (DPMs or *delegacias*). The DPMs were created in response to pressure from feminist groups demanding that violence against women be addressed. The first groups were formed in Rio de Janeiro and São Paulo, where the first DPM was established in 1985 (Hautzinger 1997). The female officers at each station are conventionally trained police, with no specialized training or qualifications for serving at the DPM except for the fact that they are women. There are more than 250 DPMs in Brazil today (Hautzinger 2002). Although domestic violence complaints were the original mission of the DPMs, these account for only 80% of the caseloads (Hautzinger 2002). Human Rights Watch (1995) reports that despite the presence of DPMs, "many rural and urban women have found police to be unresponsive to their claims and have encountered open hostility when they attempted to report domestic violence."

The U.S. record of recidivism (or repeat offenses) indicates how badly our prison system is working. Data analyzed by the Pew Center on the States (2011) found that the three-year return-to-prison rate for inmates released in 1999 was slightly higher than the recidivism rate for inmates released in 2004, 45.4% versus 43.3%. Released offenders returned to prison for committing a new crime or for a technical violation (not reporting to their parole officer or failing a drug test). Previous studies indicate that men, Blacks, non-Hispanics, and prisoners with longer prior records were more likely to be rearrested. Younger prisoners were also more likely to reoffend than were older prisoners (Langan and Levin 2002). The Bureau of Justice Statistics released data for 2007, noting that 15.5% of 1.2 million parolees returned to incarceration that year (Glaze and Bonczar 2009).

The Death Penalty

Seven states executed 35 inmates in 2014. For the year, there were 3,035 inmates serving death sentences. The majority of death row inmates were White (43%), followed by Blacks (42%) and Hispanics (13%). Since 1976, a total of 1,394 prisoners have been executed (Death Penalty Information Center 2014).

The death penalty was instituted as a deterrent to serious crime. The penalty applies only to capital murder cases, where aggravating circumstances are present. However, research indicates that capital punishment has no deterrent effect on committing murder. In fact, states with the death penalty have murder rates significantly higher than states without the death penalty. Kappeler and his colleagues (2000) explained that only a small proportion of people charged with murder can be sentenced to death. For example, between 1980 and 1989, 206,710 murders were reported to the police, but during the same period, only 117 executions were carried out. This is about 1 execution for every 1,767 murders committed during the same period (Kappeler et al. 2000).

Worldwide, 139 countries have abolished the use of the death penalty. In 2013, 778 were executed around the world in at least 22 countries. Eighty percent of these executions were in three countries: Iran, Iraq, and Saudi Arabia. The number of executions in China, believed to be in the thousands, cannot be confirmed (Amnesty International 2014).

Opponents of the death penalty point out the racial disparities in its application. The most significant studies of racial disparities point to the race of the victims as the critical factor in sentencing. Those convicted of committing a crime against a White person are more often sentenced to death. Data reported by the Death Penalty Information Center (2012) reveal that the majority of victims in death penalty cases were White (76%), followed by Blacks (15%). Nationally, only 50% of murder victims are White. In their analysis of 1990–1999 California death penalty cases, Michael Radelet and Glenn Pierce (2005) reported that those who killed a non-Hispanic African American were 56% less likely to be sentenced to death

Lessons From Death Row
Inmates

than were those who killed non-Hispanic Whites. The difference increases to 67% when comparing those sentenced to death for killing Whites versus those sentenced for killing Hispanics.

COMMUNITY, POLICY, AND SOCIAL ACTION

U.S. Department of Justice

We may perceive our criminal justice system as a single system when, actually, we have 51 different criminal justice systems: 1 federal and 50 state systems. The federal system is led by the U.S. Department of Justice. Headed by the Attorney General of the United States, the Department of Justice comprises many separate component organizations, including the FBI; the Drug Enforcement Administration (DEA); the Bureau of Alcohol, Tobacco, Firearms and Explosives; U.S. Citizenship and Immigration Services, which controls the border and provides services to lawful immigrants; the Antitrust Division, which promotes and protects the competitive process in business and industry; and the Bureau of Prisons, which oversees correctional operations and programs (U.S. Department of Justice 2002).

Funding for the U.S. Department of Justice and its organizations comes from federal legislation. The 1994 Violent Crime Control and Law Enforcement Act was the largest crime bill in history, providing funds for 100,000 new officers, $9.7 billion for prisons, and $6.1 billion for prevention programs. Under the Violence Against Women Act, the Office on Violence Against Women, administered by the Department of Justice, has awarded more than $6 billion in grant funds to U.S. states and territories. These grants have helped state, tribal, and local governments and community-based agencies to train personnel, establish domestic violence and sexual assault units, assist victims of violence, and hold perpetrators accountable (Office on Violence Against Women 2010).

Juvenile Justice and Delinquency Prevention Programs

The U.S. Department of Justice also supports the Office of Juvenile Justice and Delinquency Prevention. As its mission, the office attempts to provide national leadership, coordination, and resources to prevent and respond to juvenile delinquency and victimization. The office is guided by the Juvenile Justice and Delinquency Prevention Act of 1974 reauthorized by Congress in 2002 (U.S. Congress, 2002).

The office sponsors more than 15 programs targeting juveniles and their communities. The Tribal Youth Program is part of the Indian Country Law Enforcement Initiative to support tribal efforts to prevent and control juvenile delinquency. The Child Protection Division administers programs related to crimes against children, such as the National Center for Missing and Exploited Children and the Internet

Crimes Against Children Task Force. Recently the office has been promoting and studying the positive influence of mentoring on at-risk and delinquent youth. It sponsors a 32-site demonstration program to develop and test program models that incorporate advocacy and teaching roles for mentors.

Faith-based and community organizations have also been involved in delinquency prevention programs. One such program is the Blue Nile rites-of-passage program based in Harlem's Abyssinian Baptist Church (established before President George W. Bush's initiative). Since 1994, the program has relied on a community-based mentoring component to address the spiritual, cultural, and moral character development of African American youth (Harlem Live 1999). In general, the program was designed to have "a positive impact on the family relationships, self-esteem, sexual behaviors, drug use, peer and sibling relationships, and the religious and social values of the youth" (Irwin 2002:30). Darrell Irwin (2002) says that faith-based initiatives contain much of what has been found to be valuable in traditional mentoring programs, with the church as a backdrop. In the Harlem program, students are assigned to a mentor, either a church minister or a congregation member. During weekly meetings, mentors work with their partnered youth, emphasizing problem-solving and decision-making skills. In addition, the mentors introduce the youth to different educational and cultural activities as examples of potential community interactions. The program also includes a media literacy component where students learn how to film, edit, direct, and produce their own videos (Harlem Live 1999).

The New American Prison

In an effort to reduce the costs of incarceration to state and federal correctional agencies, the idea of private correctional institutions has gained momentum. The perception that public prisons were deteriorating and overcrowded helped to encourage the growth of private prisons in the 1980s (Pratt and Maahs 1999). Private prisons incarcerate about 7% of the sentenced adult population, usually housing low-risk offenders. Globally, Australia has the highest proportion (17%) of prisoners in private prisons, followed by the United Kingdom (10%) (L. Roth 2004).

It has been argued that private correctional institutions save taxpayers money, providing more services with fewer resources; studies reveal a slight advantage to private prisons and demonstrate a reduction in per-inmate cost over time (Larason Schneider 1999). State correction officials are also responding to the problem of chronic prison overcrowding. For example, one third of Hawaii's 6,000 state inmates are jailed in private prisons in Arizona, Kentucky, Mississippi, and Oklahoma because Hawaii does not have enough room in its own state facility (S. Moore 2007). Studies have indicated that the savings from private prisons are likely to come from lower wages and benefits, fewer staff, more efficient uses of staff, or a combination of these factors (Camp and Gaes 2002).

 Private Prisons

Scott Camp and Gerald Gaes (2002) found that private prisons did not perform better than public ones and in some cases did worse. According to the researchers, one of the most reliable indicators of prison operations is the rate at which inmates test positive for use of drugs or alcohol. If substance abuse is high, it indicates a pattern of poor security practices. For the private institutions, tests showed no drug use in 34% of the facilities and low to high drug use in 66% of the facilities. Nearly 62% of public prisons showed no evidence of drug use. In their analysis of another important performance measure, William Bales et al. (2005) found no significant difference in recidivism rates between public and private prisoner offenders. There were no significant differences among three groups in their study: adult males, adult females, and youth offender males.

Passed in 1996, the Prison Litigation Reform Act requires prisoners to exhaust all internal and administrative remedies before they can file federal lawsuits to challenge the conditions of their confinement or to report civil rights violations. The act was intended to prevent frivolous or unfounded lawsuits, but it has made it impossible for prisoners with valid complaints to be heard. Prisoners cannot file lawsuits for mental or emotional injury unless they can also show that physical injury occurred. Prisoners are required to pay for their own court filing fees; monthly installments can be taken out of their prison commissary account (American Civil Liberties Union [ACLU] 1999). The act also prohibits prison officials from settling lawsuits by agreeing to make changes in unconstitutional prison conditions. The ACLU and its National Prison Project have challenged the constitutionality of the Prison Litigation Reform Act, claiming that it "slams the courthouse door on society's most vulnerable members" (ACLU 1999). Despite its questionable constitutionality, many government leaders and courts have applauded the act.

Community Approaches to Law

Community Oriented Policing Services, or COPS, was created in response to the Violent Crime Control and Law Enforcement Act of 1994. The goal of the program is to shift from traditional law enforcement to community-oriented policing services, a change that includes putting law enforcement officers within a community and emphasizing crime prevention rather than law enforcement (COPS 2003). As stated on the COPS website, "Community policing is a law enforcement philosophy that focuses on community partnerships, problem-solving and organizational transformation" (COPS 2014). Researchers found that "police administrators have hailed community oriented policing as the preferred strategy for the delivery of services" (Novak, Alarid, and Lucas 2003:57).

One of the central premises of community policing is the relationships among the police, citizens, and other agencies. Since 1981, the National Night Out program has worked to strengthen police–community partnerships in anticrime efforts. Usually scheduled in August, National Night Out activities first involved just turning on the front porch lights of houses, but they now include block parties, cookouts,

IN FOCUS

A PUBLIC HEALTH APPROACH TO GUN CONTROL

The most deadly U.S. shooting occurred on April 16, 2007, when Virginia Polytechnic Institute and State University student Cho Seung-Hui shot and killed 32 people, including himself. In 2005, a Virginia court had declared Cho mentally ill and a danger to himself and sent him for psychiatric treatment. A month before the shooting, he purchased two semiautomatic pistols and 50 rounds of ammunition. Under federal law, Cho should have been prohibited from purchasing a gun after the Virginia court declaration. Federal law prohibits anyone who has been "adjudicated as a mental defective," as well as those who have been involuntarily committed to a mental health facility, from purchasing a gun.

Since the shooting at Virginia Tech, there have been several other deadly incidents. In July 2011, confessed killer Anders Behring Breivik killed 77 in Norway in two attacks, a bombing in downtown Oslo and a shooting massacre at a youth camp. A year later, James Holmes opened fire in a movie theater in Aurora, Colorado, during a premiere of *The Dark Knight Rises*. Holmes killed 12 and injured 56 others. Holmes amassed his weapons over several months, purchasing much of his ammunition via the Internet. In December 2012, gunman Adam Lanza killed 26 people, 20 of them children between the ages of 5 and 10 years, at Sandy Hook Elementary School in Newtown, Connecticut. The guns used by Lanza were legally registered to his mother Nancy, also one of his victims. Each tragedy reignited the debate over the regulated sale of firearms in the United States.

According to David Hemenway (2004),

Gordon M. Grant / Splash News/Newscom

The 2012 Sandy Hook Elementary school shooting reignited the debate over gun control. Many parents of the Sandy Hook victims lent their support to national and state campaigns to prohibit the sale and manufacturing of certain types of semi-automatic guns and magazines with more than 10 rounds of ammunition.

The United States has more firearms in civilian hands than any other high income nation. About 25 percent of adults in the United States personally own a firearm. Many gun owners have more than one firearm; some 10 percent of adults own over 75 percent of all firearms in the country. The percentage of households with a firearm has declined in the past two decades; about one in three households now contains a firearm. (p. 85)

He notes that public health approaches have reduced the burden of infectious disease, tobacco-related illness, and motor vehicle injuries, suggesting that a similar approach could be successfully applied to reducing gun violence, focusing on the impact of gun violence on one's community, and encouraging collaboration, research, and comprehensive policies. Hemenway (2004) explains what would be necessary for a public health approach to gun control:

Like the approach to reducing motor vehicle injuries, a public health approach to curtailing problems caused by firearms suggests pursuing a wide variety of policies while maintaining the ability of law-abiding Americans to use guns responsibly. This approach emphasizes the importance of obtaining accurate, detailed and comparable information each year on the extent and nature of the problem. For each motor vehicle death in the United States, the Fatality Analysis Reporting System collects data on more than one hundred variables. This information suggests interventions and permits evaluation of which policies are effective and which are not.

A major problem is that the detailed national information about firearm injuries does not exist. For example, whether most unintentional firearm injuries occur at home or away from home, or with long guns or handguns, is unknown. Many groups have backed the creation of a national violent death reporting system to provide detailed information on all homicides, suicides, and unintentional firearm deaths.

Although firearms are among the most lethal consumer products, killing tens of thousands of civilians each year, firearm manufacturing is one of the least-regulated industries in the United States. No federal regulatory body has specific authority over firearm manufacturing, which is exempt from regulation by the Consumer Product Safety Commission.

A public health approach would create incentives for firearm manufacturers to make products that reduce rather than increase the burden on law enforcement. Rather than producing and promoting firearms that appear primarily designed for criminal use, such as those who do not retain fingerprints, manufacturers could produce guns with unique, tamper resistant serial numbers. They could also make guns that "fingerprint" each bullet to permit authorities to match bullet and firearm with a high degree of accuracy.

Policies common in other developed countries— registration of handguns, licensing of owners, and background checks for all gun transfers—could reduce the U.S. homicide rate substantially by making it harder for adolescents and criminals to obtain handguns.

The public health approach to reducing gun violence emphasizes the need for prevention as well as punishment, recognizes that alternations in the product and the environment are more likely to be effective than attempts to change individual behavior, and urges the pursuit of multiple strategies to tackle the problem. The public health community understands the importance of involving the entire community and sees roles for many groups, including educational institutions, religious organizations, medical associations and the media.

SOURCE: Hemenway 2004.

VOICES IN THE COMMUNITY

MAX KENNER

The brainchild of Max Kenner, the Bard Prison Initiative (BPI) was created in 1999 to address the educational needs of prisoners and to provide them with the opportunity and the means to attain higher education while remaining within the correctional system.

To understand the logic behind such a program as BPI, one must revisit the 1970s, a time when the federal government looked favorably upon college in prison programs. Since then, numerous studies have shown that college in prison programs reduce the rate of recidivism, lower the number of violent incidents that occur within prisons, reestablish broken relationships between incarcerated parents and their children, and create a general sense of hope among inmates. Despite these beneficial consequences, in 1994, President Clinton signed the Violent Crime Control and Law Enforcement Act into law, essentially abrogating federal support and funding for existing programs. As a result, of the 350 programs that had arisen, only three remained.

"The prison system is so large," Kenner muses, "because it locks people up at a young age, and when they return home, they are less equipped to work, to attend school, and to function as social beings." These deficiencies result in an increased chance that released prisoners will commit another crime of a greater magnitude, thereby paving the road back to prison, but this time for a much longer sentence.

AP Photo/Rich Pedroncelli

Most state correctional systems offer some sort of educational programming. However, only a third offer college courses or degrees.

As an undergraduate of Bard College, Kenner immersed himself in the prevailing culture of social justice advocacy on campus. In 1999, he and a group of like-minded individuals made the unsettling discovery that of the 72,000 men and women in the New York State prison system, four out of every five inmates were from New York City. Armed with this finding, and an increasing frustration with governmental divestment from education in social services, the group set out to tackle the issue of educating prison inmates. "We felt that if we were really going to commit ourselves to some kind of effort to improve social justice it should be broad-based, and it should be based on public institutions," explains Kenner.

With that in mind, Kenner embarked on a mission to make Bard College an institutional home that would

---

parades, and neighborhood walks involving community members and police officers (National Night Out 2003). The community plays an important role in ensuring its own safety. In community policing, "problem solving requires that police and the community work together in identifying neighborhood problems, and that the community assumes greater 'guardianship' of the neighborhood" (Greene and Pelfrey 1997:395).

allow either faculty or students to gain access to prisons by lending its transcript services and by offering credit-bearing courses and degrees to prison inmates.

After the national collapse of the college in prison programs, however, there was an incredible distrust among people in corrections who wanted to see the colleges come back and people in higher education who wanted colleges in the prison. According to Kenner, colleges only wanted to offer courses if they could make a profit or if they could do so under ideal circumstances. Some colleges were simply not interested.

It took Kenner one and a half years to begin working with prisons. He was able to organize student volunteer programs that allowed students to conduct writing, GED, literacy, and theology workshops within the prison. "By the spring of my senior year, we had some 40 students volunteering at the prison on a weekly basis. Many of them said that it was the single most profound and influential thing that they had done at their time at Bard," says Kenner.

Upon graduation, Kenner made a proposal to Bard College President Leon Botstein, requesting that the college provide him with an office and grant him access to its transcripts so that they could begin offering college credit to prison inmates. The only stipulation was that Kenner would have to find a way to raise money to support the program.

Following graduation, Kenner was given a salaried position by Episcopal Social Services (EPS). "The Bard Prison Initiative officially started as a partnership between EPS and Bard College," says Kenner, "and five months later, in 2001, we began offering credit bearing courses to 17 students."

Currently, BPI offers two educational programs to inmates. Anyone with a GED can apply for the pre-college program and those with a higher level of education can apply for the associate's degree program. In the fall [of 2005], BPI will begin offering a bachelor's program that is consistent with the degree conferred to Bard College students. Those who have successfully completed the associate's degree program in two or three years can then reapply for admission into the bachelor's degree program.

Kenner hopes that the programs that have been implemented thus far will remain active and prove to be self-sustaining. He remains a passionate advocate for the return of college in prison programs and will continue to play an integral role in enhancing their opportunities.

BPI currently enrolls 300 incarcerated men and women in five prisons across New York state. The curriculum offerings include more than 60 courses each semester. By 2013, 300 degrees had been awarded to BPI graduates. Through the Consortium for the Liberal Arts in Prison, Bard College is providing support to college-in-prison programs in other states and schools (Bard Prison Initiative 2014).

SOURCE: Excerpt from Malik 2005. Reprinted with the permission of www.EducationUpdate.com

COPS sponsors grants and initiatives in selected communities, offering specialized training and programs to police professionals, such as technological innovations (mobile computing, computer-aided dispatch, automated fingerprint identification systems) or policing methods. In addition, the program supports innovative strategies linking police with their communities. COPS highlighted the Metropolitan Nashville Police Department's El Protector Program as one of the best strategies for working with communities whose members have limited English proficiencies. The program, established in 2004, includes two full-time officers who speak fluent Spanish. Assigned to precinct areas with the highest Latino populations, the officers work with community members and business leaders to reduce DUIs, traffic fatalities, and domestic violence.

It is difficult to assess the effectiveness of community policing methods because many of these community approaches have not been sufficiently implemented (MacDonald 2002). Jihong Zhao, Matthew Scheider, and Quint Thurman (2002) report that an additional problem is that much of the research designed to assess COPS programs is limited to the individual programs or cities. However, based on their analysis of COPS programs in 6,100 cities, the researchers discovered that COPS hiring and innovative programs resulted in significant reductions in local violent and nonviolent crime rates in cities with populations greater than 10,000. In addition, an increase of $1 in grant funding per resident for hiring contributed to a decline of 5.26 violent crimes and 21.63 property crimes per 100,000 residents. However, COPS grants had no significant impact on violent and property crime rates in cities with fewer than 10,000 residents. Data also indicate how the COPS program accelerated the establishment of new community policing programs and tactics, such as late-night recreation programs, victim assistance programs, and efficiencies in police work in funded cities (Roth and Ryan 2000).

Prison Advocacy and Death Penalty Reform

Several national, state, and local organizations are committed to reforming our prison system and advocating prisoners' rights. Most of their work comes in the form of advocacy, educational campaigns, and litigation.

JESSICA RINALDI/REUTERS/Newscom

Since it was established in 1992, the Innocence Project has rated more than 300 men and women through DNA testing. Larry Fuller was released in 2006 after spending 25 years in prison.

In the early 2000s, a network of student and community activists mobilized to end the use of prisons for profit. The group, Not With Our Money, successfully mobilized against Sodexho Marriott, a food service provider that owned more than 10% of Corrections Corporation of America (CCA), one of the largest owners and operators of U.S. private prisons. Efforts to pressure university administrators to end their food service contracts with Sodexho Marriott were successful at several colleges and universities. Since protests against Sodexho Marriott began, its parent company, Sodexho Alliance, divested all its interest in CCA (Bigda 2001).

State and local grassroots organizations, such as Coloradans Against the Death Penalty,

SOCIOLOGY AT WORK

PROBATION AND PAROLE OFFICERS

Timisha Gilbert–Class of 2006

Undergraduate Major: Sociology

Probation and parole officers work with and monitor offenders to reduce the risk of reoffending or committing another crime. Probation officers, also referred to as community supervision officers in some states, supervise individuals who have been placed on community probation instead of being sent to prison. On the other hand, parole officers monitor offenders who have been released from jail or prison. Both probation and parole officers supervise offenders through direct contact with the offenders and their families. They also oversee drug testing and electronic monitoring of offenders (U.S. Bureau of Labor Statistics 2014).

Timisha Gilbert works as a community corrections officer, a combined probation and parole officer in the Pacific Northwest. During her senior undergraduate year, she completed an internship with the organization and was hired into an entry-level community corrections officer position upon graduation. She describes her current job as "managing a caseload of high-risk offenders released from jails and prisons to complete a term of community supervision. I am required to hold offenders accountable while on supervision to ensure they abide by sentences imposed by the Court, while also promoting change through programming and other interventions."

Probation and parole work requires a bachelor's degree. Candidates should be at least 21 years of age, have no felony convictions, and submit to drug testing. Most employers require applicants to pass a series of oral, written, and psychological exams. Timisha says that she uses her sociological imagination regularly. "Using different ideas and theoretical conclusions to develop case plans has been helpful. Every offender has chosen to engage in criminal behavior for various reasons, and by reflecting on different theoretical perspectives, I am able to develop case plans for effective case supervision."

She offers the following advice to undergraduate Sociology majors:

Think outside the box. A degree in Sociology can be used in many different ways and for various organizations. Each career field has many different aspects and levels where your degree will be useful. Finally, do what you enjoy and continue to seek out opportunities for continued learning and advancement.

Timisha is currently enrolled in a master of science program in Criminal Justice.

Mississippians for Alternatives to the Death Penalty, and the Texas Coalition to Abolish the Death Penalty, support prisoners' rights and legislation to abolish the death penalty in their states.

One organization that has accepted the mission of correcting wrongful convictions is the Innocence Project. Established in 1992 by attorneys Barry Scheck and Peter Neufeld, the Innocence Project is a nonprofit legal clinic at the Benjamin N. Cardozo School of Law at Yeshiva University in New York. The clinic is dedicated to "exonerating the innocent through postconviction DNA testing" (Innocence Project 2007). As of December 2014, the project had exonerated 325 individuals. These cases highlight the problems of misidentification, corrupt scientists and police, overzealous prosecutors, inept defense attorneys, and the influence of poverty and race in the criminal justice system. The Innocence Project is currently working to establish the Innocence Network, a group of law and journalism schools and public defender offices that assist inmates trying to prove their innocence, even if their cases do not involve biological or DNA evidence. Several states have established their own innocence or justice projects.

The Innocence Project and similar organizations consistently draw the public's attention when an innocent inmate is released. In 1993, Darryl Howard was convicted of the 1991 murder of a mother and her daughter in North Carolina. He was released in 2014 based on new DNA evidence and charges of prosecutorial misconduct uncovered by the Innocence Project. DNA evidence excluded Howard, but identified another suspect. Howard was released after serving nearly 20 years of his sentence.

CHAPTER REVIEW

13.1 Explain the difference between biological, psychological, and sociological theories of crime

Biological and psychological theories of crime address how crime is determined by individual characteristics or predispositions but do not explain why crime rates vary in certain areas. Sociological theories attempt to address these reasons.

13.2 Identify how the different sociological perspectives examine crime

Functionalists argue that society sets goals and expectations, but people feel strain when they do not have the access or resources to achieve these goals. Under this strain, individuals are more likely to commit crime. Social control theorists ask why someone *doesn't* commit crime. Conflict theorists believe an act is not inherently criminal; society defines it that way. Theorists argue that criminal laws exist to preserve the interests and power of specific groups. In feminist scholarship, patriarchal power relations shape gender differences in crime, pushing women into criminal behavior through role entrapment, economic marginalization, and victimization or as a survival response. Interactionists examine the process that defines certain individuals and acts as criminal.

13.3 Summarize the different types of crime

Violent crimes are acts that involve force or threat of force against others. Property crime (three fourths of all crime in the United States) consists of taking money or property without force or threat of force. Juvenile crime refers to youth in trouble with the law. White-collar crime includes crimes committed by someone of high social status, for financial gain, or in a particular organization.

13.4 Explain how race/ethnicity is an important predictor of offender or victim status

A number of studies confirm that regardless of the seriousness of the crime, racial and ethnic minorities are more likely to be arrested or incarcerated than their White counterparts. Research indicates that some individuals are more prone than others to become victims. Victimization rates are substantially higher for the poor, the young, males, Blacks, single people, renters, and central city residents.

13.5 Describe the transformation of American policing

American policing has gone through substantial changes during the past several decades. Traditional models emphasized high visibility and the use of force and arrests as deterrents. These models reinforce an "us" versus "them" division. Police departments are now incorporating new methods based on the community and problem-solving approaches.

13.6 Explain whether private prisons are more effective than public prisons

Research indicates that private prisons do not perform better than public prisons. There is no significant difference in recidivism rates. In one study, drug use among prisoners was higher in private prisons than public ones.

KEY TERMS

cybercrime, 370

felonies, 356

index crimes, 365

juvenile crime, 369

juvenile delinquent, 369

juvenile status offender, 369

labeling theory, 363

misdemeanors, 356

property crime, 369

racial profiling, 372

strain theory, 358

violent crime, 367

white-collar crime, 370

STUDY QUESTIONS

1. Define the different types of crime considered by criminologists and sociologists.

2. Compare and contrast the explanations of crime offered by strain and social control theorists. According to these theories, is crime motivated by money or greed?

3. Examine how crime exists to preserve the interests and power of specific groups.

4. What is unique about the experiences of female offenders and prisoners? How has our criminal justice system responded? What else needs to be done?

5. Explain how crime is a learned behavior. Are there any crimes that do not fit this perspective?

6. Identify the three sources of crime data in the United States. How would you assess the reliability of these sources?

7. Is the function of our prisons to punish or rehabilitate? Review the evidence for each.

$SAGE edge™

Sharpen your skills with SAGE edge at **edge.sagepub.com/leonguerrero5e**

SAGE edge provides a personalized approach to help you accomplish your coursework goals in an easy-to-use learning environment.

Urbanization

Cities have always maintained an allure of better living and opportunities. But an examination of our cities and their surrounding areas reveals a "profound duality" (Stanback 1991). Although our urban areas are shining examples of economic and social progress, they also harbor significant social problems such as poverty, crime, crowding, pollution, and collapsing infrastructures. Moreover, opportunities and resources are unevenly distributed in cities: Some neighborhoods have safer streets and better services and may offer a better quality of life than others do (Massey 2001). "Cities in different countries with different socioeconomic and political systems often face quite similar problems, although their scales, trends, or causes differ from place to place" (Kim and Gottdiener 2004:172).

Though it is still referred to as America's Motor City, Detroit has a new nickname, "most miserable city" (Badenhausen 2013). The colossal economic failure of Detroit has brought renewed attention to the relationship between economic, social, and political forces and the health and structure of urban spaces. Detroit was an industrial giant in the beginning of the 20th century, headquarters for automobile giants General Motors, Ford, and Chrysler. The city's population peaked in the 1950s at 1.8 million. But as housing developments were established in Detroit's suburban areas, residents began to flee. Automobile manufacturing expanded into different states, and as competition grew with Japanese automakers, the three automakers collectively lost 40% of the U.S. automobile market share. Rising and persistent unemployment was followed

by declining tax revenues, declining property values, and urban blight. The Great Recession of 2007–2009 crushed the city's hope for an economic recovery. In 2014, Detroit's population was estimated at 700,000. In 2013, the city filed for bankruptcy, seeking protection from an $18 billion debt, the largest filing in U.S. history (Davey and Williams Walsh 2013).

Before we begin our study of urbanization and its related social problems, we will first review two sociological fields of study. Both remind us that cities don't just happen overnight; rather, social and demographic factors help shape our urban areas and their problems. Our urban areas are produced by economic, political, and cultural forces operating at international, national, and local levels (Kim and Gottdiener 2004).

URBAN SOCIOLOGY AND DEMOGRAPHY

In the 1920s, sociologists from the University of Chicago examined their city and the impact of city life and its problems on its residents. Their research provided the basis for urban study and for understanding the determinants of urbanization. **Urban sociology** examines the social, political, and economic structures and their impact within an urban setting. Rural sociology is the study of the same structures within a rural setting.

The first studies on urbanization or urban sociology adopted a functionalist approach, comparing a city to a biological organism. The growth of a city was likened to the development of a social organism, with each part of the city serving a specific and necessary function. A city's core, for example, served as its business or industrial center; and areas outside a city were reserved for residential or commuting activity. Out of the Chicago School of Sociology came two dominant traditions in urban studies, one focusing on **human ecology** (the study of the relationship between individuals and their physical environment) and population dynamics and the second focusing on community studies and ethnographies (Feagin 1998a).

Although this chapter's primary focus is on urban problems, an essential part of urbanization is the number of residents in an area, its population. The second sociological field we will rely on is demography: the study of the size, composition, and distribution of human populations (see also Chapter 6). Demography isn't just about counting people. Demographers analyze the changes and trends in the population. Their work begins with two fundamental facts: We are born, and then we die. Recall how in Chapter 10, "Health and Medicine," we reviewed how two demographic elements, fertility and mortality, are determined by biological and social factors.

An additional demographic element is **migration**, the movement of individuals from one area to another. Migration is distinguished by the type of movement: **immigration** is the movement of people into a geographic area; **emigration** is the movement of people out of a geographic area. **Domestic migration** (the movement of people within a country) plays a large role in the population redistribution in the United

Urban sociology: Examination of social, political, and economic structures and their impact within an urban setting

Human ecology: The study of the relationship between individuals and their physical environment

Migration: The movement of individuals from one area to another

Immigration: The movement of people leaving their country of origin to move to another

Emigration: Movement of people out of a geographic area

Domestic migration: The movement of people within a country

States (Perry 2006). In the United States, about 35.9 million people moved between 2012 and 2013 to a different residence, the majority to the same county in their state (Ihrke 2014). People migrate to pursue employment opportunities, to be closer to family, to find a more temperate climate, and to seek the opportunity of a better life. Most movers have housing-related reasons: They move to a new, better, or more affordable home or apartment (Schachter 2004).

THE PROCESSES OF URBANIZATION AND SUBURBANIZATION

Urbanization, the process by which a population shifts from rural to urban, took off in the latter half of the nineteenth century (Williams 2000). Urbanization in the United States, as in other developed countries, was closely linked with economic development and industrialization. The U.S. economy in the middle of the 19th century was divided: the northern economy was characterized by a mixture of family-based agriculture, commerce, finance, and an increasing industrial base, whereas the southern economy remained dependent on agriculture (Gordon 2001). But as the industrial economy began to grow in the North and extended into the Midwest, thousands of people were attracted to these emerging urban centers, drawn by the promise of work in factories and mills (Williams 2000). Also contributing to early urban growth was the immigration of Europeans and the migration of rural Blacks and Whites from the South to northern and midwestern urban areas (Dreier 1996).

The process of global urbanization is described in waves. The first wave occurred in North America and Europe from 1750 to 1950 (United Nations Population Fund 2007), closely linked with industrialization and economic development (Kim and Gottdiener 2004). This wave involved a few hundred million people and produced urban industrial societies that now dominate the world (United Nations Population Fund 2007).

The second wave of urbanization took place during the past half-century in developing countries. Some have referred to the shift as **overurbanization**, the process where an excess population is concentrated in an urban area that lacks the capacity to provide basic services and shelter. Overurbanization is characterized by a lack of employment, housing, and education or health infrastructures for an area's residents (Kim and Gottdiener 2004). This second urbanization wave is problematic because it involves large populations of poor people—instead of hundreds of millions as in the first wave, the second wave involves billions residing mostly in Africa and Asia (United Nations Population Fund 2007). Refer to Table 14.1 for a comparison of urban populations between developed and less developed regions.

After World War II, the United States experienced another significant population shift: suburbanization. Although **suburbanization** has come to represent the outward expansion of central cities into suburban areas (N. Smith 1986), increasing population growth rates away from city centers, it has also been linked with two

Urbanization: The process by which a population shifts from rural to urban

Overurbanization: The process in which an excess population is concentrated in an urban area that lacks the capacity to provide basic services and shelter

Suburbanization: The process by which a population shifts to suburban areas

Table 14.1 Urban population distribution of the world by development groups, 1975, 2000, 2010, and 2020 (population in millions)

	1975	**2000**	**2010**	**2020**
World (total)	1,538	2,859	3,559	4,290
More developed regions	718	881	957	1,018
Less developed regions	819	1,977	2,601	3,271

SOURCE: United Nations, Department of Economic and Social Affairs 2011.

Table 14.2 U.S. population, percentage of urban residents, selected years

Year	Percentage Urban
1900	40.0
1910	45.8
1920	51.4
1930	56.2
1940	56.5
1950	64.0
1960	69.9
1970	73.5
1980	73.7
1990	75.2
2000	79.0
2010	80.7

SOURCE: U.S. Census Bureau 1995, 2012a.

Urban population: An area with 2,500 or more individuals

Urbanized area: A densely populated area with 50,000 or more residents

additional population shifts: from the Snow Belt (industrial regions of the North and Midwest) to the Sun Belt (South and Southwest) and from rural to metropolitan areas (Dreier 1996). Though many factors contributed to suburbanization, the key players were government leaders and their policies. The U.S. Congress passed the Housing Act of 1949, which encouraged construction outside city boundaries and made home purchasing easier through the Federal Housing Administration (FHA) and Veterans Affairs home mortgage loan programs. The 1956 Federal Aid Highway Act, which established the modern interstate highway system, made rural areas more accessible. President Dwight Eisenhower, a chief proponent of the act, believed in the importance of the interstate highway system. Eisenhower (1963) declared,

> More than any single action by the government since the end of the war, this one would change the face of America. . . . Its impact on the American economy— the jobs it would produce in manufacturing and construction, the rural areas it would open up—was beyond calculation. (pp. 548–49)

The U.S. Census Bureau defines an **urban population** as an area with 2,500 or more individuals. An **urbanized area** is a densely populated area with 50,000 or more residents, and a metropolitan statistical area is a densely populated area with 100,000 or more people. U.S. Census data indicate a rapid increase in the urban population, especially after World War II (Table 14.2). For 2010, the three largest metropolitan statistical areas were New York City, Los Angeles, and Chicago

Table 14.3   Ten largest U.S. metropolitan statistical areas, 2010

Metropolitan Area	Population in Millions
New York City–northern New Jersey–Long Island [NY-NJ]	18,897
Los Angeles–Long Beach–Santa Ana [CA]	12,829
Chicago–Naperville–Joliet [IL-IN-WI]	9,461
Dallas–Ft. Worth–Arlington [TX]	6,372
Philadelphia–Camden–Wilmington [PA-NJ-DE-MD]	5,965
Houston–Sugar Land–Baytown [TX]	5,947
Washington–Arlington–Alexandria [DC-VA-MD-WV]	5,582
Miami–Ft. Lauderdale–Pompano Beach [FL]	5,565
Atlanta–Sandy Springs–Marietta [GA]	5,269
Boston–Cambridge–Quincy [MA-NH]	4,552

SOURCE: U.S. Census Bureau 2012c.

(U.S. Census Bureau 2012a). The largest area was New York City–northern New Jersey–Long Island, with 1,889,700 people. A complete list of the 10 largest metropolitan statistical areas is presented in Table 14.3. The New York–Newark area remains one of the world's largest megacities (10 million residents or more). Refer to Table 14.4 for the complete list of megacities.

POPULATION GROWTH AND COMPOSITION

Changes in the fertility, mortality, and migration rates of a population affect its composition and its biological and social characteristics. For example, **age distribution**, the distribution of individuals by age, is particularly important because it provides a community with some direction in its social and economic planning, assessing its education, health, housing, and employment needs. For example, the driving behavior of the members of the Millennial generation (those born between 1983 and 2000) may change the future of transportation (U.S. PIRG Education Fund 2013). Millennials are the first generation to embrace mobile Internet technologies, which is changing the way young Americans relate to each other, but also changing the way they choose to live. They drive less than older generations and are more likely to adopt non-driving forms of transportation. In comparison with Baby Boomers and Generation X'ers, Millennials are twice as likely to express a desire to live in a walkable urban area (U.S. PIRG Education Fund 2013).

Age distribution: The distribution of individuals by age

Table 14.4   Largest megacities in the world—1950, 2000, 2014, and 2030 (population in millions)

1950	Pop.	2000	Pop.	2014	Pop.	2030 Predicted	Pop.
New York–Newark, USA	12.3	Tokyo, Japan	34.4	Tokyo, Japan	37.8	Tokyo, Japan	37.1
Tokyo, Japan	11.3	Ciudad de Mexico (Mexico City), Mexico	18.1	Delhi, India	24.9	Delhi, India	36.1
		New York–Newark, USA	17.8	Shanghai, China	23.0	Shanghai, China	30.7
		São Paulo, Brazil	17.1	Ciudad de Mexico (Mexico City), Mexico	20.8	Mumbai, India	27.8
		Mumbai, India	16.1	São Paulo, Brazil	20.8	Beijing, China	27.7
		Shanghai, China	13.2	Mumbai, India	20.7	Dhaka, Bangladesh	27.3
		Calcutta, India	13.1	Osaka, Japan	20.1	Karachi, Pakistan	24.8
		Delhi, India	12.4	Beijing, China	19.5	Cairo, Egypt	24.5
		Buenos Aires, Argentina	11.8	New York–Newark, USA	18.5	Ciudad de Mexico (Mexico City), Mexico	23.8
		Los Angeles–Long Beach–Santa Ana, USA	11.8	Cairo, Egypt	18.4	São Paulo, Brazil	23.4

SOURCE: United Nations Population Division, Department of Economic and Social Affairs, 2014.

NOTE: In 1950, there were only two megacities in the world. By 2014, their number had increased to 28 (though only the top 10 are listed here). By 2030, 39 mega cities are predicted to exist.

Demographers have noted how the **ethnic composition** (the composition of ethnic groups within a population) affects social and human services. In 2007, the U.S. Census Bureau announced that one in three Americans were ethnic minorities, about 101 million. Roberto Suro and Audrey Singer (2002) explain how the Latino population has spread out further and faster across the nation than any previous wave of immigrants. In 2012(b), the U.S. Census Bureau announced that Hispanics were the largest and fastest-growing minority group in the United States, numbering 52 million in 2011.

Housing, education, health, and public transportation demands are affected by the rate of Latino population growth. For example, cities and areas with

Ethnic composition:
The composition of groups within a population

large established Latino communities (e.g., New York, Chicago, Miami, Southern California) should prepare for a growing Latino population characterized by low-wage workers, large families, and significant numbers of adults with little English proficiency (Suro and Singer 2002). In California, researchers from the University of California–Los Angeles Medical School recommended shifting health care services because Hispanic Californians tend to live longer than non-Hispanics and are less likely to die from heart disease or cancer (Murphy 2003).

The increasing number of ethnic Americans and their age distribution has caught demographers' attention. When data for the 2007 U.S. Census were announced, researchers noted that younger Americans were more ethnically diverse than were older generations—the average age of non-Hispanic Whites was 40.5 years, whereas among Hispanics, the average age was 27.4 years. This age gap may lead to competing political and social agendas. Communities may be divided between older Americans advocating social security, lower taxes, and better health care and younger ethnically diverse Americans demanding better education, jobs, and social services (Roberts 2007).

SOCIOLOGICAL PERSPECTIVES ON POPULATION AND URBANIZATION

Functionalist Perspective

Early functionalists were critical about the transition from simple to complex social communities. Émile Durkheim described this transition as a movement from mechanical solidarity to organic solidarity. Under **mechanical solidarity**, individuals in small simple societies are united through a set of common values, beliefs, and customs and a simple division of labor. Most individuals are engaged in the same type of economic activity or labor. In contrast, Durkheim argued, **organic solidarity** is the result of increasing industrialization and the growth of large complex societies, where individuals are linked through a complex division of labor. Under organic solidarity, individuals begin to share the responsibility for the production of goods and services, each with a specific role in production. New relationships are created according to what people can do or provide for each other. For example, most of us do not raise the food for our meals. We depend on others to grow, harvest, deliver, and sell our food and groceries, and others depend on us for our specific labor activity. Durkheim believed that as a result of industrialization, the social bonds that unite us will eventually weaken, leading to social problems.

Although industrialization and urbanization have been functional, creating a more efficient, interdependent, and productive society, they have also been problematic. Because of the weakening of social bonds and an absence of norms, society begins to lose its ability to function effectively. As our social bonds with each other have loosened, our sense of obligation or duty to one another has declined.

Mechanical solidarity: Union of individuals through a set of common values, beliefs, and customs and a simple division of labor

Organic solidarity: Union of individuals through a complex division of labor

TAKING A WORLD VIEW

GLOBAL URBANIZATION AND POPULATION GROWTH

In its 2007 report, the United Nations Population Fund predicted that "at the global level, all future population growth will [thus] be in towns and cities" (p. 6). More than half the world's population was living in urban areas by 2008, approximately 3.3 billion individuals. In contrast, the world's rural population will decline by about 28 million between 2005 and 2030. Urban population growth is expected to occur in developing nations such as Africa and Asia, with slower expansion expected in Latin America and in the Caribbean. Most of the growth is attributed to natural increases (more births than deaths) rather than migration. In the developed world, the urban population is expected to grow very little, from 870 million to 1 billion.

There are many negative consequences of urban population growth for individuals, nations, and the world: increased demand for social and human services; increased economic and political burdens, particularly for poorer developing countries; and global environmental degradation (Desai 2004). Some segments of the population are more vulnerable than others are. By 2030, 60% of all urban dwellers will be younger than age 18. Cities need to ensure that appropriate levels of basic services, education, housing, and medical care are available for these youth; if not, life on these urban streets will threaten the quality of youths' health, education, safety, and future (United Nations Population Fund 2007).

Despite its dire message, the United Nations Population Fund (2007) concludes, "Urban and national governments, together with civil society, and supported by international organizations, can take steps now that will make a huge difference for the social, economic and environmental living conditions of a majority of the world's population" (p. 3). Suggesting the need for more proactive and creative approaches, the organization recommends strategies to improve the social conditions of the poor, promote gender equality, and ensure

B MATHUR/REUTERS

In its 2007 report, the United Nations Population Fund predicted that "at the global level, all future population growth will [thus] be in towns and cities" (p. 6). Urban population growth is expected to occur in developing nations such as Africa and Asia, with slower expansion expected in Latin America and in the Caribbean.

environmental sustainability. A major component of the recommendations is to empower women and increase the level of reproductive health services available to families, believing that these interventions will influence individuals' fertility preferences (the number of children and the timing of births) and their ability to meet them. Such a strategy "empowers the exercise of human rights and gives people greater control over their lives" (United Nations Population Fund 2007:70).

  Chinese Urbanization

Urbanization can lead to social problems such as crime, poverty, violence, and deviant behavior. Functional solutions to these problems may encourage reinforcing or re-creating social bonds through such existing institutions as churches, families, and schools or instituting societal changes through political or economic initiatives. For example, under mechanical solidarity, the strong social bonds linking an individual to society (through one's family and friends) deter criminal behavior. A person would not think of committing a criminal act because it would be inherently wrong or would harm the individual's relationship with other members of society. Under organic solidarity, criminal laws, police, and prison systems serve as formal structures to deter criminal activity.

Conflict and Feminist Perspectives

Since the late 1960s, a new perspective on urban study has emerged. Referred to as the **critical political-economy perspective** or **socio-spatial perspective**, this approach uses a conflict perspective to focus on how cities are formed on the basis of racial, gender, or class inequalities. From this perspective, cities are shaped by powerful social and political actors from the private and public sectors, working within the modern capitalistic structure (Feagin 1998b). Social problems are natural to the system, rising from the unequal distribution of power between politicians and taxpayers, the rich and the poor, the homeowner and the renter, or Whites and Blacks.

Residential segregation is defined as the neighborhood clustering or separation of groups by racial, ethnic, or economic characteristics within a geographic area. Residential segregation is a form of social organization that enables differential access to resources and opportunities, such as public services, schools, and employment opportunities (Dickerson 2008), advantaging one group over another. From this perspective, residential segregation is not accidental, but is the product of institutional discrimination, city governments, zoning laws, mortgage redlining policies, tax bases, and school systems that perpetuate racialized socioeconomic inequalities (Hanlon 2011; Judd and Swanstrom 2004).

Sociologists offer three primary explanations for the persistence of Black–White segregation: housing market discrimination, differences in socioeconomic status, and preferences for specific neighborhood racial composition (Massey and Denton 1993; Charles 2003). Martha Mahoney (1997) explains:

> For whites, residential segregation is one of the forces giving race a "natural" appearance: "good" neighborhoods are equated with whiteness, and "black" neighborhoods are equated with joblessness. This equation allows whiteness to remain a dominant background norm, associated with positive qualities for white people, at the same time that it allows unemployment and underemployment to seem like natural features of black communities. (p. 330)

Critical political-economy perspective: An approach using a conflict perspective to focus on city formation based on racial, gender, or class inequalities (also referred to as socio-spatial perspective)

Socio-spatial perspective: An approach using a conflict perspective to focus on city formation based on race, gender, or class inequalities (also referred to as the critical political-economy perspective)

Residential segregation: The neighborhood clustering or separation of groups by racial, ethnic, or economic characteristics within a geographic area

 Suburban Discrimination

Within this tradition, scholars also examine the role of capitalism and capitalists in shaping cities (Feagin 1998b). Land-use decisions are made by politicians and businesspeople (Gottdiener 1977), real estate developers and financiers (Molotch 1976), or coalitions between public officials and private citizens (Rast 2001). Joe Feagin (1998b) presented a theory of urban ecology that accented the role of class structure and powerful land-oriented capitalist actors in shaping the location, development, and decline of U.S. cities. Land speculators shape the internal structure of cities by identifying and packaging particular parcels of land for business or residential use. As Feagin (1998b) describes it,

> powerful land-interested capitalists have contributed substantially to the internal physical structure and patterning of cities themselves. The central areas of cities such as San Francisco have been intentionally remade, in the name of private profit, by combinations of speculators and other capitalists, such as developers. (p. 154)

Although women play a pivotal role in urban life, theories about urbanization have taken a gender-blind approach (Women's International Network News 1999). Urban studies have not systematically considered cities as sites of institutionalized patriarchy (Garber and Turner 1995) and have not legitimately considered the role of women in urban development. In the 1880s, women activists advocated quality housing, public health and sanitation services, food safety, and health and social services in emerging cities (Parker 2011). Feminist urbanists have argued for the development of a comprehensive field of theory and research that acknowledges the role of women in urban structures (Masson 1984).

By incorporating feminist theory in patriarchy and urban studies, we can understand an additional dimension of urban life, namely the complex ways in which cities reproduce and challenge patriarchy (Appleton 1995) and the problems this creates. Cities are places where gender is experienced and constituted. As Judith Garber and Robyne Turner (1995) explain,

> urban environments are constructed around the delivery of public services and the development of policies. These shape women's ability to cope with complex urban locations, largely through the responsiveness of public and private organizations to the needs of diverse groups of women and children. (p. xxiii)

Turner (1995) argues that the living conditions of lower-income, inner-city women have been affected by the economic restructuring of cities and the patterns of downtown development. Woman-headed households increasingly make up the majority of inner-city households. Turner explains that although low-income women may find inner-city housing less costly and more accessible than housing in the suburbs is, urban living also presents a unique set of challenges in transportation, housing, employment, services, and safety. Inner-city women have less control over their living situations than suburban women do. City development decisions are made by those in power, often men, whereas the decisions affect women, the young, and the elderly. Turner (1995) concludes, "It is important to recognize the implications for women, as the heads of households, in the debate on economic restructuring, land based economies, and the portrayal of political power" (pp. 287–88).

Interactionist Perspective

Georg Simmel ([1903] 1997) was the first sociologist to explain how city life is also a state of mind. In his 1903 essay, "The Metropolis and Mental Life," Simmel described how life in a small town is self-contained; interactions with others are routine and rather ordinary. But a city's economic, personal, and intellectual relationships cannot be defined or confined by its physical space; rather, they are as extensive as the number of interactions between its residents. City dwellers must interact with a variety of people for goods and services and for personal and professional relationships. City living stimulates the intellect and individuality of its residents (Karp, Stone, and Yoels 1991). Elijah Anderson (2004) described how urban public settings (like markets, restaurants, parks), which he referred to as cosmopolitan canopies, encourage people to treat others with a certain level of civility or at least simply to behave themselves. These canopies "allow people of different backgrounds the chance to slow down and indulge themselves, observing, pondering . . . testing or substantiating stereotypes and prejudices" (p. 21).

But how well are city dwellers connected with their neighbors? The answer is that they may not be as connected as Simmel or Anderson predicted. The way a city is constructed might actually interfere with social interaction. Our dependency on automobiles compartmentalizes neighborhood relations (we only know neighbors on our block or street) and interferes with street life (no space for ball games, block parties, bike riding, and joggers) (Gottdiener 1977). Home and residential designs limit our face-to-face contact with our neighbors. Without porches, there is no place to sit out front and visit with one's neighbors; without sidewalks or local parks, families find it less appealing to take walks around their neighborhood and less easy to meet with neighbors.

Tridib Banerjee and William Baer (1984) discovered that how we define our cities is linked to

© Shaun Lombard/iStock

Does urban living (and the preoccupation with personal technology) unite or divide residents?

 Social Capital

what we value or use within them. What goods and services do people use in their community? Is it the coffee shop, the local dry cleaner, or the neighborhood grocery store? Or is it the local park, the bicycle lanes, or the athletic center down the street? The researchers asked residents of several Southern California cities to draw maps of their residential areas and discovered that illustrations by middle- and upper-income individuals contained more details and area than illustrations by lower-income people did. Upper-income groups included amenities such as tree-lined streets, wooded areas, and golf courses, whereas middle- and low-income groups included commercial and retail locations, such as gas stations, discount stores, or drug stores. Corporate symbols were commonly used to define landmarks in middle- and low-income illustrations. Banerjee and Baer concluded that income was the single most important variable in explaining the quality of residential experiences and residents' judgments about what constitutes a "good place" to live.

Based on his examination of the transformation of European cities from industrial centers to recreational destinations, Mathis Stock (2006) concluded that a city may be defined by conflicting constituent groups (residents vs. tourists) and the vastly different experiences of the city they cohabit. The transformation of cities such as Paris, Venice, and Florence into tourist destinations is often intentional, with city leaders and businesses embracing the symbols of tourism—the language, images, practices, and customs—in their cities. To entice visitors to their city, they promote their city's annual festivals and package them along with well-known cultural and historical sites as part of a cultural heritage experience. This transformation has its detractors, who, though acknowledging the revenue benefit of tourism, question whether this process has stripped these historical European cities of their authentic identities and subordinated native residents as a result. In 2009, Venetians held a mock funeral as a sign of protest for their city, complete with a fake coffin floating down the Grand Canal. The number of historic center residents dropped from 74,000 in 1993 to 60,000 in 2009; the decline is blamed on rising rents and increasing numbers of tourists that pushed locals onto the mainland (Donadio 2009).

For a summary of the different sociological perspectives, see Table 14.5.

What Does It Mean to Me?

Can't a person find some personal space? Symbolic interactionists have noted that urban dwellers are able to create a "public privacy" while living in a demanding urban world (Karp et al. 1991). Using props such as a newspaper or a smart phone, individuals send messages that they aren't interested in talking with others. You may bump into people while walking on a busy street but never stop to say, "Excuse me." The proportion of unlisted phone numbers is greater in the city than in small towns or suburban areas (Karp et al. 1991). Your coffee barista may have memorized your morning coffee order, but does your barista know your name or any other personal information? How do you create and maintain your public privacy?

Table 14.5   Summary of sociological perspectives: Cities and Suburbs

	Functional	Conflict/Feminist	Interactionist
Explanation of urbanization and its social problems	This perspective focuses on the weakening of social bonds and the functions and dysfunctions of urbanization.	Both perspectives focus on how cities are formed on the basis of racial, gender, or class inequalities.	City living is a state of mind. Urban living and its related social problems are socially defined.
Questions asked about urbanization and its social problems	How does urbanization enhance or destroy our social bonds? In what ways does urbanization affect existing institutions such as churches, families, and schools? How can we strengthen our social bonds?	Do one's race, gender, and social class determine the quality of urban living? How can we address the needs of all urban dwellers? How does one urban group gain power over the others?	How is urban living defined? How can we establish common ideas on urban life and its social problems?

THE CONSEQUENCES OF URBANIZATION

Along with suburbanization came the decentralization, some may even say the demise, of U.S. cities. Inner cities became repositories for low-income individuals and families, as the suburbs enjoyed higher tax bases and fewer social programs (Massey and Eggers 1993). Researchers have suggested that the poor economic outcomes of racial minorities, particularly African Americans, are partly the result of patterns of housing prejudice and discrimination that have prevented minority groups from moving at the same pace as the suburbanization of employment (Massey 2001; Pastor 2001). According to Douglas Massey and Mitchell Eggers (1993),

> the simultaneous proliferation of poverty and affluence created a situation in which social problems among those at the bottom of the income hierarchy multiplied rapidly at a time when more and more people had the means to escape these maladies. (p. 313)

Many of the social problems we discuss in this text seem to be magnified in urban areas. In this next section, we will review specific social problems plaguing urban areas: quality housing, crowding, homelessness, gentrification, and urban sprawl and transportation.

Urban Living Environment

Many aspects of urban life—quality of air and drinking water, sanitation and fire services, and the availability and affordability of health care—have well-established connections to the health of urban dwellers (Cohen and Northridge 2000). For example, India's cities are characterized by "teeming hovels of dirt and garbage, overcrowded and noisy lanes, and proliferation of slums" (Siddiqui and Pandey 2003:590). India's urban centers are home to more than a quarter of India's total population. Deprived of the basic amenities of water, sewage, and waste disposal facilities, India's urban residents are subject to unsafe and unhealthy living conditions.

One area that is often overlooked is the quality of housing. Substandard housing (homes with severe or moderate structural problems such as malfunctioning plumbing or heating) is a major U.S. public health issue (Krieger and Higgins 2002), particularly among urban dwellers and people of color. Housing quality has been associated with morbidity from infectious diseases, chronic illnesses, injuries, poor nutrition, and mental disorders (Krieger and Higgins 2002). Disparities in quality housing have remained unchanged since the 1970s. Approximately 7.5% of non-Hispanic Blacks and 6.3% of Hispanics live in moderately substandard housing compared with 2.8% of Whites (Jacobs 2011).

Interior residential density refers to the number of individuals per room in a dwelling. The criterion for **crowding** is more than one person per room in the household. In the United States, household crowding is more likely to be found among poor, immigrant, or urban families. Research indicates that children who live in more crowded homes have greater behavioral problems in the classroom. Crowding also leads to greater conflict between parents and children. In crowded homes, parents have been found to be more critical of and less responsive to their children (Evans, Saegert, and Harris 2001). Crowding is also related to infectious disease transmission such as tuberculosis and other respiratory diseases.

William Clark, Marinus Deurloo, and Frans Dieleman (2000) argue that household crowding is linked to inequalities in housing consumption. The researchers explain that the rising income of a large segment of U.S. society has led to increases in the overall quality of housing in the United States. But at the same time, growing income inequalities create affordability and crowding problems for very-low-income households. Affluent households demand better-quality and larger houses, increasing their consumption of livable space, pushing housing outside of inner-city boundaries. Clark et al. explain that as middle-class families move to the suburbs, they leave behind inner cities plagued with increased density and housing shortages.

Cities with large numbers of immigrants—such as those in such states as California, Texas, Arizona, and Florida—are especially subject to crowding. A study based in Southern California reveals that households of Hispanics who immigrated in the 1970s are 212 times more likely to be overcrowded than are those of earlier Hispanic immigrants or White immigrants (Myers and Lee 1996). Clark et al. (2000) also report that in metropolitan areas with high levels of recent immigration, overcrowding is higher than in nonimmigrant areas. Poor immigrant households experience the most crowding and have the most difficulty in transitioning to better, more affordable housing. Studies suggest that competition for housing in cities with many immigrants may increase the cost of housing and can lead to a

Interior residential density: The number of individuals per room in a dwelling

Crowding: Defined as more than one person per room in the household

 Overcrowding and Illness

housing squeeze. Cultural norms may also play a role in encouraging crowding among Hispanic immigrant homes.

Crowding is also a global issue, in countries experiencing rapid population growth. For example, the population of Lagos, Nigeria, has doubled over 15 years to 21 million (Rosenthal 2012). City residents typically live in apartments, 7- by 11-foot rooms described as "Face Me, Face You." Up to 50 people may share a kitchen, toilet, and sink (Rosenthal 2012).

Homelessness

By its very nature, homelessness is impossible to measure with 100% accuracy (National Coalition for the Homeless 2002). Most estimates are based on head counts in shelters, on the streets, or at soup kitchens. These estimates do not include those who live in temporary or unstable housing (e.g., those who move in with friends or relatives). Most public and private sources agree that the number of homeless people is at least in the hundreds of thousands, not counting those who live with relatives or friends (Choi and Snyder 1999). There are several national estimates of homelessness. The U.S. Department of Housing and Urban Development (2014) estimated that 578,424 people were homeless on a given night. The majority (69%) were staying in residential (shelter) programs, while the rest (31%) were in unsheltered locations.

Michael S. Williamson/The Washington Post via Getty Images

Homelessness is impossible to measure with 100% accuracy (National Coalition for the Homeless 2002). This field researcher collects information from a homeless man.

 Hiding Homelessness

 Affordable Housing Shortage

Commuting

Table 14.6   Time spent traveling to work, 2011

One-way travel time	Percentage of Workers
Less than 10 minutes	13.4
10–14 minutes	14.3
15–19 minutes	15.5
20–24 minutes	14.8
25–29 minutes	6.1
30–34 minutes	13.7
35–44 minutes	6.4
45–59 minutes	7.5
60+ minutes	8.1

SOURCE: McKenzie 2013.

Figure 14.1   Residence-to-work pattern by commute time, 2011

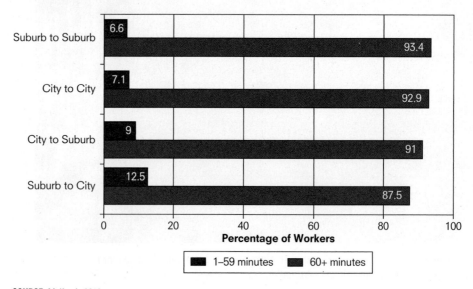

SOURCE: McKenzie 2013.

EXPLORING **social problems**

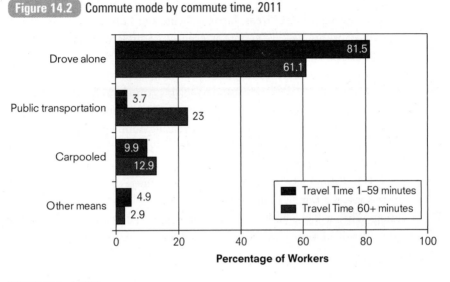

Figure 14.2 Commute mode by commute time, 2011

- Drove alone: 81.5 / 61.1
- Public transportation: 3.7 / 23
- Carpooled: 9.9 / 12.9
- Other means: 4.9 / 2.9

Legend:
- ■ Travel Time 1–59 minutes
- ■ Travel Time 60+ minutes

X-axis: Percentage of Workers (0, 20, 40, 60, 80, 100)

SOURCE: McKenzie 2013.

WHAT DO YOU THINK?

The national average travel time to work (one way) was 25.5 minutes in 2011 (McKenzie 2013). Workers in the New York and Washington, DC, metro areas had the two longest travel times, 34.9 minutes and 34.5 minutes, respectively. The percentage of workers by one-way travel time is presented in Table 14.6.

Those who commuted from suburbs to a city for work were more likely to have a 60+ minute commute compared to other home/workplace categories (refer to Figure 14.1).

The mode of commuter transportation varied by time travel (refer to Figure 14.2). Workers commuting 60+ minutes or longer relied on carpools or public transportation more than workers with commute times under an hour. However, for both groups, driving alone was the most popular transportation mode.

How would you define a "long" commute? How important is it for you to live in close proximity to where you work (or go to school)?

Nearly one quarter of all homeless were children under the age of 18. About 37% of the homeless were families. For information about the U.S. homeless population, refer to this chapter's Exploring Social Problems feature.

Globally, the highest concentrations of homeless people tend to be located in urban settings and segregated in some of the traditionally poorest areas (Toro 2007). In contrast to the United States, European countries experience lower rates of homelessness because their social welfare system guarantees some level of income, health care, and housing for all citizens. Japan is facing a rapidly growing problem of homelessness because its welfare system is even more underdeveloped than that of the United States (Toro 2007).

Before the mid-1970s, the majority of the homeless were older, single males with substance abuse or physical or mental problems (Choi and Snyder 1999). Their individual disabilities or personal pathologies were likely to have caused their homelessness. Since the mid-1970s, however, the increasing number of homeless men, women, and families indicates that more than individual disabilities or personal characteristics are causing homelessness (Choi and Snyder 1999).

The U.S. Conference of Mayors (2013) identified several interrelated causes of homelessness for families and single adults: unemployment and lack of affordable housing. When asked what three things cities should do to address homelessness, the mayors identified more mainstream assisted housing, more or better-paying employment opportunities, and permanent supportive housing for people with disabilities.

Gentrification

In their report "Dealing With Neighborhood Change," Maureen Kennedy and Paul Leonard (2001) reveal that **gentrification**, "the process of neighborhood change which results in the replacement of lower-income residents with higher-income ones, has changed the character of hundreds of urban neighborhoods in America over the last 50 years" (p. 1). Gentrification has occurred in waves: the urban renewal efforts in the 1950s and 1960s and the "back-to-the-city" movement of the late 1970s and 1980s. Gentrification is a global experience, with renewal efforts documented in Tokyo, London, Mexico City, Cape Town, Paris, Shanghai, and Sydney, as well as in many other countries and cities (N. Smith 2002). Gentrification continues today.

The researchers describe gentrification as a "double edged sword." Officials and developers point to the increasing real estate values, tax revenues, and commercial activity that take place in revitalized communities. But is there a price for these capital and economic improvements? The most contentious by-product of gentrification is the involuntary displacement of a neighborhood's low-income residents. No consistent data exist on the number of individuals who have been displaced through gentrification, yet the evidence suggests that where housing markets are tight (or limited), the amount of displacement is likely to be greater and the impacts on those displaced more serious (Kennedy and Leonard 2001).

Gentrification: The process of neighborhood change from lower- to higher-income residents

Gentrification is most often associated with the disproportionate pressure it puts on marginalized poor, elderly, or minorities. The benefits of neighborhood revitalization are not equally distributed. Research reveals how gentrification is more economically successful in higher-income neighborhoods than in minority or low-income neighborhoods. Residents of higher-income gentrified neighborhoods experience greater integration and economic benefit than residents of low-income neighborhoods that gentrify (Hwang and Sampson 2014). For example, Richard Barrett and his colleagues (2008) reported a negative association between gentrification and the health of low-income residents. The researchers concluded that neighborhood economic vitalization encourages more expensive service providers to move into the neighborhood, thus disrupting or eliminating low-income residents' access to low-cost health care. In a study of public education outcomes, Micere Keels, Julia Burdick-Will, and Sara Keene (2013) concluded that neighborhood revitalization had no effect on public school revitalization. The researchers found no significant difference in reading and math test scores between students enrolled in schools in gentrified neighborhoods compared to students enrolled in un-gentrified neighborhood schools. Their research casts doubt on the idea that low-income children will benefit from gentrification.

Though overall U.S. home values dropped between 2008 and 2011, values of homes in close-in or mixed-use neighborhoods held or increased their value. Demand for walkable urban places, with amenities of mixed housing types, destinations within walking distance, and public transportation options, increased above demand for homes in suburban areas with large home lots, ample parking, and driving as the primary means of transportation (Leinberger and Alfonzo 2012). In their analysis of sample neighborhoods in the Washington, DC, metropolitan area, Christopher Leinberger and Mariela Alfonzo (2012) documented how residents of more walkable places have lower transportation costs and higher transit access, but higher housing costs. Residents of walkable places are more affluent than residents of places with poor walkability. Leinberger (2012) reported how similar class and cost patterns are present in other urban areas, such as Seattle, Washington; Denver, Colorado; Columbus, Ohio; and Atlanta, Georgia.

Urban Sprawl and Transportation

As urban areas spread out, they create a phenomenon referred to as **urban sprawl**. Urban sprawl began with land development after World War II. Sprawl is defined as the process in which the spread of development across the landscape outpaces population growth (Ewing, Pendall, and Chen 2002). Sprawl creates four conditions for an urban area: a population that is widely dispersed in low-density developments; rigidly separated homes, shops, and workplaces; a network of roads marked by huge blocks and poor access; and a lack of well-defined activity centers, such as downtowns or town centers (Ewing et al. 2002). Sprawl increases stress on urban livability as goods and services, along with economic and educational opportunities, become less accessible to inner-city residents (W. A. Johnson 2007; Powell 2007).

Urban sprawl: The process in which the spread of development across the landscape outpaces population growth

Bicycles are ubiquitous in the Netherlands. There are an estimated 13 million bikes for the country's 16 million residents. The Dutch have established a vast network of efficient and safe bike paths.

As sprawl increases, so do the number of miles traveled, the number of vehicles owned per household, traffic fatality rates, air pollution (Corvin 2001; Ewing et al. 2002), and, eventually, our risk of asthma, obesity, and poor health. On average, an American spends 443 hours per year behind the wheel (Crenson 2003). Public transportation usage is higher in metro areas. The New York–northern New Jersey–Long Island metro area had the highest percentage of workers who commuted to work via public transportation, 30.5% (McKenzie and Rapino 2011). New suburban residential developments don't include sidewalks, and automobiles are needed to get from place to place.

The Centers for Disease Control and Prevention report that urban sprawl increases our time on the road and decreases our time spent exercising, including walking, jogging, or riding a bike (Corvin 2001). Residents who live in spread-out areas spend fewer minutes each month walking and weigh about 6 pounds more on average than do those who live in densely populated areas (Stein 2003).

Americans spend more than 100 hours per year commuting to work (U.S. Census Bureau 2005). On average, an American worker's daily commute is about 25 minutes (one-way commute time), and 75% of workers drive alone to work (McKenzie and Rapino 2011). Only 5% of commuters travel to work using public transportation. Residents from larger cities tend to have longer commutes: New York (38 minutes); Chicago (33 minutes); Newark, New Jersey (31 minutes); and Riverside, California (31 minutes) (U.S. Census Bureau 2005). Long commutes are also a global experience, particularly for poor disadvantaged workers. For example, commuting to Brazil's largest industrial city, São Paulo, can take as much as four hours each way. São Paulo commuters are mostly minimum-wage laborers, commuting daily from their working-class poor suburbs to the city's factories.

- -

What Does It Mean to Me?

Examine the public transportation system for your college city. First, is one available? Second, assess its effectiveness. Does the system serve all areas of your community? How much does it cost to use the system? How does the system serve disadvantaged populations—elderly, poor, or disabled residents? Does the system provide discounted fares for students?

- -

IN FOCUS

LIVING CAR FREE

North Americans are known for their love affair with, maybe even addiction to, their automobiles (Boddy 2000). Though the average number of persons per household has declined, 3.16 in 1969 to 2.66 in 2009, the number of vehicles has increased in the same time period from 1.16 to 1.92 (U.S. Department of Energy 2010). Despite rising fuel prices, U.S. housing and work patterns make it hard for suburban commuters to change their driving habits (Ohlemacher 2007). As of December 2014, the highest recorded average price for a gallon of regular gas was $4.43 in 2008.

However, many European countries and cities have found innovative and community-friendly ways to deal with gas prices consistently higher than $6.00 per gallon. For example, most of the 4,700 residents of Vauban, Germany, live car free. The rate of Vauban car ownership is 150 per 1,000 inhabitants compared with 640 per 1,000 residents in the United States. How does Vauban do it? Extensive city planning and innovative public policy. The city was built with an extensive system of bike paths and few parking spots. Parking spots for vehicles are available in a garage at the edge of the community for €17,500 (more than $20,000 per year). Vauban city planners have also encouraged residents to use public transportation such as tramways and buses. Many of the city's streets were designed to be too narrow for cars (de Pommereau 2006).

Car use is discouraged in many different ways throughout the world. In Germany, there is a yearly car

In 2007, the city of Paris introduced Vélib', a self-service bicycle transit system. From more than 700 locations throughout the city, individuals can rent bikes by the hour. There are 230 miles of cycling lanes in Paris.

tax based on the automobile engine size—the bigger the engine, the higher the tax. Several European cities maintain fleets of bikes for public use to encourage bike riding as a transportation alternative. European Union countries, such as France, Italy, and Germany, have closed off parts of their city centers to cars for a day or permanently. In 1983, Bogotá, Colombia, initiated a program called *ciclovía* (bike path). Designated streets are closed to cars every Sunday, encouraging residents to jog, walk, or ride their bikes on the streets and revitalizing their neighborhoods as a result. One and a half million people are said to turn out for the Sunday *ciclovía* (Wood 2007).

Car-free zones have also been embraced in several U.S. cities. New York, San Francisco, Kansas City, Atlanta, Philadelphia, Cleveland, Chicago, St. Louis, and El Paso have begun promoting car-free days in public parks, designated neighborhoods, and green spaces. Since 2010, the city of Los Angeles has sponsored CicLAvias, a car-free event spanning about 10 miles of city roads and streets. Advocates argue that these car-free practices promote family activities, active lifestyles, and closer communities (Wood 2007).

VOICES IN THE COMMUNITY

MAGIC JOHNSON

Since his retirement from the Los Angeles Lakers, Earvin "Magic" Johnson has become a commercial developer opening state-of-the-art multiplex theaters including restaurants, retail, personal service, and Starbucks locations. Johnson's company, Magic Johnson Enterprises, specifically targets business opportunities in minority inner-city and suburban neighborhoods.

At the opening of a 12-screen multiplex, the Magic Johnson Theatres, in South Central Los Angeles, Johnson was confident that such a business would succeed in inner cities because African Americans make up about 13% of the moviegoing audience (Dretzka 1995). Johnson said,

We're the No. 1 movie goers of any (minority) group but you can't find any theaters in your neighborhood. That's why our theaters are doing so much business. We have great numbers, and for everybody in the neighborhood, it means more to them than just a

Since retiring from professional basketball, Magic Johnson has become a commercial and real estate developer in minority inner-city and suburban neighborhoods.

theater. It's a pride situation, bringing the community together. (quoted in Dretzka 1995:1)

The Magic Johnson Theatres cost an estimated $11 million and feature an art deco lobby with a large concession stand and a two-level parking garage. The Johnson Development Corporation has also opened theaters in Atlanta,

---

The overall reduction in driving, particularly by the Millennial generation, provides an opportunity to transform U.S. transportation policies. U.S. PIRG (2013) recommended increasing programs that could encourage Americans to drive less (public transportation systems, bicycling and pedestrian infrastructures) and creating a strategic plan for the repair and maintenance of existing transportation infrastructure (highways and bridges).

. . . .

What Does It Mean to Me?

Could you go car free? Why or why not? Explain your dependence (or lack of dependence) on an automobile.

. . . .

 Magic Johnson Enterprises

Houston, Cleveland, and Harlem. The five theater complexes grossed $30 million in revenue in 2002 (Johnson 2003).

Johnson brought his understanding of the inner-city community to the business. In his movie concessions, knowing that inner-city children grew up drinking Kool-Aid, Johnson sells flavored sodas. "Used to be we couldn't afford to go to dinner and the movie afterward. I told Loew's [his theater partner], 'Black people are going to eat dinner at the movies,'" says Johnson (quoted in Wilborn 2002). As a result, in addition to hot dogs and popcorn, the concessions sell chicken wings and buffalo shrimp.

At his theaters, no gang colors or hanging out in large groups is allowed. Before each movie, a clip of Johnson is played, reminding his audiences: "So we got a few policies that apply to everyone. They are not meant to disrespect. They're there so we can all have a good time. So if you have a problem, leave it in the street" (Wilborn 2002).

Johnson has joined Howard Schultz, chief executive officer of Starbucks, in a franchise deal. Their partnership opened more than 100 stores. Their first location was in Ladera Center, a few miles away from the Los Angeles International Airport. The location is one of the biggest grossing in the Starbucks chain. Schultz explains that through the partnership, "we could create unique opportunities for the community—employment opportunities, opportunities for vendors—and also some hope and aspiration about a leading consumer brand doing business in underserved communities, and perhaps other companies would follow us in" (Johnson 2003:77).

Johnson's business philosophy is simple: "All of my businesses deal with people, customer service, and entertainment because that's what I'm good at. Everything flows together from that, and all the companies help each other" (quoted in E. Smith 1999:80).

In 2002, Johnson established a technology initiative program, currently operating in 11 states and the District of Columbia. Attempting to address the digital divide (refer to Chapter 11, "The Media") affecting poor and minority children, the program establishes Community Empowerment Centers providing youth and community members access to computer technology, training, and experience. The centers also support the Magic of Reading Program, providing students access to books and literacy programs. As of 2014, the centers provided direct services to 255,000 students in 16 urban markets.

COMMUNITY, POLICY, AND SOCIAL ACTION

U.S. Department of Housing and Urban Development (HUD)

The federal agency responsible for addressing the nation's housing needs and improving and developing the nation's communities is HUD. Created in 1965 as part of President Lyndon Johnson's War on Poverty, HUD was given the authority to enforce fair housing laws and to administer a variety of federal programs to provide a decent, safe, and sanitary living environment for every American (HUD 2003b; Martinez 2000).

HUD's history extends back to the National Housing Act of 1934 and to the 1937 amendment that created the U.S. Housing Authority for low-rent housing. HUD's efforts to encourage home ownership are rooted in the Housing Act of 1949, a declaration that all Americans have the right to become homeowners. Despite its expressed goal of creating "well planned and integrated residential neighborhoods," the Housing Act did not improve housing conditions for nonminority households (Martinez 2000). The goals of the Housing Act of 1949 were reaffirmed in the Fair Housing Act of 1968, authorizing the Federal Housing Administration (FHA) to make sure that home ownership was affordable and accessible for every U.S. family, including minorities and the poor (Martinez 2000). HUD continues its housing mission, expanding services to elderly residents and overseeing health care facilities and lead hazard control.

In addition, HUD has been a major player in influencing land-use decisions in urban areas (Williams 2000), spurring economic growth and development in distressed communities (HUD 2003b). HUD's major urban initiatives have included the Housing and Urban Development Act of 1970, which established a national growth policy that emphasized new community and inner-city development; the Housing and Community Development Act of 1974, which established community development block grants; and the Omnibus Budget Reconciliation Act of 1993, which created the first enterprise zones to stimulate economic development in distressed areas. Enacted in 2000, the Community Renewal and New Markets Initiative reinforced HUD's focus on fostering economic opportunity, enhancing the quality of life, and building a stronger sense of community in impoverished inner-city neighborhoods (Williams 2000).

With oversight provided by HUD, the renewal communities, empowerment zones, and enterprise communities program took an innovative approach to revitalization that targets inner cities and rural areas. The program brought communities together through public and private partnerships to attract the social and economic investment necessary for sustainable economic and community development (HUD 2003c). Each program integrated four principles: a strategic vision for change, community-based partnerships, economic opportunity, and sustainable community development. The program began with the assumption that local communities can best identify and develop local solutions to the problems they face (HUD 2003c). The empowerment zones and renewal communities program ended in December 2013.

Urban Revitalization Programs

The HOPE VI program was established by Congress in 1992. Originally called the Urban Revitalization Demonstration Program, from 1993 to 2006 HOPE VI spent nearly $6.2 billion to tear down public housing facilities and revitalize others into larger modern townhomes and detached homes with the goal of creating mixed-income communities in inner cities. Community and service programs are also established as part of the funding. In 2008, six housing authorities in four states (Illinois, Texas, Washington, and Wisconsin) were awarded a total of $97 million (HUD 2009).

The HOPE VI program was created based on recommendations from the National Commission on Severely Distressed Public Housing (HUD 2003a). The commission recommended revitalization in three areas: physical improvements, management improvements, and social and community services to address residents' needs. Program grants pay for demolition of distressed public housing and rehabilitation or new construction. The program has been criticized for worsening the local housing situation because not all demolished units are replaced and program data reveal that not all residents return to the redeveloped HOPE VI sites.

Although the program's primary focus is on the quality of housing units, HUD officials reported that the HOPE VI program has made an impact on its residents through community and supportive programs for residents. When the program was honored in 2000 by the Institute for Government Innovation, HOPE VI officials reported that nearly 3,500 public housing residents had left welfare and more than 6,500 residents had found new jobs as a result of the program (Institute for Government Innovation 2000).

The Obama administration established the Neighborhood Revitalization Initiative (NRI) in 2008, a collaborative effort with the Departments of HUD, Education, Health and Human Services, Justice, and the Treasury. The interagency strategy was promoted as an interdisciplinary, place-based, locally led and data-driven solution to the interconnected challenges of neighborhood revitalization. The initiative includes two new programs—Choice Neighborhoods and Promise Neighborhoods. Promise Neighborhoods is a neighborhood revitalization program to improve the educational and developmental outcomes of children and youth. The program utilizes place-based community change efforts, identifying and mobilizing community residents, leaders, public and private businesses and local organizations to lead and transform neighborhoods. At the end of 2012, the program was implemented in 21 states and the District of Columbia.

Creating Sustainable Communities

Tyler Norris (2001) chronicled the emergence and importance of the sustainable community movement. Since the early 1960s, thousands of public–private partnerships have been formed to work for economic development, educational improvement, environmental protection, health care, social issues, and other issues critical to communities. An array of private and public community groups form these partnerships. These alliances have been identified by several names and terms: *healthy communities*, *sustainable communities*, *livable communities*, *safe communities*, *whole communities*, and *smart growth*. Much of the improvement in public

Table 14.7   Best practices for sustainable communities

	Best Practice
1.	Define community broadly, using not only physical space but also community of interest (e.g., youth assets).
2.	Make the community's vision reflect the core values of all its members.
3.	Define health as the optimum state of well-being—physical, mental, emotional, and spiritual.
4.	Address the quality of life as experienced by all residents.
5.	Invite diverse participation and promote widespread community ownership.
6.	Focus on system change to address how people live and work together.
7.	Use local assets and resources to build capacity.
8.	Measure and report your progress and outcomes to keep citizens informed and to keep partners accountable.

SOURCE: Adapted from Norris 2001.

health, community revitalization, and quality of life can be attributed to these alliances. The best partnerships, according to Norris, bring together traditional leaders and community members often not included in the decision-making process. A summary of best practices from successful sustainable communities is presented in Table 14.7.

Examples of sustainable communities include the following:

- Highlander Research and Education Center, New Market, Tennessee. The center was established in 1932, working primarily on social change and education in the areas of labor, civil rights, and Appalachian issues. In the 2000s, the center defined its focus on four broad, interconnected issues—economic justice, racial justice, environmental justice, and democratic participation—that it believed were critical to making progress toward a more just and humane society. Current programs include an internship program, a children's justice camp, a capacity-building/leadership program, and cultural programs. Each program serves as an invaluable resource to community groups in Appalachia and in the South.

- Greensburg GreenTown, Greensburg, Kansas. After an EF5 tornado leveled the town of Greensburg in 2007, residents, city officials, and businesses made a commitment to rebuild their city sustainably. GreenTown documents and coordinates the community's green building projects. The program offers green tours, allowing visitors to see examples of public, single-family residential, multifamily residential, and commercial construction. GreenTown also provides technical assistance to individuals, community groups, businesses, and local governments wishing to adopt similar green building strategies.

SOCIOLOGY AT WORK

NONPROFIT WORK

Mairead Shutt—Class of 2001
Undergraduate Major: Sociology
Undergraduate Minor: Business

In describing what it means to live a life of moral and civic responsibility, Anne Colby and her colleagues (2003, p. 7) say, "If today's college graduates are to be positive forces in this world, they need not only to possess knowledge and intellectual capacities but also to see themselves as members of a community, as individuals with a responsibility to contribute to their communities."

Because of their personal interest or commitment to similar goals, college graduates are often drawn to nonprofit organizations, organizations that are neither for-profit businesses or government agencies. Nonprofits include hospitals, private schools, churches, social welfare organizations, and charitable organizations (Taylor 2010; Butler 2009). Many of the community-based homeless programs are nonprofits. Operations are funded by grants from the government, but also from private donations.

A bachelor's degree may be required for some entry positions; some management or administrative positions require a master's degree in Business, Public Policy, or a related field. An often-cited downside to nonprofit work is the salary, which is typically lower than for comparable positions in the for-profit world. The type of work you can do varies widely from direct client service to recruiting volunteers to program operations or fundraising.

Mairead Shutt is a relationship manager for a medium-sized environmental education nonprofit organization. She is responsible for donor development and stewardship. "My primary goal, on a day-to-day basis, is to engage donors at a highly personal level; partner with Board Members to engage donors, and stay engaged with our education programs and the impact these programs are having on students, teachers, and the community."

After completing her BA in Sociology and working in several nonprofits, Mairead went back to school to earn an MBA. She continues to use sociology in her work with donors. She says,

My foundation in sociology has helped me to see the people I interact with through my profession (including my colleagues, the students and teachers my organization serves, and the donors I communicate with) as unique individuals, as well as people that are impacted by a larger social system that helps inform their world views, opportunities, and preferences. This has allowed me to excel at working with diverse groups of people, keeping an open mind about people's experience and personal history, and communicating effectively. My sociology training is also valuable to me at work because it helped me to combine both qualitative and quantitative data, research, and analysis to understand the big picture of a situation, problem, or opportunity. Today, I regularly combine hard data and metrics with more qualitative assessments to measure fundraising progress and to evaluate goals.

Mairead offers three excellent suggestions to undergraduate Sociology majors.

(1) It is acceptable to need time and space to explore and learn about the world before knowing exactly what you would like to do for the rest of your life. Don't beat yourself up if you don't have the answer by your senior year. (2) Take on as many learning opportunities as you can. Volunteer for causes you are passionate about and build your network. (3) Do the math. Understand the salary ranges in different sectors. While I would never discourage anyone from a career in the nonprofit world, I would encourage graduates to go in with a solid understanding of the financial realities.

Housing and Homelessness Programs

The one community response to homelessness that most of us are familiar with is the homeless shelter. These shelters have been referred to as "Band-Aid" solutions, helping but not really fixing the problem. However, these emergency programs can provide immediate and necessary assistance and, in particular, security for families with children. If these shelters are to be truly effective, more humane and supportive shelter environments should be promoted to assist families and to better prepare them for independent living (Choi and Snyder 1999). For example, existing social and human services programs will be more effective if the homeless are able to obtain the benefits that they are already eligible for (Rossi 1989), such as Social Security, disability payments, and food stamps.

In 1987, Congress passed the Stewart B. McKinney Homeless Assistance Act, which established assistance programs for homeless individuals and families. Under this act, 20 programs were authorized to provide emergency food and shelter, transitional and permanent housing, education, mental health care, primary health care, and veterans' assistance services. In an effort to create more affordable housing, under Title II of the 1998 Cranston-Gonzalez National Affordable Housing Act, the HOME program provides grants to state and local governments to build, buy, or rehabilitate affordable housing for rent or homeownership. Working with community groups, the HOME program continues to serve low-income families.

Community efforts are important for the homeless and low-income families. The best-known community-based housing program is Habitat for Humanity International. Habitat serves primarily low- and very-low-income families with support from local volunteers, churches, and businesses, as well as from the sweat equity of future homeowners. Habitat families have incomes of about 30% to 50% of the area's median income.

Project Homeless Connect began in San Francisco in 2004 when Mayor Gavin Newsom had the idea of bringing city hall staff and programs to the homeless community. The project, replicated in more than 200 U.S cities and in Canada and Australia, attempts to reach out to a city's homeless population by delivering an array of services—social, medical, mental health, housing—all under one roof at a local venue. Quality-of-life services are also offered for the day, including haircuts, wheelchair repair, eyeglasses, and dental services. The project connects homeless men and women with program representatives and members of the community. It is staffed by more than 700 volunteers and is supported through donations from local businesses.

Although supportive services are necessary for the homeless, homelessness cannot be prevented or eliminated without enough housing for the poor. Homelessness cannot be prevented or eliminated without a livable wage, employment opportunities for inner-city residents, more efficient management of public housing projects, emergency rent assistance programs, and the expansion of low-income housing subsidies (Choi and Snyder 1999).

Project Homeless
Connect

CHAPTER REVIEW

14.1 Define demography

Demography, an essential part of urban studies, is the study of the size, composition, and distribution of human populations, as well as changes and trends in those areas. An additional demographic element is migration, the movement of individuals from one area to another.

14.2 Compare the processes of urbanization and suburbanization

Urbanization is the process by which a population shifts from rural to urban locales, expanded in the latter half of the 19th century. Suburbanization is the outward expansion of central cities into suburban areas, moving population centers away from city centers.

14.3 Explain how a population is affected by its age distribution or ethnic composition

Age distribution, or the distribution of individuals by age, is particularly important as it provides a community with some direction in its social and economic planning. Ethnic and age compositions will also affect community services and priorities.

14.4 Summarize how the sociological perspectives explain urbanization and its related social problems

Functionalists are critical about the shift from simple to complex societies, arguing that we lose our social bonds and connections to others in the process. The conflict perspective examines how cities are formed on the basis of racial, gender, or class inequalities stemming from capitalism. Social problems are natural to the system, arising from the unequal distribution of power among various groups. Feminist theorists have argued for the development of a comprehensive field of theory and research that acknowledges the role and experiences of women in urban environments. The structure of our urban public settings, along with how we use or experience them, contributes to how we define our cities.

14.5 Analyze the pros and cons of gentrification

Though gentrification involves the revitalization of an urban area, the benefits of gentrification are not evenly distributed. The quality of life and economic opportunities for lower-income or minority residents may not improve or may be negatively affected.

14.6 Describe the sustainable community movement

Since the early 1960s, thousands of public–private partnerships have been formed to work for economic development, educational improvement, environmental protection, health care, social issues, and other issues critical to communities. An array of private and public community groups form these partnerships.

KEY TERMS

age distribution, 395

critical political-economy perspective, 399

crowding, 404

domestic migration, 392

emigration, 392

ethnic composition, 396

gentrification, 408

human ecology, 392

immigration, 392

interior residential density, 404

mechanical solidarity, 397

migration, 392

organic solidarity, 397

overurbanization, 393

STUDY QUESTIONS

1. Define urbanization and suburbanization. What are some ways that urbanization and suburbanization contribute to social problems?

2. Explain the societal transition from mechanical to organic solidarity as identified by Émile Durkheim.

3. From an interactionist's perspective, how connected are you to your community? Do you define your community by what you value in it or what you use within it?

4. Access to affordable and/or quality housing is a problem facing urban and suburban dwellers. Identify the extent of each problem and identify solutions for each.

5. It is difficult to accurately measure the extent of the homeless problem in the United States. How does this disadvantage our understanding of homelessness? Of attempting to solve it?

6. How can sociology be used to encourage the expansion of car-free or pedestrian zones? Which sociological perspective(s) would best apply?

Sharpen your skills with SAGE edge at **edge.sagepub.com/leonguerrero5e**

SAGE edge provides a personalized approach to help you accomplish your coursework goals in an easy-to-use learning environment.

The Environment

LEARNING OBJECTIVES

15.1 Explain the relationship between human activity and environmental problems

15.2 Review the different sociological perspectives on environmental problems

15.3 Discuss climate change and global warming

15.4 Summarize federal and state responses to environmental problems

15.5 Compare the first wave and second wave of environmental interest groups

15.6 Assess the impact of the environmental movement

Megadisaster: A catastrophe that threatens or overwhelms an area's capacity to get people to safety, treat casualties, protect infrastructure, and control panic

Mega. That's the word used to describe recent environmental disasters that have seriously threatened and damaged our physical and social worlds. A **megadisaster** is defined as a catastrophe that threatens or overwhelms an area's capacity to get people to safety, treat casualties, protect infrastructure, and control panic (Choi 2011). On April 2010, British Petroleum's Deepwater Horizon drilling platform exploded in the Gulf of Mexico. In addition to killing 11 workers and injuring 17 others, the explosion led to the release of an estimated 4.9 million barrels of oil until July 15, 2010, when the damaged wellhead was finally capped. Officials responded quickly to the disaster, addressing the threats to wildlife and to the fishing and tourism industries along the coasts of Alabama, Florida, Louisiana, Mississippi, and Texas. Though active cleanup efforts ended in 2014, U.S. Coast Guard crews remain posted on the Gulf Coast ready to respond to new reports of oil.

In 2011, northeastern Japan was struck by a 9.0 earthquake. This megadisaster has been characterized as a natural catastrophe overlaid by a technical situation (Choi 2011): the earthquake was followed by a tsunami and damage to three nuclear reactors in Fukushima. The tsunami leveled 130,000 houses and damaged 250,000 more. About 270 railway lines, 15 expressways, 69 national highways, and 638 municipal roads were closed. Approximately 20,000 people died, most due to drowning, and thousands of residents were displaced. John Schwartz (2011) writes, "The sobering fact is that megadisasters like the Japanese earthquake can overcome the best efforts of our species to protect against them. No matter how high the levee or how flexible the foundation, disaster experts say, nature bats last" (p. 5).

ENVIRONMENTAL PROBLEMS ARE HUMAN PROBLEMS

The field of **environmental sociology** considers the interactions between our physical and natural environment on the one hand, and our social organization and behavior on the other (Dunlap and Catton 1994). Human beings are an integral part of the ecosystem (Irwin 2001). The state of the environment is also influenced by our cultural values and attitudes toward the environment, our social class, our technology, and our relationship with others (Cable and Cable 1995). When we use a sociological perspective to understand environmental problems, we acknowledge that "human activities are causing the deterioration in the quality of the environment and that environmental deterioration in turn has negative impacts on people" (Dunlap 1997:27).

Humans create environmental problems through intentional efforts to exploit or manage nature. Rivers that are dammed, straightened, or treated as sewers may create unintended downstream environmental problems (Caldwell 1997). The removal of rain forests to harvest wood or to create farmland decreases the number of plants and trees that absorb carbon dioxide, leading to higher amounts of greenhouse gases in the air. But environmental problems don't exist just because of our actions.

Our pursuit of economic development, growth, and jobs has also led to the degradation of the environment (Caldwell 1997). Russia, Indonesia, and Zambia are among the world's most polluted places. These countries and their residents (refer to Table 15.1) are exposed to organic and industrial pollutants caused by mining, manufacturing, and transportation. Although much of this pollution can be attributed to the countries' substandard infrastructures or the absence of regulatory controls, even if both were brought up to industrial country standards, "the legacy of old contamination from the past would continue to poison the local population" (Blacksmith Institute 2007:3).

Environmentalist Paul Hawken (1997) refers to the Biosphere 2 experiment to demonstrate just how vital and fragile our ecosystem is. The Biosphere 2 was a 3-acre, glass-enclosed ecosystem intended to sustain eight people for a two-year experiment, from September 1991 through September 1993. The Biosphere 2's $200 million budget was not enough to create a viable ecosystem for eight people. By the time the experiment ended, the Biosphere's air and drinking water were polluted, crops and trees had been killed by other vegetation, and 19 of the 25 small animal species the participants brought with them had died. The scientists who lived in the biosphere showed signs of oxygen starvation from living at the equivalent of an altitude of 17,500 feet. Even with scientific knowledge and planning, there are no human-made substitutions for essential natural resources. As Hawken (1997) explains,

> We have not come up with an economical way to manufacture watershed, gene pools, topsoil, wetlands, river systems, pollinators, or fisheries. Technological

Environmental sociology: Study of the interactions between our physical and natural environment and our social organization and social behavior

Table 15.1 The world's most polluted places (alphabetically by city or site), 2013

Site Name and Location	Major Pollutants and Sources
Agbogbloshie Dumpsite, Ghana	Heavy metals and particulates from e-waste recycling and processing
Chernobyl, Ukraine	Radioactive materials from 1986 nuclear reactor explosion
Citarum River Basin, Indonesia	Heavy metals and particulates from industry
Dzerzhinsk, Russia	Chemicals and toxic by-products, lead from chemical weapons, and industrial manufacturing
Hazarlbagh, Bangladesh	Chemicals and toxic by-products from tannery manufacturing
Kabwe, Zambia	Heavy metals and particulates from mining and smelting operations
Kallantan, Indonesia	Heavy metals and particulates from mining and smelting operations
Matanza-Riachuelo, Argentina	Heavy metals and particulates from chemical manufacturers
Niger River Delta, Nigeria	Oil and hydrocarbons from petroleum operations
Norilsk, Russia	Heavy metals and particulates from mining and smelting operations

SOURCE: Adapted from Blacksmith Institute and Green Cross Switzerland 2014.

fixes can't solve problems with soil fertility or guarantee clean air, biological diversity, pure water, and climatic stability; nor can they increase the capacity of the environment to absorb 25 billion tons of waste created annually by America alone. (p. 41)

SOCIOLOGICAL PERSPECTIVES ON ENVIRONMENTAL PROBLEMS

Functionalist Perspective

Whether they are looking at a social system or an ecosystem, functionalists examine the entire system and its components. Where are environmental problems likely to arise? Functionalists would answer that problems develop from the system itself. Agricultural and industrial modes of production are destabilizing forces in our ecosystem. Agriculture replaces complex natural systems with simpler artificial ones to sustain select highly productive crops. These crops require constant attention in the form of cultivation, fertilizers, and pesticides, all foreign elements to the natural environment (Ehrlich, Ehrlich, and Holdren 1973). When it first began, industrialization entered a society that had fewer people, less material well-being, and abundant natural resources. But modern industrialization uses "more resources to make few

Let the Environment Guide Our Development

A woman stands atop a mountain of rubbish in a China landfill. China generates an estimated 150 million tons of rubbish per year, with as much as 400 million tons estimated by 2020.

people more productive," and as a result, "more people are chasing fewer natural resources" (Hawken 1997:40). As much as agriculture, industrialization, and related technologies have improved the quality of our lives, we must deal with the negative consequences of waste, pollution, and the destruction of our natural resources. Human activities have become a dominant influence on the Earth's climate and ecosystems (Kanter 2007).

Biologists Paul Ehrlich and Anne Ehrlich (1990) contend that the impact of any human group on the environment is the product of three different factors. First is the population, second is the average person's consumption of resources or level of affluence, and third is the amount of damage caused by technology. They present a final formula: Environmental Damage = (People) × (Level of Affluence) × (Technological Damage). A high rate of population growth or consumption can lead to a "hasty application" of new technologies in an attempt to meet new and increasing demands. "The larger the absolute size of the population and its level of consumption, the larger the scale of the technology must be, and, hence, the more serious are the mistakes that are made" (Ehrlich, Ehrlich, and Holdren 1973:15). "What matters to the environment," writes Robert Engelman (2009), "are sums of human pulls and pushes, the extractions of resources and the injections of waste" (p. 24).

There is no simple way to stop the escalation of environmental problems. Halting population growth would be a good start but by itself could not solve the problem.

The United Nations announced in 2011 that the world's population had reached 7 billion, with 10 billion predicted for 2100 (UN News Centre 2011). Reducing technology's impact on the environment might be useful, but not if our population and affluence are allowed to grow. According to Ehrlich et al. (1973), the only way to address environmental problems is to simultaneously attack all components.

Conflict Perspective

Public discourse on environmental problems is often framed in terms of costs and interests. Do you save the spotted owl habitat or hundreds of logging jobs? Should you close a factory or save the river where its waste is being dumped? The proposed $7 billion Keystone XL pipeline from Alberta, Canada, to the gulf of Texas was the center of our national debate over energy independence, economic growth, and climate change. While supporters refer to the pipeline as a jobs creator and describe it as a means to reduce our dependency on foreign oil, environmentalists warn that transporting raw tar sands oil over 2,000 miles is unsafe and ultimately would prove harmful for people, wildlife, water, and the climate (Natural Resources Defense Council 2014). From this sociological perspective, environmental problems are created by humans competing for power, income, and their own interests.

Our capitalist economic system has been identified as a primary source of the conflict over polluting (or conserving) our natural world. Competing political, economic, and environmental interests ensure that this conflict will continue. J. Clarence Davies (1970) argues that the capitalist system encourages pollution, simply because air and water are treated as infinite and free resources. Polluters don't really consider who or what is being affected by environmental problems. If a paper mill is polluting the river, it doesn't affect the paper mill itself but, rather, affects the users of the water or the residents downstream. If a power plant is polluting the air, the plant doesn't pay for the cost of using the air, but pays only the cost of cleaning up a polluted area (Davies 1970).

Environmental problems occasionally make life unpleasant and inconvenient, but most Americans will tolerate this in exchange for the benefits and comforts associated with a developed industrial economy (Tobin 2000). Environmental damage, pollution, and degradation have become acceptable consequences of doing business. A higher standard of living has been confused with consumption: more is better. As Henri Lefebvre ([1971] 2000) argues, the objective of a consumer capitalist society is to satisfy real or imagined material needs. Television and print media overwhelm us with products and services and tell us that we cannot live without them. Politicians encourage lower taxes so that we have more money to spend. But increased consumption requires increased production and energy, which in turn leads to environmental damage. David Korten (1995) explains,

> About 70 percent of this productivity growth has been in . . . economic activity accounted for by the petroleum, petrochemical, and metal industries;

chemical intensive agriculture; public utilities; road building; transportation; and mining . . . the industries that are most rapidly drawing down natural capital, generating the bulk of our toxic waste, and consuming a substantial portion of our renewable energy. (pp. 37–38)

What Does It Mean to Me?

Hawken (1993) contends that we should be able to put an economic value on our renewable (forests, fisheries) and nonrenewable (coal, oil) natural resources. He advocates **natural capitalism**, the awareness of the value of nature as a system, no different than assessing the value of human or financial capital. We are able to attach a dollar amount to a tree once it is cut down for its timber, but what is its value as a living part of our ecosystem? What is the price tag on nature?

Polluters target those with the least amount of power. Race, says Robert Bullard (1999), is the most important factor in determining whether an individual drinks dirty water or lives next to a toxic site. He (Bullard 1994) defines **environmental racism** as "any environmental policy, practice or directive that differentially affects or disadvantages individuals, groups, or communities based on race or color" (p. 98). Environmental racism is institutionalized through the government, our legal system, and economic forces (Bullard 1999). Research consistently indicates that low-income people and people of color are exposed to greater environmental risks than are those who live in White or affluent communities. Low-income people and people of color suffer higher levels of environmentally generated diseases and death as a result of their elevated risk (Ringquist 2000). Environmental racism has been expanded to include members of other disadvantaged communities, examining heightened environmental risk based on race, class, gender, education, and political power.

What Does It Mean to Me?

Major U.S. corporations have joined the environmental movement. Walmart, for example, has implemented a no-package waste program, sells seafood from certified sustainable fisheries, and is transitioning its trucking fleet to vehicles that run on biofuels generated from the waste grease collected from stores' delis. According to Jared Diamond (2009), while Walmart and other corporations are motivated by money and efficiency, they are also interested in creating an earth-friendly, public-pleasing image. Should we be skeptical about these corporations' earth-friendly initiatives? Does this change the way you think about them?

Natural capitalism: The awareness of the economic value of nature

Environmental racism: Environmental policy or practice that disadvantages people based on race or color

Feminist Perspective

The feminist perspective argues that a masculine worldview is responsible for the domination of nature, the domination of women, and the domination of minorities

(Scarce 1990), acknowledging that the connection between the environment and women is one of shared oppression (Chircop 2008). Ecofeminism may be the dominant feminist perspective for explaining the relationship between humans and the environment (Littig 2001). Ecofeminism was introduced in 1974 in an effort to bring attention to the power of women to bring about an ecological revolution, using the starting point as women's experiences. Ecofeminists argue that "men driven by rationalism, domination, competitiveness, individualism, and a need to control, are most often the culprits in the exploitation of animals and the environment" (Scarce 1990:40). According to ecofeminists, "respect for nature generally promotes human welfare, and genuine respect for all human beings tends to protect nature" (Wenz 2001:190). Other feminist approaches include the feminist critique of natural science, feminist analyses of specific environmental issues (work, garbage, consumption), and feminist contributions to sustainable development (Littig 2001).

Cynthia Hamilton (1994) argues that environmental conflicts mirror social injustice struggles in other areas—for women, for people of color, for the poor. In environmental movements, Hamilton explains, what motivates activist women is the need to protect home and children. As the home is defined as the woman's domain, her position places her closest to the dangers of hazardous waste, providing her with an opportunity to monitor illnesses and possible environmental causes within her family and among her neighbors. As Hamilton sees it, these women are responding not to "'nature' in the abstract but to their homes and the health of their children" (p. 210).

The Love Canal disaster has been credited with changing public policy regarding toxic waste clean up. New legislation emerged holding polluters responsible for their actions. In addition, Love Canal marks the beginning of the environmental justice movement in the United States, inspiring other citizen groups to advocate for safe and healthy neighborhoods.

The modern **environmental justice** movement emerged out of citizen protests at Love Canal, near Niagara Falls, New York (Newman 2001). The movement is based on the principle that "all peoples and communities are entitled to equal protection of environmental and public health laws and regulations" (Bullard 1994). For many years, the movement has effectively brought racial and economic discrimination in waste disposal, polluting industries, access to services, and the impacts of transportation and city planning to the public's attention (Morland and Wing 2007).

At the center of Love Canal's citizens' protest movement was a group of local women who called themselves "housewives turned activists." Lois Gibbs and

Environmental justice: Social justice movement based on the principle that all individuals and communities are entitled to equal protection of environmental and public health laws and regulations

 The Love Canal Disaster

Debbie Cerillo formed the Love Canal Homeowners Association in 1978. Concerned about the number of miscarriages, birth defects, illnesses, and rare forms of cancer among their families and neighbors, the women worked with Beverly Paigen, a research scientist, to document the health problems in their community (Breton 1998). The information they collected became known as "housewife data" (Newman 2001). The women held demonstrations, wrote press releases, distributed petitions, and provided testimony before state and federal officials (Newman 2001). In 1978, Love Canal was declared a disaster area, some 800 residents were evacuated and relocated, and the site was cleaned up. Gibbs went on to form the Center for Health, Environment and Justice and continues to work on behalf of communities fighting toxic waste problems. More information about Love Canal is presented in the section titled "Hazardous Waste Sites and Brownfields."

Interactionist Perspective

Theorists working within the interactionist perspective address how environmental problems are created and defined. Riley Dunlap and William Catton (1994) explain, "Environmental sociologists have a long tradition of highlighting the development of societal recognition and definition of environmental conditions as 'problems'" (p. 20). Environmental problems do not materialize by themselves (Irwin 2001). As John Hannigan (1995:55) describes, the successful construction of an environmental problem requires six factors: the scientific authority for and validation of claims; the existence of "popularizers" (activists, scientists) who can frame and package the "problem" to journalists, political leaders, and other opinion makers; media attention that frames the problem as novel and important (such as the problems of rain forest destruction or ozone depletion); the dramatization of the problem in symbolic or visual terms; visible economic incentives for taking positive action; and the emergence of an institutional sponsor who can ensure legitimacy and continuity of the problem.

Social constructionists do not deny that real environmental problems exist. Rather, their interest is in "the process through which environmental claims-makers influence those who hold the reins of power to recognize definitions of environmental problems, to implement them and to accept responsibility for their solution" (Hannigan 1995:185). This perspective helps us understand how environmental concerns vary over time and how some problems are given higher priority than others.

According to Darryn Anne DiFrancesco and Nathan Young (2010), visual communication plays a critical role in many environmental issues, helping to advance or promote a problem to the public. But "global climate change, despite its status as one of the most talked-about and pivotal environmental challenges of our time, appears to lack key visual symbols or metaphors" (p. 531). The authors examined

Calculate Your Ecological Footprint

newspaper images of climate change published over a six-month period in Canada's two national newspapers, *The Globe* and *The National Post*, in 2008 and discovered that Canada's climate change story is told primarily using benign human imagery, focusing on politicians (for example, Canada's environment minister, John Baird) rather than on scientists or ordinary citizens. Emotive images, such as a polar bear mother with her cub, were rare in their sample. They conclude that the national print media in Canada were not interested in playing up the emotional aspects of the climate change debate. "In our view, the dearth of the clear imagery around global climate change makes it more difficult for ordinary citizens to visualize potential impacts and consequences, and to link (often) abstract language claims to real world and to everyday life" (p. 531).

For a summary of sociological perspectives on the environment, see Table 15.2.

Table 15.2 Summary of sociological perspectives: The environment

	Functional	Conflict/Feminist	Interactionist
Explanation of environmental problems	Environmental problems are dysfunctions of modern living, the result of agricultural and industrial modes of production.	Problems are created by humans competing for power, income, and their own interests. Our capitalist economic system has been identified as a primary source of the conflict over polluting (or conserving) our physical and natural worlds. According to the feminist perspective, a masculine worldview is responsible for the domination of nature, the domination of women, and the domination of other minorities.	Theorists from this perspective address how environmental problems are created and defined.
Questions asked about the environment and environmental problems	How are environmental problems related to our modes of production or to our patterns of consumption? Are environmental problems inevitable consequences of modern living?	How do environmental problems emerge from our capitalist economic system or from a patriarchal society? Which particular groups are at risk for experiencing environmental problems or their impacts?	How are environmental problems created? What factors are included in the process? How is a problem legitimized? What individuals or groups play a role in the process?

September 16, 2012

This 2012 NASA image shows the extent of record low Arctic sea ice melt. The yellow line marks the sea ice boundaries from the early 1980s. The loss of sea ice affects our global climate and the movement of ocean waters. Too much or too little sea ice also has consequences for wildlife and people who reside in the Arctic.

SOCIAL PROBLEMS AND THE ENVIRONMENT

Climate Change

Climate change refers to any significant change in the measures of climate (temperature, precipitation, or wind patterns) lasting for an extended period of time. **Global warming**, the ongoing rise in the global average temperature near the Earth's surface, contributes to climate change. There are also natural causes of climate change, such as ocean changes, volcanic eruption, or changes in the Earth's orbit.

To sustain life on Earth, a certain amount of surface heat is required. Heat becomes trapped through the buildup of greenhouse gases—water vapor, carbon dioxide, and other gases—making the Earth's average temperature a comfortable and sustainable 60 degrees Fahrenheit (Environmental Protection Agency [EPA] 2003b). Over the past century, the Earth's surface temperature has risen by about 1.4 degrees Fahrenheit (EPA 2012). The problem is the accumulation of specific greenhouse gases—carbon dioxide, methane, and nitrous oxide—primarily attributable to human activity during the past 50 years (EPA 2012).

The decade 2000–2009 was the warmest on record for the globe. The global combined land and ocean surface temperature was 0.96 degrees Fahrenheit above the 20th-century average (56.9 degrees Fahrenheit, for the period 1901–2000). In comparison, for the 1990s decade, the combined land and ocean surface temperature was 0.65 degrees Fahrenheit above the 20th-century average (National Oceanic and Atmospheric Administration [NOAA] 2010). The Intergovernmental Panel on Climate Change (IPCC) projects that climate change should increase by 2.2 to 11.5 degrees Fahrenheit over the next 100 years (EPA 2012). According to the World Meteorological Organization, 2014 was the hottest year on record worldwide. Michel Jarraud, the organization's secretary-general, reported that "14 of the 15 warmest years on record have all occurred in the 21st century. There is no standstill in global warming" (quoted in Ford 2014).

Since the Industrial Revolution, concentrations of carbon dioxide have increased nearly 30%, methane concentrations have increased by 145%, and nitrous oxide concentrations have increased 15% (Ehrlich and Ehrlich 1996). Fossil fuels used to run cars and trucks, heat homes and businesses, and power factories are responsible for about 98% of carbon dioxide emissions, 24% of methane emissions, and 18% of nitrous oxide emissions. Agriculture, deforestation, landfills, and mining also add

Climate change: The perceptible climate trends over time; also referred to as global warming

Global warming: The ongoing rise in the global average temperature

 Climate Change: Watching the World Change

Table 15.3 Total fossil fuel carbon dioxide emissions, 2013

Country	Per Capita Emissions in Metric Tons of Carbon Dioxide
China	9,977
United States	5,233
India	2,407
Russian Federation	1,812
Japan	1,246
Germany	759
South Korea	616
Iran	611
Saudi Arabia	519
Canada	503

SOURCE: Adapted from Global Carbon Atlas 2014.

to the amount of emissions. China and the United States have the highest fossil fuel carbon dioxide emissions worldwide (a list of the top 10 countries is provided in Table 15.3).

Although they are unable to predict specifically what will happen, where it will happen, and when it will happen, scientists have identified how our health, agriculture, resources, forests, and wildlife are vulnerable to the changes brought about by climate change. Soil moisture may decline in many regions; rainstorms may become more frequent; winters may be colder and longer. Changing regional climates could alter forests, crop yields, and water supplies. Sea levels could rise 2 feet along most of the U.S. coast. In its 2007 report, IPCC (Kanter and Revkin 2007) predicted that the most severe effects would be felt in poor countries and areas facing existing dangers from climate and coastal hazards. Poor households are especially vulnerable to climate change because they lack resources or services to protect themselves and their communities against the threats from changing conditions or crises. Human activity was also identified as the main cause of warming since 1950 (Kanter and Revkin 2007).

During his presidency, George W. Bush downplayed the problem of climate change, referring to the lack of scientific evidence confirming its causes and consequences. In March 2001, President Bush announced that the United States would not support the Kyoto Protocol, which was drawn up in 1997 to implement the United Nations Framework Convention on Climate Change. The treaty limits the emissions of greenhouse gases by an average of 5.2% below 1990 levels. According to Bush, the Kyoto regulations would have become too burdensome for U.S. industry at a time when businesses were struggling with a slowing economy. In addition, the president noted that leading world polluters, India and China, were exempted from the treaty.

In his second term, Bush began to reverse his position. In 2005, he agreed for the first time that human action was responsible for climate change, and in 2007, the president called for a long-term plan for cutting greenhouse gas emissions in the United States and throughout the world. Acknowledging how science has "deepened our understanding of climate change," the president called for other countries to set national targets to reduce greenhouse gas emissions in 10 and 20 years (Stolberg 2007).

Shortly after taking office, President Barack Obama observed that climate change, if left unchecked, would result in an irreversible catastrophe. While the United States has not yet ratified the Kyoto treaty, during the United Nations Climate Change Conference in 2009, the United States joined an international agreement to curtail greenhouse gas emissions. The nonbinding agreement, dubbed the Copenhagen Accord, brought together industrial and developing nations, such as the United States, China, India, Brazil, and South Africa. The accord calls for limiting the rise in global temperatures to no more than 3.6 degrees Fahrenheit and for economic support for emerging countries to develop low-carbon energy systems, to adapt to climate change, and to protect tropical forests (Broder 2010). The nations' leaders acknowledged that climate change is "one of the greatest challenges of our time. . . . We recognize the critical impacts of climate change and the potential impacts of response measures on countries particularly vulnerable to its adverse effects and stress the need to establish a comprehensive adaptation programme including international support" (United Nations 2009). In 2010, the Obama administration announced the formation of a National Climate Service agency to work with the NOAA's National Weather Service and National Ocean Service. Funding for the new agency was blocked by congressional lawmakers in 2011.

Air Quality

Particulate or particle pollution:
Air pollution caused by the combustion of fossil fuels—the burning of coal, diesel, gasoline, and wood; particulate matter includes road dust, diesel soot, ash, wood smoke, and sulfate aerosols that are suspended in the air

The quality of the air we breathe is subject to pollution from two sources: particulate matter and smog. Research has linked air pollution to acute and chronic illnesses (e.g., burning eyes and nose, asthma) as well as death. Air pollution also leads to environmental and property damage.

Particulate or particle pollution is caused by the combustion of fossil fuels—the burning of coal, diesel, gasoline, and wood. Particulate matter includes road dust, diesel soot, ash, wood smoke, and sulfate aerosols that are suspended in the air (Natural Resources Defense Council [NRDC] 1996). The EPA is concerned about small particulate matter, 10 micrometers in diameter or smaller, because these smaller

A man rides his bike past a coal fired powerplant in Fuxin, China. In 2012, Chinese officials selected Fuxin as the site of a national tourist attraction, promising to clean up the city and transform its reliance on coal.

particles are able to pass through the throat and nose and enter the lungs, causing respiratory problems (EPA 2007a).

Particulate pollution caused by traffic and diesel engines is a growing problem in many European Union cities. The World Health Organization (WHO) set the acceptable air quality standard at 10 micrograms of particles per cubic meter. However, nowhere in Europe is this standard being met—at the lower end of the spectrum are Paris and London (16 micrograms per cubic meter), and at the highest are cities such as Warsaw (34), Turin (41), and Milan (38) (Rosenthal 2007). The standard in the United States is 15 micrograms per cubic meter.

Smog or ground-level ozone has been referred to as a public health crisis, affecting people in nearly every U.S. state (Clean Air Network 2003). Smog is formed when nitrogen oxides emitted from electric power plants and automobiles react with organic compounds in the presence of sunlight and heat. Our reliance on automobiles has been blamed for much of the increase in smog levels.

The EPA monitors smog levels throughout the nation. The EPA sets federal eight-hour smog standards and collects data on the number of days that exceed the standard. A day is considered unhealthy if smog levels exceed the eight-hour standard. The EPA reported that 2002 was the worst recorded smog season; the eight-hour health standard was exceeded 8,818 times nationwide. The states with the highest number of unhealthy ozone days were California, Texas, and Tennessee (Clean Air

Smog or ground-level ozone: Air pollution formed when nitrogen oxides emitted from electric power plants and automobiles react with organic compounds in the presence of sunlight and heat

Network 2003). In 2008, the EPA revised national air quality standards, the first time standards have been tightened since 1997. Nationally, ground-level ozone concentrations in 2013 were among the lowest since 2002 (EPA 2010, 2014a).

Scientists report that one of every three people in the United States is at a higher risk of experiencing ozone-related health effects. Those most vulnerable to the health effects of smoggy air are children, people who work or exercise regularly outdoors, the elderly, and people with respiratory diseases. Short-term effects of smog mostly attack the lungs and lung functioning, irritating the lungs, reducing lung function, aggravating asthma, and inflaming and damaging the lining of the lungs (EPA 1999).

During the past two decades, the prevalence of asthma has increased globally, suggesting growing problems associated with indoor and outdoor air quality. Among children, who tend to be outdoors more than adults, asthma is the most common chronic disorder worldwide (WHO 2006), the leading cause of missing school, and the leading cause of hospitalization (Eisele 2003). In the same way that the ozone damages human health, it affects the health of other animals and vegetation and damages buildings (C. Palmer 1997).

Hazardous Waste Sites and Brownfields

The story of Love Canal awakened the world to chemical dumping hazards (Breton 1998). During the 1940s and 1950s, the Hooker Electrochemical Company dumped 20,000 tons of chemicals into the Love Canal in Niagara Falls, New York (Center for Health, Environment and Justice 2001). In 1953, after filling the canal and covering it with dirt, the company sold the land to the Board of Education for a dollar. Homes and an elementary school were built next to the canal. By the late 1970s, dioxin and benzene chemicals began seeping through backyards and basements. Because of the efforts of the Love Canal Homeowners Association, state and federal agencies responded by cleaning the area and relocating many residents. In 1995, the Occidental Chemical Corporation (which bought out the Hooker Electrochemical Company) agreed to pay the government $129 million to cover the costs of the incident.

As a result of the Love Canal incident, the EPA created the Superfund program to clean hazardous waste sites. Hazardous materials may come from chemical manufacturers, electroplating companies, petroleum refineries, and common businesses such as dry cleaners, auto repair shops, hospitals, and photo processing centers (EPA 2003a). Sites may be placed on the national priority list (NPL) by their state if they meet specific hazard and cleanup criteria. As of December 2014, 1,322 NPL sites had been identified; of these, 385 sites had been removed from the list after cleanup efforts were completed (EPA 2014b).

Toxic sites continue to be identified today. The Childproofing Our Communities Campaign is a collaboration of groups concerned about children's environmental health. The campaign focuses on where children spend most of their time: in school. In its 2001 report, the campaign identified more than 1,100 public schools within a half-mile radius of known contaminated sites in California, Massachusetts,

TAKING A WORLD VIEW

HOME SWEET LANDFILL

China and the United States produce more waste than any other countries in the world. Traditional waste disposal includes incineration and landfills. Most U.S. waste, about 251 million tons per year, is sent to landfills. Each American creates 4.38 pounds of trash per day (EPA 2014c). Landfills have been identified as one of the largest emitters of greenhouse gases, primarily methane (an odorless, colorless gas caused by the decomposition of animal and plant matter).

Yet, in many countries, many individuals and families call landfills their homes. In Mexico, landfill residents are called *pepenadores*. To make money, they scavenge through garbage piles, finding items (appliances, metals, or clothing) that can be reused or sold. Meals are harvested from discarded waste, and they build their homes using scrap material. Matthew Power (2006) explains, "Household and industrial trash has become for the world's poor a more viable source of sustenance than agriculture and husbandry" (p. 62).

In his article "The Magic Mountain," Power (2006) focuses on life on Payatas, a 50-acre landfill in Quezon City, the Philippines. Here the scavengers are called *mangangalahigs*, which translated means "chicken scratchers," describing the way they pick through piles of trash. Payatas has been called the "second Smoky Mountain." The first Smoky Mountain was a landfill site in Manila that supported about 30,000 men, women, and children who lived on the landfill. In 1995, the Philippine government closed the site, moving residents to temporary housing. However, over time, some Smoky Mountain residents moved to Payatas and resumed their lives as mangangalahigs.

Power (2006) claims that so much garbage is piled at the Payatas dump that it would take 3,000 trucks a day for 11 years to move it all to another landfill. He writes,

> As trucks dump each new load with a shriek of gears and a sickening glorp of wet garbage, the

Those who live on or scavenge from landfills are at high risk for death or disease. Landfills are unsafe environments, producing methane gas, and leachate, a toxic fluid that is produced from compressed trash.

> scavengers surge forward, tearing open plastic bags, spearing cans and plastic bottles with choreographed efficiency. . . . The ability to discern value at a glimpse, to sift the useful out of the rejected with as little expenditure of energy as possible, is the great talent of the scavenger. (p. 62)

Scavengers can make as much as 150 pesos a day, about $3 for their work on the dump.

Scientists have collected global evidence identifying the unhealthy consequences of landfills on human health. An increased risk of adverse health effects (e.g., low birth weight, respiratory illnesses, birth defects, and certain types of cancers) has been found near individual landfill sites and in several multisite and multicountry studies (Vrijheid 2000).

A zero-waste movement is growing in the United States. Consumers and businesses are encouraged not to use polystyrene foam containers or any packaging that is not biodegradable. Several cities have initiated yard waste composting collection and expanded their collection of recyclable household items beyond the traditional paper, glass, and aluminum to include tires, batteries, and household appliances (Kaufman 2009).

Michigan, New Jersey, and New York. The campaign estimates that more than 600,000 students attend classes in schools near contaminated land (Center for Health, Environment and Justice 2001). In a state-by-state survey of laws and regulations regarding the siting of new school construction, the campaign reported that only 14 states restrict siting schools on or near hazardous or toxic waste sites, five states have cleanup standards for contaminated soil, and eight states have funding available for the cleanup process (Center for Health, Environment and Justice 2009).

In 2002, President Bush signed the Brownfields Revitalization Act, which authorized up to $250 million annually for the cleanup of brownfields. **Brownfields** are abandoned or underused industrial or commercial properties where expansion or redevelopment is complicated by the presence or potential presence of hazardous substances, pollutants, or contaminants. There are more than 450,000 sites throughout the United States. Redevelopment efforts have included restoring waterfront parks and converting landfills to golf courses, as well as commercial and business expansion (EPA 2003a).

Water Quality and Supply

A 2003 study conducted by the Pew Oceans Commission revealed a crisis in U.S. waters caused by pollution and fishing practices (Weiss 2003). The commission expressed concern about runoff from agricultural fields, lawns, and roads. Oil from gas stations and nutrients from agricultural fields disrupt the balance of river and ocean ecosystems, leaving very little dissolved oxygen in the waters. A dead zone in the Gulf of Mexico near the mouth of the Mississippi River stretches more than 5,000 miles long. With not enough oxygen for survival, there is little marine life within the zone. There are 200 dead zones in U.S. waters (the Gulf dead zone is the largest) and an estimated 400 to 1,000 dead zones worldwide (B. Palmer 2014).

Toxic substances are turning up with greater frequency in groundwater, the source of drinking water for one of every two Americans (Ehrlich and Ehrlich 1996). The EPA (2009a) reports, "While tap water that meets federal and state standards generally is safe to drink, threats to water quality and quantity are increasing." Our drinking water is monitored in more than 55,000 community water systems for more than 80 known contaminants, including arsenic, nitrates, human and animal fecal waste, and legionella (the cause of Legionnaire's Disease).

As the conflict perspective warns, economic activity also contributes to environmental damage. Hydraulic fracturing, or fracking, is the process of extracting natural gas from shale rock layers underground. A combination of water, sand, and chemicals is injected into the shale rock to release the gas. The process is controversial for its environmental impact on our water supply: first for the use of water in the extraction process and second for the chemicals that may contaminate the groundwater supply. The state of Vermont was the first U.S. state to ban fracking.

According to the United Nations, approximately 780 million people do not have access to a decent source of drinking water and 2.5 billion do not have access to

Brownfields:
Abandoned or underused industrial or commercial properties where hazardous substances, pollutants, or contaminants are present or potentially present

 Toxic Water

Waste and Recycling

In 2012, Americans generated 251 million tons of trash. Per person per day, this equates to 4.38 pounds of trash or municipal solid waste (MSW). The types of MSW we discarded are presented in Figure 15.1. Identify the top three MSW materials discarded in 2012.

Approximately 65% of the trash ends up in 1,500 landfills and incinerators; the rest of the material is recovered or recycled (refer Figure 15.2). In 2012, Americans recycled and composted 87 million tons of MSW.

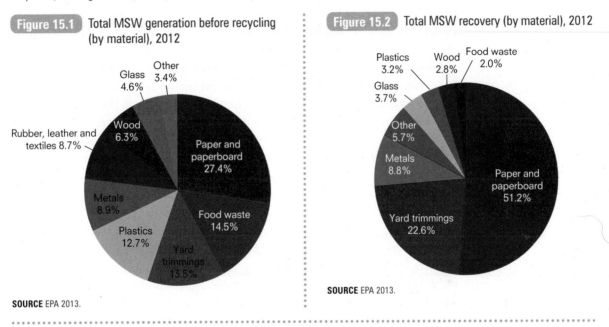

Figure 15.1 Total MSW generation before recycling (by material), 2012

Other 3.4%
Glass 4.6%
Wood 6.3%
Rubber, leather and textiles 8.7%
Paper and paperboard 27.4%
Metals 8.9%
Plastics 12.7%
Food waste 14.5%
Yard trimmings 13.5%

SOURCE EPA 2013.

Figure 15.2 Total MSW recovery (by material), 2012

Plastics 3.2%
Wood 2.8%
Food waste 2.0%
Glass 3.7%
Other 5.7%
Metals 8.8%
Paper and paperboard 51.2%
Yard trimmings 22.6%

SOURCE EPA 2013.

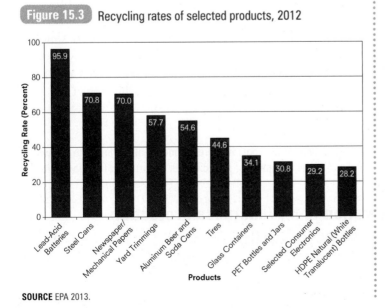

Figure 15.3 Recycling rates of selected products, 2012

Recycling Rate (Percent)

Lead-Acid Batteries 95.9
Steel Cans 70.8
Newspaper/ Mechanical Papers 70.0
Yard Trimmings 57.7
Aluminum Beer and Soda Cans 54.6
Tires 44.6
Glass Containers 34.1
PET Bottles and Jars 30.8
Selected Consumer Electronics 29.2
HDPE Natural (White Translucent) Bottles 28.2

Products

SOURCE EPA 2013.

WHAT DO YOU THINK?

The EPA (2013, p.10) explains the value of recycling:

Some waste products are recycled at a higher rate (refer to Figure 15.3).

Recycling has environmental benefits at every stage in the life cycle of a consumer product—from the raw material with which it's made to its final method of disposal. By utilizing used, unwanted, or obsolete materials as industrial feedstocks or for new materials or products, Americans can each do our part to make recycling, including composting work. Aside from reducing GHG [greenhouse gas] emissions, which contribute to global warming, recycling, including composting also provides significant economic and job creation impacts.

What items do you regularly recycle? How did you learn about recycling?

proper sanitation (Centers for Disease Control and Prevention 2014). Representatives from 100 countries at the World Water Forum recognized water as a basic human need. Other countries and organizations, including the WHO, have recognized water as a basic human right.

Only 1% of the world's water can be used for drinking. Nearly 97% of the water is salty or undrinkable; the other 2% is in ice caps and glaciers (EPA 2003b). Freshwater comes from surface water sources (lakes, rivers, and streams) and groundwater sources (wells and underground aquifers). About 66% of people get their drinking water from surface water sources. Large metropolitan areas rely on surface water, whereas small communities and rural areas depend on groundwater sources. In recent years, there has been growing concern about the availability of freshwater sources. Because of pollution, increasing urbanization, and sprawling development, we may be running out of freshwater.

Almost 30 million residents in seven western states (Colorado, Utah, Wyoming, New Mexico, Nevada, Arizona, and California) rely on the Colorado River for their drinking water. The river basin covers 240,000 square miles in the United States and a portion of northwestern Mexico. So much of the river is diverted for drinking and agricultural use that by the time it reaches the Sea of Cortez, it isn't much more than a trickle. A 2007 report by the National Research Council on the Colorado River concluded that the combination of limited water supplies, increasing population demands, warmer temperatures, and the prospect of future droughts is likely to cause conflict among existing and future water users. The report predicted that this would "inevitably lead to increasingly costly, controversial, and unavoidable trade-offs among water managers, policy makers, and their constituents" (National Academies 2007).

Since 2011, the state of California has been gripped by a severe drought, impacting the lives of many Californians through lost agricultural jobs, shrinking lakes and rivers, dead or dying lawns, and in some cases, dry toilets and washing machines. State leaders have had to make tough choices to meet the increasing demands on the state's limited water supply. The scientific community was split on whether the atmospheric conditions were due to natural variability or related to human-caused climate change. Some scientists attributed the drought to atmospheric conditions. Unusually warm temperatures and persistent ridges of high-pressure air over the northeastern Pacific prevented winter storms from reaching California during its typical 2013 and 2014 rainy seasons. The storms also bypassed Oregon and Washington (Than 2014).

· ·

What Does It Mean to Me?
Where does your drinking water come from? Is there a concern about limits to the water supply? Contact your local water company or public works department for information.

· ·

Land Conservation and Wilderness Protection

Efforts in land conservation and wilderness protection seem to be successful largely because of federal protection policies. Since adopting the 1964 Wilderness Act,

Congress has designated more than 106 million acres as "wilderness areas" through the National Wilderness Preservation System (2004). Under the act, timber cutting, mechanized vehicles, mining, and grazing activities are restricted. Human activity is limited to primitive recreation activities. The wilderness lands are protected for their ecological, historical, scientific, and experiential resources. The areas range in size from the smallest, Pelican Island, Florida (5 acres), to the largest, Wrangell–St. Elias, Alaska (almost 10 million acres of land).

The Endangered Species Act of 1973 attempts to preserve species of fish, wildlife, and plants that are of "aesthetic, ecological, educational, historical, recreational and scientific value to the Nation and its people." The act has been controversial because it preserves the interests of the species above economic and human interests. For example, if endangered species are present, the act will restrict what landowners can do on their land (C. Palmer 1997). Currently, 2,000 U.S. and foreign animal and plant species have been listed as endangered or threatened, with recovery plans approved or implemented for 1,138 species (U.S. Fish and Wildlife Service 2012). Although federal funding for the Endangered Species Act expired in October 1992, Congress has appropriated funds in each fiscal year to support the program.

The National Park System includes 397 national parks covering more than 84 million acres. Unlike the National Wilderness Preservation System, the National Park System allows and supports recreational activities. However, human activity in the form of motorized access, road and highway developments, logging, and pollution threatens the health of several national parks. The Great Smoky Mountains National Park is the most visited national park, with about 10 million visitors each year (National Parks Conservation Association 2003). The park features an ecosystem of rare plants and wildlife along with historical structures representing southern Appalachian culture, all of which are endangered according to the National Parks Conservation Association. The park has been listed as "endangered" for several years, primarily because of chronic air pollution problems. The pollution has been attributed to coal-fired power plants and other industrial sources. Local developers are allowed to build right up to the park's boundaries.

COMMUNITY, POLICY, AND SOCIAL ACTION

Federal Responses

The government's first response to the environment was directed at cleaning the nation's polluted water, air, and land. In 1969, Congress adopted the National Environmental Policy Act (NEPA), a comprehensive policy statement on our environment. For the first time in our nation's history, the government was committed to maintaining and preserving the environment (Caldwell 1970). The EPA, established in 1970, is charged with providing leadership in the nation's environmental science, research, education, and assessment efforts (EPA 2004). As the chief environmental agency, the EPA sets national standards and delegates to states and tribes the responsibility for issuing permits and monitoring and enforcing compliance. Beginning in the 1980s, the agency shifted its policies from cleanup to pollution management or prevention through market-based and collaborative mechanisms with business and industry and environmental strategic planning (Mazmanian and Kraft 1999). Additional environmental legislation, some of which we have already reviewed, includes the following:

- The Land and Water Conservation Fund Act and the Wilderness Act of 1964. In our discussion on land conservation, we already reviewed the Wilderness Act. The Land and Water Conservation Fund Act provides the necessary funds and assistance to states in planning, acquiring, and developing recreational lands and natural areas. The act also regulates admission and special user fees at national recreational areas. These two acts have been referred to as the "initial building blocks of environmental action" (Caulfield 1989:31).
- The Clean Air Act of 1970 regulates air emissions from area, stationary, and mobile sources. The act helped establish maximum pollutant standards. In 1990, the Clean Air Act was amended to address acid rain, ground-level ozone, ozone depletion, and air toxins. In 2003, seven state attorneys general filed a lawsuit against the EPA, accusing the agency of neglecting to update air pollution standards. The suit seeks regulations on carbon dioxide emissions, which are not listed under the Clean Air Act (Lee 2003). In 2007, the U.S. Supreme Court found in favor of the seven states, ruling that greenhouse gases are air pollutants covered by the Clean Air Act (EPA 2009b).
- The Clean Water Act followed in 1972. This act established standards and regulations regarding the discharge of pollutants into the waters of the United States. The EPA was authorized to implement pollution control programs, setting wastewater standards and water-quality standards for all contaminants in surface waters.
- The Endangered Species Act of 1973 created a program for the conservation of threatened and endangered plants and animals and their habitats.
- Under the Toxic Substances Control Act of 1976, the EPA has the authority to track 75,000 industrial chemicals being produced or imported into the United States.
- The Food Quality Protection Act of 1996 modified earlier statutes and created a single, health-based standard for all pesticides in foods.

In its strategic plan for 2014–2018, the EPA identified five goals: addressing climate change and improving air quality, protecting America's water supply, cleaning up communities and supporting sustainable development, ensuring the safety of chemicals and preventing pollution, and protecting human health and the environment through law enforcement and compliance.

State and Local Responses

The EPA highlights work done by states in "developing and implementing a range of programs and strategies that are cost-effectively reducing greenhouse gases, improving air quality, enhancing economic development and increasing the nation's energy security" (EPA 2007b). Calling state action "a key component of the U.S. response to climate change," the agency notes that 35 states and Puerto Rico have completed or implemented action plans for reducing greenhouse gas emissions or enhancing greenhouse gas capture.

Recognizing that there are no real borders for carbon emissions and becoming increasingly frustrated with the slow progress of federal legislation on the matter (Broder 2007), many state leaders formed regional coalitions to combat climate change. For example, the Regional Greenhouse Gas Initiative (RGGI) is a cooperative effort by northeastern and mid-Atlantic states to determine a regional strategy for controlling greenhouse gas emissions. In 2006, the Clean and Diversified Energy Initiative was signed by governors of 19 western states, along with those from American Samoa, Guam, and the Northern Mariana Islands. The goal of their initiative is to identify and produce affordable, sustainable, and environmentally responsible energy for the western states and islands.

Cities throughout the nation have embraced sustainability goals, along with environmentally responsible planning and consumption. In 2005, the U.S. Conference of Mayors endorsed the U.S. Mayors Climate Protection Agreement. Through the agreement, the mayors agreed to strive to meet or exceed Kyoto Protocol targets for reducing global warming pollution. More than 600 mayors have signed the agreement.

Two major U.S. cities made news for their environmental vision and leadership. Declaring New York City the "first environmentally sustainable twenty-first-century city," then-mayor Michael R. Bloomberg proposed a master plan to reduce energy consumption in six areas by 2030: land, transportation, water, energy, air quality, and climate change. Much of the plan would require state approval. One of the most contentious strategies involved the city's transportation burdens. Calling it "congestion pricing," Bloomberg proposed charging a fee for vehicles entering the city from 6 a.m. to 6 p.m. on weekdays—$8 for cars and $21 for trucks. The pricing plan would have reduced traffic congestion and improved air quality, as it has in parts of London and Singapore (Lueck 2007). Despite approval from the New York City Council, the state legislature failed to pass the pricing plan.

On the West Coast, San Francisco was the first city in the nation to ban the use of petroleum-based shopping bags. These plastic shopping bags take many years to degrade, meanwhile contaminating our land and water and endangering animal and marine life. Nearly 90% of all U.S. shopping bags are plastic. Beginning in 2007, plastic bags were to be replaced with biodegradable plastic bags or recyclable bags in San Francisco grocery and drug stores. Several countries, including Bhutan, Bangladesh, and China, have banned the use of nonbiodegradable plastic bags. Other countries, such as Germany and Ireland, charge a nominal fee for plastic shopping bags.

 Handling Smog

Environmental Interest Groups

Organizations concerned with the protection of the environment have played an important role in American politics since the foundation of the Sierra Club in 1892. The first wave of environmental interest groups included the National Audubon Society (1905), the National Parks Conservation Association (1919), and the National Wildlife Federation (1935). These groups were concerned with land conservation and the protection of specific sites and wildlife species. These first-wave groups depended on member support and involvement. These organizations remain among the most influential groups in the environmental movement (Ingram and Mann 1) and saved the University of New Hampshire $10,000 in waste (989).

As public attention shifted to the problems of environmental pollution, a second wave of environmental groups emerged during the 1960s and 1970s. These new organizations focused their efforts on fighting pollution. In general, the second wave of environmental groups adopted an ecological approach to our natural environment, recognizing the interrelationship between all living things and using science as a tool for understanding and protecting the environment. The Environmental Defense Fund (1967) and the Natural Resources Defense Council (1970) were started with funding support from the Ford Foundation. Both organizations relied on litigation as their instrument of reform. Other second-wave groups include Friends of the Earth, the Environmental Policy Institute, and Environmental Action. After the 1970s, environmental groups began to direct their appeals to policy makers rather than to the general public (Ingram and Mann 1989).

Although each group is committed to the environment, each has adopted its own cause, from broad environmental themes to such specific problems as toxic pollution or land conservation. The groups also have different strategies and tactics. Environmental groups may attempt to influence political policy, litigate environmental disputes, form coalitions with other environmental or interest groups, or endorse specific political candidates (Ingram and Mann 1989). Some, such as the Sea Shepherd Conservation Society, which rams and sinks whaling vessels throughout the world's oceans, adopt "in-your-face" tactics.

Now more than 75 years old, the National Wildlife Federation has eleven field offices and 47 state affiliates, including Washington, DC, and the Virgin Islands. The affiliates operate at the grassroots level by working to educate, encourage, and facilitate conservation efforts at the state level. One such organization is the Arkansas Wildlife Federation, established in 1936 by a group of sportsmen. The federation's goal has been to serve as a leader in educating people about conservation issues and in encouraging responsible stewardship of the state's natural resources. The federation, which represents a variety of constituents—hunters, sportsmen, hikers, anglers, and campers (Arkansas Wildlife Federation 2003a)—sponsors a variety of educational and community activities and projects. Seminars are offered to the public covering issues such as forest management, wetlands and water management, hunting, and fishing. The federation sponsors annual conservation achievement awards to

 Green Schools Initiative

honor citizens and organizations dedicated to natural resource endeavors. The organization also sponsors political candidate forums where citizens can ask candidates about their positions on various conservation and environmental issues (Arkansas Wildlife Federation 2003b).

A new environmental interest group is the Earth Island Institute, founded in 1982 by David Brower, who was the first executive director of the Sierra Club and cofounder of Friends of the Earth. The institute supports more than 100 projects worldwide, pledging to support campaigns "dedicated to conserving, preserving, and restoring the ecosystems on which our civilization depends" (Earth Island Institute 2010). The organization also honors youth for their environmental community work. Among those recognized in 2013 was Alex Freid, a University of New Hampshire student. At the end of his freshman year, Freid was stunned by the amount of good and usable items discarded when students moved out of their dorm rooms and apartments. He was inspired to establish the Post-Landfill Action Network or PLAN, a nonprofit cooperative network that helps college students create zero-waste solutions on their campuses. Within three years, PLAN diverted more than 100 tons of reusable waste from landfills and saved the University of New Hampshire $10,000 in waste disposal costs (Brower Youth Awards 2013).

Environmental Justice Movement

Sherry and Charles Cable (1995) argue that the grassroots environmental movement has improved the lives of many individuals and has spread environmental awareness among the public. In contrast to national environmental organizations, grassroots organizations usually consist of working-class participants, people of color, and women. Although experienced organizers or community activists lead some groups, many grassroots groups are led by inexperienced but passionate leaders. In the fight against environmental racism, these grassroots environmental groups have given a voice to communities of color (Epstein 1995) and have redefined environmental protection as a basic right (Bullard and Johnson 2000).

Grassroots organizations emphasize environmental justice, acting in the belief that some injustice has been committed by a corporation, business, or industry and that appropriate action should be taken to correct, improve, or remove the injustice(s). Environmental justice is defined as "the fair treatment and meaningful involvement of all people regardless of race, color, national origin, or income with respect to the development, implementation, and enforcement of environmental laws, regulations and policies" (Bullard and Johnson 2000:558). The movement embraces a holistic approach in creating environmental health policies and regulations: ensuring community-based collaborative partnerships, enhancing public participation in environmental decisions, promoting community empowerment, and ensuring community-based sustainable economic development (Bullard and Johnson 2000).

IN FOCUS

LOCAL AND SUSTAINABLE FOOD

After cars, our food system uses more fossil fuel than any other sector of the economy, about 19% (Pollan 2008). According to the Worldwatch Institute, food in the average American meal travels about 1,500 miles from farm to home. Food is brought into most communities via trucks, trains, or airplanes in refrigerated or storage containers. The 1,500-mile meal is said to consume as much as four times the energy and produce four times as much greenhouse gas emissions as a locally grown meal (Ketcham 2007). In addition to energy expended for transport, concern has been expressed over the amount of fossil fuel energy used in producing the food products brought to our table. In 2009, the Swedish National Food Administration began requiring the reporting of carbon dioxide emissions associated with the production of specific foods. For example, one serving per week of beef from dairy cows produces 120 kilograms of carbon dioxide emissions per year. The information will appear on some grocery items and restaurant menus throughout the country (Rosenthal 2009).

In response, environmentalists and foodies (people who have an avid interest in the latest food fads)

Local farmer's markets, like this one in Seattle, Washington, help support local farmers and encourage seasonal food consumption.

throughout the United States and elsewhere in the world have adopted what is referred to as the 100-Mile Diet. For a week, a month, a year, or life, the rules of the diet are simple: you may only consume food grown and produced within a 100-mile radius of your home. Called locavores, these 100-mile eaters advocate the value in being able to know the source of your food, supporting the local

---

These organizations have tackled a variety of environmental problems and have sought justice for housing, transportation, air quality, and economic development issues (Bullard 1994). In 2011, responding to the nuclear fallout from the Fukushima nuclear plant, citizen monitoring groups were formed across Japan. Men and women armed with dosimeters began taking radiation readings near their homes. The organized effort grew out of a perceived lack of government response and citizens' disbelief in the government's insistence that the nuclear fallout would not pose a threat or contaminate food sources (Tabuchi 2011).

Sociologists Riley Dunlap and Angela Mertig (1992) note that the environmental movement is among the few movements that have "significantly changed society" (p. xi). Nicolas Freudenberg and Carol Steinsapir (1992:33–35) identify seven achievements of grassroots organizations:

economy, and eating fresh and healthy food in season. They argue, "The distance from which our food comes represents our separation from the knowledge of how and by whom what we consume is produced, processed and transported" (Locavores 2007). This is not a diet for fast-food junkies.

Canadians Alisa Smith and J. B. MacKinnon first coined the term *100-Mile Diet* when they began a yearlong local food experiment in Vancouver, British Columbia. The couple discovered several food items that they had to live without for most or part of the year, such as chocolate, coffee, and wheat. (Most locavores make exceptions for these items, including salt and spices.) Unable to purchase local bread and wheat for baking, for one lunch meal, MacKinnon, the family chef, fashioned bread out of turnip slices. But the couple found success (eventually finding a local supplier of wheat) and satisfaction in their diet. Their experience helped fuel broader interest in the benefits of a 100-mile diet.

One way to support local agriculture is through community-supported agriculture (CSA), a partnership between community members and an independent local farm. The CSA movement began in Japan almost 30 years ago with a group of women who were concerned about pesticides, the increase in processed foods, and their country's shrinking rural population. Community members purchase seasonal shares, for about $300 to $400, which entitles them to weekly food allowances throughout the growing season. According to FoodRoutes .org, independent local farms encourage biodiversity by diversifying the local landscape and natural environment. The CSA arrangement is beneficial to the farmer and to his or her customers. Customers receive fresh produce and have the satisfaction of supporting a local business. Customers can help at the farm and provide input and suggestions to their farmer. Instead of spending time marketing produce, farmers can focus their efforts on growing quality produce and working with their community members.

Alongside first graders from Bancroft Elementary School in Washington, DC, Michelle Obama broke ground on an organic vegetable garden on the South Lawn of the White House. This is the first garden at the White House since Eleanor Roosevelt's World War II victory garden. The garden was planted with a variety of lettuces, greens, and herbs as well as a patch of berries. At the planting, Mrs. Obama expressed her interest in promoting healthy eating and local food, particularly from the more than 1 million community gardens throughout the country.

1. A number of environmentally hazardous facilities have been controlled by cleaning up contaminated sites, blocking the construction of new facilities, and upgrading corporate pollution control equipment.

2. Grassroots organizations have forced businesses to consider the environmental consequences of their actions.

3. These groups encourage preventative approaches to environmental problems, such as reducing or limiting the use of environmental contamination.

4. The grassroots movement has expanded citizens' right to participate in environmental decision making.

5. Grassroots organizations have served as psychological and social support networks for victims and their families.

VOICES IN THE COMMUNITY

CHAD PREGRACKE

Chad Pregracke started his career as an environmental activist in his own backyard. A native of Hampton, Illinois, he spent most of his life on the shores of the Mississippi River as a resident, shell diver, and commercial fisherman. Pregracke often saw garbage floating on the river or caught within its banks.

Chad Pregracke, founder of Living Lands and Waters, sits atop on of his river clean-up barges.

> I woke up like that many times—loving the natural world and hating the despicable mess. I saw the garbage on the river, and it didn't look right. It may have been commonplace, but I didn't like it and I didn't accept it. And the more garbage sites I noticed, the more it made me want to do something about it. (Pregracke and Barrow 2007:12–13)

He admits that his attempts to organize and fund his first river cleanup were less than perfect. He recalls how he did everything wrong. He didn't have a clear message, didn't have a plan, and didn't talk to the right people at local agencies. But he persevered and received funding from his first corporate sponsor, the Alcoa Corporation. Pregracke started cleaning up the river in 1997, collecting 45,000 pounds of debris from its shores. In 1998, Pregracke established his nonprofit organization, Living Lands and Waters (LLW), dedicated to cleaning up the Mississippi River.

Since its establishment, LLW has removed 4 million pounds of trash from the Mississippi and its tributary rivers Missouri and Ohio. The cleanup efforts are staffed primarily by community volunteers. Their annual haul of trash includes items such as refrigerators, tires, bowling balls, baby dolls, and Styrofoam. In August 2005, Pregracke and his crew provided assistance with cleanup and rebuilding efforts in New Orleans after Hurricane Katrina struck the area. In 2007, the MillionTrees Project was established to encourage the planting and growth of 1 million native hardwood nut-bearing trees throughout the Midwest.

Pregracke is modest in describing his life's mission:

> I've been on a mission to clean up the rivers. It was a simple concept then and it's a simple concept now, but doing it has been far from simple or easy. I realize that we're not solving all the problems or necessarily saving America's rivers—we're simply doing our part, just as I hope you're doing yours. (Pregracke and Barrow 2007:282–83)

> We all make a difference, even if we don't intend to, and it's either negative or positive. My question to you is, how big a difference do you want to make? I can't say how big a difference I've made or will continue to make, but I know this—I will plant a lot of trees and leave a cleaner river. (Pregracke and Barrow 2007:288)

For his work, Pregracke was named 2013 CNN Hero of the Year. For more information about Living Lands and Waters, visit the organization's website at http://www.livinglandsandwaters.org.

6. The movement has brought environmental concerns and action to working-class and minority Americans.

7. The grassroots movement has influenced how the general public thinks about the environment and public health.

Radical Environmentalists

Rik Scarce (1990) explains that radical environmentalists want to preserve our biological diversity. This isn't just a question of preserving the living things in our ecosystem, such as plants and animals; nonliving entities such as mountains, rivers, and oceans must also be protected. Radical groups confront problems through direct action, such as picketing an office building, breaking the law, or performing acts of civil disobedience. Other radical environmentalists may destroy machinery, property, or equipment used to build roads, kill animals, or harvest trees. Most "eco-warriors" act on their own and without the leadership of an organizational hierarchy.

Scarce (1990) says radical environmentalists adopt lifestyles that have minimal impact on the environment: they don't own cars, they adopt vegetarian diets, and they avoid occupations that involve the destruction of the environment. Although they are committed to their issues, radical environmentalists recognize that on their own, they will never be able to end the practices they protest. Their actions usually attract media attention, creating a groundswell of public support for their particular issues. Or their actions are done in concert with mainstream efforts; for example, radicals might stage tree sittings in Oregon to delay the cutting of timber until courts can hear a more mainstream group's request for injunction.

Tree sitting is a form of protest targeting timber companies at the point of production, slowing or even stopping tree cutting. Scarce (1990) explains how tree sitters make their protest in areas with active cutting, finding and choosing trees that will make the right statement. The trees they choose are the tallest, most impressive, and clearly visible from a road, or those that overlook a recently cut area. Although we may think of tree sitting as a lonely activity, tree sitters require a support group for assistance, food, and clothing, including the hauling of waste (including human) from the site. The group will carry about 250 pounds of gear and provisions—food, water, clothing, and platform materials—as far as 10 miles to their intended site. Suspended about 80 to 150 feet off the ground, the 2.5- by 6-foot wooden platform becomes the tree sitter's home for days, weeks, or months. Julia "Butterfly" Hill sat in a 600-year-old California redwood tree for 738 days, withstanding eviction threats and legal action from the Pacific Lumber Company, which owned the tree. Tree sitting has been effective in bringing public and media attention to the practices of timber and logging companies and in rallying support for the tree sitter's message. In several cases, agreements have been made with lumber companies to divert logging to other areas or to pursue viable logging programs.

Is Your School Green?

Several hundred green U.S. elementary and secondary schools have been established nationally, supported by state grants, legislation, and partners such as the Sierra Club and the National Wildlife Federation. Schools like the Environmental Charter High School in Los Angeles and the Growing Up Green Charter School in Long Island City, Queens, New York, offer students more than an environmental issues curriculum. These private, charter, and traditional public schools have adopted a focus that goes beyond the environment, addressing politics, social justice, environmental careers, social activism, and community involvement (Navarro and Bhanoo 2010). In 2012, New York City instituted a school composting program for 230 school buildings in Manhattan, Brooklyn, and Staten Island. In addition to creating composting material for farmers and local landscapers, the program creates cost savings (reducing the amount of food that goes to waste) and helps develop a new generation of conservationists (Baker 2014).

"Universities are huge institutions with huge carbon footprints, but they are also laboratories for concepts of sustainability," says Michael Crow, president of Arizona State University (Deutsch 2007:A21). Colleges and universities are taking the environmental lead by constructing green buildings, purchasing alternative energy, incorporating local and sustainable food products, and investing in efforts to make campuses carbon neutral. Their efforts include the following (Deutsch 2007; Lipka 2006):

- Bowdoin and Evergreen State Colleges purchase 100% of their energy from renewable sources or pay for energy offsets from solar or wind power.
- Arizona State University distributes free bus passes to every student, employee, and faculty member.
- Dickinson College students operate an organic garden, using some of the produce in their campus dining hall.
- Students at Central Oregon Community College and the University of Kentucky voted to pay additional fees to cover their institutions' clean-energy purchases.
- University of California–Irvine, University of Massachusetts–Amherst, Montana State University, and Eastern Tennessee State University are just some of the schools that have established a local chapter of the Real Food Challenge, an organization that promotes just and sustainable food systems on college campuses and in their communities.

Crow was among the first university presidents who signed the American College and University Presidents' Climate Commitment. The presidents acknowledge their role in leading environmental responsibility in their campuses and broader communities. The commitment, signed by more than 600 college and university presidents, includes a pledge to develop and implement a plan to achieve carbon neutrality on their campuses. Ninety college dorms are certified in Leadership in Energy and Environmental Design (LEED), the national standard for green design (Wilson 2009).

Writer Sara Lipka (2006) portrays college students as the "watchdogs for sustainability." She explains,

> Armed with Internet research, they are investigating institutional operations like energy use, food purchasing, investments, transportation, and waste disposal. They are pushing administrators to approve new projects and set higher goals for sustainability. National networks are helping students share strategies with one another and organize sophisticated, often successful proposals for campus innovations and reforms. (Lipka 2006:11)

Similar environmental programs have been established in elementary and secondary schools across the country. To learn more about what you can do to protect the environment, refer to Table 15.4.

Table 15.4 Living green: Tips for college and university students

	Tips
1.	Practice the three *R*s: Reduce, Reuse, and Recycle.
2.	Use less ink and paper. If possible, print on both sides of the page. Think twice about whether you need a hard copy of a webpage or document. Could you bookmark a page or save a file on your computer?
3.	Limit your use of disposable products. This includes cups, plates, and paper napkins. The next time you grab a handful of napkins at your dining hall or in a restaurant, ask yourself if you really need that many. One might be enough.
4.	Use compact fluorescent light bulbs in your dorm room or apartment. They may cost more, but they will last longer and save you money.
5.	Walk, bike, and limit the use of your car.
6.	Carry a refillable water bottle. Stop using bottled water.
7.	Buy recycled products; this includes paper for printing.
8.	Use refillable binders instead of notebooks. Or go electronic and take all your notes on your laptop.
9.	Buy used clothing and furniture. It is a great way to save money, and it is a great thing to do for the environment.
10.	Share your message: Tell others how you are living green on your campus.

SOURCE: Adapted from Rockler-Gladen 2007.

SOCIOLOGY AT WORK

RESEARCH

Tiffany Fackler—Class of 2009

Undergraduate Major:
Sociology, Anthropology

Undergraduate Minor: Human Services

As discussed in Chapter 4's Sociology at Work feature, your coursework in research methods and statistics provides you with important data analytic skills. Such skills are requisite for occupations such as market or survey research. Many organizations and businesses routinely require data collection and analyses as part of their operations. Employees may be responsible for all or part of the research process—data collection, analysis, and reporting.

As an undergraduate, Tiffany Fackler completed an internship related to law enforcement. Her experience eventually led her to her current position as a criminal analyst for several state agencies.

Daily I am working with law enforcement agents both tactically and strategically to ensure that they are being provided accurate information regarding subjects and subject matter. I run information through, pull from and input data into databases, create link analysis charts, write intelligence reports and assist with making connections among individuals conducting illegal activities.

Sociology is an important part of Tiffany's work life.

Utilizing sociology at work occurs even when I am not realizing I am using it. The job requirements in their nature require the use of sociology. Every day there is analysis of social behavior, where it comes from, the development of social behavior, organizations and institutions. Within the law enforcement and intelligence realm there are always changes occurring with social order. In order to appropriately report on social order and disorder, utilizing empirical investigation and critical analysis is imperative.

She says, "I truly believe that regardless of what position you hold after graduation, sociology can always be utilized."

Tiffany's primary source of career information was her adviser, though she also utilized her university's career services office and reviewed résumé writing for federal employment. She is currently enrolled in a master's program in leadership and business ethics.

CHAPTER REVIEW

15.1 Explain the relationship between human activity and environmental problems

Daily human activity, economic development, cultural values, social class, and technology all affect the health of the environment. Environmental sociology considers the interactions between our physical and natural environments and our social organization and behavior.

15.2 Review the different sociological perspectives on environmental problems

From a functionalist perspective, agriculture, industrialization, and related technologies may have improved our quality of life, but they have also led to waste, pollution, and the destruction of natural resources. Conflict theorists suggest that environmental problems are created by humans competing for power, income, and their own interests in a capitalist system. Feminists argue that a masculine worldview is responsible for the domination of nature, women, and minorities. One strand of thought, ecofeminism, believes that men are the primary culprits in the exploitation of animals and the environment. Interaction theorists address how environmental problems are created, defined, and often contested.

15.3   Discuss climate change and global warming

The terms are often used interchangeably but are two different environmental events. Climate change refers to any significant change in the measures of climate (temperature or precipitation) lasting for an extended period of time. Global warming refers to the ongoing rise in the global average temperature near the Earth's surface.

15.4   Summarize federal and state responses to environmental problems

Efforts in land conservation and wilderness protection seem to be successful largely because of federal protection policies and legislation. Examples, among many, are the Wilderness Act, the Endangered Species Act, and the formation of the Environmental Protection Agency (EPA).

15.5   Compare the first wave and second wave of environmental interest groups

Environmental organizations have played an important role in American politics since the foundation of the Sierra Club in 1892. First-wave groups (such as the National Audubon Society) were concerned with land conservation and the protection of specific sites and species, and they rely on member support and involvement. A second wave of environmental groups, which emerged during the 1960s and 1970s, includes the Environmental Defense Fund and the Natural Resources Defense Council. They focus on fighting pollution, and they adopt an ecological approach, recognizing the interrelationship between all living things and using science as a tool for understanding and protecting the environment.

15.6   Assess the impact of the environmental movement

The environmental movement has had a significant impact in controlling hazardous facilities, urging businesses to consider environmental impact, encouraging preventative approaches to problems, expanding citizens' rights to participate in decision making, bringing concerns and action to working-class and minority Americans, and influencing how the general public thinks about the environment.

KEY TERMS

brownfields, 438

climate change, 432

environmental justice, 429

environmental racism, 428

environmental sociology, 424

global warming, 432

megadisaster, 422

natural capitalism, 428

particulate or particle pollution, 434

smog or ground-level ozone, 435

STUDY QUESTIONS

1. Explain the association of human action and environmental problems.

2. From a functionalist perspective, how has human behavior and our way of life contributed to environmental problems?

3. Explain how women contributed to the environmental justice movement.

4. Identify the six factors related to the construction of an environmental problem. From this perspective, how has climate change been defined as a social problem? Or hasn't it?

5. How have interest groups and grassroots movements contributed to the success of the environmental movement?

6. What are the strategies of radical environmentalists?

$SAGE edge™

Sharpen your skills with SAGE edge at **edge.sagepub.com/leonguerrero5e**

SAGE edge provides a personalized approach to help you accomplish your coursework goals in an easy-to-use learning environment.

16

War and Terrorism

The secure life that many Americans took for granted changed on the morning of September 11, 2001 (Hoge and Rose 2001); we now live in a subtly different country (Danner 2011). It is a country whose public and political discourse has been preoccupied with war, terrorism, suicide bombs, torture, patriotism, and human loss. There is an awareness of war and terrorism in other countries and ultimately concern over whether these conflicts will threaten U.S. national security. Sociologists acknowledge that "war is never an isolated act" (Clausweitz 1984:78) and that the consequences are felt and experienced beyond specific battlefields and borders.

A decade after 9/11, a wave of revolutionary demonstrations and protests swept across the Arab world. It began in Tunisia on December 17, 2010, when a police officer took away Mohamed Bouazizi's vegetable cart because Bouazizi didn't have a license to sell his goods. After his confrontation with the police and after local officials refused to hear his complaint, Bouazizi set himself on fire in front of the provincial headquarters. Bouazizi's martyrdom spurred a "people's revolution" (Abouzeid 2011). Tunisians took to the streets in protest, ultimately leading to the end of President Zine El Abidine Ben Ali's authoritarian rule. The Arab Spring extended to other countries where citizens participated in public demonstrations, some relatively peaceful, to protest the hardships and cruelties under ruling regimes. Ruling governments were overthrown in Egypt, Libya, and Yemen.

Revolutionary demonstrations and protests continued into 2014. On September 26, hundreds of students gathered in central Hong Kong,

demanding an end to Chinese oppression and control. These protests have been referred to as the Umbrella Revolution, after the umbrellas used by protesters to shield themselves from tear gas and later as shelter from the pouring rain. Forced to disband by the end of the year, the student protestors vowed to continue their anti-government campaign. In sharp contrast, the Islamic State in Iraq and Greater Syria (ISIS) made headlines in the same year for releasing graphic video of the beheading of foreign captives, including U.S. journalists James Foley and Steven Sotloff and U.S. aid worker Peter Kassig. Formerly al-Qaeda in Iraq, ISIS has become known for its brutal and brazen tactics. President Obama pledged to degrade and ultimately destroy ISIS.

DEFINING CONFLICT

War

Genocide: The systematic targeting of members of an ethnic or a religious group

Politicide: The systematic targeting of specific groups because of their political beliefs

War is a violent political instrument (Walter 1964). It is a violent activity between armed combatants, one side hoping to impose its will on the other. Whether or not war has been declared by its leadership, war involves armed conflict between two or more states or military forces. The majority of today's wars are civil wars (fought within, not between, countries), and most often, they take place in the poorest countries.

The United Kingdom, France, and Russia have fought the most international armed conflicts since the end of World War II (refer to Table 16.1). The most conflict-prone countries (including civil wars) have been Myanmar (also known as Burma), India, and Ethiopia (Human Security Report Project 2011).

Table 16.1 Countries that have experienced the highest number of state-based armed conflicts, 1946 to 2008

Country	Number of Wars
United Kingdom	25
France	22
Russia	19
United States	17
India	14
Ethiopia	10
Myanmar (Burma)	10
China	9

SOURCE: Human Security Report Project 2011.

What Does It Mean to Me?

In 2014, polls revealed that more Americans believe the country is less safe now than before the September 11, 2001, attacks (Murray 2014). Are you concerned about a terrorist attack on U.S. soil? Do you believe we are at risk of an attack from domestic or foreign terrorists? Explain the reason for your answer.

Since 1945, there have been 140 civil wars throughout the world, killing approximately 20 million people and displacing about 67 million. Civil wars typically occur in developing countries and are fought by small, poorly trained, poorly armed forces that avoid major military engagements, but frequently target civilians (Human Security Report Project 2005). **Genocide** (the systematic targeting of ethnic or religious groups) and **politicide**

The Rise of ISIS

(targeting specific groups because of their political beliefs) have been part of many civil wars. In the competition for political power and economic resources, ethno-political conflict and violence were at the heart of the wars in Cambodia (1977–1979), Rwanda (1994), Somalia (1991–2000), and Western Sudan (2003–present). In 1994, 800,000 Tutsis were massacred by the majority Hutu ethnic group in Rwanda.

. . . .

What Does It Mean to Me?

War and violence are not the only means to achieve one's goals. Nelson Mandela, the late president of South Africa, was revered as a global symbol of peace and nonviolence. His personal path to peace began with forgiving those who imprisoned him for 27 years. Is it easier to wage war with others than to find a nonviolent way to address a conflict?

. . . .

U.S. Conflicts

"The United States was born of violence and revolution," writes Ken Cunningham (2004), "violence against the native population and among and against the various European imperial powers" (p. 556). Our nation's birth was marked by a war—the American Revolution of 1775 to 1783. In 1776, the Declaration of Independence was adopted, a public statement of a new nation's independence from Great Britain and its rights to "life, liberty, and the pursuit of happiness." The British were defeated in 1783. More than 4,000 lives were lost in the revolution against the British.

More than 3 million Americans fought in the Civil War (1861–1865). The bloodiest battle on U.S. soil led to more than 600,000 casualties, about 2 percent of the Northern and Southern population at the time.

The American Revolution was followed by the War of 1812 (1812–1815) and the Mexican War (1846–1848), both part of the economic and continental expansion of the United States. The effort was justified under the principle of manifest destiny. U.S. leaders felt it was their mission to extend freedom and democracy to others. At the end of the Mexican War, the United States acquired the northern part of Mexico, later dividing the area into Arizona, California, Nevada, New Mexico, and Utah. A **revolution** constitutes an overthrow of the existing government or political structure. Revolutions do not always lead to violent conflict.

The Civil War (1861–1865) between northern and southern states has been referred to as the bloodiest battle on U.S. soil. Although we tend to think that the war was waged solely over the issue of slavery, it was also based on deep economic, political, and social differences between the two groups of states. During his second inaugural address in 1865, President Abraham Lincoln said, "One of them would make war rather than let the nation survive, and the other would accept war rather than let it perish, and the war came." More than 600,000 died.

Revolution: An overthrow of the existing government or political structure

Beginning with the Spanish–American War (1898), U.S. troops and soldiers began to wage war in other countries, mostly responding to tyranny, oppression, and communism. The Spanish–American War was fought to liberate Cuba from Spain and to protect U.S. interests in Cuban sugar, tobacco, and iron industries. U.S. participation during World War I (1917–1918) and World War II (1940–1945) helped establish its dominance as a worldwide military force. That accomplishment, however, came at a great cost: the United States had heavy losses, 53,000 deaths in World War I and 400,000 deaths in World War II. In the latter war, the United States and its allies claimed victory against Germany, Japan, and Italy. After the North Korean People's Army invaded the Republic of Korea, the United States joined UN forces in the Korean War (1950–1953). No winner of the war has ever been declared. An armistice was agreed upon in 1953, forever separating North and South Korea. Fifty years after the invasion, Communist and UN soldiers still guard their sides of the demilitarized zone in Panmunjom. The United States fought against North Vietnamese Communists in the jungles of South Vietnam from 1964 to 1973. Although U.S. troops had begun withdrawing from Vietnam in 1969, the formal cease-fire was declared in January 1973.

U.S. engagement in Middle East wars began with the Persian Gulf War of 1990 to 1991. The United States was joined by UN forces to liberate Kuwait from Iraqi forces. Operations Desert Shield and Desert Storm were the first display of high-tech warfare: cruise missiles, stealth fighters, and precision-guided munitions. Iraq accepted the terms for the cease-fire in April 1991. After September 11, 2001, U.S. forces attacked Afghanistan in an effort to destroy al-Qaeda forces and to locate their leader, Osama bin Laden. The first war of the 21st century was the U.S. war against Iraq (2003–2011) and Afghanistan (2003–2014). Though the U.S. combat mission in Afghanistan officially ended in 2014, a new phase of U.S. military operations was established in 2015. More than 9,000 U.S. troops support the NATO-led Resolute Support Mission to combat-train, advise, and assist Afghan national security forces (White House 2014). As of December 11, 2014, the number of reported military casualties (killed in action or non-hostile deaths) was 4,425 for Operation Iraqi Freedom and 2,354 for Operation Enduring Freedom in Afghanistan. A listing of U.S. wars and casualties is presented in Table 16.2. The list does not include the numerous American Indian Wars, the conflicts between American settlers and the U.S. federal government and the indigenous populations of North America.

Terrorism

Terrorism: The unlawful use of force to intimidate or coerce compliance with a particular set of beliefs; can be either domestic (based in the United States) or foreign (supported by foreign groups threatening the security of U.S. nationals or U.S. national security)

Terrorism is a specific form of conflict. According to the U.S. federal code, **terrorism** is "the unlawful use of force or violence against persons or property to intimidate or coerce a government, the civilian population, or any segment thereof, in furtherance of political or social objectives" (28 C.F.R. Section 0.85). Todd Sandler (2011) offers the following definition of terrorism: "the premeditated use or threat to use violence by individuals or subnational groups to obtain political or social objectives through the intimidation of a large audience beyond that of the immediate victims" (p. 280).

Table 16.2 America's wars and casualties (dates indicate U.S. troop involvement)

War	Participants	Deaths in Service
American Revolution 1775–1783	Unknown	4,435
War of 1812 1812–1815	286,730	2,260
Mexican War 1846–1848	78,718	13,283
Civil War, Union Only 1861–1865	2,213,363	364,511
Spanish–American War 1898–1902	306,760	2,446
World War I 1917–1918	4,734,991	116,516
World War II 1941–1945	16,112,566	405,399
Korean War 1950–1953	5,720,000	36,576
Vietnam War 1964–1973	8,744,000	58,209
Persian Gulf War 1990–1991	2,322,000	382

SOURCE: U.S. Department of Veterans Affairs 2007.

Political terrorism expert Grant Wardlaw (1988) states, "Terrorism is a phenomenon that is increasingly coming to dominate our lives." The effects of terrorism are widespread:

It influences the way governments conduct their foreign policy and corporations transact their business. It causes changes to the structure and role of our security forces and necessitates huge expenditures on measures to protect public figures, vital installations, citizens and perhaps in the final analysis, our system of government. It affects the way we travel, the places we visit and the manner in which we live our daily lives. (Wardlaw 1988:206)

Domestic terrorism is defined as terrorism supported or coordinated by groups or individuals based in a country. The venue and targets are also in the same country. Domestic terrorist groups are likely to be found in large countries and are found more often in democracies than in authoritarian states (Human Security Report Project 2005). **International terrorism** is defined as terrorism supported or coordinated by foreign groups threatening the security of another nation or its citizens. For example, international terrorism can occur outside the United States but may be directed at U.S. targets. Acts of terrorism have occurred on every continent, and perpetrators come from diverse religious and ethnic groups; however, Islamic governments and networks have committed the most extreme acts of terror (Booth and Dunne 2002). Though in terms of the number killed, international terrorism poses far less of a threat than do other forms of political violence or violent crime, it is an important human security issue (Human Security Report Project 2005). Al-Qaeda and ISIS have come to symbolize terrorism in the 21st century.

Paul Pillar (2001) explains that there are five elements of terrorism: First, terrorism is a premeditated act. It requires intent and prior decision to commit an act of terrorism. Terrorism doesn't happen by accident; rather, it is the result of an individual's or a group's policy or decision. Second, terrorism is purposeful; it is political in its motive to change or challenge the status quo. Religiously oriented or national terrorists are driven by social forces or shaped by circumstances specific to their particular religious or nationalistic experiences (Reich 1998). According to Max Abrahms (2012), terrorist groups have process and outcome goals. **Process goals** are aimed to sustain the group and its activities by securing financial support, gaining media attention, and boosting group morale. **Outcome goals** are the group's stated political ends, which require the cooperation of the target authority or government. Third, terrorism is not like a war in which both sides can shoot at one another. Terrorism targets noncombatants, such as civilians who cannot defend themselves against the violence. The direct targets of terrorist activity are not the main targets. Fourth, terrorism is usually carried out by subnational groups or clandestine agents. If uniformed military soldiers attack a group, it is considered an act of war; an attack conducted by nongovernmental perpetrators is considered terrorism. Individuals acting alone may also commit terrorism. Finally, terrorism includes the threat of violence. It does not involve only terrorist acts that may have occurred; it also involves the potential for future attacks.

Terrorist activity has changed little over the years. Six basic tactics account for 95% of all incidents: bombings, assassinations, armed assaults, kidnappings, hijackings, and other kinds of hostage seizures. As Brian Jenkins (1988) states, "terrorists blow up things, kill people, or seize hostages. Every terrorist attack is merely a variation on these three activities" (p. 257).

Domestic terrorism: Terrorism supported or coordinated by groups or individuals based in a country

International terrorism: Terrorism supported or coordinated by foreign groups threatening the security of U.S. nationals or the national security of the United States

Process goals: Related to terrorism, goals aimed to sustain the group and its activities by securing financial support, gaining media attention, and boosting group morale

Outcome goals: Related to terrorism, the group's stated political ends, which require cooperation of the target authority or government

. . . .

What Does It Mean to Me?

In 2014, polls revealed that more Americans believe the country is less safe now than before the September 11, 2001, attacks (Murray 2014). Are you concerned about a terrorist attack on U.S. soil? Do you believe we are at risk of an attack from domestic or foreign terrorists? Explain the reason for your answer.

. . . .

SOCIOLOGICAL PERSPECTIVES ON WAR AND TERRORISM

Functionalist Perspective

Functionalists examine how conflicts help maintain the social order, creating and reinforcing social, religious, or national boundaries. War creates social stability by letting everyone know what side they are on: the good guys versus the bad guys or us versus them. There are norms and boundaries in war: Individuals will know what their roles are, what they should believe in, how they should respond in case of an attack, and how they should interact with members of the other side. But unlike war, the social boundaries in terrorist activities are less certain. In some cases, the identity of terrorists and their goals may never be known.

War provides a "safety valve" function, giving marginalized or oppressed groups a means to express their discontent or anger. Acts of terrorism, according to Martha Crenshaw (1998), are selected as a course of action from a range of alternatives. Groups may choose terrorism because the other methods may be expected not to work or may be too time-consuming for the group. Radical groups choose terrorism when they want immediate action and when they want their message to be heard. As they act, they spread their group's message, strengthening the social bonds between group members while recruiting new members for their cause.

The social structure contributes to conflict. For example, a country's education and age structure are demographic characteristics that help us understand the current situation in the Greater Middle East (Spindel 2011). Educational attainment in these countries is rising, and as a result, so are citizen demands and expectations for resolving the countries' social problems. The age structure of the population has been identified as a central component in the Arab Spring. Unlike in Western countries, the majority of residents are under 25 years of age—52% in Egypt, 55.2% in Syria, and 54.4% in Jordan. In Germany, 25% of the population is under 25 years of age.

Finally, warfare establishes power and domination. The victor is able to acquire the "spoils of war"—a country's land, people, and resources. Beyond those tangible fruits of victory, the winning side gets to make new rules or impose its rules about appropriate political, social, and economic structures.

Conflict Perspective

From this perspective, war is not natural; it is a product of oppression and domination. Conflict may be based on disputes over resources or land. Modern conflict theorists have focused on how war is used to promote economic and political interests. In 1961, President Dwight D. Eisenhower cautioned the nation about the **military-industrial complex**, the growing collaboration of the government, the military, and the armament industry. Years earlier, Eisenhower (1953) warned,

> Every gun that is made, every warship launched, every rocket fired, signifies in the final sense a theft of those who hunger and are not fed, those who are cold and are not clothed. The world in arms is not spending money alone. It is spending the sweat of its laborers, the genius of its scientists, the hopes of its children.

He explained that the complex had a corrupting influence—economic, political, and spiritual—in every city, state, and federal office of government. A decision to go to war could be motivated not by ideals to preserve or promote freedom, but to ensure the economic well-being of the defense contractor. For example, during the Iraq war, the role of oil services firm Halliburton and its subsidiary company, KBR, was closely scrutinized. Critics identify that Halliburton had an unfair advantage with no-bid military contracting because of its relationship with Vice President Dick Cheney. Cheney served as Halliburton's CEO from 1996 to 1998 and briefly in 2000. In 2007, federal investigators alleged that Halliburton was responsible for $2.7 billion in contractor waste and overcharging in Iraq.

Social scientists have noted the far-reaching and devastating impact of U.S. militarism for Americans and the rest of the world. Cunningham (2004) identifies a "vast, entrenched, bureaucratic national security apparatus" that reaches into all areas of American life and politics, including businesses, universities, primary and secondary schools, the media, and popular culture. U.S. militarism also reaches into foreign countries, through its direct military intervention and war and covert operations (conducted by the Central Intelligence Agency [CIA], the National Security Agency [NSA], and other agencies).

Feminist Perspective

From this perspective, war is considered a primarily male activity that enhances the position of males in society. "War is a patriarchal tool always used by men to create new structures of dominance and to subjugate a large mass of people" ("The Events" 2002:96). In our military system, decision-making and economic power are held primarily by men; as a result, international relations and politics are played out on women's bodies (Cuomo 1996). According to Cynthia Enloe (1990), local and global sexual politics shape and are shaped through the presence of national and

Military-industrial complex: Collaboration of the government, the military, and the armament industry

Women in the Military

In 2013, the Pentagon removed its ban on women serving in combat. Full implementation is expected by January 2016.

international U.S. military bases—through the symbolism of the U.S. soldier, the reproduction of family structures on bases, and systems of prostitution that coexist alongside bases. As she explains, "bases are artificial societies created out of unequal relations between men and women of different races and classes" (Enloe 1990:2).

Men reserve the right to make war themselves and claim that they fight wars to protect vulnerable people, such as women and children, who are viewed as not being able to protect themselves (Tickner 2002). During wars, women are charged with caring for their husbands, their sons, and the victims of war. The ideal of the "caretaking woman" helps exclude women from public and political institutions by reminding them that their first responsibility is to the family. According to Laura Kaplan (1994), this ideal "helps co-opt women's resistance to the war by convincing women that their immediate responsibility to ameliorate the effects of war takes precedence over organized public action against war" (p. 131).

Communication scholar Mary Douglas Vavrus (2013) examined the gendered propaganda in Lifetime's drama *Army Wives*. The popular program aired from 2007 to 2013, depicting the stories of four Army wives and one Army husband whose family members were deployed in Afghanistan and Iraq. Through a feminist analysis of 81 episodes, Douglas Vavrus documented a pervasive message of militarism and gendered labor; "first, that soldiers are fighting over there to protect us, over here . . . second, that wives properly bear the responsibility for the home front while their husbands are deployed to other lands" (p. 98). The women in the program have a feminine approach to the war—building schools or leading medical missions—while their husbands are risking their lives in military missions. The wives were portrayed as long-suffering, supportive, and patriotic. "For the mothers and spouses on the program, standing in the way of either their children or their deploying husbands and wives—either to complain or worry visibly—is to prevent children and spouses from reaching their heroic self-actualization that awaits each soldier in theater" (p. 99).

Interactionist Perspective

Interactionists focus on the social messages and meaning of war and conflict. *Terrorism* is a word with intrinsically negative connotations. According to political scientist Crenshaw (1995), the word "projects images, communicates messages, and creates myths that transcend historical circumstances and motivate future generations" (p. 12). In addition, the concept serves as "an organizing concept that both describes the phenomenon as it exists and offers a moral judgment" (Crenshaw 1995:9). As Jenkins (1980) explains,

> what is called terrorism thus seems to be dependent on one's point of view. Use of the term implies a moral judgment; and if one party can successfully attach the label terrorist to its opponent, then it has indirectly persuaded others to adopt its moral viewpoint. (p. 10)

Crenshaw (1995) cautions that once political concepts such as terrorism are constructed, "they take on a certain autonomy, especially when they are adopted by news media, disseminated to the public, and integrated into a general context of norms and values" (p. 9). Use of the word *terrorism* promotes condemnation of the actors and may reflect an ideological or political bias (Gibbs 1989). Terrorism is a social construct.

Terrorism is particularly useful for agenda setting (Crenshaw 1998) by the terrorist group and its target. If the reasons behind the violence are articulated clearly, terrorists can put their issues on the public agenda. Instantly, the public is aware of the group and its cause. The act may make some sympathetic to the group or could elicit anger and calls for retaliation. But the target—such as the U.S. government—can also use terrorism to set its own agenda. According to Crenshaw (1998), "conceptions of terrorism affect the ways in which governments define their interests, and also determine reliance on labels or their abandonment when politically convenient" (p. 10). When the problem is labeled *terrorism* or a group is labeled *terrorists*, a set of predetermined preferred solutions begins to emerge. When these terms depict the group as "fanatical and irrational," making attempts at diplomacy or compromise seem impossible, the inference is that the U.S. government has nothing left to do but retaliate with force. But the labeling doesn't stop: such defensive actions are often "appropriate" and "legitimate" expressions of "self-defense," but not "terrorism."

David Altheide (2006) explains how decision makers and politicians promote and use the public's beliefs and assumptions about terrorism to achieve certain goals. He refers to this as the **politics of fear**. The politics of fear promotes attacking a target, limits civil liberties, and anticipates further victimization. Altheide warns how fear promotes fear, changing our behavior and perspective. Sarah Oates (2006), in her analysis of the role of terrorism coverage in the 2004 presidential/parliamentary election campaigns in Russia, Great Britain, and the United States, concluded that terrorism played an emotive role for American and Russian voters. American and Russian voters identified terrorism as the most important issue in the election, leading them to vote for the candidate they perceived as "stronger" against the threat of terrorism, regardless of the candidate's specific policies or political views. Oates reported that terrorism did not play a role in the Great Britain election, as it was mentioned in only 10% of all British news segments in her sample, whereas it was mentioned in 25% of all U.S. election news segments. In Great Britain, the primary issues were the lack of public support for the country's involvement in the Iraq war and the state of Great Britain's economy. For more about the fear of terrorism, refer to this chapter's Exploring Social Problems feature.

For a summary of sociological perspectives, see Table 16.3.

Politics of fear: How decision makers and politicians promote and use the public's beliefs and assumptions about terrorism to achieve certain goals

Table 16.3 Summary of sociological perspectives: War and conflict

	Functional	Conflict/ Feminist	Interactionist
Explanation of war and conflict	Functionalists examine how war and terrorism help maintain the social order.	War and terrorism may be based on conflict over resources, territory, and power. From a feminist perspective, war is considered a primarily male activity that enhances the position of males in society.	An interactionist focuses on the social messages and meaning of war and terrorism.
Questions asked about war and conflict	What functions do war and terrorism serve? For terrorist groups? For the targets of terrorism? For groups in conflict? For revolutionaries?	What groups are in conflict and why?	How do our conceptions of war and conflict shape political and diplomatic responses? How do they shape our own behavior?

The Fear of Terrorism

Figure 16.1 Percentage very concerned about the rise of Islamic extremism in the United States, by political party affiliation

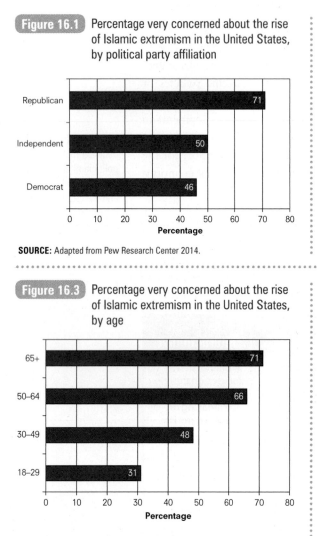

SOURCE: Adapted from Pew Research Center 2014.

Figure 16.2 Percentage very concerned about the rise of Islamic extremism in the United States, by educational attainment

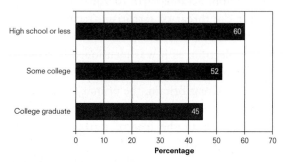

SOURCE: Adapted from Pew Research Center 2014.

Figure 16.3 Percentage very concerned about the rise of Islamic extremism in the United States, by age

SOURCE: Adapted from Pew Research Center 2014.

Figure 16.4 Percentage who believe government is doing not too/not at all well in reducing the threat of terrorism, by political party affiliation, 2014

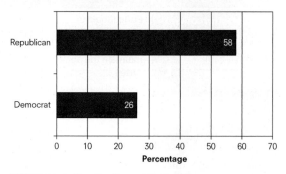

SOURCE: Adapted from Pew Research Center 2014.

WHAT DO YOU THINK?

During the 2014 midterm congressional elections, voters identified their primary concern as the state of our national security and our defenses against Islamic terrorism. The Pew Research Center conducted a national poll, asking Americans to report how concerned they were about the threat of Islamic extremism reaching the United States. Poll results are presented in Figures 16.1 to 16.3, summarizing concern by political party affiliation, education, and age.

Based on these figures, who is most concerned about Islamic terrorism?

Note how public opinion on whether the government is not doing enough to reduce the threat is also divided by political party affiliation (Figure 16.4).

Using your sociological imagination, why are these groups most concerned about terrorism? How might the politics of fear play a role in their perceptions about terrorism?

THE PROBLEMS OF WAR AND TERRORISM

The Impact of War and Terrorism

Psychological Impact

According to Crenshaw (1983), small incremental societal changes in trust, social cohesion, and integration occur as a result of terrorism. Terrorism has a particular impact in small or homogeneous societies. Research on the long-term impact of terrorism is limited, although some case studies have been conducted in Northern Ireland, where residents have lived with domestic terrorism since the late 1960s. (See this chapter's Taking a World View discussion for more about the Irish Republican Army [IRA].)

War takes a psychological toll, particularly for soldiers involved in battle. Mental health experts have identified posttraumatic stress disorder (PTSD) as a common aftereffect of battle. Those suffering from PTSD feel depressed and detached and have nightmares and flashbacks of their war experience. This anxiety disorder may occur with related issues, such as depression, substance abuse, cognition problems, and other problems of physical or mental health (National Center for PTSD 2003a). About 7% to 8% of the general U.S. population will experience PTSD symptoms in their lifetimes.

Vietnam veterans were particularly hard-hit because of extensive war-related trauma: serving hazardous duty, witnessing death and harm to self or others, and being on frequent or prolonged combat missions. The estimated lifetime prevalence of PTSD among Vietnam veterans is 30.9% for men and 26.9% for women. An additional 22.5% of men and 21.2% of women have had partial PTSD sometime in their lives (National Center for PTSD 2003b).

It is estimated that between 11% and 20% of Iraq and Afghanistan veterans will have PTSD. These service members are also at risk for depression, excessive drinking, and violence (U.S. Department of Veterans Affairs 2014a). Based on a national survey of Iraq and Afghanistan veterans, the Washington Post-Kaiser Family Foundation found that 52% say their physical or mental health is worse than before the wars. Forty-one percent experience outbursts of anger. More than half of those surveyed reported knowing a service member who has attempted or committed suicide (Clement 2014).

The rate of suicide among these veterans has been described as an epidemic, prompting legislation and funding for programs to address PTSD and other mental illness among the veterans. Much of the response was due to the release of a 2012 Department of Veterans Affairs study that estimated that 22 veterans kill themselves every day. The 22-veterans statistic has been challenged by scholars and journalists, who argue that the department included suicide among veterans who did not serve in the recent conflicts, thus overestimating the number and rate of suicides.

For information on the Iraq war's impact on veterans, turn to this chapter's In Focus feature.

 FRONTLINE's "A Soldier's Heart"

Marine Cpl. Larry Bailey II (pictured here with his father Larry) is recovering from injuries he received after tripping a rooftop bomb in Afghanistan. Iraq and Afghanistan war veterans are able to survive wounds that in past wars would have been fatal.

Economic Impact

President George W. Bush pledged that the United States would win the fight against terrorism, "whatever it takes, whatever it costs." Although the United States now has a smaller army and is using technologies that are less human intensive, military expenditures have been increasing, and with those increases comes the greater likelihood of waste, inefficiency, and "good old fashioned pork," according to opponents (Knickerbocker 2002).

The final cost of the Iraq war is estimated to be more than $2 trillion (and unlike past U.S. wars, the Iraq war is being paid almost entirely with debt). The expenditures have been justified as necessary to maintain a high state of military readiness and ground force strength, enhance the combat capabilities of U.S. armed forces, continue the development of capabilities to maintain U.S. superiority against potential threats, and continue the department's support of service members and their families. Though some believe that these additional defense expenses are necessary to win the global war on terrorism, others have criticized the escalation in military expenditures.

In 2002, the U.S. Department of Veterans Affairs (VA) guaranteed two years of free care to returning combat veterans for any combat-related medical condition. The cost of these benefits, as well as that of providing long-term disability support for soldiers and veterans and their families, may strain the department's budget and government resources. Policy analysts blame the lack of planning by the VA, noting that the administration did not expect the conflict to last as long as it has and did not predict the nature and extent of mental and physical injuries for its active-duty and retired personnel (Donn and Hefling 2007). In 2014, an internal VA audit revealed that more than 100,000 veterans received inadequate medical care or no care at all in several veteran health facilities across the country. Top VA administrators resigned, and President Obama signed a bill to reform the VA system. Between 2001 and 2013, the U.S. spent $23.6 billion for medical care and $28.9 billion for disability benefits for Iraq and Afghanistan veterans (Bilmes 2013).

A comparison of U.S. war expenditures with other countries is presented in Table 16.4.

 The Hidden Cost of the Iraq War

IN FOCUS

THE HIDDEN COSTS OF WAR

Of the 2.5 million U.S. forces deployed in Iraq and Afghanistan, almost half have sought care and assistance from the U.S. Department of Veterans Affairs. Government, health, and veterans service administrators have observed how different the needs of Iraq war veterans are from those of veterans of past wars and conflicts.

Because of the nature of the conflict itself, forces deployed in Iraq have had more contact with the enemy and more exposure to terrorist attacks than did troops in the earlier Iraq war (O'Connor 2004). The frequency and intensity of operations for active and reserve members increased during the height of the recent wars, with multiple deployments and overseas assignments for soldiers. Estimates range from one in six to one in three soldiers and Marines seeking help for mental health problems or PTSD as a result of their Iraq experiences. Between 80% and 85% of military personnel have witnessed or been part of traumatic events (Vedantam 2006).

About 280,000 female soldiers, Marines, and airmen have been deployed to Iraq or Afghanistan (Chandrasekaran 2014), 11% of the overall force. The U.S. Department of Veteran Affairs (2014b) estimates that 20% of women Iraq and Afghanistan veterans have been diagnosed with PTSD. Research on this population has indicated higher rates of PTSD and depression for female compared with male veterans, higher incidences of sexual trauma, and lower rates of accessing health care services (U.S. Department of Veterans Affairs 2012). At the release of its 2012 report on sexual assault in the military, the Department of Defense was criticized for failing to protect its female soldiers. In 2012, there were 26,000 cases of unwanted sexual contact. Sexual trauma can have adverse ramifications on a veteran's quality of life, negatively impacting physical health, psychological well-being, employment, and interpersonal relationships. President Obama requested a comprehensive review of the department's prevention practices and response protocols to sexual assault. After implementing support, education, and training programs and improving accountability measures, the number of cases declined to 19,000 in 2014.

More wounded soldiers are returning home alive from Iraq. In the past, many would not have survived traumatic brain injuries (TBIs) as a result of improvised explosive device (IED), bomb, or rocket attacks. This shockwave injury is caused when the brain is literally shaken in the soldier's skull, damaging brain tissue. Warfare and medical technology have increased survival rates, however, by making it possible to treat and mobilize wounded soldiers more quickly and closer to combat zones. TBI has been referred to as the signature injury of the Iraq war, much like Agent Orange poisoning was for the Vietnam War. Doctors at the U.S. Army's Walter Reed hospital screened all incoming patients between January 2003 and January 2005 and discovered that 60% of all wounded soldiers had some form of TBI (Zoroya 2005). TBI symptoms include severe headaches, impaired memory, and sensitivity to light and sound. These symptoms may be temporary or permanent.

Do you recall President Eisenhower's warning? Billions of dollars spent on the war means that other programs are not receiving any funding. The National Priorities Project, a nonprofit, nonpartisan organization, analyzes the impact of federal spending policies on city and state funding and budgets. Since the

Table 16.4 Top 10 military spenders, 2013

Country	Expenditures (in Billions of Dollars)	% of Gross Domestic Product
United States	640	3.8
China	188	2.0
Russia	87.8	4.1
Saudi Arabia	66.9	9.3
France	61.2	2.2
U.K.	57.9	2.3
Germany	48.8	1.4
Japan	48.6	1.0
India	47.4	2.5
South Korea	33.9	2.8

SOURCE: Adapted from Stockholm International Peace Research Institute 2014.

beginning of the Iraq war, the project has tracked the expanding war budget along with increasing budget cuts in nonsecurity (nonwar) discretionary spending. Based on its 2008 budget, the Bush administration proposed cutting $13 billion from social service and education programming—for example, a 35% budget cut in Community Development Block Grants, a 6% cut in the Head Start program, a 40% cut in the Low Income Home Energy Assistance Program, and 6% in special education programming. At the same time, the administration requested an additional $100 billion for war-related spending (National Priorities Project 2007).

The Budget Control Act of 2011 mandates reductions in federal spending, including defense spending. In 2012, President Obama and Defense Secretary Leon Panetta announced a new strategic military plan and the goal to reduce the budget by $259 billion over the next decade.

Environmental Impact

One of the most serious, yet overlooked, by-products of war is the mass destruction of ecosystems, also referred to as **ecocide** (Adley and Grant 2003).

During the Vietnam War, the United States used chemical and biological agents, such as the herbicide Agent Orange, to destroy food crops and defoliate forestlands.

Ecocide: Mass destruction of ecosystems

Herbicides were used from 1962 to 1969, covering 43% of South Vietnam's arable land and 44% of its forestland at least once, and in many cases two or more times (Falk 1973). The application rate was 13 times the dose recommended for domestic use by the U.S. Food and Drug Administration. More than 1.3 million individuals were poisoned or contaminated. The military justified this environmental destruction in order to deny the Vietnamese army protective cover and to cut off the food supply to peasants and soldiers. The contamination of soil and food crops due to Agent Orange continues to threaten the health of the Vietnamese (Adley and Grant 2003). Another method of clearing vegetation and forests in Vietnam was the use of the Rome plow. The plow is a heavily armored Caterpillar bulldozer used to clear several hundred yards on each side of the main roads. It was estimated that about 2,000 acres (3 square miles) were cleared per day until the end of the war. The croplands and forests of Vietnam were damaged, along with rare tree and animal species (Falk 1973).

Other examples of environmental degradation and destruction resulting from war include the burning of oil wells in Kuwait (1991), the health risks associated with the use of depleted uranium weapons in Iraq (since the first Gulf War in 1991), and the destruction of the mountain gorilla habitat in Rwanda (1994) (Adley and Grant 2003).

Waging a war is also a dirty business, as military activities produce harmful waste and debris. Fuel deposits, ammunition dumps, paint, tires, grease, unexploded munitions, and gunpowder contribute to the contamination of land and water (Jorgenson, Clark, and Givens 2012). Military campaigns also consume large amounts of fossil (and nuclear) fuel in planes, ships, and tanks. It is estimated that the U.S. military uses 1.3 billion gallons of oil annually in Middle East alone (Klare 2007).

Efforts to prevent and redress wartime environmental degradation and destruction have not been successful. The primary issue has been accountability—how should a nation be punished for ecocide? The environmental destructiveness of war and conflict has been acknowledged by world leaders, and in 1992 the Rio Declaration on Environment and Development (signed by all member states of the United Nations) required states to "respect international law providing protection for the environment in times of armed conflict and cooperate in its further development, as necessary" (United Nations 1992).

Political Impact

Terrorism can effect change in two political areas: the overall distribution of political power and government policies (Crenshaw 1983). Terrorism may result in radical changes in the power relationships within a state, involving shifts in who governs and under what rules. As a target of terrorism, the U.S. government has also experienced a redistribution of power as federal and state agencies have sought to improve intelligence gathering and security procedures. Institutional changes have occurred, with each major intelligence agency improving its antiterrorism activities, culminating in the creation of the Department of Homeland Security. In extreme cases, terrorism may lead to the replacement of one government by another.

Government policies usually have two goals: to destroy the terrorist group and to protect potential targets from attack. Policies may include foreign policy efforts seeking the cooperation and support of international allies. After September 11, the U.S. government attempted to destroy terrorist groups and to ensure U.S. security through a series of executive orders, regulations, and laws. The U.S. Senate Intelligence Committee released a blistering report on the Central Intelligence Agency's post-9/11 interrogation program. The 2014 report revealed how in a system of covert prisons, CIA officials authorized the use of coercive interrogation tactics—sleep deprivation, humiliation, waterboarding, sensory deprivation, and extreme cold—to obtain information from detainees who were suspected terrorists. The release of the report led to a mixture of condemnation and support from world leaders.

In 2001, Congress passed the PATRIOT Act, which established a separate counterterrorism fund, expanded government authority to gather and share evidence with wire and electronic communications, allowed agencies to detain suspected foreign terrorists, and provided for victims of terrorism. Constitutional and civil rights attorneys have been critical of the PATRIOT Act, alarmed that it would erode individual liberties and increase law enforcement abuses. Often cited is the act's disregard for the principles of political freedom, due process, and the protections of privacy—all principles at the core of a democratic society (Cole and Dempsey 2002). More than 330 cities, towns, and counties, as well as four states, have passed resolutions critical of the federal antiterrorism law (Egan 2004). Two provisions of the act have caused particular concern among citizens. One is the provision that empowers authorities to search people's homes without notification. A second clause allows government officials the right to review a person's library, business, and medical records.

What Does It Mean to Me?

President Obama proposed a 2015 budget that included $535 billion for the Department of Defense. What is your opinion of military spending? Are we spending too much or not enough? What do our military expenditures say about the values of our country? Of our role as a global leader?

The Next Threat

Domestic Terrorism

Michael Leiter, then-director of the National Counterterrorism Center, told the 2011 U.S. House Intelligence Committee that his number-one priority was identifying men and women intent on doing harm in the United States. This included concern with al-Qaeda's efforts to recruit Americans for their own efforts (Mulrine 2011).

TAKING A WORLD VIEW

IRELAND AND THE DECOMMISSIONING OF THE IRA

The trouble with the Irish is the English.

—A line from a popular Irish song
(quoted in Whittaker 2002)

In August 2007, the British Army ended Operation Banner, a 38-year security operation in Northern Ireland. Violence and bloodshed first began in 1969, the result of confrontations between Nationalist and Unionist (or Loyalist) forces. The Nationalist or Catholic groups were led by the IRA and its splinter groups. In 1970, the Provisional IRA was created (*provisional* to honor the provisional government declared by the leaders of the 1916 Easter Rising in Dublin). The Provisional IRA formed to defend the Catholic community and to throw out the British army and police (Wilkinson 1993). The Unionist or Protestant forces represented the Ulster Defence Association and its splinter groups: the Ulster Volunteer Force, the Red Hand Commandos, and the Ulster Freedom Fighters. Ulster Protestants saw themselves as Britons, loyal to the Protestant crown. These groups represent "Orange Extremism," as described by Paul Wilkinson (1993). Orange extremism has also been blamed for provoking the open conflict in the late 1960s and for creating the conditions in which the Provisional IRA could grow. The division between the groups emphasized their polarization in religion, politics, and economics (Whittaker 2002).

Between them, both sides amassed an impressive armory of rifles, homemade machine guns, grenade throwers, antitank weapons, and explosives. Bombing seemed to be a favorite tactic of both sides. In more than 30 years of conflict, 3,500 civilians have been killed and some 30,000 have been injured, and there has been a loss of property amounting to millions of pounds (Whittaker 2002). IRA terrorists also have taken their own lives without attempting to harm others. There was a chain suicide of 11 IRA members who starved themselves to death in a Belfast prison in 1981. The IRA used the hunger strikes and deaths to its organizational advantage, "to reap emotive propaganda, to restore the flow of cash and weapons from the previously dwindling U.S. sources, and to regroup and rearm" (Wilkinson 1993). Many Irish Americans embraced members of the IRA as freedom fighters and supported their cause politically and financially.

In 1998, both sides accepted the Good Friday Agreement, a 65-page document that sought to define relationships within Northern Ireland, between Northern Ireland and the Republic, and between Ireland, England, Scotland, and Wales. The agreement acknowledges that the people of Northern and Southern Ireland are the only ones with the power to bring about a united Ireland. Through the agreement, new government institutions were set in place. A cabinet-style Executive of Ministers, with members in proportion to party support, allows the participation of all groups (Ahern 2003). The new government, composed of unionists and nationalists, was established with the first elections for the new Northern Ireland Assembly in June 1998.

A number of political obstacles slowed down the implementation of the agreement, including difficulties over the total disarmament of the Provisional IRA and the dismantling of British military installations in Nationalist areas (Ahern 2003). After experiencing sectarian squabbling, the assembly failed to hold a session for five years (2001–2006); however, elections were held in March 2007 to reestablish the Northern Ireland Assembly and determine how many members from unionist (Protestant) and nationalist (Catholic) parties would be represented (Lyall and Quinn 2007). Self-rule was restored in Belfast in May 2007.

In 2012, Queen Elizabeth was photographed shaking hands with Martin McGuinness, a former IRA commander, a historic moment in Anglo–Irish relations. McGuinness serves as deputy first minister in Northern Ireland's provincial government.

 New Terrorist Recruits

On April 19, 1995, the worst domestic terrorism attack occurred around 9:00 a.m. in Oklahoma City, Oklahoma. A rental truck loaded with a mixture of fertilizer and fuel oil exploded in front of the Alfred P. Murrah Federal Building. The blast blew off the front side of the nine-story building, killing 169 and injuring hundreds more. The attack was conducted by Timothy McVeigh and Terry Nichols, motivated by antigovernment sentiment over the failed 1993 federal raid on the Branch Davidian compound in Texas. The bombing occurred on the second anniversary of the Branch Davidian incident. McVeigh was executed for his crime in 2001; Nichols is serving a life sentence.

Louis J. Freeh (2001), former director of the Federal Bureau of Investigation (FBI), identified three types of domestic groups operating in the United States: right-wing extremists, left-wing and Puerto Rican extremists, and special interest extremists. Right-wing groups, such as the World Church of the Creator, Aryan Nations, and the Southeastern States Alliance, advocate the principles of racial supremacy and tend to embrace antigovernment or antiregulatory beliefs. They have also been characterized as hate groups. The Southern Poverty Law Center (2014) identified 939 active hate groups in the United States in 2013.

Left-wing groups want to bring about revolutionary change, adopting a socialist doctrine, and see themselves as protectors of the people. Groups in this category include terrorist or separatist groups seeking Puerto Rico's independence from the United States and anarchists and extremist socialist groups such as the Workers World Party, Reclaim the Streets, and Carnival Against Capitalism. Many of these anarchist groups were blamed for the damage caused at the 1999 World Trade Organization meeting in Seattle, Washington.

Special interest groups want to resolve specific issues, rather than effect political change. These groups are at the fringes of animal rights, pro-life, environmental, antinuclear, and other political and social movements. Animal rights and environmental groups, such as the Animal Liberation Front (ALF) and the Earth Liberation Front (ELF), have recently increased their activities. Activists from these groups usually use arson and incendiary devices equipped with timers to target government and company facilities. The FBI says that these groups are responsible for more than 1,800 criminal acts and more than $110 million in damages (FBI 2009).

In 2014, Attorney General Eric Holder announced that he would reconvene the task force on domestic terrorism. In his announcements, Holder referred to the 2013 Boston Marathon bombing and the 2009 and 2014 shootings at Fort Hood as examples of "the danger we face from these homegrown threats."

Nuclear Weapons

The nuclear weapons age began on July 16, 1945, when the United States exploded the first nuclear bomb in Alamogordo, New Mexico. Three weeks later, an atomic bomb was used on the city of Hiroshima, Japan, killing 100,000 residents. Three days later, an atomic bomb was used on the city of Nagasaki, Japan, killing about

 Bioterrorism

74,000 and injuring 75,000. During the 1950s and 1960s, the United States was engaged in a "cold war" with Russia and other nuclear countries, locked in a stalemate over who would be the first to launch a nuclear attack. In 1963, the countries agreed to sign a partial test ban treaty, banning nuclear tests in the atmosphere, under water, and in space, and a nonproliferation treaty was signed in 1968, prohibiting nonnuclear countries from possessing or developing nuclear weapons. In 1996, President Bill Clinton was the first world leader to sign the Comprehensive Nuclear Test Ban Treaty, which prohibits all nuclear test explosions in all environments. However, the treaty has yet to be ratified by the U.S. Senate. All North Atlantic Treaty Organization (NATO) members, except for the United States, have ratified the treaty.

Days after the 1945 bombing of Nagasaki, Japan, the Japanese surrendered to the Allied forces, officially ending World War II. The atom bomb killed more than 70,000 residents and destroyed 70% of the city's industrial core.

Nuclear weapons are still held by more than eight nations in the world. Suspected weapons have been identified in China (250), France (300), India (80–100), North Korea (<10), Pakistan (90–100), Russia (8,484) the United Kingdom (225), and the United States (7,506) (Center for Arms Control and Non-Proliferation 2014). In 2010, Iran's president Mahmoud Ahmadinejad announced that his country was a "nuclear state." Though his claims could not be independently verified, nuclear watchdog groups and experts say it would take several years for Iran to produce a nuclear weapon. The United States has called for United Nations–backed sanctions to discourage Iran from pursuing its weapons development program.

In 2010, Obama and Russian president Dmitry Medvedev signed a treaty to reduce American and Russian strategic nuclear arsenals by 30%, to the lowest levels since the early years of the Cold War. The United States and Russia possess 95% of the world's nuclear weapons. The treaty is subject to ratification by lawmakers in both countries and according to Obama and Medvedev sets the stage for further nuclear weapons reduction. Obama has pledged not to develop any new nuclear weapons.

COMMUNITY, POLICY, AND SOCIAL ACTION

The National Commission on Terrorist Attacks Upon the United States, also known as the 9-11 Commission, was an independent bipartisan commission created by congressional legislation. The 9-11 Commission was charged with documenting and preparing a full account of the September 11 terrorist attacks. Throughout 2003 and 2004, hearings were held investigating Osama bin Laden's network, the performance of the intelligence community, emergency preparedness and response, and national policy coordination. The commission concluded that U.S. intelligence gathering by the FBI and CIA was inadequate, fragmented, and poorly coordinated.

In 2002, Bush established the Department of Homeland Security. (Before September 11, the U.S. Commission on National Security in the 21st Century [2001] had recommended the creation of a National Homeland Security Agency, responsible for planning, coordinating, and integrating all U.S. agencies responsible for security.) The primary mission of the department is to prevent terrorist attacks and reduce the vulnerability of the United States to terrorism through coordination with component agencies: U.S. Secret Service, U.S. Coast Guard, U.S. Citizenship and Immigration Services, U.S. Immigration and Customs Enforcement, U.S. Customs and Border Protection, the Federal Emergency Management Agency, and the Transportation Security Administration. The Department of Homeland Security is also responsible for the Homeland Security Advisory System, which informs the public of the current level of terrorist threat.

As a nation, the United States has used several approaches to combat and to reduce the risk of war and conflict: diplomacy, economic sanctions, and military force. Usually, war is justified as being the last resort in circumstances where there are severe domestic rights violations or international aggression by an offending state (Garfield 2002).

Political Diplomacy

According to Christopher Harmon (2000), "political will, more than new laws or new direction[s] in international politics, is the most important component of an enhanced effort against foreign supported terrorism" (p. 236). Political diplomacy includes articulating policy to foreign leaders, persuading them, and reaching agreements with them (Pillar 2001). Wars reshape diplomacy; victory becomes the goal of foreign policy, and diplomatic relationships are adjusted to achieve it (Mandelbaum 2003). Political scientist Stephen Van Evera (2006) argues that the United States must develop and use its power to make peace.

Relationship building and persuasion are at the heart of U.S. diplomatic efforts. As the lead foreign affairs agency, the Department of State attempts to formulate, represent, and implement the president's foreign policy (U.S. Department of State 2003). The secretary of state is the president's principal adviser on foreign policy and represents the United States abroad in foreign affairs. Primarily, the department manages diplomatic relations with other countries and international institutions (such as the United Nations, NATO, the World Bank, and the International Monetary Fund [IMF]). The Department of State conducts negotiations and concludes agreements and treaties with other countries on issues ranging from trade to nuclear weapons. The United States maintains diplomatic relations with more than 180 countries (U.S. Department of State 2003). Diplomacy is conducted by the secretary of state and by foreign service officers, immigration officers, FBI special agents, intelligence officers, transportation specialists, defense attachés, and other officials (Pillar 2001).

In contrast with the hard-line diplomacy embraced by George W. Bush's administration, President Obama's diplomacy has been described as a **soft-power approach**, where a nation-state is perceived as having values, motives, and actions that should be emulated (Nye 2008). A nation-state with soft power leads with noncoercive persuasion through its attitudes toward international norms, embracing the rules of law and demonstrating respect for diversity and cultural history (Hayden 2011). Political scientist Joseph Nye (2008) describes soft power as: "If I can get you to do what I want, then I do not have to force you to do what you do not want" (p. 95). The president serves as the chief diplomat, setting the tone and agenda for political diplomacy. Obama's 2009 speech at the Al-Azhar University in Cairo, Egypt, has been described as a significant diplomatic address, as the president openly acknowledged the plight of the Palestinians and Israel's relationship with the United States. Public diplomacy scholar Craig Hayden (2011) writes,

> The speech was a signal that the United States would take a more balanced approach to acknowledge the particular perspectives of the Middle East crises. The speech was also important as a function of public diplomacy in the manner of its delivery, its location and the way it signaled the course of U.S. foreign policy in the region. (p. 791)

Obama's soft-power approach has been praised for improving the U.S.'s status as the world's most admired country, yet has been criticized for not being effective or strong enough.

The Use of Economic Sanctions

For many years, the United States and the United Nations have used nonviolent approaches in the form of economic sanctions to punish or pressure countries that have violated U.S. laws or values. Sanctions are considered an alternative to diplomacy or military force. Economic sanctions, in the form of trade embargoes and the termination of development assistance, are the most commonly applied form of sanctions, and they have the most significant public health consequences. These sanctions are intended to weaken a rival's economy, to disrupt their economic and military capabilities.

U.S. sanctions were used against Iraq in 1990 to force its withdrawal from Kuwait and against Yugoslavia (1991–1996) and Serbia and Montenegro (1992–1996) during the Serbian war (Marks 1999). Recent U.S. sanctions have been imposed against Iraq, Iran and North Korea in an effort to discourage terrorist activity or the accumulation of weapons of mass destruction. According to Richard Haas (1997), "economic sanctions are popular because they offer what appears to be a proportional response to challenges in which the interests at stake are less than vital" (p. 75). Sanctions can also serve as a signal of official displeasure with a country's behavior or action.

Soft-power approach: Where a nation-state is perceived as having values, motives, and actions that should be emulated

VOICES IN THE COMMUNITY

AUNG SAN SUU KYI

Between 1989 and 2010, Daw Aung San Suu Kyi was a political prisoner in Myanmar (also known as Burma). For more than 15 years during this period, she was detained under house arrest as the Burma junta declared martial law. As reported by Amnesty International (2012), many of Myanmar's citizens live in poverty and suffer from human rights violations. Political and social dissent is controlled by arrests, torture, and imprisonment. The number of political prisoners in Myanmar is estimated at 1,995 (Amnesty International 2012).

Suu Kyi served as chairperson of the National League for Democracy (NLD), promoting democracy in the military-ruled country. The organization was banned during her arrest. The military authorities consented to her release in 2010. In 2012, Suu Kyi along with 44 other NLD candidates ran for seats in Myanmar's parliament. Suu Kyi won her seat. Eighty percent of the parliamentary seats are still held by members of the military-backed ruling party.

After the election, Suu Kyi traveled to Oslo, Norway, to collect her Nobel Peace Prize. She had received the honor in 1991 but due to her imprisonment had not been able to receive her award.

During the 2012 ceremony, Suu Kyi (2012) spoke of her goal for a free, secure, and just society in Myanmar. She spoke of the effectiveness of reform in her country:

Aung San Suu Kyi was a political prisoner for 15 years in her own country of Myanmar. After her release in 2010, she was elected in 2012 to serve as a representative in the Myanmar parliament, as a member of the National League for Democracy.

We can say that reform is effective only if the lives of the people are improved and in this regard, the international community has a vital role to play. Development and humanitarian aid, bi-lateral agreements and investments should be coordinated and calibrated to ensure that these will promote social, political and economic growth that is balanced and sustainable. The potential of our country is enormous. This should be nurtured and developed to create not just a more prosperous but also a more harmonious, democratic society where our people can live in peace, security and freedom.

Many attempts have focused on cutting aid to countries sponsoring or supporting terrorism. The problem is that most terrorist states do not receive significant aid from the United States, and based on past experience, sanctions have only made target countries and nations more angry and impassioned against the United States (Flores 1981). Shaheen Ayubi et al. (1982) concluded that economic sanctions in U.S. foreign policy may not be effective in their objectives and have often failed to achieve their political purposes. For example, sanctions applied against Cuba since 1960 failed to destabilize the Castro regime.

Sanctions may not hurt dictators and terrorists, but they may increase suffering and death among civilians (Garfield 2002), and research suggests that economic coercion may worsen public health, economic conditions, educational attainment, and the development of a civil society in the sanctioned country (Peksen 2009). According to Dursun Peksen and A. Cooper Dury (2009), "the majority of economic sanctions, so far, have been a blunt economic instrument that hits the whole target economy without any or very few discriminatory measures to lessen the negative impact on civilians" (p. 408). For example, a report issued in 1993 by the Harvard Center for Population and Development Studies maintained that sanctions exacerbated malnutrition in Haiti and increased child deaths caused by misgovernment (Neier 1993).

One approach has been to freeze only economic assets while continuing to provide food and medical aid through private agencies (Neier 1993). However, although only economic sanctions were directed against Iraq in the early 1990s, the Harvard Study Team (1991) reported that essential goods—food, medicine, and infrastructure support—were not reaching those in need. All health facilities surveyed reported major drug shortages. Children were most vulnerable, dying of preventable diseases and starvation. The chance of dying before age 5 in Iraq more than doubled, from 54 per 1,000 between 1984 and 1989 to 131 per 1,000 between 1995 and 1999 (Ali and Shah 2000).

Military Response

Military action is based on the idea that the most effective way to defeat an enemy is by the destruction of the enemy's armies, equipment, transport systems, industrial centers, and cities.

Military intervention has also been defined as a form of **humanitarian intervention**. Canada's International Commission on Intervention and State Sovereignty (2001) suggested that humanitarian intervention should be defined as a responsibility to protect. According to the commission, there are three aspects of this responsibility: how to prevent humanitarian crises in the first place, under which conditions and in what way to intervene, and how to maintain peace after a military conflict and rebuild the country. There have been approximately 20 instances of humanitarian intervention since the end of the Cold War. In 2011, evoking the responsibility to protect, the United Nations approved NATO military intervention in Libya to

Humanitarian intervention: A responsibility to protect, including three aspects: how to prevent humanitarian crises in the first place, under which conditions and in what way to intervene, and how to maintain peace after a military conflict and rebuild the country

protect civilians from being killed by the armed military forces of Libyan leader Colonel Muammar Gaddafi. Gaddafi had threatened to purge Libya of its civilian protestors. The intervention lasted about six months and led to the collapse of Gaddafi's 42-year-old regime, the leader's death, and the installation of a transitional government. Humanitarian warfare continues to be deliberated from ethical, political, and legal perspectives (Zajadlo 2005), as its implementation challenges a basic principle of sovereign power. When does another country have the right to intervene in the business of another?

Retaliation has been the most important counterterrorist use of U.S. military force. The United States first used it against Libya in 1986, responding to the April 4 bombing of a nightclub in Berlin where 2 Americans were killed and 71 were wounded. One hundred military aircraft were used to attack military targets in and around Tripoli and Benghazi in Libya (Pillar 2001). After September 11, 2001, U.S. troops were deployed to destroy Taliban operations based in Afghanistan.

According to Pillar (2001), evidence suggests that military retaliation does not serve as an effective deterrent to terrorism. First, terrorists who threaten the United States present few suitable military targets. It is tough to attack an enemy that can't be located. Many terrorist groups lack any high-value targets, whose destruction would be costly to their organization. Second, a military attack against a terrorist group may serve political and organizational goals of the terrorist leaders. Such attacks may increase recruiting, sympathy, and resources for terrorist groups. And finally, there is no evidence that terrorists will respond peacefully after a retaliatory attack. Terrorists may also respond by fighting back.

Antiwar and Peace Movements

Antiwar movements have been characterized as reactive, occurring only in response to specific wars or the threat of war. Though every 20th-century war conducted by the United States elicited organized protest and opposition (Chatfield 1992), the public's response to the Iraq and Afghanistan wars was described as apathetic. The lack of public outrage or protest over the wars was attributed to several factors: the social construction of a common enemy (terrorism), the pervasive rhetoric of patriotism and nationalism, and an overall decline in civic and political engagement. The Bush administration's policy banning media coverage of fallen soldiers' caskets was blamed for shielding the public from the personal toll of these wars. (The ban was lifted in 2009.)

Peace movements represent organized coalitions that are "fundamentally concerned with the problems of war, militarism, conscription, and mass violence, and the ideals of internationalism, globalism and non-violent relations between people" (Young 1999:228). According to Nigel Young (1999), there are different peace traditions: groups that provide ideas and initiatives for the entire peace movement. For example, the tradition of liberalism and internationalism attempts to prevent war through reformed behavior of states: peace plans, treaties, international law, and arbitration between all groups. Another tradition, anticonscriptionism, links the peace movement with individual civil rights.

Women as Peacemakers

Another peace tradition is feminist antimilitarism. Peace movements within this tradition are united by the ideal of a distinctive role for women on the issue of peace and female unity across national boundaries (Young 1999). Feminist antimilitary groups first began in the early 1900s. In 1914, Jane Addams, founder of Hull House, led a women's peace parade in New York to protest World War I. Addams, along with Carrie Chapman Catt, the main strategist and leader for the women's suffrage movement, and other women activists, formed the Women's Peace Party in 1915. Later that year, the party was renamed the Women's International League for Peace and Freedom. The organization exists today, with chapters in Africa, Asia, South Asia, the Middle East, Europe, and the Americas. Its current global mission includes building and strengthening relationships and movements for justice, peace, and radical democracy.

Women have mobilized for peace in other parts of the world: Mothers and Grandmothers of the Plaza de Mayo (Argentina) protested against the political killings and kidnapping of children during the Argentine Dirty War; the Greenham Common Women (England) called for the decommissioning of nuclear arms; and Women in Black (worldwide) are committed to peace with justice, highlighting women's different experience of war.

College Activists

There is a tradition of student involvement in politics in the United States (Altbach and Peterson 1971). Paul Knott (1971) explains that college students before World War II were mainly upper-middle-class students who treated their education as a privilege. Except for a few campuses, most undergraduates showed little social consciousness and were unwilling to challenge or question the status quo. But increasing diversity on college campuses—in students' ages, gender, and ethnic backgrounds—helped increase social awareness and infused students with a greater sense of empowerment. Student activism was at its peak in the 1960s and 1970s, supporting the civil rights movement and later protesting the Vietnam War. During the late 1970s, campuses institutionalized many of the gains made in the previous decade: establishing women's centers, Black student unions, and gay and lesbian organizations and ensuring that student government had a greater role in university operations (Vellela 1988).

Though college students have often been a central force of peace movements, the college student population is less politicized as a whole than it was 45 years ago. According to the University of California–Los Angeles (UCLA) annual survey of freshmen, 60% of students viewed "keeping up with politics" as "very important" or "essential" in 1966 compared with only 32.8% in 2011 (Pryor et al. 2011).

SOCIOLOGY AT WORK

WORKING AND VOLUNTEERING ABROAD

Michael Clark—Class of 2013

Undergraduate Majors: Sociology, Piano Performance

Pollster John Zogby describes millennials as the "first global generation," with 60% owning a passport and many expecting to work abroad at some point in their careers (Steiner 2014). There are a host of job and internship opportunities abroad for a recent graduate: teaching, cultural and au pair positions, volunteer work, student internships, short-term contract work, and government or corporate placements (Lacey 2006). An estimated 6.8 million Americans live abroad (excluding those in military service), the highest numbers residing in North, Central and South America and in Europe (U.S. Department of State 2014).

During 2014–2015, Sociology alum Michael Clark traveled and worked through Europe as a volunteer for World Wide Opportunities on Organic Farms (WWOOF). Michael is quick to say that his undergraduate study abroad experiences inspired his year abroad. According to the Institute for International Education of Students, students were more likely to enter an international career if they completed an internship abroad and studied in a non-English-speaking country (Lacey 2006).

When asked how he applies sociology to his WWOOF work, Michael replied,

> I am drawn particularly to those sociological projects which examine consumption, globalization, and stratification. As a WWOOF volunteer, I apply such a framework to interpret the stories and experiences of these small, organic farmers, such that I may contextualize them within the larger, globalized system of food production. Like George Ritzer, I regard a variety of

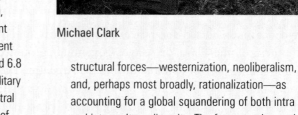

Michael Clark

structural forces—westernization, neoliberalism, and, perhaps most broadly, rationalization—as accounting for a global squandering of both intra and inter-culture diversity. The farmers who work with WWOOF, then, represent an encouraging source of opposition to these very forces. It is understandable, then, that my sociological training compels me to learn more about the slow-food movement, and other related campaigns.

Michael describes several career strategies that helped him narrow his own future prospects:

> I find it useful to learn as much as I can about those career trajectories which are interesting and available to me. Consequently, I have spent a great deal of time reading journal articles, books, and essays, from across a diverse body of disciplines. I have also spent a considerable amount of time reflecting on how my own skills and passions might address global social problems, such as stratification, environmental degradation, and the rationalization/westernization of indigenous cultures.

After his year as a WWOOFer, Michael will return to the states and hopes to enroll in a PhD Sociology program.

Courtesy of Michael Clark

Some argue, however, that progressive student activism didn't stop after the Vietnam War era (Vellela 1988). Student activism is on the rise, but it doesn't reproduce the civil rights and war protests of the 1960s and 1970s. Students are engaged in a broad range of issues: women's rights, discrimination, homophobia, immigration, the homeless, labor unions, and political action groups.

What Does It Mean to Me?

How important is keeping up with politics to you? How well informed are you about local and national political issues? Are you a registered voter? How have you been educated about your rights as a voter? About local and national issues?

The new wave of peace activism builds on existing networks established by the student anticorporate movement, which focused on economic justice related to sweatshop labor and unionization on campuses (refer to Chapter 9, "Work and the Economy"). The current wave of peace activism includes a diverse set of schools: rural southern schools (Appalachian State University in North Carolina, University of Southern Mississippi), historically Black colleges (Morehouse College, University of Georgia), community colleges from Hawaii to Massachusetts, and urban public universities (City University of New York and University of Illinois–Chicago), as well as high schools and middle schools. Student groups have held teach-ins, vigils, and fasts to call attention to a variety of issues (Featherstone 2003).

Although most recent peace activism has protested against the war in Iraq, this sentiment has not been universal. Student peace groups have been sensitive to the message that they send (Featherstone 2003). Peace groups are linking their opposition to war to the campaign for social justice, dealing with racism, economic inequality, and sexism at home. Student protestors seem to have learned from the protests of the 1960s, wanting to prevent the kind of alienation experienced by Vietnam War veterans.

CHAPTER REVIEW

16.1 Explain the difference between war and terrorism

War is a violent but legitimate political instrument between armed combatants. Terrorism is the unlawful use of force to intimidate or coerce compliance with a particular set of beliefs and can be either domestic (based in the United States) or foreign (supported by foreign groups threatening the security of U.S. nationals or U.S. national security).

16.2 Explain how the different sociological perspectives examine social problems related to war and terrorism

Functionalists examine how war and terrorism help maintain the social order, creating and reinforcing boundaries. Modern conflict theorists have focused on how war is used to promote economic and political interests, such as replacing social program funding with military expenditures. From the feminist perspective, war is considered a primarily male activity that enhances the position of males in society. Feminist theorists focus on the gender rhetoric used in war. Interactionists focus on the social messages and meaning of war and conflict.

16.3 Define the politics of fear

The politics of fear is how decision makers and politicians promote and use the public's beliefs and assumptions about terrorism to achieve certain goals. The politics of fear changes our behavior and our perspective.

16.4 Identify the effects of war and terrorism

A common aftereffect of war is the experience of posttraumatic stress disorder (PTSD). The needs of Iraq war veterans are different from veterans of other wars. The United States is the world's largest military spender. Ecocide is the mass destruction of ecosystems due to war. Examples include the use of Agent Orange to defoliate South Vietnam's forests during the Vietnam War.

16.5 Assess the effectiveness of economic sanctions

Economic sanctions such as trade embargoes, which are the most commonly applied form, may affect the civilian population more than specific leaders or terrorists. Many counterterrorism attempts have focused on cutting off aid to countries sponsoring or supporting terrorism. However, most such states do not receive significant aid from the United States, and sanctions may only worsen living conditions in the targeted country.

KEY TERMS

domestic terrorism, 462

ecocide, 472

genocide, 458

humanitarian intervention, 481

international terrorism, 462

military-industrial complex, 464

outcome goals, 462

politicide, 458

politics of fear, 467

process goals, 462

revolution, 459

soft-power approach, 479

terrorism, 460

STUDY QUESTIONS

1. From a functionalist's perspective, how do war and terrorism serve a "safety valve" function?

2. How does the military-industrial complex contribute to war and conflict?

3. From an interactionist perspective, how has the war on terrorism been socially constructed?

4. Identify the psychological, economic, and political impacts of war and conflict.

5. Explain warfare as a humanitarian intervention.

6. What role have college students and activists played in antiwar and peace movements?

$SAGE edge™

Sharpen your skills with SAGE edge at **edge.sagepub.com/leonguerrero5e**

SAGE edge provides a personalized approach to help you accomplish your coursework goals in an easy-to-use learning environment.

PART IV

Individual Action and Social Change

Since its inception, sociology has been considered a means to understand and improve what is wrong with the world. Early sociological thinking emerged from the late 18th and early 19th centuries during periods of dramatic social, economic, and political change, such as the Industrial Revolution, the French Revolution, and the Enlightenment period. The first sociological thinkers, Karl Marx, Émile Durkheim, and Max Weber, were preoccupied with these social changes and the problems they created for society. These thinkers spent their lives studying these problems and attempted to develop programs that would help solve them (Ritzer 2000).

Sociology provides us with the means to examine the social structure or "machinery" that runs our lives. In his book *Invitation to Sociology*, sociologist Peter Berger (1963) likens our human experience to that of puppets on a stage:

We located ourselves in society and thus recognize our own position as we hang from subtle strings. For a moment we see ourselves as puppets . . . . Unlike the puppets, we have the possibility of stopping in our movements, looking up and perceiving the machinery by which we have been moved. In this act lies the first step towards freedom. (p. 176)

Freedom comes first in identifying the social "machinery" that controls us and second in recognizing that the way society controls us is fundamentally different from the way strings control puppets. We have the power to transform or alter that machinery; we have the power to create social change and to address our social problems.

Social Problems and Social Action

In our first chapter, I introduced you to three connections that would be made throughout this text. The first was the connection between sociology and social problems. We began with two concepts offered by C. Wright Mills: personal troubles and public issues. Mills explained that personal troubles transform into public issues when we recognize that troubles exist not because of individual characteristics or traits but because of social forces. This book has not focused on "nuts, sluts, and perverts" (Liazos 1972) as the source of our social problems. Rather, using our sociological imagination, we've examined how social forces shape social problems in U.S. society. We have relied on four sociological perspectives—functionalist, conflict, feminist, and interactionist—to guide us through each chapter and each set of problems. These four perspectives provide a unique look at social problems and, as a consequence, offer insights about how we may solve them.

According to a functionalist, all society's needs are met by its social institutions (family, education, politics, religion, and economics). Working interdependently, these institutions ensure social order. When society experiences significant social change (e.g., the Industrial Revolution, war), the social order is particularly susceptible to social problems (e.g., crime, poverty, or violence). Social problems do not emerge from individuals; rather, problems emerge when the order is disrupted or tested.

Functionalist solutions focus on restoring the social order, repairing the broken institutions, and avoiding dramatic social change.

Like the functionalists, conflict and feminist theorists examine social problems at the macro or societal level. For conflict theorists, social problems are the result of social, economic, or political inequalities inherent in our society. Feminist perspectives consider how gender inequalities lead to social problems. Whereas functionalists assume that order is normal for society, the conflict and feminist theorists believe that conflict over resources and power is the status quo. From this perspective, how does one eliminate social problems? The existing social order needs to be replaced with a more equitable society. Midrange solutions attempt to redefine opportunity and power structures to include the participation of marginalized individuals or groups.

The interactionist perspective focuses on social problems at the micro or individual level. According to this perspective, we create our reality through social interaction. Social problems are created by the labels we attach to individuals and their situations (e.g., the "welfare mom" or a "crack addict"). In addition, problematic behavior is learned from others; for example, interactionists believe that criminal behavior is learned from other criminals. Social problems are not objective realities. Rather, they are subjectively constructed by religious, political, and social leaders who influence our opinions and conceptions of what is a social problem. This perspective leads us to many different solutions: changing the labeling process (being careful of who is being labeled and what the label is), resocialization for deviant or inappropriate behavior (if the behavior was learned, it can be unlearned), and recognizing the social construction of social problems (acknowledging that it is a subjective process).

What Does It Mean to Me?

Throughout this text, you have been introduced to four sociological perspectives. Which sociological perspective do you agree with most? Which perspective best explains the reasons and solutions for social problems?

UNDERSTANDING SOCIAL MOVEMENTS

The past 16 chapters have revealed how we continue to experience many social problems—and bear in mind that not every social problem could be addressed in the pages of this text. Yet, considering the past decade, strong evidence suggests that problems such as crime, drug abuse, and poverty have been minimized because of effective social policies and solutions. We tend to think of the government as the only effective agent of social change because politicians pass new laws and policies. But the government is not the only agent of social change. In each chapter, I introduced you to individuals, groups, and communities that have attempted to address a particular social problem. All in their own way are making the second connection, the one between social problems and their solutions.

 Racial Women, Embracing Tradition

Our nation's history is filled with groups of people who attempted to promote change or prevent it from taking place (Harper and Leicht 2002). **Social movements** are defined as conscious, collective, organized attempts to bring about or resist large-scale change in the social order (J. Wilson 1973). In today's society, almost every critical public issue leads to a social movement supporting change (and an opposing countermovement to discourage it) (Meyer and Staggenbord 1996). Social movements are the most potent forces of social change in our society (Sztompka 1994). Social movements lead the way for social reform and policies by first identifying and calling attention to social problems.

Social movements are classified by two factors. First, how much change is intended by the social movement: is it limited or radical change? And second, what is the scope of the intended change: is it a group of people or an entire society? Sociologists Charles Harper and Kevin Leicht (2002) distinguish between two dimensions of social movements in their book *Exploring Social Change: America and the World*. The first dimension identifies how much change is intended by the movement, distinguishing between reform and revolutionary movements. According to Harper and Leicht, **reform movements** try to bring about limited social change by working within the existing system, usually targeting social structures such as education or medicine and directly targeting policy makers. Examples of reform movements are pro-choice or anti-abortion groups. On the other hand, **revolutionary social movements** seek fundamental changes of the system itself. These types of social movements, such as the U.S. civil rights movement or the antiapartheid movement in South Africa, consider the political system the key to system change.

The second dimension of social movements identified by Harper and Leicht (2002) is instrumental versus expressive, addressing the scope of intended change. **Instrumental movements** seek to change the structure of society; examples are the civil rights movement and the environmental movement. **Expressive movements** attempt to change individuals and individual behavior. Based on these dimensions, John Wilson (1973) specified four types of social movements: reformative, transformative, alternative, and redemptive (see Table 17.1).

New social movements theory emphasizes the distinctive features of recent social movements. New social movements first appeared in cultural and radical feminist movements in the late 1960s, in some radical sections of the environmental movement in the 1970s, in parts of the peace movement of the late 1970s through the mid-1980s, and in radical sections of the gay rights movement since the 1980s (Plotke 1995).

John Hannigan (1991) and David Plotke (1995) distinguish between new social movements and early social movements. First, new movements have different ideologies than did earlier movements. Instead of fighting for human rights, such as voting or freedom of speech, new movements are framed around concerns about cultural and community rights, such as the right to be different, to choose one's lifestyle, and to be protected from particular risks like nuclear or environmental hazards

Social movements: Conscious, collective, organized attempts to bring about or resist large-scale change in the social order

Reform movements: An attempt to bring about limited social change by working within the existing system

Revolutionary social movements: Attempts to create fundamental change in the system itself

Instrumental movements: An attempt to change the structure of society

Expressive movements: An attempt to change individuals and individual behavior

New social movements theory: Theory emphasizing the distinctive features of recent social movements

Table 17.1   Types of social movements

	Instrumental	Expressive
Reform	*Reformative:* Partial change within the social structure via policy reform *Examples:* Labor movement, NAACP, antiabortion	*Alternative:* Partial change in individuals via individual reform *Examples:* Christian evangelism, temperance movement
Revolutionary	*Transformative:* Total change of the social structure *Examples:* Bolsheviks, Islamic fundamentalism	*Redemptive:* Total change in the individuals *Examples:* Millenarian movements, cults, the People's Temple

(Hannigan 1991). These movements have been described as identity movements, focused on cultural issues rather than economic or political power. New social movements promote a "more diverse and citizen-oriented set of interests" (Dalton, Kuechler, and Büklin 1990:3). Second, new social movements distrust formal organizations. Consequently, they tend to be small-scale, informal organizations. Finally, whereas previous movements were identified with the economic oppression of workers or minorities, new social movements are associated with a new middle class of "younger, social and cultural specialists" (Plotke 1995). Instead of acting on behalf of their own interests, this new middle class acts on behalf of groups who cannot act on their own.

· ·

What Does It Mean to Me?

How has your level of social activism changed since you've enrolled in college?

· ·

HOW DO SOCIAL MOVEMENTS BEGIN?

Social scientists offer several explanations of how social movements emerge. Individual explanations focus on the psychological dispositions or motivations of those drawn to social movements. Women and men are depicted as either frustrated or calculating actors in political or social movements. Empirical studies have not consistently supported these explanations, demonstrating that individual predispositions are insufficient to account for collective action in social movements. In addition, such theories tend to deflect attention from the real causes of discontent and injustice in our social and political structures (Wilson and Orum 1976).

Social movements do not generally arise from a stable social context; rather, they arise from a changing social order (Lauer 1976). Social movements arise from the

 Greensboro Lunch Counter Sit-ins

IN FOCUS

STUDENT ACTIVISM

College and university students have always played an important role in addressing social problems. According to longtime social activist Ralph Nader (1972), it is up to students "to prod and to provoke, to research and to act" (p. 23). The time in college is a fertile opportunity for social activism (Munson 2010). While at this particular life transition point, students experience significant change in their daily routines and their social networks. Ziad Munson (2010) explains, "To become active in a social movement, people must change their routines to accommodate the demands of activism; they need to incorporate new habits and activities that make them a part of a movement" (p. 774). When social networks are reconfigured, college students are open to new ideas and new worldviews. When regular routines are disrupted, this creates space for (new) social activism.

Student action has led to significant social change. For example, voting drives led by 17- and 18-year olds produced the Twenty-Sixth Amendment of the U.S. Constitution, granting voting rights to those 18 years of age and older (Nader 1972). The driving force behind the Twenty-Sixth Amendment came from youth who raised questions about the legitimacy of a representative government that asked 18- to 20-year-olds to fight in the Vietnam War but denied them the right to vote on war-related issues (Close Up Foundation 2004). Norvald Fimreite, a graduate student at the University of Western Ontario, was the first to report unusual levels of mercury residues in fish caught in the Great Lakes (Nader 1972). Fimreite's data led to a worldwide alert about the problems of mercury and other chemicals in the fish we eat.

Nader believes student activists can accomplish quite a lot:

> Take the corporate polluter. Sit-ins and marches will not clean up rivers and the air that he fouls. He is too powerful and there are too many like him. Yet, the student has unique access to resources that can

AP Photo/Russell Contreras

Dolores Ramos (right) joined her Highland High School classmates to protest New Mexico's Partnership for Assessment of Readiness for College and Careers examination. The standardized exam is part of the new Common Core standards. On their March 2015 exam day, hundreds of high school students left their classrooms and refused to take the exam.

> be effective in confronting the polluter. University and college campuses have the means for detecting the precise nature of the industrial effluent, through chemical and biological research. Through research such as they perform every day in the classroom, students can show the effect of the effluent on an entire watershed, and thus alert the community to real and demonstrable dangers to public health—a far more powerful way to arouse public support for a clean environment than a sit-in. Using the expertise of the campus, students can also demonstrate the technological means available for abating the discharge, and thus meet the polluter's argument that he can do nothing to control his pollution. By drawing on the knowledge of economists, students can counter arguments that an industry will go bankrupt or close down if forced to install pollution controls. Law and political science students can investigate the local, state, or federal regulations that may apply to the case, and publicly challenge the responsible agencies to fulfill their legal duties. p. 21)

Handbook for Activists

structure itself, primarily the result of social and economic deprivation. People are not acting just because of their suffering. They are likely to act when they experience **relative deprivation**, a perceived gap between what they expect and what they actually get. James Davies (1974) argued that social movements are likely to occur when a long period of economic and social improvement is followed by a period of decline. Relative deprivation theory has been used to explain the development of urban protests among African Americans during the 1960s, which were initiated by middle-class African Americans who perceived social and economic gaps between Black and White Americans (Harper and Leicht 2002). But relative deprivation alone isn't enough to create a social movement.

Neil Smelser (1963) explains that six structural conditions are necessary for the development of collective behaviors and social movements. These conditions operate in an additive fashion. First, particular structures in society are more likely to generate certain kinds of social movements than others. For example, societies with racial divisions are more likely to develop racial movements. Second, people will become dissatisfied with the current structure only if the structure is perceived as oppressive or illegitimate. Third, there must be growth of a generalized belief system. People need to share an ideology, a set of ideas, that defines the sources of the structural problems or strains and the solutions necessary to alleviate them. The civil rights movement was based on the ideology that racism was the source of restricted opportunities for minorities (Harper and Leicht 2002). Fourth, dramatic events sharpen and concretize issues. These events may initiate or exaggerate people's dissatisfaction with the current structure or redefine their beliefs about the sources of the structural problems. Examples of dramatic or precipitating events include the 1968 Watts riots in relation to the Black Power phase of the civil rights movement and the 1979 Three Mile Island nuclear disaster in relation to the antinuclear power movement (Harper and Leicht 2002). Fifth, the movement gains momentum with the mobilization of leaders and members for the movement. At this time, the social movement also begins to take the shape of a formal organization. Finally, forces in society (the existing political structure or countermovements) respond to the social movement either by accepting or by suppressing it. One of the important features of Smelser's theory is his emphasis on the relationship between the social movement and society itself, a powerful force in

More than 200,000 people participated in the March on Washington demonstrations in March 1963. This march, along with other nonviolent protests and marches, brought to the nation's attention the need for basic civil rights for all Americans, regardless of race. The U.S. Congress passed landmark legislation in the 1960s: the Civil Rights Act of 1964, the Voting Rights Act of 1965, and the Civil Rights Act of 1968 (also known as the Fair Housing Act).

U.S. Information Agency

Relative deprivation:
A perceived gap between what people expect and what they actually get

Sermons and Civil Rights

shaping the development, the direction, and, ultimately, the success of the movement (Harper and Leicht 2002).

According to **resource mobilization theory**, no social movement can succeed without resources. John McCarthy and Mayer Zald (1977) argue that human and organizational resources must be mobilized to create a social movement. A social movement requires human skills in the form of leadership, talent, and knowledge, as well as an organizational infrastructure to support its work.

On the other hand, the **political process model** emphasizes the relationship between a mobilized social movement and a favorable structure of political opportunities. Social movements are seen as rational attempts by excluded groups to mobilize their political leverage to advance their interests. Social movements are political phenomena, attempting to change social policy and political coalitions, in this view. Political structures enhance the likelihood of a successful social movement by being receptive to change or by being more or less vulnerable at different points in time. For example, Doug McAdam (1982) noted that the efforts of the civil rights movement were enhanced by the expansion of the Black vote and the shift of Black voters to the Democratic Party. Without favorable support from the political structure, the civil rights movement might not have succeeded.

Social movements gain strength when they develop symbols and a sense of community, which generates strong feelings and helps direct this energy into organized action. People will form a social movement when they develop "a shared understanding of the world and of themselves that legitimate[s] and motivate[s] collective action" (McAdam, McCarthy, and Zald 1996:6). McAdam (1982) explains that resource mobilization must include cognitive liberation. Much like Karl Marx's concept of class consciousness, **cognitive liberation** begins when members of an aggrieved group begin to consider their situation as unjust. They must recognize their situation. The second part of cognitive liberation is the group's sense that its situation can be changed. Finally, those who considered themselves powerless begin to believe that they can make a difference (Piven and Cloward 1979). Individuals must move through all three stages to become cognitively liberated. They must organize, act on political opportunities, and instigate change: "In the absence of these necessary attributions, oppressive conditions are likely, even in the face of increased resources, to go unchallenged" (McAdam 1982:34).

The Occupy Wall Street movement (or Occupy for short) was described as the first worldwide postmodern uprising (Brucato 2012). What began with hundreds of protestors in Zuccotti Park, New York, spread to more than 900 cities globally (Adam 2011) and hundreds of college and university encampments across the United States. The movement had been described as a new model for organizing and protesting: a gathering of multiple groups with diverse issues and causes, developing politics through interaction and participatory structures and lacking a clear beginning and ending (Brucato 2012). Some scholars, like political scientist Sidney

Resource mobilization theory: Theory about conditions for success of social movements

Political process model: Model of relationship between social movements and structures of political opportunities

Cognitive liberation: The recognition of one's situation as unjust

Tarrow (2011), noted how Occupy closely mirrored the second wave of feminism. Tarrow writes,

> Although the leaders of the new women's movement had policies they wanted on the agenda, their foremost demand was for recognition of, and credit for, the gendered reality of everyday life. Likewise, when the Occupy Wall Street activists attack Wall Street, it is not capitalism as such they are targeting, but a system of economic relations that has lost its way and failed to serve the public.

While Occupy became "a means of channeling legitimate anger toward productive ends, the progressive transformation of society" (Langman 2013:520), most have dismissed it as a protest, never achieving movement status due to its lack of central leadership, an organizational structure, and a single issue to unite protestors.

· ·

What Does It Mean to Me?

What do you think will be the next social movement?

· ·

HOW HAVE REFORM MOVEMENTS MADE A DIFFERENCE?

"The interest of many scholars in social movements stems from their belief that movements represent an important force for social change" (McAdam, McCarthy, and Zald 1988:727); yet, "the study of the consequences of social movements is one of the most neglected topics in literature" (Giugni 1999:xiv–xv). Early in human history, most social change was the result of chance or trial and error (Mannheim 1940), but in modern history, social movements have been the basic avenues by which social change takes place (Harper and Leicht 2002).

According to Harper and Leicht (2002), the most dramatic social, cultural, economic, and political transformations come from revolutions. Successful revolutions are rare and dramatic events, such as the early revolutions in France (1789), Russia (1917), and China (1949), and they include the political transformations in South America, Eastern Europe, and the former Soviet Union during the 1980s.

Most social movements that we're familiar with are reform movements that focus on either broad or narrow social reforms. They produce significant change, but in gradual or piecemeal ways (Harper and Leicht 2002). The most important U.S. reform movements in the first half of the 20th century focused on grievances related to social class, such as the labor movements of the early 1900s, which helped ensure safer working conditions, eliminated child labor, and provided substantial increases in wages and benefits. After World War II, a new type of reform movement, which included the civil rights movement, the student movement, the feminist movement, the gay liberation movement, and ethnic/racial movements, addressed inequalities

 Why Social Movements Should Ignore Social Media

 Eve Ensler: Happiness in Body and Soul

TAKING A WORLD VIEW

NONGOVERNMENTAL ORGANIZATIONS AS A SOURCE OF CHANGE

Nongovernmental organizations (NGOs) have been called a "positive force in domestic and international affairs, working to alleviate poverty, protect human rights, preserve the environment, and provide relief worldwide" (McGann and Johnstone 2006:65). The term refers to private, voluntary, civil society, and nonprofit organizations advocating on behalf of a range of issues: poverty, human rights, the environment, and social justice. NGOs also represent industry associations, religious organizations, and obscure causes (Paul 2000).

NGOs are known for their innovative campaigns and mobilization strategies, especially for their ability to work outside traditional government structures and political networks. Notable NGO activity includes the collection of labor, antiglobalization, and environmental groups that converged on the 1999 World Trade Organization meeting. NGOs exerted their global influence on the United Nations Conference on Environment and Development (1992) and Fourth World Conference on Women (1995).

There is no definitive count of the number of domestic and international NGOs. In 2014, there were an estimated 35,000 international NGOs (with programs in multiple countries), an increase from the 400 international NGOs reported in 1900 (Paul 2000). For example, Amnesty International, an activist group campaigning for human rights, has more than 3 million members in 150 countries. The number of NGOs has grown, especially in Central and Eastern Europe, India, and developing countries in Africa and Latin America.

---

based on social status rather than social class (Harper and Leicht 2002). Successful reform movements generate change in three areas:

1. *Culture.* Reform movements educate people and change beliefs and behaviors. Change can occur in our culture, identity, and everyday life (Taylor and Whittier 1995). By changing the ways individuals live, movements may effect long-term changes in society (Meyer 2000). The women's movement has established a clear record of cultural change. The women's movement changed the way women viewed themselves and altered our language, our schools, the workplace, politics, the military, and the media.

2. *New organizations or institutions.* Movements lead to the creation of new organizations that continue to generate change. Through these new organizations, social movements may influence ongoing and future initiatives by altering the structure of political support, limiting resources to challengers, and changing the values and symbols used by supporters and challengers. David Meyer (2000) argues that by changing participants' lives, "movements alter the personnel available for subsequent challenges" (p. 51).

   From the women's movement, the National Organization for Women (NOW) was created in 1966, along with the Women's Equity Action League

(1968), the National Women's Political Caucus (1971), the National Women's Law Center (1972), and the Feminist Majority Foundation (1987). NOW is the largest organization of feminist activists in the United States, with more than 500,000 members and 550 chapters in all 50 states. The organization continues its advocacy and legislative efforts in guaranteeing equal rights for women, ensuring abortion rights and reproductive freedom, opposing racism, and ending violence against women.

3. *Social policy and legislation.* Successful social policies have been nurtured by partnerships between the government and social movements (Skocpol 2000). Movements generally organize and mobilize themselves around specific policy demands (Meyer 2000), attempting to minimize or eliminate social problems. Public policy can do many things: new laws can be enacted or old ones may be struck down, social service programs can be created or ended, and taxes can be used to discourage bad behaviors (cigarette or alcohol taxes) or encourage other behaviors (tax breaks to build enterprise zones) (Loseke 2003).

For reform movements, the relationship between desired and actual change varies (Lauer 1976). So far, the women's movement has not achieved the passage of the Equal Rights Amendment (ERA), first proposed in 1923. As of 2012, 35 of the necessary 38 states had ratified the ERA. The women's movement has made progress in revising laws pertaining to violence against women, creating family-friendly business practices, and enhancing women's roles in the military, clergy, sports, and politics.

MAKING THE LAST CONNECTION

In the 1960s anti-segregation protests expanded beyond the south. In this photo ministers picket in front of New York City's F.W. Woolworth store to protest lunch counter segregation practices in the company's southern stores.

It was a Sunday evening, January 31, 1960, when four freshmen at North Carolina Agriculture and Technical College stayed up late talking about ending segregation in the South. They were extraordinarily poorly positioned to effect political or social change on campus, much less in the United States: young, Black, by no means affluent, and generally disconnected from the major centers of power in America. On Monday morning Ezell Blair Jr., Franklin McCain, Joseph McNeill, and David Richmond dressed in their best clothes to visit the Woolworth's in downtown Greensboro. After buying some school supplies, they sat at the lunch counter and waited for service. They spent the rest of their day there.

The following day, 27 other Black students joined them and on Wednesday twice as many. By Thursday, a few sympathetic White students from nearby schools

VOICES IN THE COMMUNITY

CAMILA VALLEJO

In May 2011, Chilean high school and college students began participating in coordinated marches, sit-ins, and strikes. Their efforts have included thousands of individuals, in protests described as the largest since the days of the dictatorship of General Augusto Pinochet. The students were mobilized by the Student Confederation of Chile (CONFECH, a group of all the student unions from public and some private universities), and the oldest union, the Student Federation of the University of Chile (FECH) (Goldman 2012). Camila Vallejo, a 23-year-old geography student from the University of Chile, emerged as the most prominent and charismatic leader of the student movement. When the protests began, Vallejo was FECH's elected president.

The young protestors had one primary issue: education reform. While Chile may have the highest income per capita in the region, it ranks as one of the most unequal countries in the world. According to Francisco Goldman (2012), a university education in Chile is proportionally the most expensive—$3,400 a year for tuition—while the average annual salary for a Chilean citizen is $8,500. Most college students take out bank loans and incur years of debt to pay for their education. While President Sebastián Piñera characterized education as a consumer good, Vallejo and her fellow protestors defined it as a fundamental right, advocating how "the university should be the motor of change in society" (Goldman 2012:23).

The student protests have been credited with the resignation of two education ministers, both ineffectual against the students (Goldman 2012). But what began as a student movement has expanded to other Chilean citizen and worker groups. Vallejo explains, "Something very powerful that has come out of the heart of this movement is that people are really questioning the economic policies of the country. People are not tolerating the way a small number of economic groups benefit from the system" (quoted in Moss Wilson 2012:5). The youth, according to Vallejo, have "revived and dignified politics" (quoted in Franklin 2011a). "It is always

Camila Vallejo joined protestors in Santiago, Chile, demanding a new national system for secondary education. In 2013, Vallejo was elected as a representative of La Florida, Santiago in the Chilean House of Deputies.

the youth that make the first move . . . we don't have family commitments, this allows us to be freer. We took the first step but we are no longer alone, the older generations are now joining this fight" (Vallejo, quoted in Franklin 2011b).

Vallejo has been honored in other countries (Germany, the United Kingdom, and the United States) for her leadership and protest work. In 2013, Vallejo was elected a member of the Chilean congress, winning 44% of the vote in the Santiago district of La Florida. She ran as a member of the Communist Party.

 Camila Vallejo's Motivation and Inspiration

had enlisted and, with the lunch counter at Woolworth's filled, a few started a sit-in at another lunch counter down the street. By the end of the week, city officials offered to negotiate a settlement and, on Saturday night, 1,600 students rallied to celebrate this victory. News of the sit-in campaigns spread throughout the South and then elsewhere across the United States, spurring other activists to emulate their efforts. Sit-ins to desegregate lunch counters and restaurants, stores and libraries, and even buses swept the South. A new organization, the Student Non-Violent Coordinating Committee (SNCC), was formed in April 1960. SNCC would become a leading force in the civil rights movement, setting much of the agenda for liberal politics in the United States during the early 1960s, precipitating the passage of the Voting Rights Act of 1965 and politicizing student activists across the United States (Meyer 2000:33).

Yes, solutions to social problems are complex and, as Mills advised, ultimately require attention to large social forces and structures, such as those targeted by social movements. But social movements don't appear overnight. Social movements begin with individual efforts such as those taken by college students Blair, McCain, McNeill, and Richmond. Grassroots organizations with strong community and local leadership, such as those on the front line of the modern environmental movement, have also proven effective in addressing social problems.

Some may believe that individual efforts don't amount to much, leading only to short-term solutions or effectively helping one person or one family at a time. But according to David Rayside (1998), the impact of any social movement should be measured over the long term. The isolated effort of thousands of individuals and groups "creates changes in social and political climates, which then enable particular groups to make more specific inroads into public policy and institutional practice" (p. 390).

The last connection presented in this text is the connection between social problems and your community. Throughout the country, college students have affirmed their commitment to community service. In 2006, according to UCLA's annual survey of entering college freshmen, one in four freshmen surveyed believed that it was important to be involved in their community. About 80% of freshmen had participated in community service during their senior year in high school, and 67% of them believed that they would continue volunteering in college (Engle 2006). High school students are also increasing their involvement in community service. School districts in every state except Wyoming, North Dakota, and South Dakota require community service.

President Obama and Michelle Obama have consistently highlighted the importance of volunteer service and its value for the nation. In 2009, President Obama launched the United We Serve initiative, calling for a "sustained, collaborative and focused effort to promote service as a way of life for all Americans" (Corporation for National and Community Service 2009). In the same year, Congress designated September 11 as the National Day of Service and Remembrance, and Obama signed the Edward M. Kennedy Serve America Act, which tripled the number of intensive service opportunities in the AmeriCorps program from 75,000 positions annually to 250,000 by 2017. Refer to this chapter's Exploring Social Problems feature for more information about how others are politically engaged.

Who Is Politically Engaged?

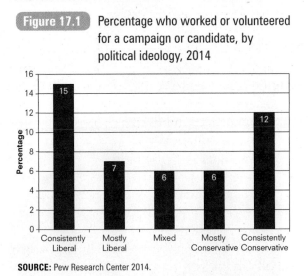

Figure 17.1 Percentage who worked or volunteered for a campaign or candidate, by political ideology, 2014

SOURCE: Pew Research Center 2014.

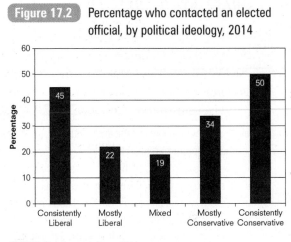

Figure 17.2 Percentage who contacted an elected official, by political ideology, 2014

SOURCE: Pew Research Center 2014.

Figure 17.3 Percentage who attended a campaign event, by political ideology, 2014

SOURCE: Pew Research Center 2014.

WHAT DO YOU THINK?

The Pew Research Center surveyed 10,013 adults in 2014, asking about their political engagement. Political engagement may be operationalized in many different ways—voting, contributing to a candidate, working for a campaign, or attending a political rally.

The Pew researchers concluded that engagement tends to be a U-shaped pattern, with higher levels of engagement at the right and left of the ideological spectrum and lower levels in the center. Notice this pattern in Figures 17.1 through 17.3.

The researchers acknowledge that other factors are correlated with political engagement, such as age and education. Hypothesize the relationship between these other demographic factors and political engagement. As education increases, does the likelihood of political engagement increase or decrease? Explain the reason for your answers.

 United We Serve

SOCIOLOGY AT WORK

GRADUATE STUDY

Barbara Prince–Class of 2012

Undergraduate Majors:
Sociology, Anthropology

Undergraduate Minor: Art History

A master's or doctorate degree in Sociology is essential for employment in higher education, industry, government, or other nonprofit or research settings.

There are two types of master's degree programs. The first type is a traditional program that leads to a PhD in Sociology, with a primary career emphasis on academic employment. Most PhD programs also offer a master's degree track. The second type is a professional or applied program that prepares graduates for research, policy, management, and service occupations. These programs are also referred to as terminal degree programs, as there is no expectation to progress to a PhD program (Spalter-Roth and Van Vooren 2011). Master's programs usually take two to three years and may include a culminating independent project or a thesis as part of the degree requirement.

A doctorate in philosophy (PhD) is the highest degree awarded in Sociology. A PhD program requires at least five to six years of study beyond the bachelor's degree. According to the American Sociological

Courtesy of Barbara Prince

If you think there is nothing that you can do to effect change, you've not been paying attention. The first step is to recognize that you can make a difference. Thomas Ehrlich (2000:xxvi) identifies how

> a morally and civically responsible individual recognizes him or herself as a member of a larger social fabric and therefore considers social problems to be at least partly his or her own; such an individual is willing to see the moral and social dimensions of issues, to make and justify informed moral and civic judgments and to take action when appropriate.

You do not have to believe in quick fixes, universal solutions, or change to the entire world to solve social problems. You do not have to join a national organization.

Who Is Politically Engaged?

Figure 17.1 Percentage who worked or volunteered for a campaign or candidate, by political ideology, 2014

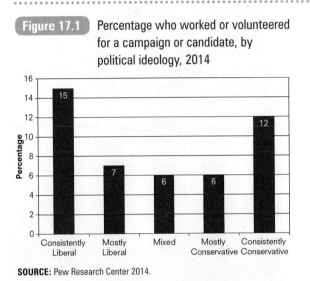

SOURCE: Pew Research Center 2014.

Figure 17.2 Percentage who contacted an elected official, by political ideology, 2014

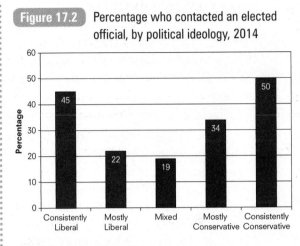

SOURCE: Pew Research Center 2014.

Figure 17.3 Percentage who attended a campaign event, by political ideology, 2014

SOURCE: Pew Research Center 2014.

WHAT DO YOU THINK?

The Pew Research Center surveyed 10,013 adults in 2014, asking about their political engagement. Political engagement may be operationalized in many different ways—voting, contributing to a candidate, working for a campaign, or attending a political rally.

The Pew researchers concluded that engagement tends to be a U-shaped pattern, with higher levels of engagement at the right and left of the ideological spectrum and lower levels in the center. Notice this pattern in Figures 17.1 through 17.3.

The researchers acknowledge that other factors are correlated with political engagement, such as age and education. Hypothesize the relationship between these other demographic factors and political engagement. As education increases, does the likelihood of political engagement increase or decrease? Explain the reason for your answers.

 United We Serve

SOCIOLOGY AT WORK

GRADUATE STUDY

Barbara Prince–Class of 2012

*Undergraduate Majors:
Sociology, Anthropology*

Undergraduate Minor: Art History

A master's or doctorate degree in Sociology is essential for employment in higher education, industry, government, or other nonprofit or research settings.

    There are two types of master's degree programs. The first type is a traditional program that leads to a PhD in Sociology, with a primary career emphasis on academic employment. Most PhD programs also offer a master's degree track. The second type is a professional or applied program that prepares graduates for research, policy, management, and service occupations. These programs are also referred to as terminal degree programs, as there is no expectation to progress to a PhD program (Spalter-Roth and Van Vooren 2011). Master's programs usually take two to three years and may include a culminating independent project or a thesis as part of the degree requirement.

    A doctorate in philosophy (PhD) is the highest degree awarded in Sociology. A PhD program requires

Courtesy of Barbara Prince

at least five to six years of study beyond the bachelor's degree. According to the American Sociological

If you think there is nothing that you can do to effect change, you've not been paying attention. The first step is to recognize that you can make a difference. Thomas Ehrlich (2000:xxvi) identifies how

> a morally and civically responsible individual recognizes him or herself as a member of a larger social fabric and therefore considers social problems to be at least partly his or her own; such an individual is willing to see the moral and social dimensions of issues, to make and justify informed moral and civic judgments and to take action when appropriate.

You do not have to believe in quick fixes, universal solutions, or change to the entire world to solve social problems. You do not have to join a national organization.

Association, over 200 colleges and universities offer PhD programs. A program application usually requires an undergraduate transcript, a personal statement on why you are interested in pursuing doctoral work, faculty recommendations, and scores from the Graduate Record Examination (GRE).

Once you decide to pursue graduate work in sociology, work with your adviser to identify which path—master's or PhD—is for you. Barbara Prince declared her sociology major in her sophomore year, yet knew nothing about careers in sociology. "I just knew that I loved the topics and found the field very interesting. I did know about going to graduate school by the end of my sophomore year, though, because it was something my mentor was always mentioning and very supportive of me pursuing." In her senior year, Barbara worked as an intern for her mentor. The experience, says Barbara, "was designed to expose me to what I would call the invisible work of being a professor. For example, my responsibilities included helping organize a conference, preparing class and review materials, and assisting with grant writing and execution."

After graduating with a bachelor's degree in Sociology and Anthropology, Barbara earned a master's degree in Sociology and is currently enrolled in a PhD program.

I am always using sociology at work in the literal sense since I am working as a graduate research assistant in sociology. . . . I am engaging my sociological imagination to help form my research questions and what I am interested in researching. My sociological imagination also helps me as a graduate research assistant and student to explore alternative explanations for social problems.

For those who are planning to go to graduate school, Barbara offers straightforward advice: "Start planning early, make as many connections as you can, and find a champion mentor." And for those on the job market, she recommends, "Be unapologetic about your sociology major. The skills you learn in sociology, such as the sociological imagination and critical thinking, are what all jobs are looking for in an employee. Even if someone doesn't know what sociology is, I guarantee they want what sociology teaches."

To begin, you can join other college and university students who have chosen to become personally involved in their community. Most efforts are small and practical, but as one college student says, "I can't do anything about the theft of nuclear grade weapons materials in Azerbaijan, but I can clean up the local pond, help tutor a troubled kid, or work at a homeless shelter" (Levine and Cureton 1998:36).

What does it take to start making that connection with your community? The second step is to explore opportunities for service on your campus and in your community. Take the chapters in this text or the material presented by your instructor to consider what social problems you are passionate about. Determine what issues you'd like to address and determine what individuals or groups you'd like to serve. Even though you may be in your college community for only four or five years, act as if you're there for life: take an interest in what happens in your community

(Hollender and Catling 1996). Whatever your interests are, you can be sure that there are people and programs in your community who share them. And if they don't exist, what would it take to create such a program?

The third step is to do what you enjoy doing. When you know what you like, when you know what you can contribute, you will find the right connection. Whatever your talent, your community program will appreciate your contribution. It could be that you are an excellent writer; if so, you could help with a program's monthly newsletter, develop an informational brochure, or design the program's website. Do you enjoy working with others? Volunteer to work with clients, to answer phones, or to help at a rally. In addition to providing invaluable service to the program, recognize the experience and skills that you will gain from your efforts.

And what is the final step? Go out and do it. It doesn't have to last an entire semester or school year; you could just volunteer for a weekend or a day. Change doesn't happen automatically; it begins with individual action. As Paul Rogat Loeb (1994) explains, the hard questions must come from us:

> We need to ask what we want in this nation and why; how should we run our economy, meet human needs, protect the Earth, achieve greater justice? . . . The questions have to come from us, as we reach out to listen and learn, engage fellow citizens who aren't currently involved, and spur debate in environments that are habitually silent.

Sociologist Michael Burawoy (2004) advocates **public sociology,**

> a sociology that seeks to bring sociology to the publics beyond the academy, promoting dialogue about issues that affect the fate of society, placing the values to which we adhere under a microscope. . . . The variety of publics stretches from our students to the readers of our books, from newspaper columns to interviews, from audiences in local civic groups such as churches or neighborhoods, to social movements we facilitate. The possibilities are endless. (p. 104)

Charles Lemert (1997) reminds us of the most valuable sociological lesson:

> Sociology . . . is different for all because each [must] find a way to live in a world that threatens even while it provides. Grace is never cheap. In the end, what remains is that we all have a stake in the world. Like it or not, life is always life together. Social living is the courage to accept what we cannot change in order to do what can be done about the rest. (p. 191)

Put your sociological imagination to work to see where change is possible. Do you have the courage?

Public sociology:
Sociology that promotes a dialogue outside the academy with a variety of public audiences

CHAPTER REVIEW

17.1 Explain the relationship between sociology, social movements, and social change

Sociology provides us with the means to examine the social structure or "machinery" that runs our lives. Social movements are conscious, collective, organized attempts to bring about or resist large-scale change in the social order. They are the most potent forces of social change in our society.

17.2 Distinguish between reform and revolutionary movements

Social movements are classified by two factors: the scope and the depth of change. Instrumental movements seek to change the structure of society itself, whereas expressive movements attempt to change individuals. While reform movements try to bring about limited social change by working within the existing system, revolutionary social movements seek fundamental changes of the system itself.

17.3 Compare cognitive liberation and collective consciousness

Like Marx's theory of collective consciousness, cognitive liberation begins only when members of an aggrieved group start to consider their situation unjust, to believe the situation can be changed, and to believe they can make a difference. For Marx, collective consciousness eventually leads to social revolution, a transformation of the social structure.

17.4 Identify the three areas of change for successful reform movements

Reform movements educate people and change our culture, our beliefs and behaviors. Movements lead to the creation of new organizations that continue to generate change. Movements generally organize and mobilize themselves around specific policy demands, attempting to minimize or eliminate social problems.

KEY TERMS

cognitive liberation, 497

expressive movements, 493

instrumental movements, 493

new social movements theory, 493

political process model, 497

public sociology, 506

reform movements, 493

relative deprivation, 496

resource mobilization theory, 497

revolutionary social movements, 493

social movements, 493

STUDY QUESTIONS

1. How does each sociological perspective identify the potential and sources for social change?

2. Identify and explain the four dimensions of social movements.

3. What is meant by the following statement: "Social movements arise from the structure itself, primarily the result of social and economic deprivation"?

4. Explain the relationship between cognitive liberation and social movements.

5. Successful reform movements generate change in three areas. Identify and explain these three areas of change.

6. Would you characterize the Occupy movement as a social movement? Why or why not?

$SAGE edge™

Sharpen your skills with SAGE edge at **edge.sagepub.com/leonguerrero5e**

SAGE edge provides a personalized approach to help you accomplish your coursework goals in an easy-to-use learning environment.

Distributive power: Power over other individuals or groups

Domestic migration: The movement of people within a country

Domestic terrorism: Terrorism supported or coordinated by groups or individuals based in a country

Double standard of aging: Separate standards of aging for men and women; men are judged in our culture according to what they can do (their competence, power, and control), but women are judged according to their appearance and beauty

Drug abuse: The use of any drug or medication for unintended purposes, which can lead to clinically significant impairment or distress

Drug addiction: Physical or psychological dependence on a drug or medication

Dysfunctions: Negative consequences of social structures

Ecocide: Mass destruction of ecosystems

Emigration: Movement of people out of a geographic area

Environmental justice: Social justice movement based on the principle that all individuals and communities are entitled to equal protection of environmental and public health laws and regulations

Environmental racism: Environmental policy or practice that disadvantages people based on race or color

Environmental sociology: Study of the interactions between our physical and natural environment and our social organization and social behavior

Epidemiology: Study of patterns in the distribution and frequency of sickness, injury, and death and the social factors that shape them

Episodic high-risk drinking: Infrequently drinking a large quantity of alcohol in a short period

Ethnic attrition: Individuals choosing not to self-identify as a member of a particular ethnic group

Ethnic composition: The composition of groups within a population

Ethnic groups: Groups of people who are set off to some degree from other groups by displaying a unique set of cultural traits, such as their language, religion, or diet

Ethnocentrism: The belief that one's own group values and behaviors are right

Exclusion: The practice of prohibiting or restricting the entry or participation of groups in society

Expressive movements: An attempt to change individuals and individual behavior

Expulsion: The removal of a group by direct force or intimidation

Extended families: Two or more adult generations, related by blood, who live together in a single household

Family: Social unit based on kinship relations, a construct of meaning and relationships both emotional and economic

Fecundity: The maximum number of children that could be born, based on the number of women of childbearing age in a population

Felonies: Crimes that are serious offenses, punishable by more than one year's imprisonment or death

Femicide: The killing of women; the term is used in contrast to the literal meaning of *homicide* as the killing of men

Feminist perspective: A theoretical perspective that defines gender (and sometimes race or social class) as a source of social inequality, group conflict, and social problems

Fertility: The level of childbearing for an individual or a population

Food insecure: Lacking in access to sufficient food for all family members

Foreign born: Anyone who is not a U.S. citizen at birth

Functionalist perspective: A theoretical perspective that examines the functions or consequences of the structure of society; functionalists use a macro perspective, focusing on how society creates and maintains social order

Gender: Social construction of masculine and feminine attitudes and behaviors

Gender mainstreaming: The integration of the gender perspective into every stage of the policy process (design, implementation, monitoring, and evaluation)

Gendered division of labor: Assignment of different tasks to men and women

Genocide: The systematic targeting of members of an ethnic or a religious group

Gentrification: The process of neighborhood change from lower- to higher-income residents

Gerontology: The study of aging and the elderly

Global warming: The ongoing rise in the global average temperature

Globalization: A process of increasing transborder connectedness; the basis may be economic, political, environmental, or social

GLOSSARY

1.5 generation: Individuals who immigrated to the United States as a child or an adolescent

Absolute poverty: Lack of basic necessities

Acute illnesses: Illnesses that strike suddenly and disappear quickly

Age distribution: The distribution of individuals by age

Ageism: Prejudice or discrimination based on someone's age

Alcoholism: Alcohol dependence, characterized by the symptoms of craving, loss of control, physical dependence, and tolerance

Alienation: Separation from one's true self; alienation occurs on multiple levels—from one's work, the product of one's work, other workers, and one's human potential

Anomie: State of normlessness

Applied research: Pursuit of knowledge for program application or policy evaluation

Assimilation: A process in which minority group members become part of the dominant group, losing their original group identity

Basic research: Exploration of the causes and consequences of a social problem

Bisexuality: Sexual orientation toward either sex

Boomerangers: Young adults who leave home for college, but return after graduation because of either economic constraints (they may be unemployed or underemployed) or personal choice

Bourgeoisie: Capitalist ruling class; owners of businesses

Brownfields: Abandoned or underused industrial or commercial properties where hazardous substances, pollutants, or contaminants are present or potentially present

Class consciousness: Awareness of one's social position

Climate change: The perceptible climate trends over time; also referred to as global warming

Cognitive liberation: The recognition of one's situation as unjust

Cohabiting: Sexual partners, not married to each other, but residing in the same household

Conflict perspective: A theoretical perspective that considers how society is held together by power and coercion for the benefit of those in power (based on social class, gender, race, or ethnicity)

Critical political-economy perspective: An approach using a conflict perspective to focus on city formation based on racial, gender, or class inequalities (also referred to as socio-spatial perspective)

Crowding: Defined as more than one person per room in the household

Cultural capital: Cultural skills and knowledge passed on to youth by their parents and through their social and economic position

Culture of poverty: A set of norms, values, and beliefs that encourage and perpetuate poverty

Cybercrime: A form of white-collar crime that involves Internet fraud and abuse

Decriminalization: Reduction of the kinds of behavior included under the law

De facto segregation: A subtle process of segregation that is the result of other processes, such as housing segregation, rather than because of an official policy

Deindustrialization: Systematic disinvestment in manufacturing and production capacities

Demography: The study of the size, composition, and distribution of human populations

Dependent variable: The variable to be explained

Devaluation of women's work: When the higher societal value placed on men than on women is reproduced within the workplace

Differential association: The learning of behaviors and norms from the groups we have contact with

Digital divide: The gap separating individuals who have access to and understanding of new forms of technology from those who do not

Digital literacy: An individual's ability to appropriately use digital tools and skills to identify, manage, evaluate, analyze, and synthesize digital sources; to construct new knowledge; and to communicate with others

Disengagement theory: Theoretical perspective that defines aging as a natural process of withdrawal from active participation in social life

Heteronormativity: The promotion of heterosexual, married, monogamous, White, and upper-middle-class norms

Heterosexism: The privileging of heterosexuality over homosexuality

Heterosexuality: Sexual orientation toward the opposite sex

Homophobia: An irrational fear or intolerance of homosexuals

Homosexuality: Sexual orientation toward the same sex

Horizontal segregation: The separation of men and women into different industries and occupations

Household: An economic and residential unit

Human agency: The active role of individuals in creating their social environment

Human capital: Job-related skills acquired through education and work experience

Human capital theory: Theory that attributes gender income differences to differences in the kind and amount of human capital men and women acquire

Human ecology: The study of the relationship between individuals and their physical environment

Humanitarian intervention: A responsibility to protect, including three aspects: how to prevent humanitarian crises in the first place, under which conditions and in what way to intervene, and how to maintain peace after a military conflict and rebuild the country

Hypothesis: Statement of a relationship between variables

Immigration: The movement of people leaving their country of origin to move to another

Impression management: Creating a favorable impression of oneself to others

Incidence rate: The number of new cases of disease within a population during a specific period

Income: Money earned for one's work

Independent variable: The variable expected to account for the cause of the dependent variable

Index crimes: Crimes including murder, rape, robbery, assault, burglary, motor vehicle theft, arson, and larceny

Individual discrimination: Prejudiced actions against minority members by individuals; may include avoiding contact or physical or verbal attacks

Industrial Revolution: Economic shift from family to market production

Infant mortality: Rate of infant deaths per 1,000 live births

Institutional discrimination: Discrimination practiced by political or social institutions

Institutionalized heterosexuality: The set of ideas, institutions, and relationships that define the heterosexual family as the societal norm

Instrumental movements: An attempt to change the structure of society

Interactionist perspective: A micro-level perspective that highlights what we take for granted: the expectations, rules, and norms that we learn and practice without even noticing; interactionists maintain that through our interaction, social problems are created and defined

Interior residential density: The number of individuals per room in a dwelling

International terrorism: Terrorism supported or coordinated by foreign groups threatening the security of U.S. nationals or the national security of the United States

Juvenile crime: Criminal acts performed by juveniles

Juvenile delinquent: A youth who engages in criminal behavior

Juvenile status offender: A juvenile who has violated a law applying only to minors

Labeling theory: Theory stating that individuals and acts are defined or labeled as criminal

Labor migration: The movement of people from one country to another for employment

Latent functions: Unintended and often hidden consequences

Legalization: Removal from control of the law

LGBT: Term used to refer to lesbians, gays, bisexuals, and transgender individuals as a group

Life chances: Access provided by social position to goods and services

Life course perspective: A theoretical perspective that considers the entire course of human life (from childhood, adolescence, and adulthood to old age) as social constructions that reflect the broader structural conditions of society

Macro level of analysis: Societal level of analysis

Manifest functions: Intended and recognized consequences

Master status: An identity that determines how others view individuals and how individuals view themselves

Mechanical solidarity: Union of individuals through a set of common values, beliefs, and customs and a simple division of labor

Media: Technological processes that facilitate communication

Media literacy: The ability to assess and analyze media messages

Medicalization: Process through which a condition or behavior becomes defined as a medical problem

Megadisaster: A catastrophe that threatens or overwhelms an area's capacity to get people to safety, treat casualties, protect infrastructure, and control panic

Micro level of analysis: Individual level of analysis

Migration: The movement of individuals from one area to another

Military-industrial complex: Collaboration of the government, the military, and the armament industry

Misdemeanors: Crimes that are minor offenses, punishable by a fine or less than one year's imprisonment

Modernization theory of aging: Theoretical perspective that links the role and status of the elderly with their labor contribution or their relationship to the means of production

Morbidity: Study of illnesses and disease

Mortality: Incidence of death in a population

Multicultural literature: Literature that focuses on people of color, religious minorities, regional cultures, the disabled, or the aged

Multiracial: Mixed or multiple race

Native: Anyone born in the United States or a U.S. island area or born abroad of a U.S. citizen parent

Natural capitalism: The awareness of the economic value of nature

Neglect: Failure to provide for a child's basic needs

New social movements theory: Theory emphasizing the distinctive features of recent social movements

Nuclear family: Family consisting of parents and their children

Objective reality: Actual existence of a particular condition

Occupational sex segregation: The degree to which men and women are concentrated in occupations that predominantly employ workers of one sex

Organic solidarity: Union of individuals through a complex division of labor

Organizational child: A child prepared by education for a bureaucratic adult world

Outcome goals: Related to terrorism, the group's stated political ends, which require cooperation of the target authority or government

Overurbanization: The process in which an excess population is concentrated in an urban area that lacks the capacity to provide basic services and shelter

Particulate or particle pollution: Air pollution caused by the combustion of fossil fuels—the burning of coal, diesel, gasoline, and wood; particulate matter includes road dust, diesel soot, ash, wood smoke, and sulfate aerosols that are suspended in the air

Patriarchy: Society in which the powerful (often men) dominate the powerless (often women)

Physical abuse: Nonaccidental physical injury, from bruising to death

Pluralism: Each ethnic or racial group maintains its own culture (cultural pluralism or multiculturalism) or a separate set of social structures and institutions (structural pluralism)

Political process model: Model of relationship between social movements and structures of political opportunities

Politicide: The systematic targeting of specific groups because of their political beliefs

Politics of fear: How decision makers and politicians promote and use the public's beliefs and assumptions about terrorism to achieve certain goals

Population aging: The increase in the number or proportion of older individuals in the population

Poverty guidelines: Used to determine family or individual eligibility for relevant federal programs

Poverty threshold: The original federal poverty measure, based on the economy food plan

Power: The ability to achieve one's goals despite resistance from others

Power elite: A select group possessing true power

Prejudice: A negative attitude based on the attributes of an individual

Prestige: Social respect or standing

Prevalence rate: Total number of cases involving a specific health problem during a specific period

Process goals: Related to terrorism, goals aimed to sustain the group and its activities by securing financial support, gaining media attention, and boosting group morale

Proletariat: The working class in a capitalist economy

Property crime: Criminal acts that involve the taking of money or property from another without force or the threat of force against the victims; burglary, larceny, theft, motor vehicle theft, and arson are examples of property crimes

Public sociology: Sociology that promotes a dialogue outside the academy with a variety of public audiences

Qualitative methods: Research methods designed to capture social life as participants experience it

Quantitative methods: Research methods that rely on the collection of statistical data and require the specification of variables and scales collected through surveys, interviews, or questionnaires

Race: Group or population sharing a set of genetic characteristics and physical features

Racial profiling: The use of race or ethnicity by law enforcement consciously or unconsciously as a basis of judgment for criminal suspicion

Racism: The belief in the inferiority of certain racial or ethnic groups, often accompanied by discrimination

Reform movements: An attempt to bring about limited social change by working within the existing system

Refugees: Persons who are unable or unwilling to return to their country of origin due to persecution or fear of persecution on account of race, religion, nationality, membership in a particular social group, or political opinion

Relative deprivation: A perceived gap between what people expect and what they actually get

Relative poverty: Failure to achieve society's average income or lifestyle

Residential segregation: The neighborhood clustering or separation of groups by racial, ethnic, or economic characteristics within a geographic area

Resource mobilization theory: Theory about conditions for success of social movements

Revolution: An overthrow of the existing government or political structure

Revolutionary social movements: Attempts to create fundamental change in the system itself

Role strain: Strain experienced when the demands of one's role exceed one's ability and resources to fulfill that role

Scientific management: Analysis and implementation of the best way to complete a task

Second generation: Those born in the United States to one or more foreign-born parents

Segregation: Physical and social separation of ethnic or racial groups

Service revolution: Economic shift toward service and information occupations

Sex: Physiological distinctions between male and female

Sexism: Prejudice or discrimination based solely on someone's sex

Sexual orientation: The classification of individuals according to their preference for emotional-sexual relationships and lifestyle

Sick role: Set of behaviors regarding actions and treatment of ill persons

Smog or ground-level ozone: Air pollution formed when nitrogen oxides emitted from electric power plants and automobiles react with organic compounds in the presence of sunlight and heat

Social capital: Investments in social relationships and networks distributed unequally by social class

Social construction of reality: The world regarded as a social creation

Social constructionism: Subjective definition or perception of conditions

Social inequality: Unequal distribution of resources, services, and positions

Social innovation: Policy, program, or advocacy that features an untested or a unique approach

Social institutions: A stable set of statuses, roles, groups, and organizations that provides a foundation for addressing fundamental societal needs; an example of a social institution is the family

Social media: Media that are based on conversation and interaction with individuals online

Social movements: Conscious, collective, organized attempts to bring about or resist large-scale change in the social order

Social policy: Enactment of a course of action through a formal law or program

Social problem: A social condition that has negative consequences for individuals, our social world, or our physical world

Social stratification: The ranking of individuals into social strata or groups

Sociological imagination: The ability to link our personal lives and experiences with our social world

Sociology: The systematic study of individuals and social structures

Socio-spatial perspective: An approach using a conflict perspective to focus on city formation based on race, gender, or class inequalities (also referred to as the critical political-economy perspective)

Soft-power approach: Where a nation-state is perceived as having values, motives, and actions that should be emulated

Species being: A human being's true self

Stereotype threat: The risk of confirming in oneself a characteristic that is a negative stereotype

Stigma: A discrediting attribute

Strain theory: Robert K. Merton's theory that predicts that criminal behavior is likely to occur when individuals are unable to achieve social and material goals because of insufficient access or resources

Subjective reality: Attachment of meanings to our reality

Suburbanization: The process by which a population shifts to suburban areas

Sweatshop: A workplace that violates more than one federal or state labor law; the term has come to include exploitation of workers, for example, in workplaces with no livable wages or benefits, poor and hazardous working conditions, and possible verbal or physical abuse

Symbolic interactionism: Theoretical perspective that examines how we use language, words, and symbols to create and maintain our social reality

Terrorism: The unlawful use of force to intimidate or coerce compliance with a particular set of beliefs; can be either domestic (based in the United States) or foreign (supported by foreign groups threatening the security of U.S. nationals or U.S. national security)

Theory: A set of assumptions and propositions used for explanation, prediction, and understanding

Tracking: Designation of academic courses for students based on presumed aptitude

Transgender: Individuals whose gender identity is different from that assigned to them at birth

Transnational: Immigrants who maintain social, economic, and cultural ties across international borders

Underemployment: Employment under less-than-optimal conditions regarding pay, skill, or working hours

Urban population: An area with 2,500 or more individuals

Urban sociology: Examination of social, political, and economic structures and their impact within an urban setting

Urban sprawl: The process in which the spread of development across the landscape outpaces population growth

Urbanization: The process by which a population shifts from rural to urban

Urbanized area: A densely populated area with 50,000 or more residents

Variables: A property of people or objects that can take on two or more values

Vertical segregation: The separation of men and women in workplace hierarchies; lower-ranking positions are dominated by women, while management ranks are dominated by men

Violent crime: Criminal acts that involve force or the threat of force against others and include aggravated assault, murder, rape, and robbery

Wealth: The value of one's personal assets

White-collar crime: Crimes committed by someone of high social status, for financial gain, or in a particular organization

Chapter 1

Adams, Bert and R. A. Sydie. 2001. *Sociological Theory*. Thousand Oaks, CA: Pine Forge.

Advisory Committee on Student Financial Assistance. 2006. *Mortgaging Our Future: How Financial Barriers to College Undercut America's Global Competitiveness*. Washington, DC: Advisory Committee on Student Financial Assistance.

AIDS United. 2014. *Now Is the Time: 2013 Annual Report*. Washington, DC: AIDS United.

Akintola, Olagoke. 2010. "Perceptions of Rewards Among Volunteer Caregivers of People Living With AIDS Working in Faith-Based Organizations in South Africa: A Qualitative Study." *Journal of the International AIDS Society* 13:22.

Ballantine, Jeanne and Keith Roberts. 2012. *Our Social World, Condensed Version*. 2nd ed. Thousand Oaks, CA: Sage Publications.

Ballesteros, P., J. L. Estrada, G. Barriga, F. Molinar, M. C. Hernandez, L. Huerta, G. Cocho, and C. Villarreal. 2006. "Comparative Analysis of Gender Differences in HIV-1 Infection Dynamics." *AIP Conference Proceedings* 854(1):48–50.

Berger, Peter and Thomas Luckmann. 1966. *The Social Construction of Reality*. Garden City, NY: Anchor.

Bernard, Jessie. 1982. *The Future of Marriage*. 2nd ed. New Haven, CT: Yale University Press. (Original work published 1972)

Callan, Patrick and Joni Finney. 2002. "State Policies for Affordable Higher Education." Pp. 10–11, 13 in *Losing Ground: A National Status Report on the Affordability of American Higher Education*. San Jose, CA: National Center for Public Policy and Higher Education.

Centers for Disease Control and Prevention. 2007. "Basic Information." Retrieved May 7, 2010 (http://www.cdc.gov/hiv/topics/basic/index .htm).

Centers for Disease Control and Prevention. 2012. "HIV in the United States." Retrieved March 9, 2012 (http://www.cdc.gov/hiv/resources/ factsheets/us.htm).

Centers for Disease Control and Prevention. 2013. "HIV in the United States: At a Glance." Retrieved July 30, 2014 (http://www.cdc.gov/ hiv/statistics/basics/ataglance.html).

Centers for Disease Control and Prevention. 2014. "HIV/AIDS: Basic Statistics." Retrieved September 27, 2014 (http://www .cdc.gov/hiv/basics/statistics.html).

Chakrapani, Venkatesan, Peter Newman, Murali Shunmugam, Alan McLuckie, and Frederick Melwin. 2007. "Structural Violence Against Kothi-Identified Men Who Have Sex With Men in Chennai, India: A Qualitative Investigation." *AIDS Education and Prevention* 19(4):346–64.

Chodorow, Nancy. 1978. *The Reproduction of Mothering: Psychoanalysis and the Sociology of Gender*. Berkeley: University of California Press.

College Board. 2014. "Trends in College Pricing 2013." Retrieved July 30, 2014 (https://trends .collegeboard.org/sites/default/files/college-pricing-2013-full-report-140108.pdf).

Collins, Patricia Hill. 1990. *Black Feminist Thought: Knowledge, Consciousness, and Empowerment*. Boston: Unwin Hyman.

Coser, L. 1956. *The Functions of Social Conflict*. New York: Free Press.

Dahrendorf, Ralf. 1959. *Class and Class Conflict in Industrial Society*. Stanford, CA: Stanford University Press.

Dugger, Celia. 2009. "As Donors Focus on AIDS, Child Illnesses Languish." *New York Times*, October 30, p. A8.

Durkheim, Émile. 1973. "The Dualism of Human Nature and Its Moral Condition." Pp. 149–63 in *Emile Durkheim on Morality and Society*, edited by R. Bellah. Chicago, IL: University of Chicago Press. (Original work published 1914)

Education Trust. 2009. *Priced Out: How the Wrong Financial-Aid Policies Hurt Low-Income Students*. Washington, DC: Education Trust.

Ellis, R. A. 2003. *Impacting Social Policy: A Practitioner's Guide to Analysis and Action*. Pacific Grove, CA: Thomson Brooks/Cole.

Feagin, Joel. 2002. "Social Justice and Sociology: Agendas for the Twenty-First Century: Presidential Address." *American Sociological Review* 66:1–20.

Fine, Gary Alan. 2006. "The Chaining of Social Problems: Solutions and Unintended Consequences in the Age of Betrayal." *Social Problems* 53(1):3–17.

Frankfort-Nachmias, Chava and Anna Leon-Guerrero. 2013. *Social Statistics for a Diverse Society*. Thousand Oaks, CA: Sage Publications.

Fumaz, C. R., J. A. Munoz-Moreno, A. L. Ballesteros, R. Paredes, M. J. Ferrer, A. Salas, D. Fuster, E. Masmitja, N. Perez-Alvarez, G. Gomez, C. Tural, and B. Clotet. 2007. "Influence of the Type of Pegylated Interferon on the Onset of Depressive and Neuropsychiatric Symptoms in HIV-HCV Coinfected Patients." *AIDS Care* 19(1):138–45.

Habitat for Humanity. 2004. "Millard Fuller." Retrieved May 7, 2010 (http://www.habitat.org/ how/millard.html).

Heiner, Robert. 2002. *Social Problems: An Introduction to Critical Constructionism*. New York: Oxford University Press.

Herbert, Bob. 2011. "The Human Cost of Budget Cutting." *New York Times*, February 20, p. 11.

Hytrek, Gary and Kristine Zentgraf. 2007. *America Transformed: Globalization, Inequality and Power*. New York: Oxford University Press.

Institute for College Access & Success. 2014. "Student Debt and the Class of 2013."

Retrieved December 28, 2014 (http://project onstudentdebt.org/files/pub/classof2013.pdf).

International AIDS Society. 2011. "A Day in the Life of Judy Auerbach." Retrieved December 28, 2014 (http://blog.iasociety.org/ post/2011/09/23/A-Day-in-the-Life-of-Judy-Auerbach-IAS-Member-and-Vice-President-of-Research-and-Evaluation-at-the-San-Francisco-AIDS-Foundation.aspx).

Irwin, Alan. 2001. *Sociology and the Environment*. Cambridge, England: Polity Press.

Kaplan, Laura Duhan. 1994. "Women as Caretaker: An Archetype That Supports Patriarchal Militarism." *Hypatia* 9(2):123–33.

Katzer, Jeffrey, Kenneth Cook, and Wayne Crouch. 1998. *Evaluating Information: A Guide for Users of Social Science Research*. 4th ed. Boston: McGraw-Hill.

Lemert, Charles. 1997. *Social Things: An Introduction to the Sociological Life*. Lanham, MD: Rowman & Littlefield.

Lichtenstein, Bronwen. 2004. "AIDS as a Social Problem: The Creation of Social Pariahs in the Management of an Epidemic." Pp. 316–34 in *Handbook of Social Problems: A Comparative International Perspective*, edited by George Ritzer. Thousand Oaks, CA: Sage Publications.

Loseke, Denise. 2003. *Thinking About Social Problems*. New York: Aldine de Gruyter.

Loseke, Denise and Joel Best. 2003. *Social Problems: Constructionist Readings*. New York: Aldine De Gruyter.

Madoo Lengermann, Patricia and Jill Niebrugge-Brantley. 2004. "Contemporary Feminist Theory." Pp. 436–80 in *Sociological Theory*, edited by George Ritzer and Douglas Goodman. Boston: McGraw-Hill.

Mapping Pathways. 2011. "Addressing Social Drivers of HIV/AIDS: Q&A with Judith Auerbach." Retrieved September 1, 2014 (http://mappingpathways.blogspot.com/ 2011/09/addressing-social-drivers-of-hivaids-q.html).

Marx, Karl. 1972. "Theses on Feuerbach." In *The Marx-Engels Reader*, edited by Robert C. Tucker. New York: Norton.

Mead, George Herbert. 1962. *Mind, Self, and Society: From the Standpoint of a Social Behaviorist*. Chicago, IL: University of Chicago Press. (Original work published 1934)

Merton, Robert. 1957. *Social Theory and Social Structure*. Glencoe, IL: Free Press.

Mills, C. Wright. 2000. *The Sociological Imagination*. New York: Oxford University Press. (Original work published 1959)

National Center for Public Policy and Higher Education and Public Agenda. 2010. "Squeeze Play 2010: Continued Public Anxiety on Cost, Harsher Judgments on How Colleges Are Run." Retrieved May 7, 2010 (http:// www.publicagenda.org/pages/squeeze-play-2010#CollidingChart).

NPR. 2014. "Balancing College Dreams With Financial Realities." Retrieved July 31, 2014 (http://www.npr.org/2014/03/17/290759615/balancing-college-dreams-with-the-reality-of-finances).

Pew Research Center. 2014. "Middle Easterners See Religious and Ethnic Hatred as Top Global Threat." Retrieved December 21, 2014 (http://www.pewglobal.org/2014/10/16/middle-easterners-see-religious-and-ethnic-hatred-as-top-global-threat/).

Ritzer, George. 2000. *Sociological Theory*. New York: McGraw-Hill.

Ritzer, George. 2008. *Sociological Theory*. New York: McGraw Hill.

Sambisa, William, Sian Curtis, and Vinod Mishra. 2010. "AIDS Stigma as an Obstacle to Uptake of HIV Testing: Evidence From a Zimbabwean National Population-Based Survey." *AIDS Care* 22:170–86.

Schneider, Anne and Helen Ingram. 1993. "Social Construction of Target Populations: Implications for Politics and Policy." *American Political Science Review* 87(2):334–47.

Schroedel, Jean R. and Daniel R. Jordan. 1998. "Senate Voting and Social Construction of Target Populations: A Study of AIDS Policy Making, 1987–1992." *Journal of Health Politics, Policy and Law* 23(1):107–31.

Schutt, Russell. 2012. *Investigating the Social World: The Process and Practice of Research*. Thousand Oaks, CA: Sage Publications.

Simoni, Jane, Karina Walters, Kimberly Balsam, and Seth Meyers. 2006. "Victimization, Substance Abuse, and HIV Risk Behaviors Among Gay/Bisexual/Two-Spirit and Heterosexual American Indian Men in New York City." *American Journal of Public Health* 96(12):2240–45.

Smith, Dorothy. 1987. *The Everyday World as Problematic: A Feminist Sociology*. Boston: Northeastern University Press.

Spalter-Roth, Roberta and Nicole Van Vooren. 2008. *What Are They Doing With a Bachelor's Degree in Sociology?* Washington, DC: American Sociological Association.

Spector, Malcolm and John Kituse. 1987. *Constructing Social Problems*. New York: Aldine de Gruyter.

Tabi, Marian and Robert Vogel. 2006. "Nutritional Counseling: An Intervention for HIV Positive Patients." *Journal of Advance Nursing* 54(6):676–82.

Tong, Rosemarie. 1989. *Feminist Thought: A Comprehensive Introduction*. Boulder, CO: Westview Press.

Turner, Jonathan. 1998. *The Structure of Sociological Theory*. 6th ed. Belmont, CA: Wadsworth.

UNAIDS. 2014. "Fact Sheet 2014." Retrieved July 30, 2014 (http://www.unaids.org/en/media/unaids/contentassets/documents/factsheet/2014/20140716_FactSheet_en.pdf).

U.S. Bureau of Labor Statistics. 2014. "How to Become a Sociologist." Retrieved August 9, 2014 (http://www.bls.gov/ooh/life-physical-and-social-science/sociologists.htm#tab-4).

Zetterberg, Hans. 1964. "The Practical Use of Sociological Knowledge." *Acta Sociologica* 7:57–72.

Part II

Shapiro, Thomas. 2004. *Great Divides: Readings in Social Inequality in the United States*. New York: McGraw-Hill.

Chapter 2

AAC&U. 2013. "Critical Thinking VALUE Rubric." Retrieved August 20, 2014 (http://www.aacu.org/value/rubrics/pdf/CriticalThinking.pdf).

Abramovitz, Mimi. 1996. *Regulating the Lives of Women: Social Welfare Policy From the Colonial Times to the Present*. Boston: South End Press.

Alvarez, Lizette. 2012. "No Savings Are Found From Welfare Drug Tests." *New York Times*, April 18, p. A14.

Arnold, Althea, Sheila Crowley, Elina Bravve, Sarah Brundage, and Christine Biddlecombe. 2014. *Out of Reach 2014*. Washington, DC: National Low Income Housing Coalition.

Banfield, Edward. 1974. *The Unheavenly City Revisited*. Boston: Little, Brown.

Besharov, D. 2002."The Past and Future of Welfare Reform." Retrieved May 9, 2010 (http://www.aei.org/article/14781).

Bhargava, D. and J. Kuriansky. 2002. "Defining Who's Poor: Families Suffer as the Government Continues to Rely on the Outdated Measure of the Poverty Line." Retrieved August 30, 2003 (http://www.wowonline.org/ourprograms/fess/state-resources/NY/MEDIA/9-22-02,%20Defining%20who's%20poor%20Families%20suffer%20as%20the%20governme.pdf).

Blank, Rebecca. 2011. "The Supplemental Poverty Measure: A New Tool for Understanding Poverty." *Pathways* (Fall):10–14.

Bornstein, David. 2011. "Out of Poverty, Family Style." Retrieved April 18, 2012 (http://opinionator.blogs.nytimes.com/2011/07/14/out-of-poverty-family-style/#).

Brady, David, Andrew Fullerton, and Jennifer Moren Cross. 2010. "More Than Just Nickels and Dimes: A Cross-National Analysis of Working Poverty in Affluent Democracies." *Social Problems* 57:559–85.

Braveman, Paula. and Eleuther Tarimo. 2002. "Social Inequalities in Health Within Countries: Not Only an Issue for Affluent Countries." *Social Science and Medicine* 54:1621–35.

Bricker, Jesse, Arthur Kennickell, Kevin Moore, and John Sabelhaus. 2012. *Changes in U.S. Family Finances From 2007 to 2012: Evidence From the Survey of Consumer Finances*. Washington, DC: Federal Reserve System.

Briefel, R., Jonathan Jacobson, Nancy Clusen, Teresa Zavitsky, Miki Satake, Brittany Dawson, and Rhoda Cohen. 2003. *The Emergency Food Assistance System: Findings From the Client Survey: Executive Summary* (Food Assistance and Nutrition Research Report, No. 32). Washington, DC: U.S. Department of Agriculture, Economic Research Service.

Burak, Esra. 2011. "Spotlight on Family Independence Initiative." *Pathways* (Summer):27–28.

Cammisa, Ann Marie. 1998. *From Rhetoric to Reform? Welfare Policy in American Politics*. Boulder, CO: Westview Press.

Center for Women Policy Studies. 2002. *From Poverty to Self Sufficiency: The Role of Postsecondary Education in Welfare Reform*. Washington, DC: Center for Women Policy Studies.

Center on Budget and Policy Priorities. 2012. "Chartbook: SNAP Helps Struggling Families Put Food on the Table." Retrieved April 14, 2012 (http://www.cbpp.org/cms/index.cfm?fa=view&id=3744).

Center on Budget and Policy Priorities. 2013a. "Policy Basics: Introduction to the Supplemental Nutrition Assistance Program (SNAP)." Retrieved August 6, 2014 (http://www.cbpp.org/cms/index.cfm?fa=view&id=2226).

Center on Budget and Policy Priorities. 2013b. "Census: SNAP Lifted 4 Million People Out of Poverty in 2012 and Reduced Hardship for Millions More." Retrieved August 5, 2014 (http://www.offthechartsblog.org/census-snap-lifted-4-million-people-out-of-poverty-in-2012-and-reduced-hardship-for-millions-more/).

Children's Defense Fund. 2014. *The State of America's Children 2014*. Washington, DC: Children's Defense Fund.

Christopher, Karen. 2005. "The Poverty Line Forty Years Later: Alternative Poverty Measures and Women's Lives." *Race, Gender & Class* 12:34–52.

Clemetson, Lynette. 2003. "Poor Workers Finding Modest Housing Unaffordable, Study Says." *New York Times*, September 9, p. A15.

Cockerman, William. 2004. "Health as a Social Problem." Pp. 281–97 in *Handbook of Social Problems: A Comparative International Perspective*, edited by George Ritzer. Thousand Oaks, CA: Sage Publications.

Coleman-Jensen, Alisha, Mark Nord and Anita Singh. 2013. *Household Food Security in the United States in 2012*. Washington, DC: U.S. Department of Agriculture.

Confessore, Nicholas. 2012. "Super PAC for Gingrich to Get $5 Million Infusion." *New York Times*, January 24, pp. A1, A16.

Conley, Dalton. 1999. *Being Black, Living in the Red: Race, Wealth, and Social Policy in America*. Berkeley: University of California Press.

DeNavas-Walt, Carmen and Bernadette Proctor. 2014. *Income and Poverty in the United States: 2013* (Current Population Reports, P60-249). Washington, DC: U.S. Census Bureau.

DeNavas-Walt, Carmen, Bernadette Proctor, and Jessica Smith. 2007. *Income, Poverty and Health Insurance Coverage in the United States: 2006* (Current Population Reports, P60-233). Washington, DC: U.S. Government Printing Office.

DeNavas-Walt, Carmen, Bernadette Proctor, and Jessica Smith. 2012. *Income, Poverty and Health Insurance Coverage in the United States:*

2011 (Current Population Reports, P60–243). Washington, DC: U.S. Government Printing Office.

Domhoff, G. William. 2002. *Who Rules America? Power and Politics.* Boston: McGraw-Hill.

Dowd, Tim and John Horowitz. 2011. "Income Mobility and the Earned Income Tax Credit: Short-Term Safety Net or Long-Term Income Support." *Public Finance Review* 39: 619–52.

Drake, Bruce. 2013. "Americans See Growing Gap Between Rich and Poor." Retrieved August 19, 2014 (http://www.pewresearch.org/fact-tank/2013/12/05/americans-see-growing-gap-between-rich-and-poor/).

European Commission. 1985. "85/8/EEC: Council Decision of 19 December 1984 on Specific Community Action to Combat Poverty" (No. 31985D0008). Retrieved June 4, 2010 (http://eur-lex.europa.eu/smartapi/cgi/sga_doc?smartapi!celexapi!prod!CELEX numdoc&lg=EN&numdoc=31985 D0008&model=guichett).

Federal Interagency Forum on Child and Family Statistics. 2007. *America's Children 2007.* Washington, DC: U.S. Government Printing Office.

Fessler, Pam. 2012. "Struggling Families Lift Themselves Out of Poverty." Retrieved July 31, 2012 (http://www.npr.org/2012/07/13/155103662/struggling-families-lift-themselves-out-of-poverty).

Fraser, Nancy. 1989. *Unruly Practices: Power, Discourse, and Gender in Contemporary Social Theory.* Minneapolis: University of Minnesota Press.

Fischer, Will and Barbara Sard. 2013. "Chart Book: Federal Housing Spending Is Poorly Matched to Need." Retrieved November 13, 2014 (http://www.cbpp.org/cms/index.cfm?fa=view&id=4067#Four).

Freeman, Lance. 2002. "America's Affordable Housing Crisis: A Contract Unfulfilled." *American Journal of Public Health* 92(5): 709–13.

Freidman, P. 2000. *The Earned Income Tax Credit* (Issue Notes, Vol. 4, No. 4, April). Washington, DC: Welfare Information Network.

Fry, Richard and Rakesh Kochhar. 2014. "America's Wealth Gap Between Middle-Income And Upper-Income Families Is Widest on Record." Retrieved December 24, 2014 (http://www.pewresearch.org/fact-tank/2014/12/17/wealth-gap-upper-middle-income/).

Funiciello, Theresa. 1993. *Tyranny of Kindness: Dismantling the Welfare System to End Poverty in America.* New York: Atlantic Monthly Press.

Gans, Herbert. 1971. "The Uses of Poverty: The Poor Pay All." *Social Policy* 2:20–24.

Gans, Herbert. 1995. "The Uses of Poverty: The Poor Pay All." Pp. 308–314 in *Down to Earth Sociology,* edited by James Henslin. New York: Free Press.

Gilbert, Dennis. 2003. *The American Class Structure in an Age of Growing Inequality.* Belmont, CA: Thomson Wadsworth.

Gilens, Martin. 1999. *Why Americans Hate Welfare: Race, Media, and the Politics of Antipoverty Policy.* Chicago, IL: University of Chicago Press.

Gilman, Michelle Estrin. 2012. "The Return of the Welfare Queen." *Journal of Gender, Social Policy, & the Law* 22:247–279.

Goffman, Erving. 1951. "Symbols of Class Status." *British Journal of Sociology* 2: 294–304.

Gordon, Linda. 1994. *Pitied but Not Entitled.* New York: Free Press.

Grovum, Jake. 2014. "States Resist Food Stamp Cuts." Retrieved August 7, 2014 (http://www.usatoday.com/story/news/nation/2014/03/17/stateline-food-stamps/6538141/).

Hachen, David. 2001. *Sociology in Action.* Thousand Oaks, CA: Pine Forge.

Handler, Joel and Yeheskel Hasenfeld. 1991. *The Moral Construction of Poverty: Welfare Reform in America.* Newbury Park, CA: Sage Publications.

Harrington, Michael. 1963. *The Other America: Poverty in the United States.* Baltimore, MD: Penguin Books.

Harris, K. M. 1993. "Work and Welfare Among Single Mothers in Poverty." *American Journal of Sociology* 99:317–52.

Hart Research Associates. 2013. *It Takes More Than a Major: Employer Priorities for College Learning and Student Success.* Washington, DC: Hart Research Associates.

Henderson, Debra, Ann Tickamyer, and Barry Tadlock. 2005. "The Impact of Welfare Reform on the Parenting Role of Women in Rural Communities." *Journal of Children & Poverty* 11:131–47.

Hennessy, Judith. 2005. "Welfare, Work, and Family Well-Being: A Comparative Analysis of Welfare and Employment Status for Single Female-Headed Families Post-TANF." *Sociological Perspectives* 48(1):77–104.

Hildebrandt, Eugenie and Sheryl Kelber. 2012. "TANF Over Time: The Tale of Three Studies." *Policy, Politics and Nursing Practice* 13:130–141.

Holzer, Harry, Diane Whitmore Schanzenbach, Greg Duncan, and Jens Ludwig. 2008. "The Economic Costs of Childhood Poverty in the United States." *Journal of Children and Poverty* 14:41–61.

Iceland, John. 2003. *Poverty in America.* Berkeley: University of California Press.

Johnson, Lyndon. 1965. *Public Papers of the Presidents of the United States: Lyndon B. Johnson, 1965* (Vol. 2, entry 301, pp. 635–40). Washington, DC: U.S. Government Printing Office.

Jones, Arthur and Daniel Weinberg. 2000. *The Changing Shape of the Nation's Income Distribution 1947–1998* (Current Population Reports, P60-204). Washington, DC: Government Printing Office.

Keister, Lisa and Stephanie Moller. 2000. "Wealth Inequality in the United States." *Annual Review of Sociology* 26:63–81.

Kreiger, Nancy, David Williams, and Nancy Moss. 1997. "Measuring Social Class in U.S. Public Health Research: Concepts, Methodologies and Guidelines." *Annual Review of Public Health* 18:341–378.

Kulongoski, Theodore. 2007. Press Release, April 24, 2007. Retrieved July 4, 2007 (http://governor.oregon.gov/Gov/P2007/press_042407.shtml).

Lafer, Gordon. 2002. *Let Them Eat Training: The False Promise of Federal Employment Policy Since 1980.* Ithaca, NY: Cornell University Press.

Levernier, William, Mark Partridge, and Dan Rickman. 2000. "The Causes of Regional Variations in U.S. Poverty: A Cross-County Analysis." *Journal of Regional Science* 40:473–97.

Lewis, Oscar. 1969. *On Understanding Poverty: Perspectives From the Social Sciences.* New York: Basic Books.

Li, Shi, Hiroshi Sato, and Terry Sicular. 2013. *Rising Inequality in China: Challenges to a Harmonious Society.* New York: Cambridge University Press.

Lieberman, Robert C. 1998. *Shifting the Color Line: Race and the American Welfare State.* Cambridge, MA: Harvard University Press.

Llobrera, Joseph and Bob Zahradnik. 2004. *A Hand Up: How State Earned Income Tax Credits Help Working Families Escape Poverty in 2004.* Washington, DC: Center on Budget and Policy Priorities.

Magin, Janis. 2006. "For 1,000 or More Homeless in Hawaii, Beaches Are the Best Option." *New York Times,* December 5, A16.

Magnet, Myron. 2000. *The Dream and the Nightmare: Sixties' Legacy to the Underclass.* New York: Encounter Books. (Original work published 1993)

Mann, Michael. 1986. *The Sources of Social Power: A History of Power From the Beginning to A.D. 1760,* Vol. 1. New York: Cambridge University Press.

Marable, Manning. 2000. *How Capitalism Underdeveloped Black America.* Cambridge, MA: South End Press.

Marger, Martin. 2002. *Social Inequality: Patterns and Processes.* Boston: McGraw-Hill.

Marmot, Michael. 2004. *Status Syndrome: How Our Position on the Social Gradient Affects Longevity and Health.* London: Bloomsbury.

McCall, Leslie. 2002. *Complex Inequality: Gender, Class, and Race in the New Economy.* New York: Routledge.

McNamee, Stephen and Robert K. Miller. 2014. *The Meritocracy Myth.* New York: Rowman & Littlefield.

Mills, C. Wright. 2000. *The Sociological Imagination.* New York: Oxford University Press. (Original work published 1959)

Morgen, Sandra, Joan Acker, and Jill Weigt. 2010. *Stretched Thin: Poor Families, Welfare Work, and Welfare Reform.* New York: Cornell University Press.

National Center for Children in Poverty. 2001. "Child Poverty Fact Sheet: June 2001." Retrieved September 27, 2003 (http://cpmcent.columbia.edu/dept/nccp/ycpf).

Nelson, Kathyrn, Mark Treskon, and Danilo Pelletiere. 2004. *Losing Ground in the Best of Times: Low Income Renters in the 1990s.* Washington, DC: National Low Income Housing Coalition.

Neubeck, Kenneth and Noel Cazenave. 2001. *Welfare Racism: Playing the Race Card Against America's Poor.* New York: Routledge.

Nichols, Austin. 2011. "Poverty in the United States, September 13, 2011." Retrieved January 26, 2012 (http://www.urban .org/UploadedPDF/412399-Poverty-in-the-United-States.pdf).

Norris, Donald and Lyke Thompson. 1995. "Introduction." Pp. 1–18 in *The Politics of Welfare Reform*, edited by D. Norris and L. Thompson. Thousand Oaks, CA: Sage Publications.

Oliver, Melvin L. and Thomas M. Shapiro. 1995. *Black Wealth/White Wealth.* New York: Routledge.

Patterson, James T. 1981. *America's Struggle Against Poverty, 1900–1980.* Cambridge, MA: Harvard University Press.

Pew Research Center. 2008. "Inside the Middle Class: Bad Times Hit the Good Life." Retrieved May 7, 2010 (http://pewsocialtrends.org/ assets/pdf/MC-Middle-class-report.pdf).

Piven, Frances Fox. 2002. "Globalization, American Politics, and Welfare Policy." Pp. 27–42 in *Lost Ground: Welfare Reform and Beyond*, edited by R. Albelda and A. Withorm. Cambridge, MA: South End Press.

Piven, Frances Fox and Richard A. Cloward. 1993. *Regulating the Poor: The Functions of Public Welfare.* New York: Vintage Books.

Pugh, Tony. 2007. "Housing Bleaker for Nation's Poor, Study Finds." *News Tribune*, July 15, A13.

Quadagno, Jill. 1994. *The Color of Welfare Reform: How Racism Undermined the War on Poverty.* New York: Basic Books.

Rainwater, Lee and Timothy M. Smeeding. 2003. *Poor Kids in a Rich Country: America's Children in Comparative Perspective.* New York: Russell Sage.

Ruggles, P. 1990. *Drawing the Line: Alternative Poverty Measures and Their Implications.* Washington, DC: Urban Institute Press.

Savage, Howard A. 1999. *Who Could Afford to Buy a House in 1995?* (U.S. Census Bureau Current Housing Reports, H121/99-1). Washington, DC: U.S. Census Bureau.

Sernau, Scott. 2001. *Worlds Apart: Social Inequalities in a New Century.* Thousand Oaks, CA: Pine Forge.

Sherman, Arloc, Robert Greenstein, and Kathy Ruffing. 2013. "Contrary to 'Entitlement Society' Rhetoric, Over Nine-Tenths of Entitlement Benefits Go to Elderly, Disabled or Working Households." Retrieved August 6, 2014 (http://www.cbpp.org/ cms/?fa=view&id=3677).

Short, Kathleen. 2001. *Experimental Poverty Measures: 1999* (Current Population Reports, Consumer Income, P60-216). Washington, DC: U.S. Census Bureau.

Short, Katherine. 2011. *The Research Supplemental Poverty Measure: 2010* (P60–241). Washington DC: U.S. Census Bureau.

Sicular, Terry. 2013. "The Challenge of High Inequality in China." *Inequality in Focus* 2:1–5.

Smeeding, Timothy, Katherine Ross, and Michael O'Conner. 1999. *The Economic Impact of the Earned Income Tax Credit (EITC): Consumption, Savings, and Debt.* Syracuse, NY: Syracuse University, Center for Policy Research.

Sulzberger, A. G. 2011. "States Adding Drug Test as Hurdle for Welfare." Retrieved January 28, 2012 (http://www.nytimes.com/2011/10/11/ us/states-adding-drug-test-as-hurdle-for-welfare.html?pagewanted=all).

UNICEF Office of Research. 2013. *Child Well-Being in Rich Countries: A Comparative Overview.* Florence, Italy: UNICEF Office of Research.

U.S. Bureau of Labor Statistics. 2014. "A Profile of the Working Poor, 2012" (Report 1047). Retrieved August 5, 2014 (http://www.bls.gov/ cps/cpswp2012.pdl).

U.S. Conference of Mayors. 2014. *Hunger and Homelessness Survey: A Status Report on Hunger and Homelessness in America's Cities.* Washington DC: U.S. Conference of Mayors.

U.S. Congressional Budget Office. 2011. *Trends in the Distribution of Household Income Between 1979 and 2007.* Washington, DC: Congressional Budget Office.

U.S. Department of Health and Human Services. 2006. "Welfare Reform: Deficit Reduction Act of 2005." Retrieved March 11, 2007 (http://www .acf.hhs.gov/programs/ofa/drafact.htm).

U.S. Department of Health and Human Services. 2012. "Temporary Assistance for Needy Families Information Memorandum." Retrieved July 24, 2012 (http://www.acf.hhs .gov/programs/ofa/policy/im-ofa/2012/ im201203/im201203.html).

U.S. Department of Health and Human Services. 2014. "2014 Poverty Guidelines." Retrieved November 13, 2014 (http://aspe.hhs.gov/ poverty/14poverty.cfm).

Weaver, R. Kent. 2000. *Ending Welfare as We Know It.* Washington, DC: Brookings Institution Press.

Weil, Alan and Kenneth Feingold. 2002. "Introduction." Pp. xi–xxxi in *Welfare Reform: The Next Act*, edited by A. Weil and K. Feingold. Washington, DC: Urban Institute.

Weitz, Rose. 2001. *The Sociology of Health, Illness, and Health Care: A Critical Approach.* Belmont, CA: Wadsworth/Thompson Learning.

White House. 2010. "President Obama Announces Members of the White House Council for Community Solutions." Retrieved April 18, 2012 (http://www.whitehouse.gov/ the-press-office/2010/12/14/president-obama-announces-members-white-house-council-community-solution).

White House. 2013. "Remarks by the President on Economic Mobility." Retrieved August 19, 2014 (http://www.whitehouse.gov/ the-press-office/2013/12/04/remarks-president-economic-mobility).

Williams, Laura. 2012. *Housing Landscape 2012.* Washington, DC: Center for Housing Policy.

Wolff, Edward. 2006. "Changes in Household Wealth in the 1980s and 1990s in the US." Pp. 107–50 in *International Perspectives on Household Wealth*, edited by E. Wolff. Corwall, England: MPG Books.

Wong, Edward. 2013. "Survey in China Shows a Wide Gap in Income." *New York Times*, July 30, p. A9.

Wood, Robert, Quinn Moore, and Anu Rangarajan. 2008. "Two Steps Forward, One Step Back: The Uneven Economic Progress of TANF Recipients." *Social Service Review* 82:3–28.

World Bank. 2009. "Overview: Understanding, Measuring and Overcoming Poverty." Retrieved May 7, 2010 (http://web.worldbank.org/ WBSITE/EXTERNAL/TOPICS/EXTPOVERTY/ 0,,contentMDK:20153855~menuPK: 373757~pagePK:148956~piPK:216618~ theSitePK:336992,00.html).

World Bank. 2012. "New Estimates Reveal Real Drop in Extreme Poverty 2005–2010." Retrieved November 8, 2012 (http://econ .worldbank.org/WBSITE/EXTERNAL/ EXTDEC/0,,contentMDK: 23129612~pagePK:64165401~piPK:6416 5026~theSitePK:469372,00.html).

Zedlewski, Shelia and Pamela Loprest. 2003. "Welfare Reform: One Size Doesn't Fit All." *Christian Science Monitor, Electronic Edition*, August 25. Retrieved May 7, 2010 (http:// www.urban.org/url.cfm? ID=900648).

Zucchino, David. 1999. *Myth of the Welfare Queen.* New York: Touchstone/Simon & Schuster.

Chapter 3

Allport, Gordon. 1954. *The Nature of Prejudice.* Garden City, NY: Doubleday.

American Council on Education and American Association of University Professors. 2000. *Does Diversity Make a Difference? Three Research Studies on Diversity in College Classrooms, Executive Summary.* Washington, DC: American Council on Education and American Association of University Professors.

Association of American Colleges and Universities. 2000. "More Colleges and Universities Require Students to Take Diversity Classes." Retrieved May 13, 2007 (http://www.aacu-edu.org/ news_room/2000archive/irvinesurveypr.cfm).

Baghdjian, Alice and Albert Schmieder. 2014. "Swiss Vote to Set Limits on Immigration from EU." Retrieved August 27, 2014 (http://www .reuters.com/article/2014/02/09/us-swiss-vote-immigration-idUSBREA180H220140209).

Bauman, Zygmunt. 2000. *Globalisation: The Human Consequences.* Cambridge, England: Polity Press.

Benhabib, Seyla. 2012. "The Morality of Migration." Retrieved August 27, 2014 (http:// opinionator.blogs.nytimes.com/2012/07/29/ stone-immigration/).

Bendick, Mark, Jr., Mary Lou Egan, and Suzanne M. Lofhjelm. 1998. *The Documentation and Evaluation of Antidiscrimination Training in the United States.* Washington, DC: Bendick and Egan Economic Consultants.

Bernstein, Mary and Marcie De la Cruz. 2009. "'What Are You?' Explaining Identity as a Goal of the Multiracial Hapa Movement." *Social Problems* 56:722–45.

Bowman, Nicholas. 2011. "Promoting Participation in a Diverse Democracy: A Meta-Analysis of College Diversity Experiences and Civic Engagement." *Review of Educational Research* 81:29–68.

Brown, Anna and Eileen Patten. 2014a. "Statistical Portrait of the Foreign-Born Population in the United States, 2012." Retrieved August 28, 2014 (http://www.pewhispanic .org/2014/04/29/statistical-portrait-of-the-foreign-born-population-in-the-united-states-2012/).

Brown, Anna and Eileen Patten. 2014b. "Statistical Portrait of Hispanics in the United States, 2012." Retrieved August 28, 2014 (http://www .pewhispanic.org/2014/04/29/statistical-portrait-of-hispanics-in-the-united-states-2012/)

Brown, Hana. 2013. "Racialized Conflict and Policy Spillover Effects: The Role of Race in the Contemporary U.S. Welfare State." *American Journal of Sociology* 119:394–443.

Budrys, Grace. 2003. *Unequal Health: How Inequality Contributes to Health or Illness.* Lanham, MD: Rowman & Littlefield.

Byrd, W. Michael and Linda Clayton. 2002. *An American Health Dilemma: Race, Medicine, and Health Care in the United States, 1900–2000.* New York: Routledge.

Camarota, Steven. 2007. "Immigrants in the United States, 2007: A Profile of America's Foreign-Born Population." Retrieved May 10, 2010 (http://www.cis.org/articles/2007/back1007 .html).

Camarota, Steven. 2009. "Immigration's Impact on U.S. Workers." Retrieved May 10, 2010 (http:// www.cis.org/node/1582#20).

Camarota, Steven and Karen Jensenius. 2009. "Trends in Immigrant and Native Employment." Retrieved May 10, 2010 (http://www.cis.org/ articles/2009/back509.pdf).

Carby, Hazel. 1985. "White Woman Listen! Black Feminism and the Boundaries of Sisterhood." Pp. 389–403 in *The Empire Strikes Back: Race and Racism in Seventies Britain*, edited by Paul Gilroy. London: Hutchinson.

Castles, Stephen and Mark Miller. 1998. *The Age of Migration.* New York: Guilford Press.

Center for Immigration Studies. 2009. "Immigration History." Retrieved May 10, 2010 (http://www .cis.org/ImmigrationHistory).

Chaudry, Ajay, Randy Capps, Juan Manuel Pedroza, Rosa Maria Castaneda, Robert Santos, and Molly Scott. 2010. *Facing Our Future: Children in the Aftermath of Immigration Enforcement.* Washington DC: Urban Institute.

Chávez, Maria. 2011. *Everyday Injustice: Latino Professionals and Racism.* New York: Rowman & Littlefield.

Collin, Jeff and Kelley Lee. 2003. *Globalization and Transborder Health Risk in the U.K.* London: Nuffield Trust.

Collins, Patricia Hill. 2000. *Black Feminist Thought: Knowledge, Consciousness, and the Politics of Empowerment.* New York: Routledge.

Conner, Phillip, D'vera Cohn, and Anna Gonzalez-Barrera. 2013. "Changing Patterns of Global Migration and Remittances." Retrieved September 3, 2014 (http://www

.pewsocialtrends.org/2013/12/17/changing-patterns-of-global-migration-and-remittances/).

Cooperative Children's Book Center. 2014. "Children's Books By and About People of Color Published in the United States." Retrieved August 25, 2014 (http://ccbc.education.wisc .edu/books/pcstats.asp#black).

DaCosta, Kimberly. 2007. *Making Multiracials.* Stanford, CA: Stanford University Press.

Dave, Paresh. 2014. "Vandals Put Noose on Old Miss Statue of James Meredith; He Speaks Out." Retrieved August 22, 2014 (http:// www.latimes.com/nation/nationnow/la-na-nn-james-meredith-statue-ole-miss-noose-race-20140218-story.html).

Day, Phyllis. 2009. *A New History of Social Welfare.* Boston: Pearson.

Del Barco, Mandalit. 2012. "In Pursuit of Recognition: An Undocumented Immigrant's Resilient Fight." Retrieved December 29, 2014 (http://www.npr.org/2012/12/25/167526579/ in-pursuit-of-recognition-undocumented-immigrant-s-resilient-fight).

DeNavas-Walt, Carmen and Bernadette Proctor. 2014. *Income and Poverty in the United States: 2013* (Current Population Reports, P60-249). Washington, DC: U.S. Census Bureau.

Denson, Nida. 2009. "Do Curricular and Cocurricular Diversity Activities Influence Racial Bias? A Meta-Analysis." *Review of Educational Research* 79:805–838.

Donadio, Rachel. 2010a. "Race Riots Grip an Italian Town, and a Mafia Role Is Investigated." *New York Times*, January 11, pp. A1, A7.

Donadio, Rachel. 2010b. "Looking Past the Façade of Italian City After Riots." *New York Times*, January 13, p. A6.

Du Bois, W. E. B. 1996. "Darkwater." P. 532 in *The Oxford W. E. B. Du Bois Reader*, edited by Eric Sunquist. New York: Oxford University Press.

Duncan, Brian and Stephen Trejo. 2011. "Intermarriage and the Intergenerational Transmission of Ethnic Identity and Human Capital for Mexican Americans." *Journal of Labor Economics* 29(2):195–227.

Düvell, Franck. 2005. "Globalization of Migration Control." Pp. 23–46 in *Crossing Over: Comparing Recent Migration in the United States and Europe*, edited by Holger Henke. Oxford, England: Lexington Books.

Farley, John. 2005. *Majority–Minority Relations.* Upper Saddle River, NJ: Pearson-Prentice Hall.

Feagin, Joe. 1999. "Excluding Blacks and Others From Housing: The Foundation of White Racism." *Cityscape* 4(3):79–91.

Feagin, Joe and Pinar Batur. 2004. "Racism in Comparative Perspective." Pp. 316–34 in *Handbook of Social Problems: A Comparative International Perspective*, edited by George Ritzer. Thousand Oaks, CA: Sage Publications.

Foner, Nancy. 2000. *From Ellis Island to JFK: New York's Two Great Waves of Immigration.* New York: Russell Sage.

Fry, Richard. 2005. *The High Schools Hispanics Attend: Size and Other Key Characteristics.* Washington, DC: Pew Hispanic Center.

Fry, Richard and Paul Taylor. 2013. "Hispanic High School Graduates Pass Whites in Rate of College Enrollment: High School Drop-out Rate at Record Low. Retrieved September 20, 2014 (http://www.pewhispanic.org/2013/05/09/ hispanic-high-school-graduates-pass-whites-in-rate-of-college-enrollment/).

Gabard, Donald and Terry Cooper. 1998. "Race: Constructs and Dilemmas." *Administration & Society* 30:339–56.

Gagné, Patricia and Richard Tewksbury. 2003. *The Dynamics of Inequality: Race, Class, and Sexuality in the United States.* Upper Saddle River, NJ: Prentice Hall.

Galagan, Patricia. 1993. "Navigating the Differences." *Training and Development* 47(4):28–33.

Gordon, Milton. 1964. *Assimilation in American Life.* New York: Oxford University Press.

Greenhouse, Linda. 2003. "Justices Back Affirmative Action by 5 to 4, but Wider Vote Bans a Racial Point System." *New York Times*, June 24, pp. A1, A25.

Greenhouse, Linda. 2007. "Justices, 5–4, Limit Use of Race for School Integration Plans." *New York Times*, June 29, pp. A1, A20.

Grieco, Elizabeth. 2010. "Race and Hispanic Origin of the Foreign-Born Population in the United States: 2007." Retrieved May 10, 2010 (http:// www.census.gov/prod/2010pubs/acs-11.pdf).

Grinde, D. A. 2001. "ALANA/Ethnic Studies Assessment." Retrieved May 13, 2007 (http:// www.diversityweb.org/research_and_trends/ research_evaluation_impact/curriculum_ development/alana.cfm).

Gyory, Andrew. 1998. *Closing the Gate: Race, Politics and the Chinese Exclusion Act.* Chapel Hill: University of North Carolina Press.

Harris, G. L. A. 2009. "Revising Affirmative Action in Leveling the Playing Field: Who Have Been the Beneficiaries Anyway?" *Review of Public Personnel Administration* 29: 354–372.

Harris, Violet. 1990. "African American Children's Literature: The First One Hundred Years." *Journal of Negro Education* 59:540–555.

Harris, Violet. 1996. "Continuing Dilemmas, Debates and Delights in Multicultural Children's Literature." *The New Advocate* 9:107–122.

Heilman, Madeline E., Caryn J. Block, and Peter Stahatos. 1997. "The Affirmative Action Stigma of Incompetence: Effects of Performance Information Ambiguity." *Academy of Management Journal* 40:603–25.

Herring, Cedric and Sharon Collins. 1995. "Retreat From Equal Opportunity? The Case of Affirmative Action." Pp. 163–81 in *The Bubbling Cauldron: Race, Ethnicity, and the Urban Crisis*, edited by Michael Smith and Joe Feagin. Minneapolis: University of Minnesota Press.

Human Rights Watch. 2009. *Forced Apart (By the Numbers): Non-citizens Deported Mostly for Nonviolent Offenses.* New York: Human Rights Watch.

Hytrek, Gary and Kristine Zentgraf. 2007. *America Transformed: Globalization, Inequality and Power.* New York: Oxford University Press.

Idelson, Holly. 1995. "A 30-Year Experiment." *Congressional Quarterly Weekly Report* 53(22):1579.

Jaspin, Eliot. 2006. *Buried in the Bitter Waters: The Hidden History of Racial Cleansing in America.* New York: Basic Books.

Johnson, Lyndon. 1965. *Public Papers of the Presidents of the United States: Lyndon B. Johnson, 1965* (Vol. 2, entry 301, pp. 635–40). Washington, DC: U.S. Government Printing Office.

Kalev, Alexandra, Frank Dobbin, and Erin Kelly. 2006. "Best Practices or Best Guesses? Assessing the Efficacy of Corporate Affirmative Action and Diversity Policies." *American Sociological Review* 71:589–617.

Kaplan, W. and B. Lee. 1995. *The Law of Higher Education: A Comprehensive Guide to Legal Implications of Administrative Decision Making.* San Francisco: Jossey-Bass.

Korgen, Kathleen, J. Mahon, and Gabe Wang. 2003. "Diversity of College Campuses Today: The Growing Need to Foster Campus Environments Capable of Countering a Possible Tipping Effect." *College Student Journal* 37:16–26.

Kotlowski, Dean. 1998. "Richard Nixon and the Origins of Affirmative Action." *Historian* 60(3):523–42.

Krogstad, Jens Manuel and Jeffrey S. Passel. 2014. "5 Facts About Illegal Immigration in the U.S." Retrieved December 28, 2014 (http://www.pewresearch.org/fact-tank/2014/11/18/5-facts-about-illegal-immigration-in-the-u-s/).

Lee, Erika. 2006. "A Nation of Immigrants and a Gatekeeping Nation: American Immigration Law and Policy." Pp. 5–35 in *A Companion to American Immigration,* edited by Reed Ueda. Cornwall, England: Blackwell.

Levy, Charles. 1973. "The Value Base of Social Work." *Journal of Education for Social Work* 9:34–42.

Liptak, Adam. 2012. "Court Splits Immigration Law Verdicts; Upholds Hotly Debated Centerpiece, 8–0." *New York Times,* June 26, pp. A1, A13.

Liptak, Adam. 2014. "Court Backs Michigan on Affirmative Action." Retrieved November 15, 2014. (http://www.nytimes.com/2014/04/23/us/supreme-court-michigan-affirmative-action-ban.html).

Marger, Martin. 2002. *Social Inequality: Patterns and Processes.* Boston: McGraw-Hill.

McGary, Howard. 1999. *Race and Social Justice.* Oxford, England: Blackwell.

Migrant Clinicians Network. 2009. "Environmental and Occupational Health." Retrieved May 10, 2010 (http://www.migrantclinician.org/clinical_topics/environmental-and-occupational-health.html).

Muttarak, Raya, Heather Hamill, Anthony Heath, and Christopher McCrudden. 2013. "Does Affirmative Action Work? Evidence From the Operation of Fair Employment Legislation in Northern Ireland." *Sociology* 47:560–579.

Myers, John P. 2005. *Minority Voices.* Boston: Pearson Education.

Myers, Walter Dean. 2014. "Where Are the People of Color in Children's Books?" *New York Times,* March 16, pp. 1, 6.

National Conference of State Legislatures. 2011. "2011 Immigration-Related Laws and Resolutions in the States (Jan. 1–Dec. 7, 2011)." Retrieved February 5, 2012 (http://www.ncsl.org/issues-research/immigration/state-immigration-legislation-report-dec-2011.aspx).

Odell, Patricia, Kathleen Korgen, and Gabe Wang. 2005. "Cross-Racial Friendships and Social Distance Between Racial Groups on a College Campus." *Innovative Higher Education* 29(4):291–305.

Ohlemacher, Stephen. 2006. "Race Matters, and Minorities Still Suffer, Report Says." *News Tribune,* November 14, pp. A6–A7.

Ole Miss/University of Mississippi News. 2014. "Statement from the University of Mississippi, February 17." Retrieved August 22, 2014 (http://news.olemiss.edu/statement-from-the-university-of-mississippi/#.U_dPm1ZN0YU).

Omi, Michael and Howard Winant. 1994. *Racial Formation in the United States: From the 1960s to the 1990s.* New York: Routledge.

Ore, Tracy E., ed. 2003. *The Social Construction of Difference and Inequality: Race, Class, Gender, and Sexual Orientation.* Boston: McGraw-Hill.

Parker-Pope, Tara. 2013. "Black Women's Poorer Fate in Breast Cancer Cases Is Tied to Later Diagnoses." *New York Times,* July 24, A10.

Passel, Jeffrey and D'Vera Cohn. 2012. *U.S. Foreign-Born Population: How Much Change From 2009 to 2010?* Washington, DC: Pew Hispanic Center.

Parker-Pope, Tara. 2013. "Black Women's Poorer Fate in Breast Cancer Cases Is Tied to Later Diagnoses." *New York Times,* July 24, A10.

Pew Research Center. 2013. "Second Generation Americans: A Portrait of the Adult Children of Immigrants." Retrieved December 29, 2014 (http://www.pewsocialtrends.org/2013/02/07/second-generation-americans/).

Pew Research Center. 2014. "Race in America: Tracking 50 Years of Demographic Trends." Retrieved August 28, 2014 (http://www.pewsocialtrends.org/2013/08/22/race-demographics/).

Pincus, Fred. 2003. *Reverse Discrimination: Dismantling the Myth.* Boulder, CO: Lynne Rienner.

Preston, Julia. 2007. "Immigration Is at Center of New Laws Around U.S." *New York Times,* August 6, p. A12.

Preston, Julia 2009. "White House Plan on Immigration Includes Legal Status." *New York Times,* November 14, p. A10.

Preston, Julia. 2012a. "Immigration Ruling Leaves Issues Unresolved." *New York Times,* June 27, p. A14.

Preston, Julia. 2012b. "Young Immigrants, in America Illegally, Line Up for Reprieve." *New York Times,* August 14, A8, A12.

Preston, Julia and John Cushman, Jr. 2012. "Obama to Permit Young Migrants to Remain in U.S." *New York Times,* June 16, pp. A1, A16.

Purves, Alan and Richard Beach. 1972. *Literature and the Reader.* Urbana, IL: National Council Of Teachers of English.

Redfield, Robert. 1958. "Race as a Social Phenomenon." Pp. 66–71 in *Race: Individual and Collective Behavior,* edited by E. Thompson and E. C. Hughes. Glencoe, IL: Free Press.

Restrepo, Dan and Ann Garcia. 2014. "The Surge of Unaccompanied Children From Central America: Root Causes and Policy Solutions." Retrieved September 6, 2014 (http://www.americanprogress.org/issues/immigration/report/2014/07/24/94396/the-surge-of-unaccompanied-children-from-central-america-root-causes-and-policy-solutions/).

Rosenbaum, Sara and Joel Teitelbaum. 2004. "Addressing Racial Inequality in Health Care." Pp. 135–50 in *Policy Challenges in Modern Health Care,* edited by D. Mechanic, L. Rogut, D. Colby, and J. Knickman. New Brunswick, NJ: Rutgers University Press.

Samers, Michael. 2003. "Invisible Capitalism: Political Economy and the Regulation of Undocumented Immigration in France." *Economy and Society* 32:555–83.

Schemo, Diana Jean. 2001. "U. of Georgia Won't Contest Ruling on Admissions Policy." *New York Times,* November 10, p. A8.

Schwartzman, Luis. 2007. "Does Money Whiten?" *American Sociological Review* 72(2):940–63.

Shook, Natalie and Russell Fazio. 2008. "Interracial Roommate Relationships: An Experimental Field Test of the Contact Hypothesis." *Psychological Science* 19:717–23.

Shuford, John. 2001. "Four DuBoisian Contributions to Critical Race Theory." *Transactions of the Charles S. Peirce Society* 37(3):301–37.

Smith, Jessica and Carla Medalia. 2014. *Health Insurance Coverage in the United States: 2013.* Washington, DC: U.S. Census Bureau.

Springer, Ann D. 2005. "Update on Affirmative Action in Higher Education: A Current Legal Overview, January 2005." Retrieved February 20, 2012 (http://www.aaup.org/issues/diversity-affirmative-action/update-2005).

Suárez-Orozco, Carola, Hirokazu Yoshikawa, Robert Teranish, and Marcelo Suárez-Orozco. 2011. "Growing Up in the Shadows: The Developmental Implications of Unauthorized Status." *Harvard Educational Review* 81(3):438–72.

Swink, Dawn. 2003. "Back to Bakke: Affirmative Action Revisited in Educational Diversity." *BYU Education and Law Journal* 1:211–57.

Tavernise, Sabrina. 2012. "Whites Account for Under Half of Births in U.S." *New York Times,* May 17, pp. A1, A20.

Tsang, Chiu-Wai Rita and Tracy Dietz. 2001. "The Unrelenting Significance of Minority Statuses: Gender, Ethnicity, and Economic Attainment Since Affirmative Action." *Sociological Spectrum* 21:61–80.

United Nations. 2009. *International Migration 2009.* Retrieved May 10, 2010 (http://www.un.org/esa/population/publications/2009Migration_Chart/ittmig_wallchart09.pdf).

United Nations. 2013. *International Migration Report 2013*. New York: United Nations.

United We Stand. 2014. "Sofia Campos – Board Chair – Boston/California." Retrieved September 3, 2014 (http://unitedwedream.org/sofia-campos-board-chair-bostoncalifornia/).

Urbina, Ian. 2014. "Using Jailed Migrants as a Pool of Cheap Labor." Retrieved August 28, 2014 (http://www.nytimes.com/2014/05/25/us/using-jailed-migrants-as-a-pool-of-cheap-labor.html?_r=0).

U.S. Bureau of Labor Statistics. 2013. "Fatal Occupational Injuries Incurred by Foreign-Born Workers, 2008–2012." Retrieved August 28, 2014 (http://www.bls.gov/iif/oshwc/cfoi/foreign_b.pdf).

U.S. Census Bureau. 2005. "Directive No. 15, Race and Ethnic Standards for Federal Statistics and Administrative Reporting." Retrieved November 9, 2012 (http://wonder.cdc.gov/wonder/help/populations/bridged-race/Directive15.html).

U.S. Census Bureau. 2012a. "Housing Vacancies and Homeownership: Annual Statistics 2011." Retrieved November 10, 2012 (http://www.census.gov/housing/hvs/data/ann11ind.html).

U.S. Census Bureau. 2012b. "Most Children Younger Than Age 1 Are Minorities, Census Bureau Reports." Retrieved May 22, 2012 (http://www.census.gov/newsroom/releases/archives/population/cb12- 90.html).

U.S. Census Bureau. 2012c. "U.S. Census Bureau Projections Show a Slower Growing, Older, More Diverse Nation a Half Century From Now." Retrieved August 22, 2014 (http://www.census.gov/newsroom/releases/archives/population/cb12-243.html).

U.S. Census Bureau. 2014a. Table PEPASR6H Annual Estimates of the Resident Population by Sex, Age, Race and Hispanic Origin for the United States: April 1, 2010 to July 1, 2013 Population Estimates. Retrieved August 22, 2014 (http://factfinder2.census.gov/faces/tableservices/jsf/pages/productview.xhtml?pid=PEP_2013_PEPASR6H&prodType=table).

U.S. Census Bureau. 2014b. Table 3.17 Year of Entry of the Foreign-Born Population by Sex and World Region of Birth: 2012. Retrieved August 22, 2014 (http://www.census.gov/population/foreign/data/cps2012.html).

U.S. Customs and Border Protection. 2014. "Southwest Border Unaccompanied Alien Children." Retrieved August 29, 2014 (http://www.cbp.gov/newsroom/stats/southwest-border-unaccompanied-children).

U.S. Department of State. 2014. "FY13 Refugee Admissions Statistics." Retrieved August 22, 2014 (http://www.state.gov/j/prm/releases/statistics/228666.htm).

U.S. Immigration and Customs Enforcement. 2011. "FY2011: ICE Announces Year-End Removal Numbers, Highlights Focus on Key Priorities Including Threats to Public Safety and National Security." Retrieved February 5, 2012 (http://www.ice.gov/news/releases/1110/111018washingtondc.htm).

Van Ausdale, Debra and Joe R. Feagin. 2001. *The First R: How Children Learn Race and Racism*. Lanham, MD: Rowman & Littlefield.

White House. 2012. "Remarks by the President on Immigration." Retrieved June 16, 2012 (http://www.whitehouse.gov/the-press-office/2012/06/15/remarks-president-immigration).

White House. 2014. "Fact Sheet: Immigration Accountability Executive Action." Retrieved November 28, 2014 (http://www.whitehouse.gov/the-press-office/2014/11/20/fact-sheet-immigration-accountability-executive-action).

Wilgoren, J. 2000. "Affirmative Action Plan Is Upheld in Michigan." *New York Times*, December 14, p. A32.

Williams, Richard, Reynold Nesiba, and Eileen Diaz McConnell. 2005. "The Changing Face of Inequality in Home Mortgage Lending." *Social Problems* 52(2):181–208.

Wittig, Michele and Sheila Grant-Thompson. 1998. "The Utility of Allport's Conditions of Intergroup Contact for Predicting Perceptions of Improved Racial Attitudes and Beliefs." *Journal of Social Issues* 54(4):795–812.

Woodhouse, Shawn. 1999. "Faculty Perceptions of the Impact of Affirmative Action on Employment Practices in the University of Missouri System." PhD dissertation, University of Missouri, Columbia, MO.

Woodhouse, Shawn. 2002. "The Historical Development of Affirmative Action: An Aggregated Analysis." *Western Journal of Black Studies* 26(3):155–59.

Yardley, Jim. 2002. "The Ten Percent Solution." *New York Times Magazine*, April 14, pp. 28–31.

Yee, Shirley. 2001. "The Past, Present, and Future of Affirmative Action: AHA Roundtable, January 1998—Introduction." *NWSA Journal* 10(3):135–41.

Zhou, Min. 2004. "Assimilation, the Asian Way." Pp. 139–53 in *Reinventing the Melting Pot: The New Immigrants and What It Means to Be American*, edited by Tamar Jacoby. New York: Basic Books.

Chapter 4

AAUP. 2013. *Graduating to a Pay Gap: The Earnings of Women and Men One Year After College Graduation*. Washington, DC: AAUP.

Acosta, R. Vivian and Linda Jean Carpenter. 2009. "Thirty Seven Years Later, Title IX Hasn't Fixed It All." *Academe* July–August:22–4.

Bem, Sandra Lipsitz. 1993. *The Lenses of Gender: Transforming the Debate on Sexual Inequality*. New Haven, CT: Yale University Press.

Berger, Peter. 1963. *Invitation to Sociology: A Humanistic Perspective*. New York: Anchor Books.

Böhnisch, L. 2003. *The Delimitation of Masculinity: Confusions and Formations of Being a Man During Societal Transition*. Opladen, Germany: Leske + Budrich.

Bonvillian, Nancy. 2006. *Women and Men: Cultural Constructs of Gender*. New York: Prentice Hall.

Charles, Maria. 2003. "Deciphering Sex Segregation: Vertical and Horizontal Inequalities in Ten National Labor Markets." *Acta Sociologica* 46(4): 267–87.

Charles, Maria and David Grusky. 2004. "The Four Puzzles of Sex Segregation." Pp. 3–37 in *Occupational Ghettos: The Worldwide Segregation of Women and Men*, edited by Maria Charles and David Grusky. Stanford, CA: Stanford University Press.

Dey, Judy Goldberg and Catherine Hill. 2007. *Behind the Pay Gap*. Washington, DC: AAUW Educational Foundation.

Durkheim, Émile. 2007. "The Division of Labor and Marriage." Pp. 41–44 in *Before the Second Wave: Gender in the Sociological Tradition*, edited by Barbara Finlay. Upper Saddle River, NJ: Pearson Prentice Hall.

Elber, Lynn. 2012. "Doc McStuffins' TV Show Gives Black Girls, Aspiring Doctors Hope." Retrieved July 10, 2012 (http://www.huffingtonpost.com/2012/06/12/doc-mcstuffins-tv-show-give-black-doctors-hope_n_1590683.html).

Elliot, Jane. 2005. "Comparing Occupational Segregation in Great Britain and the United States: The Benefits of Using a Multi-group Measure of Segregation." *Work, Employment and Society* 19(1):153–74.

England, Paula. 2001. "Gender and Access to Money: What Do Trends in Earnings and Household Poverty Tell Us?" Pp. 131–53 in *Reconfigurations of Class and Gender*, edited by Janine Baxter and Mark Western. Stanford, CA: Stanford University Press.

Ewert, Stephanie. 2012. *What It's Worth: Field of Training and Economic Status in 2009* (P70–129). Washington, DC: U.S. Census Bureau.

Farley, John. 2005. *Majority–Minority Relations*. Upper Saddle River, NJ: Pearson Prentice Hall.

Fluke, Sandra. 2012. Testimony transcript. Retrieved September 6, 2014 (http://abcnews.go.com/images/Politics/statement-Congress-letterhead-2nd%20hearing.pdf).

Garber, Greg. 2002. "Landmark Law Faces New Challenges Even Now." Retrieved May 11, 2010 (http://espn.go.com/gen/womenandsports/020619title9.html).

Inter-Parliamentary Union. 2014. "Women in National Parliaments." Retrieved September 3, 2014 (http://www.ipu.org/wmn-e/classif.htm).

Kliff, Sarah. 2012. "Meet Sandra Fluke: The Woman You Didn't Hear at Congress' Contraceptives Hearing." Retrieved September 3, 2014 (http://www.washingtonpost.com/blogs/wonkblog/post/meet-sandra-fluke-the-woman-you-didnt-hear-at-congress-contraceptives-hearing/2012/02/16/gIQAJh57HR_blog.html).

Korgen, Kathleen Odell, Jonathan White, and Shelley White. 2011. *Sociologists in Action: Sociology, Social Change, and Social Justice*. Thousand Oaks, CA: SAGE.

Kuhlmann, Ellen and Ellen Annandale. 2012. *The Palgrave Handbook of Gender and Healthcare*. London: Palgrave Macmillan.

Marger, Martin. 2008. *Social Inequality: Patterns and Processes*. Boston: McGraw-Hill.

Maume, David J. 1999. "Occupational Segregation and The Career Mobility of White Men and Women." *Social Forces* 77:1433–59.

May, Caroline. 2012. "Met Law Student and Feminist Hero Sandra Fluke." Retrieved September 6, 2014 (http://dailycaller .com/2012/03/03/meet-law-student-and-contraception-advocate-sandra-fluke/).

McFarland, Kay and Donna Rhoades. 1998. "Gender-Related Values and Medical Specialty Choice." *American Psychiatry* 22:236–39.

Mishel, Lawrence, Jared Bernstein, and Sylvia Allegretto. 2007. *The State of Working America: 2006/2007*. Ithaca, NY: ILR Press.

National Coalition for Women and Girls in Education. 2012. *Title IX at 40*. Washington, DC: National Coalition for Women and Girls in Education.

National Committee on Pay Equity. 2014. "The Wage Gap Over Time." Retrieved March 29, 2015 (http://www.pay-equity.org/info-time .html).

National Women's Law Center. 2002a. *The Battle for Gender Equity in Athletics: Title IX at Thirty*. Washington, DC: National Women's Law Center.

National Women's Law Center. 2002b. "Quick Facts on Women and Girls in Athletics." Retrieved May 11, 2010 (http://lobby.la.psu .edu/_107th/135_Title%20IX/Organizational_ Statements/NWLC/NWLC_Quick_Facts_on_ Women_and_Girls_in_Athletics_June_2002 .pdf).

National Women's Law Center. 2012. "Debunking the Myths About Title IX and Athletics." Retrieved March 18, 2012 (http://www.nwlc .org/resource/debunking-myths-about-title-ix-and-athletics).

National Women's Law Center. 2013. *The Wage Gap by State for Women Overall*. Washington, DC: National Women's Law Center.

National Women's Law Center. 2014a. *FAQ About the Wage Gap*. Washington, DC: National Women's Law Center.

National Women's Law Center. 2014b. *The Wage Gap Over Time*. Washington, DC: National Women's Law Center.

Pear, Robert. 2012. "Senate Rejects Steps Targeting Coverage of Contraception." Retrieved May 2, 2012 (http://www.nytimes .com/2012/03/02/us/politics/senate-kills-gop-bill-opposing-contraception-policy. html?pagewanted=all).

Pelosi, Nancy. 2007. "Pelosi Commemorates Women's History Month." Retrieved February 20, 2013 (http://www.democraticleader.gov/ news/press/pelosi-commemorates-womens-history-month).

Perales, Francisco. 2013. "Occupational Sex-Segregation, Specialized Human Capital and Wages: Evidence From Britain." *Work, Employment and Society* 24:600–620.

Ridgeway, Cecilia L. and Lynn Smith-Lovin. 1999. "The Gender System and Interaction." *Annual Review of Sociology* 25:191–216.

Riska, Elianne. 2010. "Coronary Health Disease: Gendered Public Health Discourses."

Pp. 158–171 in *The Palgrave Handbook of Gender and Healthcare*, edited by Ellen Kuhlman and Ellen Annandale. Basingstoke, England: Palgrave.

Rose, Stephen J. and Heidi I. Hartmann. 2004. *Still a Man's Labor Market: The Long-Term Earnings Gap*. Washington, DC: Institute for Women's Policy Research.

Roth, Louise Marie. 2006. *Selling Women Short: Gender and Money on Wall Street*. Princeton, NJ: Princeton University Press.

Scambor, Christian and Elli Scambor. 2008. "Men and Gender Mainstreaming: Prospects and Pitfalls of a European Strategy." *Journal of Men's Studies* 16:301–15.

Simões, Solange and Marlise Matos. 2009. "Modern Ideas, Traditional Behaviors, and the Persistence of Gender Inequality in Brazil." *International Journal of Sociology* 38:94–100.

Stolberg, Sheryl Gay. 2003. "Working Mothers Swaying Senate Debate, as Senators." *New York Times*, June 7, pp. A1, A11.

Stolberg, Sheryl Gay. 2009. "Obama Signs Equal-Pay Legislation." Retrieved May 11, 2010 (http://www.nytimes.com/2009/01/30/us/ politics/30ledbetter-web.html).

Tickner, J. Ann 2002. "Gendering World Politics: Issues and Approaches in the Post–Cold War Era." *Political Science Quarterly* 117(2):336–37.

United Nations. 2006a. "Executive Summary: Ending Violence against Women: From Words to Action. Study of the Secretary-General." Retrieved May 11, 2010 (http://www .un.org/womenwatch/daw/vaw/launch/english/ v.a.w-exeE-use.pdf).

United Nations Girls Education Initiative. 2013a. *Teaching and Learning: Achieving Quality for All: Gender Summary*. New York: United Nations Girls Education Initiative.

United Nations Girls Education Initiative. 2013b. *Annual Report 2013*. New York: United Nations Girls Education Initiative.

U.S. Bureau of Labor Statistics. 2011. "College Enrollment and Work Activity of 2011 High School Graduates." Retrieved March 18, 2012 (http://www.bls.gov/news.release/hsgec .nr0.htm).

U.S. Department of Education. 2014. "U.S. Department of Education Releases List of Higher Education Institutions With Open Title IX Sexual Violence Investigations." Retrieved September 20, 2014 (http://www.ed.gov/ news/press-releases/us-department-education-releases-list-higher-education-institutions-open-title-i).

U.S. Department of Labor, Women's Bureau. 2014. "Leading Occupations." Retrieved September 3, 2014 (http://www.dol .gov/wb/stats/leadoccupations.htm).

Wang, Wendy, Kim Parker, and Paul Taylor. 2013. "Breadwinner Moms." Retrieved September 8, 2014 (http://www.pewsocialtrends.org/2013/ 05/29/breadwinner-moms/).

Wharton, Amy. 2004. "Gender Inequality." Pp. 156–71 in *Handbook of Social Problems: A Comparative International Perspective*, edited by George Ritzer. Thousand Oaks, CA: Sage Publications.

Wildman, Stephanie and Adrienne Davis. 2000. "Language and Silence: Making Systems of Privilege Visible." Pp. 50–60 in *Readings for Diversity and Social Justice*, edited by Maurianne Adams, Warren Blumenfeld, Rosie Castañeda, Heather Hackman, Madeline Peters, and Ximena Zúñiga. New York: Routledge.

World Health Organization. 2013. *Global and Regional Estimates of Violence Against Women: Prevalence and Health Effects of Intimate Partner Violence and Non-partner Sexual Violence*. Italy: World Health Organization.

Chapter 5

American Psychological Association. 2008. *Just the Facts About Sexual Orientation and Youth: A Primer for Principals, Educators and School Personnel*. Washington, DC: American Psychological Association.

Anderson, Eric. 2011. "Updating the Outcome: Gay Athletes, Straight Teams, and Coming Out on Educationally Based Sports Teams." *Gender & Society* 25:250–268.

Badgett, M. V. Lee and Mary King. 1997. "Lesbian and Gay Men Occupational Strategies." Pp. 73–86 in *HomoEconomics: Capitalism, Community and Lesbian and Gay Life*, edited by A. Gluckman and B. Reed. New York: Routledge.

Bailey, J. Michael and Alan Bell. 1993. "Familiality of Female and Male Homosexuality." *Behavior Genetics* 23:313–22.

Bailey, J. Michael and Richard Pillard. 1991. "A Genetic Study of Male Sexual Orientation." *Archives of General Psychiatry* 48:1089–96.

Belkin, Aaron. 2003. "Don't Ask, Don't Tell: Is the Gay Ban Based on Military Necessity?" *Parameters* Summer:108–19.

Belkin, Aaron, Morten Ender, Nathaniel Frank, Stacie Furia, George Lucas, Gary Packard, Jr., Tammy Schultz, Steven Samuels, and David Segal. 2012. *One Year Out: An Assessment of DADT Repeal's Impact on Military Readiness*. Los Angeles: Palm Center, University of California Los Angeles.

Bevacqua, Maria. 2004. "Feminist Theory and the Question of Lesbian and Gay Marriage." *Feminism and Psychology* 14(1):36–40.

Bringle, Robert and Julie Hatcher. 1999. "Reflection in Service Learning: Making Meaning of Experience." *Educational Horizons* 77:179–85.

Bronski, Michael. 1998. *The Pleasure Principle: Sex, Backlash, and the Struggle for Gay Freedom*. New York: Bedford/ St. Martin's Press.

Bumiller, Elisabeth. 2002. "The Most Unlikely Story Behind a Gay Rights Victory." *New York Times*, June 27, p. A19.

Bumiller, Elisabeth. 2012. "Uneventful Year in Military After Key Change for Gays." *New York Times*, September 30, p. A17.

Burke, Matthew. 2013. "Bill Would Upgrade Records of Those Discharged Under DADT." Retrieved September 19, 2014 (http://

www.stripes.com/news/us/bill-would-upgrade-records-of-those-discharged-under-dadt-1.226901).

Card, Claudia. 1996. "Against Marriage and Motherhood." *Hypatia* 11:1–23.

Cass, V. C. 1979. "Homosexual Identity Formation: A Theoretical Model." *Journal of Homosexuality* 4:219–35.

Chen, Jialu. 2012. "Dan Savage on 'It Gets Better' and Surging Santorum." Retrieved May 9, 2012 (http://www.motherjones.com/media/2012/02/dan-savage-interview-it-gets-better-rick-santorum).

Chibbaro, Lou. 2013. "U.S. Professional Sports Called the 'Last Closet.'" Retrieved September 8, 2014 (http://www.washingtonblade.com/2013/08/28/u-s-professional-sports-called-the-last-closet-lgbt-sports-issue/).

Chou, W. S. 2001. "Homosexuality and the Cultural Practices of Tongzhi in Chinese Societies." *Journal of Homosexuality* 4:27–46.

Collins, Jason. 2014. "Parting Shot: Jason Collins Announces NBA Retirement in His Own Words." Retrieved December 31, 2014 (http://www.si.com/nba/2014/11/19/jason-collins-retirement-nba).

D'Augelli, Anthony. 1998. "Developmental Implications of Victimization of Lesbian, Gay and Bisexual Youths." Pp. 187–210 in *Understanding Prejudice Against Lesbians, Gay Men and Bisexuals*, edited by G. M. Herek. Thousand Oaks, CA: Sage Publications.

D'Augelli, Anthony, Scott Hershberger, and Neal Pilkington. 1998. "Lesbian, Gay, and Bisexual Youths and Their Families: Disclosure of Sexual Orientation and Its Consequences." *American Journal of Orthopsychiatry* 68:361–71.

Dubé, E. M. 2000. "The Role of Sexual Behavior in the Identification Process of Gay and Bisexual Men." *Journal of Sex Research* 48:139–62.

Feller, Ben. 2009. "Obama Inks Defense Bill With Hate Crimes Provision." Retrieved November 1, 2009 (http://abcnews.go.com/Business/wireStory?id=8938866).

Ferguson, Ann. 2007. "Gay Marriage: An American and Feminist Dilemma." *Hypatia* 22(2):39–57.

Gates, Gary and Frank Newport. 2012. "Special Report: 3.4% of U.S. Adults Identify as LGBT." Retrieved November 15, 2012 (http://www.gallup.com/poll/158066/special-report-adults-identify-lgbt.aspx).

Gettleman, Jeffrey. 2010. "After U.S. Evangelicals Visit, Uganda Considers Death for Gays." *New York Times*, January 4, pp. A1, A9.

Greenhouse, Linda. 2003. "Texas Sodomy Law Held Unconstitutional—Scathing Dissent." *New York Times*, June 27, pp. A1, A17.

Human Rights Campaign. 2013. "Employment Non-discrimination Act." Retrieved February 21, 2013 (http://www.hrc.org/laws-and-legislation/federal-legislation/employment-non-discrimination-act).

Human Rights Campaign. 2014a. "Marriage Equality and Other Relationship Recognition Laws." Retrieved September 4, 2014 (http://hrc-assets.s3-website-us-east-1.amazonaws.com/files/assets/resources/marriage-equality_8-2014.pdf).

Human Rights Campaign. 2014b. "Parenting Laws: Joint Adoption." Retrieved September 8, 2014 (http://hrc-assets.s3-website-us-east-1.amazonaws.com/files/assets/resources/joint_adoption_6-10-2014.pdf#__utma=149406063.1462250260.1409760603.140986 1482.1410189195.4&__utmb=149406063.10.9.1410189670276&__utmc=149406063&__utmx=-_utmz=149406063.1410189195.4.4.utmcsr=google|utmccn=(organic)|utmcmd=organic|utmctr=(not%20 provided)&__utmv=-&__utmk=3118128).

Human Rights Campaign. 2014c. "Parenting Laws: Second Parent or Stepparent Adoption." Retrieved September 8, 2014 (http://hrc-assets.s3-website-us-east-1.amazonaws.com/files/assets/resources/second_parent_adoption_6-10-2014.pdf).

Human Rights Campaign. 2014d. *Beyond Marriage Equality: A Blueprint for Federal Non-discrimination Protections.* Washington, DC: Human Rights Campaign.

Hunter, Nan. 1995. "Marriage, Law and Gender: A Feminist Inquiry." Pp. 107–22 in *Sex Wars: Sexual Dissent and Political Culture*, edited by L. Duggan and N. D. Hunter. New York: Routledge.

Katz, Jonathan Ned. 2003. "The Invention of Heterosexuality." Pp. 136–48 in *The Social Construction of Difference and Inequality: Race, Class, Gender, and Sexuality*, edited by Tracy E. Ore. Boston: McGraw-Hill.

Katz, Marsha and Helen LaVan. 2004. "Legal Protection From Discrimination Based on Sexual Orientation: Findings From Litigation." *Employee Responsibilities and Rights* 16(4):195–209.

Lambda Legal. 2003. "Landmark Victory." Retrieved July 8, 2003 (http://www.lambdalegal.org/news/pr/dc_20030626_landmark-ruling-for-gay-civil-rights-us-supreme-court.html).

Lehne, Gregory K. 1995. "Homophobia Among Men: Supporting and Defining the Male Role." Pp. 325–36 in *Men's Lives*, edited by M. Kimmel and M. Messner. Boston: Allyn & Bacon.

Levs, Josh. 2012, October 2. "California Governor OKs Ban on Gay Conversion Therapy, Calling it 'Quackery.'" Retrieved September 8, 2014 (http://www.cnn.com/2012/10/01/us/california-gay-therapy-ban/).

Lind, Amy. 2004. "Legislating the Family: Heterosexist Bias in Social Welfare Policy Frameworks." *Journal of Sociology and Social Welfare* 31(4):21–35.

Marullo, Sam. 1996. "The Service Learning Movement in Higher Education: An Academic Response to Troubled Times." *Sociological Imagination* 33:117–37.

McCarthy, Justin. 2014. "Same-Sex Marriage Support Reaches New High at 55%." Retrieved September 20, 2014 (http://www.gallup.com/poll/169640/sex-marriage-support-reaches-new-high.aspx).

Michael, Robert, John Gagnon, Edward Laumann, and Gina Kolata. 1994. *Sex in America: A Definitive Survey*. Boston: Little, Brown.

Movement Advancement Project, Family Equality Council, and Center for American Progress. 2012. "Securing Legal Ties for Children Living in LGBT Families." Retrieved July 21, 2012 (http://www.lgbtmap.org/file/securing-legal-ties.pdf).

Mustanski, Brian, Meredith Chivers, and J. Michael Bailey. 2002. "A Critical Review of Recent Biological Research on Human Sexuality." *Annual Review of Sex Research* 13:89–140.

O'Connell, Martin and Sarah Feliz. 2011. *Same-Sex Couple Household Statistics From the 2010 Census* (SEHSD Working Paper 2011–26). Washington, DC: U.S. Census Bureau.

Patterson, Charlotte and Richard Redding. 1996. "Lesbian and Gay Families With Children: Implications of Social Science Research for Policy." *Journal of Social Issues* 52(3):29–50.

Radkowsky, M. and Lawrence J. Siegel. 1997. "The Gay Adolescent: Stressors, Adaptations, and Psychological Interventions." *Clinical Psychology Review* 17:191–216.

Redding, R. E. 2008. "It's Really About Sex: Same-Sex Marriage, Lesbigay Parenting and the Psychology of Disgust." *Duke Journal of Gender, Law and Policy* 15:127–87.

Rivers, Ian and Daniel Carragher. 2003. "Social-Developmental Factors Affecting Lesbian and Gay Youth: A Review of Cross-National Research Findings." *Children and Society* 17(5):374–85.

Robinson, Paul. 1976. *The Modernization of Sex: Havelock Ellis, Alfred Kinsey, William Masters and Virginia Johnson.* New York: Harper & Row.

Rosenbloom, Stephanie. 2006. "Is This Campus Gay-Friendly?" *New York Times*, September 14, pp. S1–S2.

Savage, Charles and Sheryl Gay Stolberg. 2011. "In Turnabout, U.S. Says Marriage Act Blocks Gay Rights." *New York Times*, February 24, pp. A1, A18.

Savage, Dan. 2010. "Give 'Em Hope." Retrieved March 9, 2012 (http://www.thestranger.com/seattle/SavageLove?oid=4940874).

Schneider, Beth. 1986. "Coming Out at Work: Bridging the Private/Public Gap." *Work and Occupations* 13(4):463–87.

Schumm, W. R. 2006. "Empirical and Theoretical Perspectives from Social Science on Gay Marriage and Child Custody Issues." *St. Thomas Law Review* 18:425–75.

Servicemembers Legal Defense Network. 2007. "Fact Sheet: Foreign Military Services Which Allow Open Service." Retrieved June 10, 2007 (http://sldn.3cdn.net/877fa9ce3ef2a2b2bc_wrm6bngt7.pdf).

Shalikashvili, John. 2007. "Second Thoughts on Gays in the Military." *New York Times*, January 2, p. A19.

Stacey, Judith and Timothy Biblarz. 2001. "(How) Does the Sexual Orientation of Parents Matter?" *American Sociological Review* 66:159–83.

Tavernise, Sabrina. 2011. "New Numbers, and Geography, for Gay Couples." *New York Times*, August 25, pp. A1, A4.

Vidal, Gore. 1988. "Someone to Laugh at the Squares With." In *At Home: Essays, 1982–1988*, edited by G. Vidal. New York: Random House.

Ward, Brian, James Dahlhamer, Adena Galinsky, and Sarah Joestl. 2014. *Sexual Orientation and Health Among U.S. Adults: National Health Interview Survey, 2013* (National Health Statistics Report No. 77). Hyattsville, MD: National Center for Health Statistics.

Chapter 6

Berger, Joseph. 2012. "A Shift From Nursing Homes to Managed Care at Home." *New York Times*, February 24, p. A20.

Binstock, Robert. 2005. "Old-Age Policies, Politics and Ageism." *Generations* 29:73–78.

Binstock, Robert. 2006. "Older People and Political Engagement: From Avid Voters to 'Cooled-Out Marks.'" *Generations* 30:24–30.

Butler, Robert. 1969. "Ageism: Another Form of Bigotry." *Gerontologist* 9(3):243–46.

Bytheway, William. 1995. *Ageism*. Buckingham, England: Open University Press.

Calasanti, Toni and Kathleen Slevin. 2001. *Gender, Social Inequalities, and Aging*. Walnut Creek, CA: AltaMira Press.

Calasanti, Toni, Kathleen Slevin, and Neal King. 2006. "Ageism and Feminism: From 'Et Cetera' to Center." *NWSA Journal* 18(1):13–30.

Campbell, A. 2003. *How Policies Make Citizens: Senior Political Activism and the American Welfare State*. Princeton, NJ: Princeton University Press.

Center for Information and Research on Civic Learning and Engagement. 2012. "Youth Turnout: At Least 49%, 22–23 Million Under-30 Voted." Retrieved November 16, 2012 (http://www.civicyouth.org/youth-turnout-at-least-49-22-23-million-under-30-voted/).

Centers for Medicare and Medicaid Services. 2012. "NHE Fact Sheet." Retrieved March 11, 2012 (https://www.cms.gov/NationalHealthExpendData/25_NHE_Fact_Sheet.asp).

Clark, Robert, Richard Burkhauser, Marilyn Moon, Joseph Quinn, and Timothy M. Smeeding. 2004. *Economics of an Aging Society*. Malden, MA: Blackwell.

Cowgill, Donald. 1974. "The Aging of Populations and Societies." *The Annals of the American Academy of Political and Social Science* 415:1–18.

Curl, Angela and M. C. Hokenstad. 2006. "Reshaping Retirement Policies in Post-industrial Nations: The Need for Flexibility." *Journal of Sociology and Social Welfare* 33(2):85–106.

DeNavas-Walt, Carmen and Bernadette Proctor. 2014. *Income and Poverty in the United States: 2013* (Current Population Reports, P60-249). Washington, DC: U.S. Census Bureau.

DeNavas-Walt, Carmen, Bernadette Proctor, and Jessica Smith. 2012. *Income, Poverty and Health Insurance Coverage in the United States: 2011* (Current Population Reports, P60–243). Washington, DC: U.S. Government Printing Office.

Dennis, Helen and Kathryn Thomas. 2007. "Ageism in the Workplace." *Generations* 31:84–89.

Duncan, Colin and Wendy Loretto. 2004. "Never the Right Age? Gender and Age-Based Discrimination in Employment." *Gender, Work and Organizations* 11(1):95–115.

Encore.org. 2014. "About us." Retrieved September 14, 2014 (http://www.encore.org/learn/aboutus).

Encore.org. 2013. "Barbara Young." Retrieved September 14, 2014 (http://www.encore.org/barbara-young).

Feder, Judith and Robert Friedland. 2005. "The Value of Social Security and Medicare to Families." *Generations* 29:78–85.

Fisher, Anne. 2004. "Older, Wiser, Job-Hunting." *Fortune* 149(3):46.

Freedman, Rita. 1986. *Beauty Bound*. Lexington, MA: D. C. Heath.

Frey, William. 2007. *Mapping the Growth of Older America: Seniors and Boomers in the Early 21st Century*. Washington, DC: Brookings Institution.

Frey, William. 2011. "America Reaches Its Demographic Tipping Point." Retrieved March 11, 2012 (http://www.brookings.edu/opinions/2011/0826_census_race_frey.aspx).

Glionna, John. 2011a. "Retired Scientists Say It's Their Job." *Tacoma News Tribune*, July 17, p. AA1.

Glionna, John. 2011b. "Retired Scientists Still Say They Want to Help at Japan Nuclear Plant." Retrieved March 11, 2012 (http://latimesblogs.latimes.com/world_now/2011/12/japans-march-11-earthquake-and-tsunami-fukushima-daiichi-nuclar-power-plant-radioactive-fallout.html).

Goffman, Erving. 1986. *Stigma: Notes on the Management of Spoiled Identity*. New York: Touchstone. (Original work published 1963)

Goodman, John C. 1998. "Why Your Grandchildren May Pay a 55 Percent Payroll Tax." *Wall Street Journal*, October 7, p. A22.

Hagestad, Gunhild and Peter Uhlenberg. 2005. "Should We Be Concerned About Age Segregation? Some Theoretical and Empirical Explorations." *Research on Aging* 28(6):638–53.

Handy, Jocelyn and Doreen Davy. 2007. "Gendered Ageism: Older Women's Experiences of Employment Agency Practices." *Asia Pacific Journal of Human Resources* 45:85–99.

He, Wan, Manisha Sengupta, Victoria Velkoff, and Kimberly DeBarros. 2005. *65+ in the United States: 2005* (P23-209). Washington, DC: U.S. Census Bureau.

Hoyert, Donna and Jiaquan Xu. 2012. *Deaths: Preliminary Data for 2011*. (National Vital Statistics Reports, Vol. 61, No. 6.) Washington, DC: Centers for Disease Control and Prevention.

Howell, Karen. 2011. "Integrated Care Benefits Seniors and Government Budgets." *The Globe and Mail*, July 13, p. A7.

Hurd Clarke, Laura. 2000. "Older Women's Body Image and Embodied Experience: An Exploration." *Journal of Women and Aging* 12:77–97.

Issa, Philip and Sheila Zedlewski. 2011. "Poverty Among Older Americans, 2009." Retrieved May 2, 2012 (http://www.urban.org/uploadedpdf/412296-Poverty-Among-Older-Americans.pdf).

Jones, Jeffrey. 2014. "In U.S. 14% of Those Aged 24 to 34 Are Living With Parents." Retrieved September 5, 2014 (http://www.gallup.com/poll/167426/aged-living-parents.aspx).

Keeter, Scott, Juliana Horowitz, and Alec Tyson. 2008. "Young Voters in the 2008 Election." Retrieved March 11, 2012 (http://pewresearch.org/pubs/1031/young-voters-in-the-2008-election).

Kessler, Eva-Marie, Katrin Rakoczy, and Ursula M. Staudinger. 2004. "The Portrayal of Older People in Prime Time Television Series: The Match With Gerontological Evidence." *Ageing & Society* 24:531–52.

Kincannon, Charles, Wan He, and Loraine West. 2005. "Demography of Aging in China and the United States and the Economic Well-Being of Their Older Populations." *Journal of Cross Cultural Gerontology* 20:243–55.

Levenson, A. J. 1981. "Ageism: A Major Deterrent to the Introduction of Curricula in Aging." *Gerontology and Geriatrics Education* 1:11–62.

Levin, Jack and William Levin. 1980. *Ageism: Prejudice and Discrimination Against the Elderly*. Belmont, CA: Wadsworth.

Levy, B. and E. Langer. 1994. "Aging Free From Negative Stereotypes: Successful Memory in China and Among the American Deaf." *Journal of Personality and Social Psychology* 66(6):989–97.

Luo, Ye, Jun Xu, Ellen Granberg, and William Wentworth. 2012. "A Longitudinal Study of Social Status, Perceived Discrimination, and Physical and Emotional Health Among Older Adults." *Research on Aging* 34(3):275–301.

Mabry, J. Beth and Vern Bengston. 2005. "Disengagement Theory." Pp. 113–17 in *Encyclopedia of Ageism*, edited by E. Palmore, L. Branch, and D. Harris. New York: Haworth Press.

McConatha, Jasim, Frauke Schnell, Karin Volkwein, Lori Riley, and Elizabeth Leach. 2003. "Attitudes Toward Aging: A Comparative Analysis of Young Adults From the United States and Germany." *International Journal of Aging and Human Development* 57(3):203–15.

Miller, Darryl, Teresita Leyell, and Julianna Mazachek. 2004. "Stereotypes of the Elderly in U.S. Television Commercials From the 1950s to the 1990s." *International Journal of Aging and Human Development* 58(4):315–40.

Moody, Harry. 2006. *Aging: Concepts and Controversies*. 5th ed. Thousand Oaks, CA: Pine Forge.

Moon, Marilyn. 1999. "Growth in Medicare Spending: What Will Beneficiaries Pay?" Retrieved March 16, 2003 (http://www.urban.org/publications/407788.html).

Murphy, Sherry, Jiaquan Xu, and Kenneth Kochanek. 2012. *Deaths: Preliminary Data for 2010*. Washington, DC: Centers for Disease Control and Prevention.

National Center for Health Statistics. 2009. *Health, United States, 2008 With Chartbook*.

Hyattsville, MD: National Center for Health Statistics.

Nelson, Todd. 2002. *Ageism: Stereotyping and Prejudice against Older Adults.* Cambridge, MA: MIT Press.

Nelson, Todd. 2005. "Ageism: Prejudice Against Our Feared Future Self." *Journal of Social Issues* 61(2):207–21.

OASDI Trustees. 2007. *The 2007 Annual Report of the Board of Trustees of the Federal Old-Age and Survivors Insurance and Federal Disability Insurance Trust Funds.* Washington, DC: U.S. Government Printing Office.

Ohlemacher, Stephen. 2007. "The First Baby Boomer Applies for Social Security." *Seattle Times,* October 16, pp. A1, A11.

Packer, Dominic and Alison Chasteen. 2006. "Looking to the Future: How Possible Aged Selves Influence Prejudice Toward Older Adults." *Social Cognition,* 24:218–47.

Pampel, Fred C. 1998. *Aging, Social Inequality, and Public Policy.* Thousand Oaks, CA: Pine Forge.

Peterson, Robin T. and Douglas T. Ross. 1997. "A Content Analysis of the Portrayal of Mature Individuals in Television Commercials." *Journal of Business Ethics* 15:425–33.

Pope, Elizabeth. 2012. "Found: Older Volunteers to Fill Labor Shortage." *New York Times,* March 8, p. F9.

Raab, Barbara. 2013. "From Nanny to National Organizer: Helping Domestic Workers Stand Up for Their Rights." Retrieved September 14, 2014 (http://www.nbcnews.com/feature/in-plain-sight/nanny-national-organizer-helping-domestic-workers-stand-their-rights-f2D11767824).

Rampell, Catherine and Matthew Saltmarsh. 2009. "A Reluctance to Retire Means Fewer Openings." Retrieved May 11, 2010 (http://www.nytimes.com/2009/09/03/business/03retire.html?pagewanted=all&_r=0).

Rhee, Nari. 2012. *Black and Latino Retirement (In)security.* Berkeley: University of California, Center of Labor Research and Education.

Robinson, Kristen. 2007. *Trends in Health Status and Health Care Use Among Older Women, Aging Trends, No. 7.* Hyattsville, MD: National Center for Health Statistics.

Sanders, Marlene. 2002. "Older Women and the Media." *Women in Action* 3(September):56.

Saucier, Maggi. 2004. "Midlife and Beyond: Issue for Aging Women." *Journal of Counseling and Development* 82:420–25.

Slackman, Michael. 2011. "Bullets Stall Youthful Push for an Arab Spring." *New York Times,* March 18, pp. A1, A10.

Social Security Administration. 2014a. "Social Security Facts." Retrieved September 13, 2014 (http://www.ssa.gov/news/press/basicfact.html).

Social Security Administration. 2014b. "A Summary of the 2014 Annual Reports." Retrieved September 13, 2014 (http://www.ssa.gov/oact/trsum/).

Social Security and Medicare Boards of Trustees. 2007. "The Summary of the 2007 Annual

Reports." Retrieved May 11, 2010 (http://www.ssa.gov/OACT/TRSUM/index.html).

Sontag, Susan. 1979. "The Double Standard of Aging." Retrieved February 11, 2007 (http://www.unz.org/Pub/SaturdayRev-1972sep23-00029?View=PDFPages).

Spalter-Roth, Roberta and Nicole Van Vooren. 2008. "What Are They Doing With a Bachelor's Degree in Sociology?" Washington, DC: American Sociological Association.

Street, Debra and Jeralynn Sittig Crossman. 2006. "Greatest Generation or Greedy Geezers? Social Spending Preference and the Elderly." *Social Problems* 53(1):75–96.

Thornton, James. 2002. "Myths of Aging or Ageist Stereotypes." *Educational Gerontology* 28:301–12.

Turner, B. 1996. *The Body and Society: Explorations in Social Theory.* Thousand Oaks, CA: Sage Publications.

U.S. Census Bureau. 2011. "Household Data, Annual Averages, 3. Employment Status of the Civilian Noninstitutional Population by Age, Sex, and Race." Retrieved March 11, 2012 (http://www.bls.gov/cps/cpsaat03.pdf).

U.S. Census Bureau. 2012. *The 2012 Statistical Abstract.* Retrieved March 11, 2012 (http://www.census.gov/compendia/statab/2012/tables/12s0007.pdf).

Werner, Carrie. 2011. *The Older Population: 2010.* 2010 Census Brief No. C2010BR-09. Washington, DC: U.S. Census Bureau.

West, Loraine, Samantha Cole, Daniel Goodkind, and Wan He. 2014. *65+ in the United States: 2010.* Washington, DC: U.S. Census Bureau.

Wilson, Duff. 2007. "Aging: Disease or Business Opportunity?" *New York Times,* April 15, pp. BU1, 7–8.

Xu, Qingwen and Julian Chow. 2011. "Exploring the Community-Based Service Delivery Model: Elderly Care in China." *International Social Work* 43:374–87.

Yang, Frances and Sue Levkoff. 2005. "Ageism and Minority Populations: Strengths in the Face of Challenge." *Generations* 29:42–48.

Zaidi, Asghar. 2006. *Poverty of Elderly People in EU25.* Retrieved May 11, 2010 (http://www.euro.centre.org/data/1156245035_36346.pdf).

Part III

Newman, David. 2006. *Sociology: Exploring the Architecture of Everyday Life.* Thousand Oaks, CA: Pine Forge.

Chapter 7

AARP. 2002. "Facts About Grandparents Raising Children." Retrieved August 28, 2002 (http://www.aarp.org/congacts/grandparents/grandfacts).

Alvarez, Lizette. 2009. "Wartime Soldier, Conflicted Mom: Overseas and Back Home, Torn Between Service and Family." *New York Times,* September 27, pp. 1, 22.

Amato, Paul. 2000. "The consequences of divorce for adults and children." *Journal of Marriage and Family* 62:1269–87.

Amato, Paul and Danelle DeBoer. 2001. "The Transmission of Marital Instability Across Generations: Relationship Skills or Commitment to Marriage?" *Journal of Marriage and Family* 63:1038–51.

Amato, Paul R. and Bruce Keith. 1991. "Parental Divorce and the Well-Being of Children: A Meta-Analysis." *Journal of Marriage and the Family* 53:895–915.

Anderson, Kristin. 1997. "Gender, Status, and Domestic Violence: An Integration of Feminist and Family Violence Approaches." *Journal of Marriage and the Family* 59(3):655–79.

Andres, Manon and Rene Moelker. 2011. "There and Back Again: How Parental Experiences Affect Children's Adjustments in the Course of Military Deployments." *Armed Forces & Society* 37:418–47.

Annie E. Casey Foundation. 1998. *Kids Count Special Report: When Teens Have Sex: Issues and Trends.* Baltimore, MD: Annie E. Casey Foundation.

Armas, Genaro. 2002. "Census Shows More Grandparents Are Raising Their Grandchildren." *News Tribune,* July 8, pp. A1, A6.

Avellar, Sarah and Pamela Smock. 2005. "The Economic Consequences of the Dissolution of Cohabitating Unions." *Journal of Marriage and the Family* 67(2):315–27.

Beck, Ulrich. 1992. *Risk Society: Towards a New Modernity.* Thousand Oaks, CA: Sage Publications.

Bengston, Vern L. 2001. "Beyond the Nuclear Family: The Increasing Importance of Multigenerational Bonds." *Journal of Marriage and the Family* 63(1):1–17.

Bent-Goodley, Tricia. 2005. "Culture and Domestic Violence: Transforming Knowledge Development." *Journal of Interpersonal Violence* 20(2):195–203.

Bethea, Lesa. 1999. "Primary Prevention of Child Abuse." *American Family Physician* 59(6):1577–86.

Bianchi, Suzanne, John Robinson, and Melissa Milkie. 2006. *Changing Rhythms of American Family Life.* New York: Russell Sage.

Branzel, Amy. 2005. "Queering Citizenship? Same-Sex Marriage and the State." *GLQ: A Journal of Lesbian and Gay Studies* 11:171–204.

Breines, Winifred and Linda Gordon. 1983. "The New Scholarship on Family Violence." *Signs* 8:490–531.

Brooks Conway, Morgan, Teresa Christensen, and Barbara Herlihy. 2003. "Adult Children of Divorce and Intimate Relationships: Implications for Counseling." *Family Journal* 11(4):364–73.

Brown, Allie. 2010. "From Sex Abuse Victim to Legal Advocate." Retrieved May 11, 2010 (http://www.cnn.com/2010/LIVING/01/07/cnnheroes.ward/).

Brownmiller, S. 1975. *Against Our Will: Men, Women, and Rape.* New York: Bantam Books.

Buckley, Cara. 2007. "Despite Alternatives, Many Newborns Are Abandoned." *New York Times,* January 13, p. A14.

Bumpass, Larry. 1998. "The Changing Significance of Marriage in the United States." Pp. 63–82 in *The Changing Family in Comparative Perspective: Asia and the United States*, edited by K. Oppenheim Mason, N. Tsuya, and M. Choe. Honolulu, HI: East-West Center.

Bumpass, Larry and Hsien-Hen Lu. 2000. "Trends in Cohabitation and Implications for Children's Family Contexts in the United States." *Population Studies* 54(1):29–41.

Card, J. 1999. "Teen Pregnancy Prevention: Do Any Programs Work?" *Annual Review of Public Health* 20:257–85.

Catalano, Shannon. 2012. "Intimate Partner Violence, 1993-2010." Retrieved September 13, 2014 (http://www.bjs.gov/content/pub/pdf/ipv9310.pdf).

Centers for Disease Control and Prevention. 2013. "National Marriage and Divorce Rate Trends." Retrieved September 13, 2014 (http://www.cdc.gov/nchs/nvss/marriage_divorce_tables.htm).

Chase Goodman, Catherine and Merril Silverstein. 2006. "Grandmothers Raising Grandchildren: Ethnic and Racial Differences in Well-Being Among Custodial and Coparenting Families." *Journal of Family Issues* 27(11):1605–26.

Cherlin, Andrew, Kathleen Kiernan, and P. Lindsay Chase-Lansdale. 1995. "Parental Divorce in Childhood and Demographic Outcomes in Young Adulthood." *Demography* 32:299–318.

Child Welfare Information Gateway. 2006. *Long-Term Consequences of Child Abuse and Neglect*. Washington, DC: U.S. Department of Health and Human Services, Administration for Children and Families.

Child Welfare Information Gateway. 2007. *Recognizing Child Abuse and Neglect: Signs and Symptoms*. Retrieved May 26, 2010 (http://www.childwelfare.gov/pubs/factsheets/signs.cfm).

Clarke, Linda and Ceridwen Roberts 2004. "The Meaning of Grandparenthood and Its Contribution to the Quality of Life of Older People." Pp. 188–208 in *Growing Older: Quality of Life*, edited by Alan Walker and Catherine Henessey. Open University Press.

Copeland, Anne P. and Kathleen. M. White. 1991. *Studying Families*. Newbury Park, CA: Sage Publications.

Crewe, Sandra Edmonds. 2012. "Guardians of Generations: African American Grandparent Caregivers for Children of HIV/AIDS Infected Parents." *Journal of Family Strengths* 12 (1):1–20.

Dafoe Whitehead, Barbara and David Popenoe. 2005. *The State of Our Unions: The Social Health of Marriage in America, 2005*. Retrieved May 11, 2010 (http://www.stateofourunions.org/pdfs/SOOU2005.pdf).

Demo, David H. 1992. "Parent-Child Relations: Assessing Recent Changes." *Journal of Marriage and the Family* 54:104–17.

DeParle, Jason and Sabrina Tavernise. 2012. "Unwed Mothers Now a Majority in Births in 20's." *New York Times*, February 18, pp. A1, A14.

Dodson, Lisa, Tiffany Manuel, and Ellen Bravo. 2002. *Keeping Jobs and Raising Families in Low-Income America: It Just Doesn't Work*. Cambridge, MA: Radcliffe Public Policy Center and 9 to 5 National Association of Working Women.

Ellis, Renee and Tavia Simmons. 2014. "Coresident Grandparents and Their Grandchildren: 2012" (P20-576). Retrieved January 10, 2015 (http://www.census.gov/content/dam/Census/library/publications/2014/demo/p20-576.pdf).

Engels, Fredrich. 1902. *The Origin of Family, Private Property, and the State*. New York: International Publishers.

Erera, Pauline Irit. 2002. *Family Diversity: Continuity and Change in the Contemporary Family*. Thousand Oaks, CA: Sage Publications.

Eurostat. 2009. "Population, Eurostat Yearbook 2009." Retrieved December 29, 2009 (http://epp.eurostat.ec.europa.eu/cache/ITY_OFFPUB/KS-HA-09-001-01/EN/KS-HA-09-001-01-EN.PDF).

Fields, Jason. 2003. *America's Families and Living Arrangements: 2002* (Current Population Reports, P20-547). Washington, DC: U.S. Census Bureau.

Furstenberg, Frank. 2007. *Destinies of the Disadvantaged: The Politics of Teen Childbearing*. New York: Russell Sage.

Furstenberg, Frank F., Jeanne Brooks-Gunn, and S. Philip Morgan. 1987. *Adolescent Mothers in Later Life*. Cambridge, England: Cambridge University Press.

Garcia-Moreno, Claudia, Henrica Jansen, Mary Ellsberg, Lori Heise, and Charlotte Watts. 2006. "Prevalence of Intimate Partner Violence: Findings From the WHO Multi-country Study on Women's Health and Domestic Violence." *The Lancet* 368:1260–69.

Gelles, Richard and Peter Maynard. 1987. "A Structural Family Systems Approach to Intervention in Cases of Family Violence." *Family Relations* 33(2): 270–76.

Goldman, Jill, Marsha Salus, Deborah Wolcott, and Kristie Kennedy. 2003. *A Coordinated Response to Child Abuse and Neglect: The Foundation for Practice*. Washington, DC: Office on Child Abuse and Neglect, Health and Human Services.

Goodwin, Paula Y., William D. Mosher, and Anjani Chandra. 2010. *Marriage and Cohabitation in the United States: A Statistical Portrait Based on Cycle 6 (2002) of the National Survey of Family Growth* (Vital Health Statistics, Series 23, No. 28). Washington, DC: National Center for Health Statistics.

Gubernskaya, Zoya. 2010. "Changing Attitudes Toward Marriage and Children in Six Countries." *Sociological Perspectives* 53(2):179–200.

Hanson, Marci and Eleanor Lynch. 1992. "Family Diversity: Implications for Policy and Practice." *Topics in Early Childhood Special Education* 12(3):283–305.

He, Wan, Manisha Sengupta, Victoria Velkoff, and Kimberly De Barros. 2005. *65+ in the United States, 2005* (P23-209). Washington, DC: U.S. Department of Commerce, Economics and Statistics Administration, U.S. Census Bureau.

Hetherington, E. Mavis and John Kelly. 2002. *For Better or for Worse: Divorce Reconsidered*. New York: Norton.

Hiew, Chock C. 1992. "Separated by Their Work: Families With Fathers Living Apart." *Environment and Behavior* 24:206–25.

Hoffman, Saul. 1998. "Teenage Childbearing Is Not So Bad After All . . . Or Is It? A Review of the New Literature." *Family Planning Perspectives* 30(5):236–39, 243.

Hoffman, Saul. 2006. *By the Numbers: The Public Cost of Adolescent Childbearing*. Washington, DC: The National Campaign to Prevent Teen Pregnancy.

Jensen, Peter, David Martin, and Henry Watanabe. 1996. "Children's Response to Separation During Operation Desert Storm." *Journal of the American Academy of Child and Adolescent Psychiatry* 35:433–41.

Jetter, Alexis. 2000. "Uppity Women: Wynona Ward." Retrieved May 11, 2010 (http://www.msmagazine.com/feb00/uppitywomen.asp).

Johnson, Shannon, Michelle Sherman, Jeanne Hoffman, Larry James, Patti Johnson, and John Lochman. 2007. *The Psychological Needs of U.S. Military Service Members and Their Families: A Preliminary Report* (Presidential Task Force on Military Deployment Services for Youth, Families and Service Members). Washington, DC: American Psychological Association.

Kelch-Oliver, Karia. 2011. "African American Grandchildren Raised in Grandparent-Headed Families: An Exploratory Study." *The Family Journal* 19:396–406.

Kim, Eunjeong and King Davis. 2003. "Conceptualizing Unmarried Motherhood in South Korea: The Role of Patriarchy and Confucianism in the Lives of Women." *Journal of Social Work Research and Evaluation* 4:107–20.

Kirby, Douglas. 2007. "Abstinence, Sex and STD/HIV Education Programs for Teens: Their Impact on Sexual Behavior, Pregnancy and Sexually Transmitted Disease." *Annual Review of Sex Research* 18:143–77.

Kreider, Rose. 2005. *Number, Timing and Duration of Marriage and Divorces: 2001* (Current Population Reports, P70-97). Washington, DC: U.S. Census Bureau.

Kreider, Rose. 2010. "Increase in Opposite-Sex Cohabiting Couples from 2009 to 2010 in the Annual and Economic Supplement (ASED) to the Current Population Survey (CPS)." Retrieved March 16, 2012 (http://www.census.gov/population/www/socdemo/Inc-Opp-sex-2009-to-2010.pdf).

Kreider, Rose and Diana Elliot. 2009. *America's Families and Living Arrangements: 2007* (Current Population Reports, P20-561). Washington, DC: U.S. Census Bureau.

Kreider, Rose and J. Fields. 2002. *Number, Timing, and Duration of Marriages and Divorces: Fall 1996* (Current Population Reports, P70-80). Washington, DC: U.S. Census Bureau.

Lang, Susan. 1993. "Findings Refute Traditional Views on Elder Abuse." *Human Ecology* 21(3):30.

Lenski, Gerhard and Jean Lenski. 1987. *Human Societies*. New York: McGraw-Hill.

Levai, Marion, Sheldon Kaplan, Karen Daly, and George McIntosh. 1994. "The Effect of the Persian Gulf Crisis on the Psychiatric Hospitalization of Navy Children and Adolescents." *Child Psychiatry and Human Development* 24:245–54.

Levendosky, Alytia and Sandra Graham-Bermann. 2000. "Behavioral Observations of Parenting in Battered Women." *Journal of Family Psychology* 14:80–94.

Levendosky, Alytia, Shannon Lynch, and Sandra Graham-Bermann. 2000. "Mothers' Perceptions of the Impact of Woman Abuse on Their Parenting." *Violence Against Women* 6(3):247–71.

Little, Kristin, Mary Malefyt, and Alexander Walker. 1998. "A Tool for Communities to Develop Coordinated Responses." In *Promising Practices Initiative of the STOP Violence Against Women Grants Technical Assistance Project.* Retrieved August 29, 2002 (http://www.vaw.umn.edu/Promise/PP3).

MacKinnon, Carol E., Zolinda Stoneman, and Gene H. Brody. 1984. "The Impact of Maternal Employment and Family Form on Children's Sex Role Stereotypes and Mothers' Traditional Attitudes." *Journal of Divorce* 8:51–60.

Manning, Wendy and Antwan Jones. 2006. "Cohabitation and Marital Dissolution." Paper presented at the Annual Meeting of the Population Association of America, April, Los Angeles, CA.

Manning, Wendy and Pamela Smock. 2002. "First Comes Cohabitation and Then Comes Marriage? A Research Note." *Journal of Family Issues* 23(8):1065–87.

Martin, Joyce, Brady Hamilton, Michelle Osterman, Sally Curtin, and T. J. Matthews. 2013. *Births: Final Data for 2012.* Washington, DC: U.S. Department of Health and Human Services, Centers for Disease Control and Prevention.

Mays, Jennifer. 2006. "Feminist Disability Theory: Domestic Violence Against Women With a Disability." *Disability & Society* 21:147–58.

National Center on Elder Abuse. 2002a. "Frequently Asked Questions: What Is Elder Abuse?" Retrieved May 27, 2010 (http://www.ncea.aoa.gov/NCEAroot/Main_Site/FAQ/Questions.aspx).

National Center on Elder Abuse. 2002b. *Sentinels: Reaching Hidden Victims—Final Report, May 2002.* Washington, DC: National Center on Elder Abuse.

National Marriage Project. 2009. "State of Our Unions: The Marriage Report 2009." Retrieved January 7, 2010 (http://www.stateofourunions.org/2009/si-cohabitation.php).

National Marriage Project. 2011. *The State of Our Unions.* Charlottesville, VA: National Marriage Project.

National Marriage Project. 2013. *The State of Our Unions: 2012.* Charlottesville, VA: National Marriage Project.

National Partnership for Women and Families. 2009. "Paid Leave." Retrieved May 11, 2010 (http://www.nationalpartnership.org/site/PageServer?pagename=issues_work_paidleave).

Navaie-Waliser, Maryam, Penny Feldman, David Gould, Carol Levine, Alexis Kuebris, and Karen Donelan. 2002. "When the Caregiver Needs Care: The Plight of Vulnerable Caregivers." *American Journal of Public Health* 92(3):409–13.

New Jersey Safe Haven Protection Act. 2007. "FAQ's." Retrieved January 14, 2007 (http://www.njsafehaven.org/faq.html).

Organisation for Economic Co-operation and Development. 2010. Retrieved February 21, 2012 (http://www.oecd.org/els/soc/41920080.pdf).

Popenoe, David. 1993. "American Family Decline, 1960–1990: A Review and Appraisal." *Journal of Marriage and the Family* 55:527–55.

Povoledo, Elisabetta. 2007. "Updating an Old Way to Leave the Baby on the Doorstep." *New York Times*, February 28, p. A4.

Powell, Brian, Catherine Bolzendahl, Claudia Geist, and Lara Carr Steelman. 2010. *Counted Out: Same-Sex Relations and Americans' Definitions of Family.* New York: Russell Sage.

Radcliffe Public Policy Center. 2000. *Life's Work: Generational Attitudes Toward Work and Life Integration.* Cambridge, MA: Radcliffe Public Policy Center.

Ray, Rebecca, Janet Gornick, and John Schmitt. 2010. "Who Cares? Assessing Generosity and Gender Equality in Parental Leave Policy Designs in 21 Countries." *Journal of European Social Policy* 20:196–216.

Roberts, Sam. 2007. "51% of Women Are Now Living Without a Spouse." *New York Times*, January 16, pp. A1, A19.

Rubin, Lillian. 1995. *Families on the Fault Line: America's Working Class Speaks About the Family, the Economy and Ethnicity.* New York: Harper Perennial.

Rutter, Michael and Marta Tienda. 2005. "The Multiple Facets of Ethnicity." Pp. 50–59 in *Ethnicity and Causal Mechanisms*, edited by Michael Rutter and Marta Tienda. New York: Cambridge University Press.

Sang-Hun, Choe. 2009. "Group Resists Korean Stigma for Mothers on Their Own." *New York Times*, October 8, p. A6.

Silk, Jessica and Diana Romero. 2013. "The Role of Parents in Teen Pregnancy Prevention: An Analysis of Programs and Policies." *Journal of Family Issues* 35:1339–62.

Simons, Ronald L. 1996. *Understanding Differences Between Divorced and Intact Families: Stress, Interaction, and Child Outcomes.* Thousand Oaks, CA: Sage Publications.

Smith, Dorothy. 1993. "The Standard North American Family: SNAF as an Ideological Code." *Journal of Family Issues* 14(1):50–65.

SmithBattle, Lee. 2007. "'I Wanna Have a Good Future': Teen Mothers' Rise in Educational Aspirations, Competing Demands, and Limited School Support." *Youth & Society* 38(3):348–71.

Smock, Pamela J. 1994. "Gender and Short Run Economic Consequences of Marital Disruption." *Social Forces* 73:243–62.

Somers, Cheryl and Mariane Fahlman. 2001. "Effectiveness of the 'Baby Think It Over' Teen Pregnancy Prevention Program." *Journal of School Health* 71(5):188–207.

Stacey, Judith. 1996. *In the Name of the Family: Rethinking Family Values in the Post-modern Age.* Boston: Beacon Press.

State of California, Economic Development Department. 2014. *Paid Family Leave: Ten Years of Assisting Californians in Need.* Sacramento, CA: State of California, Economic Development Department.

Tjaden, Patricia and Nancy Thoennes. 2000. *Extent, Nature and Consequences of Intimate Partner Violence* (NCJ 18186). Washington, DC: National Institute of Justice, U.S. Department of Justice.

Trail Ross, Mary Ellen and Lu Ann Aday. 2006. "Stress and Coping Among African American Grandparents Who Are Raising Their Grandchildren." *Family Issues* 27:912–32.

U.S. Bureau of Justice Statistics. 2012. "Intimate Partner Violence in the U.S." Retrieved March 16, 2012 (http://bjs.ojp.usdoj.gov/content/intimate/victims.cfm#age12).

U.S. Bureau of Labor Statistics. 2014. "Occupational Outlook Handbook: Paralegals and Legal Assistants." Retrieved December 23, 2014 (http://www.bls.gov/ooh/legal/paralegals-and-legal-assistants.htm).

U.S. Census Bureau. 1999. *Statistical Abstract of the United States: 1999* (Table No. 91). Washington, DC: U.S. Census Bureau.

U.S. Department of Health and Human Services; Administration for Children and Families; Administration on Children, Youth and Families; Children's Bureau. 2013. *Child Maltreatment 2012.* Washington, DC: U.S. Department of Health and Human Services; Administration for Children and Families; Administration on Children, Youth and Families; Children's Bureau.

U.S. Department of Justice. 2011. "Elder Abuse and Mistreatment." Retrieved September 27, 2014 (http://ojp.gov/newsroom/factsheets/ojpfs_elderabuse.html).

Uunk, Wilfred. 2004. "The Economic Consequences of Divorce for Women in the European Union: The Impact of Welfare State Arrangements." *European Journal of Population* 20(3):251–85.

van der Lippe, Tanja, Annet Jager, and Yvonne Kops. 2006. "Combination Pressure: The Paid Family Balance of Men and Women in European Countries." *Acta Sociologica* 49:303–19.

Vespa, Jonathan, Jamie Lewis, and Rose Kreider. 2013. *America's Families and Living Arrangements: 2012* (P20-750). Washington, DC: U.S. Census Bureau.

Videon, Tami. 2002. "The Effects of Parent–Adolescent Relationships and Parental Separation on Adolescent Well-Being." *Journal of Marriage and Family* 64(2):489–504.

Ward, Wynona. 2002. "Transcript: Wynona Ward—Have Justice Will Travel." Retrieved May 11, 2010 (http://www.pbs.org/now/transcript/transcript_ward.html).

Weaver, Heather, Gary Smith, and Susan Kippax. 2005. "School-Based Sex Education Policies and Indicators of Sexual Health Among Young People: A Comparison of the Netherlands, France,

Australia and the United States." *Sex Education* 5:171–88.

Wolfinger, Nicholas. 2005. *Understanding the Divorce Cycle: The Children of Divorce in Their Own Marriages.* Cambridge, UK: Cambridge University Press.

Chapter 8

Aber, J. L., Joshua Brown, and Christopher C. Henrich. 1999. *Teaching Conflict Resolution: An Effective School-Based Approach to Violence Prevention.* Washington, DC: National Center for Children in Poverty.

Adams, Mike S. and T. D. Evans. 1996. "Teacher Disapproval, Delinquent Peers, and Self-Reported Delinquency: A Longitudinal Test of Labeling Theory." *Urban Review* 28(3): 199–211.

American Association of University Women. 1992. *How Schools Shortchange Girls: The AAUW Report.* New York: American Association of University Women.

American Association of University Women. 2001. *Hostile Hallways: Bullying, Teasing, and Sexual Harassment in School.* Washington, DC: American Association of University Women.

American Council on Education. 2012. "Undergraduate Degrees Conferred, by Field of Study and Gender: 2009–10." Retrieved September 19, 2014 (http://www .acenet.edu/news-room/Pages/Graduate-Degrees-Conferred-by-Field-of-Study-and-Gender-2009-10.aspx).

Ansalone, George. 2001. "Schooling, Tracking and Inequality." *Journal of Children and Poverty* 7(1):33–49.

Ansalone, George. 2004. "Educational Opportunity and Access to Knowledge: Tracking in the U.S. and Japan." *Race, Gender & Class* 11(3):140–52.

Ansell, Nicola. 2008. "Substituting for Families? Schools and Social Reproduction in AIDS-Affected Lesotho." *Antipode* 40:802–24.

Barnett, W. Steven, Megan Carolan, James Squires, and Kirsty Clarke Brown. 2013. *The State of Preschool 2013: State Preschool Yearbook.* New Brunswick, NJ: National Institute for Early Education Research.

Berliner, David and Bruce Biddle. 1995. *The Manufactured Crisis: Myths, Frauds, and the Attack on America's Public Schools.* Reading, MA: Addison-Wesley.

Bjork, Christopher and Ryoko Tsuneyoshi. 2005. "Education Reform in Japan: Competing Visions for the Future." *Phi Delta Kappan* April:619–26.

Bohan, Janis and Glenda M. Russell. 1999. "Support Networks for Lesbian, Gay and Bisexual Students." Pp. 279–94 in *Coming Into Her Own: Educational Successes in Girls and Women*, edited by S. N. Davis, M. Crawford, and J. Sebrechts. San Francisco: Jossey-Bass.

Bourdieu, Pierre. 1977. "Cultural Reproduction and Social Reproduction." Pp. 71–84 in *Power and Ideology in Education,* edited by J. Karabel and

A. H. Halsey. Oxford: Oxford University Press.

Bumiller, Elisabeth. 2002. "Bush Calls Ruling About Vouchers a 'Historic' Move.'" *New York Times,* July 2, pp. A1, A15.

Centers for Disease Control and Prevention. 2014. "Trends in Prevalence of Behaviors That Contribute to Violence on School Property National YRBS: 1991–2013." Retrieved September 25, 2014 (http://www .cdc.gov/healthyyouth/yrbs/pdf/trends/ us_violenceschool_trend_yrbs.pdf).

College Board. 2013. *2013 College-Bound Seniors Total Group Profile Report.* Retrieved November 6, 2014 (http://media.collegeboard .com/digitalServices/pdf/research/2013/ TotalGroup-2013.pdf).

College Entrance Examination Board. 1999. *Reaching the Top: A Report of the National Task Force on Minority High Achievement.* New York: College Entrance Examination Board.

Center for Research on Education Outcomes. 2013. *National Charter School Study 2013.* Stanford, CA: Center for Research on Education Outcomes.

Dinkes, Rachel, Jana Kemp, Katrina Baum, and Thomas Snyder. 2009. *Indicators of School Crime and Safety: 2009* (NCES 2010-012/NCJ 228478). U.S. Departments of Education and Justice. Washington, DC: U.S. Government Printing Office.

Downey, Douglas, Paul von Hippel, and Beckett Broh. 2004. "Are Schools the Great Equalizer? Cognitive Inequality during the Summer Months and the School Year." *American Sociological Review* 69:613–35.

Equal Employment Opportunity Commission. 2001. "Facts about Sexual Harassment." Retrieved May 14, 2010 (http://www.eeoc.gov/facts/ fs-sex.html).

Field, Kelly. 2012. "College Groups React to Obama's Higher-Education Budget With Praise and Caution." Retrieved May 24, 2012 (http:// chronicle.com/article/College-Groups-React-With/130775/).

Fineran, Susan. 2002. "Sexual Harassment Between Same-Sex Peers: Intersection of Mental Health, Homophobia, and Sexual Violence in Schools." *Social Work* 47(1):65–74.

Finn, Chester. 1997. "The Politics of Change." Pp. 226–50 in *New Schools for a New Century: The Redesign of Urban Education*, edited by Diane Ravitch and Joseph Viteritti. New Haven, CT: Yale University Press.

Flannery, Daniel. 1997. *School Violence: Risk, Preventive Intervention, and Policy.* New York: ERIC Clearing House on Urban Education (ERIC Document Reproduction Services No. ED416272).

Freeman, Kendralin and Dennis Condron. 2011. "Schmoozing in Elementary School: The Importance of Social Capital to First Graders." *Sociological Perspectives* 54:521–46.

Garcia, David. 2008. "The Impact of School Choice on Racial Segregation in Charter Schools." *Educational Policy* 22:805–29.

"Goals 2000: Reforming Education to Improve Student Achievement." 1998. Retrieved May 18, 2010 (http://www.ed.gov/pubs/ G2KReforming/index.html).

Good, Thomas L. and Jennifer S. Braden. 2000. *The Great School Debate: Choice, Vouchers, and Charters.* Mahwah, NJ: Lawrence Erlbaum.

Hallinan, Maureen. 1994. "Tracking: From Theory to Practice." *Sociology of Education* 67(2):79–91.

Hallinan, Maureen. 2003. "Ability Grouping and Student Learning." Pp. 95–124 in *Brookings Papers on Educational Policy*, edited by Diane Ravitch. Washington, DC: Brookings Institute, Brown Center on Educational Policy.

Halpern, Robert. 2003. *Making Play Work: The Promise of After School Programs for Low-Income Children.* New York: Columbia University Press.

Henry, Gary, Craig Gordon, and Dana Rickman. 2006. "Early Education Policy Alternatives: Comparing Quality and Outcomes of Head Start and State Prekindergarten." *Educational Evaluation and Policy Analysis* 28:77–99.

Hill, Catherine, Christianne Corbett, and Andresse St. Rose. 2010. *Why So Few? Women in Science, Technology, Engineering and Mathematics.* Washington, DC: AAUW.

Hill, Catherine and Holly Kearl. 2011. *Crossing the Line: Sexual Harassment at School.* Washington, DC: AAUW.

Holland, Dorothy C. and Margaret A. Eisenhart. 1990. *Educated in Romance: Women, Involvement, and College Culture.* Chicago: University of Chicago Press.

Hu, Winnie. 2012. "10 States Are Given Waivers From Education Law." *New York Times,* February 10, p. A13.

Human Rights Watch. 2001. *Hatred in the Hallways: Violence and Discrimination Against Lesbian, Gay, Bisexual, and Transgender Students in U.S. Schools.* New York: Human Rights Watch.

Jacobs, Jerry A. 1996. "Gender Inequality and Higher Education." *Annual Review of Sociology* 22:153–85.

Johnson, Jean, Jon Rochkind, Amber Ott, and Samantha DuPont. 2009. *With Their Whole Lives Ahead of Them.* San Francisco: Public Agenda.

Johnson, Robert C. and Debra Viadero. 2000. "Unmet Promise: Raising Minority Achievement." *Education Week* 17(43):1.

Kahlenberg, Richard. 2002. "Socioeconomic Integration." Presented at 20th Annual Magnet Schools of America Conference. Retrieved May 18, 2010 (http://www.tcf.org/list.asp? type=NC&pubid=906).

Kanter, Rosabeth Moss. 1972. "The Organization Child: Experience Management in a Nursery School." *Sociology of Education* 45:186–211.

Kennedy, Sheila. 2001. "Privatizing Education." *Phi Delta Kappan* 82(6):450–57.

King, Rachel. 2006. "Outsourcing: Beyond Bangalore." *Business Week Online.* December 11:6–6.

Kingery, Paul M., B. E. Pruitt, G. Heuberger, and J. A. Brizzolara. 1993. "School Violence Reported by Adolescents in Rural Central Texas." Texas A&M University, College Station, TX. Unpublished manuscript.

Kirp, David. 2014. "Rage Against the Common Core." *New York Times,* December 28, Review 19.

Kirsch, Irwin, Ann Jungeblut, Lynn Jenkins, and Andrew Kolstad. 2002. *Adult Literacy in America: A First Look at the Results of the National Adult Literacy Survey*. Retrieved May 18, 2010 (http://nces.ed.gov/pubs93/93275.pdf).

Kopp, Wendy. 2001. *One Day, All Children: The Unlikely Triumph of Teach for America and What I Learned Along the Way*. New York: PublicAffairs.

Kosciw, Joseph, Emily Greytak, Mark Bartkiewicz, Madelyn Boesen, and Neal Palmer. 2012. *The 2011 National School Climate Survey: The Experiences of Lesbian, Gay, Bisexual and Transgender Youth in Our Nation's Schools*. New York: GLSEN.

Kozol, Jonathan. 1991. *Savage Inequalities: Children in America's Schools*. New York: Harper Perennial.

Kozol, Jonathan. 2005. *The Shame of the Nation: The Restoration of Apartheid Schooling in America*. New York: Crown.

Laird, J., S. Lew, M. DeBell, and C. Chapman. 2006. *Dropout Rates in the United States: 2002 and 2003* (NCES 2006-062). U.S. Department of Education. Washington, DC: National Center for Education Statistics.

Lareau, Annette. 2003. *Unequal Childhoods: Class, Race, and Family Life*. Berkeley: University of California Press.

Lin, Nan. 2011. *Social Capital: A Theory of Social Structure and Action*. Cambridge, England: Cambridge University Press.

Linn, Marcia and Cathy Kessel. 1996. "Success in Mathematics: Increasing Talent and Gender Diversity Among College Majors." Pp. 83–100 in *Issues in Mathematics Education, Conference of the Mathematical Sciences*. Vol. 6, *Research in Collegiate Mathematics Education II*, edited by J. Kaput, A. H. Schoenfeld, and E. Dubinsky. Providence, RI: American Mathematical Society.

Literacy Volunteers of America. 2002. "Facts on Literacy in America." Retrieved September 5, 2003 (http://www.literacy volunteers.org/about/faqs/facts.html).

Marger, Martin. 2008. *Social Inequality: Patterns and Processes*. Boston: McGraw-Hill.

Maruyama, G. 2003. "Disparities in Educational Opportunities and Outcomes: What Do You Know and What Can We Do?" *Journal of Social Issues* 59(3):653–76.

Meier, Deborah. 1995. *The Power of Their Ideas*. Boston: Beacon Press.

Mickelson, Roslyn and Everett, Bobbie. 2008. "Neotracking in North Carolina: How High School Courses of Study Reproduce Race and Class-Based Stratification." *Teachers College Record* 110(3):535–70.

Mori, Rie. 2002. "Entrance Examinations and Remedial Education in Japanese Higher Education." *Higher Education* 43:27–42.

National Commission on Excellence in Education. 1983. *A Nation at Risk: The Imperatives for Educational Reform*. Washington, DC: U.S. Department of Education.

National Girls Collaborative Project. 2014. "About NGCP." Retrieved April 9, 2015 (http://www.ngcproject.org/about-ngcp).

Organisation for Economic Co-operation and Development. 2013. *OECD Skills Outlook 2013: First Results from the Survey of Adult Skills*. Paris, France: OECD Publishing.

Organisation for Economic Co-operation and Development. 2014. *Education at a Glance 2014: OECD Indicators*. Paris, France: OECD Publishing.

Ono, Hiroshi. 2001. "Who Goes to College? Features of Institutional Tracking in Japanese Higher Education." *American Journal of Education* 109(2):161–95.

Phillips, Meredith. 2011. "Parenting, Time Use, and Disparities in Academic Outcomes." Pp. 207–28 in *Whither Opportunity? Rising Inequality, Schools and Children's Life Chances*, edited by Greg Duncan and Richard Murnane. New York: Russell Sage.

ProLiteracy Worldwide. 2006. *The State of Adult Literacy 2006*. New York: ProLiteracy Worldwide.

Ravitch, Diane. 1997. "Somebody's Children: Educational Opportunity for All American Children." Pp. 251–73 in *New Schools for a New Century: The Redesign of Urban Education*, edited by D. Ravitch and J. P. Viteritti. New Haven, CT: Yale University Press.

Ravitch, Diane and Joseph P. Viteritti. 1997. "Introduction." Pp. 1–16 in *New Schools for a New Century: The Redesign of Urban Education*, edited by D. Ravitch and J. P. Viteritti. New Haven, CT: Yale University Press.

Reardon, Sean. 2011. "The Widening Academic Achievement Gap Between the Rich and the Poor: New Evidence and Possible Explanations." Pp. 91–116 in *Whither Opportunity: Rising Inequality, Schools and Children's Life Chances*, edited by G. Duncan and R. Murnane. New York: Russell Sage.

Riegle-Crumb, C., Farkas, G., & Muller, C. 2006. "The Role of Gender and Friendship in Advanced Course Taking." *Sociology of Education* 79(3):206–228.

Robers, Simone, Jana Kemp, Amy Rathbun, Rachel Morgan, and Thomas Snyder. 2014. *Indicators of School Crime and Safety: 2013* (NCES 2014-042/NCJ 243299). Washington, DC: U.S. Department of Education, National Center for Education Statistics, and U.S. Department of Justice, Bureau of Justice Statistics.

Rohlen, Thomas. 1983. *Japan's High Schools*. Berkeley: University of California Press.

Sacks, Peter. 2009. "Tearing Down the Gates: Confronting the Class Divide in American Education." *Liberal Education* 95:14–19.

Sadker, David and Karen Zittleman. 2009. *Still Failing at Fairness: How Gender Bias Cheats Girls and Boys in School and What We Can Do About It*. New York: Simon & Schuster.

Sadker, Myra and David Sadker. 1994. *Failing at Fairness: How Our Schools Cheat Girls*. New York: Simon & Schuster.

Sallie Mae and Ipsos. 2012. *How America Pays for College 2012*. Retrieved July 24, 2012 (https://www1.salliemae.com/NR/rdonlyres/75C6F178-9B25-48F5-8982-41F9B3F35BF6/0/HowAmericaPays2012.pdf).

Saporito, Salvatore and Annette Lareau. 1999. "School Selection as a Process: The Multiple Dimensions of Race in Framing Educational Choice." *Social Problems* 46:418–39.

Schemo, Diana Jean. 2002. "Few Exercise New Right to Leave Failing Schools." *New York Times*, August 28, pp. A1, A14.

Schmid, Randolph. 2010. "Teachers Give Girls Math Anxiety, Study Says." *News Tribune*, January 26, p. A6.

Schofield, Janet Ward. 2010. "International Evidence on Ability Grouping With Curriculum Differentiation and the Achievement Gap in Secondary Schools." *Teachers College Record* 112(5):1492–1528.

Shaw, Margaret. 2001. *Promoting Safety in Schools: International Experience and Action* (Bureau of Justice Assistance Monograph, NCJ 186937). Washington, DC: U.S. Department of Justice.

Silverman, Linda Kreger. 1986. "What Happens to the Gifted Girl?" Pp. 43–89 in *Critical Issues in Gifted Education*. Vol. 1, *Defensible Programs for the Gifted*, edited by C. J. Maker. Rockville, MD: Aspen.

Smith, Dorothy E. 2000. "Schooling for Inequality." *Signs* 25(4):1147–51.

Smith, R. S. 1995. "Giving Credit Where Credit Is Due: Dorothy Swaine Thomas and the 'Thomas Theorem.'" *American Sociologist* 26(4):9–29.

Spencer, Steven J., Claude M. Steele, and Diane M. Quinn. 1999. "Stereotype Threat and Women's Math Performance." *Journal of Experimental Social Psychology* 35:4–28.

Stambach, Amy and Natalie Crow Becker. 2006. "Finding the Old in the New: On Race and Class in US Charter School Debates." *Race, Ethnicity and Education* 9:159–82.

Steele, Claude M. 1997. "A Threat in the Air: How Stereotypes Shape Intellectual Identity and Performance." *American Psychologist* 52:613–29.

Steele, Claude M. and Joshua Aronson. 1995. "Stereotype Threat and the Intellectual Test Performance of African Americans." *Journal of Personality and Social Psychology* 69(5):797–811.

Stombler, Mindy and Patricia Yancey Martin. 1994. "Bringing Women In, Keeping Women Down." *Journal of Contemporary Ethnography* 23(2):150–84.

Sum, Andrew, Irwin Kirsch, and Robert Taggart. 2002. *The Twin Challenges of Mediocrity and Inequality: Literacy in the U.S. From an International Perspective*. Princeton, NJ: Educational Testing Service.

Taylor, Paul, Kim Parker, Richard Fry, D'Vera Cohn, Wendy Wang, Gabriel Velasco, and Daniel Dockterman. (2011). *Is College Worth It? College Presidents, Public Assess Value, Quality and Mission of Higher Education*. Washington, DC: Pew Social and Demographic Trends.

Thomas, William I. and Dorothy Swaine Thomas. 1928. *The Child in America: Behavior Problems and Programs*. New York: Knopf.

Traub, James. 2000. "What No School Can Do." *New York Times Magazine*, January 16, pp. 52–57, 68, 81, 90–91.

United Nations Educational, Scientific and Cultural Organization. 2013. *Adult and Youth Literacy: National, Regional and Global Trends, 1985–2015*. Montreal, Canada: United Nations Educational, Scientific and Cultural Organization.

U.S. Census Bureau. 2012. "The 2012 Statistical Abstract, Education." Retrieved November 6, 2014 (http://www.census.gov/compendia/statab/2012/tables/12s0232.pdf),

U.S. Census Bureau. 2013. "2013 American Community Survey 1-Year Estimates: Educational Attainment." Retrieved September 28, 2014 (http://factfinder2.census.gov/faces/tableservices/jsf/pages/productview.xhtml?pid=ACS_13_1YR_S1501&prodType=table).

U.S. Census Bureau. 2014. CPS Historical Time Series Tables, Table A-2. Retrieved September 25, 2014 (http://www.census.gov/hhes/socdemo/education/data/cps/historical/).

U.S. Department of Education. 2007. *The Nation's Report Card: America's High School Graduates: Results From the 2000 NAEP High School Transcript Study*. Washington, DC: U.S. Department of Education.

U.S. Department of Education. 2010. *A Blueprint for Reform: The Reauthorization of the Elementary and Secondary Education Act*. Washington, DC: U.S. Department of Education.

U.S. Department of Education, National Center for Education Statistics. 2014. "Fast Facts: Charter Schools." Retrieved September 25, 2014 (http://nces.ed.gov/fastfacts/display.asp?id=30).

U.S. Department of Health and Human Services. 2005. *Head Start Impact Study: First Year Findings*. Washington, DC: U.S. Department of Health and Human Services.

Wall, Shavaun, Elizabeth Timberlake, Michaela Farber, Christine Sabatino, Harriett Liebow, Nancy Smith, and Nancy Taylor. 2000. "Needs and Aspirations of the Working Poor: Early Head Start Program Applicants." *Families in Society* 81(4):412–21.

Warren, David. 2012. "Statement by NAICU President David L. Warren on President Obama's Higher Education Proposals." Retrieved May 24, 2012 (http://www.naicu.edu/news_room/statement-by-naicu-president-david-1-warren-on-president-obamas-higher-education-proposals).

Washington, Valora and Ura J. Oyemade Bailey. 1995. *Project Head Start: Models and Strategies for the Twenty-First Century*. New York: Garland.

White House. 2012. "Fact Sheet: President Obama's Blueprint for Keeping College Affordable and Within Reach for All Americans." Retrieved May 24, 2012 (http://www.whitehouse.gov/the-press-office/2012/01/27/fact-sheet-president-obama-s-blueprint-keeping-college-affordable-and-wi).

Wiland, Harry and Dale Bell. 2006. *Edens Lost & Found: How Ordinary Citizens Are Restoring Our Great American Cities*. White River Junction, VT: Chelsea Green.

Zernike, K. 2010. "Annual Poll of Freshmen Shows Effect of Recession." *New York Times*, January 21, p. A23.

Zigler, Edward and Susan Muenchow. 1992. *Head Start: The Inside Story of America's Most Successful Educational Experiment*. New York: Basic Books.

Chapter 9

Abell, Hilary. 1999. "Endangering Women's Health for Profit: Health and Safety in Mexico's Maquiladoras." *Development in Practice* 9(5):595–601.

Armas, Genaro. 2004. "Outearning Men Women's Toughest Job." *News Tribune*, June 4, p. 7.

Avendaño, Ana and Jonathan Hiatt. 2012. "Worker Self-Organization in the New Economy: The AFL-CIO's Experience in Movement Building With Community-Labour Partnerships." *Labour, Capital and Society* 45:66–95.

Bacon, David. 2011. "The Rebirth of Solidarity on the Border." Retrieved April 8, 2012 (http://www.cipamericas.org/archives/4697).

Bahnisch, Mark. 2000. "Embodied Work, Divided Labour: Subjectivity and the Scientific Management of the Body in Frederick W. Taylor's 1907 'Lecture on Management.'" *Body & Society* 6(1):51–68.

Barboza, David. 2010. "After Suicides, Scrutiny of China's Grim Factories." Retrieved November 6, 2014 (http://www.nytimes.com/2010/06/07/business/global/07suicide.html?pagewanted=all).

Bernanke, Ben. 2009. "Four Questions About the Financial Crisis." Retrieved May 13, 2010 (http://www.federalreserve.gov/newsevents/speech/bernanke20090414a.htm).

Bernstein, Jared. 1997. "Low-Wage Labor Market Indicators by City and State: The Constraints Facing Welfare Reform" (EPI Working Paper No. 118). Washington, DC: Economic Policy Institute.

Bernstein, Jared, Heidi Hartmann, and John Schmitt. 1999. *The Minimum Wage Increase: A Working Woman's Issue* (EPI Issue Brief No. 133). Washington, DC: Economic Policy Institute.

Bertrand, Marianne and Sendhil Mullainathan. 2003. "Are Emily and Greg More Employable Than Lakisha and Jamal? A Field Experiment in Market Discrimination" (NBER Working Paper No. 9873). Cambridge, MA: National Bureau of Economic Research.

Bluestone, Barry and Bennett Harrison. 1982. *The Deindustrialization of America*. New York: Basic Books.

Bosman, Julie. 2009. "Minus a Paycheck, Jobless Flock to Do Good." *New York Times*, March 16, pp. A1, A18.

Brady, David and Michael Wallace. 2001. "Deindustrialization and Poverty: Manufacturing Decline and AFDC Reciprocity in Lake County, Indiana 1964–93." *Sociological Forum* 16(2):321–58.

Braverman, Harry. 1974. *Labor and Monopoly Capital: The Degradation of Work in the Twentieth Century*. New York: Monthly Review Press.

Brenner, Joanna. 1998. "On Gender and Class in U.S. Labor History." *Monthly Review: An Independent Socialist Magazine* 50(6):1–15.

Budig, Michelle. 2002. "Male Advantage and the Gender Composition of Jobs: Who Rides the Glass Escalator?" *Social Problems* 49(2):258–77.

Business Alliance for Local Living Economies. 2012. "About BALLE." Retrieved April 9, 2012 (http://www.livingeconomies.org/aboutus).

Byrne, Geraldine and Robert Heyman. 1997. "Understanding Nurses' Communication With Patients in Accident and Emergency Departments Using a Symbolic Interactionist Perspective." *Journal of Advanced Nursing* 26:93–100.

Campos, Paul. 2013. "Sonia Sotomayor Debate: Should Unhappy Lawyers Blame Themselves?' Retrieved April 9, 2015 (http://ideas.time.com/2013/01/28/sonia-sotomayor-debate-should-unhappy-lawyers-blame-themselves/).

Carley, Michael. 2000. "Urban Partnerships, Governance and Regeneration of Britain's Cities." *International Planning Studies* 5(3):273–97.

Carnevale, Anthony, Tamara Jayasundera, and Ban Cheah. 2012. *The College Advantage: Weathering the Economic Storm, Executive Summary*. Retrieved August 27, 2012 (http://www9.georgetown.edu/grad/gppi/hpi/cew/pdfs/CollegeAdvantage.ExecutiveSummary.081512.pdf).

Cook, Nancy. 2009. "What Mancession?" Retrieved May 13, 2010 (http://www.newsweek.com/id/206917).

Co-op America. 2003. "What Is a Sweatshop?" Retrieved April 26, 2003 (http://www.sweatshops.org/educated/issue.html).

Darity, William A. 2003. "Employment Discrimination, Segregation and Health." *American Journal of Public Health* 93(2):226–32.

DeJong, Gordon F. and Anna Madamba. 2001. "A Double Disadvantage? Minority Group, Immigrant Status, and Underemployment in the United States." *Social Science Quarterly* 82(1):117–30.

DeNavas-Walt, Carmen and Bernadette Proctor. 2014. *Income and Poverty in the United States: 2013* (Current Population Reports, P60-249). Washington, DC: U.S. Census Bureau.

Dobbs, Lou. 2004. "Coming Up Empty." *U.S. News & World Report*, January, 26:46.

Economic Policy Institute. 2012. "The Great Recession." Retrieved June 20, 2012 (http://stateofworkingamerica.org/great-recession/).

Economist. 2009. "Women and Work: We Did It!" Retrieved May 14, 2010 (http://www.economist.com/displayStory.cfm?story_id=E1_TVTSQQRJ&source=login_payBarrier).

Ehrenreich, Barbara. 2001. *Nickel and Dimed: On (Not) Getting By in America*. New York: Metropolitan Book/Henry Holt.

Eitzen, D. Stanley and Maxine Baca Zinn. 2006. "Globalization: An Introduction." Pp. 1–11 in

Globalization: The Transformation of Social Worlds, edited by D. Stanley Eitzen and Maxine Baca Zinn. Belmont, CA: Wadsworth.

England, Paula and Irene Browne. 1992. "Trends in Women's Economic Status." *Sociological Perspectives* 35(1):17–51.

Esbenshade, Jill. 2008. "Going Up Against the Global Economy: New Developments in the Anti-Sweatshops Movement." *Critical Sociology* 34:453–70.

Equal Employment Opportunity Commission. 2013. "Charge Statistics VY1997 Through FY 2013." Retrieved October 4, 2014 (http://eeoc.gov/eeoc/statistics/enforcement/charges.cfm).

Eurostat. 2012. "Unemployment Statistics, February 2012." Retrieved April 8, 2012 (http://epp.eurostat.ec.europa.eu/statistics_explained/index.php/Unemployment_statistics).

Eurostat. 2014. "Unemployment Statistics." Retrieved October 5, 2014 (http://epp.eurostat.ec.europa.eu/statistics_explained/index.php/Unemployment_statistics).

Fantasia, Rick and Kim Voss. 2004. *Hard Work: Remaking the American Labor Movement.* Berkeley: University of California Press.

Filion, Kai. 2009. "Fact Sheet for 2009 Minimum Wage Increase—Minimum Wage Issue Guide." Retrieved May 13, 2010 (http://www.epi.org/publications/entry/mwig_fact_sheet/).

Foo, Lora Jo. 1994. "The Vulnerable and Exploitable Immigrant Workforce and the Need for Strengthening Worker Protection Legislation." *Yale Law Review* 103(8):2179–212.

Frank Fox, Mary and Sharlene Hesse-Biber. 1984. *Women at Work.* Palo Alto, CA: Mayfield.

Frontline. 2002. "Accounting Lessons." Retrieved May 1, 2003 (http://www.pbs.org/wgbh/pages/frontline/shows/regulation/lessons/).

Fussell, Elizabeth. 2000. "Making Labor Flexible: The Recomposition of Tijuana's Maquiladora Female Labor Force." *Feminist Economics* 6(3):59–79.

General Accounting Office (GAO). 1994. "Garment Industry: Efforts to Address the Prevalence and Conditions of Sweatshops" (GAO/HEHS-95-29, November). Retrieved May 13, 2010 (http://www.gao.gov/archive/1995/he95029.pdf).

Gluck, Sherna Berger. 1987. *Rosie the Riveter Revisited: Women, the War, and Social Change.* Boston: Twayne.

Gorman, Maryann. 2001. "The White Dog's Tale" *YES!* Magazine, Spring 2001.

Gruben, William C. 2001. "Was NAFTA Behind Mexico's High Maquiladora Growth?" *CATO Journal* 18(2):263–75.

Hall, Richard. 1994. *Sociology of Work: Perspectives, Analyses, and Issues.* Thousand Oaks, CA: Pine Forge.

Hirschhorn, Larry. 1984. *Beyond Mechanization: Work and Technology in a Post-industrial Age.* Cambridge, MA: MIT Press.

Human Rights Campaign. 2015. "Employment Non-Discrimination Act." Retrieved April 9, 2015 (http://www.hrc.org/resources/entry/employment-non-discrimination-act).

Information for Decision Making. 2000. "Minimum Wage Legislation and Living Wage Campaigns." Retrieved April 20, 2003 (http://www.financeprojectinfo.org/MWW/minimum.asp#effects).

International Labor Rights Forum. 2011. "Factory Profiles." Retrieved April 11, 2012 (http://www.laborrights.org/creating-a-sweatfree-world/fairness-in-flowers/factory-profiles).

Jagoda, Agnieszka. 2013. "Deskilling as the Dark Side of the Work Specialization." *International Journal of Academic Research* 5:331–34.

Kalleberg, Arne. 2011. *Good Jobs, Bad Jobs.* New York: Russell Sage.

Lazes, Peter and Jane Savage. 2000. "Embracing the Future: Union Strategies for the 21st Century." *Journal for Quality and Participation* 23(4):18–24.

Lederer, Edith. 2012. "UN: 2.4 Million Human Trafficking Victims." Retrieved April 8, 2012 (http://abcnews.go.com/US/wireStory/24-million-human-trafficking-victims-16066837#.T4IzzWAz3hM).

Levering, Robert and Milton Moskowitz. 2007. "The 100 Best Companies to Work For." *Fortune* 155(1):94.

Lindquist, Diane. 2001. "Rules Change for Maquiladoras." *Industry Week* 250(1):23–26.

Luce, Stephanie. 2012. "Living Wage Policies and Campaigns: Lessons From the United States." *International Journal of Labour Research* 4:111–26.

Maryland Department of Labor, Licensing and Regulation. 2011. "Maryland's Living Wage Frequently Asked Questions." Retrieved April 8, 2012 (http://www.dllr.state.md.us/labor/prev/livingwagefaqs.shtml#1).

McDonald, Paula, Diane Guthire, Lisa Bradley, and Jane Shakespeare-Finch. 2005. "Investigating Work–Family Policy Aims and Employee Experiences." *Employee Relations* 27: 478–494.

McMahon, Brian, Richard Roessler, Phillip Rumrill, Jessica Hurley, Steven West, Fong Chan, and Linnea Carlson. 2008. "Hiring Discrimination Against People With Disabilities Under the ADA: Characteristics of Charging Parties." *Journal of Occupational Rehabilitation* 18:122–32.

Mishel, Lawrence, Jard Bernstein, and Heidi Shierholz. 2009. *State of Working America 2008/2009.* Washington, DC: Economic Policy Institute.

Moffatt, Allison. 2005. "Murder, Mystery and Mistreatment in Mexican Maquiladoras." *Women and Environments International Magazine* 66/67:19–21.

Mollick, Andre Varella and Jorge Ibarra-Salazar. 2013. "Productivity Effects on the Wage Premium of Mexican Maquiladoras." *Economic Development Quarterly* 27:208–20.

Mosisa, Abraham. 2002. "The Role of Foreign-Born Workers in the U.S. Economy." *Monthly Labor Review* 125(5):3–15.

National Committee on Pay Equity. 2014. "The Wage Gap Over Time: In Real Dollars, Women See a Continuing Gap." Retrieved September 3, 2014 (http://www.pay-equity.org/info-time.html).

National Institute for Occupational Safety and Health (NIOSH). 2003. "Stress at Work." Retrieved May 13, 2010 (http://www.cdc.gov/niosh/docs/99-101/).

Newburger, Eric and Thomas Gryn. 2009. *The Foreign-Born Labor Force in the United States: 2007* (American Community Survey Reports, ACS-10). Washington, DC: U.S. Census Bureau.

Parenti, Michael. 1988. *Democracy for the Few.* 5th ed. New York: St. Martin's.

Phillips. Lucy. 2006. "Battle of the Bulge." *People Management* 12:20–21.

Pollina, Ronald. 2003. "Can We Maintain the American Dream?" *Economic Development Journal* 2(3):54–58.

Rampell, Catherine. 2010. "Women Now Majority in American Workplaces." *New York Times,* February 6, p. A10.

Reskin, Barbara and Irene Padavic. 1994. *Women and Men at Work.* Thousand Oaks, CA: Pine Forge Press.

Reuter, Alison. 2005. "Subtle but Pervasive: Discrimination Against Mothers and Pregnant Women in the Workplace." *Fordham Urban Law Journal* 33:110–50.

Ritzer, George. 1989. "Sociology of Work: A Metatheoretical Analysis." *Social Forces* 67(3):593–604.

Ritzer, George. 2000. *Sociological Theory.* Boston: McGraw-Hill.

Rodriguez, Eunice. 2001. "Keeping the Unemployed Healthy." *American Journal of Public Health* 91(9):1403–12.

Rubin, Stanford and Richard Roessler. 2008. *Foundations of the Vocational Rehabilitation Process.* Austin, TX: Pro-Ed.

Schmidt, Diane and Gilbert Duenas. 2002. "Incentives to Encourage Worker-Friendly Organizations." *Public Personnel Management* 31(3):293–309.

Schur, Lisa, Douglas Kruse, and Peter Blanck. 2005. "Corporate Culture and the Employment of Persons With Disabilities." *Behavioral Sciences and the Law* 2:3–20.

Shin, Sang-Hyup. 2009. "A Study on the Economic Benefits of Globalization: Focusing on the Poverty and Inequality Between the Rich and the Poor." *International Area Studies Review* 12:191–214.

Shockley, Kristin and Tammy Allen. 2012. "Motives for Flexible Work Arrangement Use." *Community, Work & Family* 15:217–31.

Student Labor Action Project. 2007. "About SLAP." Retrieved May 13, 2010 (http://www.jwj.org/projects/slap.html).

Sullivan, Cath and Susan Lewis. 2001. "Home-Based Telework, Gender and the Synchronization of Work and Family: Perspectives of Teleworkers and Their Co-residents." *Gender, Women and Organization* 8:123–45.

Sullivan, Teresa. 2004. "Work-Related Social Problems." Pp. 193–208 in *Handbook of Social Problems: A Comparative International Perspective,* edited by George Ritzer. Thousand Oaks, CA: Sage Publications.

Swanger, Joanna. 2007. "Feminist Community Building in Ciudad Juárez: A Local Cultural Alternative to the Structural Violence of Globalization." *Latin American Perspectives* 34 (2):108–23.

Sweatshop Watch. 2000. "Student Organizing." Retrieved September 5, 2004 (http://swatch.igc.org/swatch/codes/).

Sweatshop Watch. 2003. "Frequently Asked Questions." Retrieved April 15, 2003 (http://www.sweatshopwatch.org/swatch/questions).

Taylor, Frederick W. 1911. *The Principles of Scientific Management.* New York: Harper.

Toossi, Mitra. 2005. "Labor Force Projections to 2014: Retiring Boomers." *Monthly Labor Review November 2005.* Washington, DC: Bureau of Labor Statistics.

Toossi, Mitra. 2012. "Employment Outlook: 2010–2020: Labor Force Projections to 2020: A More Slowly Growing Workforce." Retrieved October 9, 2014 (http://www.bls.gov/opub/mlr/2012/01/art3full.pdf).

Uchitelle, Louis. 2006. "Raising the Floor on Pay: States Leap Ahead of Congress in Acting on Minimum Wage." *New York Times*, December 20, pp. C1, C15.

UNICEF. 2012. "Nominal Wages for Women is Roughly 20% Lower Than Men's." Retrieved October 9, 2014 (http://www.unicef.org/factoftheweek/index_39100.html).

UNITE HERE. 2012. "Who We Are." Retrieved April 9, 2012 (http://www.unitehere.org/about/).

United Nations Office on Drugs and Crime, Anti–Human Trafficking Unit. 2006. *Trafficking in Persons: Global Patterns.* New York: United Nations Office on Drugs and Crime.

U.S. Bureau of Labor Statistics. 2009. "Census of Fatal Occupational Injuries—Current and Revised Data." Retrieved January 10, 2010 (http://www.bls.gov/iif/oshwc/cfoi/cfch0007.pdf).

U.S. Bureau of Labor Statistics. 2012. "Civilian Labor Force Participation Rates by Age, Sex, Race and Ethnicity." Retrieved April 8, 2012 (http://www.bls.gov/emp/ep_table_303.htm).

U.S. Bureau of Labor Statistics. 2013a. "Table 4. Fastest Growing Occupations, 2012 and Projected 2022." Retrieved October 5, 2014 (http://www.bls.gov/news.release/ecopro.t04.htm).

U.S. Bureau of Labor Statistics. 2013b. "Employer-Reported Workplace Injuries and Illness – 2012." Retrieved October 5, 2014 (http://www.bls.gov/news.release/pdf/osh.pdf).

U.S. Bureau of Labor Statistics. 2014a. "The Employment Situation—September 2014." Retrieved October 5, 2014 (http://www.bls.gov/news.release/empsit.nr0.htm).

U.S. Bureau of Labor Statistics. 2014b. "Women in the Labor Force: A Databook." Retrieved October 9, 2014 (http://www.bls.gov/cps/wlf-databook-2013.pdf).

U.S. Bureau of Labor Statistics. 2014c. "Labor Force Characteristics of Foreign-Born Workers Summary." Retrieved October 9, 2014 (http://www.bls.gov/news.release/forbrn.nr0.htm).

U.S. Bureau of Labor Statistics. 2014d. "Characteristics of Minimum Wage Workers 2013." Retrieved November 20, 2014 (http://www.bls.gov/cps/minwage2013.pdf).

U.S. Bureau of Labor Statistics. 2014e. "Census of Fatal Occupational Injuries Summary, 2013." Retrieved October 5, 2014 (http://www.bls.gov/news.release/cfoi.nr0.htm).

U.S. Bureau of Labor Statistics. 2014f. "Union Members Summary." Retrieved October 4, 2014 (http://www.bls.gov/news.release/union2.nr0.htm).

U.S. Census Bureau. 1951. *Statistical Abstract of the United States* (Table 203). Washington, DC: U.S. Census Bureau.

U.S. Census Bureau. 1960. *Statistical Abstract of the United States* (Table 274). Washington, DC: U.S. Census Bureau.

U.S. Census Bureau. 1966. *Statistical Abstract of the United States* (Table 319). Washington, DC: U.S. Census Bureau.

U.S. Department of Labor. 2002. "Minimum Wage Laws in the States." Retrieved May 13, 2010 (http://www.dol.gov/esa/minwage/america.htm).

U.S. Department of Labor, Women's Bureau. 2014 "Latest Annual Data." Retrieved October 9, 2014 (http://www.dol.gov/wb/stats/recentfacts.htm#earnings).

Weber, Max. 1978. "Bureaucracy." Pp. 956–1005 in *Economy and Society*, Vols. 1 and 2, edited by Guenther Roth and Claus Wittich. Berkeley: University of California Press. (Original work published 1925)

Weidenbaum, Murray. 2006. "Globalization: Wonder Land or Waste Land?" Pp. 53–60 in *Globalization: The Transformation of Social Worlds*, edited by D. Stanley Eitzen and Maxine Baca Zinn. Belmont, CA: Wadsworth.

Weller, Christian and Adam Hersh. 2006. "Free Markets and Poverty." Pp. 69–73 in *Globalization: The Transformation of Social Worlds*, edited by D. Stanley Eitzen and Maxine Baca Zinn. Belmont, CA: Wadsworth.

Yergin, Daniel. 2006. "Globalization Opens Door to New Dangers." Pp. 30–31 in *Globalization: The Transformation of Social Worlds*, edited by D. Stanley Eitzen and Maxine Baca Zinn. Belmont, CA: Wadsworth.

Zeitlin, Irving. 1997. *Ideology and the Development of Sociological Theory.* Englewood Cliffs, NJ: Prentice Hall.

Zhou, Min. 1993. "Underemployment and Economic Disparities Among Minority Groups." *Population Research and Policy Review* 12:139–57.

Chapter 10

American Diabetes Association. 2003. "Type 2 Diabetes." Retrieved March 27, 2008 (http://www.diabetes.org/diabetes-basics/type-2/facts-about-type-2.html).

American Diabetes Association. 2012. "Diabetes Statistics." Retrieved April 11, 2012 (http://www.diabetes.org/diabetes-basics/diabetes-statistics/?loc=DropDownDB-stats).

American Diabetes Association. 2014. "Statistics About Diabetes." Retrieved October 12, 2014 (http://www.diabetes.org/diabetes-basics/statistics/).

Association of American Medical Colleges. 2010. "America Needs a More Diverse Physician Workforce." Retrieved November 23, 2014 (https://www.aamc.org/download/87306/data/physiciandiversityfacts.pdf).

Barclay, David. 2012. "Impact of 'Sick' and 'Recovery' Roles on Brain Injury Rehabilitation Outcomes." *Rehabilitation Research and Practice* 1–10.

Beatrice, Dennis. 1996. "States and Health Care Reform: The Importance of Program Implementation." Pp. 183–206 in *Strategic Choices for a Changing Health Care System*, edited by S. Altman and U. Reinhardt. Chicago, IL: Health Administration Press.

Becker, Gary S. and Casey B. Mulligan. 1994. *On the Endogenous Determination of Time Preference.* Discussion Paper No. 94-2, Economics Research Center/National Opinion Research Center, July.

Beckles, Gloria and Benedict Truman. 2011. "Education and Income—United States, 2005–2009." *CDC Health Disparities and Inequalities Report United States*, 2011: 13–15.

Belluck, Pam. 2012. "Medicaid Expansion May Lower Death Rates, Study Says." *New York Times*, July 26, p. A13.

Braveman, P. and E. Tarimo. 2002. "Social Inequalities in Health Within Countries: Not Only an Issue for Affluent Countries." *Social Science and Medicine* 54:1621–35.

Buse, Uwe. 2006. "A Woman's Fight to Save the Poor from Black Fever." *Spiegel Online*, December 21.

Calnan, Michael. 1987. *Health & Illness: The Lay Perspective.* London, England: Tavistock.

Centers for Medicare and Medicaid Services. 2012. "NHE Fact Sheet." Retrieved April 11, 2012 (http://www.cms.gov/Research-Statistics-Data-and-Systems/Statistics-Trends-and-Reports/NationalHealthExpendData/NHE-Fact-Sheet.html).

Centers for Medicare and Medicaid Services. 2014a. "Historical." Retrieved October 12, 2014 (http://www.cms.gov/Research-Statistics-Data-and-Systems/Statistics-Trends-and-Reports/NationalHealthExpendData/NationalHealthAccountsHistorical.html).

Centers for Medicare and Medicaid Services. 2014b. "NHE Fact Sheet." Retrieved November 20, 2014 (http://www.cms.gov/Research-Statistics-Data-and-Systems/Statistics-Trends-and-Reports/NationalHealthExpendData/NHE-Fact-Sheet.html).

Citizens Council on Health Care. 2003. "Summary of Minnesota's 1992 Health Care Reform Law." Retrieved May 20, 2010 (http://www.cchconline.org/privacy/mncaresumm.php3).

Cockerman, William C. 2004. "Health as a Social Problem." Pp. 281–97 in *Handbook of Social Problems: A Comparative International Perspective*, edited by George Ritzer. Thousand Oaks, CA: Sage Publications.

Cockerman, William C. and Michael Glasser. 2001. "Epidemiology." Pp. 1–2 in *Readings in Medical Sociology*, edited by W. Cockerman and M. Glasser. Upper Saddle River, NJ: Prentice Hall.

Collins, Karen S., Dora L. Hughes, Michelle M. Doty, Brett L. Ives, Jennifer N. Edwards, and Katie Tenney. 2002. *Diverse Communities, Common Concerns: Assessing Health Care*

Quality for Minority Americans: Findings From the Commonwealth Fund 2001 Health Care Quality Survey. New York: Commonwealth Fund.

Congressional Budget Office. 2012a. Updated Estimates for the Insurance Coverage Provisions of the Affordable Care Act. Washington, DC: Congressional Budget Office.

Congressional Budget Office. 2012b. "Estimates for the Insurance Coverage Provision of the Affordable Care Act Updated for the Recent Supreme Court Decision." Retrieved February 21, 2013 (http://www.cbo.gov/publication/43472).

Conrad, Peter. 2001a. "General Introduction." Pp. 1–6 in The Sociology of Health and Illness: Critical Perspectives, edited by P. Conrad. New York: Worth.

Conrad, Peter. 2001b. "The Social and Cultural Meanings of Illness." Pp. 91–93 in The Sociology of Health and Illness: Critical Perspectives, edited by P. Conrad. New York: Worth.

Cooper, Michael. 2012. "Many Governors Still Unsure About Medicaid Expansion." New York Times, July 15, p. 14.

Davis, Karen, Cathy Schoen, Stephen C. Schoenbaum, Michelle M. Doty, Alyssa L. Holmgren, Jennifer L. Kriss, and Katherine K. Shea. 2007. Mirror, Mirror on the Wall: An International Update on the Comparative Performance of American Health Care. Washington, DC: Commonwealth Fund.

DeNavas-Walt, Carmen, Bernadette Proctor, and Jessica Smith. 2012. Income, Poverty and Health Insurance Coverage in the United States: 2011 (Current Population Reports, P60–243). Washington, DC: U.S. Government Printing Office.

Erie Family Health Center. 2014. "About Erie." Retrieved November 23, 2014 (http://www.eriefamilyhealth.org/about-erie).

Finkelstein, Amy, Sarah Taubman, Bill Wright, Mira Bernstein, Jonathan Gruber, Joseph Newhouse, Heidi Allen, Katherine Baicker, and the Oregon Health Study Group. 2011. The Oregon Health Insurance Experiment: Evidence From the First Year. Retrieved July 3, 2012 (http://www.oregonhealthstudy.org/en/researchers/Oregon_Health_Insura nce_Experiment.pdf).

Goffman, Erving. 1961. Asylums: Essays on the Social Situation of Mental Health. New York: Pantheon.

Goodnough, Abby. 2012. "Massachusetts Aims to Cut Growth of Its Health Costs." New York Times, August 1, p. A14.

Greil, Arthur, Julia McQuillan, and Kathleen Slauson-Blevins. 2011. "The Social Construction of Infertility." Sociology Compass 5:736–46.

Grossman, Michael and Robert Kaestner. 1997. "Effects of Education on Health." Pp. 69–123 in The Social Benefits of Education, edited by J. Behrman and N. Stacey. Ann Arbor: University of Michigan Press.

Hamilton, J. A. 1994. "Feminist Theory and Health Psychology: Tools for an Egalitarian, Women-Centered Approach to Women's Health." Pp. 56–66 in Reframing Women's Health: Multidisciplinary Research and Practice, edited by A. Dan. Thousand Oaks, CA: Sage Publications.

Haney, D. 2003. "Big Study Dispels More Myths About Estrogen." News Tribune, March 18, p. A3.

Hargreaves, Margaret, Carolyne Arnold, and William Blot. 2006. "Community Health Centers." Pp. 485–94 in Multicultural Medicine and Health Disparities, edited by D. Satcher and R. Pamies. New York: McGraw-Hill.

Heffernan, Tim. 2005. "Victoria Hale: Exec of the Year." Retrieved March 11, 2007 (http://www.keepmedia.com/pubs/Esquire/2005/12/01/1078555).

Holahan, John and Stacey McMorrow. 2013. "What Drove the Recent Slowdown in Health Care Spending Growth and Can it Continue?" Retrieved October 12, 2014 (http://www.rwjf.org/content/dam/farm/reports/reports/2013/rwjf405861).

Hoyert, Donna and Jiaquan Xu. 2012. "Deaths: Preliminary Data for 2011" (National Vital Statistics Reports, Vol. 61, No 6). Washington, DC: Centers for Disease Control and Prevention.

Institute for Health Metrics and Evaluation. 2013. The State of US Health: Innovations, Insights, and Recommendations From the Global Burden of Disease Study. Seattle, WA: IHME.

Jasso-Aguilar, Rebeca and Howard Waitzkin. 2011. "Multinational Corporations, the State, And Contemporary Medicine." Health Sociology Review 20:245–57.

Kaiser Family Foundation. 2014. "The Uninsured: A Primer – Key Facts About Health Insurance on the Eve of Coverage Expansions." Retrieved November 20, 2014 (http://kff.org/uninsured/report/the-uninsured-a-primer-key-facts-about-health-insurance-on-the-eve-of-coverage-expansions/).

Kleinfield, N. R. 2006. "Modern Ways Open India's Doors to Diabetes." New York Times, September 13, pp. A1, A12.

Kolata, Gina. 2007. "A Surprising Secret to Long Life: Stay in School." New York Times, January 3, p. A1.

Krieger, Nancy, D. R. Williams, and N. Moss. 1997. "Measuring Social Class in U.S. Public Health Research: Concepts, Methodologies, and Guidelines." Annual Review of Public Health 18:341–78.

Lambert, Bruce L., Richard L. Street, Donald J. Cegala, David H. Smith, Suzanne Kurtz, and Theo Schofeld. 1997. "Provider–Patient Communication, Patient-Centered Care, and the Mangle of Practice." Health Communication 9(1):27–43.

Link, Bruce and Jo Phelan. 2001. "Social Conditions as Fundamental Causes of Disease." Pp. 3–17 in Readings in Medical Sociology, 2nd ed., edited by W. Cockerman and M. Glasser. Upper Saddle River, NJ: Prentice Hall.

Lipska, Kasia. 2014. "A Global Diabetes Epidemic." New York Times, April 27, Review, p. 5.

Liptak, Adam. 2012. "Justices, by 5–4, Uphold Health Care Law; Roberts in Majority; Victory for Obama." New York Times, June 29, pp. A1, A12.

Lock, Margaret. 1993. Encounters With Aging: Mythologies of Menopause in Japan and North America. Berkeley: University of California Press.

Long, Sharon, Karen Stockley, and Heather Dahlen. 2012. Health Reform in Massachusetts as of Fall 2010: Getting Ready for the Affordable Care Act & Addressing Affordability. Washington, DC: Urban Institute.

Lowrey, Annie. 2012. "In Hopeful Sign, Health Spending Is Flattening Out." New York Times, April 29, pp. 1, 19.

Lurie, Nicole and Tamara Dubowitz. 2007. "Health Disparities and Access to Health." Journal of the American Medical Association 297(10):1118–21.

MacDorman Marian, T. J. Mathews, Ashna Mohangoo, and Jennifer Zeitlin. 2014. "International Comparisons of Infant Mortality and Related Factors: United States and Europe, 2010" (National Vital Statistics Reports, Vol. 63, No 5). Hyattsville, MD: National Center for Health Statistics.

Magnus, Stephen and Stephen Mick. 2000. "Medical Schools, Affirmative Action and the Neglected Role of Social Class." American Journal of Public Health 90:1197–1201.

Markens, Susan. 1996. "The Problem of 'Experience': A Political and Cultural Critique of PMS." Gender and Society 10:42–58.

Marmot, Michael. 2005. "Social Determinants of Health Inequalities." Lancet 365: 1099–104.

Martin, Joyce, Brady Hamilton, Michelle Osterman, Sally Curtin, and T. J. Matthews. 2013. "Births: Final Data for 2012." (National Vital Statistics Report, Vol. 62, No. 9.) Washington, DC: Centers of Disease Control and Prevention.

Mather, Barbara. 2012. "The Social Construction and Reframing of Attention-Deficit/Hyperactivity Disorder." Ethical Human Psychology & Psychiatry 14:15–26.

Mathers, Jonathan and Jayne Parry. 2009. "Why Are There So Few Working-Class Applicants to Medical Schools? Learning From the Success Stories." Medical Education 43:219–28.

McCarthy, Justin. 2014. "As New Enrollment Period Starts, ACA Approval at 37%." Retrieved November 23, 2014 (http://www.gallup.com/poll/179426/new-enrollment-period-starts-aca-approval.aspx).

Medicine360. 2014. "Our Mission." Retrieved October 11, 2014 (http://www.medicines360.org/who-is-m360/m360-mission/).

Men's Health Network. 2002. "The Men's Disease Awareness and Prevention Project." Retrieved December 8, 2002 (http://www.menshealthnetwork.org/Programareas/Prevention).

Mirowsky, John and Catherine Ross.. 2005. "Education, Learned Effectiveness, and Health." London Review of Education 3:205–20.

Murphy, Michael, Martin Bobak, Amanda Nicholson, Michael Marmot, and Richard Rose. 2006. "The Widening Gap in Mortality by Educational Level in the Russian Federation, 1980–2001." American Journal of Public Health 96(7):1293–99.

Murphy, Sherry, Jiaquan Xu, and Kenneth Kochanek. 2012. "Deaths: Preliminary Data for 2010." *National Vital Statistics Reports* 60:4.

National Center for Health Statistics. 2014. *Health, United States, 2013 With Special Feature on Prescription Drugs.* Washington, DC: Centers for Disease Control and Prevention.

Obama, Barack. 2009. "Remarks by the President to a Joint Session of Congress on Health Care." Retrieved May 20, 2010 (http://www .whitehouse.gov/the_press_office/Remarks-by-the-President-to-a-Joint-Session-of-Congress-on-Health-Care).

Obama, Barack. 2010. "On Behalf of My Mother." Retrieved May 20, 2010 (http://www .whitehouse.gov/blog/2010/03/23/behalf-my-mother).

Oberlander, Jonathan. 2002. "The U.S. Health Care System: On a Road to Nowhere." *Canadian Medical Association Journal* 167(2):163–68.

Oregon Health Study. 2012. "About the Study." Retrieved July 3, 2012 (http://www .oregonhealthstudy.org/en/about/index.php).

Organisation for Economic Co-operation and Development. 2014. *Health Statistics 2014 – Frequently Requested Data.* Retrieved October 12, 2014 (http://www.oecd.org/health/ health-systems/oecd-health-statistics-2014- frequently-requested-data.htm).

Parsons, Talcott. 1951. *The Social System.* New York: Free Press.

Pear, Robert. 2002. "Pennsylvania Struggles to Repair Model Prescription Aid Program." *New York Times,* July 13, pp. A1, A8.

Pear, Robert. 2007. "Governors Worry Over Money for Child Health Program." *New York Times,* February 25, p. A15.

Pear, Robert. 2012. "Recession Holds Down Health Spending." *New York Times,* January 10, p. A16.

Peck, B. Mitchell and Sonya Conner. 2011. "Talking With Me or Talking at Me? The Impact of Status Characteristics on Doctor–Patient Interaction." *Sociological Perspectives* 54:547–67.

Peterson, Suni, Martin Heesacker, and Robert C. Schwartz. 2001. "Physical Illness: Social Construction or Biological Imperative?" *Journal of Community Health Nursing* 18(4):213–22.

Pew Hispanic Center. 2009. *Between Two Worlds: How Young Latinos Come of Age in America.* Retrieved May 20, 2010 (http://pewhispanic .org/files/reports/117.pdf).

Reid, T. R. 2009. *The Healing of America: A Global Quest for Better, Cheaper, and Fairer Health Care.* New York: Penguin Press.

Roberts, Sam. 2010. "Census Figures Challenge Views of Race and Ethnicity." *New York Times,* January 22, p. A13.

Roth, Kimberlee. 2006. "A Love of Science and a Vision to Save Millions of Lives Make Her Day." Retrieved March 11, 2007 (http://uk.ashoka .org/node/920).

Sack, Kevin. 2009. "With Health Care for Nearly All, Massachusetts Now Faces Costs." *New York Times,* March 16, pp. A1, A13.

Sack, Kevin. 2010. "From the Hospital Room to Bankruptcy Court." *New York Times,* November 25, pp. A1, A21.

Sacks, Heather, Todd Kutyla, and Sharon Silow-Carroll. 2002. *Toward Comprehensive Health Coverage for All: Summaries of 20 State Planning Grants* (U.S. Health Resources and Services Administration, Report 577). Washington, DC: Commonwealth Fund.

Saraceno, Benedetto and Shekhar Saxena. 2004. "Bridging the mental health research gap in low- and middle-income countries." *Acta Psychiatrica Scandinavica* 110:1–3.

Saul, Stephanie. 2008. "In Sour Economy, Some Scale Back on Medications." *New York Times,* October 22, pp. A1, A18.

Seabury, Seth, Amitabh Chandra, and Anupam Jena. 2013. "Trends in the Earnings of Male and Female Health Care Professionals in the United States, 1987–2010." *JAMA Internal Medicine* 173:1748–50.

Sievert, Lynnette, Lynn Morrison, Daniel Brown, and Angela Reza. 2007. "Vasomotor symptoms Among Japanese-American and European-American women living in Hilo, Hawaii." *Menopause* 14:261–69.

Singer, Natasha. 2007. "Is the 'Mom Job' Really Necessary?" *New York Times,* October 4, pp. E1, E3.

Smith, Jessica and Carla Medalia. 2014. *Health Insurance Coverage in the United States: 2013.* Washington, DC: U.S. Census Bureau.

Starr, Paul. 1982. *The Social Transformation of American Medicine.* New York: Basic Books.

Street, R. L. 1991. "Information-Giving in Medical Consultations: The Influence of Patients' Communicative Styles and Personal Characteristics." *Social Science and Medicine* 32:541–48.

Szasz, Thomas. 1960. "The Myth of Mental Illness." *American Psychologist* 15:113–18.

UNICEF. 2012. *The State of the World's Children 2012: Children in an Urban World.* New York: UNICEF.

U.S. Bureau of Labor Statistics. 2014a. "Census of Fatal Occupational Injuries Summary, 2013." Retrieved October 5, 2014 (http://www.bls.gov/ news.release/cfoi.nr0.htm).

U.S. Bureau of Labor Statistics. 2014b. "Physicians and Surgeons." Retrieved January 19, 2015 (http://www.bls.gov/ooh/healthcare/physicians-and-surgeons.htm).

U.S. Census Bureau. 2002. "Motherhood: The Fertility of American Women, 2000." *Population Profile of the United States: 2000* (Internet Release). Retrieved February 22, 2003 (http:// www.census.gov/population/pop-profile/2000/ chap04.pdf).

U.S. Health Resources and Services Administration. 2014a. "The Affordable Care Act and Health Centers." Retrieved November 23, 2014 (http://bphc.hrsa.gov/about/ healthcenterfactsheet.pdf).

U.S. Health Resources and Services Administration. 2014b. "What Is a Health Center?" Retrieved November 23, 2014 (http:// bphc.hrsa.gov/about/index.html).

Waldron, Ingrid. 2001. "What Do We Know About Causes of Sex Differences in Mortality? A Review of the Literature." Pp. 37–49 in *The Sociology of Health and Illness: Critical Perspectives,* edited by A. Dan. New York: Worth.

Weitz, Rose. 2001. *The Sociology of Health, Illness, and Health Care: A Critical Approach.* Belmont, CA: Wadsworth/Thompson Learning.

Werth, Barry. 2013. "A Tale of Two Drugs." Retrieved November 23, 2014 (http://www .technologyreview.com/featuredstory/520441/ a-tale-of-two-drugs/)

Wilkinson, Richard G. 1996. *Unhealthy Societies: The Afflictions of Inequality.* London: Routledge.

Chapter 11

Alexander, Alison and Jarice Hanson. 1995. *Taking Sides: Clashing Views on Controversial Issues in Mass Media and Society.* Guilford, CT: Dushkin.

Altheide, David L. 1997. "The News Media, the Problem Frame, and the Production Fear." *Sociological Quarterly* 38(4):647–68.

Bagdikian, Ben. 1997. *The Media Monopoly.* Boston: Beacon Press.

Ball-Rokeach, Sandra and Muriel Cantor, eds. 1986. *Media, Audience, and Social Structure.* Beverly Hills, CA: Sage Publications.

Barner, Mark. 1999. "Sex-Role Stereotyping in FCC-Mandated Children's Educational Television." *Journal of Broadcasting and Electronic Media* 43:551–64.

Barnes, Kassandra, Raymond Marateo, and S. Pixy Ferris. 2007. "Teaching and Learning With the Net Generation." *Innovate: Journal of Online Education* 3(4):1–8.

Baron, David. 2006. "Persistent Media Bias." *Journal of Public Economics* 90:1–36.

Bash, Dana and Tom Cohen. 2013. "Officials Cite Thwarted Plots, Oversight in Defending Surveillance." Retrieved December 26, 2014 (http://www.cnn.com/2013/06/18/politics/ nsa-leaks/).

Black, Allison. 2010. "Gen Y: Who They Are and How They Learn." *Educational Horizons* 88(2):92–101.

Blumberg, Stephen, Julian Luke, Nadarajasundaram Ganesh, Michael Davern, Michel Boudreaux, and Karen Soderberg. 2011. *Wireless Substitution: State-Level Estimates From the National Health Interview Survey, January 2007–June 2010.* Washington, DC: U.S. Department of Health and Human Services.

Boswell, Wendy and Julie Olson-Buchanan. 2007. "The Use of Communication Technologies After Hours: The Role of Work Attitudes and Work–Life Conflict." *Journal of Management* 33:592–610.

Branton, Regina and Johanna Dunaway. 2008. "English- and Spanish-Language Media Coverage of Immigration: A Comparative Analysis." *Social Science Quarterly* 89:1006–22.

Center for Media and Public Affairs. 2012. "About the Center for Media and Public Affairs." Retrieved April 21, 2012 (http://www.cmpa .com/about.htm).

Central Intelligence Agency. 2012. "Internet Users." Retrieved April 21, 2012 (https://www.cia.gov/library/publications/the-world-factbook/rankorder/2153rank.html).

Chomsky, Noam. 1989. *Necessary Illusions: Thought Control in Democratic Societies*. Boston: South End Press.

CNN Money. 2011. "Industries." Retrieved April 20, 2012 (http://money.cnn.com/magazines/fortune/fortune500/2011/industries/145/index.html).

Committee to Protect Journalists. 2014. "Home page." Retrieved December 26, 2014 (http://www.cpj.org).

Considine, David, Julie Horton, and Gary Moorman. 2009. "Teaching and Reading the Millennial Generation Through Media Literacy." *Journal of Adolescent and Adult Literacy* 52:472–81.

Coser, Lewis. 1974. *Greedy Institutions: Patterns of Undivided Commitment*. New York: Free Press.

Croteau, David and William Hoynes. 2000. *Media Society: Industries, Images, and Audiences*. Thousand Oaks, CA: Pine Forge Press.

Croteau, David and William Hoynes. 2001. *The Business of Media: Corporate Media and the Public Interest*. Thousand Oaks, CA: Pine Forge Press.

Davis, Geena. 2006. "Where Are the Girls?" Retrieved July 25, 2007 (http://www.commonsenseblog.org/archives/2006/02/where_are_the_g.php).

Drori, Gili. 2004. "The Internet as a Global Social Problem." Pp. 433–50 in *Handbook of Social Problems: A Comparative International Perspective*, edited by George Ritzer. Thousand Oaks, CA: Sage Publications.

Epstein, Edward Jay. 1981. "The Selection of Reality." Pp. 119–32 in *What's News*, edited by E. Abel. San Francisco: Institute for Contemporary Studies.

Eschholz, Sarah, Jana Bufkin, and Jenny Long. 2002. "Symbolic Reality Bites: Women and Racial/Ethnic Minorities in Modern Film." *Sociological Spectrum* 22:299–334.

European Commission. 2014. "Media Literacy." Retrieved December 7, 2014 (http://ec.europa.eu/culture/policy/audiovisual-policies/literacy_en.htm).

Federal Communications Commission. 2004. "About the FCC." Retrieved May 13, 2010 (http://www.fcc.gov/aboutus.html).

Federal Trade Commission. 2011. "Facebook Settles FTC Charges That It Deceived Consumers by Failing to Keep Privacy Promises." Retrieved April 22, 2012 (http://ftc.gov/opa/2011/11/privacysettlement.shtm).

Fenner, Grant and Robert Renn, 2004. "Technology-Assisted Supplemental Work: Construct Definition and a Research Framework." *Human Resource Management* 43:179–200.

Fonner, Kathryn and Michael Roloff. 2010. "Why Teleworkers Are More Satisfied With Their Jobs Than Are Office-Based Workers: When Less Contact Is Beneficial." *Journal of Applied Communication Research* 38:336–61.

Fox, Susannah and Lee Rainie. 2014. "The Web at 25 in the U.S." Retrieved December 7, 2014 (http://www.pewinternet.org/2014/02/27/the-web-at-25-in-the-u-s/).

Galtung, Johan and Mari Ruge. 1973. "Structuring and Selecting News." Pp. 67–72 in *The Manufacture of News*, edited by S. Cohen and J. Young. London: Constable.

Gans, Herbert. 1979. *Deciding What's News: A Study of CBS Evening News, NBC Nightly News, Newsweek, and Time*. New York: Pantheon.

Gibson, Katie. 2009. "Undermining Katie Couric: The Discipline Function of the Press." *Women and Language* 32:51–59.

Glassner, Barry. 1997. *The Culture of Fear: Why Americans Are Afraid of the Wrong Things*. New York: Basic Books.

Goffman, Erving. 1959. *The Presentation of Self in Everyday Life*. New York: Penguin Books.

Governors Highway Safety Association. 2014. "Distracted Driving Laws." Retrieved October 18, 2014 (http://www.ghsa.org/html/stateinfo/laws/cellphone_laws.html).

Guillén, Mauro and Sandra Suárez. 2005. "Explaining the Global Digital Divide: Economic, Political and Sociological Drivers of Cross-National Internet Use." *Social Forces* 84(2):681–708.

Gunkel, David J. 2003. "Second Thoughts: Towards a Critique of the Digital Divide." *New Media and Society* 5(4):499–522.

Gurevitch, Michael and Mark R. Levy. 1985. *Mass Communication Review Yearbook*. Vol. 5. Beverly Hills, CA: Sage Publications.

International Women's Media Foundation. 2010. *Global Report on the Status of Women in the News Media*. Washington, DC: IWMF.

Kellner, Douglas M. 1995. *Media Culture: Cultural Studies, Identity, and Politics Between the Modern and the Postmodern*. New York: Routledge.

Kelly, Joe and Stacy Smith. 2006. *Where the Girls Aren't: Gender Disparity Saturates G-Rated Films*. Duluth, MN: Dads and Daughters Foundation.

Kelly, K., K. Clark, and L. Kulman. 2004. "Trash TV." *U.S. News and World Report* 136(6):48–51.

Klite, P., R. A. Bardwell, and J. Salzman. 1997. "Local TV News: Getting Away With Murder." *Harvard International Journal of Press/Politics* 2:102–12.

Lazarus, Wendy and Francisco Mora. 2000. *Online Content for Low-Income and Underserved Americans: The Digital Divide's New Frontier*. Santa Monica, CA: Children's Partnership.

Leonardi, Paul, Jeffrey Treem, and Michelle Jackson. 2010. "The Connectivity Paradox: Using Technology to Both Decrease and Increase Perceptions of Distance in Distributed Work Arrangements." Journal of Applied Communication Research 38:85–105.

Livingstone, Sonia, Elizabeth Van Couvering, and Nancy Thumin. 2004. *Adult Media Literacy: A Review of the Research Literature on Behalf of Ofcom* London: Office of Communications.

Martin Allan. 2006. "Literacies for the Digital Age." Pp. 3–25 in *Digital Literacies for Learning*, edited by Allan Martin and Dan Madigan. London: Facet Publishing.

McChesney, Robert and John Nichols. 2010. *The Death and Life of American Journalism: The Media Revolution That Will Begin the World Again*. Philadelphia: First Nation Books.

McNair, B. 1998. *The Sociology of Journalism*. London: Oxford University Press.

Media Awareness Network. 2004. "What Is Media Literacy?" Retrieved May 13, 2010 (http://www.media-awareness.ca/english/teachers/media_literacy/what_is_media_literacy.cfm).

Miller, Claire Cain and Brad Stone. 2009. "News Without Newspapers." *New York Times*, April 13, pp. B1, B4.

Miller, Mark Crispin. 2002. "What's Wrong With This Picture?" *The Nation* 274(1):18–22.

Naoum, Chris. 2012. "The Future of Privacy in a Social Media and Networking World." Retrieved April 22, 2012 (http://broadbandbreakfast.com/2012/04/the-future-of-privacy-in-a-social-media-and-networking-world/).

National Safety Council. 2010. "National Safety Council Estimates That at Least 1.6 Million Crashes Each Year Involve Drivers Using Cell Phones and Texting." Retrieved May 13, 2010 (http://www.nsc.org/Pages/NSCestimates16millioncrashescausedbydriversusingcellphonesandtexting.aspx).

Neupane, Shiwani. 2014, "Women's Feature Service: Mapping the Struggles of Feminism in India." Retrieved December 14, 2014 (http://passblue.com/2014/09/01/womens-feature-service-mapping-the-struggles-of-women-in-india/).

Newspaper Association of America. 2012. "Newspaper Circulation Volume." Retrieved October 18, 2014 (http://www.naa.org/Trends-and-Numbers/Circulation-Volume/Newspaper-Circulation-Volume.aspx).

Nguyen, Jimmy. 2011. "Internet Privacy Class Actions: How to Manage Risks From Increasing Attacks Against Online and Social Media." *Computer & Internet Lawyer* 28(9):8–11.

Parekh, Angana. 2001. "Bringing Women's Stories to a Reluctant Mainstream Press." *Nieman Reports* 55(4):90–92. Retrieved December 14, 2014 (http://niemanreports.org/articles/bringing-womens-stories-to-a-reluctant-mainstream-press/).

Pérez-Peña, Richard. 2009. "As Cities Go From Two Newspapers to One, Some Talk of Zero." *New York Times*, March 12, pp. A1, A17.

Peterson, T. 1981. "Mass Media and Their Environments: A Journey Into the Past." Pp. 13–32 in *What's News*, edited by E. Abel. San Francisco: Institute for Contemporary Studies.

Pew Internet & American Life Project. 2012. *Digital Differences*. Retrieved April 22, 2012 (http://pewinternet.org/~/media/Files/Reports/2012/PIP_Digital_differences_041312.pdf).

Pew Research Center. 2011. "Views of the News Media: 1985–2011, Press Widely Criticized, but Trusted More Than Other Information Sources."

Retrieved October 18, 2014 (http://www.people-press.org/files/legacy-pdf/9-22-2011%20Media%20Attitudes%20Release.pdf).

Pew Research Internet Project. 2013. "Broadband Technology Fact Sheet." Retrieved October 18, 2014 (http://www.pewinternet.org/fact-sheets/broadband-technology-fact-sheet/).

Porter, William E. 1981. "The Media Baronies: Bigger, Fewer, More Powerful." Pp. 97–118 in What's News, edited by E. Abel. San Francisco: Institute for Contemporary Studies.

Postman, N. 1989. Amusing Ourselves to Death. London: Methuen.

Powell, Kimberly and Lori Abels. 2002. "Sex Role Stereotypes in TV Programs Aimed at the Preschool Audience: An Analysis of Teletubbies and Barney and Friends." Women and Language 25(1):14–22.

Project for Excellence in Journalism. 2004. The State of the News Media 2004. Retrieved March 21, 2004 (http://www.stateofthemedia.org/2004/execsum.pdf).

Project for Excellence in Journalism. 2011. The State of News Media 2011. Retrieved November 30, 2012 (http://stateofthemedia.org/overview-2011/).

Project for Excellence in Journalism. 2012. The State of News Media 2012. Retrieved April 22, 2012 (http://stateofthemedia.org/).

Rideout, Victoria, Ulla Foehr, and Donald Roberts. 2010. Generation M²: Media in the Lives of 8- to 18-Year-Olds. Washington, DC: Kaiser Family Foundation.

Rivadeneyra, Rocío and L. Monique Ward. 2005. "From Ally McBeal to Sábado Gigante: Contributions of Television Viewing to the Gender Role Attitudes of Latino Adolescents." Journal of Adolescent Research 20:453–75.

Schorr, Daniel. 1998. "Mother Teresa and Diana." Christian Science Monitor 90(193):15.

Schudson, M. 1986. "The Menu of Media Research." Pp. 43–48 in Media, Audience, and Social Structure, edited by S. Ball-Rokeach and Muriel Cantor. Beverly Hills, CA: Sage Publications.

Scott, Mark. 2014. "British Court Rules in Favor of Electronic Surveillance." New York Times, December 6, p. A6.

Servon, Lisa. 2002. Bridging the Digital Divide: Technology, Community, and Public Policy. Boston: Blackwell.

Seymour-Ure, C. 1974. The Political Impact of Mass Media. Beverly Hills, CA: Sage Publications.

Shaw, Daniel L. and Maxwell E. McCombs. 1997. The Emergence of American Political Issues: The Agenda Setting Function of the Press. St. Paul, MN: West.

Signorielli, Nicole and Margaret Lears. 1992. "Children, Television, and Conceptions About Chores: Attitudes and Behaviors." Sex Roles 27:157–70.

Smith, Stacy, Marc Choueiti, and Katherine Pieper. 2014. "Gender Bias Without Borders: An Investigation of Female Characters in Popular Films Across 11 Countries." Retrieved December 6, 2014 (http://seejane.org/wp-content/uploads/gender-bias-without-borders-executive-summary.pdf).

Sullivan, Teresa. 2014. "Greedy Institutions, Overwork, and Work-Life Balance." Sociological Inquiry 84:1–15.

Thoman, Elizabeth and Tessa Jolls. 2004. "Media Literacy: A National Priority for a Changing World." Retrieved January 11, 2015 (http://www.medialit.org/reading-room/media-literacy-national-priority-changing-world).

Tucker, Patrick. 2009. "Newspapers Face the Final Edition." The Futurist September–October:8–9.

United Nations Development Programme. 2001. Human Development Report 2001: Making New Technologies Work for Human Development. New York: United Nations Development Programme.

U.S. Bureau of Labor Statistics. 2014. "Software Developers." Retrieved January 17, 2015 (http://www.bls.gov/ooh/computer-and-information-technology/software-developers.htm).

U.S. Census Bureau. 2010. Statistical Abstract of the United States. Washington, DC: U.S. Census Bureau.

Van den Bulck, J. 2000. "Is Television Bad for Your Health? Behavior and Body Image of the Adolescent 'Couch Potato.'" Journal of Youth and Adolescence 29(3):273–88.

Vartanova, Elena. 2002. "Digital Divide and the Changing Political/Media Environment of Post-socialist Europe." International Communication Gazette 64:449–65.

Wade, Marcia. 2008. "Business News: Media Monopolies." Black Enterprise 39:28.

Warschauer, M. 2003. Technology and Social Inclusion. Cambridge, MA: MIT Press.

Wasburn, Philo and Mara Wasburn 2011. "Media Coverage of Women in Politics: The Curious Case of Sarah Palin." Media, Culture & Society 33:1027–41.

Women's Feature Service. 2014. "About Us." Retrieved April 11, 2015 (http://www.wfsnews.org/aboutus.html).

Wright, Kevin, Bryan Abendschein, Kevin Wombacher, Michaela O'Connor, Megan Hoffman, Molly Dempsey, Christopher Krull, Audrey Dewes, and Audrey Shelton. 2014. "Work-Related Communication Technology Use Outside of Regular Work Hours and Work Life Conflict: The Influence of Communication Technologies on Perceived Work Life Conflict, Burnout, Job Satisfaction, and Turnover Intentions." Management Communication Quarterly 28:507–30.

Part IV

Hawken, Paul. 1993. The Ecology of Commerce: A Declaration of Sustainability. New York: HarperCollins.

Krugman, Paul. 2014. "Why We Fight Wars." New York Times, August 17. Retrieved November 28, 2014 (http://www.nytimes.com/2014/08/18/opinion/paul-krugman-why-we-fight.html).

Chapter 12

Abatemarco, Diane, Bernadette West, Vesna Zec, Andrea Russo, Persis Sosiak, and Vedran Mardesic. 2004. "Project Northland in Croatia: A Community Based Adolescent Alcohol Prevention Intervention." Journal of Drug Education 34(2):167–78.

Abramsky, Sasha. 2003. "The Drug War Goes Up in Smoke." The Nation 277(5):25–28.

Alcohol Policies Project. 2001. "National Poll Shows 'Alcopop' Drinks Lure Teens." Retrieved May 21, 2010 (http://www.cspinet.org/booze/alcopops_press.htm).

Allen, Mike, William Donohue, Amy Griffin, Dan Ryan, and Monique Mitchell Turner. 2003. "Comparing the Influence of Parents and Peers on the Choice to Use Drugs: A Meta-Analysis of the Literature." Criminal Justice and Behavior 30:162–86.

Alleyne, Vanessa. 2007. "Locked Up Means Locked Out: Women, Addiction and Incarceration." Women & Therapy 29:181–94.

American Lung Association. 2006. "Smoking Fact Sheet." Retrieved February 21, 2007 (http://www.lungusa.org/site/pp.asp?c=dvLUK900E&b=39853).

American Medical Association. 2004. "Girlie Drinks . . . Women's Diseases." Retrieved April 27, 2007 (http://www.cslep.org/CSLEP/publications/girlie_drinks_survey.pdf).

Becker, Howard. 1963. Outsiders: Studies in the Sociology of Deviance. New York: Free Press.

Beckett, Katherine. 1995. "Fetal Rights and 'Crack Moms': Pregnant Women in the War on Drugs." Contemporary Drug Problems 22:587–612.

Benavie, Arthur. 2009. Drugs: America's Holy War. New York: Routledge Press.

Boyd, Carol, Sean E. McCabe, and Hannah d'Arcy. 2003. "Ecstasy Use Among College Undergraduates: Gender, Race, and Sexual Identity." Journal of Substance Abuse Treatment 24:209–15.

Brower, Aaron. 2002. "Are College Students Alcoholics?" Journal of American College Health 50:253–55.

Bush-Baskette, Stephanie. 1998. "The War on Drugs as a War Against Black Women." In S. Miller (Ed.), Crime Control and Women: Feminist Implication of Criminal Justice Policy (pp. 113–29). Thousand Oaks, CA: Sage Publications.

Bush-Baskette, Stephanie and Vivian Smith. 2012. "Is Meth the New Crack for Women in the War on Drugs? Factors Affecting Sentencing Outcomes for Women and Parallels Between Meth and Crack." Feminist Criminology 7:48–69.

Butler, Edward R. 1993. "Alcohol Use by College Students: A Rite of Passage Ritual." NASPA Journal 31(1):48–55.

Caetano, Raul, Catherine Clark, and Tammy Tam. 1998. "Alcohol Consumption Among Racial/Ethnic Minorities: Theory and Research." Alcohol Health and Research World 22(4):233–38.

CDC Foundation. 2014. "What Is Public Health?" Retrieved January 10, 2015 (http://www.cdcfoundation.org/content/what-public-health).

Centers for Disease Control and Prevention. 2014a. "Secondhand Smoke (SHS) Facts." Retrieved November 22, 2014 (http://www.cdc.gov/tobacco/data_statistics/fact_sheets/secondhand_smoke/general_facts/).

Centers for Disease Control and Prevention. 2014b. "More Than a Quarter-Million Youth Who Had Never Smoked a Cigarette Used E-cigarettes in 2013." Retrieved November 22, 2014 (http://www.cdc.gov/media/releases/2014/p0825-e-cigarettes.html).

Chauvin, Chantel. 2012. "Social Norms and Motivations Associated With College Binge Drinking." *Sociological Inquiry* 82:257–81.

Clapp, John, Audrey Shillington, and Lance Segars. 2000. "Deconstructing Contexts of Binge Drinking Among College Students." *American Journal of Drug and Alcohol Abuse* 26(1):139–54.

Collins, R. Lorraine and Lily McNair. 2003. "Minority Women and Alcohol Use." Retrieved May 21, 2010 (http://pubs.niaaa.nih.gov/publications/arh26-4/251-256.htm).

Community Anti-Drug Coalitions of America. 2014. "Alameda County's Safe Medication Disposal Ordinance – 1st in the U.S.!" Retrieved November 22, 2014 (http://www.cadca.org/content/alameda-county-safe-medication-disposal-ordinance-1st-us).

Crispo, A., P. Brennan, K. H. Jockel, A. Schaffrath-Rosario, H. E. Wichmann, F. Nyberg, L. Simonato, F. Mereletti, F. Forastiere, P. Boffetta, and S. Darby. 2004. "The Cumulative Risk of Lung Cancer Among Current, Ex- and Never-smokers in European Men." *British Journal of Cancer* 91:1280–86.

Crutchfield, Robert and Walter R. Gove. 1984. "Determinants of Drug Use: A Test of the Coping Hypothesis." *Social Science & Medicine* 18:503–509.

Cussen, Meaghan and Walter Block. 2000. "Legalize Drugs Now! An Analysis of the Benefits of Legalized Drugs." *American Journal of Economics and Sociology* 59(3):525–36.

Desilver, Drew. 2014. "Feds May Be Rethinking the Drug War, But States Have Been Leading the Way." Retrieved November 28, 2014 (http://www.pewresearch.org/fact-tank/2014/04/02/feds-may-be-rethinking-the-drug-war-but-states-have-been-leading-the-way/).

Drug Policy Alliance. 2003. "Women and the War on Drugs." Retrieved May 21, 2010 (http://www.drugpolicy.org/communities/women).

Durkin, Keith, Timothy Wolfe, and Gregory Clark. 2005. "College Students and Binge Drinking: An Evaluation of Social Learning Theory." *Sociological Spectrum* 25:255–72.

European Lung Association. 2006. "First Ever EU Figures on Passive Smoking Deaths." Retrieved May 21, 2010 (http://www.european-lung-foundation.org/uploads/Document/WEB_CHEMIN_285_1142589119.pdf).

Federal Bureau of Investigation. 2013. "Crime in the United States 2012." Retrieved November 22, 2014 (http://www.fbi.gov/about-us/cjis/ucr/crime-in-the-u.s/2012/crime-in-the-u.s.-2012/persons-arrested/persons-arrested).

Fellner, Jamie. 2000. *Punishment and Prejudice: Racial Disparities in the War on Drugs* (Vol. 2, No. 2). New York: Human Rights Watch.

Filmore, K. M., J. M. Golding, E. V. Leino, M. Motoyoshi, C. Shoemaker, H. Terry, C. Ager, and H. Ferrer. 1997. "Patterns and Trends in Women's and Men's Drinking." Pp. 21–48 in *Gender and Alcohol*, edited by R. W. Wilsnack and S. C. Wilsnack. New Brunswick, NJ: Rutgers Center of Alcohol Studies.

Frone, Michael R. 2004. "Alcohol, Drugs and Workplace Safety Outcomes: A View From a General Model of Employee Substance Use and Productivity." Pp. 127–56 in *The Psychology of Workplace Safety*, edited by J. Barling and M. R. Frone. Washington, DC: American Psychological Association.

Goode, Erich. 2004. "Drug Use as a Global Social Problem." Pp. 494–520 in *Handbook of Social Problems: A Comparative International Perspective*, edited by G. Ritzer. Thousand Oaks, CA: Sage Publications.

Gunawan, Imana. 2014. "Savings Lives, One Needle at a Time." *Seattle Weekly News*, March 11. Retrieved November 22, 2014 (http://www.seattleweekly.com/home/951641-129/saving-lives-one-needle-at-a).

Hawkins, Elizabeth and C. June La Marr. 2012. "Pulling for Native Communities: Alan Marlatt and the Journeys of the Circle." *Addiction Research and Theory* 20:236–42.

Herd, Denise and Joel Grube. 1996. "Black Identity and Drinking in the U.S.: A National Study." *Addiction* 91(6):845–57.

Hesselbrock, Michie N. and Victor M. Hesselbrock. 1997. "Gender, Alcoholism, and Psychiatric Comorbidity." Pp. 49–71 in *Gender and Alcohol*, edited by R. W. Wilsnack and S. C. Wilsnack. New Brunswick, NJ: Rutgers Center of Alcohol Studies.

Hetzer, Hannah. 2014. "Uruguay Unveils Details for World's First National Legal Marijuana Market." Retrieved November 28, 2014 (http://www.huffingtonpost.com/hannah-hetzer/uruguay-marijuana-market_b_5275735.html).

Hoffman, John and Cindy Larison. 1999. "Worker Drug Use and Workplace Drug Testing Programs: Results From the 1994 National Household Survey on Drug Use." *Contemporary Drug Problems* 26:331–54.

Holmes, Malcolm and Judith Antell. 2001. "The Social Construction of American Indian Drinking: Perceptions of American Indian and White Officials." *Sociological Quarterly* 42(2):151–73.

Inciardi, James. 1999. "American Drug Policy: The Continuing Debate." Pp. 1–8 in *The Drug Legalization Debate*, edited by James Inciardi. Thousand Oaks, CA: Sage Publications.

Iwamoto, Derek, Stephanie Takamatsu, and Jeanette Castellanos. 2012. "Binge-Drinking and Alcohol Related Problems Among U.S. Born Asian Americans." *Cultural Diversity & Ethnic Minority Psychology* 18:219–27.

Jacobs, Andrew. 2010. "China Turns Drug Rehab Into a Punishing Ordeal." *New York Times*, January 8, p. A4.

Jacobson, Jodie and Paul Sacco. 2012. "Employee Assistance Program Services for Alcohol and Other Drugs Problems: Implications for Increased Identification and Engagement in Treatment." *The American Journal on Addiction* 21:468–75.

Kaplan, Howard, Steven Martin, and Cynthia Robbins. 1984. "Pathways to Adolescent Drug Use: Self-Derogation, Peer Influence, Weakening of Social Controls, and Early Substance Abuse." *Journal of Health and Social Behavior* 25:270–89.

Klingner, Donald, Gary Roberts, and Valerie Patterson. 1998. "The Miami Coalition Surveys of Employee Drug Use and Attitudes: A Five-Year Retrospective." *Public Personnel Management* 27(2):201–22.

Lederman, Linda, Lea Stewart, Fern Goodhart, and Lisa Laitman. 2003. "A Case Against 'Binge' as a Term of Choice: Convincing College Students to Personalize Messages About Dangerous Drinking." *Journal of Health Communications* 8:79–91.

Leonard, K. E. and J. C. Rothbard. 1999. "Alcohol and the Marriage Effect." *Journal of Studies on Alcohol* (Suppl. 13):139–46.

Leventhal, Howard and Paul Cleary. 1980. "The Smoking Problem: A Review of the Research and Theory in Behavioral Risk Modification." *Psychological Bulletin* 88:370–405.

Levy, Kira, Kevin O'Grady, Eric Wish, and Amelia Arria. 2005. "An In-Depth Qualitative Examination of Ecstasy Experience: Results of a Focus Group With Ecstasy-Using College Students." *Substance Use & Misuse* 40:1427–41.

Lewinsohn, Peter, Richard Brown, John Seeley, and Susan Ramsey. 2000. "Psychosocial Correlates of Cigarette Smoking Abstinence, Experimentation, Persistence and Frequency During Adolescence." *Nicotine and Tobacco Research* 2:121–31.

MacDonald, Scott, Samantha Wells, and T. Cameron Wild. 1999. "Occupational Risk Factors Associated With Alcohol and Drug Problems." *American Journal of Drug and Alcohol Abuse* 25(2):351–69.

Marshall, Carolyn. 2007. "Drinks With Youth Appeal Draw Growing Opposition." *New York Times*, April 13, p. A12.

McBride, Duane, Yvonne Terry, and James Inciardi. 1999. "Alternative Perspectives on the Drug Policy Debate." Pp. 9–54 in *The Drug Legalization Debate*, edited by James Inciardi. Thousand Oaks, CA: Sage Publications.

McGrath, Shelly, Catherine Marcum, and Heith Copes. 2012. "The Effects of Experienced, Vicarious, and Anticipated Strain on Violence and Drug Use Among Inmates." *American Journal of Criminal Justice* 37:60–75.

Motel, Seth. 2014. "6 Facts About Marijuana." Retrieved November 28, 2014 (http://www.pewresearch.org/fact-tank/2014/11/05/6-facts-about-marijuana/).

Murphy, Shilo. 2014. Interview on Talking StickTV. Retrieved November 22, 2014 (https://www.youtube.com/watch?v=Whai20LhV_s).

National Clearinghouse for Alcohol and Drug Information. 2003a. "Intensive Outpatient

Treatment for Alcohol and Other Drug Abuse: The Treatment Needs of Special Groups." Retrieved May 21, 2010 (http://www.health.org/govpubs/bkd139/8g.aspx).

National Clearinghouse for Alcohol and Drug Information. 2003b. "Cigarettes and Other Nicotine Products." Retrieved August 2, 2003 (http://www.drugabuse.gov/infofacts/tobacco.html).

National Institute on Alcohol Abuse and Alcoholism. 2003a. "The Creation of the National Institute on Alcohol Abuse and Alcoholism." Retrieved March 21, 2008 (http://www.niaaa.nih.gov/AboutNIAAA/OrganizationalInformation/History.htm).

National Institute on Alcohol Abuse and Alcoholism. 2003b. "NIAAA's Purpose." Retrieved July 31, 2003 (http://pubs.niaaa.nih.gov/publications/HealthDisparities/Purpose&Vision.html).

National Institute on Alcohol Abuse and Alcoholism. 2005. "Alcoholism: Natural History and Background." Retrieved May 21, 2010 (http://pubs.niaaa.nih.gov/publications/HealthDisparities/Alcoholism1.htm).

National Institute on Alcohol Abuse and Alcoholism. 2014. "Alcohol Facts and Statistics." Retrieved November 22, 2014 (http://pubs.niaaa.nih.gov/publications/AlcoholFacts&Stats/AlcoholFacts&Stats.htm).

National Institute on Drug Abuse. 1998. "Tobacco Addiction." Retrieved August 2, 2003 (http://www.nida.nih.gov/ResearchReports/Nicotine/addictive.html).

National Institute on Drug Abuse. 2002. *Marijuana Abuse* (NIH Publication No. 02-3859, October). Rockville, MD: National Institute on Drug Abuse.

National Institute on Drug Abuse. 2003a. "NIDA Info Facts: MDMA (Ecstasy)." Retrieved May 21, 2010 (http://www.drugabuse.gov/Infofax/ecstasy.html).

National Institute on Drug Abuse. 2003b. "Drug Addiction Treatment Methods." Retrieved August 2, 2003 (http://www.drugabuse.gov/infofacts/treatmeth.html).

National Institute on Drug Abuse. 2006. "Cigarettes and Other Tobacco Products." Retrieved May 21, 2010 (http://www.drugabuse.gov/infofacts/tobacco.html).

Office of National Drug Control Policy. 2003. "Enabling Legislation." Retrieved May 21, 2010 (http://www.whitehousedrugpolicy.gov/about/legislation.html).

Office of National Drug Control Policy. 2006. "Marijuana Overview." Retrieved February 21, 2007 (http://www.whitehousedrugpolicy.gov/drugfact/marijuana/index.html#extentofuse).

Office of National Drug Control Policy. 2014. "How Illicit Drug Use Affects Business and the Economy." Retrieved November 22, 2014 (http://www.whitehouse.gov/ondcp/ondcp-fact-sheets/how-illicit-drug-use-affects-business-and-the-economy).

PBS. 2000. "Frontline: Drug Wars." Retrieved August 2, 2003 (http://www.pbs.org/wgbh/pages/frontline/shows/drugs).

Pennell, Susan, Joe Ellett, Cynthia Rienick, and Jackie Grimes. 1999. *Meth Matters: Report on Methamphetamine Users in Five Western Cities.* Washington, DC: U.S. Department of Justice, Office of Justice Programs, National Institute of Justice.

Perry, Cheryl, Carolyn Williams, Kelli Komro, Sara Veblen-Mortenson, Melissa Stigler, Karen Munson, Kian Farbakhsh, Resa Jones, and Jean Forster. 2002. "Project Northland: Long-Term Outcomes of Community Action to Reduce Adolescent Alcohol Use." *Health Education Research* 17:117–32.

Plant, M. A., P. Miller, and M. L. Plant. 2005. "Trends in Drinking, Smoking and Illicit Drug Use Among 15- and 16-Year Olds in the UK (1995–2003)." *Journal of Substance Use* 10(6):331–39.

Prinstein, Mitchell and Shirley Wang. 2005. False Consensus and Adolescent Peer Contagion: Examining Discrepancies Between Perceptions and Actual Reported Levels of Friends' Deviance and Health Risk Behaviors." *Journal of Abnormal Child Psychology* 33:293–306.

Reinarman, Craig and Harry G. Levine. 1997. *Crack in America: Demon Drugs and Social Justice.* Berkeley: University of California Press.

Roberts, Dorothy. 1991. "Punishing Drug Addicts Who Have Babies: Women of Color, Equality, and the Right of Privacy." *Harvard Law Review* 104(7):1419–82.

Roman, Paul and Terry Blum. 2002. "The Workplace and Alcohol Problem Prevention." *Alcohol Research and Health* 26(1):49–57.

Saad, Lydia. 2014. "Majority Continues to Support Pot Legalization in U.S." Retrieved November 28, 2014 (http://www.gallup.com/poll/179195/majority-continues-support-pot-legalization.aspx).

Scalia, John. 2001. *Federal Drug Offenders, 1999, With Trends 1984–1999* (August 2001, NCJ 187285). Washington, DC: U.S. Department of Justice, Office of Justice Programs.

Silbering, Robert. 2001. "The 'War on Drugs': A View From the Trenches." *Social Research* 68(3):890–96.

Social Issues Research Center. 1998. *Social and Cultural Aspects of Drinking.* Retrieved May 21, 2010 (http://www.sirc.org/publik/drinking3.html#_VPID_5).

Substance Abuse and Mental Health Services Administration. 2003a. "Benefits and Costs." Retrieved July 31, 2003 (http://www.samhsa.gov/DrugFreeWP/Benefits.html).

Substance Abuse and Mental Health Services Administration. 2003b. "Drug Free Workplace Programs." Retrieved July 31, 2003 (http://www.gov/DrugFreeWP/Legal.html).

Substance Abuse and Mental Health Services Administration. 2014. *Results From the 2013 National Survey on Drug Use and Health: Summary of National Findings.* Rockville, MD: SAMHSA.

Sutherland, Edwin. 1939. *Principles of Criminology.* 3rd ed. Philadelphia: J. B. Lippincott.

Tanner, Lindsey. 2003. "Underage Drinkers Consume 20 Percent of Booze, Study Says." *News Tribune,* February 26, p. A7.

Task Force of the National Advisory Council on Alcohol Abuse and Alcoholism. 2010. "A Snapshot of High-Risk College Drinking Consequences." Retrieved May 2, 2012 (http://www.collegedrinkingprevention.gov/StatsSummaries/snapshot.aspx).

Tavernise, Sabrina. 2014. "E-Cigarettes Top Smoking Among Youths, Study Says." *New York Times,* December 17, A21.

Trevino, Roberto and Alan Richard. 2002. "Attitudes Toward Drug Legalization Among Drug Users." *American Journal of Drug and Alcohol Abuse* 28(1):91–108.

United Nations Office on Drugs and Crime. 2006. "Who Is Doing Drugs?" Retrieved June 27, 2007 (http://www.unodc.org/unodc/drug_demand_who.html).

United Nations Office on Drugs and Crime. 2012a. *Cannabis: A Short Review.* New York: United Nations Office on Drugs and Crime.

United Nations Office on Drugs and Crime. 2012b. *World Drug Report 2011.* New York: United Nations Office on Drugs and Crime.

United Nations Office on Drugs and Crime. 2014. *World Drug Report 2014.* Vienna, Austria: United Nations Office on Drugs and Crime.

U.S. Bureau of Labor Statistics. 2014. "Epidemiologists." Retrieved January 10, 2015 (http://www.bls.gov/ooh/life-physical-and-social-science/epidemiologists.htm).

U.S. Department of Labor. 2003. "Working Partners: Small Business Workplace Kit: Facts and Figures." Retrieved May 21, 2010 (http://www.dol.gov/asp/programs/drugs/workingpartners/Screen15.htm).

U.S. Department of Labor. 2007. "Workplace Substance Abuse." Retrieved May 2, 2012 (http://www.osha.gov/SLTC/substanceabuse/index.html).

U.S. Department of Labor. 2014. "How Does Substance Abuse Impact the Workplace?" Retrieved November 22, 2014 (http://www.dol.gov/elaws/asp/drugfree/benefits.htm).

Vaughn, Christy. 2002. "Ecstasy: More Deadly Than Many Young People Know." Retrieved August 2, 2003 (http://www.health.org/newsroom/rep/182.aspx).

Washington Post. 2014. "Congress Should Reform the Mandatory Minimum Sentences for Drug Offenses." Retrieved November 22, 2014 (http://www.washingtonpost.com/opinions/congress-should-reform-the-mandatory-minimum-sentences-for-drug-offenses/2014/07/23/df845d68-1125-11e4-9285-4243a40ddc97_story.html).

Wechsler, Henry. 1996. "Alcohol and the American College Campus." *Change* 28(4):20–25.

Weisheit, Ralph and Kathrine Johnson. 1992. "Exploring the Dimensions of Support for Decriminalizing Drugs." *Journal of Drug Issues* 92(22):53–75.

Weitzman, Elissa, Alison Folkman, Kerry Folkman, and Henry Wechsler. 2003. "The Relationship of Alcohol Outlet Density to Heavy and Frequent Drinking and Drinking-Related Problems Among College Students at Eight Universities." *Health and Place* 9:1–6.

Wheaton, Blair. 1990. "Life Transitions, Role Histories, and Mental Health." *American Sociological Review* 55:209–23.

Williams, Carolyn and Cheryl Perry. 1998. "Lesson From Project Northland: Preventing Alcohol Problems During Adolescence." *Alcohol Health and Research World* 22(2):107–16.

Wilsnack, Richard W. and Sharon C. Wilsnack. 1992. "Women, Work, and Alcohol: Failures of Simple Theories." *Alcoholism: Clinical and Experimental Research* 16:172–79.

Wilsnack, Sharon C., Nancy D. Vogeltanz, Albert D. Klassen, and T. Robert Harris. 1997. "Childhood Sexual Abuse and Women's Substance Abuse: National Survey Findings." *Journal of Studies on Alcohol* 58:264–71.

Winter, Greg. 2003. "Study Finds No Sign That Testing Deters Student Drug Use." *New York Times*, May 17, pp. A1, A12.

World Health Organization. 2004. *Global Status Report on Alcohol 2004*. Singapore: World Health Organization.

World Health Organization. 2014. "Tobacco Fact Sheet." Retrieved November 22, 2014 (http://www.who.int/entity/mediacentre/factsheets/fs339/en/index.html).

Yamaguchi, Ryoko, Lloyd Johnston, and Patrick O'Malley. 2003. "Relationship Between Student Illicit Drug Use and School Drug-Testing Policies." *Journal of School Health* 73(4):159–64.

Ziemelis, Andris, Ronald Buckman, and Abdulaziz Elfessi. 2002. "Prevention Efforts Underlying Decreases in Binge Drinking at Institutions of Higher Education." *Journal of American College Health* 50(5):238–52.

Chapter 13

Ackerman, William V. 1998. "Socioeconomic Correlates of Increasing Crime Rates in Smaller Communities." *Professional Geographer* 50(3):372–87.

Adler, Freda. 1975. *Sisters in Crime*. New York: McGraw-Hill.

Adler, Freda, Gerhard Mueller, and William Laufer. 1991. *Criminology*. New York: McGrawHill.

Agnew, Robert. 1992. "Foundation for a General Strain Theory of Crime and Delinquency." *Criminology* 30:47–88.

Akers, Ronald and Christine Sellers. 2009. *Criminological Theories: Introduction and Evaluation*. Los Angeles, CA: Roxbury.

Albrecht, Hans-Jorg. 2001. "Post-adjudication Dispositions in Comparative Perspective." Pp. 293–30 in *Sentencing and Sanctions in Western Countries*, edited by Michael Tonry and Richard Frase. New York: Oxford University Press.

Alexander, Michelle. 2010. *The New Jim Crow: Mass Incarceration in the Age of Colorblindness*. New York: New Press.

American Civil Liberties Union. 1999. "Prisoners' Rights" (ACLU Position Paper). New York: American Civil Liberties Union.

Amnesty International. 2014. "Death Sentences and Executions 2013." Retrieved April 12, 2015 (http://www.amnestyusa.org/research/reports/death-sentences-and-executions-2013).

Anderson, C. 2003. "Prison Populations Challenge Already Cash-Strapped States." *News Tribune*, July 28, p. A7.

Apuzzo, Matt and Michael Schmidt. 2014. "U.S. to Continue Racial Profiling in Border Policy." *New York Times*, December 6, A1, A14.

Bales, William, Laura Bedard, Susan Quinn, David Ensley, and Glen Holley. 2005. "Recidivism of Public and Private State Inmates in Florida." *Criminology and Public Policy* 4(1):57–82.

Bard Prison Initiative. 2014. "What We Do." Retrieved April 12, 2015 (http://bpi.bard.edu/what-we-do/).

Barnett, Cynthia. n.d. *The Measurement of White Collar Crime Using Uniform Crime Reporting (UCR) Data*. Washington, DC: U.S. Government Printing Office.

Becker, Sarah and Jill McCorkel. 2011. "The Gender of Criminal Opportunity: The Impact of Male Co-Defenders on Women's Crime." *Feminist Criminology* 6:79–110.

Beckett, Katherine and Theodore Sasson. 2000. *The Politics of Injustice*. Thousand Oaks, CA: Pine Forge Press.

Bigda, Carolyn. 2001. "College Students Oppose Private Prisons." Retrieved May 17, 2010 (http://www.dollarsandsense.org/archives/2001/0901bigda.html).

Blumstein, Alfred and Richard Rosenfeld. 1998. "Explaining Recent Trends in U.S. Homicide Rates." *The Journal of Criminal Law and Criminology* 88(4):1175–216.

Braithwaite, John. 1989. *Crime, Shame and Reintegration*. Cambridge, England: Cambridge University Press.

Brownstein, Henry. 2001. *The Social Reality of Violence and Violent Crime*. Boston: Allyn & Bacon.

Caldeira, Teresa and James Holston. 1999. "Democracy and Violence in Brazil." *Society for Comparative Study of Society and History* 41(4):691–729.

Camp, Scott and Gerald Gaes. 2002. "Growth and Quality of U.S. Private Prisons: Evidence From a National Survey." *Criminology and Public Policy* 1(3):427–50.

Cao, Liqun, Anthony Troy Adams, and Vickie Jensen. 2000. "The Empirical Status of the Black-Subculture-of-Violence Thesis." Pp. 47–62 in *The System in Black and White*, edited by M. Markowitz and D. Jones-Brown. Westport, CT: Praeger.

Carson, E. Ann. 2014. "Prisoners in 2013" (NCJ 247282). Retrieved December 26, 2014 (http://www.bjs.gov/content/pub/pdf/p13.pdf).

Chambliss, William. 1988. *Exploring Criminology*. New York: Macmillan.

Chesney-Lind, Meda and Lisa Pasko. 2004. *The Female Offender: Girls, Women, and Crime*. Thousand Oaks, CA: Sage Publications.

Community Oriented Policing Services. 2003. "A Guide to the COPS Office." Retrieved May 17, 2010 (http://www.cops.usdoj.gov/Default.asp?Item=35).

Community Oriented Policing Services. 2014. "About." Retrieved January 1, 2015 (http://www.cops.usdoj.gov/Default.asp?Item=35).

Cooper, Alexia and Erica Smith. 2011. *Homicide Trends in the United States, 1980–2008* (NCJ 236018). Washington, DC: U.S. Bureau of Justice Statistics.

Cross, Beverly. 2001. "A Time for Action." In Tammy Johnson, Jennifer Emiko Boyden, and William J. Pittz (eds.), *Racial Profiling and Punishment in U.S. Public Schools: How Zero Tolerance Policies and High Stakes Testing Subvert Academic Excellence and Racial Equity*. Applied Research Centre 5. http://www.arc.org/erase/downloads/profiling.pdf.

Cullen, Francis and Robert Agnew. 2011. *Criminological Theory: Past to Present*. New York: Oxford University Press.

Davis, Robert, B. Taylor, and R. Titus. 1997. "Victims as Agents: Implications for Victim Services and Crime Prevention." Pp. 167–79 in *Victims of Crime*, edited by R. Davis, A. Lurigio, and W. Skogan. Thousand Oaks, CA: Sage Publications.

Death Penalty Information Center. 2012. "Facts About the Death Penalty." Retrieved May 13, 2012 (http://www.deathpenaltyinfo.org/documents/FactSheet.pdf).

Death Penalty Information Center. 2014. "Facts About the Death Penalty." Retrieved January 1, 2015 (http://www.deathpenaltyinfo.org/documents/FactSheet.pdf).

Durose, Matthew, Alexia Cooper, and Howard Synder. 2014. "Recidivism of Prisoners Released in 30 States in 2005: Patterns From 2005 to 2010." Washington, DC: U.S. Department of Justice.

Eith, Christine and Matthew Durose. 2011. *Contacts Between Police and the Public, 2008* (NCJ 234599). Washington, DC: U.S. Bureau of Justice Statistics.

Elliot, Delbert S., Suzanne Ageton, and Rachelle Canter. 1979. "An Integrated Perspective on Delinquent Behavior." *Journal of Research in Crime and Delinquency* 16:3–27.

Erickson, Kai. 1964. "Notes on the Sociology of Deviance." Pp. 9–21 in *The Other Side: Perspectives of Deviance*, edited by Howard Becker. New York: Free Press.

Federal Bureau of Investigation. 1989. *White Collar Crime: A Report to the Public*. Washington, DC: Government Printing Office.

Federal Bureau of Investigation. 2011. "Financial Crime Reports to the Public." Retrieved December 26, 2014 (http://www.fbi.gov/stats-services/publications/financial-crimes-report-2010-2011).

Federal Bureau of Investigation. 2014a. "Full Time Law Enforcement Employees." Retrieved December 26, 2014 (http://www.fbi.gov/about-us/cjis/ucr/crime-in-the-u.s/2011/crime-in-the-u.s.-2011/tables/table_74_full-time_law_enforcement_employees_by_population_group_percent_male_and_female_2011.xls).

Federal Bureau of Investigation. 2014b. "2013 Law Enforcement Officers Killed and Assaulted."

Retrieved December 26, 2014 (http://www.fbi.gov/about-us/cjis/ucr/leoka/2013/officers-feloniously-killed/felonious_topic_page_-2013).

Flavin, Jeanne. 2001. "Feminism for the Mainstream Criminologist: An Invitation." *Journal of Criminal Justice* 29:271–85.

Gaes, Gerald, Timothy Flannagan, Laurence Motiuk, and Lynn Stewart. 1999. "Adult Correctional Treatment." Pp. 361–426 in *Crime and Criminal Justice: A Review of Research*, Vol. 26, *Prisons*, edited by Michael Tonry and Joan Petersilia. Chicago, IL: University of Chicago Press.

Galbraith, M. Susan. 2004. "So Tell Me, Why Do Women Need Something Different?" *Journal of Religion & Spirituality in Social Work* 23:197–212.

Glaze, Lauren and Thomas Bonczar. 2009. *Probation and Parole in the United States, 2007 Statistical Tables* (NCJ 224707). Washington, DC: U.S. Bureau of Justice Statistics.

Glaze, Lauren and Danielle Kaeble. 2014. "Correctional Populations in the United States, 2013" (NCJ248479). Washington, DC: U.S. Department of Justice.

Goldstein, Herman. 1990. *Problem-Oriented Policing*. Boston: McGraw-Hill.

Greene, J. R. and W. V. Pelfrey. 1997. "Shifting the Balance of Power Between Police and Community: Responsibility for Crime Control." Pp. 393–423 in *Critical Issues in Policing: Contemporary Readings*, edited by R. Dunham and G. Alpert. Prospect Heights, IL: Waveland Press.

Guerino, Paul, Paige Harrison, and William Sabol. 2011. *Prisoners in 2010* (NCJ 236096). Washington, DC: U.S. Bureau of Justice Statistics.

Haney, Craig and Philip Zimbardo. 1998. "The Past and Future of U.S. Prison Policy: Twenty-Five Years After the Stanford Prison Experiment." *American Psychologist* 53:709–27.

Hannon, Lance and James Defronzo. 1998. "The Truly Disadvantaged, Public Assistance, and Crime." *Social Problems* 45(3):383–92.

Harlem Live. 1999. "The Blue Nile Rites of Passage." Retrieved August 7, 2003 (http://www.bluenile passage.org/).

Harrell, Erika and Michael Rand. 2010. *Crime Against People With Disabilities, 2008* (NCJ 231328). Washington, DC: U.S. Bureau of Justice Statistics.

Hautzinger, Sarah. 1997. "'Calling a State a State': Feminist Politics and the Policing of Violence Against Women in Brazil." *Feminist Issues* 15(1):3–30.

Hautzinger, Sarah. 2002. "Criminalizing Male Violence in Brazil's Women's Police Stations: From Flawed Essentialism to Imagined Communities." *Journal of Gender Studies* 11(3):243–51.

Hemenway, David. 2004. "A Public Health Approach to Firearms Policy." Pp. 85–98 in *Policy Challenges in Modern Health Care*, edited by David Mechanic, Lynn B. Rogut, David Colby, and James Knickman. New Brunswick, NJ: Rutgers University Press.

Henrichson, Christian and Ruth Delaney. 2012. *The Price of Prisons: What Incarceration Costs Taxpayers*. Washington, DC: VERA Institute of Justice.

Hirschi, Travis. 1969. *Causes of Delinquency*. Berkeley: University of California Press.

Huggins, M. 1997. "From Bureaucratic Consolidation to Structural Devolution: Police Death Squads in Brazil." *Policing and Society* 7:207–34.

Human Rights Watch. 1995. "Global Report on Women's Human Rights 1990 to 1995." Retrieved July 30, 2003 (http://www.hrw.org/about/projects/womrep/General-187.htm#P2966_897325).

Human Rights Watch. 1997. *Police Brutality in Urban Brazil*. Retrieved May 18, 2010 (http://www.hrw.org/reports/1997/brazil/).

Human Rights Watch. 1999. *Punishment and Prejudice: Racial Disparities in the War on Drugs*. New York: Human Rights Watch.

Human Rights Watch. 2000. *The Impact of the War on Drugs on U.S. Incarceration*. New York: Human Rights Watch.

Human Rights Watch. 2009. "Lethal Force: Police Violence and Public Security in Rio de Janeiro and Sao Paulo." Retrieved February 16, 2010 (http://www.hrw.org/en/node/86987/section/1).

Human Rights Watch. 2012. *Old Behind Bars: The Aging Prison Population in the United States*. New York: Human Rights Watch.

Human Rights Watch. 2014. "Brazil." Retrieved January 1, 2015 (http://www.hrw.org/world-report/2014/country-chapters/brazil).

Innocence Project. 2007. "What Is the Innocence Project?" Retrieved May 18, 2010 (http://www.innocenceproject.org/Content/9.php).

Irwin, Darrell. 2002. "Alternatives to Delinquency in Harlem: A Study of Faith-Based Community Mentoring." *Justice Professional* 15(2):29–36.

Jensen, Vickie. 2001. *Why Women Kill: Homicide and Gender Equality*. Boulder, CO: Lynne Rienner.

Joseph, J. 2000. "Overrepresentation of Minority Youth in the Juvenile Justice System: Discrimination or Disproportionality of Delinquent Acts? Status of the Black-Subculture-of-Violence Thesis." Pp. 227–40 in *The System in Black and White*, edited by M. Markowitz and D. Jones-Brown. Westport, CT: Praeger.

Justice Policy Institute. 2008. "Substance Abuse Treatment and Public Safety." Retrieved May 18, 2010 (http://www.justicepolicy.org/images/upload/08_01_REP_DrugTx_AC-PS.pdf).

Kappeler, Victor, Mark Blumberg, and Gary Potter. 2000. *The Mythologies of Crime and Criminal Justice*. Prospect Heights, IL: Waveland Press.

Kaufman, Joanne, Cesar Rebellon, Sherod Thaxton, and Robert Agnew. 2008. "A General Strain Theory of Racial Differences in Criminal Offending." *Australian and New Zealand Journal of Criminology* 41:421–37.

LaFree, Gary and Gwen Hunnicutt. 2006. "Female and Male Homicide Victimization Trends." Pp. 195–239 in *Gender and Crime: Patterns of Victimization and Offending*, edited by

K. Heimer and C. Krusttschnitt. New York: New York University Press.

Langan, Patrick and David Levin. 2002. *Recidivism of Prisoners Released in 1994* (NCJ 193427). Washington, DC: U.S. Department of Justice, Office of Justice Programs.

Larason Schneider, A. 1999. "Public–Private Partnerships in the U.S. Prison System." *American Behavioral Scientist* 43(1):192–208.

Laub, John. 1983. "Urbanism, Race, and Crime." *Journal of Research of Crime and Delinquency* 20:183–98.

Laub, John. 1997. "Patterns of Criminal Victimization in the United States." Pp. 9–26 in *Victims of Crime*, edited by R. Davis, A. Lurigio, and W. Skogan. Thousand Oaks, CA: Sage Publications.

Lemert, Edwin M. 1967. *Human Deviance, Social Problems, and Social Control*. Englewood Cliffs, NJ: Prentice Hall.

Liska, Allen. 1992. *Social Threat and Social Control*. Albany: SUNY Press.

Lopez, Mark Hugo and Michael Light. 2009. "A Rising Share: Hispanics and Federal Crime." Retrieved January 18, 2015 (http://www.pewhispanic.org/2009/02/18/a-rising-share-hispanics-and-federal-crime/).

MacDonald, J. 2002. "The Effectiveness of Community Policing in Reducing Urban Violence." *Crime and Delinquency* 48(4):592–618.

Malik, Nazneen. 2005. "The Bard College Prison Initiative." *Education Update* 10(9):19.

Mitchell, Michael and Charles Wood. 1999. "Ironies of Citizenship: Skin Color, Police Brutality, and the Challenge of Democracy in Brazil." *Social Forces* 77(3):1001–20.

Moore, Mark. 1999. "Security and Community Development." Pp. 293–337 in *Urban Problems and Community Development*, edited by R. F. Ferguson and W. T. Dickens. Washington, DC: Brookings Institution.

Moore, Solomon. 2007. "States Export Their Inmates as Prisons Fill." *New York Times*, July 31, pp. A1, A14.

Morash, Merry, Timothy Byrum, and Barbara Koons. 1998. *Women Offenders: Programming Needs and Promising Practices*. Washington, DC: National Institute of Justice.

Morenoff, Jeffrey. 2005. "Racial and Ethnic Disparities in Crime in the United States." Pp. 139–73 in *Ethnicity and Causal Mechanisms*, edited by M. Rutter and M. Tienda. New York: Cambridge University Press.

Naffine, Ngaire. 1996. *Feminism and Criminology*. Philadelphia: Temple University Press.

National Night Out. 2003. "The History of NATW and National Night Out." Retrieved May 18, 2010 (http://www.nationaltownwatch.org/nno/history.html).

Norris, Clive, Nigel Fielding, Clark Kemp, and Jane Fielding. 1992. "Black and Blue: An Analysis of the Influence on Being Stopped by the Police." *British Journal of Sociology* 43(2):207–24.

Novak, Kenneth, Leanne Alarid, and Wayne Lucas. 2003. "Exploring Officers' Acceptance of Community Policing: Implications for Policy Implementation." *Journal of Criminal Justice* 31:57–71.

Office on Violence Against Women. 2010. "About the Office." Retrieved May 18, 2010 (http://www.ovw.usdoj.gov/overview.htm).

Pew Center on the States. 2011. *State of Recidivism: The Revolving Door of America's Prisons.* Washington, DC: Pew Charitable Trusts.

Planty, Michael, Lynn Langton, Christopher Krebs, Marcus Berzofsky, and Hope Smiley-McDonald. 2013. "Female Victims of Sexual Violence 1994–2010" (NCJ 240655). Retrieved December 26, 2014 (http://www.bjs.gov/content/pub/pdf/fvsv9410.pdf).

Pratt, Travis and Jeff Maahs. 1999. "Are Private Prisons More Cost-Effective Than Public Prisons? A Meta-Analysis of Evaluation Research Studies." *Crime and Delinquency* 45(3):358–71.

Puzzanchera, Charles. 2013. "Juvenile Arrests 2011." Retrieved December 26, 2014 (http://www.ojjdp.gov/pubs/244476.pdf).

Radelet, Michael and Glenn Pierce. 2005. "The Impact of Legally Inappropriate Factors on Death Sentencing for California Homicides 1990–1999." *Santa Clara Law Review* 49:1–47.

Reiman, Jeffrey. 1998. *The Rich Get Richer and the Poor Get Prison.* Boston: Allyn & Bacon.

Rich, John and Marguerite Ro. 2002. *A Poor Man's Plight: Uncovering the Disparity in Men's Health.* Battle Creek, MI: W. K. Kellogg Foundation.

Rosen, Jeffrey. 2010. "Could Keeping Convicts From Violating Probation or Their Terms of Release Be the Answer to Prison Overcrowding?" *New York Times Magazine,* January 10, pp. 36–39.

Roth, Jeffrey and Joseph Ryan. 2000. "The COPS Program After 4 Years—National Evaluation." Retrieved May 18, 2010 (http://www.ncjrs.gov/pdffiles1/nij/183644.pdf).

Roth, Lenny. 2004. "Privatisation of Prisons." Retrieved January 1, 2015 (http://www.parliament.nsw.gov.au/prod/parlment/publications.nsf/0/ED4BA0B9D18C2546CA256EF9001B3ADA).

Sabol, William, Heather West, and Matthew Cooper. 2009. *Prisoners in 2008* (NCJ 228417). Washington, DC: U.S. Department of Justice, Office of Justice Programs.

Sampson, Robert J. and William Julius Wilson. 1995. "Towards a Theory of Race, Crime, and Urban Inequality." Pp. 37–54 in *Crime and Inequality,* edited by John Hagen and Ruth Peterson. Palo Alto, CA: Stanford University Press.

Sanders, W. 1981. *Juvenile Delinquency: Causes, Patterns, and Reactions.* New York: Holt, Rinehart and Winston.

Savage, Charlie. 2012. "U.S. to Expand Its Definition of Rape in Statistics." *New York Times,* January 7, pp. A10, A15.

Simon, Thomas, James Mercy, and Craig Perkins. 2001. *Injuries From Violent Crime, 1992–1998* (NCJ 168633). Washington, DC: U.S. Department of Justice, Office of Justice Programs.

Smith, Erica and Alexia Cooper. 2013. "Homicide in the U.S. Known to Law Enforcement, 2011." Retrieved December 26, 2014 (http://www.bjs.gov/content/pub/pdf/hus11.pdf).

Stafford, Mark C. 2004. "Juvenile Delinquency." Pp. 480–93 in *Handbook of Social Problems: A Comparative International Perspective,* edited by George Ritzer. Thousand Oaks, CA: Sage Publications.

Steffensmeier, Darrell and Emilie Allan. 1996. "Gender and Crime: Toward a Gendered Theory of Female Offending." *Annual Review of Sociology* 22:459–87.

Stoutland, Sara. 2001. "The Multiple Dimensions of Trust in Resident/Police Relations in Boston." *Journal of Research in Crime and Delinquency* 38(3):226–56.

Sutherland, Edwin H. 1949. *White Collar Crime.* New York: Dryden Press.

Tonry, Michael. 2004. "Crime." Pp. 465–79 in *Handbook of Social Problems: A Comparative International Perspective,* edited by George Ritzer. Thousand Oaks, CA: Sage Publications.

Tonry, Michael and David P. Farrington. 1995. "Strategic Approaches to Crime Prevention." Pp. 1–20 in *Crime and Justice: A Review of Research.* Vol. 19, *Building a Safer Society—Strategic Approaches to Crime Prevention,* edited by Michael Tonry and David P. Farrington. Chicago: University of Chicago Press.

Truman, Jennifer. 2011. *Criminal Victimization, 2010* (NCJ 235505). Washington, DC: U.S. Bureau of Justice Statistics.

Truman, Jennifer and Lynn Langton. 2014. "Criminal Victimization, 2013" (NCJ 247648). Retrieved December 26, 2014 (http://www.bjs.gov/content/pub/pdf/cv13.pdf).

Turk, Austin. 1969. *Criminality and Legal Order.* Chicago: Rand McNally.

Turk, Austin. 1976. "Law as a Weapon in Social Conflict." *Social Problems* 23:276–91.

U.S. Bureau of Justice Statistics. 2003a. "Crime Characteristics." Retrieved July 8, 2003 (http://www.ojp.usdoj.gov/bjs/cvict_c.htm).

U.S. Bureau of Justice Statistics. 2003b. "State and Local Law Enforcement Statistics." Retrieved July 14, 2003 (http://www.ojp.usdoj.gov/bjs/sandlle.htm).

U.S. Bureau of Labor Statistics. 2014. "Probation Officers and Correctional Treatment Specialists." Retrieved January 18, 2015 (http://www.bls.gov/ooh/community-and-social-service/probation-officers-and-correctional-treatment-specialists.htm).

U.S. Congress. 2002. "Public Law 107-273, Title II Juvenile Justice." Retrieved May 18, 2010 (http://ojjdp.ncjrs.org/about/PL_107_273.html).

U.S. Department of Justice. 2002. "DOJ Seal—History and Motto." Retrieved May 18, 2010 (http://www.usdoj.gov/jmd/ls/dojseal.htm).

U.S. Department of Justice. 2014. *Guidance for Federal Law Enforcement Agencies Regarding the Use of Race, Ethnicity, Gender, National Origin, Religion, Sexual Orientation or Gender Identity.* Washington, DC: U.S. Department of Justice.

Walmsley, Roy. 2012. World Female Imprisonment List. Retrieved December 26, 2014 (http://www.prisonstudies.org/sites/prisonstudies.org/files/resources/downloads/wfil_2nd_edition.pdf).

Walmsley, Roy. 2014. World Prison Population. Retrieved January 1, 2015 (http://www.prisonstudies.org/sites/prisonstudies.org/files/resources/downloads/wppl_10.pdf).

Walsh, Anthony and Lee Ellis. 2007. *Criminology: An Interdisciplinary Approach.* Thousand Oaks, CA: Sage Publications.

Weitzer, Ronald and Steven A. Tuch. 2002. "Perceptions of Racial Profiling: Race, Class and Personal Experience." *Criminology* 40:435–57.

White House. 2013. "Remarks by the President on Trayvon Martin." Retrieved January 18, 2015 (http://www.whitehouse.gov/photos-and-video/video/2013/07/19/president-obama-speaks-trayvon-martin#transcript).

Wilson, William Julius. 1996. *When Work Disappears: The World of the New Urban Poor.* New York: Knopf.

Wolf, J. 2000. "War Games Meets the Internet: Chasing 21st Century Cybercriminals With Old Laws and Little Money." *American Journal of Criminal Law* 28:95–117.

Wolfgang, Marvin and Franco Ferracuti. 1967. *The Subculture of Violence: Towards an Integrated Theory in Criminology.* New York: Tavistock.

World Health Organization. 2005. *WHO Multi-country Study on Women's Health and Domestic Partner Violence Against Women: Summary Report of Initial Results on Prevalence, Health Outcomes and Women's Responses.* Geneva, Switzerland: World Health Organization.

Zhao, Jihong, Matthew Scheider, and Quint Thurman. 2002. "Funding Community Policing to Reduce Crime: Have COPS Grants Made a Difference?" *Criminology and Public Policy* 2(1):7–32.

Chapter 14

Appleton, Lynn M. 1995. "The Gender Regimes in American Cities." Pp. 44–59 in *Gender in Urban Research,* edited by J. A. Garber and R. S. Turner. Thousand Oaks, CA: Sage Publications.

Badenhausen, Kurt. 2013. "Detroit Tops 2013 List of Most Miserable Cities." Retrieved January 14, 2015 (http://www.forbes.com/sites/kurtbadenhausen/2013/02/21/detroit-tops-2013-list-of-americas-most-miserable-cities/).

Banerjee, Tridib and William C. Baer. 1984. *Beyond the Neighborhood Unit: Residential Environments and Public Policy.* New York: Plenum Press.

Barrett, Richard E., Young Ik Cho, Kathryn E. Weaver, Kirak Ryu, Richard T. Campbell, Thereese A. Dolecek, and Richard B. Warnecke. 2008. "Neighborhood Change and Distant Metastasis at Diagnosis of Breast Cancer." *Annals of Epidemiology* 18(1):43–47.

Boddy, Sharon. 2000. "Car-Free and Carefree." *E Magazine* 11(2):14–18.

Butler, Amy. 2009. "Wages in the Nonprofit Sector: Management, Professional and Administrative Support Jobs." Retrieved January 17, 2015 (http://www.bls.gov/opub/mlr/cwc/wages-in-the-nonprofit-sector-management-professional-and-administrative-support-occupations.pdf).

Charles, Camille Zubrinsky. 2003. "The Dynamics of Racial and Residential Segregation." *Annual Review of Sociology* 29: 167–207.

Choi, Namkee G. and Lidia J. Snyder. 1999. *Homeless Families With Children: A Subjective Experience of Homelessness.* New York: Springer.

Clark, William A. V., Marinus C. Deurloo, and Frans M. Dieleman. 2000. "Housing Consumption and Residential Crowding in U.S. Housing Markets." *Journal of Urban Affairs* 22(1):49–64.

Cohen, Hillel W. and Mary E. Northridge. 2000. "Getting Political: Racism and Urban Health." *American Journal of Public Health* 90(6): 841–43.

Colby, Anne, Thomas Ehrlich, Elizabeth Beaumont, and Jason Stephens. 2003. *Educating Citizens: Preparing America's Undergraduates for Lives of Moral and Civic Responsibility.* Menlo Park, CA: Carnegie Foundation for the Advancement of Teaching/Jossey-Bass.

Corvin, A. 2001. "Urban Sprawl Creates Belly Sprawl, CDC Suggests." *News Tribune*, November 2, p. A11.

Crenson, Matt. 2003. "He Wants to Reclaim Towns for Pedestrians." *Christian Science Monitor*, October 15. Retrieved May 22, 2010 (http://www.csmonitor.com/2003/1015/p13s02-lihc.html).

Davey, Monica and Mary Williams Walsh. 2013. "Billions in Debt, Detroit Tumbles Into Insolvency." Retrieved January 17, 2015 (http://www.nytimes.com/2013/07/19/us/detroit-files-for-bankruptcy.html?pagewanted=all&_r=0).

de Pommereau, Isabelle. 2006. "New German Community Models for Car-Free Living." *Christian Science Monitor* 99(18):1, 11.

Desai, Sonalde. 2004. "Population Change." Pp. 69–86 in *Handbook of Social Problems: A Comparative International Perspective*, edited by G. Ritzer. Thousand Oaks, CA: Sage Publications.

Dickerson, Niki. 2008. "Occupational and Residential Segregation: The Confluence of Two Systems of Inequality." *Labor Studies Journal* 33:393–411.

Donadio, Rachel. 2009. "Mock Funeral for Venice Dramatizes Flight of Residents From City's Heart." *New York Times*, November 15, p. 10.

Dreier, Peter. 1996. "America's Urban Crisis: Symptoms, Causes, and Solutions." Pp. 79–141 in *Race, Poverty, and American Cities*, edited by J. C. Boger and J. W. Wegner. Chapel Hill: University of North Carolina Press.

Dretzka, G. 1995. "Filling Void, Real and Symbolic Ex-Laker 'Magic,' Sony Bring First-Run Movies, Hope to South-Central L.A." *Chicago Tribune*, July 21, Business section, p. 1.

Eisenhower, Dwight. 1963. *Mandate for Change 1953–1956.* Garden City, NY: Doubleday.

Evans, Gary W., Susan Saegert, and Rebecca Harris. 2001. "Residential Density and Psychological Health Among Children in Low-Income Families." *Environment and Behavior* 33(2):165–80.

Ewing, Reed, Rolf Pendall, and Don Chen. 2002. *Measuring Urban Sprawl and Its Impact.* Washington, DC: Smart Growth America.

Feagin, Joe R. 1998a. "Introduction." Pp. 1–24 in *The New Urban Paradigm*, edited by J. R. Feagin. Lanham, MD: Rowman & Littlefield.

Feagin, Joe R. 1998b. "Urban Real Estate Speculation." Pp. 133–58 in *The New Urban Paradigm*, edited by J. R. Feagin. Lanham, MD: Rowman & Littlefield.

Garber, Judith A. and Robyne S. Turner. 1995. "Introduction." Pp. x–xxvi in *Gender in Urban Research*, edited by J. A. Garber and R. S. Turner. Thousand Oaks, CA: Sage Publications.

Gordon, John S. 2001. "The Business of America." *American Heritage* 52(4):6–59.

Gottdiener, Mark. 1977. *Planned Sprawl: Private and Public Interests in Suburbia.* Beverly Hills, CA: Sage Publications.

Hanlon, James. 2011. "Unsightly Urban Menaces and the Rescaling of Residential Segregation in the United States." *Journal of Urban History* 37:732–56.

Hwang, Jackelyn and Robert Sampson. 2014. "Divergent Pathways of Gentrification: Racial Inequality and the Social Order of Renewal in Chicago Neighborhoods." *American Sociological Review* 79:726–51.

Ihrke, David. 2014. *Reason for Moving: 2012 to 2013: Population Characteristics (P20-574).* Washington, DC: U.S. Census Bureau.

Institute for Government Innovation. 2000. "Awards Recipients: Hope VI Mixed Finance Public Housing." Retrieved May 22, 2010 (http://www.innovations.harvard.edu/awards.html?id=3853).

Jacobs, David. 2011. "Environmental Health Disparities in Housing." *American Journal of Public Health* 101: S115–S122.

Johnson, Roy S. 2003. "It Must Be Magic." *Savoy*, February, pp. 70–71, 72–78, 80.

Johnson, William A. 2007. "Sprawl and Civil Rights: A Mayor's Reflections." Pp. 103–23 in *Growing Smarter: Achieving Livable Communities, Environmental Justice and Regional Equity*, edited by R. Bullard. Cambridge, MA: MIT Press.

Judd, Dennis and Todd Swanstrom. 2004. *City Politics: Private Power and Public Policy.* Lebanon, IN: Addison-Wesley.

Karp, David, Greg Stone, and William Yoels. 1991. *Being Urban: A Sociology of City Life.* London: Greenwood.

Keels, Micere, Julia Burdick-Will, and Sara Keene. 2013. "The Effects of Gentrification on Neighborhood Public Schools." *City and Community* 12:238–59.

Kennedy, Maureen and Paul Leonard. 2001. "Dealing With Neighborhood Change: A Primer on Gentrification and Policy Choices" (Discussion paper). Washington, DC: Brookings Institution Center on Urban and Metropolitan Policy and Policy Link.

Kim, Chigon and Mark Gottdiener. 2004. "Urban Problems in Global Problems." Pp. 172–92 in *Handbook of Social Problems: A Comparative International Perspective*, edited by G. Ritzer. Thousand Oaks, CA: Sage Publications.

Krieger, James and Donna L. Higgins. 2002. "Housing and Health: Time Again for Public Health Action." *American Journal of Public Health* 92(5):758–68.

Leinberger, Christopher. 2012. "Now Coveted: A Walkable, Convenient Place." *New York Times*, May 27, pp. 6–7.

Leinberger, Christopher and Mariela Alfonzo. 2012. *Walk This Way: The Economic Promise of Walkable Places in Metropolitan Washington, D.C.* Washington, DC: Brookings Institution.

Mahoney, Martha. 1997. "The Social Construction of Whiteness." Pp. 330–33 in *Critical White Studies: Looking Behind the Mirror*, edited by R. Delgado and J. Stefanic. Philadelphia: Temple University Press.

Martinez, S. 2000. "The Housing Act of 1949: Its Place in the Realization of the American Dream of Homeownership." *Housing Policy Debate* 11(2):467–87.

Massey, Douglas. 2001. "Residential Segregation and Neighborhood Conditions on U.S. Metropolitan Areas." Pp. 391–434 in *America Becoming: Racial Trends and Their Consequences*, Vol. 1, edited by N. Smelser, W. J. Wilson, and F. Mitchell. Washington, DC: National Academy Press.

Massey, Douglas and Nancy Denton. 1993. *American Apartheid and Segregation and the Making of the Underclass.* Cambridge, MA: Harvard University Press.

Massey, Douglas and Mitchell Eggers. 1993. "The Spatial Concentration of Affluence and Poverty During the 1970s." *Urban Affairs Quarterly* 29(2):299–315.

Masson, D. 1984. "Les Femmes dans les Structures Urbanies: Apercu d'un Nouveau Champ de Recherché." *Canadian Journal of Political Science* 17:753–82.

McKenzie, Brian. 2013. "Out of State and Long Commutes: 2011, ACS-20." Washington, DC: U.S. Census Bureau.

McKenzie, Brian and Melanie Rapino. 2011. *Commuting in the United States: 2009* (ACS-15). Washington, DC: U.S. Census Bureau.

Molotch, H. 1976. "The City as a Growth Machine." *American Journal of Sociology* 82:309–32.

Murphy, Dean E. 2003."New Californian Identity Predicted by Researchers." *New York Times*, February 17, p. A13.

Myers, Dowell and Seong Woo Lee. 1996. "Immigration Cohorts and Residential Overcrowding in Southern California." *Demography* 33:51–65.

National Coalition for the Homeless. 2002. "How Many People Experience Homelessness?" Retrieved June 10, 2003 (http://www.nationalhomeless.org/factsheets/How_Many.html).

Norris, Tyler. 2001. "Civic Gemstones: The Emergent Communities Movement." *National Civic Review* 90(4):307–18.

Ohlemacher, Stephen. 2007. "In Nation of Sprawl, We're All Just Single Dots in Our Cars." *News Tribune*, June 14, p. A3.

Parker, Brenda. 2011. "Material Matters: Gender and the City." *Geography Compass* 5/6:433–47.

Pastor, M. 2001. "Geography and Opportunity." Pp. 435–68 in *America Becoming: Racial Trends and Their Consequences*, Vol. 1, edited by N. J. Smelser, W. J. Wilson, and F. Mitchell. Washington, DC: National Academy Press.

Perry, Marc. 2006. *Domestic Net Migration in the United States: 2000 to 2004* (Current Population Reports, P25-1135). Washington, DC: U.S. Census Bureau.

Powell, John. 2007. "Race, Poverty and Urban Sprawl: Access to Opportunities Through Regional Strategies." Pp. 51–71 in *Growing Smarter: Achieving Livable Communities, Environmental Justice and Regional Equity*, edited by R. Bullard. Cambridge, MA: MIT Press.

Rast, J. 2001. "Manufacturing Industrial Decline: The Politics of Economic Change in Chicago, 1955–1998." *Journal of Urban Affairs* 23(2):175–90.

Roberts, Sam. 2007. "New Demographic Racial Gap Emerges." *New York Times*, May 17, p. A19.

Rosenthal, Elisabeth. 2012. "Nigeria's Population Is Soaring in Preview of a Global Problem." *New York Times*, April 15, pp. 1, 12.

Rossi, Peter. 1989. *Down and Out in America: The Origins of Homelessness.* Chicago: University of Chicago Press.

Schachter, J. 2004. *Geographical Mobility: 2002 to 2003* (Current Population Reports, P20-549). Washington, DC: U.S. Census Bureau.

Siddiqui, Roomana and Janak Pandey. 2003. "Coping With Environmental Stressors by Urban Slum Dwellers." *Environment and Behavior* 35:589–604.

Simmel, Georg. 1997. "The Metropolis and Mental Life." Pp. 174–86 in *Simmel on Culture: Selected Writings*, edited by D. Frisby and M. Featherstone. London: Sage Publications. (Original work published 1903)

Smith, Eric L. 1999. "The Magic Touch." *Black Enterprise*, May, pp. 74–82.

Smith, Neil. 1986. "Gentrification, the Frontier, and the Restructuring of Urban Space." Pp. 15–34 in *Gentrification of the City*, edited by N. Smith and P. Williams. Boston: Allen & Unwin.

Smith, Neil. 2002. "New Globalism, New Urbanism: Gentrification as Global Urban Strategy." *Antipode* 34(3):427–50.

Stanback, Thomas M., Jr. 1991. *The New Suburbanization: Challenge to the Central City.* Boulder, CO: Westview Press.

Stein, Rob. 2003. "Waistlines Sprawl With Suburbs, Study Finds." *News Tribune,* August 29, p. A3.

Stock, Mathis. 2006. "European Cities: Toward a Recreational Turn?" *Studies in Culture, Polity and Identities* 7(1):1–19.

Suro, Roberto and Audrey Singer. 2002. *Latino Growth in Metropolitan America: Changing Patterns, New Locations* (Brookings Institution Center on Urban and Metropolitan Policy and Pew Hispanic Center, Survey Series). Washington, DC: Brookings Institution.

Taylor, Marisa. 2010. "A Career in Nonprofit." Retrieved January 17, 2015 (http://www.wsj.com/articles/SB10001424052748703946504575470081491461608).

Toro, Paul. 2007. "Toward an International Understanding of Homelessness." *Journal of Social Issues* 63(3):461–81.

Turner, Robyne S. 1995. "Concern for Gender in Central-City Development." Pp. 271–88 in *Gender in Urban Research*, edited by J. A. Garber and R. S. Turner. Thousand Oaks, CA: Sage Publications.

United Nations, Department of Economic and Social Affairs. 2011. "World Urbanization Prospects, the 2011 Revision." Retrieved May 18, 2012 (http://esa.un.org/unpd/wup/CD-ROM/Urban-Rural-Population.htm).

United Nations Population Division, Department of Economic and Social Affairs. 2014. *World Urbanization Prospects: The 2014 Revision, Highlights*. Retrieved December 20, 2014 (http://esa.un.org/unpd/wup/Highlights/WUP2014-Highlights.pdf).

United Nations Population Fund. 2007. *The State of World Population: Unleashing the Potential of Urban Growth.* New York: United Nations Population Fund.

U.S. Census Bureau. 1995. "Urban and Rural Populations 1900 to 1990." Retrieved May 21, 2010 (http://www.census.gov/population/censusdata/urpop0090.txt).

U.S. Census Bureau. 2005. "Americans Spend More Than 100 Hours Commuting to Work Each Year." Retrieved October 12, 2007 (http://www.census.gov/Press-Release/www/releases/archives/american_community_survey_acs/004489.html).

U.S. Census Bureau. 2012a. "Housing Vacancies and Homeownership, Annual Statistics: 2011." Retrieved May 28, 2012 (http://www.census.gov/housing/hvs/).

U.S. Census Bureau. 2012b. "Most Children Younger Than Age 1 Are Minorities, Census Bureau Reports." Retrieved December 10, 2012 (http://www.census.gov/newsroom/releases/archives/population/cb12-90.html).

U.S. Census Bureau. 2012c. *Statistical Abstract of the United States.* Washington, DC: U.S. Census Bureau.

U.S. Conference of Mayors. 2013. *Hunger and Homelessness Survey: A Status Report on Hunger and Homelessness in America's Cities*. Washington, DC: U.S. Census Bureau.

U.S. Department of Energy. 2010. "Fact #618: April 12, 2010, Vehicles per Household and Other Demographic Statistics." Retrieved May 17, 2012 (http://www1.eere.energy.gov/vehiclesandfuels/facts/2010_fotw618.html).

U.S. Department of Housing and Urban Development. 2003a. "About HOPE VI." Retrieved May 22, 2010 (http://www.hud.gov:80/offices/pih/programs/ph/hope6/about/index.cfm).

U.S. Department of Housing and Urban Development. 2003b. "HUD's History." Retrieved March 11, 2003 (http://portal.hud.gov/portal/page/portal/HUD/about/hud_history).

U.S. Department of Housing and Urban Development. 2003c. "Welcome to the Community Renewal Initiative." Retrieved June 24, 2004 (http://www.hud.gov/offices/cpd/economic development/programs/rc/index.cfm).

U.S. Department of Housing and Urban Development. 2009. "About HOPE VI." Retrieved May 22, 2010 (http://www.hud.gov/offices/pih/programs/ph/hope6/about/index.cfm#4b).

U.S. Department of Housing and Urban Development. 2014. *The 2014 Annual Homeless Assessment Report (AHAR) to Congress*. Washington, DC: U.S. Department of Housing and Urban Development.

U.S. PIRG Education Fund. 2013. *A New Direction: Our Changing Relationship With Driving and the Implications for America's Future.* Washington D.C.: U.S. PIRG Education Fund.

Wilborn, P. 2002. "Magic Johnson Now Winning at Business; Politics Could Be Next." *Cincinnati Enquirer On Line Edition,* May 26. Retrieved October 8, 2002 (http://enquirer.com/editions/2002/05/26/spt_Magic_ johnson_now.html).

Williams, Donald C. 2000. *Urban Sprawl: A Reference Handbook.* Santa Barbara, CA: ABC-CLIO.

Women's International Network News. 1999. "Women and the Urban Environment." *Women's International Network News* 25(1):60–61.

Wood, Daniel. 2007. "On the Rise in American Cities: The Car-Free Zone." *Christian Science Monitor* 99(109):1, 12.

Chapter 15

Arkansas Wildlife Federation. 2003a. "About the Arkansas Wildlife Federation." Retrieved May 18, 2010 (http://www.arkansaswildlifefederation.org/history.html).

Arkansas Wildlife Federation. 2003b. "Arkansas Wildlife Federation Education Projects." Retrieved May 18, 2010 (http://www.arkansaswildlife federation.org/programs/education.html).

Baker, Al. 2014. "At City Schools, a Program Turns Good Food Into Perfectly Good Compost." New York Times, June 23, A17.

Blacksmith Institute. 2007. *The World's Most Polluted Places.* New York: Blacksmith Institute.

Blacksmith Institute and Green Cross Switzerland. 2014. *The World's Worst 2013: The Top Ten Toxic Threats.* New York: Blacksmith Institute.

Breton, Mary Joy. 1998. *Women Pioneers for the Environment.* Boston: Northeastern University Press.

Broder, John. 2007. "Governors Join in Creating Regional Pacts on Climate Change." *New York Times,* November 15, p. A16.

Broder, John. 2010. "Climate Goal Is Supported by China and India." *New York Times,* March 10, p. A9.

Brower Youth Awards. 2013. "Alex Freid, Durham, NH." Retrieved December 30, 2014 (http://

www.broweryouthawards.org/winner/alex-freid/).

Bullard, Robert. 1994. *Dumping in Dixie: Race, Class, and Environmental Quality.* Boulder, CO: Westview Press.

Bullard, Robert. 1999. "Dismantling Environmental Racism in the USA," *Local Environment* 4: 5–19.

Bullard, Robert and Glenn Johnson. 2000. "Environmental Justice: Grassroots Activism and Its Impact on Public Policy Decision Making." *Journal of Social Issues* 56: 555–578.

Cable, Sherry and Charles Cable. 1995. *Environmental Problems, Grassroots Solutions: The Politics of Grassroots Environmental Conflict.* New York: St. Martin's.

Caldwell, Lynton C. 1970. *Environment: Challenge to Modern Society.* Garden City, NY: Natural History Press.

Caldwell, Lynton C. 1997. "Environment as a Problem for Policy." P. 118 in *Environmental Policy: Transnational Issues and National Trends*, edited by L. Caldwell and R. Bartlett. Westport, CT: Quorum Books.

Caulfield, Henry. 1989. "The Conservation and Environmental Movements: A Historical Analysis." Pp. 13–56 in *Environmental Politics and Policy*, edited by J. Lester. Durham, NC: Duke University Press.

Center for Health, Environment and Justice. 2001. *Poisoned Schools: Invisible Threats, Visible Actions.* Falls Church, VA: Child Proofing Our Communities Campaign.

Center for Health, Environment and Justice. 2009. *Safe School Siting Toolkit.* Falls Church, VA: Center for Health, Environment and Justice.

Centers for Disease Control and Prevention. 2014. "Global Water, Sanitation, and Hygiene." Retrieved December 25, 2014 (http://ecowatch .com/2014/08/08/devil-in-the-deep-blue-sea-dead-zones/).

Chircop, Andrea. 2008. "An Ecofeminist Conceptual Framework to Explore Gendered Environmental Health Inequalities in Urban Settings and to Inform Healthy Public Policy." *Nursing Inquiry* 15:135–47.

Choi, Charles. 2011. "Mega-quakes and Mega-disasters: Will US Heed Wake-up Call in Japan?" Retrieved June 14, 2012 (http://www .csmonitor.com/Science/2011/0328/Mega-quakes-and-mega-disasters-Will-US-heed-wake-up-call-in-Japan).

Clean Air Network. 2003. *Danger in the Air: Unhealthy Levels of Smog in 2002.* Washington, DC: U.S. Public Interest Research Group Education Fund.

Davies, J. Clarence. 1970. *The Politics of Pollution.* New York: Pegasus.

Deutsch, Claudia. 2007. "College Leaders Push for Carbon Neutrality." *New York Times*, June 13, p. A21.

Diamond, Jared. 2009. "Will Big Business Save the Earth?" *New York Times*, December 6, p. I2.

DiFrancesco, Darryn Anne and Nathan Young. 2010. "Seeing Climate Change: The Visual Construction of Global Warming in Canadian National Print Media." *Cultural Geographies* 18:517–36.

Dunlap, Riley. 1997. "The Evolution of Environmental Sociology: A Brief History and Assessment of the American Experience." Pp. 21–39 in *The International Handbook of Environmental Sociology*, edited by M. R. Redclift and G. Woodgate. Cheltenham, England: Edward Elgar.

Dunlap, Riley and William Catton. 1994. "Struggling With Human Exemptionalism: The Rise, Decline, and Revitalization of Environmental Sociology." *American Sociologist* 25(1):5–30.

Dunlap, Riley and Angela Mertig. 1992. *American Environmentalism: The U.S. Environmental Movement, 1970–1990.* Washington, DC: Taylor & Francis.

Earth Island Institute. 2010. "About Us." May 18, 2010 (http://www.earthisland.org/index.php/ aboutUs/).

Ehrlich, Paul and Anne Ehrlich. 1990. *The Population Explosion.* New York: Touchstone/ Simon & Schuster.

Ehrlich, Paul and Anne Ehrlich. 1996. *Betrayal of Science and Reason: How Anti-environmental Rhetoric Threatens Our Future.* Washington, DC: Island Press.

Ehrlich, Paul, Anne Ehrlich, and John Holdren. 1973. *Human Ecology: Problems and Solutions.* San Francisco: W. H. Freeman.

Eisele, K. 2003. "With Every Breath You Take." Retrieved May 18, 2010 (http://www.nrdc .org/onearth/03win/asthma1.asp).

Engelman, Robert. 2009. "Population Sustainability." *Scientific American Earth 3.0* 19:22–29.

Environmental Protection Agency. 1999. *Smog—Who Does It Hurt? What You Need to Know About Ozone and Your Health* (EPA-452/K-99-001). Washington, DC: Environmental Protection Agency.

Environmental Protection Agency. 2003a. "EPA Announces $73.1 Million in National Brownfields Grants in 37 States and Seven Tribal Communities." Retrieved August 26, 2003 (http://www.epa.gov/brownfields/news/ pr062003.htm).

Environmental Protection Agency. 2003b. *Water on Tap: What You Need to Know.* Washington, DC: Environmental Protection Agency.

Environmental Protection Agency. 2004. "About EPA." Retrieved May 18, 2010 (http://www .epa.gov/epahome/aboutepa.htm).

Environmental Protection Agency. 2007a. "Particulate Matter." Retrieved May 18, 2010 (http://www.epa.gov/air/particles/index .html).

Environmental Protection Agency. 2007b. "State Actions." Retrieved October 24, 2007 (http:// www.epa.gov/climatechange/wycd/statean dlocalgov/state.html).

Environmental Protection Agency. 2009a. "Water on Tap: A Consumer's Guide to the Nation's Drinking Water." Retrieved May 18, 2010 (http://www.epa.gov/safewater/wot/pdfs/ book_ waterontap_full.pdf).

Environmental Protection Agency. 2009b. "Endangerment and Cause or Contribute Findings for Greenhouse Gases Under Section

202(a) of the Clean Air Act." Retrieved May 27, 2010 (http://www.epa.gov/climatechange/ endangerment.html).

Environmental Protection Agency. 2010. *Our Nation's Air: Status and Trends Through 2008.* Washington, DC: Environmental Protection Agency.

Environmental Protection Agency. 2013. *Municipal Solid Waste Generation, Recycling and Disposal in the United States: Facts and Figures for 2012.* Washington, DC: Environmental Protection Agency.

Environmental Protection Agency. 2014a. "Air Quality Trends." Retrieved December 27, 2014 (http://www.epa.gov/airtrends/aqtrends .html).

Environmental Protection Agency. 2014b. "National Priorities List." Retrieved December 27, 2014 (http://www.epa.gov/superfund/sites/npl/).

Environmental Protection Agency. 2014c. "Municipal Solid Waste." Retrieved December 27, 2014 (http://www.epa.gov/epawaste/ nonhaz/municipal/).

Epstein, Barbara. 1995. "Grassroots Environmentalism and Strategies for Social Change." *New Political Science* 32(Summer):1–24.

Ford, Dana. 2014. "2014 May Be the Hottest Year on Record." Retrieved December 27, 2014 (http://www.cnn.com/2014/12/03/world/ climate-change-report/).

Freudenberg, Nicolas and Carol Steinsapir. 1992. "Not in Our Backyard: The Grassroots Environmental Movement." Pp. 27–35 in *American Environmentalism: The U.S. Environmental Movement, 1970–1990*, edited by Riley Dunlap and Angela Mertig. Washington, DC: Taylor & Francis.

Global Carbon Atlas. 2014. "Emissions." Retrieved December 24, 2014 (http://www .globalcarbonatlas.org/?q=en/emissions).

Hamilton, Cynthia. 1994. "Concerned Citizens of South Central L.A." Pp. 207–19 in *Unequal Protection*, edited by Robert Bullard. San Francisco: Sierra Club Books.

Hannigan, John. 1995. *Environmental Sociology: A Social Constructionist Perspective.* London: Routledge.

Hawken, Paul. 1993. *The Ecology of Commerce: A Declaration of Sustainability.* New York: HarperCollins.

Hawken, Paul. 1997. "Natural Capitalism." *Mother Jones* 22(2):40–58.

Ingram, Helen and David Mann. 1989. "Interest Groups and Environmental Policy." Pp. 135–57 in *Environmental Politics and Policy*, edited by J. Lester. Durham, NC: Duke University Press.

Irwin, Alan. 2001. *Sociology and the Environment.* Cambridge, England: Polity Press.

Kanter, James. 2007. "U.N. Warns of Rapid Decay of Environment." *New York Times*, October 26, p. A8.

Kanter, James and Andrew Revkin. 2007. "Scientists Detail Climate Changes, Poles to Tropics." *New York Times*, April 7, pp. A1, A5.

Kaufman, Leslie. 2009. "Nudging Recycling From Less Waste to None." *New York Times*, October 20, pp. A1, A17.

Ketcham, Christopher. 2007. "The Hundred Mile Diet." Retrieved May 18, 2010 (http://www.thenation.com/article/hundred-mile-diet).

Korten, David. 1995. *When Corporations Rule the World.* West Hartford, CT: Kumarian Press.

Lee, J. 2003. "7 States to Sue EPA Over Standards on Air Pollution." *New York Times*, February 21, p. A24.

Lefebvre, Henri. 2000. *Everyday Life in the Modern World.* London: Athlone Press. (Original work published 1971)

Lipka, Sara. 2006. "Students Call for Action on Campuses." *Chronicle of Higher Education* 53(9):11.

Littig, Beate. 2001. *Feminist Perspectives on Environment and Society.* Harlow, England: Prentice Education.

Locavores. 2007. "Locavores." Retrieved May 18, 2010 (http://locavores.com/).

Lueck, Thomas J. 2007. "The Mayor Draws a Blueprint for a Greener City." *New York Times*, April 23, p. A18.

Mazmanian, Daniel and Michael Kraft. 1999. "The Three Epochs of the Environmental Movement." Pp. 3–42 in *Toward Sustainable Communities: Transition and Transformations in Environmental Policy*, edited by D. Mazmanian and M. Kraft. Cambridge, MA: MIT Press.

Morland, Kimberly and Steve Wing. 2007. "Food Justice and Health in Communities of Color." Pp. 171–88 in *Growing Smarter: Achieving Livable Communities, Environmental Justice and Regional Equity*, edited by Robert Bullard. Cambridge, MA: MIT Press.

National Academies. 2007. "Press Release February 21, 2007." Retrieved May 18, 2010 (http://www8.nationalacademies.org/onpinews/newsitem.aspx?RecordID=11857).

National Oceanic and Atmospheric Administration (NOAA). 2010. "State of the Climate Global Analysis: Annual 2009." Retrieved May 18, 2010 (http://www.ncdc.noaa.gov/sotc/?report=global&year=2009&month=13).

National Parks Conservation Association. 2003. "New List of America's Ten Most Endangered National Parks Highlights Widespread Problems." Retrieved May 18, 2010 (http://www.npca.org/media_center/press_releases/2003/page-27599890.html).

Natural Resources Defense Council. 1996. "Particulate Pollution." Retrieved March 24, 2008 (http://www.nrdc.org/air/pollution/qbreath.asp).

National Resources Defense Council. 2014. "Stopping the Keystone XL Pipeline." Retrieved December 25, 2014 (http://www.nrdc.org/energy/keystone-pipeline/).

National Wilderness Preservation System. 2004. "Fast Facts at a Glance." Retrieved May 18, 2010 (http://www.wilderness.net/index.cfm?fuse=NWPS&sec=fastFacts).

Navarro, Mireya and Sindya Bhanoo. 2010. "Teaching Green, Beyond Recycling." *New York Times*, January 11, p. A12.

Newman, Rich. 2001. "Making Environmental Politics: Women and Love Canal Activism." *Women's Studies Quarterly* 1–2:65–84.

Palmer, Brian. 2014. "Devil in the Deep Blue Sea: How Many Dead Zones are Out There?" Retrieved December 25, 2014 (http://ecowatch.com/2014/08/08/devil-in-the-deep-blue-sea-dead-zones/).

Palmer, Clare. 1997. *Environmental Ethics.* Santa Barbara, CA: ABC-CLIO.

Pollan, Michael. 2008. "Farmer in Chief." *New York Times Magazine*, October 12, pp. 63–71, 92.

Power, Matthew. 2006. "The Magic Mountain." *Harper's Magazine,* December, pp. 57–68.

Pregracke, Chad and Jeff Barrow. 2007. *From the Bottom Up: One's Man Crusade to Clean America's Rivers.* Washington, DC: National Geographic.

Ringquist, Evan J. 2000. "Environmental Justice: Normative Concerns and Empirical Evidence." Pp. 232–56 in *Environmental Policy*, edited by N. Vig and M. Kraft. Washington, DC: Congressional Quarterly Press.

Rockler-Gladen, Naomi. 2007. "Green Tips for College Students." Retrieved May 18, 2010 (http://collegeuniversity.suite101.com/article.cfm/green_tips_for_college_students).

Rosenthal, Elisabeth. 2007. "Parents and Health Experts Try to Ease Italy's Pollution." *New York Times*, June 12, p. A3.

Rosenthal, Elisabeth. 2009. "Sweden Looks to Diet to Cut Global Warming." *New York Times*, October 23, pp. A1, A6.

Scarce, Rik. 1990. *Eco-warriors: Understanding the Radical Environmental Movement.* Chicago, IL: Noble Press.

Schwartz, John. 2011. "The Best-Laid Plans." *New York Times*, March 13, pp. 1, 5.

Stolberg, Sheryl Gay. 2007. "Bush Proposes Goal to Reduce Greenhouse Gas." *New York Times*, June 1, pp. A1, A12.

Tabuchi, Hiroko. 2011. "Citizens' Testing Finds 20 Radioactive Hot Spots Around Tokyo." *New York Times*, October 15, pp. A1, A3.

Than, Ker. 2014. "Causes of California Drought Linked to Climate Change, Stanford Scientist Says." Retrieved December 24, 2014 (http://news.stanford.edu/news/2014/september/drought-climate-change-092914.html).

Tobin, Richard. 2000. "Environment, Population, and the Developing World." Pp. 326–49 in *Environmental Policy,* edited by N. Vig and M. Kraft. Washington, DC: Congressional Quarterly Press.

United Nations. 2009. "Draft Decision-/CP.15." Retrieved February 27, 2010 (http://unfccc.int/resource/docs/2009/cop15/eng/l07.pdf).

UN News Centre. 2011. "As World Passes 7 Billion Milestone, UN Urges Action to Meet Key Challenges." *UN News Service*, October 31. Retrieved December 12, 2012 (http://www.un.org/apps/news/story.asp?NewsID=40257#.UMZc3pPjncY).

U.S. Fish and Wildlife Service. 2012. "Summary of Listed Species Populations and Recovery Plans." Retrieved June 14, 2012 (http://ecos.fws.gov/tess_public/pub/Boxscore.do).

Vrijheid, Martine. 2000. "Health Effects of Residence Near Hazardous Waste Landfill Sites: A Review of Epidemiologic Literature."

Environmental Health Perspectives I (108, Suppl. 1):101–12.

Weiss, Kenneth. 2003. "Life in U.S. Ocean Waters in Death Spiral, Study Says." *News Tribune*, June 5, p. A3.

Wenz, Peter. 2001. *Environmental Ethics Today.* New York: Oxford University Press.

Wilson, Charles. 2009. "When Your Dorm Goes Green and Local." Retrieved May 18, 2010 (http://www.nytimes.com/2009/09/27/magazine/27Ecodorm-t.html?_r=0).

World Health Organization. 2006. "Asthma." Retrieved May 18, 2010 (http://www.who.int/mediacentre/factsheets/fs307/en/index.html).

Chapter 16

Abouzeid, Rania. 2011. "Bouazizi: The Man Who Set Himself and Tunisia on Fire." Retrieved August 1, 2012 (http://www.time.com/time/magazine/article/0,9171,2044723,00.html).

Abrahms, Max. 2012. "The Political Effectiveness of Terrorism Revisited." *Comparative Political Studies* 45:366–93.

Adley, Jessica and Andrea Grant. 2003. "The Environmental Consequences of War." Retrieved July 12, 2012 (http://www.sierraclub.ca/national/postings/war-and-environment.html).

Ahern, Bertie. 2003. "In Search of Peace: The Fate and Legacy of the Good Friday Agreement." *Harvard International Review* Winter:26–31.

Ali, Mohamed and Iqbal Shah. 2000. "Sanctions and Childhood Mortality in Iraq." *Lancet* 355(9218):1851–57.

Altbach, Philip and Patti Peterson. 1971. "Before Berkeley: Historical Perspectives on American Student Activism." *The ANNALS of the American Academy of Political and Social Science* 395:1–14.

Altheide, David. 2006. "Terrorism and the Politics of Fear." *Cultural Studies—Critical Methodologies* 6:415–39.

Amnesty International. 2012. "Myanmar (Burma) Human Rights." Retrieved June 25, 2012 (http://www.amnestyusa.org/our-work/countries/asia-and-the-pacific/Myanmar).

Ayubi, Shaheen, R. E. Bissell, N. Korsah, and L. Lerner. 1982. *Economic Sanctions in U.S. Foreign Policy.* Philadelphia: Foreign Policy Research Institute.

Bilmes, Linda J. 2013. "The Financial Legacy of Iraq and Afghanistan: How Wartime Spending Decisions Will Constrain Future National Security Budgets." HKS Faculty Research Working Paper Series RWP13-006.

Booth, Ken and Tim Dunne. 2002. *Worlds in Collision: Terror and the Future of Global Order.* New York: Palgrave Macmillan.

Center for Arms Control and Non-Proliferation. 2014. "Fact Sheet: Global Nuclear Weapons Inventories in 2014." Retrieved December 14, 2014 (http://armscontrolcenter.org/issues/nuclearweapons/articles/fact_sheet_global_nuclear_weapons_inventories_in_2014/).

Chandrasekaran, Rajiv. 2014. "A Legacy of Pain and Pride." Retrieved December 11, 2014 (http://www.washingtonpost.com/sf/national/2014/03/29/a-legacy-of-pride-and-pain/).

Chatfield, Charles. 1992. *The American Peace Movement*. New York: Twayne.

Clausewitz, Karl. 1984. *On War* (translated by Michael Howard and Peter Paret). Princeton, NJ: Princeton University Press.

Clement, Scott. 2014. "Iraq and Afghanistan: The Physical and Mental Toll, by the Numbers." Retrieved December 13, 2014 (http://www.washingtonpost.com/news/post-nation/wp/2014/03/31/iraq-and-afghanistan-the-physical-and-mental-toll-by-the-numbers/).

Cole, David and James X. Dempsey. 2002. *Terrorism and the Constitution*. New York: New Press.

Crenshaw, Martha. 1983. "Introduction: Reflections on the Effects of Terrorism." Pp. 1–37 in *Terrorism, Legitimacy, and Power*, edited by Martha Crenshaw. Middletown, CT: Wesleyan University Press.

Crenshaw, Martha. 1995. *Terrorism in Context*. University Park: Pennsylvania State University Press.

Crenshaw, Martha. 1998. "The Logic of Terrorism: Terrorist Behavior as a Product of Strategic Choice." Pp. 7–24 in *Origins of Terrorism: Psychologies, Ideologies, States of Mind*, edited by W. Reich. Washington, DC: Woodrow Wilson International Center for Scholars and Cambridge University Press.

Cunningham, Kenneth. 2004. "Permanent War? The Domestic Hegemony of the New American Militarism." *New Political Science* 26(4):551–67.

Cuomo, Chris. 1996. "War Is Not Just an Event: Reflections on the Significance of Everyday Violence." *Hypatia* 11(4):30–45.

Danner, Mark. 2011. "After September 11: Our State of Exception." Retrieved July 2, 2012 (http://www.nybooks.com/articles/archives/2011/oct/13/after-september-11-our-state-exception/?pagination=false).

Donn, Jeff and Kimberly Hefling. 2007. "Wounded Vets Return to Empty Pockets." *News Tribune*, September 30, pp. A6–A7.

Douglas Vavrus, Mary. 2013. "Lifetime's Army Wives, or I Married the Media-Military-Industrial Complex." *Women's Studies in Communication* 36:92–112.

Egan, Timothy. 2004. "Sensing the Eyes of Big Brother, and Pushing Back." *New York Times*, August 8, p. 16.

Eisenhower, Dwight. 1953. Speech to the American Society of Newspaper Editors, April 16, 1953, Washington, DC. Retrieved May 22, 2010 (http://www.eisenhower.archives.gov/all_about_ike/speeches/chance_for_peace.pdf).

Enloe, Cynthia. 1990. *Bananas, Beaches, and Bases: Making Feminist Sense of International Politics*. Berkeley: University of California Press.

"The Events of 11 September (2001) and Beyond." 2002. *International Feminist Journal of Politics* 4(1):95–113.

Falk, Richard. 1973. "Environmental Warfare and Ecocide—Facts, Appraisal, and Proposals." *Security Dialogue* 4:80–96.

Featherstone, Liza. 2003. "Students Wrestle With War." *The Nation* 273(20):18–20.

Federal Bureau of Investigation. 2009. "New Most Wanted Terrorist." Retrieved May 22, 2010 (http://www.fbi.gov/page2/apri109/wanted042109.html).

Flores, D. A. 1981. "Note: Export Controls and the US Effort to Combat International Terrorism." *Law and Policy in International Business* 13(2):521–90.

Freeh, Louis J. 2001. "Threat of Terrorism to the United States." Testimony Before the U.S. Senate Committees on Appropriations, Armed Services, and Select Committee on Intelligence, May 10, 2001. Retrieved May 22, 2010 (http://www.fbi.gov/news/testimony/threat-of-terrorism-to-the-united-states).

Garfield, Richard. 2002. "Economic Sanctions, Humanitarianism, and Conflict After the Cold War." *Social Justice* 29(3):94–107.

Gibbs, Jack P. 1989. "Conceptualization of Terrorism." *American Sociological Review* 54:329–40.

Haas, Richard. 1997. "Sanctioning Madness." *Foreign Affairs* November/December:74–85.

Harmon, Christopher. 2000. *Terrorism Today*. New York: Routledge.

Harvard Study Team. 1991. "The Effect of the Gulf Crisis on the Children of Iraq." *New England Journal of Medicine* 325(13):977–80.

Hayden, Craig. 2011. "Beyond the 'Obama Effect': Refining the Instruments of Engagement Through U.S. Public Diplomacy." *American Behavioral Scientist* 55:784–802.

Hoge, James F., Jr., and Gideon Rose. 2001. "Introduction." Pp. ix–xiv in *How Did This Happen? Terrorism and the New War*, edited by J. F. Hoge, Jr., and G. Rose. New York: PublicAffairs.

Human Security Report Project. 2005. *Human Security Report 2005: War and Peace in the 21st Century*. New York: Oxford University Press.

Human Security Report Project. 2011. *Human Security Report 2009/2010: The Causes of Peace and the Shrinking Costs of War*. New York: Oxford University.

International Commission on Intervention and State Sovereignty. (2001). *The Responsibility to Protect*. Ottawa, Canada: International Development Research Center.

Jenkins, Brian M. 1988. "Future Trends in International Terrorism." Pp. 246–66 in *Current Perspectives on International Terrorism*, edited by R. Slater and M. Stohl. New York: St. Martin's Press.

Jorgenson, Andrew, Brett Clark and Jennifer Givens. 2012. "The Environmental Impacts of Militarization in Comparative Perspective: An Overlooked Relationship." *Nature and Culture* 7: 314–37.

Kaplan, Laura D. 1994. "Woman as Caretaker: An Archetype That Supports Patriarchal Militarism." *Hypatia* 9(2):123–33.

Klare, Michael. 2007. "The Pentagon v. Peak Oil." Retrieved December 30, 2014 (http://www.tomdispatch.com/post/174810/michael_klare_the_pentagon_as_global_gas_guzzler).

Knickerbocker, Brad. 2002. "Return of the Military-Industrial Complex?" *Christian Science Monitor* 94(52):2.

Knott, Paul D. 1971. *Student Activism*. Dubuque, IA: William C. Brown.

Lacey, Jill. 2006. "Working Abroad: Finding International Internships and Entry-Level Jobs." *Occupational Outlook Quarterly* Fall:2–18.

Lyall, Sarah and Eamon Quinn. 2007. "At the Polls, Northern Ireland Tries to Resurrect Self-Rule." *New York Times*, March 8, p. A9.

Mandelbaum, Michael. 2003. "Diplomacy in War Time: New Priorities and Alignments." Pp. 255–68 in *How Did This Happen? Terrorism and the New War*, edited by J. F. Hoge, Jr., and G. Rose. New York: PublicAffairs.

Marks, Stephen. 1999. "Economic Sanctions as Human Rights Violations: Reconciling Political and Public Health Imperatives." *American Journal of Public Health* 89(10): 1509–13.

Mulrine, Anna. 2011. "No. 1 Priority for U.S. Security: Domestic Terrorism, Threat Report Says." Retrieved June 20, 2012 (http://www.csmonitor.com/USA/2011/0210/No.-1-priority-for-US-security-domestic-terrorism-threat-report-says).

Murray, Mark. 2014. "ISIS Threat: Fear of Terror Attack Soars to 9/11 High, NBC News/WSJ Poll Finds." Retrieved December 13, 2014 (http://www.nbcnews.com/politics/first-read/isis-threat-fear-terror-attack-soars-9-11-high-nbc-n199496).

National Center for PTSD. 2003a. "What Is Posttraumatic Stress Disorder?" Retrieved August 15, 2003 (http://www.ncptsd.org/facts/general/fs_what_is_ptsd.html).

National Center for PTSD. 2003b. "Epidemiological Facts About PTSD." Retrieved June 6, 2010 (http://www.ptsd.va.gov/professional/pages/epidemiological-facts-ptsd.asp).

National Priorities Project. 2007. "Federal Budget Year in Review 2007." Retrieved May 22, 2010 (http://www.nationalpriorities.org/yearinreview2007).

Neier, Aryeh. 1993. "Watching Rights." *The Nation* 257(19):683.

Nye, Joseph. 2008. "Public Diplomacy and Soft Power." *Annals of the American Academy of Political and Social Science* 616:94–109.

Oates, Sarah. 2006. "Comparing the Politics of Fear: The Role of Terrorism News in Election Campaigns in Russia, the United States and Britain." *International Relations* 4: 425–37.

O'Connor, Anahad. 2004. "The Reach of War: The Soldiers." *New York Times*, July 1. Retrieved June 6, 2010 (http://www.nytimes.com/2004/07/01/world/reach-war-soldiers-1-6-iraq-veterans-found-have-stress-related-disorder.html).

Peksen, Dursun. 2009. "Better or Worse? The Effect of Economic Sanctions on Human Rights." *Journal of Peace Research* 46: 59–77.

Peksen, Dursun and A. Cooper Drury. 2009. "Economic Sanctions and Political Repression: Assessing the Impact of Coercive Diplomacy on Political Freedoms." *Human Rights Review* 10:393–411.

Pew Research Center. 2014. "Growing Concern About Rise of Islamic Extremism at Home and Abroad." Retrieved December 14, 2014 (http://www.people-press.org/2014/09/10/growing-concern-about-rise-of-islamic-extremism-at-home-and-abroad/).

Pillar, Paul R. 2001. *Terrorism and U.S. Foreign Policy.* Washington, DC: Brookings Institution Press.

Pryor, John, Linda DeAngelo, Laura Palucki Blake, Sylvia Hurtado, and Serge Tran. 2011. *The American Freshman: National Norms Fall 2011.* Los Angeles, CA: Higher Educational Research Institute.

Reich, Walter. 1998. "Understanding Terrorist Behavior: The Limits and Opportunities of Psychological Inquiry." Pp. 261–80 in *Origins of Terrorism: Psychologies, Ideologies, States of Mind,* edited by W. Reich. Cambridge, MA: Woodrow Wilson International Center for Scholars and Cambridge University Press.

Sandler, Todd. 2011. "New Frontiers of Terrorism Research: An Introduction." *Journal of Peace Research* 48:279–86.

Southern Poverty Law Center. 2012. "Hate Map 2011." Retrieved June 28, 2012 (http://www.splcenter.org/get-informed/hate-map).

Spindel, Chad. 2011. "The People Want to Topple the Regime: Exploring the Arab Spring in Egypt, Syria and Jordan." *Sage Open* October–December 2011. doi: 10.1177/2158244011428648.

Steiner, Julian. 2014. "America's First Globals: The Millennial Generation." *Foreign Service Journal* 91:55.

Stockholm International Peace Research Institute. 2014. *SIPRI Yearbook 2014: 4. Military Expenditure and Arms Production.* Retrieved November 11, 2014 (http://www.sipri.org/yearbook/2014/04).

Suu Kyi, Aung Saa. 2012. "Nobel Lecture June 12, 2012." Retrieved June 25, 2012 (http://nobel peaceprize.org/en_GB/laureates/laureates-1991/aung-san-2012/).

Tickner, J. Ann. 2002. "Feminist Perspectives on 9/11." *International Studies Perspectives* 3:333–50.

United Nations. 1992. "The Rio Declaration on Environment and Development." Retrieved July 12, 2012 (http://www.unesco.org/education/information/nfsunesco/pdf/RIO_E.PDF).

U.S. Commission on National Security in the 21st Century. 2001. "Road Map for National Security: Imperative for Change." Retrieved May 22, 2010 (http://govinfo.library.unt.edu/nssg/Reports/reports.htm).

U.S. Department of State. 2003. "Diplomacy: The State Department at Work." Retrieved May 22, 2010 (http://www.state.gov/r/pa/ei/rls/dos/4078.htm).

U.S. Department of State. 2014. "Bureau of Consular Affairs." Retrieved November 30, 2014 (http://travel.state.gov/pdf/ca_fact_sheet.pdf).

U.S. Department of Veterans Affairs. 2007. "Factsheet: America's Wars." Retrieved June 6, 2010 (http://www1.va.gov/opa/publications/factsheets/fs_americas_wars.pdf).

U.S. Department of Veterans Affairs. 2012. "Strategies for Serving Women Veterans." Retrieved December 14, 2014 (http://www.va.gov/opa/publications/Draft_2012_Women-Veterans_StrategicPlan.pdf).

U.S. Department of Veterans Affairs. 2014a. "Mental Health Effects of Serving in Afghanistan and Iraq." Retrieved December 11, 2014 (http://www.ptsd.va.gov/public/PTSD-overview/reintegration/overview-mental-health-effects.asp).

U.S. Department of Veterans Affairs. 2014b. "Traumatic Stress in Women Veterans." Retrieved December 13, 2014 (http://www.ptsd.va.gov/public/PTSD-overview/women/traumatic-stress-female-vets.asp).

Van Evera, Stephen. 2006. "Assessing U.S. Strategy Against the War on Terror." *Annals of the American Academy of Political and Social Science* 607:10–26.

Vedantam, Shankar. 2006. "Veterans Report Mental Illness." *Washington Post*, March 1, p. A01.

Vellela, Tony. 1988. *New Voices: Student Activism in the 80s and 90s.* Boston: South End Press.

Walter, E. V. 1964. "Violence and the Process of Terror." *American Sociological Review* 29(2):248–57.

Wardlaw, Grant. 1988. "State Response to International Terrorism." Pp. 206–45 in *Current Perspectives on International Terrorism,* edited by R. Slater and M. Stohl. New York: St. Martin's Press.

White House. 2014. "FACT SHEET: Wales Summit – NATO's Changing Role in Afghanistan." Retrieved November 11, 2014 (http://www.whitehouse.gov/the-press-office/2014/09/04/fact-sheet-wales-summit-nato-s-changing-role-afghanistan)

Whittaker, David. 2002. *Terrorism: Understanding the Global Threat.* London: Longman.

Wilkinson, Paul. 1993. "The Orange and the Green: Extremism in Northern Ireland." Pp. 105–23 in *Terrorism, Legitimacy, and Power,* edited by M. Crenshaw. Middleton, CT: Wesleyan University Press.

Young, Nigel. 1999. "Peace Movements in History." Pp. 228–36 in *Approaches to Peace,* edited by D. P. Barash. New York: Oxford University Press.

Zajadlo, Jerzy. 2005. "Legality and Legitimization of Humanitarian Intervention: New Challenges in the Age of the War on Terrorism." *American Behavioral Scientist* 48:653–670.

Zoroya, Greg. 2005. "Key Iraq Wound: Brain Trauma." Retrieved June 6, 2010 (http://www.usatoday.com/news/nation/2005-03-03-brain-trauma-lede_x.htm).

Part V

Berger, Peter. 1963. *Invitation to Sociology.* New York: Doubleday.

Ritzer, George. 2000. *Sociological Theory.* New York: McGraw-Hill.

Chapter 17

Adam, Karla. 2011. "Occupy Wall Street Protests Go Global." Retrieved July 24, 2012 (http://www.washingtonpost.com/world/europe/occupy-wall-street-protests-continue-world-wide/2011/10/16/gIQAcJ1roL_story.html).

Brucato, Ben. 2012. "The Crisis and the Way Forward: What We Can Learn From Occupy Wall Street." *Humanity & Society* 36:76–84.

Burawoy, Michael. 2004. "Public Sociologies: A Symposium From Boston College: Introduction." *Social Problems* 51:103–30.

Close Up Foundation. 2004. *The 26th Amendment: Pathway to Participation.* Alexandria, VA: Close Up Foundation.

Corporation for National and Community Service. 2009. "President Obama Joins President Bush in Call to Service." Retrieved May 21, 2010 (http://www.nationalservice.gov/about/newsroom/releases_detail.asp?tbl_pr_id=1555).

Dalton, Russell, Manfred Kuechler, and Wilhelm Bürklin. 1990. "The Challenge of New Movements." Pp. 3–20 in *Challenging the Political Order,* edited by Russell Dalton and Manfred Kuechler. New York: Oxford University Press.

Davies, James. 1974. "The J-Curve and Power Struggle Theories of Collective Violence." *American Sociological Review* 87:363–87.

Ehrlich, Thomas. 2000. *Civic Responsibility and Higher Education.* New York: The ACE Series on Higher Education.

Engle, Shaena. 2006. "More College Freshmen Committed to Social and Civic Responsibility, UCLA Survey Reveals." Retrieved May 19, 2010 (http://newsroom.ucla.edu/portal/ucla/More-College-Freshmen-Committed-6754.aspx?RelNum=6754).

Franklin, Jonathan. 2011a. "Camila Vallejo—Latin America's 23-Year–Old New Revolutionary Folk Hero." Retrieved August 26, 2012 (http://www.guardian.co.uk/world/2011/oct/08/camila-vallejo-latin-america-revolutionary).

Franklin, Jonathan. 2011b. "Chile's Commander Camila, the Student Who Can Shut Down a City." Retrieved August 26, 2012 (http://www.guardian.co.uk/world/2011/aug/24/chile-student-leader-camila-vallejo).

Giugni, Marco. 1999. "Introduction." Pp. xiii–xxxiii in *How Social Movements Matter,* edited by M. Giugni, D. McAdam, and C. Tilly. Minneapolis: University of Minnesota Press.

Goldman, Francisco. 2012. "They Made Her an Icon, Which Is Impossible to Live Up To." *New York Times Magazine,* April 8, pp. 22–27, 46.

Hannigan, John. 1991. "Social Movement Theory and the Sociology of Religion: Toward a New Synthesis." *Sociological Analysis* 52(4):311–31.

Harper, Charles and Kevin Leicht. 2002. *Exploring Social Change: America and the World.* Upper Saddle River, NJ: Prentice Hall.

Hollender, Jeffrey and Linda Catling. 1996. *How to Make the World a Better Place.* New York: W. W. Norton.

Langman, Lauren. 2013. "Occupy: A New New Social Movement." *Current Sociology* 61: 510-524.

Lauer, Robert H. 1976. "Introduction: Social Movements and Social Change: The Inter-relationships." Pp. xi–xxviii in *Social Movements and Social Change*, edited by R. Lauer. Carbondale: Southern Illinois University.

Lemert, Charles. 1997. *Social Things: An Introduction to the Sociological Life*. Lanham, MD: Rowman & Littlefield.

Levine, Arthur and Jeanette Cureton. 1998. *When Hope and Fear Collide: A Portrait of Today's College Student*. San Francisco: Jossey-Bass.

Liazos, Alexander. 1972. "Nuts, Sluts, and Perverts: The Sociology of Deviance." *Social Problems* 20:103–20.

Loeb, Paul Rogat. 1994. *Generation at the Crossroads*. New Brunswick, NJ: Rutgers University Press.

Loseke, Denise. 2003. *Thinking About Social Problems*. New York: Aldine de Gruyter.

Mannheim, Karl. 1940. *Man and Society in an Age of Reconstruction*. New York: Harcourt Brace.

McAdam, Doug. 1982. *Political Process and the Development of Black Insurgency*. Chicago: University of Chicago Press.

McAdam, Doug, John McCarthy, and Mayer Zald. 1988. "Social Movements." Pp. 695–737 in *Handbook of Sociology*, edited by N. Smelser. Newbury Park, CA: Sage Publications.

McAdam, Doug, John McCarthy, and Mayer Zald. 1996. *Comparative Perspectives on Social Movement: Political Opportunities, Mobilizing Structures, and Cultural Framings*. Thousand Oaks, CA: Sage Publications.

McCarthy, John and Mayer Zald. 1977. "Resource Mobilization and Social Movements: A Partial Theory." *American Journal of Sociology* 82:1212–41.

McGann, James and Mary Johnstone. 2006. The Power Shift and the NGO Credibility. *International Journal of Not for Profit Law* 8:65–77.

Meyer, David. 2000. "Social Movements: Creating Communities of Change." Pp. 33–55 in *Feminist Approaches to Social Movements, Community, and Power*, Vol. 1, edited by R. Teske and M. A. Tetreault. Columbia: University of South Carolina Press.

Meyer, David and Suzanne Staggenbord. 1996. "Movements, Countermovements, and the Structure of Political Opportunity." *American Journal of Sociology* 101(6):1628–60.

Moss Wilson, William. 2012. "Just Don't Call Her Che." *New York Times*, January 29, p. 5.

Munson, Ziad. 2010. "Mobilizing on Campus: Conservative Movements and Today's College Students." *Sociological Forum* 25:769–86.

Nader, Ralph. 1972. *Action for a Change*. New York: Grossman.

Paul, James A. 2000. "NGOs and Global Policy-Making." Retrieved May 19, 2010 (http://www.globalpolicy.org/component/content/article/177/31611.html).

Pew Research Center. 2014. "Political Polarization in the American Public." Retrieved November 2, 2014 (http://www.people-press.org/2014/06/12/political-polarization-in-the-american-public/).

Piven, Francis and Richard Cloward. 1979. *Poor People's Movements: Why They Succeed, How They Fail*. New York: Vintage Books.

Plotke, David. 1995. "What's So New About New Social Movements?" Pp. 113–36 in *Social Movements: Critique, Concepts, Case-Studies*, edited by S. Lyman. New York: New York University Press.

Rayside, David. 1998. *On the Fringe: Gays and Lesbians in Politics*. Ithaca, NY: Cornell University Press.

Skocpol, Theda. 2000. *The Missing Middle*. New York: Norton.

Smelser, Neil. 1963. *Theory of Collective Behavior*. New York: Free Press.

Spalter-Roth, Roberta and Nicole Van Vooren. 2011. "Are Master's Programs Closing? What Makes for Success in Staying Open?" Retrieved November 30, 2014 (http://www.asanet.org/research/are_masters_programs_closing_databrief.pdf).

Sztompka, Piotr. 1994. *The Sociology of Social Change*. New York: John Wiley & Sons.

Tarrow, Sidney. 2011. "Why Occupy Wall Street Is Not the Tea Party of the Left." Retrieved November 2, 2014 (http://www.foreignaffairs.com/articles/136401/sidney-tarrow/why-occupy-wall-street-is-not-the-tea-party-of-the-left).

Taylor, Verta and Nancy Whittier. 1995. "Analytical Approaches to Social Movement Culture: The Culture of the Women's Movement." Pp. 163–87 in *Social Movements and Culture*, edited by H. Johnson and B. Klandermans. Minneapolis: University of Minnesota Press.

Wilson, John. 1973. *Introduction to Social Movements*. New York: Basic Books.

Wilson, Kenneth and Anthony Orum. 1976. "Mobilizing People for Collective Political Action." *Journal of Political and Military Sociology* 4:187–202.

INDEX